# The Sharecropper Boy Goes Back Home

## A MEMOIR OF A PERSONAL JOURNEY
## BEGINNING WITH THE GREAT DEPRESSION

# Jim White

outskirts
press

## DEDICATION

*To my beautiful wife, Gloria, who came into my life late but has brought joy and fun to me. Your joie de vivre approach compensates for my tendency to be overly serious. Also, I want to dedicate this work to my parents, Haskell H. and Macie Bell Mitchell White, who kept our family of eight children well fed and reasonably comfortable throughout a devastating recession that brought many residents to their knees.*

# Introduction

## "The Sharecropper Boy Goes Back Home"

MY LIFE STARTED as a "Sharecropper Boy" and through hard work and lots of luck reached the point that I was in charge of a national program for a cabinet level Federal Agency, something I never anticipated in my wildest dreams. During the long stretch of time during that period, life was full of extreme "highs" and "lows" but was never dull. I've been urged for years by friends and relatives to write an account of those years.

In fact, about 30 years ago I did write a few chapters of a memoir on a brand new Macintosh computer I purchased soon after arriving at Purdue University, where I had my last "career." In 1983, when I began this career, I had never touched a computer. Therefore, I wrote the first long and detailed "Users Guide" to the new system on my old Royal Manual typewriter. I knew that I must give up this "old friend" and become familiar with a strange new machine called the computer. That would be required if I were to teach people around the world how to access the huge volume of chemical information available on this new computerized system. This could only be done with computers.

In my early ignorance of the vagaries of computers, however, I failed to protect or "save" the personal work I had started on my Memoir. Then one early morning as I was typing away, I received the dreaded symbol of a BOMB exploding. This meant the computer's hard drive had crashed, taking with it those priceless words of wisdom I had slaved over. I kept the discs containing those words, hoping some day a "rescue" disc would be able to resurrect them. That never happened. The "rescue discs" I tried never provided anything but symbols and gibberish. In any event, I finally gave up and tossed the corrupted discs in the trash can. And the idea of writing a Memoir was postponed until I reached the age of 89!

Therefore, this presentation is based on long ago memories. I kept no notes or diaries over the years. Unlike some newspaper writer friends who saved copies of everything they wrote, I saved hardly any of my writing. I have some examples that people saved and gave to me. Part of this failure to save my writing for posterity was based on the thought that my writing would improve with added experience and knowledge. The world and I will never know if that were true, unless someone has a better reason than I to pore over microfilm (possibly preserved) at the various newspapers at which I labored during the years I was a newspaper reporter.

The same goes for most of the articles I wrote for wire services and magazines, as well as speeches I wrote for various officials including a Secretary of Agriculture. One thing I am sure of: my writing changed drastically, and not for the better, when I began writing those heavy tomes you can still find in the Code of Federal Register (CFR) or in various other (mostly educational) writings at NC

State University, University of Illinois, Purdue University, the U.S. Department of Agriculture, the U.S. Environmental Protection Agency, and the U.S. Department of Energy. Unfortunately, my breezy, irreverent style of newspaper writing definitely was not appropriate for government publications. So, sadly that style of writing gradually dissipated from my repertoire and at my age I'm not likely to get it back.

Although this memoir is primarily about the personal journey of my life, I've tried to reflect impressions of the world during this period: the great depression, World War II and the "greatest generation" period, plus the tremendous opportunities we have enjoyed with increased knowledge and technology developed during my lifetime.

In my opinion not all of the changes we've experienced are for the good. The Federal Government has become too large and controls too much of our lives. And perhaps even worse, so-called journalists no longer even appear to recognize "journalist ethics" such as objectivity that we once aspired to achieve. Civility also seems to have disappeared with today's culture. Debating ideas now too often dissolves into shouting matches. Once considered by my peers as a liberal, (I voted for Democrat Adlai Stevenson) my views have remained fairly stable but the political world around me has changed drastically.

Let's hope that our nation will eventually return to a state envisioned by our forefathers: a nation based on Christian/Jewish principles of hope, security, respect, freedom, and opportunities for everyone. And as individuals, I hope we can return to a society where we debate ideas with civility rather than engaging in diatribes against each other when we disagree.

Because of my failure to keep notes or a diary during my long life, I have only myself to blame for any errors (either factual or editorial) in this accounting of "The Sharecropper Boy Goes Back Home." Because of their projected length, I have divided these Memoirs into 12 parts. These are outlined below.

# Table of Contents

Introduction ...................................................................................................... i

PART 1:  Beginning of a Personal Journey ............................................... 1

PART 2:  World War II and its Effect on the White Family ........................... 49

PART 3:  Coming Home from the Navy: Work or College? ........................... 81

PART 4:  I "Accidentally" Find my Career--Journalism ............................... 121

PART 5:  Career Change to Educational Journalism and Another Degree ............... 157

PART 6:  The Move to the Nation's Capital as Federal Information Officer ............. 187

PART 7:  My Career Takes Another Turn: Working with USDA, EPA, & DOE .......... 265

PART 8:  The Real Battle Begins with the Big "C" ....................................... 329

PART 9:  Starting Life Anew, Cancer Free, and an Invitation from
Purdue University ....................................................................... 383

PART 10: Anatomy of an Old House Restoration ....................................... 447

PART 11: Soon to be an Innkeeper ......................................................... 475

PART 12: Life After Closing the Inn ........................................................ 527

Note about White House Inn Recipes ..................................................... 585

Acknowledgments ............................................................................... 587

# PART 1

## Beginning of a Personal Journey

# CHAPTER 1
## The Big Surprise!

MY MOTHER, MACIE Belle Mitchell White, became pregnant for the eighth time in 1925 and the "surprise" was baby Jim born on May 10, 1926, at the "Hancock Place," owned then by Haskell H. and Macie Mitchell White. I was baby No. 8 and was delivered by Dr. Benjamin Neely Miller, a great family physician for York County and the eastern part of Cherokee County, SC. Either he or Dr. T.A. Campbell, who practiced mainly in eastern Cherokee County, delivered all eight of the H. H. White children.

Dr. Miller, who studied at Davidson College, University of the South, and University of Maryland, also delivered children for the Mitchell, Whitesides, White, Wilburn, Love, McGill, Smith, and other families of that time period and area. No ordinary "country" doctor, he was highly trained and competent. He continually improved his medical training and education by traveling to famous educational institutions for further study. His training and education enabled him to deal competently with outbreaks of diphtheria, malaria fever, rheumatic fever, scarlet fever, typhoid fever, and other often deadly diseases prevalent at that time.

He also did surgery, both at hospitals and residences. He delivered many babies, set broken bones, and sewed up cuts. On at least one occasion he had to put in over 80 sutures on a man who had been in a knife fight.

One story of Dr. Miller's surgery involved a family member of mine. One day Dr. Miller received a call from Will Mitchell in Kings Creek. My "Uncle Willie" told Dr. Miller he was worried because his young son, William Morrow Mitchell, who was just learning to talk, was speaking with a lisp.

Dr. Miller said he was going past the Mitchell home later that day and would stop by and check on William Morrow. Dr. Miller looked inside William Morrow's mouth and immediately knew he was "tongue tied." Dr. Miller then suggested they go out to the back porch (for better light) where he clipped the skin holding the tongue down. "Uncle Willie" paid his son a nickel to sit still while the surgery was performed! As soon as William Morrow's mouth healed he began speaking clearly without a lisp.

More about Dr. Miller: After he graduated from medical school at the University Of The South, Sewanee, Tennessee, he decided he needed more training before taking on the arduous job of diagnosing and treating patients for a wide range of ailments. So, he spent a year at Maryland's University Hospital working with two outstanding specialists there. When it was time for him to leave, these doctors urged him to join the hospital staff. However, he had made the decision to return to South Carolina and establish his practice in the small town of Smyrna, so he declined that offer. *How many of today's doctors would make that decision?*

Most of the families in the Smyrna, Hickory Grove, Blacksburg, and Kings Creek area were seriously feeling the effects of the recession when Dr. Miller began his practice working out of the tiny village of Smyrna. I heard that his charge for delivering a baby was $2.00.

Often the families were so poor they couldn't pay any cash money, so Dr. Miller would be paid with a ham, a chicken, a few eggs, or some other farm product for his services. Dr. Miller sold these products to a friend in Smyrna and used the money to buy medicine which he supplied to patients. Regardless of whether he received anything for his services, Dr. Miller never refused to treat a patient.

# CHAPTER 2

## Practicing Medicine in the 20's and 30's

AS TYPICAL FOR that period and place, Dr. Miller originally visited his patients by horse and buggy. Sometimes the dirt roads and weather were so bad he would be forced to unhook the buggy, grab his medical bag, and mount the horse to continue on to his patient's house.

The demands were so great on Dr. Miller's time that he needed two horses to maintain his schedule of patient visits. One would rest while the other one worked. In 1908, Dr. Miller purchased his first car (a Maxwell) and this enabled him to get to his patients faster.

*Note: Information about Dr. Miller comes from personal recollection as well as from the book: "Benjamin Neely Miller, MD" written by his daughter, Martha Miller Douglas. I will be eternally grateful that his granddaughter, Addie Jane White (no relation of mine) presented a copy of this out-of-print book to me.*

No one ever told me what Dad paid Dr. Miller to deliver me but I suspect it was a ham or chicken, not cash, since the family was already suffering from the Great Depression and it's doubtful our family would have had $2.00 cash. My father always blamed Herbert Hoover for the depression. He derisively referred to "Hoover Carts" until the day he died. *These carts were wagons with automobile wheels and tires pulled by mules because the owner could not afford to operate the car.*

Dad gave President Franklin D. Roosevelt full credit for our recovery from the depression, although many economists now credit World War II for the bustling post war economy. Ironically, despite his praise for Roosevelt, Dad never took advantage of any of the special programs put into place by this President.

Returning to my early life, I was told by family members that Mother was exhausted by carrying me to term. That is understandable since she was 43 years old when I was born and had been responsible for taking care of the food, clothing, and other needs of our already large family. Mom credited much of my early care to my oldest sister, Isabel, while she recuperated. Soon afterward, Sister Isabel married Marvin Blackwell and was gone from the house. *I hope taking care of me didn't hasten her leaving!*

Another reason to think I was a "surprise" was that the family no longer owned a bassinet and I spent my earliest days in a dresser drawer. Apparently the bassinet had been given away because my brother, Frank, was six years old by this time and no further children were expected after he was born.

My earliest recollections upon being able to walk were: (1) my fear of a billy goat from a neighboring farm and (2) running through the house trying to avoid hugging and kissing by my four older (and very affectionate) sisters. I remember racing from one sister and being caught by another. Obviously they were more than a little pleased to have a baby boy in the house, someone on whom to bestow their motherly instincts. *Isn't it a shame that we don't always appreciate our blessings at the time?*

The billy goat, was somewhat of a neighborhood pet who was allowed free rein and bothered no one but me. However, when he saw me outside the house he immediately ran toward me forcing me to run back inside. If I was too far from the house, I climbed the nearest rail fence. However, in retrospect, it's obvious the goat wasn't intent on really "catching" me. He could have climbed the fence easier than I with my short legs. The goat must have had a sense of humor.

# CHAPTER 3

## Entertainment--Country Style

IN THOSE DAYS, entertainment for rural folks was really scarce, compared with today's abundance of electronic communication devices. Remember, even black and white television was not available at that time. Although we possessed a battery powered radio, our listening was limited since the battery was already worn out when we got the radio.

We could listen to the radio for a few minutes before it would give out completely. With an overnight rest, the battery would regain enough strength to operate the radio a few more minutes before running down again. Someone gave me a "crystal radio" and I spent many hours trying to get it to work but all I ever received from it were some indistinguishable sounds like the ocean or heavy winds.

So, especially when I was very young and we had company, I was often asked to provide the entertainment. The adults would call upon me to sing a current, sad song about a terrible train wreck which trapped and killed many people. Being a sensitive child from birth, I could never finish this song before breaking into tears.

The adults seemed to think that show of emotion by a child was amusing, indicating just how starved they were for entertainment. In any event, the fact that I was quick to oblige, suggests that I might have been a ham at an early age--a character-istic completely reversed as I grew older. Since I wasn't yet old enough to read, I assume Mother must have taught me the words to that song about a train wreck. She was only partially successful since I remember singing only part of the song about this tragedy before dissolving into tears.

Story telling or playing cards provided most of the entertainment for many Cherokee County farm families during the depression. But cards (except for Rook) were not allowed in our house because they suggested gambling. Story telling re-volved around "mad dogs"-- a major problem in the South at that time. *(Remember how the rabid dog terrified the small, fictional town in Alabama, featured in the book "To Kill a Mockingbird"?)* Since these stories were a bit too scary for the women folks (as well as for me) that entertainment venue was limited at our house. Therefore, guests were too often required to suffer a little boy's quavery voice singing "The twain is at the 'tation" and waiting for the tears to start.

In case anyone thinks my tears were a sign of weakness, they need to know something about our family genealogy. As mentioned earlier, Mother bore Mitchell genes. Our Mitchell family members were typically Irish and wore their emotions on their sleeves. When Mother didn't see her brothers or sisters for a couple of weeks, they would embrace, kiss, and cry--both at the beginning and ending of their time together. *I definitely inherited some of the Mitchell characteristics.*

My father was just the opposite: a taciturn, Scottish type who saw crying by a male as an extreme sign of weakness. His views on this didn't change until he was quite old when his voice might break slightly while saying the blessing at a family dinner.

As an adult, these remembrances, along with several other incidents in my early life to be mentioned later might help explain why as an adult I suffered from extreme stage fright, an abiding fear of dogs, and a nervous disposition.

Actually an incident of family kindness may have contributed to my fear of man's best friend. This happened when I was three or four and my sister, Faye, who had recently married Alfonso (Shilly) Shillinglaw, decided to take me to spend the night at their house in Blacksburg. This was my first night away from Mother and was meant to be a treat for all of us, especially Mother.

One of the highlights of the visit was to take me to see my first movie. Faye and Shilly thought I would really enjoy this movie, featuring a large male German shep-herd dog called "Rin-Tin-Tin." Attending this particular movie was considered great entertainment for youngsters at that time. Unfortunately, it did not turn out well for me.

First of all, I had no concept of a moving picture. And the large picture of a German shepherd dog that almost filled the screen scared the dickens out of me. I was so frightened by the experience that my sister and brother-in-law took me home before the movie ended and put me to bed. I couldn't go to sleep for thinking about that big dog. *I don't recall the name of the movie but the film "Frozen River" featur-ing Rin-Tin-Tin was released in 1929 when I was three years old so that might have been the one I saw.*

Concerned about my inability to go to sleep, Sister Faye remembered my love of drawing and brought a pad of paper and a pencil to my bed. I drew pictures until I fell asleep. That was the only time I was at a movie theatre until I was 15 years old but I remember that first one vividly.

# CHAPTER 4
## Loss of the Farm

AT AROUND MY fourth birthday, fortunes for the H. H. White family changed drastically. I was told only that we were moving to a new home (actually a tenant farm). I was too young then to understand the significance of this move. In fact I was somewhat pleased that I would be leaving that billy goat behind. I had no idea that we had lost our home and farm and had suddenly gone from farm owners to "sharecroppers." But the move was devastating to the family adults--especially my Dad. By way of background, Dad apparently had always dreamed of having his own farm where he could raise cotton on a large scale. This dream appeared to be within his reach when he used all the money he had saved to purchase the "Hancock Place." The farm consisted of a nice manor house, a large barn, and two tenant houses on 330 acres. *That was a large farm by Cherokee County standards at the time.*

Like other Cherokee County farmers, Dad borrowed money from the bank to put in the crop for that year. Considerable money was needed to buy seed, fertilizer, equipment, etc., and for the huge amount of labor required to get the cotton ready for market. At the time the money was borrowed, cotton was selling for 45 cents per pound. Unfortunately for cotton farmers, at harvest time the price of cotton had dropped to 5 cents per pound. Neither he, nor most of the other farmers in our area, could repay their loans.

Though he struggled to hold onto the farm, it was ultimately lost to foreclosure. Thus, his dream had turned into a nightmare from which he never fully recovered. As the final insult, the "bank holiday" imposed by the government took the remainder of the White family's meager savings, leaving him a beaten and bitter man. And it left our family virtually penniless.

Loss of the farm on what is now Rutherford Street Extended, changed the lives of the H.H. White family dramatically. We went from community leaders to sharecroppers almost overnight. I learned all that much later.

About all I remember of the move itself was the adults loading up a wagon with all our earthly goods to be pulled by a team of mules to our new location. *I suspect more than one trip was made by the adults, since the wagon would not have been able to carry an entire household of furniture, plus farm equipment, and members of the family in one wagon load. But I made only one trip.* This began a succession of moves to tenant farms in the Mt. Paran community with each one a little worse than the previous one. Finally, the family moved across the county to the old Mitchell home place at Kings Creek (to be discussed in more detail later).

Although at the time, I was not consciously aware that the family had suffered such a serious setback, probably at a subconscious level, these events may have contributed to an early lack of self confidence and an enduring case of anxiety that remained with me into adulthood. *As an indication of this, although I retired after successful and rewarding careers, am now happily married to a wonderful woman, enjoy relatively good health for my age, and have no serious money worries, I'm still a nail biter.*

# CHAPTER 5

## Our First Tenant House Experience

UPON ENTERING THE new tenant house, my attention was immediately drawn to something I had never seen before: a telephone left in the house by the previous tenants. And amazingly to me, the phone still worked. The phone was hooked to a "party line" which added to the fascination of this device to a country boy not yet in school.

I marveled over the fact that I could (for a short time) hear and talk to people I couldn't see. This thrill lasted until the phone company disconnected the line a couple of weeks later. We didn't have the money to have the telephone put in our name and I was a teenager before I had access to a phone again.

The Parker family owned our first rental property and lived nearby in their own home. A son of the Parker family (named Bill as I recall) was in college and he introduced me to "exotic" games such as tennis and golf--games I had never seen nor even heard of before. Bill would invite me to their large back yard where he would practice hitting golf and tennis balls. I spent lots of time there at his invitation, helping him retrieve the balls so he could continue the practice. I was thrilled at being part of these exciting new (to me) games.

I remember another incident that occurred soon after our move to the Parker place. It wasn't nearly as much fun as chasing balls for Bill Parker. I was exploring the woods behind our house (barefoot as usual) when I stepped on a nail protruding from an old board. As hard as I tried, I could not pull the nail from my foot. I crawled painfully back to the house where Mother removed the rusty nail and then doused my foot with kerosene oil, the standard treatment for almost all wounds at that time. There was concern by the adults that I might get "lockjaw" since there were no tetanus shots then (at least for us). Luckily after a few weeks the family could breathe easier since no "lockjaw" had appeared and the wound had healed.

While I was still 5, I got to know a beautiful 16 year old neighbor girl who lived just down the road from us. She was named Louise Byers. She was very kind and affectionate to me and became my "first love." She would talk with me for hours. I could hardly wait to grow up so I could marry her.

Then to my dismay, my oldest brother, Howard, started courting her and the next thing I knew they were married and gone from the neighborhood. Their marriage was a true love affair and resulted in eight children: five boys and three girls. My brother once jokingly said, "All I have to do is take my pants off and hang them on the bedstead and another child was on the way."

I was a lonely boy after Howard took Louise away. But just before I started school, I met a neighbor boy, Frank Neal, who lived on a nearby farm. He helped relieve my loneliness. Everyone called him "Frankie." We looked very much alike with both of us having fair skin, many freckles, and bright red hair. We began playing together and quickly became "best buddies."

# CHAPTER 6
## Starting School--in My Knickers!

WHEN I REACHED age six I prepared to enter Holly Grove Elementary School, considered one of the best Cherokee County schools. This was an exciting but scary time for me because of the opportunity to meet and get to know other children my age. *Because of the age difference between me and my siblings, I had basically been growing up like an only child.*

I recall being pretty nervous that first day of school, despite the fact that I already had a friend in my first year class. My mother, who never really considered our family to be "sharecroppers," had made "knickers" for me to wear. The fancy knickers contrasted with the clothes worn by all the other little boys who were dressed in overalls--most of which sported patches and some not overly clean by our standards. My unusual attire immediately established me as being different from the other first grade boys. In fact, I suspect it made me look like somewhat of a "dandy." I did not enjoy the other children staring at me! Obviously, many of them had never seen such a sight!

A few days after school started, at lunch time I went outside with the other children to play. Soon, a big boy known as the school's tough kid came up and began teasing me about my attire. My brother, Frank, who was younger and smaller than the other boy, saw what was happening and quickly came to my rescue. After exchanging some harsh words, they began to fight. My brother quickly gained the upper hand and the other wanted to quit. I'll never forget the scene of my "big brother" chasing and beating the larger boy who was soon reduced to tears. No one bothered me after that but I was eventually able to convince Mom to let me wear overalls so I wouldn't look that different from the other little boys.

The first grade teacher had just graduated from Winthrop College. I don't remember her name but she was very pretty and taught school only that one year. During the year, she met a young Clemson graduate and married him at the end of the school year. That ended her teaching career--at least in South Carolina during that period.

*Note: At that time, in South Carolina, women teachers who got married were not allowed to continue teaching. The reason for this harsh and sexist rule? A married woman teacher might become pregnant and a replacement would be required. It would have been scandalous if the little ones were exposed to a pregnant teacher! That may be how the term "Old Maid School Teacher" started since women teachers could not be married at that time in South Carolina.*

But that first year with the pretty young teacher was certainly a pleasant one for me. Apparently her "motherly instinct" had already kicked in because almost daily she invited me to sit on her lap while she conducted first grade classes. I was glad to oblige.

To my disappointment, when I started second grade, I had a new teacher whose motherly instincts apparently were dormant. I recall that she did not ask me (or anyone else) to sit on her lap a single time that year! I never saw my first year teacher again although I never forgot her.

# CHAPTER 7
## The Beginning of Stage Fright

THE PROCESS OF developing stage fright began for me the second or third year of school. Our teacher at that time announced plans for staging a class play. I was pleased to be chosen to play one of the "three bears." That pleasure lasted only until an early rehearsal when the other two bears failed to attend school that day.

By way of background, unlike most farming community schools of that period, Holly Grove School had an impressive stage and auditorium. The fact I might be required to rehearse alone on that big stage made me exceedingly nervous. I was also conscious that my lines would make no sense without the supporting dialog by the other two bears. Against my protests, the teacher insisted I go up on the stage alone and say my lines.

I attempted to comply with the teacher's demands, but as I had anticipated, my lines made no sense without the participation of the two missing bears. The resulting uproarious laughter of the rest of the class ended that rehearsal. It also ended any future acting for me. I vowed to myself that I would never again participate in a school play. I kept that vow during all my years in school. And, beginning that day I suffered from stage fright the rest of my life. (Note: *career wise I had to make speeches all over the USA, and had to learn how to suppress my stage fright. But I never completely overcame that fear inside*).

Our trips to Holly Grove School back then could be a problem. We had no school bus service to and from our house and no car to drive us there. So, my brother Frank and I had to walk over a mile through heavy woods before reaching the road that led to the school. *Taking the dirt road around the woods to school would have forced us to walk about twice as far.* Since I had Frank to protect me from "mad dogs" and other fearsome forest creatures, I didn't mind the walk through the forest. However, starting my third school year, Frank had graduated from elementary school and gone on to Blacksburg High School, leaving me to walk through the woods alone. This of course intensified my fear of dogs and any wild animals that might be lurking in the woods.

A group of other Holly Grove students, including Frankie Neal, almost always waited for me on the road as I emerged from the forest. As a group we would make the rest of the remaining short trek to school together assuaging my fears.

*A neat thing happened at a reunion held at the White House Inn B&B in Blacksburg which I owned and operated from 1991-1997. During the event, three elderly white haired ladies introduced themselves to me, saying they were part of the group that met me on the way to school. They laughingly said, "Jimmy, you would come running out of those woods like your life depended on it!" They had also brought along a group picture of our class that included both Frankie and me. None of us could distinguish Frankie and me from each other. I regret not getting a copy of that photo.*

Although Frankie Neal was only a few months older, he was light years ahead of me when it came to knowing the ways of the world. Obviously I had been a protected child. Frankie quickly began to educate me, starting with the "birds and bees" story--a story I simply could not accept. *I still believed that babies were delivered by stork!* He finally made a believer out of me when an event he predicted came true. This process began when Frankie brought a calendar with him to school. He showed me where he had circled the date he had caught his parents "in the act" he had described to me. He had also circled a calendar date for 9 months later.

Incredibly, on or near the second mark on the calendar, he came to school grinning like a Cheshire cat. Then he proudly told me that he had new twin siblings born almost exactly on the second calendar date. With that kind of proof, how could I not believe anything Frankie told me? Naturally he also disabused me about the existence of Santa Claus, though I never disclosed this to anyone and hung on to "Santa Claus" as long as possible.

I remember my time in the Mt. Paran community as largely pleasant. Frankie and I spent lots of time together. We also paid frequent visits to a nearby Neal family related to Frankie and also friends of my family. The thing that sticks out in my memory was the large grape arbor on their property. Mrs. Neal would usually offer us a glass of grape juice upon our arrival and then invite us to go outside and pick our own grapes from this highly productive arbor. *Since our family never stayed at any one tenant farm long enough to establish a grape arbor, the Neal's grapes and grape juice were special treats.*

Another Neal, (Vardell), a relative of Frankie and close friend of my sister Edith, was a frequent visitor to our house. I think Vardell had a bit of a crush on my pretty sister because he visited us so often. Vardell was an accomplished musician, both as singer and guitarist, and he was always willing to entertain. What I remember the most, however, is that on one of those visits, Vardell forgot to take his guitar with him when he left. I tried to play that guitar daily, but unfortunately for me he quickly came back to retrieve it. That ended my musical career.

*A final note about the Frank Neal family of Holly Grove community, Blacksburg, SC. Years later, when I returned to Blacksburg I learned that a son of Frank, Bill Neal, had become a famous chef. He died young and I never had a chance to meet him but have been fortunate enough to obtain a couple of his books. Ironically, he was probably better known in Paris, France, than in his home town.*

A sad memory from Holly Grove School involved a young girl in our class who was from a very poor family. Some students made fun of her because she wore dirty underwear to school. This treatment of the little girl offended me since I knew that this was not her fault but the fault of her family. *This hearkens to the old joke of girls being warned by their mothers to "Always wear clean underwear in case you are in an accident."* In this case, the little girl's mother was probably not even aware of what was happening. Despite my urgings to desist, some children continued to make fun of this defenseless little girl--demonstrating how cruel children can be to each other.

A final memory from that stage of my life involved a pleasant--rather than scary--story about dogs. Dad was known to have the very best hunting dogs around. The top dog in our group of hunting dogs was one called Betsy. She was a pretty little hound, friendly, and always the first to smell and flush a rabbit from its hiding place. For some reason never explained to me, Dad traded Betsy for something he must have needed badly. Since we usually went rabbit hunting (weather permitting) on most holidays, I dreaded going on the next hunt without Betsy. Then, to my joy, she showed up at our house the following Thanksgiving morning and went hunting with us. After the hunt was over, Dad returned Betsy to her new owner and she never visited us again.

During the time we lived in the Mt. Paran community, we lived in three different rental houses. The second one, just down the road from the first one, still involved a long walk through the woods to school. The third rental house was on another road with school bus service to school. The fourth and last move as sharecroppers was to the "Old Mitchell Home Place" at Kings Creek when I was about nine years old. Many more details of that period will follow.

It may seem strange for a youngster, but my major worry during those early years was that my mother would die before I was old enough to take care of myself. I sensed that her health was fragile. I attributed that to her relatively "old age" of 43 when I was born and the hard work she endured taking care of our large family.

As a result of this concern, I tried not do anything to worry Mom and perhaps shorten her life. This concern stayed with me until she died at age 68 and obviously was a strong factor in the development of my cautious personality. For example, I was always home early because I knew Mom wouldn't go to sleep until I was safely in bed. If I received an injury I tried my best to conceal it from her. This exaggerated concern probably indicated I was a "Mama's Boy" as some of my family openly suggested, and I didn't deny.

# CHAPTER 8
## Brief Introduction to H. H. White Family

BEFORE GOING FURTHER with this Memoir, it might be useful to devote some space to describe the makeup of our family with some brief observations about the various members:

The progenitor and dominant member of our family undoubtedly was our father, Haskell H. White, a handsome man with flaming red hair. He was over six feet tall and weighed a rawboned 185 pounds at maturity. A man of that size born in the 1800's was rare.

Dad was the eldest son of Andrew Campbell White and Isabella Newell Crawford. I know from historical records that my White ancestors came to America from County Antrim, Ireland. Both of my paternal grandparents died when I was quite young and I had no chance to get to know them. Dad's parents lived in the next county and since we rarely had a workable car it was difficult to visit them on a regular basis.

Also, the times we were able to visit Dad's parents were marred by the health condition of Grandmother Isabella White. My memories of her are colored by the fact that she was in the later stages of melanoma cancer. (I also suspect Mom spared me the trauma of viewing Grandmother White's cancer). The melanoma was concentrated on her nose and apparently the only treatment at that time was application of a purple ointment. The loss of much of her nose from cancer, plus the purple color, gave her face a ghastly appearance. I'm ashamed to admit that I was frightened to be around her as a little boy.

This cancer apparently was a genetic component of our family since my oldest sister, Isabel, suffered an attack of melanoma on the calf of her leg. Surgery cured her disease and she lived to be 90. Later, her eldest daughter, Mary Ann, who became a nurse anesthetist, had melanoma in an almost identical place on her leg. Despite heroic efforts to combat it, she died of the disease after a nine year battle.

I also learned in mid-life that my paternal Grandfather, Andrew Campbell White, died of prostate cancer, a disease that struck me in my mid-50's. *There is evidence that genetics can also be a factor in prostate cancer. In a later chapter, I will supply a detailed account of my personal battle with cancer and its disastrous effect on me and my family.*

On the maternal side of my family, my mother, Macie Belle Mitchell, was the daughter of Robert Hayes Mitchell and Isabella Elizabeth Morrow, whose ancestors also migrated from Northern Ireland. As already mentioned, both of my maternal grandparents died before I had a chance to get to know them.

Family members and old newspaper articles of the day portrayed Robert Hayes Mitchell as one of the most admirable men in the community. I learned that he was highly romantic and much in love with his wife. In a family letter, I read that at Grandmother Isabella Elizabeth's graveside service, Grandfather Robert broke off a small branch from a nearby cherry tree and placed it lovingly on Grandmother Mitchell's coffin with the words: "My love, I'll be joining you by the time this tree blossoms." The letter said he grieved himself to death two months later--before the cherry tree blossomed.

The family never told me much about Grandfather Mitchell's early life except that he and some brothers served in the Confederate Army. However, when I lived in York years later, a friend gave me a book which documented some very different activities after the Civil War ended. The family never mentioned these aspects of Grandfather Robert Hayes Mitchell's life to me. *However, I will discuss them in more detail in a later chapter with most of my observations based on the book.*

*In recent years I've learned much about the history of my paternal family through the efforts of a niece and nephew who uncovered many revealing facts about the White family (and to a lesser extent the Mitchell family) during genealogy searches. But in order to preserve some chronology in this narrative, I shall refrain from too many diversions at this time.*

Returning to information about my Dad, he was known as "Hass" by his friends and neighbors. When I was a youngster, he appeared to me as the toughest man ever born. As I grew, that evaluation changed, as I increasingly saw him as the quiet "common sense" leader in our farming community--whether it be Mt. Paran or Kings Creek.

As was common for that period, both Mother and Father had only about three to five years of formal education. Obviously Dad never attended a veterinary school. However, when a neighbor had a problem with any sick livestock, the neighbor would come pick up Dad so he could see, diagnose, and treat the animal, naturally at no cost except for the gas expended by the neighbor to transport Dad from home and back.

Dad also demonstrated to family and neighbors how to cut hair, repair shoes, and repair various equipment around the farm. He knew how and when to plant for maximum production which he shared with neighbors when asked. He was a quiet, modest man, and I would not have known about these activities had I not personally observed them. *He continued to cut my hair through high school, college and afterward when I was nearby. He passed this skill along to me and I trimmed the hair of almost all "drama club members" at my college. They had complained that barbers gave them a "skin head" treatment when they wanted just a trim. Dad let me use his old "barber tools" so I could give my student friends a smooth trim.*

Whether it was the red hair or not, Dad had a quick temper and was not afraid to act on it. People knew that his ordinarily good nature could change quickly with any real or perceived insult. Consequently, people treated him with great respect. *I was so sensitive and fearful of his temper that all he had to do was give me a certain "look" and I would jump to obey any "suggestion" from him.*

Our mother, Macie Belle Mitchell White, was a small, very pretty young lady of 21, who was already serious about a beau when she met Hass, three years her junior. Her personality was completely opposite to Dad's, but their personalities seemed to complement each other.

The word is that as a 90 pound beauty with dark skin and hair, Macie was the real "belle" of the community. And not just in name only! In any event, she met her true love at a house party where guests spent the night and slept on "pallets." I won't speculate on what happened but before the night was over, she was smitten by Hass White. Immediately afterwards, she broke off her relationship with the other young man and married Dad.

As was the custom of the day, the wife was expected to join the husband's church. On the first service after marriage, she dutifully went with Dad to the Baptist church he and his family attended, fully expecting to join that church in the near future. However, the minister seemed (at least to her) to address Mother personally, emphasizing the Baptist belief that anyone not totally immersed (i.e., those sprinkled) were not really baptized and were going to Hell. Of course Mother's family, all Presbyterians at that time, had been sprinkled rather than dunked.

So upset was Mother at the suggestion that she and most of her family members were going to Hell, she rose in the middle of the sermon and left the church. Dad promptly followed his bride out and they never returned to that church. They later settled the religious issue by joining the Associate Reformed Presbyterian (ARP) Church. Dad was happy with this church and eventually become an elder at the Blacksburg ARP Church. Mother's reaction to the Baptist minister was the only time I ever knew (or heard about) my sweet, loving Mother ever displaying a temper.

*Note: Ironically, all of Dad's family who migrated from Ireland to the Chester/ Lancaster/York area were originally regular Presbyterians or ARP's. Family genealogy shows that several members of our family were not only members but were ministers of those denominations. It still leaves us wondering why my father's branch of the White family left the Presbyterian Church and became Baptists. I suspect one of my family members married a persuasive Baptist.*

*Father, Mother, Grandfather Robert Hayes Mitchell and Grandmother Isabella Morrow Mitchell, Great Grandfather Klokie Mitchell, and many other relatives rest in either the Smyrna or Sharon ARP church cemeteries.*

Despite her limited formal education, Mother was extremely intelligent. She was so well organized that she did all the cooking, cleaning, sewing, and maintaining of the 10-member White household without complaint. She was an excellent seamstress and made much of the girls' clothing (as well as my knickers). She also used these skills to make beautiful quilts which were required to survive cold winters while there was no heating system in any of our rental houses. And she spent many hours before a hot wood stove each day cooking our meals or canning food for the winter. The heat was brutal in the kitchen during July and August but it was the best place to be in the winter months.

Mother almost always went about her duties with a smile on her face. Few, if any of us, were fully aware, until later, of just how much planning and work was required to maintain a happy, well fed, and relatively comfortable family--living in houses without a single modern convenience.

# CHAPTER 9
## H. H. White Family Expands Rapidly

RETURNING TO CHRONOLOGY: Once married, Mother and Father quickly expanded the family by having their first two of eight children: two girls, **Isabel and Faye;** followed by two boys, **Howard and Robert**; then two more girls, **Nell and Edith**; and finally, two more boys, **Frank and James,** in the order listed. Unfortunately, all but one of the H. H. White children inherited Dad's sensitive skin, not a good skin type to possess for field work in the South. Only Frank (who had Mom's good skin) escaped that fate. Two of us, Nell and I, got the bright red hair with all the good and bad that go with it!

More about Dad: In addition to farming, I found out that Dad had once worked as a butcher and owned his own butcher shop. At various times he also served as a rural mailman. He had to give up that latter job because of a serious back problem aggravated by the bumpy dirt roads.

Mom told me that long before I was born, Dad was also appointed for one term as Magistrate for Blacksburg and chose not to run for election when his term ended. In later years after we moved to the Mitchell home place, some influential Cherokee County politicians came to our house and persuaded Dad to run for the magistrate's job. He agreed to do so, but as it turned out, he had no chance of winning because his opponent was blind and used that handicap to his advantage for an easy victory. Dad did receive every single vote from the Kings Creek community, however, and that was more important to him than winning the election.

Dad let me travel with him while he was campaigning and we spent more quality time on those trips than at any other time. A couple of memories of that time spent with Dad follow: (1) We owned a used Ford Model T that was reliable but had some peculiarities, e.g., when we approached a tall hill, Dad would turn the car around and back up the hill (I was told that this maneuver ensured that gasoline would flow to the carburetor) and (2) once when we visited a prospective voter, the man brought out a beautiful little lamb and offered to give it to me. Knowing my nature, Dad refused to let me accept the lamb. He knew I would make a "pet" out of it, which conflicted with his motto: "Livestock are for eating--not pets."

# CHAPTER 10

## Our Last Move as Sharecroppers.

AS MENTIONED ABOVE, our last move as a sharecropping family was to the old Mitchell home place at Kings Creek, SC. It was in this farm house where Mother as well as the other children of Robert Hayes Mitchell grew up. It had been a tenant house for many years after it was bought by mother's younger brother, William Morrow Mitchell, Sr., the postmaster at Kings Creek.

The Mitchell home place was small and in bad condition as were most of the houses utilized by tenants in our poor community. Not uncommon for those days, it had no electricity, running water or heating/cooling systems. It lacked any insulation so it was hot in the summer and cold in the winter. And the two-hole toilet was located down the hill a respectable distance from the house.

Family members recall Dad spending much of the first two weeks at the Mitchell place shooting large rats, which had inhabited the house's crawl space while the house sat vacant. The spaces between the floor boards were so large that we could see the rats from above--not a reassuring sight. The size of the house was obviously inadequate for our family, having only a small parlor, living room, two bedrooms and kitchen. But we made the best of the cramped space. Sisters Nell and Edith slept in one bedroom, Robert and Frank slept in the second bedroom, Dad and Mom slept on a pallet in the living room, and I slept in an entry hall closet with no windows. (*Note: I still suffer from claustrophobia!*).

The only sources of heat were the fireplace in the living room and the wood burning stove in the kitchen. The quilts made by Mom kept us reasonably comfortable during cold winter nights! Drinking water was supplied from a well on the back porch and the outdoor toilet was supplemented by "chamber pots" when bad weather made the downhill trek too difficult. *I'll avoid references to Sears catalogs or corn cobs but acknowledge the family had no money for toilet paper! Enough said about that!*

*I digress to make a few comments about one of Mother's brothers (my Uncle Willie Mitchell) who was always an inspiration to me. He was an intellectual person in a community comprised largely of poorly educated farm people. Obviously, he earned a relatively small salary as postmaster at this tiny village. However, since many people at that time were earning nothing, Uncle Willie's guaranteed salary and intelligence allowed him to become a wealthy landowner (at least in our thinking). He used his money wisely to buy farm land at tax and foreclosure sales. His small grocery business in the same building that contained the Kings Creek Post Office supplemented his income but I was told that he lost money when he extended credit to people unable to pay him back.*

*Extremely knowledgeable and an avid reader, he was the sage of the community and willing to answer questions asked by local residents without being patronizing. He played the violin (not fiddle), and was an accomplished chess and checker player.*

*He was a truly unusual man for our backward area and was a real asset to the community. But the best thing about him was that he was an extremely nice human being. I was very flattered to learn that Uncle Willie was keeping a file of newspaper articles with my by-lines as he followed my career while I was a reporter in South Carolina. Unfortunately, I didn't follow his lead and must rely on a fading memory.*

# CHAPTER 11
## Why the H.H. White Family Ate So Well!

AS I MENTIONED, although we lacked money we did not suffer from lack of good food even during the worst of the depression. In fact, relatives living in town visited us frequently to get a square meal of Mom's famous biscuits, "macaroni pie," fried chicken, and at least six vegetable dishes for each Sunday dinner. For dessert, she would serve home baked pies and cakes.

I will always remember her rhubarb and strawberry pie which was a big favorite with everyone when these ingredients were in season. She also made apple pies which were proclaimed delicious by everyone but me. *I had given myself a terrible stomach ache by eating green apples as a youngster. This caused me to dislike apples in any form. In fact, I never got over my dislike of apples until my wife, Gloria, cajoled me into trying a Red Delicious apple cut in half, the seeds removed, and each side spread with peanut butter and raisins. She called this a "walking salad" and it walked right onto my list of good and healthy foods.*

The family accomplished this abundance of food mainly because of Dad's insistence that we plant a very large garden (of an acre or more) every year. Dad knew we needed to do this to feed our large family, relatives, and other visitors. At Dad's insistence, we planted and harvested more than we could possibly consume at the time, so that the "extra" could be used as "barter" to obtain things we needed but did not grow on our farm. In addition, Mom canned food so we would have plenty to eat over winter and until the next season's crops were available. Not all local farmers had the energy and desire to follow the example of my parents and suffered more from the depression than we did.

Dad also made sure that we always had the necessary livestock and implements to be a small but successful farm. Our livestock included two mules, two milk cows, dozens of "yard" chickens and 6 or 7 pigs. *And of course we always had several hound dogs which helped us obtain game meat.* We were always adequately equipped with the plows, wagons, scythes, hoes, shovels and other needed farm implements and Dad kept them in good shape.

Although most of our meat was supplied by the pigs, chickens and whatever game we could obtain, about every other year we would raise a calf to yearling size.

When it was butchered, we would have enough veal to provide a feast for the entire family. *By way of explanation, we obtained the calf when one of the milk cows had to be bred so she would continue to provide milk.*

It was my job to take care of this little calf until it reached the age to be butchered. I had to learn not to get too attached to the calf knowing what its eventual fate would be. I learned my lesson in that regard when Dad killed and butchered my "pet" pig causing me much heartache.

We raised a large variety of garden vegetables which included: tomatoes, all types of melons, strawberries, peanuts, rhubarb, peppers, cucumbers, beans, peas, sweet corn, and onions, as well as several cruciferous vegetables such as mustard greens, collard greens, turnip greens and cabbage, sweet and Irish potatoes, i.e., almost anything Mom wanted for the kitchen. We also grew field corn, wheat, oats, and cane. The latter enabled us not only to have feed for our livestock but to provide us with our own flour, corn meal, grits, and cane (which was made into molasses used to embellish Mom's excellent biscuits).

The harvested and shelled grains (shelling was a job for the whole family) were taken to grain mills and ground to Dad's specifications. Since we had little or no cash, the mill owners would keep an agreed upon amount of the grain as payment for their services. Obtaining molasses from the cane was an exciting event for a young boy. We would cut and strip the cane stalks, load them on the wagon pulled by our two mules and take them to the cane mill. *I would usually ride on top of the cane and suck enough of the sweet juice during the ride to make myself sick before we arrived at the cane mill.*

At the mill, the cane stalks were fed into an extractor, and the juice was captured in a large vat. A single mule walking around in a circle supplied the power to extract the juice. Once the extraction process was complete, the juice was poured into large cooking vats heated by logs. Then the process of boiling the juice began. The vats would be continually stoked with wood to keep them boiling hot, and the liquid would be stirred often with large wood stirrers and the scum on top removed.

This work would usually start before dark and continue for several hours. As the juice began to thicken to the texture of molasses, the remaining, "clean skimmings" would be removed from the surface and women family members would make a special "taffy" from these "skimmings."

It may not sound appetizing but after hours of working with the cane and juice, the resulting "taffy" made a very tasty, very sweet candy. And enough molasses would be produced to last until the next crop of cane was grown and processed. As with the grains, the operator of the cane mill would be paid with a share of delicious molasses which he could sell to cover his expenses.

Our only source of "cash" came from cotton, Dad's favorite crop. I recall that we had a five acre cotton allotment at that time. *Note: Even back then the government determined how many acres of cotton and tobacco farmers were allowed to plant!* A five acre allotment may sound like it would provide more than enough cash, since we raised almost all our own food. I will explain the fallacy of that thinking in the next chapter.

# CHAPTER 12
## Cherokee County Soil "Farmed to Death"

IT SHOULD BE pointed out that by the 1930's much Cherokee County farmland had been "farmed to death." When we arrived at the Mitchell Place and started preparing the fields for planting, we found the soil consisted primarily of red clay and rocks--not ideal for growing the things we were going to plant. The only fertile acreage available to us was some "bottom land" adjacent to Cherokee Creek. We utilized most of that for growing oats, wheat, and corn--essential food crops for us and the livestock.

Because of the larger size of the upland acreage and the intensive nature of the work required to grow and harvest it, we planted the cotton on the rocky acreage nearer the house. As the first year's cotton crop was starting to mature, we found out that in addition to the bad soil, we had another battle to fight. The dreaded cotton boll weevil had become a serious problem in Cherokee County. Despite our best efforts, these insects took a heavy toll on our cotton crop.

Controlling cotton boll weevils was difficult (nearly impossible) at that time because insecticides to combat them were not yet available. Hoeing the inhospitable soil to remove weeds was a necessary but difficult job in the rocky soil where we were growing cotton--already a labor intensive crop. *I'll never forget the shock to the elbow when hoeing around cotton stalks and the hoe strikes a hidden rock, causing sparks to fly and the arm to hurt longer.*

Picking cotton was a skill I never mastered. Dad was one of the best, fastest cotton pickers in our area. And he was by far the best one in the family. He would begin picking two rows at a time while the rest of us would pick a single row. Dad would gradually move ahead and finish two rows before any of the rest of us finished one. At the end of day, Dad would have picked 300 or more pounds while the other grownups would be lucky to have picked 200 pounds. *I never was able to pick more than 100 pounds in a day.*

Despite Dad's efforts and hard work, an acre of this weakened soil would produce only half a bale of cotton. Compare that to some other areas of the U.S., where cotton farms can run to hundreds, even thousands of acres. *By using modern farming methods this rich, fertilized and irrigated soil (e.g. in California and the Mississippi Delta) can produce two or more bales per acre!*

In our case, after the cotton ginner got his share for removing the seeds and baling the cotton and Uncle Willie received half of the remaining net, very little actual cash remained for the White family's backbreaking work. But Dad's love of raising cotton remained as long as the family was capable of planting, hoeing, picking, and hauling the cotton to the cotton gin.

From descriptions above, it should be obvious that Dad was a strong and independent individual (who scared the dickens out of me as a youngster). As tough as he was, he could be a "softy" where the female family members were concerned.

And I never heard him utter a cross word to Mother. Although the boys were careful around him, the girls could tease and pick at him. They never understood why the boys (especially this one!) had any fear of him.

My lack of closeness to Dad was probably magnified because I sensed that he was disappointed in me. It was obvious to me that he would have preferred an outdoor, hunter/fisher type boy to one who sat in the corner and read books. It seemed to bother him when he saw me reading a book. Obviously, he felt I was wasting time when I could be doing something useful with my hands. I remained undeterred, however. *At night, I would sometimes wait until Mom turned off the oil lamp near my bed and then after everyone else was asleep, I would light a candle and continue to read.*

*Apparently my feeling that Dad had always been disappointed in me was not just my child's imagination. When I was grown up and a college graduate, I was told by a relative that Dad was disappointed when he learned that I had given up my school teaching job to become a newspaper writer at about half the salary I made as a school teacher. Dad was said to exclaim: "Jim just can't do anything right!"*

Of course as I progressed in the newspaper world, my salary quickly surpassed a school teacher's salary and I was doing something I was good at and loved. Dad never understood how anyone could make a living putting words on paper. I knew he was somewhat pleased that I was able to obtain the "respectable" job of a school teacher. *Then I blew it by leaving that profession to become a frivolous newspaper reporter.* ·

# CHAPTER 13
## Trips to Blacksburg Exciting!

RETURNING TO EARLIER memories, one of the things I remember most vividly about my farm boy days were the Saturdays when we would load up the wagon and travel to the town of Blacksburg about five miles away. Once there, Dad would visit the grocery stores and barter our fresh, surplus farm products (e.g., eggs, milk, butter, ham, canned or fresh vegetables, etc.) for things we couldn't or didn't grow, such as coffee, cheese, tea, sugar, salt and the like--not to mention the macaroni that Mom used to make her wonderful "macaroni pie" (macaroni and cheese to you more sophisticated folks).

While Dad would go from store to store bartering, the rest of us would be entertained by an array of street sellers (called "barkers") selling patent medicines and other interesting items. We never bought any of these things but it was fun to listen to the banter. To us, the town square in Blacksburg had a "circus like" atmosphere in those days! It was real entertainment for me.

In the 1920's and 1930's, Blacksburg was a thriving small town with two movie theaters, a large, active railroad terminal, and two resort hotels centered around mineral springs and a small mountain called Whitaker Mountain. Earlier, the Blacksburg area had an operating gold mine and enough iron ore mines to gain the name, "Iron City." None of those mines were operational in my lifetime. However, a Barite Mine (or Bartese as some called it) located on the east side of the railroad tracks near the Kings Creek Post Office was fully operational then.

An important subject barely discussed by my family or friends was racial discrimination in the U.S., but especially in our state of South Carolina. Although racism was much worse at the time I was growing up, I was largely unaware of the racial problems which existed all around me. It wasn't a subject of discussion in our neighborhood. I did sometimes wonder about a few things but they didn't seem to be major issues in that area and time. For example, I did think it strange that on our visits to Blacksburg, Negroes walking down a sidewalk moved into the street to make room for white people.

I also wondered why my Negro playmates went to different schools from me but I rarely heard racial issues per se discussed by my family and our neighborhood. Of course, if such matters were covered by the local media, I probably would have missed them since we couldn't afford such luxuries as newspapers, magazines, and a working radio.

When I was older and entered some public places in town, e.g., to get my driver's license, I also observed that Negroes and whites had different drinking fountains but just thought that this was some sort of peculiar custom that both races preferred. I didn't know at the time that these strange customs were practiced primarily in the South. Because our nearest neighbor was a Negro family, it was natural for these children to be my playmates. Although I had heard Dad occasionally use the "N" word, he admonished us children never to use that word when addressing a Negro. And he told us that we were to treat Negroes with the same respect we did white people. And we did.

The first time I witnessed outright racism displayed in its rawest form occurred one day while our Kings Creek School was taking its lunch time break. I was standing with a group of fellow students when three Negro boys walked past. They were not bothering anyone, but one of the older, more aggressive boys at the school decided these Negro boys had no right to be walking up "our road" and "past our school." The white student decided it was up to him to teach these black boys a lesson.

So, the white student chased after and confronted the three boys. I didn't overhear the conversation but could see that my fellow student was spoiling for a fight. Although I could see they were reluctant, one of the Negro boys about the same size finally accepted the challenge to fight. They squared off and the white student led with a "haymaker" right. The Negro youngster avoided the big swing, which was supposed to end the fight, and peppered his opponent several times to the face. The white boy swung and missed again and received several more blows to the face.

It quickly became obvious that the white boy had made a mistake in seeking this fight. *Although I felt a little guilty about not supporting my fellow student, I found myself secretly cheering for the Negro boy because I thought he had every right to walk past our school on a public road.* Therefore I was not bothered much by the fact that he was giving my friend and fellow student a severe beating. After a few more swings and misses, the white boy called it quits and the Negro boys continued on up the road. I was pleased that none of the other students, who greatly outnumbered the Negro boys, offered to help their classmate.

When I arrived at the Kings Creek School, I had had no experience fighting and did not desire any such experience. However, on the first day I was there I was challenged to fight by a classmate who was a year older but about my size. Although not in the mood to fight, I "went through the motions" and was quickly thrown to the ground. This became an almost daily occurrence with the boy who later became my "best buddy," Bascomb Love. I saw that he dominated the boys his age but that he didn't challenge the much older and bigger boys who only attended school when not needed for work on the farm. Some of these boys were as much as 16 years old and tough as nails from their farm work. None of the younger boys, including Bascomb, messed with them.

I quickly realized that Bascomb needed to be recognized as the toughest kid in our class and needed to "throw me down" almost daily. I soon took the role of "peace-maker" at the school and didn't mind it much as long as it made Bascomb happy since I suffered no physical or emotional injury. We went through this routine with me pre-tending to resist but really just wanting to "get it over with" so we could resume play. Neither of us ever got angry since I understood that Bascomb needed the reputation of the toughest kid in our class and I didn't. We soon became constant companions.

# CHAPTER 14

## Our Farm Labor Force Continues to Decline

RETURNING TO THE White farm labor situation, when we moved to the Mitchell place to sharecrop for Uncle Willie, our labor force was already pretty small and about to get smaller. Oldest brother Howard had married and moved out of the house as had two older sisters, Isabel and Faye. Soon afterward, the next oldest boy, Robert, married Lena Randall of Grover, NC, and moved away. This left Dad, Frank and me to do the field work. Sisters Edith and Nell were still around but did field work only on an emergency basis, i.e. to "save" a crop. When they worked in the field, they wore large bonnets and extra clothing to protect against sunburn. Tanned skin on young ladies was not in vogue at that time!

Mother did not work in the field but stayed busy cooking and canning vegetables to last through the winter. Along with a multitude of other duties, she swept and mopped the floors of the house and even swept the yard around the exterior of the house. *Most farm people did not usually plant or maintain much shrubbery or lawns at that time.* Mom also did most of the family's laundry which was no small job when you consider that all she had to work with was a washboard and tub. And most of us were doing dirty farm work which increased her work load.

When none of us children was available and laundering needed to be done, Mom would lower a bucket into the well and then pull the full bucket of water to the surface before bringing it into the house. Once inside, she heated the water in the kitchen stove's hot water tank. When the water reached the temperature she wanted, she used it to hand wash clothing and bed linens in a washtub on the floor of the kitchen. After using a "washboard" to help her clean the clothes, she then carried the wet clothes outside to hang on lines to dry.

The washtub at our house was kept busy. In addition to its primary role in washing fabrics, it also served as our "bath tub" when we had our Saturday baths! In case you're wondering why we only took one tub bath a week, you need to know just how difficult and time consuming this task was back then. For example we had to follow the same procedure mentioned above in filling the tub with cold water. And while this was being done, more water was being heated on the wood stove and some of it added to the cold water so that every family member could take a warm bath.

This process had to be repeated several times when the tub bathing began. With several people needing to use this one tub, both fresh and hot water had to be added several times before everyone had finished taking their baths. As the youngest child, I was last in line and by then the water was not squeaky clean. Mom would add lots of fresh and hot water to try to compensate. The time and effort needed to take a tub bath led to lots of "sponge baths," which could be done in a fraction of the time and effort and was usually satisfactory for farm folks.

In those days, farm people were not as fastidious as city residents who had running water, bath tubs and showers. And this was reflected in other ways, e.g., dental care. Like many farm families of that period, we did not have a toothbrush or tooth paste in the house. I don't recall any of us ever going to the dentist while at home. The fact is, most dentists back then were mere "tooth pullers" and we could take care of that necessity by using a long string fastened to a doorknob. I remember my Dad doing that when I was losing my "baby teeth." *I met my first dentist in Boot Camp where the Navy dentist put in 11 fillings during my first visit with him. You can bet that I never again neglected my teeth.*

While on the farm, my sisters made their own toothbrushes and tooth paste. They would ask one of their brothers to cut small branches from either hickory or beech trees and bring them back to the house. The girls then used a sharp knife to make small splits in one end of the stick to make the semblance of a tooth brush. And they made a tooth paste concoction by mixing salt and baking soda.

With these homemade items, the girls would be able to present nice, white toothy smiles until they married and could afford real toothbrushes and paste. The male members of our family, along with most poor Southern males and some females, did not want to go to all this trouble and thus became early wearers of "false teeth." I never saw either of my parents with their natural teeth.

As for farm work, people who have never lived on a farm have no idea of the hard work required to prepare the soil for planting, weeding, and harvesting of farm products. On our farm this work eventually had to be done by Dad, Frank, and me.

In addition to the field crops, we had to do similar work with the large garden. We also had to do one more onerous (and sometimes odorous) chore: collect livestock manure and use it for fertilizer. And finally, it took time and work to butcher several hogs and process them into ham, bacon, and sausage--the only way we had to preserve the meat for the following months. And if this work was not done carefully and properly, the meat spoiled and had to be thrown away.

When we moved to the Mitchell home place, I was still young and not much help as a field hand although I tried. My efforts to hoe and pick cotton on land that consisted primarily of red clay and rocks must have been pitiful. And the summer heat bearing down on my red haired skin caused bad sunburn as well as painful headaches.

After seeing how difficult this work was and the painful effect it was having on me, Dad decided that my best contributions to the family lay outside the field. He assigned me several jobs that needed to be done on a regular basis. One of these was to take care of the livestock by keeping them fed and watered. I had to milk one (and sometimes two) cows in the early mornings and late afternoons. One feeding job included "slopping" the hogs. I was also expected to gather eggs from the hen house(s) and bring them into the house. One of the toughest of these jobs was drawing water from the well and carrying it to the livestock watering troughs.

With Mom's supervision I was also responsible for harvesting fresh vegetables from the garden, carrying things that needed to be cooled back and forth to the spring, and chasing down and killing chickens needed for the table.

# CHAPTER 15

## Start of My Farm Work Day

EVERY MORNING BEFORE daylight, Dad woke me up to start my chores, beginning with the first milking of the dairy cow (or cows). Dad himself would begin starting fires in the fireplace and wood stove. And if we were running short of firewood, he would go outside and begin splitting and chopping firewood while the rest of the family except me slept.

Because of the distance to the barn (about the length of a football field), I would assemble and carry everything I needed (usually a lantern and two pails--when both cows were giving milk). It was fairly easy going downhill to the barn with empty buckets, but difficult to go back up the hill carrying full buckets and the lantern without spilling any milk, but I managed it.

I began the milking process by properly positioning the cow (or cows) to be milked. This was especially important to my peace of mind for this reason: the barn backed up to a wooded area which partially blocked the sight of a swamp just beyond. Unusual for Upstate South Carolina, this swamp contained cypress trees and their "knees," strange looking appendages rising from above the surface *(similar to what you might see in old Turner Classic black and white movies). In the dark this scene could be pretty scary to a kid.*

By placing the cows just right, I was able to milk while keeping an eye on the trees and swamp. I wanted to be able to spot any wild animals (and of course "mad dogs") hiding in the swamp and waiting to pounce on me! Fear, caused by my vivid imagination, the darkness, and the mysterious swamp which lay just beyond the tree line, motivated me to become very fast and efficient at milking. And I wasted little time in gathering up the lantern and pail or pails containing fresh milk, and hustling back up the hill to Mom's kitchen.

The swamp, which seemed so foreboding in the dark, was fed by a large above ground spring which we also used to preserve foods that needed to be kept cool. Since we had no refrigerator and couldn't afford to buy ice for the ice box, Mom needed some way to keep milk, butter, and foods such as melons cool. She also used the deep well on the back porch to keep some things cool by lowering a bucket with as much food as it would hold. Since the bucket would not hold much, I was kept pretty busy carrying items to the spring and then back as needed.

I actually enjoyed spending time at the spring in broad daylight when the swamp was clearly visible and not so forbidding. In addition to the sealed food items I placed in the water, the spring itself contained a variety of live critters such as crawdads, small frogs, minnows, and other interesting creatures which I could observe and play with. Also, the tree-shaded area around the spring was also a nice place to escape the cruel summer heat.

# CHAPTER 16
## The Swamp's Near Fatal Attraction

AS INTRIGUING AS I found the swamp during daylight hours, this bucolic scene turned out to be a near "fatal attraction" for me. Although we knew the swamp was infested with mosquitoes, we thought of them primarily as an annoyance when we sat on the front porch to cool off. We had no idea that they carried a virus which could be fatal. Soon after we moved to the Mitchell place one or more of their bites sent my temperature soaring.

When Dr. Miller arrived to diagnose my ailment and start treating me, I was already going into a semi-coma that lasted a full week. My ailment turned out to be malaria. I was told later that he began treating me with quinine, at that time about the only treatment available for this serious ailment. When I regained full consciousness

I was craving ice cream and someone brought me a dish of strawberry flavored ice cream. Although I relished the ice cream, it made me sick and I couldn't tolerate that flavor for many years.

The malaria also seemed to affect my stomach adversely for a long time after I had otherwise recovered. I had trouble keeping food down and Mother went to great lengths trying to find food that would not upset my stomach. She usually succeeded by feeding me her homemade biscuits filled with cheese which my sensitive stomach would usually accept. *I still like cheese biscuits although none compares to the ones Mom made and fed me.*

As a grownup, I also learned that having had malaria made me an unacceptable blood donor until I was too old to donate blood. Since recovering from malaria as a boy, I have had only one serious reoccurrence. That was just after the completion of desert training in California while serving in a Navy amphibious group during World War II. (More about that later).

# CHAPTER 17
## My Least Liked Farm Duty

TO ANYONE WHO has read this far, it will be no surprise that the duty I dreaded the most was killing a chicken for dinner. Sometimes, when no one else was around I was forced to do this job. I tried the two most common methods of administering the coup de grace, but I was so squeamish that neither worked well for me. First, I tried chopping their heads off but found it hard to hold the chicken in place while using a hatchet to sever the head. I also tried ringing their necks as I had seen the adults do but never got the hang of it. And even when successful, I could not bear the sight of the chicken jumping around before it died.

Other than my fear of dogs (except our hounds) my sensitivity where animals were concerned was well known within the family. I well remember two events illustrating that point. One case involved a young chicken that ran from our yard into the road where it was hit by a car passing by. I saw what happened and ran to the injured chicken which had suffered the loss of an eye, a broken wing, and a large hole in its craw among other injuries.

The chicken had too many less serious injuries to count. Family members assumed we would finish off and make a meal of this chicken but I was determined to save her. I borrowed my Mother's needle and thread to sew up the hole in the craw, fashioned a splint for the wing, and bandaged the empty eye socket. I sterilized all of the chicken's injuries with kerosene, the all-in-one sterilizer at our house.

The chicken not only lived but became a pet that followed me around like a puppy. This idyllic scene lasted for several months but one day the chicken started running around in circles and dropped dead! Thank goodness, no one suggested we eat that chicken!

The second event involved a sickly, runt pig that required a lot of personal care to survive. I happily provided the little runt with that special care and attention which eventually let the little runt (I named Henry) grow into a large, handsome specimen. But he still remained a pet to me. Then as "butchering time" approached, I became concerned with what Dad would do about my pet pig. Surely, he would not shoot and cut the throat of my pet!

Finally, I got up the nerve to ask Dad what was going to happen with Henry. With no hesitation, he said: "Why of course, we'll butcher him like we do with all of the pigs." When I tried to protest, he said: "I warned you not to name or make a pet of any of our animals. I told you they are part of our food supply."

As the fateful day and hour approached, I walked far away from the house hoping not to hear any sounds of what was about to happen. Ordinarily, Dad would need only one shot with his trusty .22 long rifle to kill an animal. But when he shot my pet pig, I could have heard Henry's screams a mile away. And he had to shoot the pig two more times before he stopped screaming. By this time I had run as far as I could, trying unsuccessfully to get out of "hearing range."

When I decided it was time to return home, Dad had left my pet pig hanging by his hind legs to "bleed out" after slitting his throat. Dad was kind enough not to ask me to participate in any of the butchering process for any of the pigs that season. I eventually got over the hurt but did not eat any more pork that year. I didn't know whether or not the meat on the table was Henry!

By now you have probably discerned that I wasn't really cut out to be a farm boy. Most of my friends had no difficulty in killing animals. And they seemed free of worry and other insecurities that beset me as far as I could tell. In any event, love of reading helped me escape the farm and avoid working in cotton mills as so many of my friends and relatives did at that time. And despite the bad schooling I received early in my life, I credit reading as the reason I did well in high school, college, and graduate school.

# CHAPTER 18
## A Secret Not to Be Shared

SOMETHING UNUSUAL HAPPENED one night when my siblings were all asleep. A light sleeper myself, I heard a whispered conversation between my parents. Dad was usually too tired from his heavy work schedule to engage in much conversation before going to sleep. However, that evening my parents were speaking in a whisper about our family financial situation. It was obvious that the children were not supposed to hear this conversation.

The reason I could hear it was that I slept in the hall closet which was adjacent to the front (or living) room where my parents slept. Their soft whispered words came through the uninsulated wall clearly to my young, sharp ears. I heard my Dad whisper to Mom that the family's cash money totaled only $1.65.

Although I knew nothing about finances, I immediately sensed that this was bad news. But since I was not supposed to hear it, I never mentioned it to anyone. Neither my parents nor siblings ever knew I had overheard my parents' conversation. This concern about our financial situation by my father spoke volumes to me. It gave me the answers to questions I was afraid to ask about why we kept moving from one bad house to a worse one. In retrospect, I probably should have shared this information rather than tucking it inside my young, sensitive psyche. Instead I remained silent and hid even more behind the covers of the books I read.

My insecurities soon after these revelations became more obvious. They were reflected when Mom would send me to Uncle Willie's store to make a small purchase for her. I worried the entire time to the store and back that I had misunderstood her instructions and had bought the wrong thing. I don't recall ever making that mistake but remained fearful I might. *Had I made a mistake, Mom would not have reprimanded me but I would not have been able to live with myself, knowing our financial situation.*

When I was 10 years old "Santa Claus" brought me a bike for Christmas. It was old and worn out but I appreciated the bike as much as if it we were a new, shiny one. Since we had little money, I suspect Dad had traded something for the bike. It was so old and in such really bad shape it would surely have ended up in the junk yard if Dad had not rescued it. The worst of the bike's problems was that after I rode it a short distance, the front wheel would start to rub against the frame. This would require me to get off the bike, loosen the front wheel assembly with a wrench, then realign the wheel and tighten the front assembly as tightly as I could. Sometimes I had to repeat this procedure two or three times on the roughly three mile round-trip to Kings Creek so I began carrying the wrench with me any time I rode the bike.

Despite its flaws, I was proud to have that bike. It gave me freedom I didn't have before. I was the only one of us children to ever have a bike. This fact caused some resentment from an older brother who said I was being spoiled badly as the "baby" of the family. Santa Claus had never brought him a bike.

Perhaps he had a right to be jealous since the usual Christmas present for each of us was a stocking stuffed with some candy or other sweets, nuts, a couple of apples (and when we could afford it) an orange. Oranges were precious commodities back then and we felt fortunate to have one of these in the Christmas stocking. When children at that time were asked what they wanted for Christmas, the refrain was invariably: "Fruit, nuts, and candy."

Other than the concern that I might make a mistake, going to Kings Creek on my bicycle could be an adventure in itself. Thinking about it brings back many memories of my visits to Uncle Willie's Store and visits with my friend Bascomb Love. When I visited Uncle Willie, I always spent time with his children (my two cousins, Hayes and William Morrow Mitchell). The latter two were the only relatives I could (or wanted to) visit by bike on a regular basis. This gave me a chance to listen to Hayes as she practiced the piano, my favorite musical instrument. Also since they had a radio that worked, I would sometimes be able to listen to my favorite program, "The Lone Ranger," all the way through!

I was awed by the finery I experienced at Uncle Willie's house. Their home was a fine, large custom built brick house. Their furnishings, including the piano, were of a quality I could only dream about. Naturally their house had electricity, running water and central heat, as well as a refrigerator and electric stove. They had a maid to clean and cook for them and a gardener to care for their spacious lawn. I had difficulty even imagining living in such luxury.

Hayes and William Morrow's mother, Aunt Parmelia Mitchell, would often serve them ice cream from their refrigerator/freezer. The first time I was there at ice cream time I was offered a dish. But Mom had taught me that I should not appear too eager to accept something, so I declined, hoping my aunt would insist. Aunt Parmelia apparently was not familiar with this rule, and assumed I didn't like ice cream. She never offered me ice cream again and I was too shy to ask for it. Actually, ice cream was always my very favorite dessert and I never had enough of it until I was grown and on my own. So, I would sit there and try not to drool while Hayes and William Morrow relished their ice cream.

*I actually had such a craving for ice cream that if we had the smallest amount of snow or ice, I would gather it up in a container, fill a quart jar with milk, eggs, vanilla flavor and sugar, place the jar inside the container along with the ice or snow and salt. I would then begin to turn the smaller jar with my bare hands until the liquid had developed some icing. By that time both my hands would be frozen but I would enjoy that concoction anyway.*

# CHAPTER 19
## Many Memories of Kings Creek

OTHER THAN THE ice cream fiasco, and my fear of making a mistake, my memories of those trips to Kings Creek are largely pleasant. I recall one memorable visit to Uncle Willie's store during Christmas season, when a strange man and his little boy walked into the store. I watched in amazement when the father, with a big flourish, handed the boy a quarter and told him he could spend the whole quarter on candy for his Christmas present.

The boy went from one end of the candy counter to the other asking Uncle Willie for "one of this, two of that," etc. *I was stunned (and jealous) when I saw the large bag of candy that boy carried out of the store! At that time, lots of the candy sold for less than a penny. I had never seen anyone with that much store bought candy in my life.*

Another trip to Kings Creek and back was also memorable in a different way. As I was riding down the dirt road to town, a strange, large dog ran out and bit my right leg. Since I was going downhill I pedaled faster and the dog soon tired of the chase. I feared the dog would show up at the roadside on my way back but I never saw it again. I didn't report this small bite to the family but the incident did nothing to remove my fear of dogs. Most importantly, my bicycle did not require a stop for repairs on the way back!

Although work was hard and money non-existent, the White family did have its share of fun. There were Wednesday night church prayer meetings where the older boys and girls got together—and did not always come home with their parents. And as mentioned, we seemed to have lots of visitors, which sometimes provided me with playmates. The only musical instrument in our home, an old, worn-out hand-cranked gramophone provided music for the girls in the family to practice dancing in the little parlor. They had to make do with two or three scratchy records, but almost any record was better than playing rook or listening to "mad dog" stories.

The family also looked forward to visits by Mom's older brother, Uncle Sam Mitchell, who often stopped by the house to visit and have a hot cup of coffee. We loved to have Uncle Sam, a candy wholesaler, come visit us for several reasons. First of all, he traveled his candy route in a shiny Buick automobile and we liked to look at and admire it; second, he always had interesting stories to tell; and third, before leaving he would present each of us with a sample of candy he was delivering to retail outlets. The samples left by Uncle Sam were the only "store bought" candy we ever had while living on the farm.

Uncle Sam and his wife, Aunt Rena, owned small cafés, first in Gaffney and later in Blacksburg. Apparently Uncle Sam did not appreciate the restaurant business as much as his wife because I never saw him behind the counter and he continued his candy business. Aunt Rena was a wonderful cook and seemed to appreciate all aspects of the business, both cooking and waitressing. I had my first restaurant hamburger at the Blacksburg café. Aunt Rena had fixed the hamburger for someone who failed to pick it up and she gave it to me. Although it was cold, I thought this burger was the best thing I had tasted in my life! Fast food was virtually unknown at that time.

One final story about Uncle Sam: He had such a love of coffee that before making a trip in his car to service his candy business, he would boil a pot of coffee to the point that its consistency was a thick syrup. He would pour this very strong coffee into a jar and take it with him, along with his supply of candy. He would periodically stop, pour a little of the syrup into a cup, add some hot water, and voila, he would have his coffee. He may have been the inventor of instant coffee! The word (that I cannot confirm) was that if he could not find hot water, he would steal some from the radiator of his car. *That was before we had antifreeze in car radiators!* Uncle Sam had a reputation for liking lots of coffee, fancy cars and pretty women. He was truly a character compared to other members of the Mitchell family.

My memories of the little village of Kings Creek remain vivid to this day. I cherish the time I spent with my best friend, Bascomb Love, as well as the time I spent with two especially close cousins, William Morrow and Hayes Mitchell. Cousin Hayes always seemed to be practicing the piano. I really enjoyed listening to her play and that may be responsible for my love of the piano. *Although we are both in our 90's, when I visit her at her home these days she still plays for me just as she did when we were youngsters. In fact, she may be playing better now than she did back then. When I asked her to explain this, she said: "I'm playing for my own pleasure now."*

*Unfortunately she and I are the only surviving first cousins from the Mitchell side of our family. Her younger brother William Morrow died of cancer at a young age. The last time I visited him he summoned me close to his death bed and urged: "Jimmy, please get your prostate checked often." This turned out to be prophetic since that deadly disease later threatened my life. Bascomb and I became re-acquainted in our mid-twenties when I was a reporter for the Rock Hill Evening Herald during the period 1952-54. That story will be expanded in a later part of this manuscript.*

# CHAPTER 20
## Kings Creek School Experience

THE KINGS CREEK School was a far cry from Holly Grove School. Although it consisted of a nice, large building, it had only a single teacher for around 40 children ranging in age from 6 to 16 years. Classes were held in one large room heated by a wood stove. And it had girl and boy "outside toilets." On days when the weather was nice (i.e. heat was not needed) the teacher would let "well behaved" students go to the unheated library to read or study while she taught a class. I was always in the "well behaved" category and I read every book in the library, many of them several times.

In theory, sending well behaved students not having a lesson at the time allowed the teacher to devote more time to fewer students. In actuality, it often failed to work as planned. Left unsupervised, one student (often Bascomb) would start something and the rest would erupt in laughter. The poor, beleaguered teacher would then rush in to calm things down. Often, we would all be marched back to the big room for the rest of the day.

Although I was only nine when we moved to Kings Creek I was advanced scholastically over most of the Kings Creek students. This was probably due to my attendance at a better school (Holly Grove) and a well developed, even voracious appetite for reading. Since many of the older students had difficulty reading and understanding their bookwork, they began asking me to help them with their classroom assignments even though I was years younger than they were.

Many older children were still in grammar school, although some were as old as age 16. These poor students were not expected to ever graduate from grammar school. This was not because they were necessarily dumb. Their parents only allowed them to attend school part of the year. When the time for planting, tending, and harvesting began, their parents pulled them out of school to work on the farm. Thus, these youngsters had no expectation of ever graduating from grammar school, much less attending high school.

Sadly, some of them barely learned to read and write. In retrospect, that might help explain their occasional misbehavior. No doubt some of this misbehavior may have been caused by these students' belief that they would never be able to escape the life they now endured. This situation with the older boys posed a danger to early maturing girls at the school. They sometimes became a target for boys advanced sexually but not educationally.

My need to find reading material led me to an exciting discovery one day at the Mitchell place. For some reason I was exploring the tight crawl space underneath the house and spotted what looked like the page of a book buried in the soil. Voila, when I dug it out with my hands, I discovered it was a western adventure magazine! Something I had never seen before. Overjoyed by this unexpected discovery, I almost excavated the underpinnings of the house searching for more copies. I eventually found three or four more magazines.

Of course I eventually learned that these magazines were considered "trashy" by those more sophisticated than I. But because of the scarcity of reading material at our house and school, I cherished this trash like gold.

Although Mother encouraged my love of reading, as already indicated, Dad did not appreciate this trait. He was a thorough-going outdoorsman. If he had any spare time, which was rare, he spent it hunting and fishing. He did everything he could to make an outdoorsman out of me but was unsuccessful. Once when we were rabbit hunting, he handed me his beautiful 20 gauge double barreled Parker shotgun and told me to shoot the next rabbit we saw. Almost immediately, a rabbit running from our hunting dogs came into view. I raised the gun and fired, killing the rabbit.

Being successful in shooting a shotgun thrilled me at first. But when I saw the rabbit up close, I almost cried and had bad dreams about the little animal for months afterward. I vowed never to shoot another rabbit and never did.

On another occasion, I went with some grownups, including Dad and my brother-in-law, R.B. Turner, on a "frog gigging" expedition at night. I was o.k. until the grownups cut the legs off the frogs and tossed their still live bodies aside without killing them. I thought it was cruel to do this but assumed the frogs would die quickly. Then a couple of nights later, we went back to the same area for more "frog gigging." I immediately spotted some of the poor frogs from our last visit there. With severed back legs they were still crawling around with their front legs. That ended my "frog gigging" experience.

# CHAPTER 21
## Some Strange Happenings at School

ONE RECURRING INCIDENT that happened during breaks at the school provides another illustration of how cruel children can be. A very retarded boy (called Monkey) lived in a house close to the school. *This boy unfortunately did resemble a primate in his facial expressions and his walk.* Since he was not capable of school work, he had time on his hands. He spent much of this time building small re-creations of villages in a sandy area near his house. I suppose these were his visions of sand castles.

Some of the older school boys liked to "tease" Monkey by scattering grain among his village. Chickens in the boy's yard would rush to eat the grain and while scratching for more grain would destroy the boy's carefully constructed village. Meanwhile, the boys doing this mischief would be hiding behind bushes, laughing at the sight of Monkey trying to chase the chickens away. This laughter would cause Monkey to go into a rage; he would chase and throw rocks at the perpetrators. Several of us thought this was terrible but were not strong or brave enough to stop it from happening.

My second or third year at Kings Creek School, a young Clemson graduate who had just taken a job as Assistant Cherokee County Extension Agent visited our school to decide whether or not to establish a boys' 4-H Club there and began interviewing the older boys in an attempt to find one capable of serving as president of this club. I wasn't old enough to even join a 4-H Club at the time but he chose me, obviously ignoring the rules in order to find someone willing and able to keep the necessary club records!

Once the club was organized, the agent helped each of us select a project (such as raising a pig, calf, chickens, etc.), explained the rules, and helped me schedule some meetings and activities. The young Extension (or 4-H Club) Agent was supposed to return periodically to check on our progress. The rules called for selecting a school winner who would then compete at the County level. The County winner would be eligible to compete at various levels up to the State Championship level.

Since most of us were too poor to invest in a serious project I doubted that any of us would go beyond being the school winner. Dad told me he would buy (or trade for) a dozen small hatchlings (biddies) as my project. These were a fancy breed (I cannot recall the name). They were really beautiful and I looked forward to showing them off after they matured. We had facilities to raise the very young biddies but when they reached the size and age to be moved to a larger area, I had no place to move them except to the regular chicken house where they would be integrated with our backyard chickens. So that was where I moved them.

As it happened, the special biddies apparently were not nearly as hardy as our backyard varieties and they began to get sick and die. No doubt they had contracted a disease that our backyard chickens had developed immunity to that allowed them to survive. My little chickens began to die and pretty soon my little flock was gone. I really dreaded having to tell the 4-H agent about my failure. Not to matter, since the 4-H Club Agent, after establishing the club and helping us select a project, never again returned to the school. I never saw nor heard from him again for over 50 years! *(How I met that Agent, Mr. S.C. Stribling, after all that time is an interesting coincidence that I'll describe later).*

# CHAPTER 22
## A Chance to Learn How to Drive!

SOMETIME DURING THIS period (i.e., I was about 10-11 years old) Brother Frank came up with an idea that seemed to be a "win win" situation for both of us. Frank, who was six years older than I, drove the high school bus around the Kings Creek area, picking up students and driving them to Blacksburg High School. There wasn't a good place to park the bus near the house, so he had been parking it down the hill near the barn. He didn't mind the trek downhill to get the bus when the weather was nice. But he didn't enjoy walking down to the barn in the winter, starting the cold bus and sitting in it until it warmed up.

But he came up with an idea he thought would appeal to me. He thought (rightly) that I wouldn't mind braving any kind of weather in order to learn how to drive. So, he offered me a deal: he would teach me to drive if I would be willing to start driving the school bus from the barn area to the house. Without hesitating, I jumped at the offer! After all, I would have already been to the barn that morning to milk one or two cows. Going back to the barn to drive the bus up the hill seemed like an adventure rather than a chore to me.

Frank began the process of getting me ready to drive the bus by starting with the old Model T Ford we had acquired and which would actually run (at that time). He spent time teaching me the vagaries of driving the "T" which had the brake, accelerator, and clutch pedals in close proximity on the floor. Frank demonstrated how to drive the old Model T several times and I practiced the exercise with the engine off. Then he hand cranked the engine and told me to take a short test drive across our front yard. On my first attempt, I completely forgot the lessons. I mistook the clutch (or accelerator) pedal for the brake pedal and drove the car through a large bush.

That ended my driving lesson for that day. However, my nerves settled down and the lessons resumed the next day. After a few more lessons, I got the hang of driving the T and Frank decided I was ready to begin learning to drive the school bus. To my surprise, since the bus was much newer than our old car, it turned out easier to learn how to drive than our old Model T. Pretty soon I was making my second trip down the hill to the barn and starting the bus, which fortunately did not require hand cranking! Then I would drive it up the hill to Frank who would get on the "warmed up" bus and start his route.

During our lessons, I noted that Frank never "scraped" the gears when shifting. He taught me the same thing. However, after I began riding to Blacksburg on this same bus driven by another driver, he invariably "scraped" the gears when changing them. I still remember gritting my teeth in anticipation of the "scraping" sound. By the time I was 14, I was an accomplished driver and easily obtained my South Carolina driver's license. And I didn't "scrape" any gears when undergoing my driving test.

I thought then (and still think) that Frank was the best "big brother" in the world. In addition to teaching me how to drive, he also taught me much about life, e.g. "Fight back against a bully or he will pick on you forever." Frank explained: "Try to get in one good lick to the bully's nose. If you bloody his nose, he will leave you alone from then on." *Frank was absolutely right then but since some boys today are more inclined to use deadly force, rather than a punch to the nose, I'm not as sure as I once was.*

Frank also told me that I should protect others against bullies and I've always tried to practice that. *However, I learned that acting as a protector can sometimes get you in trouble. While I was in college and later after I graduated, I was involved in two serious fights for that reason. Both cases happened as a result of trying to save good friends from serious, perhaps even permanent injuries. After they had been beaten into submission, their attackers refused to stop. (More about these incidents later).*

As was the custom for country boys back then, my big brother also taught me to swim by tossing me into a "swimming hole" at Cherokee Creek. That may sound cruel by today's standards but Frank was always there to catch me if I started to sink. And I soon learned how to swim.

# CHAPTER 23
## Too Much Attention Added to Shyness

AS A YOUNGSTER, I was always concerned about the amount of unwanted attention I received from my "flaming red hair" and dreamed of having dark hair like my brother Frank so I could blend in with others. At that time, redheads were often singled out for merciless teasing--or at least I was. And forced to wear thick eye glasses from age 12. These teasers now had a chance to refer to both my "red hair" and my "Four Eyes." Frank's hair and skin were dark like Mother's and that's how I wanted to look. And of course he didn't need glasses.

I had successfully hidden my very bad eyesight from my parents for some time but my brother-in-law R.B. Turner gave me away. I had tried to overcome the fact that my distance vision was getting steadily worse by asking the teacher to move my seat closer and closer to the blackboard on a regular basis. Finally I was sitting on the front row and still having difficulty seeing the blackboard right in front of me. When I was 11 or 12 years old, R.B. took me to spend some time with him and my sister, Edith. They lived in Gastonia, NC, which I considered a major metropolis. At the time, R.B. was a newspaper distributor for The Charlotte News, an afternoon newspaper. He often invited me to ride with him to Charlotte to pick up the newspapers which he would drop off to groups of newspaper carriers on the way back to Gastonia. He drove a new Ford coupe and I thought he possibly had the most exciting job anyone could have.

On one of my visits to my sister's house, R.B. took me to a baseball game. He immediately noticed that I couldn't read the numbers on the batters' uniforms--even though we were seated near the batter's box. Upon our return to Kings Creek, R.B. told my parents about this and my secret was out. My parents took me to an eye doctor in Blacksburg who gave all of us a scare when he said my eyes were so bad that he might not be able to correct my vision. Fortunately, he was able to fit me with thick spectacles that allowed me to have reasonably good distance vision. But it made me more vulnerable to teasing.

As mentioned earlier, most of my school time at the Kings Creek school was spent in the school's little library. My time away from school was largely spent completing the chores Dad assigned me. When I had some spare time, I rode my bike to visit my new friend, Bascomb Love. The Loves, Wilburns, and Mitchells were the "upper crusts" of the community. These and a few other families owned and lived in what I considered fine homes near the center of the village. And they also owned new or nearly-new automobiles--either a Chevrolet or Ford. Which of these was a better car could lead to serious arguments in those days. Although the Loves were much better off financially than our family, owning their own home, good automobiles, etc., this did not affect the relationship between the two families.

The older White boys and girls often dated the Love boys and girls. In fact my "after school" social life revolved around Bascomb and his older brother, William Bird Love. They often urged me to spend the night at their house. I did not often accept these offers because I had no means of reciprocating.

# CHAPTER 24
## Putting Things Into Perspective

THE BOOK, "THE Other Side of the River," by Will Cobb and Bobby Gilmer Moss, puts the financial situation into perspective by their discussion of Mr. A. W. Love, Bascomb's uncle. The book revealed that Mr. Love, who was a trustee of the Merchants and Planters National Bank, often paid people who wanted to withdraw their money from the bank "out of his own pocket." In this way, he prevented runs on the bank by panicked customers and thus saved the bank from going under during the depression. *I have even heard that Mr. Love also saved the State from going bankrupt by extending them a loan at the height of the depression.*

Despite the large difference in economic success separating the H. H. White family and the more financially viable families mentioned above, this gap did not seem to make any difference in our social lives. In fact, I recall a young lady from one of the prominent families visiting our house on a Sunday afternoon to see Frank. When told he was taking a nap, she marched right into his bedroom. This "scandalous" act shocked my Mother.

On many occasions other pretty young ladies would stop their cars beside the road and try to "entice" Frank from the cotton field to spend a few minutes with them. Dad frowned on this act, but Frank found it hard to resist these invitations.

Like my early best friend, Frankie Neil, Bascomb Love was much more advanced socially than I. He matched my timidity toward the opposite sex with extreme boldness. He used his ingenuity to construct a small cabin on their land just across the street from the school and would often entertain girls there during the school lunch break. I didn't dare get involved in Frankie's escapades, despite his urging. Both of us graduated from grammar school in 1939 and enrolled the next school year in the Blacksburg Centralized High School as eighth graders. A lover of the game of football, I had expected to play for Blacksburg High School like my brother Frank.

I ran into some unexpected problems in my efforts to play high school football and also from my good friend Bascomb. During recess the first week at the new school, Bascomb decided it was time for him to throw me down as he did almost daily at Kings Creek. However, I decided I didn't want to be thrown down in front of all these strange new children. So, I turned the tables and threw him down. He looked at me with surprise and never asked me to wrestle him again.

Recesses were great at the new school since it gave me a chance to play "sand lot" football. We played tackle football with no helmet or other safety equipment. I discovered some things about myself during that period. Other than those "wrestling matches" with Bascomb, I really enjoyed physical contact. I found that I wasn't afraid to tackle anyone, even the football team members who sometimes joined in the recess games.

In fact, during one of the recess games, I hit a starter on the football team so hard that he was momentarily knocked unconscious. This caught the attention of the high school coaches and they immediately asked me to come out for the football team as soon as practice started. So, it appeared that my dream of playing organized football would soon be realized.

However, I found out differently when I got back home. The fact that I took a bus to and from school, created an unexpected problem for me, as far as playing sports was concerned. The problem? I lived five miles from the school and thus had to ride the school bus to and from school. The coach told me about this rule but that we could get around it if I brought a signed permission slip from my parent(s) granting me permission to miss the bus ride home. The coach said if I brought him this signed slip it would be legal for me to miss the bus and he was able and willing to take me home in his car after practice each day.

I did not anticipate any difficulty getting my parents to sign the permission slip but I couldn't have been more wrong. When I brought the permission slip home, Mom looked at it, and handed it to Dad who said: "I'm not going to sign this slip for you to play football." When I asked why, he said: "Your big brother Frank got a badly broken arm playing football. He was bigger and stronger than you, and no telling how bad you would be hurt."

End of conversation as far as Dad was concerned. Although I continued presenting the permission slip hoping he might reconsider and sign it he finally he told me sternly: "I don't want to hear the word 'football' again in this house." Not wanting to further anger him, I followed this edict to the letter. However, Dad didn't realize I had been playing tackle football without any safety equipment since my first day of school and continued to do so all the time I had been in high school and I never told him.

# CHAPTER 25

## Test Results a Surprise!

SOMETIME LATER IN my first year at Blacksburg HS, we were given a special new test which had just been developed to measure the IQ of freshmen students. The test results when compiled would be unveiled at a special assembly. Of course everyone, including me, assumed that the son of the town's physician, Dr. T.A. Campbell, would be the winner. So it was no surprise when Tommy Campbell (who later himself became an MD) was declared the winner. Then, to everyone's amazement, including mine, "Jimmy White" of Kings Creek was declared the second place winner.

I was as shocked as everyone else. As I sank down in my seat trying to escape this unwanted attention, the school principal seemed to think he needed to explain this unexpected outcome. He said: "I checked with the Librarian and it appears that Jimmy has checked out a book almost every day of the school year. I think the rest of you might want to start reading more." The more the principal talked, the more I shrank down in my seat.

*My obsession with the reading/writing world continues to this day. Just recently, my Cousin Hayes Mitchell who also rode the bus from Kings Creek to Blacksburg HS commented: "Jimmy, I still remember always seeing you reading a book coming and going to school." More about this in the next section with our move from the farm.*

Toward the end of our farming days when most of the children were gone from the farm and living on their own, Dad knew he had to earn some money away from the farm. So he took a job at a nearby barite (or bartese) mine at Kings Creek. This mine produced a product similar to mica. He still tried to operate the farm on a scaled down basis, obviously greatly "scaled down" since he worked at the mine from sunrise to sunset six days a week at the magnificent salary of a dollar a day. Frank and I were left to do the farm work.

One day at the mine, Dad was knocked from the area he was working and fell headfirst to the bottom of the mine shaft. He would probably have been killed except that his head hit the side of a 55 gallon drum, turning his body so that he didn't land directly on his head. Hitting the drum caved in one side of his face and the fall severely injured other parts of his body. He was treated by Dr. Miller and his face and body soon healed enough for him to go back to work. Remarkably, his face gradually regained its shape and he regained his good looks. Of course he never asked for nor received any compensation for the injuries. There was no OSHA in those days.

Soon after Dad's injuries healed, Frank met a dark haired Kings Mountain, NC beauty by the name of Grace Ledford, married her, and moved out of our house. Although gone from the farm, memories of Frank remained at Blacksburg High School my entire time there. Frank was a tall, handsome, young man who had an engaging smile. He was one of those people who everyone wanted as a friend. And he achieved that without any obvious effort on his part. He was also an excellent football player until his injury.

His reputation as a lothario cast a shadow over me that I never escaped! As soon as I enrolled in Blacksburg High School, many students asked me, with incredulity in their voices: "You're not Frank White's brother, are you?" That was understandable in view of the fact that I wore "coke bottle" glasses, was a "bookworm" and was too shy to converse with anyone except my Kings Creek friends. *(More about Frank's good looks and personality later)!*

Due to the loss of family members (except me) to help him with the farm, remaining injuries from his fall in the mine, plus a variety of other serious illnesses including pleurisy, Dad finally realized that the family no longer had the manpower to handle the physical work of farming and/or working in the mine. So, he began seeking alternatives to support himself, Mom and me.

# CHAPTER 26
## Yay! No More Cotton Hoeing or Picking!

ONCE HE DECIDED to give up farming, Dad realized that we had to move from Kings Creek in order for him to find a decent job. He decided that we would move to Blacksburg where we could live for awhile in a vacant house there. While Dad looked for a town job, we lived in a small house purchased later by Faye and "Shilly" Shillinglaw. Despite the precarious situation we were in, the move to a house within walking distance to the school gave me that long awaited chance to finally go out for the football team. Since I did not need a slip signed by my parents I promptly went out for the team.

Although I was neither big nor fast I easily made the team because of my willingness (eagerness) to hit other players regardless of their size or strength. As a junior, I anticipated playing two years of high school football. I never asked permission or even mentioned any of this to my Dad. However, when I would arrive home from school after practice sessions, dirty and sweaty, I knew he had to be aware of what I was doing. However, he chose to ignore this transgression, the first and only time I had ever knowingly defied his wishes. I suspect he was even proud, though he never admitted it.

Then, as I was anticipating starting in the opening game of the season, my father was offered a job as butcher for the Dover Mill Company store west of Shelby, NC. His pay was to be $15 a week, which we thought was wonderful. It would be much easier work at over twice his salary at the mine. The move to Shelby which cost me a chance to start in that first game, was another bitter-sweet time for us. It was sweet for the family but bitter for me because I knew I would never be able to play high school football. I knew that I would not be able to make the Shelby football team arriving there after the season had started with no experience.

Also, I would be in the school only one more year, since like Blacksburg, there were only 11 years of school at that time. *Ironically, they went to a 12 year school plan the next year after I graduated.*

Naturally my disappointment was tempered by the fact that Dad now had an easier and better paying job and Mom could live in a house, that though modest, had electricity, running water, and an unheated bathroom on the back porch. Dad also bought an oil stove which sat in the living room and provided sufficient heat to the entire house. With the purchase of a used refrigerator and electric stove, we now felt we were living in the lap of luxury compared to living in Kings Creek!

Things soon got even better for us financially. Before the first year was over, D.A. Beam Grocery Store in the town of Shelby offered Dad a job as butcher with a big raise to $20 per week! And, even better, the Beam store was located downtown on Lafayette St. within walking distance of our house on Cline St.

The move to Shelby did cause me another problem, however. I had received my South Carolina driver's license when I was 14 years old. When we moved to North Carolina I could no longer drive a car since you had to be at least 16 years old to get a driver's license in that state. Not being able to drive a car for the next two years was a small price to pay considering the improved financial and living conditions for the family, however.

Classes at Shelby High School were also initially difficult for me. First, of course the Shelby school had higher standards than the Blacksburg school. And starting in the middle of a term with new books and new teachers added to my problems. After a couple of months and some extra study, however, I caught up and had no further problems with the school work. I continued my habit of reading and the better equipped Shelby High School Library offered a treasure trove of books.

Because of my shyness, it took me some time to make friends at this new school. No big surprise there. At least I didn't have to compete with my popular, handsome big brother who was not known in Shelby. During this time, I also began to have more fun time away from school. I again started playing "sandlot" sports. Much of this play was with two cousins, Jay W. and Bobby White, sons of Uncle Clarence White, Dad's younger brother.

Both Jay and Bobby were accomplished athletes who taught me how to play "pepper" baseball--a game that could be played with two or three people with one pitching and one hitting and one other person to "shag" balls. The object was to take short strokes with the bat and attempt to hit the ball accurately back to the pitcher or other player(s). This was excellent for achieving control with the bat and keeping an eye on the ball until contact. I soon became adept with the bat and we could play this game for hours.

At the same time the three of us formed the basis of a "sandlot" football team (again playing tackle football without safety equipment). Although I was not a fast runner, I could hold on to any football I could touch. So, I became Jay's "go to" receiver. During one of these games, I fell and broke my left wrist. Not wanting to worry Mom or incur Dad's wrath, I failed to tell them of the injury. Finally, I could no longer hide the swelling and big knot on my wrist and my parents took me to the doctor. He examined it and said, "It has been broken but has already healed crooked. The only way I can fix it is to break it again and reset it." I decided to live with a slightly crooked wrist.

Cousin Jay White was an excellent, natural tailback who was highly sought after by the Shelby football coaches, but he resisted all efforts by the coaches and varsity players to play football for the high school. He was too busy as an ambitious businessman to devote the time required for team sports. All through high school, he worked several jobs, including working in the movie theatre on weeknights and weekends, and also managing several newspaper carriers (I was one). His crew of several delivery boys dropped off the newspapers at houses, collected the money and turned it over to Jay. He counted the money and gave us our share of the proceeds. He was making and saving too much money to waste his time on high school sports.

However, some of the high school football team members didn't accept this reason in good grace. They started a rumor that Jay was "yellow" because he wouldn't come out for the team. Members of his "sandlot" team were incensed by this and challenged a group of the high school players to an after school game.

The Saturday of the game came and both teams began warming up for the game. Once it started Jay took great pleasure in running right at and over the toughest of these players. By the end of the game, several of the high school team players were complaining we were playing "too rough." A couple of them were even crying and complaining that Jay was deliberately trying to hurt them. That game stopped the "yellow" talk and Jay continued running his various businesses.

*After graduating as an engineering student at NC State, Jay went to work for Duke Power Company. When he retired from Duke Energy he was second in command as a Vice President in charge of engineering.*

# CHAPTER 27
## Not Alone at Last

MY SOCIAL LIFE continued to be virtually non-existent in Shelby as I continued to bury myself in books. My self confidence was not helped by the fact that I had put on too much weight, my curly red locks had become straight, and I was beset by acne. And my vision continued to deteriorate, requiring me to wear even stronger glasses. I had become highly interested in girls but my self-image was so bad that I wouldn't date anyone who would go out with me!

*In time, I found there were other shy boys at the high school and I eventually became friends with a couple of the other social outcasts. We perceived Shelby High School as consisting of two social strata: (1) children of executive and professional people who were members of Cleveland Country Club and (2) children of mill hill people cruelly called "lint heads." We didn't fit either category and floated around the edges of both.*

*I still recall standing in the corner with these friends watching and admiring the "in crowd" as they danced to the Big Band music at Junior-Senior dances. The three of us feared rejection so much we never moved from our safe corner.*

*Many years later, at a Shelby High School class of 1943 reunion, however, we three "misfits" got together and discussed those past times when we seemed to be the only ones not having a good time. Ironically, the three of us had enjoyed much more success after high school than our more socially adept classmates. Of the three outcasts, one had become an MD and the other two of us had successful professional careers. And we were definitely no longer shy wall flowers.*

Through the generosity of Faye and Alfonso Shillinglaw, my summers became more interesting than any I had ever experienced. The first summer, my brother-in-law "Shilly" took me to Asheville, NC where he and my sister Faye, and their toddler, Sue, lived. He and his brother owned and operated a service station in town. They offered me a job and place to stay for the summer.

As almost everyone knows, Asheville is a beautiful city, and it was several degrees cooler than Shelby so I was happy to be there. Also, I enjoyed much of the work such as pumping gas, checking tires, and cleaning windshields. I disliked and wasn't good at fixing tires, changing oil, or anything requiring too much "dirty" work.

The following summer, the Shillinglaws again invited me to the Asheville area to live and work. This time I was invited to Biltmore which borders Asheville. The Shillinglaw brothers had sold the service station and had gone to work for Biltmore Dairy, a famous and highly successful business at that time. The two brothers were in charge of caring for the large Jersey bulls kept at Biltmore Estate's dairy farm.

As part of their compensation, both Shillinglaw families were provided cottages on the grounds of the magnificent Biltmore Estate. "Shilly" had been able to get me a job with the dairy, and I again stayed with his family. I enjoyed work there which I recall was mostly loading cases of dairy products going to outlets and unloading and disposing of returns from those outlets. Employees were allowed to consume the chocolate milk, ice cream and other "goodies" returned by the delivery people. I took full advantage of this and unfortunately gained more pounds of unneeded weight to my already rotund body.

Biltmore was an exciting place to spend the summer for this early teenage boy who had never been far from home. I went to sleep to the roars of large, Jersey bulls which are extremely aggressive and can be very dangerous. They were nothing like the sweet natured, docile Jersey milk cows we had on our farm. Bears and other large wild animals still roamed the acreage of the huge estate, adding to the excitement of living on the Estate's grounds.

Unfortunately, because of my ignorance, I never asked to visit one of the largest mansions in the world (Biltmore Estate, established by the Vanderbilt family). *It saddened me years ago to learn that Biltmore, which boasted the finest quality dairy products anywhere with its high butterfat content Jersey cow's milk, had closed its dairy operation. I have visited there as a guest in recent years and sampled their tasty wine but still miss products from that wonderful dairy.*

During the next school year, I worked at various part time jobs. For example, I worked after school and Saturdays at the J.C. Penney Store where I received a salary of 17 ½ cents per hour. At other times I worked as a service station attendant in Shelby. Again, I was o.k. at pumping gas and cleaning windshields but not so good at changing oil and other automotive tasks. My brother-in-law Clayburn Turner, who owned a garage near Blacksburg, told my Dad: "Jim won't ever make a mechanic; he doesn't like to get his hands dirty." He was right.

Even the small salaries I received at these jobs allowed me to save enough to buy a fancy new Western Flyer bicycle and retire the bike Dad had given me. I rode everywhere on that Western Flyer, as far as Blacksburg to visit my sister, Nell, and her husband, Clayburn Turner.

# CHAPTER 28
## Storm Clouds Gathering for WWII

DURING THIS TIME, of course, the storm clouds of World War II were gathering in the U.S. Then on December 7, 1941 while I was still 15 years old, Japan made its surprise attack on the Pearl Harbor Naval Base in Hawaii.

*According to the Internet, over 350 Imperial Japanese fighter planes, bombers and torpedo bombers attacked the Base and the ships anchored there. The planes came in two waves, launched from six aircraft carriers. They meant to strike a fatal blow at the U. S. Navy fleet and almost succeeded. All eight of our battleships were badly damaged and four were sunk. In addition, the Japanese damaged or sank three of our cruisers, three destroyers, a training ship and a minelayer. Even worse, 2,400 Americans lost their lives in the attack and another 1,180 others were wounded. Many Naval Base buildings were destroyed.*

This sneak attack by Japan led the U. S. to declare war on Japan the following day, December 8. Soon afterward the U. S. was at war with Japan, Germany and Italy in an all out war against the Axis. But as one Japanese General reportedly exclaimed after the successful attack: "We have awakened a sleeping giant." History proved him right as Americans rallied to the aid of their country.

Many people remember exactly when and where they were when the attack on Pearl Harbor came. All I remember was that I was home in Shelby and some friends told me about it the next day. *(We still didn't have a working radio).* I had never heard of Pearl Harbor at the time and did not know that Hawaii was considered a part of the United States of America. Although I was an avid reader, my love of reading had not yet included history and geography. That interest came much later.

Despite my ignorance of what led to World War II, our lives changed significantly once it started. Most importantly, the War soon involved two of our immediate family: my older brothers, Robert and Frank. I would be involved at a later date. *Details of all three White brothers' wartime service will follow in PART 2 of this Memoir.*

Meanwhile, in addition to saying goodbye to loved ones going off to fight for their country, World War II caused other significant changes to our culture. As men were volunteering or being drafted, they left voids in the workforce filled by the nation's women. **"Rosie the Riveter"** became the symbol of American women working in factories and shipyards during WWII. Many women served important roles by replacing male workers leaving for the military.

Images of women workers were used in government posters and commercial advertising to encourage them to volunteer for wartime service in factories. For example, ***"Rosie the Riveter"*** was the title of a song and a Hollywood movie during WWII.

Those who can recall those days know that almost everyone participated in the War in some way. Some of the participation was not voluntary. During the spring of 1942, the government introduced a rationing system because certain things were in really short supply during the war and rationing was a way to make sure that everybody got their fair share. I also suspect that this was another way to ensure that everyone contributed to the war effort and would become conscious that the nation was fighting for its way of life.

Under rules of the rationing program, families were issued ration stamps to restrict the purchase of things especially needed for the war effort. People used stamps to buy their allotted amounts of food products such as coffee, meat, sugar, fat, butter, vegetables, and certain fruit. They also had stamps that allowed them to buy limited amounts of gas, tires, clothing, and fuel oil. Ladies were no longer able to buy silk stockings because the silk was needed for making parachutes.

In 1942, smokers of **Lucky Strike Cigarettes** noticed that their Lucky Strike cigarette packs had changed from dark green and gold to white and red. This change was accompanied by radio commercials announcing that "Lucky Strike Green Has Gone To War"--meaning that the green dye used for the packaging would be used for the war effort.

The government also released posters urging Americans to "Do with less—so they'll have enough", i.e. U.S. troops. At the same time, individuals and groups conducted drives to collect scrap metal, aluminum cans, and rubber, which were recycled and used to produce armaments. Many people bought U.S. war bonds to help pay for the high cost of conducting WWII. And many of those with outside space started "Victory Gardens."

# CHAPTER 29
## Shortage of Men Leads to My First Real Job

BECAUSE MATURE MEN were in short supply I was able to get a part time job at the Shelby Post Office at age 16. This was a really good but demanding job compared to my previous ones. I owed this good job not only to the war but to our next door neighbor, Mr. Perry Noblitt, who recommended me for it.

I had much to learn in a hurry. After limited training, I had to be at the Post Office early each morning to take the place of any one of six carriers who didn't show up for work. In the unlikely event that all six regular carriers appeared, there was always inside work that needed to be done. I don't recall ever missing a day of work. This steady work at a higher salary began to change both my economic and social situations.

Within a few months I had earned and saved enough money to buy my first car, a 1936 Oldsmobile. By then I had received my North Carolina driver's license and could legally drive again. Having my own car was a major factor in improving my social life. Several popular guys became my friends and they would fix me up with double dates in order to have transportation. I knew I was being used but I was also using them to gain some social acceptance in Shelby.

As useful as the car was, gas rationing limited how much I could drive. However, friends riding with me contributed some of their allotted amount of gasoline so we could stay on the move a reasonable amount of time.

Despite being able to go to parties and going on double dates arranged by friends, I was still extremely shy around the opposite sex and totally unskilled at making "small talk." Through reading I had acquired a large "understanding" vocabulary. However, I did not have the confidence to use this ability in social situations. I was not always sure of the pronunciation of many words I had learned from reading. Rather than risk mispronouncing words, I omitted them from my vocal vocabulary. Usually I just remained mostly silent around girls--not a recipe for becoming a popular teenager.

Once at a party where I was playing the game "Post Office" for the first time, I was invited into a darkened room where a girl I didn't know well awaited. My naive nature soon became obvious. Since I was new at such games, I thought we would just spend a few minutes together in this darkened room, talk a little bit, and then rejoin the crowd. However, the girl proceeded to give me my first kiss. To my dismay, she put her tongue into my mouth! I was repelled by the whole thing.

When I emerged from the room with a stricken look on my face, a female classmate friend asked: "Did she French kiss you?" I didn't know what a "French kiss" was but reckoned I had just received one and didn't like it.

My closest friend at the time, Tommy Singleton, helped me achieve more interaction with the opposite sex by inviting me to go on double dates with him and his girlfriend, Joyce, who was very pretty as was her older sister, Gladys. Tommy and Joyce often "fixed me up" with Gladys. Tommy was eventually engaged to Joyce but they never married. I never even held hands with Gladys but was happy just to be in her company. I day dreamed that someday I might even be able to get a date with a desirable girl such as Gladys and Joyce.

Tommy had an athletic, trim body, handsome movie star features, curly strawberry blond hair, plus a line of chatter always ready to unleash on a pretty girl. He would mimic characters such as Woody Woodpecker and I recall one of his favorites: "thufferin thuccotash," uttered by Sylvester the cat! I was amazed that he was so uninhibited that he could make these comic utterances in front of girls!

*Note: Sadly, good looks are not guaranteed to last forever. Some years later, after I was working as a Federal Information Officer in Washington DC, I stopped at a service station outside Blacksburg to gas up my car. An obese, completely bald man with one blind eye, emerged from the station and filled my car with gasoline. He gave me a long look and asked: "Are you Jimmy White?" I replied: "Yes, who are you?" He told me he was my old friend, Tommy Singleton. I tried to hide my shock at his changed appearance.*

*Years later when I returned to Blacksburg, I became re-acquainted with him and by then he had become a very successful businessman. And underneath the changed exterior, he was still the same funny, personable Tommy I had known as a teenager. Unfortunately, he died young and I still miss him.*

Work at the Post Office not only allowed me to accumulate enough money to buy that second hand car: it opened up other possibilities for me. The work itself was challenging both physically and intellectually and I needed those challenges to help me mature. I had to learn all the streets and house numbers in a town of around 10,000 people. *(This was an asset to me when I returned to Shelby after graduating from college and was working as a newspaper reporter).*

Before and during the war, Shelby had six routes and twice a day service except for Saturday which had one delivery. Since it was wartime, mail was unusually heavy. In fact, we almost had to run the routes in order to make deliveries twice daily. Despite that, I much preferred the outside work, i.e., walking the routes. And it turned out to be good preparation for Boot Camp down the road! *(Note: Soon after the war, the number of routes was changed from six to twelve, and then delivery went from twice to once a day. What a deal!)*

Although I enjoyed (and needed) the physical work of delivering the mail I despised encounters with dogs which were prevalent. Shelby had no leash laws at that time. One house I served had several aggressive dogs and the owner refused to control them. He sat on the porch and seemed to enjoy my discomfort as his dogs growled and nipped at me. With the Postmaster's concurrence, I was finally allowed to stop delivery of mail to his mailbox. I was told later that when this man learned that I was in service overseas, he replied: "I hope he doesn't come back!" Fortunately, most of the people I served were appreciative and considerate.

Meanwhile, Mom, Dad and I enjoyed living at the Cline Street house. Compared to the tenant houses we lived in while "sharecropping," this house was very comfortable for three people. And I was getting ready for more exciting times in my young life as I awaited the call to serve my country.

# PART 2

# WORLD WAR II AND ITS
# EFFECT ON THE WHITE FAMILY

# CHAPTER 1

## Three White Brothers Overseas at the Same Time

MY BROTHER FRANK was the first in the H.H. White family to go to war. He became a soldier in the U. S. Army soon after war was declared. As soon as he completed his first military training he was sent to California early in 1942 to receive final training in how to drive tanks and half tracks. He would soon be sent overseas where he would serve with the Sixth Armored Division of General George Patton's Third Army until WWII ended. More about Frank's heroic service and awards will be described later.

Brother Robert was the next in our family to go to war. A few months after Frank was called, Bob went into the Army Air Corp. After receiving specialized aircraft mechanic training in Spokane, WA, Bob was sent to the Pacific. Although I don't know whether or not Bob was involved in the capture of Tinian Island from the Japanese, all I know is that he ended up there as an aircraft mechanic until the end of the war.

Bob never discussed these details with me and I only remembered later that he was at Tinian when "Enola Gay" left that island carrying the atomic bomb, "Little Boy," which was dropped on Hiroshima. Shortly afterward, a plane carrying another atomic bomb left Tinian Island for Nagasaki where the second bomb was dropped, effectively ending the war. *I regret not urging Bob to talk more about his wartime service since as an aircraft mechanic he might have worked on "Enola Gay."*

I was the last to go, to the U. S. Navy in 1944. My experiences and adventures will be detailed later in this Part.

Unlike today, the World War II era saw the entertainment industry being very supportive of the nation's war effort. Brother Frank had a firsthand experience in one Hollywood effort to promote patriotism. This particular effort was to select the "best looking soldier on the West Coast" with the winner to serve as escort for the 1941 Miss America, Miss Rosemary La Planche. *Not surprising to those of us who knew him, Frank was selected as that "best looking soldier."* Although he was already married, Frank thought it was his patriotic duty to escort Miss La Planche around Hollywood.

Like many other celebrities of that day Miss La Planche was a true patriot. In her role as Miss America, she traveled extensively with the USO, and sold war bonds wherever she went. Her sister Louise was quoted as saying: "She wrote us an excited letter about selling $50,000 worth of war bonds in a single day!"

The entertainment world went all out in producing patriotic songs and movies. Who can forget such memorable songs as "Remember Pearl Harbor," "Kiss The Boys Goodbye," "I'll Be Seeing You," "There'll Be Bluebirds Over The White Cliffs of Dover" and "Praise the Lord and Pass the Ammunition"? It took longer for Hollywood to gear up and begin releasing full scale movies about the war but early on they made many training and "propaganda" movies for the government. They also did their part by opening up the Hollywood Canteen and providing talent for USO shows which traveled overseas to entertain troops. Comedian Bob Hope was a prime example but there were many others.

More importantly, many Hollywood stars actively served in World War II. These included: Gene Autry, Eddie Albert, Ernest Borgnine, Charles Bronson, Art Carney, Tony Curtis, Douglas Fairbanks, Jr., Clark Gable, William Holden, Don Knotts, Burt Lancaster, Jack Palance, Tyrone Power, Ronald Reagan, Mickey Rooney, and Jimmy Stewart, to name a few. Many, such as Gene Kelly, signed up for active duty but were asked to use their talents to entertain the troops. And remember that great orchestra leader, Glenn Miller, lost his life when his plane went down while he was serving overseas.

Everyone I knew personally wanted to participate in WWII. *This explains my disgust at former President Bill Clinton and others who were willing to flee to Canada to avoid serving their country during the Vietnam War. Personally, I wanted to enlist starting at age 16, but with two of her sons already in war zones I could not do this to my mother. However, that burden was lifted from my shoulders when I received my draft notice at age 18. It then became my "duty" to serve.*

*My concern became: Will I be able to pass the physical?* Some of my friends and relatives expressed doubt that I could pass the physical for two reasons: I had bad eyes and stomach problems *(present since my bout with malaria)*. Mother had worked hard cooking food that I could keep down. However, there was nothing she could do about the fact that I was legally blind without glasses.

Much to the surprise of many, I passed the physical fitness test and was given a choice of the Army, Navy or Marine Corps! I chose the Navy. (Note: I used a little deception to help me pass the critical vision test. When called to take the test, I was told to walk forward until I could read the eye chart without squinting from at least three feet away. I walked closer than the three foot line and squinted. This let me read the required line without my glasses. The examiner no doubt spotted this bit of deception, but with a wink and a grin, he said, "You passed."

Like most young American boys, I would have been crushed had I failed the test to serve my country. My exuberance subsided, however, when the examiner added that I would never be able to serve in a war zone. When I asked why, he explained that if I lost my glasses in battle I would be a handicap rather than an asset to the war effort. *The Navy must have lost that paperwork because a year later I was in the Pacific War Zone on an LST waiting to participate in the invasion of Japan! All I can figure is that they really did need live bodies! The same reasoning must have applied to Frank who passed the physical despite a weakened heart caused by rheumatic fever as a youngster.*

# CHAPTER 2

## Boot Camp: My First Real Step Toward Manhood

I WAS NERVOUS about taking the long train ride surrounded by strangers heading toward Bainbridge, Maryland, where I would take "boot camp" training. After all, until then, I had been a farm boy who had never been more than a couple of hours away from home. However, I soon found myself enjoying the chance to "sightsee" along the way. I remember the train stopping at Washington, DC. From there, as I recall, we continued on to Baltimore, MD, where the train was met by Navy petty officers who transported us to Bainbridge and the dreaded "boot camp."

The first day at Bainbridge was a busy, exciting day. We were measured and issued our new Navy clothing. I'm embarrassed to say that my waist size was 38, my height was 5' 8", and I weighed 168 pounds. Not exactly a Mr. America! Then we were taken to the barbershop where our long locks were quickly removed. *I had thought my hair was already pretty short but the Navy barber did not think so and I became a "skin head."*

Finally, we were marched to our barracks where 120 of us would reside for the next 12 weeks. *(We had been scheduled for 16 weeks, but, because of the shortage of live bodies, our time in "boot" was reduced).* One of the first things I observed was that the Navy had done its best to mix disparate groups of young men together. We were about equally divided between "Rebels" and "Yankees." We represented most states in the South as well as New York, New Jersey, Maryland and Pennsylvania and a couple of New England states.

From the very first night, I found this to be an explosive mixture. A Northern boy would mock a Southern boy's accent and we would all head to the gym where the two combatants would fight it out in the ring. *This was the Navy's way of settling arguments. No fighting in the barracks but o.k. in the gym.*

Southern boys were especially upset by the language Northern boys used. The Northern boys would often use curse words (e.g. son of a bitch, bastard, etc.) in jest and not meant to be taken seriously. However, a Southern boy would take these words personally and invite the boy from the North to the ring.

A young blond haired boy from Georgia engaged in almost nightly fights for the first two weeks, defending Southern language and customs. He was far from a classic boxer but won several fights with his energy. Win or lose he flailed away, defending the honor of "Southern Womanhood." The conflicts gradually tapered off and by graduation day the two groups understood and were at peace with each other. Many even established lasting friendships.

Because "Boots" usually had no experience in military matters, we were required to salute Chief Petty Officers (CPO's) for practice in learning the proper way to salute. We needed this practice since we seldom encountered Commissioned Officers. *(Those palm up salutes you see in the movies and on TV would not cut it in the real Navy!)*

The Navy wasted little time showing us their way of doing things. Our first week there, a regular Navy non commissioned officer (Non Com) took us out early in the morning for a long run. We were told to run until we could no longer put one foot in front of the other. As we started out I settled in with the last group of runners; this was natural since I was never a fast runner. However, as the run proceeded, my group began to pass the faster runners--some of whom lay exhausted at the side of the road. As this continued, what was left of our group took the lead. Eventually, only three were left still running and I was one of the three.

The NCO in charge drove up and said: "You guys can stop now." He invited us to climb up on the truck and we were driven back to the barracks. This was a real life example of the "tortoise and hare" you read about in school.

All of us were also quickly introduced to the Navy's way of swimming and jumping into the pool from a very high tower. Strangely, we were not allowed to wear anything for these exercises--which you were required to successfully complete to remain in the Navy. Some of the recruits never made it and were removed to "we don't know where." I had no problem with the swimming itself since it had always been one of my favorite activities. But it took some getting used to the idea of swimming naked. The most daunting aspect of all this was the jumping from a high tower with no swim suit or jock strap to protect private parts.

Making sure that mine were protected, I jumped with my legs far out front. I landed almost on my back and did a couple of somersaults in the water as a result--but no damage of any kind. The jumping procedure offered a strong incentive for getting out of the way of the next jumper in a hurry: the guy lined up behind you was supposed to count out a few seconds and jump (or be pushed by the instructor). If you didn't swim rapidly from the place you landed you might become a landing pad for the next person.

The first week of Boot Camp also began the process of learning self defense--Navy style. Some of the things we were taught would not be appropriate to discuss in this memoir. However, the skill of boxing taught at Boot Camp was straightforward and had a long-time positive effect on my life. This experience bears further discussion.

On the first day of learning to box, the instructor began the session by demonstrating some punching and self defense techniques. Then he looked us over and lined us up with a practice partner roughly the same weight. So, my 168 pound 5 ft. 8 inch body was paired against a lean, lanky West Virginia boy of about that same weight. However, he was 6 ft. 2 inches tall with arm and leg lengths to match. Obviously, we were proportioned very differently--all to my practice partner's advantage.

Before we put on the gloves, the instructor told us that the point of the exercise was to practice the moves he had just shown us, i.e. how to punch effectively and to defend ourselves. He emphasized that we should hold back on our punches so that we did not injure our practice partners. I tried to follow the instructor's demonstrations of how to spar effectively while protecting myself. However, the West Virginia guy apparently did not hear the last part of the instruction. He immediately began to try to knock my head off. I defended myself as best I could but his longer reach and my limited experience made this a one sided exhibition.

The instructor obviously saw what was happening but did nothing to stop it. At the end of the session, I was bloody, bruised and disheartened while my so-called practice partner did not show a single bruise and swaggered away with a big smile on his face. However, as we headed back to the barracks I vowed to myself: "This will never happen to me again." And it never did.

# CHAPTER 3
## A Dose of Reality Leads to the Gym

AFTER DINNER THAT evening, while the rest of the guys were playing cards or having "bull sessions," I went to the gym to practice what the boxing instructor had taught us and to begin lifting weights to build up my strength. I knew it was time to replace the fat on my body with muscle.

The gym was well equipped with professional style ring, boxing gloves, jump ropes, heavy punching bags and "speed" bags, as well as regular weight lifting equipment. That night I spent much of my time beginning the process of increasing my punching power by pounding the heavy bag. *This also helped relieve the frustration from my earlier humiliation.* Then I went to the speed bag to begin working on my timing. In case your only exposure to a speed bag is seeing champion boxers showing off their incredible hand speed, let me assure you that this skill doesn't come easily. My first efforts at this were pitiful and I soon moved on to the weight lifting equipment.

I developed a nightly routine for the rest of boot camp which included: (1) doing some weight lifting as a warm up, (2) punching the heavy bag, (3) working to establish a rhythm with the speed bag, and (4) finding a willing partner to spar with me. Sensing that I was serious about learning to box, experienced boxers would often volunteer to spar with me and offer me tips for improving. None ever reacted like the West Virginia boy; the experienced boxers always "pulled their punches" to keep from hurting me.

*An interesting side note to the above: boot camps and service schools were well stocked with high level athletes. In the gym I met professional and near professional boxers and wrestlers. And when we attended football games between U.S. Service schools, we watched players who were the quality of many NFL players. Some had already played professional football, while others had competed at major colleges.*

*For example, the starting quarterback for our Bainbridge team was All American, Donald Durden of Oregon State, who was named "Rose Bowl Player Of The Game" at Durham, NC in 1942. The game was changed from Pasadena, CA to Durham because of fears of an attack by the Japanese on the West Coast of the U.S. following Pearl Harbor.*

*Durden's backup, who became the starter before the end of the season, was a recent high school tailback by the name of Charlie "Choo Choo" Justice. "Choo Choo" later became a legendary star for the University of North Carolina. As an "All American" tailback for UNC, he shared stardom with his friend, Art Weiner, his major pass catcher. Both were drafted by the NFL and played pro football but their careers were shortened by injuries.*

The only time I missed a night at the gym was when the Company Commander planned an event we were required to attend. *Ironically, I never saw my first day practice partner at the gym during the weeks we were at Bainbridge.* Soon this intense workout program began to pay off as my pants became looser and the shirts and pea coat became tighter. And I was actually gaining, rather than losing, weight.

The boxing instructor must have become aware of my dedication because at our regular sessions he began calling me up on the stage to demonstrate punches. Soon I became his regular sparring partner on stage as he added refinements to our boxing skills. The instructor had told us in advance that our last boxing lesson before we left Boot Camp would be with the person we sparred with at the first practice. I eagerly looked forward to facing the guy who had beaten me so badly that first session.

So, at that last boxing event, I did not wait for the instructor to line us up, I spotted my first boxing lesson practice partner and lined up opposite him. He moved and placed himself in front of someone else. I moved the other guy out of the way and again lined up across from him. He moved for the third time and I gave up chasing him around. I left the session knowing that I didn't have anything more to prove. He left as a coward.

Incidentally, by then a growth spurt and my daily workouts in the gym had totally changed the conformation of my body. I had gained inches in height and now had a 32 inch waistline. I also had gained muscle and weighed a solid 180 pounds.

In retrospect, I think the instructor made the right decision by not stopping the first sparring session when the West Virginia boy turned the session into an all out attack. I suspect the instructor was giving me a chance to prove myself. *He was one of the NCO's who picked us up at the end of the first big run when I was one of the three boys who ran until picked up by the truck. The events of that day may have shown him that I was not a quitter.*

While most of our time at Boot Camp involved some type of physical effort, at one point we were given the Navy's version of an I.Q. Test. This test was used to help the Navy determine our next assignment: e.g. to go to a Service School for more specialized training or be sent directly to the fleet as a seaman.

After the test was evaluated, I learned that I had received a very high score and would be heading to the Naval Training Center at San Diego, CA to attend Yeoman Service School. I was surprised at my high score. I couldn't understand why a Boot Camp friend (who I had thought was much smarter than I) received a score that was only slightly more than half of mine. He was immediately sent out to sea and I never saw or heard from him again.

Although pleased that I had scored well on the test, I didn't want to go to Yeoman School. I had heard that Yeoman School was for "sissies." But the Navy never gave us a choice. They never asked us what our preference was--they were filling the Navy's needs, not ours. Despite my reservations about Yeoman School, I finished up Boot Camp on a high note.

Before we were to leave Bainbridge for our future assignments, we were allowed a visit home. When I arrived back in Shelby many folks didn't recognize me because of the physical changes to my body. Also, other factors, e.g. my pimples were gone, the curls had returned to my red hair, and my increased self confidence, might also have had something to do with my changed personality and appearance.

My biggest problem while I was on leave was that none of my civilian clothes came close to fitting me. The waists of my civilian pants were far too big and the in-seams were too short. My Navy uniforms had been replaced and/or been drastically altered to fit my "new" body during boot camp. Thus, I had to wear my uniform during my leave since I didn't have time or money to spend on a new wardrobe.

Most of my leave time was with my family and a few friends. One such friend, who aspired to be a professional boxer, asked me to put on the gloves and spar with him. I wouldn't have dared accept his offer before joining the Navy. And he never would have asked me. However, with all the instruction I had received and my nightly visits to the gym, I was able to handle him easily. I didn't try to hurt him, however. The experience helped both of us. It helped him decide not to pursue a career as a professional boxer and it gave me the desire to continue learning more about this sport which had increased my self confidence and conditioning so much.

After leave, I returned to Bainbridge briefly and joined three other new Second Class Seamen who were put on a train heading to San Diego, CA. Since we were from different companies, we were strangers but all of us were going to training schools there. As I recall I was the only yeoman trainee of the four. A slightly older guy was leader of our group.

# CHAPTER 4
## Heading West-- but with a Detour!

HEADING WEST ON the train, I was enjoying the experience of getting to know my three new friends. And I was dazzled by the changes in scenery as we left the Mid-Atlantic states, passed through the Midwestern states and approached the Rocky Mountains. The scenery was very different from any I had ever experienced. Then I began to feel sick and the sailor in charge of our foursome summoned a Medic to check on me.

The Medic took my temperature and checked other vitals and said that I was very sick and needed to be taken off the train as soon as we were near a hospital. I vaguely remember being carried off the train on a stretcher. When I came to my senses a day or so later, I found out that I was in a Naval Hospital at Glenwood Springs, Colorado. A nurse told me I had contracted German measles and would remain in isolation until the doctors determined that I was no longer contagious. After that I would remain in the hospital until I recovered enough to board another train bound for California.

The Glenwood Springs Naval Hospital had been created from what had been an expensive, elegant resort for the very wealthy. Being alone in a room with just an occasional visit by a nurse, was not great fun for an 18 year old boy who knew not a soul in Colorado and faced going on to California on my own. But the surroundings were beyond anything I had ever experienced. Glenwood Springs is near Carbondale and Snowmass on Hwy. 70 leading to Denver. Today, it is again a tourist mecca.

My room at the hospital was large and comfortable and views of the nearby mountains were sensational. This interlude gave me an opportunity to read--something I had not had time to do in Boot Camp. After about a week, I was released from isolation and allowed to roam around the hospital. My favorite "hang out" was a cafe with a juke box where I could listen to the wonderful music of Glenn Miller, Tommy and Jimmy Dorsey, Artie Shaw and other great "big band" orchestras of that time. As enjoyable as it was, hearing this music I loved made me homesick.

After I had been at Glenwood Springs about two weeks, a hospital administrator came to my room and told me I was about to be discharged and needed to get ready to be driven to the railroad station to board a train to California that same afternoon. I was alert enough to ask him about my papers. He said: "We don't have any paperwork for you. We'll just put you on the train and you'll get off in San Diego. You won't need any paperwork." I didn't believe that the sailor in charge would let them take me off the train without papers and said: "I'm not getting on a train without papers because the Shore Patrol will put me in the brig." He thought this idea was ridiculous but I was adamant in my refusal. He left my room in a "huff."

An hour or so later, he re-appeared with an apologetic expression on his face. More importantly, he was carrying my official papers, left by the leader of the group I had been traveling with. That afternoon I was transported to the train, clutching those papers to my chest. Within 15 minutes after leaving the Glenwood Springs train station, two Shore Patrolmen approached me on the train and asked to see my papers. I breathed a big sigh of relief as they looked at and returned my paperwork.

When I got off the train in San Diego, there was no one to meet me and I had no idea where to go. I asked around and some locals were able to tell me how to find the gates to the Naval Base. I entered the Base, presented my paperwork, and was told that I had missed the company I was supposed to join but was being assigned to a new company being formed. The three guys I had traveled with from Bainbridge had been going to their school for two weeks and I never saw them during my stay at San Diego.

# CHAPTER 5
## Undeserved Leadership Role in a New Company

WHEN MY NEWLY formed company assembled for the first time, the Company Commander for our class had already been selected. This man had been just one day from receiving his "wings" and commission as a Naval Aviator when doctors discovered he had a slight heart murmur. This "washed him out" of aviation school and into the regular Navy as an enlisted man. He was understandably bitter about this and didn't try to hide it.

Before the meeting ended, we were told that the company needed four Section Chiefs. The OIC looked us over and spotted my red hair. He immediately called me forward and made me a Section Chief. I began to think: "maybe having red hair isn't so bad after all."

Although I had not sought and did not deserve the leadership position, it turned out to be a blessing. My Section Chief title spared me from toilet cleaning, and other onerous chores. My job was to supervise and approve or disapprove such work by members of my section. Being a Section Chief also spared me from participating in the 24 hour per day guard duty we were required to maintain. *The latter seemed rather silly since we weren't guarding anything but it was getting us ready for overseas duty coming soon.*

As I mentioned earlier, I still didn't like the idea of going to Yeoman School. I wanted no part of this "sissy" training. For the first and only time in my life, I considered deliberately "flunking out" of school. But that was not my nature and I couldn't force myself to do it. I also discovered that none of my classmates were "sissies." In fact, as a group, we were more physically impressive than most of the other specialists in training.

I gradually began to realize that being a yeoman actually had some tangible advantages. In fact, as I learned the duties of a yeoman I could see why other sailors actually envied the job of the yeoman. That was because commissioned officers heavily depend on their yeomen to handle the paperwork, make out leave and liberty passes, and, in many cases actually run the office when they were not present.

As an example of the above benefits, when a ship anchors at port, sailors normally receive either a "port" or "starboard" liberty pass and can enjoy liberty (if allowed) on alternate days. Since the yeoman makes out these passes, he could (and did) make out both "port" and "starboard" passes for himself. Thus he could go on liberty when he wanted provided he got his work done. He also can speed up or slow down such things as issuance of "leave" paperwork for those he likes or dislikes.

Although I studied enough to pass, I can't say I enjoyed all the courses to prepare us to be a yeoman. Learning shorthand was one of these. I thought this class fit the "sissy" category too well and I tried just hard enough to pass. The class I appreciated most was the typing class. I had taken one year of typing in high school so I at least knew the keyboard and could already type about 25 words per minute (WPM).

The Navy told us we had to increase our speed at least five WPM each week with a limited number of errors. The threats should we fail to make this progress were vague but sounded serious enough to catch my attention. By the time we left Service School I could maintain a speed of 65 WPM for five or more minutes with the allowed number of errors. And I could type 125 WPM for a timed minute or two! Don't tell me threats don't work!

*When I became a journalist, I found that being able to "touch type" at a relatively high speed was a real asset. Most newspaper reporters at that time used the old "hunt and peck" system. Although they appeared to be typing at a high rate of speed, their actual speed did not come close to the speed of an average typist using the "touch" system. Later in careers with several Federal Government agencies I had private secretaries. However, I could still type faster than most of them. So, rather than dictate letters, manuscripts, etc., I found it quicker and more efficient to type out a quick rough draft which the secretary could then turn into a pretty, error-free official piece of work.*

*The government efficiency experts really frowned on this approach and always tried to force me to get rid of my typewriter and dictate my work products to a secretary. However, I refused to remove my old Royal manual typewriter and continued to use the system that worked best for me. I seemed to "do my best thinking" through my fingers. I hasten to add that both the speed and accuracy of my typing have badly deteriorated as I've gotten older. Neither arthritic hands nor "old brains" work well in my case.*

# CHAPTER 6

## Marching to Victory

YEOMAN SCHOOL OFFERED me other opportunities worth noting. I was a music lover and had always enjoyed moving to music although my shyness then kept me from learning to dance. I was pleased to learn that marching was a highly competitive "sport" with the Service Schools at San Diego Naval Base Training Center. The various schools, e.g. radio technician, electronic specialist, yeoman, boatswain's mate (bosun), quartermaster, gunner's mate, etc., all competed for the honor as well as special privileges in the form of extra weekend leaves awarded to the winning team.

Our team was led by our tough talking company commander who acted and sounded like a commissioned officer, though he had missed being one. He obviously had previous training in marching and had a really impressive, deep, strong voice as he shouted out commands to the team. Besides the extra time off, the yeoman team had another incentive for winning: our pride. The fact that no yeoman school team had ever won this competition may actually have provided us more incentive than receiving extra leave and other prizes.

In the finals of the competition, our team was marching flawlessly and our chances of winning seemed good. Then, near catastrophe happened: our Commander called a quick double "to the rear march." All of us did the first "to the rear" command smartly and correctly. At the second command, the man in back of me failed to turn and suddenly he and I were face to face. Without hesitating, I flipped him around so quickly that apparently the judges did not see this mistake.

Despite our "screw up," we became the first yeoman school company to win the marching contest. As a flourish, our Company Commander then marched us right up to face the radio tech team which had gone out of its way to give us "wolf whistles" and toss derogatory remarks questioning our "manhood." The Commander dismissed us and we challenged the radio tech guys to say something derogatory to our faces. Since quite a few of us were larger and more physical than members of their team, they remained silent and slunk away. We had no cat calls from them after that.

Ironically, the early leader of one of the other companies was none other than the great dancer, Gene Kelly. He led his team for several practices but then we didn't see him again. We were eventually told that he was yanked out of the school and given duties entertaining the troops for the rest of WWII.

Our Company Commander deserved much credit for whipping us into shape to win the marching contest. However, that's the only praise I could give him since he remained bitter about being deprived of his commission and took this out on us lowly "non coms." As Section Chief, I was responsible for seeing that my crew remained ship shape and properly performed its duties such as standing guard, cleaning the barracks and latrines, etc. The work first had to be done to my satisfaction and then the satisfaction of the Company Commander. Rarely did we succeed in pleasing him. Even after our work had passed "spot" inspections with flying colors, he would find something he didn't like and chew me out. Finally I had all I could take from him and challenged him to meet me at the gym to settle matters. He accepted.

As mentioned earlier, I was following Navy protocol for handling serious disagreements. Any tussle inside the barracks might result in the whole company being awakened at 2 a.m. and forced to march for an hour or so before returning to bed.

So, at the agreed upon time, we met at the gym with our "corner men" and a referee. I figured I was in for a tough fight and that I would probably lose. In addition to his tough voice, he was swarthy, a little older, and appeared very fit and very confident. Although I didn't expect to win, I thought I could make it uncomfortable enough that he might have second thoughts about his actions in trying to make our lives miserable. I remembered Brother Frank's advice about how to deal with bullies: Bloody their noses!

We pulled on our gloves, climbed into the ring, shook hands, went to our corners, and waited for the referee's signal to begin. At that signal, I quickly went past the center of the ring and began to punch the guy around. It soon became apparent that the tough looking, tough talking commander was all "show." He could not defend himself and didn't come close to hitting me. When I realized that he didn't have any ability to fight and seemed paralyzed with fear, I stopped hitting, grabbed him in a bear hug, and suggested we call it quits.

He readily agreed to that. We shook hands and he said he appreciated my good sportsmanship. I thought that we parted on what appeared to be a friendly basis. However, the next day the "sneaky so-and-so," relieved me of my duties as Section Chief and assigned me guard duty that night. That told me all I needed to know about him. It was no big deal, however, since we were nearing the end of our time and I would never see him again.

Upon graduation we were all promoted from Seaman Second to Yeoman Third Class. I was grateful to be able to skip over Seaman First Class which required being able to tie about 100 different knots! That was a skill I didn't have and didn't want.

# CHAPTER 7
## Learning About Life Outside the Classroom

AS FOR MY time at San Diego, I think I learned much more about life during time outside the classroom than I did inside it. I was the only Southern farm boy in our company. And I was truly a social neophyte compared to boys from New York, New Jersey, and Pennsylvania who were in the majority.

I often heard the Yankee boys make fun of "queers" and disparage "Jews." I didn't know what they were talking about when they used the word "queer" and I could not imagine we had a Jew in our class. I thought that "queer" just meant that someone was odd. Growing up in Cherokee County, South Carolina, I had never heard the word homosexual. My more worldly shipmates explained this to me in graphic details. *To indicate just how provincial I was, I had never known a Jew, a Catholic or for that matter, a Republican. Our county was populated primarily by Scotch Irish Democrats who attended Protestant churches.*

After getting over the shock of learning about homosexuality, I asked who among our classmates were Jews. The Northern boys laughingly told me that we had at least two boys of the Jewish faith in our class. They had a hard time believing that I did not know that one of my best friends in our class, Lorch Foltz, was a Jew. The other Jew was named Goldstein, a name recognized as Jewish by everyone in the company but me. I had thought a Jew or Catholic would have some noticeable physical difference and neither of these two was noticeably different from the rest of us.

Then I learned that my other best friend in class, Mario Perez, was a Roman Catholic--something I also had not suspected. Finding out that my two best Navy friends belonged to groups I had never before knowingly encountered was a huge surprise. Fortunately, I had not made any derogatory remarks about ethnic or religious groups and thus had not inadvertently offended either of these friends. I owed this to my parents who taught us as children to be respectful of the beliefs of others.

This teaching stood me in good stead throughout my life but was not common to my part of the country. Many of my neighbors and their children made no attempt to conceal their biases.

If anything, the differences between my two new Navy friends and me may have brought us closer together. It certainly reinforced the early teaching of my parents and offered great learning experiences which added spice to my life and which I still cherish. For some reason, these two young friends of mine never became close friends with each other. So I was almost always accompanied by one or the other (but never both) to Los Angeles or its nearby suburban towns. The answer to the question of why these two friends never became friends of each other might have been caused by their different backgrounds.

My Jewish friend, Lorch Foltz, was from a wealthy family in Dallas, Texas. His family owned upscale clothing manufacturing companies which marketed their clothing lines to such stores as Neiman Marcus. My other friend, Mario Perez, was from a poor immigrant Mexican family who lived in the small town of La Brea where I met and got to know his family in person. Although Mario and his teenage sister had grown up in the USA and spoke fluent English, their parents spoke limited, broken English and conversed with each other in Spanish.

My travel with each was also very different. When I went to L.A. with Lorch Foltz, his family back in Texas would call ahead to a swanky hotel and reserve a room with two beds for the two of us in the name of Commander Lorch Foltz. *I knew that ordinary enlisted sailors like the two of us could not afford and would not be welcome at such hotels.* At best, we might be allowed to sleep on cots in the back lobby area with access to the visitor's rest rooms.

I wondered why the upscale hotel desk people never questioned Lorch about why he was not wearing a high ranking commissioned officer uniform. But I finally decided that his wealthy family's influence extended all the way to California. In any event, it was nice to enjoy this luxury for the first time in my life. In addition, the Foltz family often sent their son large boxes of "goodies" which he shared with me and other friends. However, I had to appreciate his family's kindnesses from far away Texas.

It was a totally different story with my Mexican friend, Mario Perez. Although hesitant as though I might refuse, he invited me to spend a weekend with him and his family. I readily accepted his invitation and had one of the most enjoyable weekends I had ever experienced. His family, who lived in a very modest house, seemed a bit uncomfortable at first when Mario arrived with his red haired, very fair skinned friend with a Southern drawl. That discomfort was only momentary and Mario's family quickly turned out to be sweet and loving and accepting of this strange looking and talking Southern boy. That night I slept between clean white sheets in the small guest room and awoke to the smell of freshly brewed coffee and homemade Mexican food being cooked. Although I spoke no Spanish, that did not prove to be a handicap in my friendship with the Perez family.

Love can be shown in many ways other than verbally and that is what happened in this case. The Perez family introduced me to Mexican food prepared slowly by Mama Perez. I had never seen, much less eaten, a tortilla before that time. And Mama Perez made everything from scratch. On my second visit to their home, Mama Perez spread fresh butter on hot tortillas and brought them and a cup of coffee to my bedroom. She placed the coffee on my bedside table and then hand fed me a hot, buttered tortilla. I've never tasted a tortilla as good as that one. It was the closest thing to being back home with my mother, Macie.

So, I found love--not luxury--with the Perez family. The fact that Mr. Perez brought home a laborer's salary did not appear to bother this happy family. They proudly introduced me to their Hispanic friends and neighbors and I developed a lifelong affection for Latinos. They owned an older model car and Mario and I dated some of the Hispanic girls in and around La Brea. The teenage Perez daughter was beautiful, with dark eyes and jet black hair. She attended an all girl Catholic school and once asked me to be her escort at a school dance. Before we left for the dance, she hung a St. Christopher medal around my neck and this A.R. Presbyterian boy became a Catholic for one memorable evening!

Their son and my friend, Mario, was sent overseas a short time before I was and I became like a surrogate son to this loving family. Once, fearing that I was abusing their hospitality, I failed to visit them when I had a free weekend. Mama Perez found this out and broke into tears. I realized then that I had to juggle my visits with the Perez family and others so that Mama's feelings would not be hurt.

*Although those experiences occurred many years ago, I remain grateful for the kindnesses and friendships I had with both of these young men and their wonderful, loving families. I've had no contact with the Perez family since the war because I've never been near La Brea, CA. I did spend one evening with Lorch Foltz and his wife when I was on a business trip to Dallas, TX. Lorch had become head of his family's clothing manufacturing business but otherwise was the big, friendly guy I had known back in San Diego.*

# CHAPTER 8
## A Quick Lesson in a Strange City

OCCASIONALLY, I CHOSE to hitch-hike alone to my weekend liberty destination. Sailors would usually gather in groups waiting for someone to pick them up. I felt that large groups might intimidate some drivers so I tried a different tactic. I moved away from the group and stood by myself with thumb in the air. My system worked out really well. I would usually get a ride quickly and it appeared that having red hair worked to my advantage. Often the first words I heard were: "I have a (niece, nephew or another family member) who has red hair."

On one of these "solo" excursions, I went to Santa Barbara to visit a family that had moved there from Shelby, NC, some years before. Although we were not really close friends, I thought it would be nice to visit with someone from "back home." Although invited, I did not want to stay at their house overnight. So, I went to a hotel in town and made plans to sleep there (on a cot in the back lobby). *It was common during World War II for hotels to accommodate servicemen unable to pay regular rates.*

I was shown to my cot and placed my overnight bag on it to show that it was "taken." Then, I started looking for the "head"--Navy parlance for rest room. A well dressed gentleman saw me looking around and said, "Sailor, I'll show you to the men's room." On the way, he introduced himself and said he was acting in a play currently being held in Santa Barbara. I was impressed that he was being so nice to a strange sailor.

When we reached the men's room I turned to thank him for his kindness. However, he unexpectedly entered the rest room with me. Next he tried to join me in the enclosed toilet! I suddenly remembered what my Northern Navy buddies had warned me about. I pushed him out and latched the door. That was my first personal experience with homosexuality!

*I have many bitter-sweet memories of my time in California. While there I also became good friends with two Southern sailor boys, Jeremy Yates of Arkansas and Frank Turner of Charlotte, NC. I believe I met them at the Hollywood Canteen. I had some fun times in LA with each before they were shipped out for overseas.*

When I spent time with Frank, we would usually go to Hollywood and use his older brother's apartment as our base. His brother, Jim Turner, was an actor who was billed in back home (Charlotte, NC) newspapers as "the next Randolph Scott," who was also from Charlotte and was a very popular Hollywood actor at that time. He is probably best remembered as a "tall in the saddle" Western film hero.

Although Jim Turner had had some small parts in Hollywood movies when Frank and I were there, to my knowledge he never became the big star envisioned by the Charlotte media. His younger brother Frank, himself, looked like a Hollywood leading man. He was extremely handsome and liked to show off his bronzed, muscular body at beaches we visited together. We must have made an interesting contrast walking along the beach in our bathing suits with my pale skin, freckles and red hair and his dark brown skin and jet black hair.

*Frank Turner shipped out before I did but we were able to reconnect briefly after the war while I was at Catawba College less than an hour away from Charlotte, NC, Frank's home. Then, we again lost touch when he left for San Francisco, CA to work for one of the wire services.*

The other Southern sailor I met in California, Jeremy Yates, was also shipped out soon after we met but not before we became close friends. Before leaving, Jeremy introduced me to a Jewish family named Shall. This family lived in L.A. proper and had two teenage girls. Jeremy and I developed strong friendships with them. *I still have a photo of the four of us at beautiful and spacious Griffith Park which is recognizable by the large HOLLYWOOD sign that overlooks the park.*

After Jeremy left for overseas duty, I became close friends with the entire Shall family and they began inviting me to spend weekends at their home. Mr. Shall and I had a special connection through the sport of boxing. He was a professional fight trainer and of course I had a growing interest in boxing. Mr. Shall had discovered and worked with the great welter-weight boxer, Sugar Ray Robinson, early in his career. As Sugar Ray's immense boxing talent became better known, Mr. Shall was eased out of his position by more famous trainers who could give Sugar Ray greater exposure.

Soon Sugar Ray's skills were known around the world and he eventually became World Champion boxer in two different weight classes. *(I've always thought that Sugar Ray Robinson was the best boxer, pound for pound, of anyone in the world!).* I learned much about boxing from Mr. Shall whose knowledge of the sport was far superior to mine.

*An interesting observation: during my time in California I had formed strong personal relationships with two different families, Shall and Perez, plus four Navy buddies, and all except Frank and Jeremy were members of minorities.*

# CHAPTER 9

## A Possible Romance?

I WAS NEVER romantically involved with either of the Shall girls, although I cherished their friendship. *(In retrospect, I realize that this was the first time I had ever felt completely comfortable with non-related members of the opposite sex. Obviously I had overcome much of my shyness by then and had discovered how to make "small talk").* The Shall sisters also offered me an opportunity for romance when they introduced me to their pretty, younger cousin. *(Note: big age difference: I was 18 and she was 16).*

In this case, there was an immediate strong mutual attraction--also a new experience for me. I had had a couple of "crushes" in my life but the objects of those crushes never knew it. This budding romance did not sit well with her parents, however, who apparently were more "orthodox" than their close relatives who had invited me into their home. The young lady's parents quickly let me know that they didn't want their pretty daughter involved with a sailor--and certainly not one of a different religion. So that prospect of romance was quickly nipped in the bud!

I had lots of wholesome fun with the Shall girls but had one potentially dangerous encounter when Nanette and I were returning from a picnic at Griffith Park. The bus we were riding on was full. We were standing, holding on to straps, when a group of four tough-looking Hispanic young men boarded the bus. One of them got much closer than necessary to Nanette and I could see he was making her very uncomfortable. Without thinking of possible repercussions, I shoved him away from her.

He and his friends gave me some hate stares but got off at the next stop. Nanette then told me that she recognized the four men as "Pachucos," a very dangerous gang *(perhaps like the MS-13 gangs existing today)*. I had read newspaper stories about fights between "Pachucos" and sailors and the "bad blood" between them. Nanette said she feared these might attack me for insulting their friend. She said that the "Pachuca" girls were known to hide razors in their hair.

My last contact with the Shall girls occurred when I went to L.A. to catch the train taking me for my final training at Port Hueneme, CA. By then I was assigned to ACORN 54, an amphibious outfit and had been scheduled for Marine style training before going overseas. I had written to say goodbye to the Shall family and told them when and from where I would be leaving. Not expecting anyone to be at the L.A. train station to see me off, to my surprise the Shall daughters, their pretty cousin, and an attractive girl friend of theirs were there.

The scene of four good looking young women lined up to kiss a sailor goodbye aroused wild cheering from other servicemen boarding or already on the train. I must admit I enjoyed both the cheering and the kisses. My reaction to these kisses was very different from that first one I received playing Post Office a few years earlier!

*I was sorry that my good friend, Jeremy Yates, could not be there to share in this celebration. Jeremy and I lost contact until the war ended. After returning from overseas, we were able to re-establish contact and resumed our friendship by mail. Both of us were in college and were trying to figure out a way we could get together. Then before we were able to work this out, I received a letter from his mother saying that Jeremy's car had stalled on a railroad track and he was killed by a train. I still remember his kindness and wry sense of humor.*

# CHAPTER 10

## Learning Marine Training

AFTER MY MEMORABLE "send off" from Los Angeles, I arrived at Port Hueneme, CA with little idea of what lay ahead. I found myself again surrounded by complete strangers. I was the only person from my class at San Diego assigned to ACORN 54. In case you're wondering what the acronym ACORN stands for, join the club! Despite many questions, the Navy never revealed what those letters represented. All we were told was that in battle we would follow the Marines ashore and immediately set up an organizational unit to supply what was needed. Internet searches of Acronyms provided little help. The only reference I could find for ACORN was Aviation Construction Ordinance Radar (Naval). That, obviously, did not sound like our group.

Acronym aside, shortly after we arrived at 29 Palms we were told to get ready for special desert training--the same type of training Marines receive before going overseas. We were told that this training was to prepare us for participation in the anticipated invasion of Japan. Each of us was issued an M-1 Carbine and was taught how to use it. Much of the other training was strictly physical, consisting of various types of obstacle courses with running, jumping, climbing walls, doing pull ups and pushups, etc. Although I don't recall having any particular problem with any of this training, I'll never forget the experience of crawling on my belly under live fire. *I did not have to be warned twice to keep my butt down!*

Immediately after completing this training and returning to Port Hueneme, I became ill with a very high fever and was taken to a nearby Naval Hospital where my illness was diagnosed as a recurrence of malaria fever suffered when I was 10 years old. Before that diagnosis was made, an interesting thing occurred. As I was being wheeled into the emergency room, some nurses screamed, "You're back!" I was puzzled by this since I had never been there before.

Then when I reached my room, I found out the reason for their excitement: red-haired actor Van Johnson had recently been discharged from this hospital and I was mistaken for him. That's how I ended up in Van Johnson's room and bed. When informed of the mix up, I kiddingly replied: "I'm insulted: I'm much better looking than that guy!" After a few days treatment I was returned to my unit and was told to prepare for boarding a troop ship headed for the Pacific to be part of the invasion of Japan. All of us were warned not to tell anyone, even our families, of our destination.

*Note: During WWII, one of the most well known slogans was "Loose Lips Sink Ships."* Apparently someone must have had very "loose lips," since the town of Oxnard had a big going away party for us, complete with an orchestra, food, adult beverages, and female dance partners, the night before we were to leave. In addition, hundreds of townspeople came to the dock the next morning to wave goodbye to us as we boarded the ship and sailed away to the sounds of a live band playing "Anchors Aweigh" and other patriotic music!

Boarding a troop ship did not remotely resemble boarding a peace time cruise ship. In this case, we had to climb a steep gang plank with our one hundred pound sea bags carried on our left shoulders. When we reached the top, we had to salute the flag at the bow of the ship. Then, we saluted the Officer of the Day (OD) and asked his permission to come aboard. After we were allowed to board the ship we had to continue down several ladders to our bunks.

Still in good shape from my time in the gym, I had no problem boarding the ship while carrying my sea bag consisting of everything I owned including clothing, and personal toiletries, as well as hammock and M-1 carbine which had been issued to me at 29 Palms and stayed with me until I was ready to board the ship to return home. Handling this weight was quite a chore for the smaller or out-of-shape guys. In fact, I was fearful that some of them might fall from the gang plank into the sea. As far as I know, all of them were able to complete the boarding despite some shaky moments.

There were many moist eyes (including mine) as we weighed anchor and slowly left the harbor to the sound of patriotic music by the orchestra and shouts of goodbye from the crowd gathered on the dock. I'll admit I wondered if I would ever again see the USA. Thus with a mixture of fear and excitement we headed for the open seas of the wide Pacific.

This journey would eventually include brief stops at Pearl Harbor, Enewetok and Ulithi Atolls, and Okinawa where we boarded our LST to await the signal to invade Japan. Details of this journey will follow later, after more description of how my family was being affected by the war.

# CHAPTER 11
## Horrors of War

THE FACT IS, World War II was horrible for all parents with children involved but it was especially hard on Haskell and Macie White who saw three of their four sons in combat zones at the same time. Because of her soft, sensitive nature, Mom was simply crushed by this situation.

Frank emerged as the only big hero of the three of us, receiving a Silver Star and several other commendation medals for bravery. He drove tanks and half-tracks during the entire time he was overseas, culminating in the "Battle of the Bulge." His 6th Armored Division was recognized as the fastest moving Division of the Third Army and usually accompanied General George Patton who was always out front. Frank said Patton would shout "Follow me boys!" as he raced past them in his jeep.

Patton's aggressive attitude probably brought WWII in Europe to a quicker end but it also resulted in many troops being killed or badly injured when caught behind enemy lines. Frank received a special award for "demonstrating exceptional courage" for making repeated trips behind enemy lines to carry wounded and dead soldiers on his back and return them to their units. That of course represented the military's credo of "leaving no soldier behind." Other awards for his bravery was one for running into a burning building and driving a truck loaded with ammunition through a wall of the building. His quick action saved many lives which would have been lost had the ammunition exploded inside the building.

The family learned about these and other acts of bravery from newspaper and radio accounts, as well as from the Department of the Army. Frank did not discuss his activities during the war except for one night when I asked him why he did these things. His reply: "Someone had to do them."

Loved by most of his troops, Gen. Patton was highly criticized by fellow generals for driving (or leading) his troops so fast that food and other supplies could not keep up. This became a war-time scandal in the news media and did seriously affect the physical well being of his troops. For example, Brother Frank was a muscular 215 pounder when he entered the Army but at the end of the War weighed 135 pounds. When I asked Frank about this, he said he and his troops sometimes had to survive on squirrels, rabbits, deer or anything else they could catch or scrounge.

During this period, a tank Frank was driving was blown up and only Frank and one other crew member survived. The other survivor was so badly injured that he was sent home. Frank bandaged up his own wounds (refusing offers to be put in for a Purple Heart) got into another tank and rejoined the fight. This was typical of him. Although wounded many times during his 42 months of fighting, he never allowed his officers to submit the paperwork needed to get a Purple Heart! His only regret about that was that he could have returned home a few weeks earlier had he received one or more Purple Hearts.

*Contrast that with John Kerry, former Secretary of State, who received three Purple Hearts and a Silver Star for his three months as a "Swift Boat" captain during the Vietnam War. In fact, he might have become President of the United States, except for action by his shipmates who were outraged at his claims of wounds and bravery. I was happy that the actions by former Kerry shipmates (known as "Swift Boating") may have kept him from becoming president.*

Back to a true hero, Brother Frank, in the heat of battle, the lieutenant leading Frank's unit was killed. Frank was asked to accept a "field commission" and take the Lieutenant's position. He refused to take the commission but agreed to lead the unit as a sergeant which he did until the war ended. At the end of the war in Europe, Frank was one of the first Americans to begin freeing the Jews and others awaiting gas chambers at concentration camps. This was so traumatic that he could not discuss conditions he found there but I have no doubt he had nightmares about them.

Once the concentration camps were emptied, Frank served the rest of his time in the Army as U.S. Official in Charge of a small German town where he regained some of the weight he lost during the fighting. Ironically, he ended up becoming friends of some German people he met while serving in their town.

By the time Frank returned home his weight had returned to about 160 pounds. He never regained his muscular physique and died at age 38 from a bad heart, damaged by rheumatic fever as a young boy, and further weakened by the stress of all those months and years of fighting. He left his wife, Grace, and three young children: Vickie, Lynn and Richard. And he left a void in my life never filled.

*Note: Some months after the War, the family received a paper from the War Department showing that Frank was in battle for 42 straight months. During that time, he often went long periods of time without even being able to communicate with his family by letter. Contrast that with present day servicemen who can communicate frequently with their families by telephone, email and even SKYPE, and rarely remain in a battle zone for more than a year without being able to come home for a visit.*

Although Robert never talked of his service there is no doubt in my mind that his life was also shortened by his wartime service. He died at age 55 also from a bad heart. He left his wife, Lena, and son, Robert Keith.

*My oldest brother, Howard, was probably the most naturally adventurous of the*

*H.H. White boys. He no doubt would have been the first to go into service except for the fact that he was married and already had several children then. Eventually, the number of children resulting from his marriage to a beauty named Louise Byers reached 8: five boys and three girls.*

# CHAPTER 12
## My War Zone Service--No Heroism for Me

MY TRIP TO the active war zone seemed to take forever. The top speed of this troop ship must not have topped 11 knots per hour. Our first stop was at Pearl Harbor and the awful scene of destruction caused by the Japanese bombing on December 7, 1941. We spent a few days there stocking up on food. I was so starved for fruit that I ate canned pineapple until I began breaking out in hives.

Traveling on the troop ship made me wonder if I was really in the Navy. Our bunks were stacked 4 to 5 high. If I turned over, I hit the butt of the sailor above me. If the sailor below me turned over, he hit my butt. And the heat on this over-loaded ship was almost unbearable as we neared the equator. The ship was supposed to be cooled with large fans, but none of them worked.

After some nights without sleep, I decided to try spending my nights topside. I found space under one of the ship's small boats where it was much cooler and less crowded. There was one big problem: Since it rained every night it was almost impossible to keep dry. I soon learned I could open my hammock and put it on the deck, cross my arms and stretch the hammock over me, thus diverting the water around me.

After that I slept like a baby, except for the times that our radar would detect a Japanese submarine. When the alarm sounded we would rush to our stations and begin dropping depth bombs while the ship went into zig zag maneuvers. These occasions became more frequent when our ship passed near Truk Island which was still held by the Japanese. *The powers that be decided it was simpler just to let the Japanese stay on Truk and starve, than to risk the loss of our troops by taking the island.*

We never knew whether or not we sank any submarines and we didn't stick around long enough to spot any tell tale oil slicks. In any event, our ship remained undamaged. Before arriving at Okinawa, our ultimate destination, we had two more brief intermediate stops at small islands to get brief respites from the confined quarters. One of these was Ulithi Atoll, part of the Marshall Islands in the Western Pacific. The other was Enewetak Atoll, scene of a fierce battle the previous year that cost the lives of hundreds of U.S. Marines and thousands of Japanese.

On the surface, Enewetak seemed insignificant but I learned later it provided a stepping stone for later critical assaults by the U.S. on the Marianna Islands to the North. Enewetak also later gained some fame as the site where the U.S. exploded our first hydrogen bomb. *(Ironically, newspaper articles in the year 2014 said the Marshall Islands were suing the United States for damages when the U.S. tested new bombs there after the War).*

On the way, as a 3rd class petty officer, I was lucky to be spared onerous duties such as cleaning toilets and chipping paint. Since the ship had its own yeomen, the services of the two passenger yeomen were not really essential. My fellow yeoman of ACORN 54 and I were welcome to visit and hang around the office. Since we didn't want to be in the way, we rarely stayed long but stopped by the office daily to offer our services. Rarely were we needed. Therefore, much of my day was spent in one of the small boats watching the vast expanse of ocean, day dreaming of "back home" or finding someone to spar with. Other sailors with nothing to do kept up continuous games of poker.

All of us expected to be part of the invasion force as soon as we arrived at Okinawa, already secured by the Marines. Just before leaving the troop ship to board our landing ship, I was informed that, for reasons I never understood, both of us yeomen 3rd class had been promoted to Yeoman 2nd class. I couldn't have cared less about the promotion at the time but it became important to me later!

Once anchored at Okinawa, some of us were taken from the troop ship and loaded onto LST 974, along with tanks, jeeps and other invasion equipment. The other yeoman and I were separated at this point but later renewed our friendship after being discharged.

# CHAPTER 13
## An Event that Saved Many Lives--War is Over!

AS WE AWAITED the invasion signal, we learned that one of our bombers had released an atomic bomb on Hiroshima. This was followed by a second bomb on Nagasaki, and soon after that we received the joyful news that the War in the Pacific was over!

Although Okinawa was technically "secure" at the time we arrived there, many Japanese soldiers hiding in the island's caves had either not received word the war was over or just chose to continue fighting. Every night some emerged from the caves with their weapons, ready to continue the war. Since many of the Marines had already been sent home, there was a shortage of military personnel to guard the caves. So they turned to nearby ships for help in dealing with Japanese soldiers still occupying the caves.

Those guarding the caves were ordered to shoot any Japanese soldier who came out of the cave with a weapon. Soon after I boarded the LST, I was told that it was my turn to guard the cave that night. As instructed, I loaded up my M-1 Carbine and prepared to head for shore. Just as I, along with other shipmates headed for the "cave guarding" duty were boarding the small boat to take us ashore, we were suddenly told to get back on our LST. It turned out that our ship's Captain had just received an urgent message that a huge typhoon was headed straight for Okinawa and our ship was ordered to leave Buckner Bay and head out to open sea immediately. This move was to try to avoid collisions with other ships.

Anyone familiar with an LST knows that this flat-bottomed ship rocks so much it can cause sea sickness for those inclined to have this ailment--even when anchored in port! Just imagine how it would be bounced around by huge waves caused by a typhoon. Heading out to sea that night I lashed myself in my hammock and the ship's rocking motion soon put me to sleep. I was surprised the next morning to find that we had been rammed by another ship that night during the worst of the typhoon. I slept through this event. We later heard that this typhoon and its after effects ultimately cost the lives of 15,000 people at Okinawa. In addition, almost everyone on the ship except me was deathly sea sick. My previously weak stomach remained calm and I didn't miss a meal. Obviously I was over the worst of my stomach problems.

After the typhoon subsided, we expected to return to Okinawa. However, our next orders were to proceed on to mainland Japan to occupy that country. Thank God we didn't have to go as invaders. Before we reached our destination, Ominato, Japan, a small city in the Northern Honshu area, we were told that the climate there was extremely cold, and we were issued fur lined everything: hats, jackets, pants and boots! It's interesting that Post World War II Ominato does not even appear on many maps of Japan. We were not briefed on its history and thought it was just a little out-of-the way town. But 70 years later online articles on Ominato give a different story from my recollection as a teenager. I learned that Ominato played a highly significant role in World War II as reflected by Wikipedia.

After the start of the Pacific War, Ominato became the home port of the Imperial Japanese Navy (IJN) 5th Fleet. The diversionary attack on Dutch Harbor in the Aleutian Islands during the Battle of Midway was launched from Ominato. This port city was bombed several times in the closing days of the war, followed by a large attack from August 8-10, 1945, which destroyed several ships. *American forces landed from the USS Panamint (AGC-13) to accept the surrender of the base from the Imperial Japanese Navy on 9 September 1945. The base facilities were used by the United States Navy (I guess that was us) during the Occupation of Japan and are currently in use by the Japan Maritime Self Defense Forces.*

We were not even made aware of the surrender of the base mentioned above and received no briefing on this historic event. Our group of occupiers apparently slipped into port on a little LST while these ceremonies (of which we "swabbies" were un-aware) were taking place. As we prepared to go ashore, we were ordered to unload our weapons before leaving the ship. This was to ensure that some sailor wouldn't get "trigger happy" and restart the war.

Ominato was just as cold and snowy as we had been told. This was the first time this Southern boy had ever experienced "real cold." We needed all the fur lined garments we had been issued and never saw the ground without a covering of snow while we were there. After going to our quarters (which were better than anything we had stayed in previously), we were just getting comfortably settled down when the ceiling lights started moving back and forth. That was our first experience with an earthquake and it was pretty scary. However, we soon got used to earthquakes which are common in Japan. These earthquakes were usually not severe and the Japanese pretty much ignored them, as did we after awhile.

Citizens of Ominato had expected the worst when we occupied their land. They assumed we would subject them to the same type of treatment that our military received in Japanese POW camps. However, General Douglas McArthur had taken steps to see that this would not happen. He ordered occupying troops to follow the rules of the Geneva Convention, i.e., we were not to abuse the Japanese people. With just a few exceptions, the Occupation Forces behaved extremely well and treated the Japanese with respect.

We received the same from the Japanese. We did little work there and mostly stood guard, ate and slept. We had excellent quarters in the deserted Japanese barracks and made full use of their facilities. The only worthwhile thing I remember doing while there was to gather up the trash daily, load it on one of our jeeps and go through the snow to empty the trash at a Japanese public dump. I was envied by the other guys who never got to go anywhere. I don't know why I was selected for this job but some officer must have known that, since I was from the South, I could drive almost any type of motorized vehicle. *Many of the sailors from Northern cities did not even know how to drive a car. They had used public transportation back home.*

Being a teenager, I made a game of testing my ability to get the jeep through the largest snow mounds I could find. The little 4-wheel drive jeep never failed me, despite my efforts to get stuck. I was always able to get back to our camp on time. These actions, as immature as they were, reflected that my character was changing from an uptight, cautious individual into someone who would occasionally take a chance.

A short few weeks after we occupied Ominato, we were told we were leaving to occupy another part of Japan. A group of Marines then took over occupation duties there with an impressive filmed ceremony. To our great wonderment, on our final night at Ominato, the city fathers planned a "going away" party for us. It turned out to be a surprisingly festive occasion. The town's citizens turned out in force to bid us goodbye. They provided food, drink, a band that attempted to play American "Big Band" music, and the town's prettiest young ladies to dance with us. *(Some of the sailors, who were starved for female companionship, were so smitten by the girls that they tried to figure out a way to take the girls home with them! I've heard a few succeeded).*

At the end of the party, many townspeople and sailors were teary eyed as they bade sorrowful farewells to each other! Who would have ever expected that type of emotion from people who were deadly enemies only a few weeks before?

# CHAPTER 14

## Onward to Another Occupation and Serious Duty

THE DAY AFTER the party, we boarded another LST (Number 1060 as I recall) and headed for our next occupational assignment. It was at Kisarazu, Japan, about 40 miles south of Tokyo. We were told that we would take over and operate the Kisarazu Navy Air Field for U.S. Military airplanes, among other duties. We were informed that the Japanese had just completed this new airfield in anticipation of a U.S. invasion.

However, Wikipedia reveals this Air Base was originally established in 1936 as "a base for the Imperial Japanese Navy Air Service, subordinate to the Yokosuka Naval District" just across the bay. It added that "after the end of World War II, from September 1945, the base was used by the United States Air Force." *They failed to mention that four Navy Yeomen (including yours truly) operated this air field for the Air Force!*

Since we found some partially finished new work, it appeared that the Air Base had, in fact, recently undergone modernization in preparation for the expected U.S. invasion. *(Some townspeople confirmed that!) We found some new runways, hangars, barracks and other operational infrastructure had recently been completed.*

To us, the re-modeled dormitories and other facilities seemed almost luxurious compared to what we were accustomed to back in the USA. We found the town and the area around it very different from the Northern area we first occupied. The weather was moderate and the area was much more developed with excellent railway service, residences, and active downtown stores and commercial buildings. I thought it was a very nice small city.

Unlike the situation at Ominato, we had daily contact with Japanese citizens. The Air Base employed many Japanese as cooks, wait staff, housekeepers, grounds keepers and barbers (The latter were all women)! After getting over some early shyness, we found these employees to be friendly, helpful, and efficient workers.

*The only really ill will we observed was the hatred the Koreans and Japanese had for each other! This is understandable in view of the fact that the Japanese Imperial Army forced approximately 200,000 young Korean women to become "sex slaves" to Japanese soldiers during WWII. These poor young ladies were called "comfort women." This issue festered for many years. Then Internet accounts stated that in 1992 a spokesman for the Japanese Government issued an official apology saying, "We cannot deny that the former Japanese army played a role" in abducting and detaining the "comfort girls," and "We would like to express our apologies and contrition." Then in 1998, a Japanese court ruled that the Government must compensate the women and awarded the surviving women monetary compensation.*

Now back to the story of my experiences in Kisarazu. A young Navy Lieutenant JG by the name of Minter, had been charged with organizing and operating the Air Field. He had already decided that he would utilize four Navy yeomen to handle the tower operation. I was to be one of these four. The other three were all "old salts" who had many years at sea. Because of their seniority at the Yeoman Third Class level, it was assumed that one of them would be in charge. They were disconcerted when I arrived with my newly-sewn-on Yeoman Second Class credentials.

Naturally, Lt. Minter put me in charge as the Senior N.C.O. However, I knew the only way this group could work as a team, with a neophyte like me in charge, was to forget that I outranked them. I determined that we would operate as equals. That decision removed resentment and we worked as a team with never a serious disagreement among us. Lt. Minter said that someone needed to be on duty at the tower 24 hours per day, despite the fact that we might not have a single Air Force plane land at night and only a few during daylight hours. However, he left it up to me to figure out the duty roster.

I called my group together to decide how we would provide 24 hour per day service. We discussed various plans and I told them my preference was to have one person on duty for 24 hours straight and then have three days off. *We had a cot in the work area and the person on duty could sleep most of the night. When a plane was near, the pilot would radio the tower and whoever was on duty would give them landing instructions. Sometimes not a single plane would arrive and we could sleep through the night.*

One further suggestion I offered was that when any of us were present at the base and we had nothing else to do, we might drop by the tower to help if needed. But this would not be a requirement as long as our duty system worked. All of them voted for my plan and we never had a single problem while I was there.

My reason for wanting all those days off? I wanted to learn about Japan and its people by traveling around the country on those "off days." This was especially important since we were required to be back inside the gate by 8 p.m., limiting the time each day we could be away from the base. In order to comply with base rules, I began to study maps of Japan with emphasis on the Kisarazu/Yokosuka area. I would then talk with the Japanese workers with whom I had become friendly. They would advise on how far I could go by train and get back to base before curfew. (I became especially good friends with a couple of Japanese citizens, one who was very large and wanted to be a Sumo wrestler and another who introduced me to a Japanese family).

Even with advice from Japanese friends, I was still a little apprehensive about starting one of these ventures alone so I talked with a shipmate (who planned to become a minister) and convinced him into going with me on my first train trip. We arrived at the train station, purchased our tickets, and decided we should use the "Head" (restroom) before boarding the train. We got quite a surprise! As we unzipped and started using the urinal (a trough with running water), several Japanese girls came into the rest room, looked us over, giggled, and then went into the stalls provided for women. With the look of shock on his face, my minister-to-be friend quickly zipped up his pants and ran from the station. So, I made my first train trip alone. I didn't see my friend until I returned later that day. As far as I know, he never left the base again while he was in Japan.

To ensure that I didn't miss curfew, I started with short round trips that took just a few hours. When I reached my self-imposed limit for the first leg of the trip, I would leave the train and explore that particular town until time to board a train heading back to Kisarazu. These trips were very interesting and educational to me. Many of the towns I stopped in had never seen an American in person. And I suspect none of them had ever seen someone with flaming red hair like mine. I was also a head taller than most of them.

My presence in a town often created a sensation. As soon as I got off the train and started down the street, I would begin to draw a crowd. Sometimes it appeared that the entire town was following me, pointing at my hair, and laughing.

On many occasions, I would be approached by a town official and invited to go with him to the Mayor's office. I never refused these invitations. Every Mayor was gracious and would first offer me tea (never coffee at that time). Often the Mayor would know a little English and I would utilize my very limited vocabulary supplemented by an English/Japanese dictionary and we could have some semblance of a conversation. At the end of the visit he would bow and almost always hand me a gift--usually a piece of Japanese pottery or silk. Once I was presented a Samurai sword which I sent home and kept for several years.

As I gained knowledge (and courage) I gradually increased the distance of each trip. I finally went as far as Tateyama at least twice. This city is located at the far southern tip of the Boso Peninsula, facing the Pacific Ocean to the east and south, and the entrance to Tokyo Bay on the west. Almost all of my travel in Japan was alone. For some reason none of my shipmates showed any interest in getting to know the country and its citizens. With few exceptions, most of them hung around the base and played poker or other card games.

However, on a few occasions, I went by jeep or truck with a small group of sailors to visit the big city of Tokyo. On the way, nature would call and we would leave the vehicle to satisfy that urge. We always selected a place that seemed totally vacant of people. That would change quickly when we unzipped and started to "relieve ourselves." Inevitably, we would be surrounded by Japanese women. Like in the train station, these women stared, pointed, and laughed. We eventually got used to that.

When we reached Tokyo the first time, I could not believe the devastation caused by our bombing. With a few exceptions, the buildings had been knocked down and burned. The gutters along the streets were filled with molten metal. To our amazement and a tribute to Japanese ingenuity, the famous jeweler, Mikimoto, was already operating his business in the basement of his building which had been destroyed from the ground up!

Since Mikimoto was a pioneer developer of cultured pearls, I should have made a purchase of some pearls while there. However, I didn't know enough about such things to risk money that way. *I learned that cultured pearls are actually real but the oysters producing them are induced to form the pearl by man instead of as a natural occurrence. Wikipedia explains that "Mantle cells are implanted into the gonads or other soft tissues of the mother oyster and a pearl sack grows around them."*

Driving around Tokyo, we could see that a few buildings had been deliberately spared from the worst of the bombing. The Imperial Palace and the Imperial Hotel were two historic buildings that our pilots were asked to avoid hitting with bombs.

The latter had been largely designed and built to specifications laid out by America's famous architect Frank Lloyd Wright. That these buildings were spared didn't mean that they didn't receive damage from the bombing around them. Below is an excerpt from Wikipedia:

*"During World War II, the South wing of the hotel was gutted by incendiary bombs on 25 May 1945, and the Peacock room was destroyed. The hotel asked Wright to come back and design the repairs to the hotel, but Wright refused. The hotel was commandeered for a period by the Occupation forces and managed by the U.S. Government, under the supervision of Lieutenant J. Malcolm Morris 1945 to 1952, and some of the damage was repaired during this time..."*

We were not allowed inside the Imperial Palace but we did have tea in the tea room at the Imperial Hotel. Although my shipmates had little interest in learning about the Japanese culture, they certainly enjoyed one aspect of it: the houses of "ill repute" known erroneously by GI's as "Geisha houses." True Geishas are highly trained entertainers. The girls being visited by my shipmates did not have these skills. They were sexual objects for the sailors (and others). I personally knew sailors who would visit these places where they would exchange highly prized cigarettes and chocolate for sex.

On occasion, when I wasn't traveling, I would accompany friends to one of these places (designated as "safe places" to visit). They were actually inspected by the Navy and guarded by our Shore Patrol. I knew one of these guards who took full advantage of the opportunity to enjoy free sex because of his position. He contracted diseases and was a frequent visitor/patient to the medical stations where medics treated his infections. Despite warnings of permanent damage, he continued his activities at both inspected and non-inspected facilities. On the other hand, when I went with friends to these places, I never entered any of the "back rooms" where the girls "entertained."

Incidentally, I should mention that these girls were not like our "street walkers." They had no choice in the matter and were often fairly refined young ladies. Sometimes, if a Japanese family was in dire financial need, they might send one of their daughters to such a place to earn money to keep the family from total financial ruin.

*I vividly remember spending part of Christmas Day, 1945, at one of these places with friends. I was there to have company while my friends satisfied their sexual urges. I remained true to my standards regarding sex and alcohol the entire time I was in Japan.*

In addition to learning about Japan, I became aware of other worldly things (in retrospect some of these might be considered unsavory). One of the first things I learned was that I had untapped ways of earning some money selling cigarettes. The entire time I had been away from the U.S., the Navy had been giving each of us two cartons of cigarettes a week. Since I didn't smoke, I had been giving the cartons to my shipmates who smoked. Then, soon after I began assisting Air Force pilots in landing, one asked me if I was "bartering" cigarettes with the Japanese for "yen" and other valuables.

He laughed when I told him I had been giving my Navy supplied cigarettes away. He said that many Japanese loved American cigarettes--especially Lucky Strikes! The pilot proceeded to educate me and suggested he would be happy to bring me more cigarettes than my allotment on his next trip provided I would do some bartering for him. Intrigued by this, I told him I would check around to see if I could find a market where I could exchange cigarettes for goods, e.g. cameras. *Even back then, many Japanese carried an expensive camera around their necks. That is how I learned about such prized German cameras as Zeiss Ikons, Leikas and Nikons as well as some valuable Japanese made cameras.*

My Japanese worker/friend introduced me to a man who might meet my needs. Although he was probably a "black market" operator, he became a good friend and associate. (You can readily see that my high standards are going downhill in a hurry). The next time the pilot landed, I was ready to receive cigarettes to be used in bartering. Also, I had stopped giving away my unwanted cigarettes and was accumulating a pocket full of yen and sen. (Because of inflation in that country after the war, a pocket full of yen and sen might have amounted to $20.00 at most!)

After the pilot's education, I never lacked for Japanese currency and sent home several nice cameras, two or three Samurai swords, and two Japanese rifles. I sold all of these items while in college--mostly to have money to go to dances at women's colleges around the state of North Carolina.

My Japanese "black market" friend also introduced me to a respectable merchant who had a wife and two very nice late teen daughters. Mr. Sato took me into his home at some risk. Many of the better class Japanese were fearful of losing prestige if they brought former enemy Americans into their homes. Being friendly in public was one thing; bringing an American into their home was another.

After my first visit to the Sato home, the ice was broken and for the rest of my stay in Japan I was always welcomed into the Sato family home. Kimie Sato, their youngest daughter, and I were attracted to each other and would sit with our feet hanging over the charcoal fire pit in the middle of the living room and talk. We eventually held hands--a daring thing for a respectable Japanese girl to do before marriage. Kimie had been engaged through a family arrangement as is common in Japan. Kimie's fiancé had become a "kamikaze pilot" late in the war and of course, never came home.

She said she had never even held hands with him and barely knew him. After several "dates," she gave me a light kiss which she said was her "first kiss" with a man. Once when I was visiting her I overstayed the base curfew. I didn't want to face charges for this so took an incredible risk to avoid Captain's Mast or possibly worse. I remembered a friend telling me that a large tree had fallen across the ravine that served to keep anyone from entering the base except through the gate.

I found this fallen tree and walked across it in almost total darkness. This allowed me to bypass the gate and avoid a "late sign-in." I went to bed and to sleep with no worry in the world. Early the next morning, I was awakened and taken to Shore Patrol Headquarters. I asked the SP why I was brought there and he said: "A Japanese woman was raped by a sailor last night. We noticed on the roster that you failed to check in last night."

He added that the Japanese woman victim would be brought into the room to signify whether or not I was the guilty party. I was pretty nervous while I waited for her to arrive. However, when the victim arrived and took one look at me and my red hair she immediately began shaking her head and saying: "Na, na, na, not him." I was obviously relieved but when asked why I failed to sign in I stammered and pleaded ignorance. Since failure to "sign-in" was not a serious offense, I was told I was free to go and they continued the search for the rapist. This rape by one of our military was one of only a handful of known violations against the Japanese by our servicemen during the occupation.

I continued to visit the Sato family until I left for home. But you can bet I didn't miss curfew or walk that tree across the ravine again. Before I left, Kimie and I exchanged addresses and soon after I arrived home in Shelby I received a letter from her. In the letter, she said she had traveled to Yokohama to wave goodbye to me from a cliff overlooking our ship. But of course I never saw her. We continued to exchange letters for a few more years but then the letters stopped. But I still remember the pretty Japanese girl and her family who invited a lonely young sailor into their home for that brief moment in time.

The troop ship I came back to the U.S. on was much like the one I traveled on from California to Okinawa. This time, the work crew consisted of sailors through the rank of 3rd class petty officer. But since I was now a 2nd class petty officer, I was again spared the cleaning, chipping and painting that all sailors dread. God was still blessing me.

After the long, slow journey across the Pacific, Alcatraz came into view, signaling that we were close to San Francisco. Note: Ironically a large number of police boats were circling Alcatraz as we passed by. We later learned that some prisoners had escaped Alcatraz, which was thought to be "impregnable" until then. As I recall, the prisoners were never found but were assumed dead by drowning. Soon after passing Alcatraz, we dropped anchor at Treasure Island and were able to kiss the ground of our wonderful country. After disembarking, we were given passes and told to enjoy our first and only night on liberty in beautiful San Francisco.

On the way from Japan to the U.S., I had become friends with a sailor from Utah. He told me he was a member of the Church of Jesus Christ of Latter Day Saints, i.e., a Mormon. *I had never heard of this religious group although I later learned that my father had allowed a group of Mormons to set up their sleeping tents on our farm while they were in South Carolina on a recruiting trip. When I returned to South Carolina after 50 years away, I met descendants of those Mormons who camped on land where we had lived and farmed!*

In any event, the Utah sailor invited me to accompany him to his sister's apartment in downtown San Francisco. I was happy to accept the invitation because I knew no one there. We had a fine time with his attractive sister who guided us on a walking tour around the city. My friend and I returned to our base that night thinking that we would start for home the next day. In fact, my shipmate did leave the next morning, starting his journey home but I was told I had another day in San Francisco.

Before leaving, however, he called his sister and told her that he was leaving as planned but that I had been kept over another night. She told him to tell me to come to her apartment and I accepted her invitation and we had another enjoyable evening before I said another "final" goodbye.

I got out of bed the next morning ready to head to the railroad station and leave the west coast behind. Then I was told that I had again been delayed and could have another liberty in San Francisco. I didn't dare call my friend's sister again and went on liberty by myself only to bump into her on a street downtown. Both of us were surprised and she asked: "Why didn't you call me?" I replied that I feared she would think I was "nuts."

She insisted on treating me to another night on the town and then we again said our third "final" goodbye. *This one did turn out to be final!* The next day I got on a train with about 19 other sailors heading east to New Orleans. We would spend the night in that city and then go to our separate destinations. This would be a four-day train ride from California to New Orleans.

Our group consisted of 15 white guys and 5 black guys. We had been issued chits that we could use to purchase food at stops along the way to New Orleans as well as money to stay in a hotel for one night. We had decided as a group to save our dinner chits in order to have a last, expensive meal together at a fine restaurant in New Orleans. We ate hot dogs, chips and the like at short stops along the way, in anticipation of that final celebratory meal at the best restaurant we could find.

After leaving the train station for our overnight in New Orleans we got advice from some local citizens as to where we could get the best food. So, the 20 of us, all in uniform, entered the chosen restaurant and were placed at tables. Then, the restaurant manager approached us and said: "I'm sorry, the colored boys won't be able to eat at this restaurant." I was incensed at hearing this, got up from my table and said: "Look, we've all just returned from the war; if all of us can't eat here, none of us will eat here."

Several of the other white sailors began getting up to leave with me but one of the black fellows came up and grabbed me around the shoulder and said: "Jim, we're back in the South and we'll find the same thing at any restaurant we go to. You guys go ahead and enjoy your meal here and we'll find a black restaurant which will serve us." They then said their goodbyes to us and left. That's the last time I saw any of these fellows but the meal that I ate at that restaurant was certainly not enjoyable. It left me with a bitter taste.

The following morning we would all go our separate ways. I had a train ticket that would take me north to Charleston, SC, (where I would receive my discharge papers) and a bus ticket for either Shelby or Kings Mountain. The others had tickets to their respective destinations where they would get their discharge papers. The rest of that night, the next day's train ride, and the bus ride home are just a blur to me. I do remember Brother Frank meeting my bus and with tears in his eyes said: "My Little Brother--you're not so little now!" He then drove me home.

Mom was tearfully happy to have her little boy back home and Dad even gave me a hug. I spent the next few days getting to know my family again--especially Frank and Bob who had been in harm's way for such a long time. I also visited with all my siblings and their children. All of the latter had grown considerably. And I saw some nieces and nephews for the first time. It was nice beyond words to be home.

PART 3

# Coming Home from the Navy: Work or College?

# CHAPTER 1
## What to Do: Decisions! Decisions!

WHEN I ARRIVED home after discharge from the Navy, May 16, 1946, I had no firm idea of what to do with the rest of my life. I had thought of applying for my old job at the Shelby Post Office but didn't like the idea of having the "fear of dogs" problem that carrying the mail entails. I thought about getting a job as a butcher. After all, I had some training and experience in that job while relieving Dad as the butcher at Beam's store when he was on vacation or sick. But a career as a butcher didn't inspire me.

I had learned through the service grapevine that returning veterans would be offered benefits to prepare them to return to civilian life. Those I had heard about (but with few specific details) included: (1) the GI bill which would pay some or all college expenses and (2) what was referred to at the time as the "52-20 Club." I knew more about the latter because Brother Bob, who had returned home earlier than I, was participating in it. Briefly, the government would pay a World War II veteran $20 per week for 52 weeks, while they pursued or trained for a career.

Many of the veterans used the "52-20" club as an excuse to get some rest and a small amount of money with little effort. Often they would indicate they were looking for a type of job not readily available. For example, my brother Bob had indicated that he wanted to learn to be a "shoe maker" because he knew there was no opportunity for this trade in our area. After the 52 weeks were up, many veterans who had signed up for the program would simply go back to their old jobs. Bob was one of those who went back to the mill where he worked before the war.

I personally knew a couple of veterans who spent the 52 weeks gambling at the VFW or American Legion clubs. Later one of these was tops in his college class and the other had a successful career as a writer and politician. *I'm not suggesting gambling as preparation for a career but it worked for these two!* Brother Frank, who had more time in battle than anyone else I knew, apparently had no need for the "52-20" club. Neither did I.

Apparently news about Frank's courage and awards had been recognized in the business world. As soon as he returned home, he was highly sought after by companies offering him management training jobs. He evaluated but turned down these offers and went back to his old job as a loom fixer/supervisor in a Kings Mountain cotton mill. When I asked him why, he said, "I didn't want to wear a tie and jacket every day and I can do my present job in my sleep."

After getting settled down again at my parents' little home on Cline Street (but still lacking civilian clothes that fit) I ventured downtown to Messick's Soda Shop to see if I might bump into some old friends. I had no sooner sat down with a cup of coffee when I was joined by a high school friend, Milton Hornaday, who had recently been discharged as a bombardier in the Army Air Corps. He was also still in uniform.

After exchanging some "war stories," our conversation got around to career choices. Milton asked me what I was planning to do in the future. I told him I didn't know, that I had several possibilities, but none seemed very exciting. I asked what he was going to do and he said, "I'm starting college tomorrow on the G.I. Bill. Why don't you consider doing that?" I replied: "Milton, I had a lousy education until I came to Shelby and I'm not sure that I'm college material."

I told him that I had scored well on the two I.Q. tests I had taken: the one in high school and the one the Navy gave me. But I still wasn't sure that my poor educational background would allow me to succeed in college. Milton scoffed at this, saying: "Nonsense, Jim. I went to school with you for one and a half years and have been around you enough to know that you will do well in college."

Then Milton said, "I'm going to need to hitch a ride or take a bus to Salisbury early tomorrow morning to start summer school classes at Catawba College." I had never heard of this school, but Milton explained that it was a small liberal arts college in Salisbury, NC. Knowing I had a car, Milton then suggested: "Why don't you drive me to Catawba in your car tomorrow? While there, you can look the campus over, talk to the Registrar, and he can give you expert advice about college!"

Milton also advised me that should I decide to go to college, I needed to act quickly because colleges around the country were filling up with World War II veterans. In fact he was concerned that it might already be too late to enroll in college starting that fall. I mulled over his suggestion and then said: "I'll pick you up in my car early in the morning so you can get there for your first class. Then we'll see what happens."

The next morning I picked up Milton and his luggage and we drove to Salisbury, a distance of about 70 miles. I immediately liked the looks of the neat, compact campus and drove to the Registrar's Office where Milton introduced me to the Registrar, Dr. Donald Dearborn. Milton asked me to meet him at the Student Union once my interview with Dr. Dearborn was over. Then he left for his first class.

# CHAPTER 2
## Prospects for College Being Explored!

DR. DEARBORN AND I had an interesting discussion, back and forth. I told him about concerns over my lack of a strong educational background, one-teacher schools, etc. He assured me that based on our conversation, he thought I would do well at college despite my poor educational background. He added that he would need a copy of my high school transcripts before I could be admitted, should I decide to enroll at Catawba.

He said the school was already full for the fall session (because of returning veterans) but they had one vacancy in summer school. "If your high school transcripts are good and you decide to take this spot, I'll find a way to squeeze you in this fall," he assured me.

During our conversation, Dr. Dearborn described some of the advantages that this small college might have for me. He said that the classes were small compared to the large State Universities. He explained that fewer students per class would increase my chances for interaction with professors. He added that this might be an important factor for me since it would better enable me to get any special assistance I might need.

Dr. Dearborn then took me upstairs to see the room where I might live that summer and introduced me to my potential roommate. Then, I headed to the Student Union to meet Milton. With what I learned from talking with Dr. Dearborn and after a tour of the small, neat campus with Milton I decided that Catawba College was the right fit for me. And I had no doubt my high school transcripts would be acceptable. I've never regretted the decision to enroll at Catawba College.

I think the small classes and interaction with professors were useful in providing me the self confidence I needed to succeed in college. *Fortunately, thanks to my love of reading, I never needed any special assistance!* Later that day I returned to Shelby to get a copy of my high school transcripts and to pack toiletries and the few clothes that would fit me.

Mom had saved the money I had sent her while I was in service and she gave it to me to take to college. This money would enable me to buy the school books I needed before the G.I. Bill kicked in and to purchase some new, more appropriate attire for college.

Early the next morning I left Shelby to start my new life. Mom was sad to see me go after the short time at home but happy with my decision to go to college. After looking at my high school transcripts, Dr. Dearborn was impressed. He completed my enrollment and signed me up for Freshman English and College Algebra & Trigonometry. I tried to convince him that I was weak at math despite the good grades reflected by my transcripts but he wasn't buying that. So instead of enrolling me in a general math course--which was all that was required, I ended up in the College Algebra and Trigonometry class. *I had never even heard of the latter.*

After completing all enrollment paperwork, I bought necessary text books at the college bookstore. Then I went to the dormitory room I had visited the previous day. This room was located on the second floor of the Administration Building and contained two single beds, two chairs and two small chests. The accommodations were certainly modest. The only bathroom on that floor had several showers to accommodate all the male students on that floor!

The male students (mostly veterans) would walk down the hall, covered only by a towel, to take a shower. Sometimes the towel would be draped on their shoulder. Modest they were not! When the nice woman who served as our Residence Dean met a young male in this state of undress, she merely smiled and kept walking.

Upon entering my dormitory room, which would be my residence for the summer session, I was startled to see my new roommate, Perry Lefever, standing on his hands atop his bedpost. It turned out he was an accomplished gymnast who could easily walk up and down the building's staircase on his hands. I soon learned that Perry was a truly great little athlete.

Perry had gained "Little All America" status as Tailback on Catawba's football team the previous year. Unfortunately for him, however, his small size worked against him when he suddenly had to compete against bigger, faster athletes who had returned from the war. He was unable to make the playing squad the following year. His pride wouldn't let him be a member of the practice squad, called the "Rinky Dinks," so he left football behind.

The 1946-47 team was loaded with returning veterans, most of whom had played for Service Teams and thus competed against professional and major college All Americans. That Catawba football team was rated in the top 20 teams in the nation that year and three of its team members, Ray Yagiello, M. L. Barnes and Clyde Biggers went on to star in the NFL. *I later read a newspaper report saying Yagiello was the only player in several years to play the entire game (offense and defense) for his Los Angeles NFL team.*

Catawba was selected to play in the newly-created Tangerine Bowl that year and handily won the game against previously unbeaten Maryville College of Maryville, Tennessee. The final score was 31-6 and the game was played in Orlando, Florida. The next year Catawba won its second Tangerine Bowl, defeating Marshall, 7-0.

# CHAPTER 3
## Beginning College Classes Two Days Late

IN ADDITION TO beginning my classes late, I found upon entering the College Algebra/Trigonometry class, they were already on page 43. Since I had been out of high school for three years and had not thought about or used algebra during that time the class might as well have been in Greek. I did not understand a thing the Professor was discussing. Incidentally, Dr. Dearborn, who had signed me up for this class, was teaching it! Could filling that seat possibly have anything to do with the fact that I was in this class rather than the general math class?

However, I thought if I studied hard enough I might be able to catch up with the class. But I never did. I had never failed a course in my life but suspected this record might soon change. The freshman English class was a totally different experience. I understood and enjoyed this class from day one. I already had great appreciation for English grammar, and my extensive reading had prepared me well for both the grammar and literature aspects of the class. And I quickly learned how lucky I was that the class was being taught by Dr. Raymond Jenkins, head of the English Department, and an outstanding educator.

*In my opinion based on later college and university experience, Dr. Jenkins would have been a "star" at any place he chose to teach; fortunately for me and many others, he chose small Catawba College. I thoroughly enjoyed Freshman English despite the pressure of knowing I needed an "A" in it to help compensate for what I feared would be a bad grade in College Algebra/Trig.*

Outside class, I met another ex-sailor by the name of Robert (Bob) Bright of High Point, NC. He quickly became my best college friend. Both of us had just been discharged from the Navy, but Bob had attended Catawba for one semester before enlisting and thus was able to help me get oriented. He would graduate with the class of '49 rather than my class of '50. (*Bob had a startling resemblance to the young Marlon Brando and was sometimes accosted by Brando fans seeking his autograph*).

Bob and I had many things in common. Both of us came from poor families. His father was a carpenter and mine had worked as (or with) a carpenter early in his youth but didn't choose it as a career. Both Bob and I had loving parents with little formal education but lots of common sense. Both of us were shy and under developed (both physically and socially) in high school. He had entered the Navy at 135 pounds and emerged a strong six footer weighing about 180 pounds. I had entered the Navy as a short, chubby 168 pounder and emerged as a strong 5'11" 185 pound man.

Both of us had wanted to play high school football but were deprived of that opportunity for different reasons. Over that summer, the two of us spent much time together, decided we would live off campus that fall, and would go out for the football team. We both loved to dance and spent some time almost nightly improving our dancing skills in the Student Union. Dancing well was a highly prized skill at Catawba and was a regular nightly event. We had several fine student pianists who enjoyed providing dance music; if no musician showed up we danced to "Big Band" records.

Neither at home nor in the Navy, had I ever been exposed to fine dining. When I went to dinner that first evening at Catawba, I was seated at a table with white table cloth, white cloth napkins, and a full array of silverware required for fine dining. I had no idea which fork to pick up.

Fortunately, a pretty young blond student seated nearby spotted my discomfort. She slipped over beside me, sat down, and whispered instructions on which silverware to use and when. I was forever grateful to Mary Bowyer for saving me from further embarrassment. We eventually became good study friends and on nice days would share a picnic lunch and a blanket on one of Catawba's beautiful lawns while enjoying lunch and studying.

Years after graduation, a good friend of mine (who unknown to me had a secret crush on Mary), told me he was really jealous of me, thinking Mary and I were "more than friends." He had a hard time believing that Mary and I had only a "friendship" relationship. The fact is that once I overcame shyness I have always enjoyed the company of girls whether it was on a romantic or strictly friendship basis.

# CHAPTER 4
## Boxing Comes Back into My Life

ON MY TRIPS home during the summer session, I reconnected with some friends who were boxing at small professional venues. The town of Cherryville, NC was one of the most popular of these and held "professional" boxing matches almost every weekend. Matches between Shelby and Cherryville boxers were especially interesting because of the heavy, sometimes vicious competition between young males from these two towns. The competition was for girls! A Shelby boy dating a Cherryville girl was taking his life in his own hands; it was the same for a Cherryville boy dating a Shelby girl.

One of my boxing friends lived across the street from my uncle, Clarence White, where I spent much time learning to play sandlot sports. My friend, J. R. Dixon, reminded me of my favorite boxer, Sugar Ray Robinson, long time Welterweight Champion of the World. J. R. Dixon was also a welterweight, and like Sugar Ray, was quite tall and slender for that weight class.

J.R. had set up a heavy punching bag and a "speed" bag at his parents' home and he invited me to use his equipment any time I felt like it. Another boxer friend was also fighting and winning at Cherryville and the three of us often met at J.R.'s house to work out and spar. This second friend had an older brother who was a nationally ranked boxer. At the time, the older brother was fighting main events at large venues such as Miami, Florida. He was frequently mentioned in "RING" magazine.

Almost every weekend when I came home, I would try to work in some sparring sessions with these friends. Finally, I had reached the point that they were urging me to sign up for a real (small) professional match at Cherryville. I thought seriously about doing this but realized that I had two major weaknesses that would prevent me from ever having real success as a professional boxer. The most obvious weakness was my poor eyesight. This made me vulnerable to a quick right hand. J.R. who had long arms and a quick right hand, forcefully taught me that lesson!

I soon discovered that the only way I could counter the bad eyesight problem was to stay close to the other boxer. Even then, J.R. would occasionally find an opening with his right hand. My extremely bad vision simply didn't allow me to react quickly enough against a really good boxer. Another problem I had was difficulty in keeping my weight down. My normal weight was now 190 pounds, which meant I would have to fight as a heavyweight. Although I had a large chest and frame, I had small bones and relatively short arms for that weight class. I felt I needed to be at 170 or below. This was difficult to achieve with a 46" chest and a naturally stocky build.

So, I decided not to risk serious injury and to enjoy boxing only as a hobby. I soon found a young man (also a redhead) at Catawba whose ability was similar to mine but he still hoped to become a professional some day. We sparred with each other at every opportunity. We also sparred with several football team members; in fact we sparred with anyone who had an interest in this sport.

My ability, though limited by factors I could not control, proved to be a great confidence builder for the rest of my life. And in a few instances it really came in handy. *Confidence in the ability to defend yourself shows somehow, perhaps in the way you carry yourself. And ironically, having the confidence that you can defend yourself if and when needed against almost anyone means you rarely have to prove it.*

My friend J.R. had none of my weaknesses. He was born with great eyesight and a perfect "welterweight" body. With time and professional training, I felt he could have a great future in boxing. The only match I saw him lose (and that was a debatable loss on points) he was paired against a much larger Cherryville man who must have outweighed him by 30 pounds or more. Obviously the local fight promoters either didn't weigh J.R.'s opponent or their scales were faulty. Even with that disadvantage, J.R. was able to stay away from the larger man, get in some stinging blows and leave the ring unmarked. He should have won on points but did not. The judges were local!

However, before J.R.'s reputation gained traction outside the Shelby/Cherryville area, he fell in love with a girl, married her, and never got back in the boxing ring as far as I know. I also lost touch with my other Shelby boxing friend who will go unnamed. Unfortunately, the public record showed his older brother's glory days in boxing didn't last long. In one of my issues of RING magazine (which I subscribed to for years) I read that he had been knocked out; then a few issues later, I read that he had suffered another knockout.

Many years later, I bumped into him after he had retired from boxing and returned home to Shelby. When I got close to him I immediately knew that he had taken too many blows to the head. With relatively short arms he had to absorb too many blows in order to land one of his own. It didn't take an expert to see that he was "punch drunk." This made me grateful that I had pursued this sport only as a hobby.

# CHAPTER 5
## My Summer Session Ends--No Surprises

AS I FEARED, when I received my grades at the end of the summer session, I had received an "F" in College Algebra. However, unexpectedly, I had passed trigonometry which I had thought would be more difficult than the algebra part. As I expected, I made an "A" in English. So, other than the embarrassment of making my first "F", I was o.k. scholastically. And, true to his word, Dr. Dearborn squeezed me into the Fall Session.

I had become part of World War II veterans who pretty much dominated the Catawba College campus in the 1946-47 school year, and most of the succeeding years, until we graduated. Many of these were grizzled veterans who had served several years at war.

Even neophytes like Bob Bright and me, who served only during the latter part of World War II, were much more experienced than recent high school graduates. As a result of the influx of veterans, several Catawba traditions fell by the wayside. Freshmen were supposed to wear silly little caps called "dinks" to inform everyone of their lowly status. The veterans refused to wear the "dinks" and the school didn't know what to do about it so the tradition ended--at least while the veterans were there. Another tradition was that the incoming freshman class competed with the sophomore class in a series of field events. For the first time ever, the sophomore boys had no chance against the older, stronger, mostly veteran freshmen. After the dust settled, peace returned to the campus and at least while we were there, physical class competition ceased.

Despite our similarities in background, Bob and I were very unlike in our academic likes and abilities. Bob made "A's" in higher math and "hard science" courses but struggled with English, sociology, psychology, and the like. With a minimal amount of study, I could make "A's" in the subjects that were difficult for Bob. Other than the advanced College Algebra course, the only other course I had trouble with was biology. I was again a victim of my dratted high school transcripts--and Dr. Dearborn.

This particular biology class was designed for future doctors and dentists and I should not have been in that class since I did not aspire to either. I should have been in the general biology class but Dr. Dearborn had again been influenced by my high school biology grades. Being in this class was truly a mixed blessing. I thoroughly enjoyed and did well on the study of Genetics. In fact my good understanding of this subject resulted in being asked by some future doctors and dentists to help them with "after class" tutoring.

The extensive amount of laboratory work for this biology course was really my downfall. I didn't like working with dead animals in the first place. And the smell of formaldehyde used to preserve animal specimens often drove me from the lab with a splitting headache. Being forced to skip out on the lab work didn't help my grade in biology. I was fortunate to have a lab partner willing to handle the bulk of the lab work when I was forced to leave. Otherwise, I might have received my second "F." As it was, my interest in and understanding of Genetics allowed me to receive a grade of "C" for the course.

I tried to blame my "F" in college algebra on the fact that my class was too far ahead when I entered the class and I never caught up. However, this excuse evaporated when I retook the course the following year. With Bob's efforts to "tutor" me and an understanding professor's generosity, I was able to "squeak out" a "D" on College Algebra. I now had my only "F" and my only "D" from the same course.

*Good friend Bob who made only "A's" in Catawba's math and hard science courses later enrolled in graduate school at NC State and repeated the pattern he established at little Catawba College. Apparently no math course was too hard for him to conquer. He made all "A's" in the toughest math courses NC State had to offer. I considered him a math genius-- almost like the character played by Dustin Hoffman in the movie "Rain Man."*

As planned that summer, Bob and I moved into a garage apartment just off campus for the fall session. Also, as hopeless optimists, that fall we tried out for the football team. After a week spent mostly exercising to get in football shape, we were called aside by Assistant Football Coach and Head Basketball Coach Earl (Footsy) Ruth. The Coach said: "You two guys have enough natural ability to make the practice squad but because neither of you played high school football, you'll never catch up enough with how the game is played to make the playing squad."

He added: "You can be 'tackling dummies' for the next four years if you want, but you will be risking serious injuries that may haunt you the rest of your lives. It's your choice." We decided that Coach Ruth knew more about the risks we faced and turned in our uniforms that day-- our dreams of playing organized football gone forever.

# CHAPTER 6
## Dancing Our Way Out of Shyness

INSTEAD OF NURSING our emotional wounds after our short football "careers" ended, we concentrated on improving our social skills by dancing every night in the Student Union. It should be emphasized that at that time liberal arts schools like Catawba held several "formal" dances a year, so the ability to dance well at that time was a great asset to a male student.

But Bob and I both wanted more dancing than we could get on campus and yearned for greater opportunities. These opportunities came up unexpectedly. We both soon found out that the nightly practices had paid off. Apparently news of our dancing abilities had spread to several women's colleges and we began getting invitations to attend their dances as designated "stags." Although neither of us had ever heard of this arrangement, we liked the idea of this new dancing experience and the chance to meet many attractive girls from other colleges.

Being selected for this "honor" did wonders for our self confidence as well as our social lives. Being a stag had many advantages. For example, we immediately got to meet and dance with many new and different girls. Also it freed us the expense of buying flowers and tickets to dances; and the dance sponsors would find us a free place to spend the night.

The only requirements for the stag (other than to wear a tuxedo and appear at the right time and place) were: (1) to be able to dance a variety of dances, (2) have the nerve to tap a strange male dancer on the shoulder and dance away with his date and (3) have the physical stamina to dance every number. Designated stags were advised to keep a sharp eye for a girl who needed a dancing partner, either because her date couldn't dance at all or danced so poorly that her health and well being were in danger.

Of course, under the rules, we were not supposed to dance with just the prettiest girls and best dancers. Also, it was frowned upon to dance too many times with the same girl. Sometimes this was difficult if mutual attraction was involved. But you had to be careful that the dance sponsor did not give you the "evil eye." You might find yourself removed from the stag list for that college for the rest of the year. Bob and I were able to follow the rules and were never kicked off the list.

By some unwritten rule, the stags were not supposed to know who recommended them for a particular college (or colleges). I never had any idea how I got on the list at Flora McDonald College in Red Springs, NC, as well as Greensboro College for Women (GC) and Women's College of the University of North Carolina (WUNC), both at Greensboro, NC, or Meredith or Peace College, both at Raleigh, NC to name a few. I never spotted anyone I knew at these colleges. I did know a couple of girl students at nearby Mitchell Junior College in Statesville but they never admitted being the source of my stag designation. *Although these were all women's colleges at that time, most are now co-ed. Times have been changing.*

Bob told me he never was able to figure out who recommended him to be a stag either. Although we would have liked to travel together to some of these dances, that never happened since the dance sponsors wanted only one stag at each dance. We enjoyed comparing experiences later.

I had only one unfortunate incident during the many dances where I was a stag. That unpleasant time was at Flora McDonald. I had many great times at this small college affectionately referred to as "Flossie Mac." In fact, I dated a co-ed I met there quite a few times. However, on this one occasion, my overnight sleeping arrangement didn't work out. The sponsor had arranged for me to spend the night at the home of a fairly prominent businessman in Red Springs. This man greeted me at the door and was very friendly and personable. After a brief conversation, I asked him to show me where I could change and sleep after the dance was over. He led me to a large bedroom and then said, "We might as well sleep together and not mess up another bed."

At that I picked up my overnight bag, carried it back to my car, and never stayed around to say goodbye to my expected host. I don't remember where I changed from my formal outfit after the dance, but it was probably at a restroom at the college. Then I made the long drive back to Salisbury just in time for an early breakfast at my favorite all night restaurant. *I was glad that my Navy classmates back at San Diego had explained some different sexual practices to me.*

At our first formal dance at Catawba, both Bob and I had rented tuxedos. We found out that the rented tuxes were not only expensive but did not fit well. We talked about these problems afterward and decided it made more sense to buy our own tuxes. So we headed to the big city of Charlotte where it was easy to find formal attire for sale. Both of us bought tuxedos, ties (real ones, not clip-ons), shirts, cummerbunds, cuff links, etc., that actually fit us. The cost of each was about equal to the cost of two rentals. Later, we went to the same place to buy white dinner jackets. I recall one night Bob asking: "Jim, do you realize we've worn our tuxes six out of the last seven weekends?"

We literally wore out our formal wear while at Catawba. I hasten to add that dancing was not our only activity at Catawba. Both of us studied enough to make satisfactory grades—at least to us. Neither Bob nor I or our closest friends were interested in making the "Dean's List." If we made too many "A's" we thought we were "over studying," and eased up.

*The only time after that first summer session that I had any real concern about my grades occurred years later when I was offered a graduate assistantship at the University of Illinois and learned that I would have to have a "B" average for admittance to its Master's Program. I was relieved when my Catawba transcripts showed I had a "B+" average. (Thank God for all those English courses I signed up for at college).*

# CHAPTER 7
## Advantages to Living Off Campus

OUR FIRST FULL year living off campus in a garage apartment offered many advantages. Our apartment was owned by a very nice former Catawba staff member. It was roomy, had modern appliances, and was in easy walking distance to the dining room, Student Union, and class rooms. Although I had a car, it was not required for our campus activities.

Bob and I enjoyed many of the same activities. Both of us liked sports and we had similar tastes in music, i.e., Big Band and Jazz. Our favorite band was Stan Kenton whose music was a predecessor to "modern" jazz. Then we heard Dave Brubeck and were hooked on jazz for life. We were able to receive and listen regularly to late night radio stations in New Orleans, LA and Louisville, KY. We especially enjoyed listening to music being broadcast from "The Blue Room at the Roosevelt Hotel" in New Orleans. We were fans of many bands that performed there.

Later at night we would listen to the "music of Peter Toma at The Fountain Lounge," also located in the Roosevelt Hotel. (*Fortunately, after I moved to Washington DC, my job offered me many opportunities to travel to New Orleans and stay in that grand old hotel. While there I would visit both their famous music rooms, plus the iconic Sazarac Lounge. I had learned to enjoy libations by that time. This lounge featured three drinks they claimed to invent: the Sazarac Cocktail, Bayou Swizzle and Ramos Gin Fizz.*)

Often, other Catawba students would visit us at the apartment to listen to music, especially when we had the radio tuned to the Charlotte station which featured the late night musical program, "Our Best To You." This program, starting around midnight, was designed to appeal to college students around the state. The program featured romantic music dedicated to college sweethearts. For example, "Dan from UNC" might dedicate "Moonlight Cocktail" to "Betty of Meredith College." Those were the good old days when the radio, friends, and conversation provided much of our entertainment.

Bob and I also dated some girls living off campus. Why did we not date girls living on campus? Many of them would come to breakfast with hair in curlers and without makeup. This was not an appealing sight to two young men who were beginning to gain confidence and were more discriminating where the opposite sex was concerned.

The two off campus girls we dated the most both had out-of-state boyfriends so we knew no strong romantic ties were likely to develop. The one I dated was an upper class student at Catawba who had a serious relationship with a high ranking commissioned officer she later married. No long term relationship developed between Bob and the other girl either. But we enjoyed the time we spent with these girls. Also, both of us dated girls we met when performing as stags at various colleges but distance and shortage of "gas money" (at 20 cents per gallon!) limited the amount of time we could spend with them. *(I sold cameras and other valuables brought back from Japan to obtain travel money for dances at the various colleges where I was a stag.)*

Despite having no strong romantic relationships while at Catawba, I was no longer the "wall flower" when it came to girls. In fact, most of my "study friends" were girls and I regularly met several for coffee and we would then traipse into our classrooms together and sip our coffee. Without realizing it, I was beginning to become quite comfortable with friends of the opposite sex. And my "small talk" ability was growing although it never reached the "thufferin thuccotash" level of Shelby friend, Tommy Singleton.

Bob and I even ventured to take two girls to a night club in Charlotte one evening. We bought a bottle of Taylors New York State vermouth wine and "brown bagged" it into the club. To those unfamiliar with this practice, many parts of the South at that time did not allow restaurants and clubs to serve alcoholic drinks. However, the police turned a blind eye to guests who brought alcoholic drinks into restaurants and night clubs in bottles concealed in a brown bag. Restaurants and night clubs in "dry areas" would provide "set ups" for a small extra charge so that customers could mix their own drinks. Thus the term "brown bagging" came about. Buying a bottle of wine and taking it into a night club was a daring thing for two previously nondrinking young men just learning such "sophisticated" activities.

Despite enjoying life with Bob and friends at the garage apartment, I felt that I needed to broaden my interests and friendships by living on campus. Catawba had completed a new male residence hall to be available that fall. Therefore, I applied for and was accepted into this new facility. Instead of a simple room with a "group" bathroom, the new facility consisted of two connecting rooms comprising a "suite." Each side would accommodate three students, and the rooms were connected by a study area and central bathroom. Residents there would be "living in style." Bob decided to remain off campus another year with a new apartment mate, Clinton Clark, a pre-ministerial student. The new living arrangements for the two of us did nothing to interfere with our friendship which lasted until Bob's death many years later.

As for the new facility, Catawba instituted a policy of random placement of male students, i.e., you didn't get to choose your suite mates. This policy was designed to ensure that students would be exposed to a variety of personalities and life styles. I agreed fully with this policy.

# CHAPTER 8
## New Male Residence Hall Changes My Lifestyle

MY FIRST SUITE mates were a very diverse pair: Cecil (Goofy) Gilchrist and Sam Erwin. A good athlete himself, Goofy was outgoing, personable, and spent much of his time with the "jocks" of Catawba. Sam was a quiet, introverted type who was studying for the ministry and associated mostly with pre-ministerial students. I landed somewhere in the middle of these personalities.

Sometime during the first week of the new school year, Goofy decided to have a poker party in our suite. The three suite mates and a few other guys participated in the poker party. I had resisted any type of gambling while in the Navy but decided it might be a good way to get better acquainted with minor gambling since it was part of the "on campus" life. I was surprised that Sam decided to participate.

I had only $20 to lose and lost it pretty quickly. I left the game never to play poker again. Sam had beginner's luck and won about $30. This was enough to convince him that he was a natural born poker player and he became a regular at the poker table. After that his luck changed. Soon, he had run through all his savings. Whether it was a coincidence or not, Sam also decided he didn't want to become a minister and changed from that major.

In any event, Sam and Goofy became great friends and I'm told that after graduation they got coaching positions at the same high school. Because my journalism career was taking me to many locations outside of the Salisbury area, I didn't see them many times after graduation. I attended few "Homecomings" at Catawba and lost touch with both of them. Much later, after I moved to the Washington DC area, I learned that Goofy (now known by his real name Cecil) had become a respected and well liked Recreation Director for the city of Harrisonburg, VA. In fact, *the Cecil S. Gilchrist Community Activities Center* was named for him.

Meanwhile, back to college life, the shyness continued to wear off as I broadened my activities and friendships on and off campus. I was asked to be official student photographer for the school newspaper, "The Pioneer." I used my one remaining ill gotten high quality camera brought back from Japan to take candid shots of students around campus for The Pioneer. I also submitted some candid campus shots to the yearbook, Sayakini, the school's Indian name.

It never occurred to me to try my hand at writing for either the school yearbook or newspaper, however. My self confidence in that area had not reached the point that I considered myself qualified to write for either of these two media. Just as I had thought earlier that I was not "college material," I thought only extraordinarily "smart" people could become professional writers. Obviously I still had not put myself into that category.

Ironically, Dr. Raymond Jenkins, head of the English Department, often chose my papers to be read during the class. And, while many of my fellow classmates labored for hours preparing their papers, I usually finished mine in the back of the classroom as the class was beginning. Dr. Jenkins knew it and apparently did not care because he continued to give me high grades. It hadn't taken me long to figure out that Dr. Jenkins preferred (as did I) writing that was succinct, emphasized something unusual or unique, and when possible, introduced humor into the paper.

Many of the students in our class apparently did not learn that lesson. When reviewing a book for an English class assignment, many would copy large sections of the book, writing page after page of something the rest of the class had already read. Or they would expound endlessly on a subject of their interest to the point of boredom. I quickly saw that this approach did not appeal to Dr. Jenkins or others in the class and continued my own approach. Dr. Jenkins would often begin scanning papers and start chuckling when he got to my work and would either read it himself or ask me to read it to the class. I received A's on most of my work in English classes— almost always if Dr. Jenkins was the teacher.

But this experience never translated into my thinking that I could possibly write for the campus papers--much less have a career in writing. Curiously, as far as I know, only one person who wrote for the Sayakini or The Pioneer while I was at Catawba ever earned a living as a writer. That exception was Herman Helms who became a highly regarded sportswriter for The Charlotte Observer after graduation. There may have been others but I am not aware of them.

I'm sure that Jim Foster, who contributed some feature articles to The Pioneer, used a variety of skills combined with his high intelligence to rise to the position of Vice-President in charge of Public Relations for the Daytona 500 Speedway. His writing ability no doubt contributed to his selection to that high position.

My role as school photographer for The Pioneer did give me a chance to get to know more students on a personal basis and to improve my photographic skills which later became valuable. Of course the college hired professional photographers to take formal class photos. I was neither equipped nor capable of doing that. However, I enjoyed and did a satisfactory job of taking candid pictures of students in casual scenes around campus. It turned out that the photography I did on campus was also an unexpected asset to my journalism career later.

The campus life turned out to be just the place for me. I thoroughly enjoyed my time as a college student. As mentioned earlier, I found out that I had no trouble making good grades without excessive study. (I was really taken aback when several students who had ranked 1st and 2nd in their high schools, flunked out of Catawba after the first semester). They simply could not do college level work despite hard work and apparent intelligence.

Despite my otherwise positive college experience, I was getting nowhere in terms of figuring out what I would do to earn a living upon graduation. Many Liberal Arts students have trouble deciding on a "major." I eventually gave up trying to prepare for a specific career and became an English Major without any idea where that might lead. I made that decision because: (1) English grammar was enjoyable and easy for me and (2) it gave me a legitimate excuse to continue reading a lot which still was my #1 hobby.

I selected my minors pretty much the same way. Although I had no career goals in that direction, courses such as psychology were enjoyable and educational in helping me learn more about myself and others. So psychology became a minor. After taking some courses in Spanish, I was fascinated by that language and culture and ended up making it another minor. My third minor, education, came toward the end of college when I was becoming more concerned about getting a job in a weakening job market.

Back to my regular college life, much to my surprise, after one year of college, I found myself accepted into a group of students considered the "intellectuals" around campus. Roy Grove, who later became a college professor, was the unofficial leader of the group. My extensive reading finally started paying off and my spare time became much richer and stimulating. Most of us were sophomores when we began to have our almost nightly "bull sessions." We discussed books, authors, religion, sex, sociology, psychology, i.e., all the subjects that college sophomores know so much about--or so they think.

Although none of us was a Biblical scholar, many in the group had strong views concerning the spiritual side of life. Some of these bright students questioned any belief in God. Having grown up in a Christian family but not being a student of the Bible, I usually kept quiet when the Holy Divinity was being discussed. However, I was a good listener and these discussions triggered many questions in my own mind. At one point in my life I had serious doubts about organized religion. Those doubts were certainly answered in my later life, when that will be discussed more thoroughly.

Meanwhile, I had become good friends with a student whose family lived in Liverpool, England where his State Department father was Consul General. Not wanting this college friend, John Huddleston, to be alone on campus over holidays, I often took him home with me to spend time with my family. At Catawba, John was a member of the school's acting group called "The Blue Masque." He was a naturally good actor who had strong parts in many of "The Blue Masque" productions while at Catawba. Through John, I became friends with other cast members.

One Blue Masque member I met through John kept bemoaning the fact that he could not get a decent haircut in Salisbury. He complained that despite urging the barbers to take "just a little bit off" he would emerge looking like a "skin head" on stage. That was not an appealing look unless an actor was playing the part of a Marine or Boot Camp sailor. *Remember in those days men did not go to hair stylists!* In any event, this cast member was being featured in an upcoming play, needed a trim, but was afraid to get it fearing what he might look like afterward on stage.

I had heard complaints about bad haircuts by many young men, but had not experienced it personally since my Dad had always cut my hair and understood that the shape of one's head was the largest factor in how a man's haircut should look. To assist the concerned college actor, I made what appeared to be a foolhardy suggestion: I told him I was going home for the weekend and if he could hold off until that Monday, I would borrow my Dad's barber clippers and scissors and give him a trim.

Although I had never cut anyone's hair, I was confident I had learned enough watching my Dad cut people's hair that I could give someone a decent haircut. The student eagerly agreed to that idea and the following Monday, using Dad's barber tools, I gave him a trim. He was ecstatic about the result and immediately told the rest of the Blue Masque members about it.

After that the Blue Masque cast members (even several of the girls) wanted me to give them hair trims before a play. After returning my Dad's barber tools my next trip home, I found and bought a good set of used barber's clippers and scissors. I was in great demand the rest of my time at Catawba. *I'm sure this popularity had nothing to do with the fact that I never charged anything for this service!*

Neither Milton nor I needed to attend school the second summer at college so, with both of us wanting to make some spending money, we got summer jobs with Plantation Pipeline. This company was clearing rights-of-way for their gas line running through North Carolina. We joined the crew just northeast of Shelby and helped clear right-of-way from there to Greensboro, NC, before returning to school.

Right-of-way clearing turned out to be one of the toughest jobs I ever had. It was tougher than work as a postman and tougher than Navy Boot Camp. It meant getting up ready to go to work by daylight and working until dark. Our main tool was a bush axe which we used to cut bushes and small trees up to about 2-3 inches in diameter. We walked and swung those axes from morning until dark. And we had to try to avoid disturbing yellow jackets which built their in-ground nests where we were working.

Despite the hard work, I enjoyed that summer. Much of the time, our crew was in short driving distance to Salisbury. So, many nights I showered, changed clothes and drove to Salisbury to visit friends and to date off campus coeds. I didn't get much sleep but had a good time that summer. And the walking on rough terrain and swinging a bush axe day after day helped me get in the best physical condition of my life.

After our crew reached Greensboro, we were released and I went back to Shelby to spend a few days before the start of the fall session of my sophomore year. I had said goodbye to Milton who had transferred to Western Carolina College in Cullowhee, NC. Since he fell in love with the mountains (the girl he married was a mountain girl), he remained there as an educator, and I didn't see him again for about 50 years. *But I never forgot the good advice he gave me in 1946 at Messick's Soda Shop.*

# CHAPTER 9
## An Unexpected Ending to Summer

THE FEW DAYS I spent in Shelby turned out to be quite eventful. On one of my last nights home, I went into the Shelby Cafe on Lafayette St. to have a cup of coffee. While I was there, a pretty young lady (Doris Dean Allen, of Grover, NC) who was engaged to a friend of mine (Herman Smith) sat down in the booth with me. A few minutes later, a guy I knew slightly came into the Cafe and spoke to us. After I introduced him to Doris, he took her hand and was still holding it when Herman unexpectedly entered the cafe.

Herman immediately took offense when he saw the man holding the hand of his fiancée. He jerked the guy's hand away and invited him to go outside to settle things. At the sound of fighting going on outside the restaurant, I started to get out of the booth to see what was happening. Doris Dean blocked me from getting up saying: "Jim, you didn't have anything to do with this. I don't want you to get in trouble."

After a few minutes, I decided I needed to know what was happening to my friend Herman, so I broke loose from Doris, and went outside. What I saw was really scary. Herman was on his back and his head was being pounded into the sidewalk. Not by the guy who started things by openly flirting with Doris but by one of his buddies. I never knew what happened to cause the second guy to jump on Herman.

By that time a large crowd had gathered and many were begging the man on top to stop hitting Herman, who appeared to be barely conscious and unable to defend himself. The young man hitting him was a rugged truck driver with bulging muscles he liked to display. He ignored the people in the crowd and kept pounding Herman's head into the sidewalk. Fearing that Herman might sustain permanent brain damage or even death, I knew I had to intervene.

So, I grabbed the muscular young man around the arms and pulled him off Herman. While I was doing this, the guy who went outside to "settle things" with Herman began hitting me. I held on to the aggressor, until some of the crowd took Herman back into the restaurant to check on his condition. Then I turned to the guy who had been hitting me and said in a soft voice: "You had no right to hit me when I was trying to break up the fight. Let's finish this in the alley, not the street." *Since I had an unblemished record in town, the last thing I wanted was to be involved in a street fight on the main street of Shelby!*

The guy agreed to my suggestion and I started toward the nearby alley thinking he was following. After a few steps, the guy suddenly hit me from behind as hard as he could. The blow landed on the side of my face and jaw. It succeeded only in knocking off my glasses. I was completely unhurt by this sudden attack from behind. *The fact that my opponent was not able to knock me down with an unexpected, unimpeded punch to the face and jaw probably surprised both of us.*

At that point, going to the alley was no longer an option and the street fight began. I was informed later that the guy was known as a street fighter who always tried to get his opponent down so he could beat on him from above, like what happened to Herman. So the first thing he tried was to throw me down. I didn't relish fighting on the pavement at all and instead turned to my boxing skills. I began pounding him with quick, short body blows. Soon the body blows had taken the fight out of him and he was just trying to hang on to me. I had just pushed him away to get in a knockout punch to his jaw when I was suddenly lifted up by my belt.

A quick look over my shoulder revealed that it was a Shelby policeman holding my belt. Police officers had arrived on the scene in response to an urgent call to come stop a fight in front of the Shelby Cafe. The call had been made to the police when Herman was taking his beating. The police quickly arrested all four of us and placed us in separate jail cells at the Police Department. I did not enjoy my first and only "perp" walk!

Since I was not about to alarm my mother by calling my folks to come bail me out, I was prepared to spend the night in jail--something I didn't relish. However, luck was on my side. A young lady who had witnessed my role in the fight called her father, who was a local judge, told him the story and I was soon released. The other three combatants spent the night in jail.

Since I was late getting home that night, my mother knew something was wrong. She met me at the door and Dad got out of bed to join us in the living room. I told them briefly why I was late. I spared the gory details, but Mom was still shaken by the event. Dad actually got a smile on his face and I sensed that he was proud that his "bookworm" boy had been able to defend himself.

As ordered, the fight participants, including me, appeared in court the following morning prepared to tell our versions of the story. My name was called first but the judge said: "You don't need to come up here, young man. I already know from the police and other witnesses that you were just trying to break up a fight and save a friend from a bad beating. I'm finding you 'not guilty'."

The judge listened to the other three participants tell their stories, found all of them guilty of "participating in an affray" and issued them fines. They left the court house with a "record" while I left with my record still unblemished. Although I had not sought this incident, many of my friends in Shelby were complimentary of my action and I felt that I had gained new respect in town.

I was really glad that I was in such good shape for my one and only "street fight." And I credited the hard work of cutting right-of-way all summer and the boxing workouts I engaged in with my boxer friends for my success. *Incidentally, Doris and Herman were later married. Doris played an important part in my life after I graduated from college and had not yet found a career. More about that later.*

# CHAPTER 10
## A Chance to Play Intramural Sports

BACK AT COLLEGE I continued to dance, attended many of the nightly bull sessions, and studied enough to make decent grades. Although knowing we would never be able to play on a college football team, Bob Bright and I still yearned to play competitive sports. So the two of us joined what turned out to be the top intramural basketball team on campus. Bob was the star of the team. I played regularly but was far from being a star. Head Basketball Coach Earl Ruth, who happened to watch one of our games, was so impressed by Bob's basketball ability that he asked: "Why is that guy not on our varsity basketball team?"

After the game Coach Ruth talked with Bob but when he found that Bob was already in his junior year at college and had only one year left before graduating, he said it would make no sense for Bob to try out for the team at that late date. Bob was pleased that his talent was recognized by a college coach but agreed that it was too late for him to become a college player.

One of our intramural team players was a "Little All America" football player who also played a good game of basketball. He was also a very nice person off the field. Our team was good enough that we sometimes went off campus to compete against and win against junior college teams. Mitchell College, in Statesville, NC was one of those teams. However, most of our games were against other Catawba intramural teams.

Once when we were playing another campus team, our football "Little All America" end was driving to the basket for a layup. A star Catawba football team lineman on the other team launched a "body block" on our player, who lay stunned by the unexpected, dangerous and illegal play. The lineman compounded his "dirty play" by standing in a threatening manner over our teammate. I was incensed by this and without thinking, shoved the lineman away from our player and said: "Why don't you pick on somebody your own size!"

I meant me of course but later realized that was a ridiculous statement since the football player outweighed me by probably 50 pounds. At the time, however, I felt I was the bigger man. I often wondered why the lineman didn't accept my challenge. He certainly lost face as a tough guy that day. Some friends expressed the opinion that the so-called "tough lineman" backed down because he had seen me sparring with several of his football team members, some of whom were bigger than he. In any event, I was grateful that I had risen to the challenge back at Boot Camp and had continued working to improve my physical skills since that time.

Sometime during the second or third year of college, while I was home in Shelby one weekend, I bumped into Joyce, the younger sister of Gladys, the girl I had a crush on and dated before going into the Navy. Joyce had turned into a beautiful young woman. We had a cup of coffee together that day and she volunteered that she had broken up with my old friend, Tommy, and that her sister had married the sailor she was waiting for when we spent time together. In the course of the conversation, she let me know she was unattached and would like to see me again. Since I was also unattached, we got together for some dates that were strictly on a friendship basis.

Despite the fact that she was now a fully "grown up" beautiful woman, Joyce was still like a "little sister" to me. I thought of her as still innocent and unsophisticated at that time. It saddened me that she had broken up with Tommy and had dropped out of high school in the 9th grade. She had never learned to dance so I taught her a few steps and found she was a natural at dancing. *(She later taught dancing and performed on The Arthur Murray TV Show in New York City but that's another story).*

Joyce and I had several casual dates and even went to a big dance in Charlotte. This was memorable to me because it featured the "big band" music of Stan Kenton, one of my favorite band leaders as mentioned earlier. However, no romance was possible for me because of the "little sister" image Joyce still generated--despite the fact that she was only three years younger than I. We soon lost touch and I later heard through the grapevine that she had married.

# CHAPTER 11
## Sharing a Suite with Strangers

WITH SOME NOTABLE exceptions, college became a comfortable, routine place for me. A big exception occurred my last full year of school while I (following Catawba's policy) was sharing a suite with two other young men I barely knew until then. The three of us had few things in common and did not socialize together. By then, I was much more into social activities since neither of my roommates danced or partied. But we were all compatible and an unfortunate incident brought us closer together.

One suitemate was Joe Austin, one of the top academic students on campus, and also an English major, about the only thing we had in common. The other was Ken Griffin, whose only common interest with me was the fact that both of us had grown up in a large, poor tenant farm family. Joe was muscular and had done some body building but was known primarily for his high intellect and good study habits. Ken was tall and athletic with plans to be a high school coach after graduating. Our similarities and differences made an interesting combination.

Then one night I arrived at our dorm after a date to find our suite in disarray. Joe was lying on his bed covered with blood. He had also thrown up on his bed. It was obvious that something traumatic had happened. Ken said he had been there when another student had entered our suite, along with two friends, and attacked Joe. Ken seemed addled by the incident and didn't know what to do. He had no automobile and had not called for an ambulance. Since I had a car, we helped Joe into it and took him to the Emergency Room at Salisbury Hospital.

The doctors at the hospital checked Joe out thoroughly, treated his wounds, and released him saying he needed to rest and let his wounds heal. They had found no signs that he had suffered any permanent physical damage. I got the story of what had happened on the way back from the hospital. Joe said earlier in the evening, he had walked to the corner cafe, a "hang out" for Catawba students just off campus, to get a sandwich and a Coke. While there, he was accosted by a Catawba student accompanied by two Catawba friends, one of whom was a big end on the football team. By all accounts, all had been consuming beer and one was very angry at Joe for "giving him a bad grade in English."

Joe said he told the belligerent student that he only "read and corrected" school work for Dr. Raymond Jenkins, his class teacher. Joe explained that after making corrections to papers, he turned in the work to Dr. Jenkins, who assigned the grade the student would receive. The student did not accept this explanation and shoved Joe. Then the two got into a fist fight which was quickly broken up.

Joe said he returned to our suite very upset, locked the outside door to the suite, and lay down on his bed to try to calm his nerves. Ken said when he arrived at our suite Joe had become physically ill and had thrown up. He added that a few minutes later, the three male students involved in the earlier incident came through the connecting suite unannounced into our room. *Apparently the locked outside suite door had prevented them from coming in directly so they had gone through the adjoining suite to get to our suite.*

In any event, Ken said that after the men entered our suite from the connecting study/bath area one of them immediately jumped on top of Joe and began beating him with his fists. It turned out he was the one who had earlier fought with Joe. At that point, Joe was so weak he couldn't defend himself, much less fight back. The other two men kept Ken from interfering with the fight. With no one to stop him this time, he beat Joe unmercifully before the three of them left.

By the time we returned from the hospital, campus police had arrived at our room and interviewed us. We assumed that since this was a serious matter, the Salisbury City Police would be called and that the three males who invaded our room and beat up our roommate, would be charged with a serious crime. Instead, when I inquired the next day I was told that the matter had been turned over to the Student Council to be handled internally on campus.

I had some serious reservations about the Student Council's ability to deal with a problem this serious. I wasn't overly impressed by the head of the Council. However, I could hardly believe it when the Council announced they had recommended that Joe and the guys who invaded our room were receiving virtually the same punishment: a short suspension. This even included the one who attacked Joe lying sick in his bed. The college was expected to approve the Council's recommendation.

Outraged by this miscarriage of justice, I set out to get these sentences changed. I began with a direct effort to get another hearing in which my roommate Ken and I could testify before the Council. My appeal for a hearing was denied by the Student Council. Then I wrote and started circulating a petition for a new hearing. I was able to enlist a couple of brave students to work with me, and soon had a petition with several hundred names on it calling for a re-hearing of the issue with witnesses before the Council.

I was pleased we got the result we wanted: a re-hearing where I would be Joe's advocate. *I was disappointed to learn that some of the students I previously admired would not assist with the petition because a member of the football team was one of the perpetrators and they feared retaliation.*

As leader of the petition drive, I was asked to speak for my roommate at the re-hearing. When called to speak, I lost my "stage fright" and stated that I and the petition signers were shocked at the mishandling of this case by the Council which recommended that Joe receive the same punishment as the perpetrators who invaded our room.

I then asked the head of the Student Council to explain the charges and how they reached their decision. I specifically wanted to know how they (the Council chairman) said the main charge against Joe was that he fought back when the guy angry about his bad grade accosted him off campus. He said that despite provocation, Joe should have walked away because fighting was against campus rules. "Oh, so Joe was supposed to be yellow and walk away after he was attacked?" I asked sarcastically.

Then I asked: "Why did you not penalize these three guys for drinking alcohol? Everyone who saw them said they were half drunk and this is also a violation of campus rules; plus I think that their invasion of our suite and beating Joe in his own room was a serious violation of campus rules, plus a criminal act which should have involved the police."

The chairman then replied: "We couldn't charge them with drinking since it was done off campus." Naturally I jumped on this inconsistency by pointing out that the original fracas where Joe fought back was also off campus. "So, using your own reasoning then, Joe wasn't guilty of anything since both the drinking and initial fight occurred off campus." I ended my argument by pointing out that under their own reasoning, the only issue they had left to decide was the punishment these three guys would receive for invading our room and one of them beating the hell out of a sick man lying on his bed while the other two invaders kept our other roommate from coming to Joe's aid.

At this point, the Council members went into closed session to reconsider their earlier action. The next day the Council announced they had reconsidered the issue and the perpetrator who beat up Joe would be kicked out of school; his two friends would have longer suspensions; and Joe's punishment was rescinded.

# CHAPTER 12
## Politics on a College Campus

THIS WAS MY first involvement in anything suggesting campus politics and certainly wasn't something I was seeking. Circumstances forced this action upon me and I wondered if there would be any after effects. I received some "hard stares" from a few friends of the football team member involved in the incident but no repercussions.

One other incident that involved me and school politics occurred when a member of the football team was the only candidate submitted to students as a candidate for president of the student body. This time my actions were voluntary. Although we had no personal animosity toward this player, several friends and I thought the fact that the Nominating Committee had offered us the choice of only one person was ridiculous. I decided to be a trouble maker for the second time. By then I had lost all respect for student government.

This time I was able to convince a friend, Jim Foster, that we should take some action to show our displeasure. It was already too late to select our own official candidate and launch a serious campaign. So, after some discussion, we decided that a "fake" campaign with Jim Foster as the "candidate" might make our point. And we could have fun in the process. Jim and I worked together to develop campaign material (posters and fliers) and began our satirical campaign.

Although we did not take our campaign seriously, we had a serious goal: to show how ridiculous it was for the nominating committee to offer us a single candidate, a football player with no particular qualifications, for this high position. We had some fun with the campaign as did many of our fellow students. A few close friends of the official candidate did not find any humor in our efforts but we had no serious "kick backs."

I had forgotten about this college prank until years later when Jim Foster reminded me of it at a college homecoming. I did not at first recall this event but Jim chided me by saying: "I can't believe you don't remember this. You were my campaign manager." *These events involving football team members may suggest that I had a problem with the football team. That suggestion would be wrong. Several of the team members were then and remained friends of mine. Obviously, they didn't take any of this personally. The only problem I had was that football team members seemed to be treated differently from the rest of the student body by the administration and student government.*

The summer before my junior year at Catawba also turned out to be an interesting one. I received a notice from the Navy inviting me to join the Naval Reserve and participate in a cruise. When I saw that one scheduled cruise was to Vera Cruz, Mexico, I decided to join the Naval Reserve so I could go on that cruise. By that time I had completed three years of Spanish and was yearning for an opportunity to practice with some real life Spanish speaking people. My reading and writing of Spanish was not bad but I had no confidence in my ability to speak the language.

I can't recall where, but I boarded the Navy ship (which turned out to be a destroyer) and we set sail for Vera Cruz. On the way we wore our navy fatigues and practiced firing the destroyer's big guns. Just as it was when I was on active duty, my reserve job was to load or unload large shells and stand by until they were fired and then get ready for the next ones. *Unfortunately, the military still did not provide hearing protectors, so my ears would ring for hours. Little did I know that I was adding damage to my inner ear that caused me to have tinnitus and hearing loss that gets worse every year that goes by. But at that age, who worries about such things!*

After a few days at sea, we arrived at the beautiful port city of Vera Cruz. Fortunately, Mom had saved my Navy whites and they still fit me so I was ready for liberty soon after we reached port. I went ashore at around 1:00 p.m. that first day hoping to find someone to converse with. What I found was closed doors and almost entirely empty streets. Then I remembered: "It was siesta time!" Mexican businesses close down for a couple of hours in early afternoon while people take a nap. Then the store owners, clerks, and customers return to resume business--usually into the night.

I sat around on a park bench enjoying a view of the ocean while waiting for the city to awake from its siesta. The first time I had an opportunity to use my Spanish was in a restaurant that had just re-opened. I ordered "chili con carne y cafe con leche, por favor" using my best Spanish accent. When my order arrived, it consisted of a cup of coffee and a small bowl of hot peppers! I then remembered that "chili" is an American dish. The Mexicans in Mexico didn't even know what I was asking for! Since Mexican ethnic food was virtually unknown in the Carolinas at that time I didn't know what else to order. So, I settled on a fresh fish dish which was delicious.

While there, I learned that Vera Cruz is noted for its fine seafood and took full advantage of that knowledge then and on a much later visit to that fine city which I shall describe in a later Part. We remained at anchor in Vera Cruz for three or four days before heading back to sea. During that time I went on liberty every day (remember as a yeoman I could obtain both a port and starboard pass).

During those leave times, I practiced my verbal Spanish religiously with any Mexican who would converse with me. The improvement of that aspect of the Spanish language when forced to use it was incredible. It's common knowledge that it is extremely difficult if not impossible to gain fluency in a foreign language in a classroom. I made more progress in speaking Spanish in those three days in Mexico than I did in an entire semester in college.

Since I had primarily joined the Naval Reserve to get the trip to Mexico, I immediately lost interest in being a reserve member. I never attended a single reserve meeting and heard nothing more from the Navy until they contacted me during the Korean War to see if I wanted to be recalled to service. I declined that offer.

During my junior year in college I still had no idea what my career would be. My concern about getting a job was heightened by the fact that the country was in a slight recession and the job situation was getting tighter every year. So for my last semester my junior year, I had taken some education courses, in case my only job option was teaching. As the job situation worsened, I realized that it made sense for me to sign up for all the education courses required to get a North Carolina teaching certificate before leaving school.

I was scheduled to graduate at mid-year my senior year so the process of preparing for a job had suddenly become urgent. I had completed all the required courses I needed to graduate, so I was able to complete enough education courses to obtain NC teaching certification. With one exception, all of my courses that semester were education related. The one exception was an advanced English course the college had just added for the first time. *Naturally, although I didn't need the credit, I could hardly wait to sign up for that course after it was revealed that it involved lots of diagramming. Unlike most students, I was one of those weird people who enjoyed diagramming and this course featured some problems requiring multiple pages to complete the diagramming. Oh, what fun I had!*

Like most of my fellow students, I didn't take the education classes seriously. So, my routine quickly evolved into meeting two or three girls in the coffee shop. After getting our coffee, we would casually saunter into the classroom and sit in the back row sipping our coffee while the teacher tried to hold the attention of the class. This was difficult for both the teacher and students since the subject matter was so dull. *Hopefully, education courses have improved since that time.*

The only excitement the education curriculum held for me was the "practice teaching." Before we could receive our teacher's certificate, each of us was required to go into a public school to augment or sometimes even replace the regular teacher for a specified time. Knowing the students would be ready to take advantage of us "greenhorns," this situation definitely caught and held our interest. And in my particular case at least, it made me regret not paying more attention to the education courses. I managed to struggle through the "practice teaching" but it added to my feeling that I was not cut out to be a career school teacher.

# CHAPTER 13
## The Job Search Ends with a Teaching Job

NOT HAVING ANY desire to march across the stage to receive my handshake from the President, I asked that my Catawba degree and Teacher's Certificate be mailed to me so I could immediately start my job search. After a quick local search, I thought that my best chance to find a job lay in larger cities such as Charlotte which had a big job market. Soon I was bumping into recent Catawba (and other) college graduates pounding the sidewalks and opening doors to talk with potential employers.

I filled out and left applications with many private businesses as well as Federal and State employment agencies but did not spot anyone with an urgent need for someone with my qualifications. It didn't take long for reality to set in. Few employers were looking for recent college graduates with a major in English and minors in psychology and Spanish.

Then my hopes brightened late one afternoon while I was meeting with an interviewer for a large national corporation. The interviewer and I hit it off well and both of us were enthusiastic when it appeared that my qualifications met this particular company's needs. My growing despair began to lessen. Then, he turned the card over showing the job requirements, shook his head sadly, and said, "You won't do." Then he handed me the card which on the back read: "No Redheads."

Both of us were initially puzzled about this company's apparent discrimination. Then, we understood. This was an investigator's job and they were looking for someone who would blend in with the crowd. My bright red hair caused me to stand out--rather than blend in. Thus I was unqualified for this type job. *Why didn't I think about getting a wig???*

I was very discouraged as I drove back to my parents' house. But soon after I arrived there, Catawba called to tell me that Sanford (NC) High School desperately needed an English and Spanish teacher for the semester about to begin. The college spokesman gave me the Sanford High School Principal's telephone number and suggested I call him right away. I talked with that principal who explained that the regular English and Spanish teacher was pregnant and needed to be replaced for the coming semester. After she had her baby and had recovered, she would resume her teaching career the following fall session.

When I asked the principal how they knew I was available, he said they had picked me from a list of graduates that Catawba College had sent out to North Carolina high schools. He then told me what I would be expected to do: teach five English courses ranging from the eighth through the twelfth grade, plus first and second year Spanish. After hearing their needs, I emphasized that I had never taught school before and that this schedule seemed to be pretty heavy for a neophyte like me, i.e., that I might not be able to do the program justice. He explained that it was too late to get an experienced teacher and he felt I would do an adequate job.

Then he commented that my resume had mentioned an interest in sports and asked if I would consider starting and coaching both boys and girls tennis teams. This question intrigued me. I felt that I would be reasonably competent as a coach, though I had never done this before. And it sounded like a part of the job I would really enjoy. So, I said yes, I would take on the job of teaching English and Spanish and that I was willing to start and coach the tennis teams.

I realized that I would need to find a place to stay for at least that semester and did not know a soul in Sanford or any other town nearby. So I asked the principal if he could recommend a place for me to live for the rest of the school year. He thought for a moment and then said there was a boarding house near the school run by a very nice widow who would only rent to school teachers.

He said he did not know whether or not she had a vacancy but he would check on it for me and call me back. He soon called back and said the boarding house had an opening for one male teacher and that the room would be clean and nice. And he added that the rent was very reasonable and included home cooked dinners and breakfasts. But he warned that the owner was strict about decorum. Men boarders were required to wear a dress shirt, tie and jacket for dinner meals and were expected to have good table manners. *(Thank God for Mary Bowyer and her quick help when I entered college!)*

Two days later I arrived at my new place to live for the next several months. I found another Catawba graduate and friend of mine had just arrived as a boarder. His name was Frank Shaver, known around the college campus as "Shorty" Shaver because he was only a shade above 5 feet tall. He was to be a Sanford assistant coach and history teacher.

It was a big relief to me to find a fellow Catawba graduate and friend living at the same place and working at the same school. Frank and I had been friends on campus although we did not run with the same crowd at school. *An interesting life point: I was dating a girl from Charlotte and her roommate was a cute girl under 5 feet tall. We thought this petite girl and "Shorty" might be a perfect match--at least size-wise. But the petite girl did not give Frank a chance. She took one look at him and whispered to my date: "He is too short!"*

Sanford High School was a small to medium sized school, bursting at the seams while a new, larger school building was being constructed. As a result of the crowded conditions, teachers were told not to send unruly students to the principal's office or the library. We had to deal with these students completely on our own inside the classroom. There was no place to send them as punishment.

And as was the custom in the South at that time, the school was segregated. By then, I had become a social liberal, but since I was a newcomer to Sanford, I knew better than to make a fuss about the segregation issue. And although much of my shyness with individuals and small groups was no longer a problem, I soon found out my stage fright was still present. My instinct was to leave through the window at the noisy sound of student footsteps coming down the hall to my classroom.

The schedule I encountered was overwhelming from the start. I had to prepare lesson plans each day for all five of my English classes, plus my two Spanish classes. The regular teacher had left no lesson plans for me, perhaps because as an experienced teacher, she no longer needed such plans. So, I had to struggle getting ready for each day's lesson, hoping to stay at least one day ahead of the students. I'm not sure I always succeeded.

Also, it was time-consuming to meet with potential members of my boy's and girl's tennis teams, to begin tryouts, and try to arrange a schedule at this late date. Since tennis teams were new to this school, I was completely on my own in trying to arrange matches for the spring season. I quickly discovered that very few schools the size of Sanford even had tennis teams, except for upscale schools such as Pinehurst and Southern Pines. That meant I had to start contacting larger schools hoping they might have an opening in their schedule.

My fears were soon realized. I found that many schools with tennis teams already had a full schedule. With a great deal of effort, however, I was finally able to arrange a schedule of eight matches, most of them away, as I recall. As a new, unknown coach, I had no negotiating strength, thus we had to agree to do most of the traveling. *I think some of these schools felt sorry for me and "squeezed" us into their schedules, as long as we were willing to come to their facility.*

When the winter weather eased up, I started getting the clay courts into shape, enlisting the help of any potential team members willing to give me a hand. There was nothing in the budget to hire this done professionally. Meanwhile, I was spending every night trying to get ready for my seven daily classes. Sometimes I just had to "wing it" to get through a class. And as a novice, I had not developed this skill to a great degree.

# CHAPTER 14
## Proof I Wasn't Meant to be a High School Teacher

MOST OF THE students were understanding and helpful. Others, almost always older boys, were not so accommodating. And, because the school was badly overcrowded, I soon faced the problem of having no place to send a recalcitrant student. I thought this situation was unfair to the teacher but even more so for the students who were in the classroom to learn.

I did my best to follow this rule, but when one male student continued to deliberately disrupt my second year Spanish class, I decided this situation was just too unfair to senior students who really needed to learn something in this course to prepare for college, so I took action: I sent the student out of my classroom and told him "never to return." The school administration put him somewhere. (I never asked where but he was out of my sight). The administration let me know they were not happy about it but I never apologized for my action.

This situation plus a couple of other incidents involving lack of discipline, confirmed that my career as a school teacher would be short, i.e., only for that semester. The first incident was pretty mild, consisting of a challenge by one senior male student who wanted me to meet him after class for a sparring session. I went to his house and had one such session and he never challenged me again. In fact, we became friends.

The second incident was much more serious. While walking down the hall at the end of the day, I passed by the classroom of a female teacher, and after a "double take" look realized that she was being intimidated by a burly senior tight end on the football team. He was not in any of my classes but I had heard he had received a football scholarship at a major university for that fall. When I entered the room I found the female teacher cowering in a corner with the student standing over her in a threatening manner.

My reaction was probably not the correct one for a teacher. But it worked for me that time. I immediately ran to her aid, slammed the student against the wall and challenged him to hit me. He rapidly left the room and the teacher thanked me profusely. I took no further action on the matter but the incident led me to conclude that my temperament was not suited to teaching high school students. The teacher did not pursue any action against this student either so he graduated without anything bad on his record. I later read in the newspaper that he was playing first string for the university team that had offered him the scholarship.

Coaching the tennis teams at Sanford was more rewarding than my classroom work. As I started practices, I discovered that I had been blessed by having some talented tennis players. The only problem was lack of depth. My top three male players were definitely capable of competing with players from any high school in North Carolina. Unfortunately, I could find no other real tennis players in the school and had to complete my roster with non-tennis-playing athletes.

Since I had no experience coaching tennis (and only mediocre playing ability), I quickly decided that my role as a coach would be an organizational one: keeping the courts in shape, setting up practices, establishing positions on the team, keeping up morale, coaching the team's matches, and arranging transportation to and from opposing schools. I knew better than to try to help any of my top players with their strokes.

Although I figured (rightfully as it turned out) we could win most boys' matches by counting on wins from my top three players, plus one win at doubles, this could not always be assured at the larger schools. We needed one more competitive player, which I had in the person of my No. 1 girl player--provided I was able to use her! When I was arranging matches with other schools, I would ask the coach if I could play this girl at No. 4. A few agreed but most did not.

The boys' team never lost a match when my top girl tennis player was allowed to play for them. Consequently, the boys had a winning, but not perfect season. They won all their matches with schools of comparable size but lost two matches to much larger schools. I remember Greensboro was one of those schools and Winston-Salem might have been the other. At one of these big schools we were tied and on the way to a win when my No. 4 player started "showing off" and lost to a player he should have beaten. With one more dependable player, the boys' team might have had a perfect season. Not bad for a school which had never fielded a tennis team before!

Unfortunately, the girls' team had only that one really good player and did not have a winning season. But I was proud of them for competing in all the matches. And, as I recall, their No. 1 player didn't lose a match. This young lady, although only about five feet tall, was a great athlete. Not only was she a terrific tennis player, she was an excellent center for the exceptionally good girls' basketball team. At the center position, she overcame her short height by developing a "hook shot" that could not be blocked by much taller players. *Surprisingly, girls' basketball was so popular at this town and school that the girls' team attracted more people than the boys' team.*

One final note about my tennis players: I learned later that two of my top male players, (No. 2 and No. 3) were later named North Carolina's "Male Tennis

Champions." My top female player also won the award as "North Carolina Female Tennis Champion." Since I was out-of-state when these events occurred, I cannot personally confirm these facts but having seen their talents, I have no reason to doubt the accuracy of what I was told. I know for a fact that my top girl player later established her own nationally known tennis camp.

Summarizing my brief time at Sanford High School, I was glad for the experience but equally glad when my term was up. I felt that I was not temperamentally suited to teach late teen students, especially grades 9, 10, and 11. Students at those grade ages seemed to have lost all respect for teachers. Too much time had to be spent maintaining discipline for my liking. But many 12th graders suddenly realized they needed to take high school seriously because of impending college or career goals. Consequently they showed respect for their teachers.

The eighth graders in most cases, intuitively still respected their teachers and were a pleasure to teach. I encountered one of these in Washington DC where he was interning at the Georgetown University Dental School. He said he had fond memories of our brief moment of time together.

My biggest surprise as a high school teacher was the interest students took in me and my social life. I had taken no interest at all in my teachers' lives outside the classroom. However, my social life seemed to intrigue my students. If I partied with a group of teachers, I was asked about it the next day. Sometimes I felt like I was living in a fish bowl. This phenomenon of the students' personal interest in me might have stemmed from the fact that, although I was 24 years old, I looked younger than many of the male high school students. Genetics at play?

In fact, several of my girl students tried to fix me up with their older sisters--and one succeeded. This girl showed me pictures of her sister who was a student nurse in a city about an hour away and finally convinced me I should stop by to meet her. Since I was going past that city on a visit back to Shelby, I decided to take my student's offer to arrange a meeting for us. *(Probably not one of the best decisions I've ever made)*.

My expectations were not high for my blind date with the student's sister. Boy was I shocked when she came to the door to meet me. She could have served as a double for the actress Jean Simmons! And she turned out to be as nice as she looked. We dated a few times but I met a Sanford girl about that time and this turned out to be the longest and strongest relationship I had experienced in my relatively short dating life. Thus, I did not pursue a real relationship with the student nurse.

The Sanford girl was an attractive, bright and talented young lady from a prominent family in Sanford. She was a student at a prominent School of Design near New York City. We dated when she was home on visits during the last part of my term and for the summer months. We also got together once when she traveled from her school to meet me in Charlotte. But the distance was too great for our relationship to survive and it gradually fizzled out. I heard later that she was a successful fashion designer in Manhattan; we never again met in public.

As the end of the school year approached, I knew I had to find a job that would tide me over until I could get on some kind of career track. My fellow Catawba graduate friend, Frank Shaver, also was in a similar situation, i.e., he had a contract for only one semester. But since his career track was already established to continue as a coach/teacher, his problem was easier to solve. As I recall he returned to the Salisbury area and obtained a teaching/coaching job that led to a good career in his chosen profession.

# CHAPTER 15
## At This Point I Needed a Job of Any Kind

AS FOR ME, I had to settle for any job I could find outside of the teaching profession. And I needed it now to pay the rent! After a brief job search, I went to work for a Sanford furniture store. I joined their furniture moving crew, with prospects for joining the sales/management staff at some future time. It was certainly a test of my physical strength when I had to help carry a large refrigerator up a narrow staircase and then help bring the old one back down. Also, the existing crew members tried to embarrass the school teacher by subjecting me to some of the hardest jobs.

However, my physical fitness program practiced over the years, combined with a few "tricks of the trade" I learned quickly soon turned things in my favor, and I was accepted as an equal member of the furniture moving crew. Although obviously not a proper career track with my educational background, I enjoyed the physical work and the salary allowed me to live comfortably and continue an active social life. One aspect of the job I especially appreciated was that it gave me an opportunity to purchase a used--but like new--kitchen stove and refrigerator to deliver and install in my Mom's kitchen. These appliances were the 50's style which is much in vogue today. She loved the appearance of the appliances and the fact her "little boy" bought them for her meant more to her than their looks.

Meanwhile, during the school year I had been in touch with college friend John Huddleston. A brilliant linguist, he had been enrolled in UNC Chapel Hill's prestigious "French House." This school was designed primarily for French teachers and talented graduate school students. Because of his fluency with languages, he was accepted to the school after only one year of French at Catawba. I visited him at Chapel Hill and spent some enjoyable time at the "Rathskeller" located underneath one of the businesses.

It was one of the favorite hangouts of UNC students. I still remember the risqué poem written on the wall by a UNC student. The poem may not appeal to a mature person but at the time I read it, I thought it was hilarious. I know now that there are other versions of this "poem" but here is the one I remember:

"The sexual life of the camel is not what everyone thinks,
One night in a fit of passion he made an attack on a sphinx
But the sphinx's posterior orifice
Was filled by the sand of the Nile
Which accounts for the hump on the camel
And the sphinx's inscrutable smile."

Back to the life of two immature college graduates, the last time I visited John at Chapel Hill he said he needed something to do and a place to stay that summer. I was puzzled since he had told me that his family (still overseas with the State Department) had sent him money to travel to Mexico for the summer to pursue his study of the Spanish language. He was already fluent in Spanish because he picked up the language while serving with some Puerto Rican soldiers during World War II. Consequently, he was able to skip first year Spanish and go directly to an advanced course. But he "conned" his parents into thinking that he needed the Mexico experience to round out his knowledge.

However, being something of a "playboy," John had already spent the money he was supposed to use to travel and stay in Mexico. He said he was now broke and he didn't know what he was going to do. He couldn't stay with his family since they were in England and he didn't dare ask them for more money. I invited him to stay with me in my apartment, while we figured out a way he could earn some money.

I had been forced to get an apartment since I was no longer a teacher and not eligible to continue staying at the boarding house. Although not large, my apartment would allow me room to squeeze in a second person for a limited time. When John arrived, we discussed ways he could earn money in this small town with its limited job opportunities. Since John was an experienced consumer of alcohol, and Sanford and the nearby area was "dry," he got the idea that we could make some quick money if he traveled to Fayetteville, NC, which was "wet" and brought back a load of liquor to sell for a big profit!

Speak of foolishness! Imagine the newspaper headlines: "Former Teacher-/Tennis Coach and Son of Consul General Caught In Bootlegging Scheme!" What's more, John would be using my almost new car which would surely be confiscated if he were caught carrying illegal whiskey. But those sensible considerations aside, John left early one morning for Fayetteville and I went to my job hauling furniture. I did not have a restful day.

Fortunately, John came to his senses en route and decided to buy only the "legal" limit which lessened the chances of a "bootlegging" charge and the chance that my car might be confiscated if he were stopped and checked by the Highway Patrol. He thought a small profit on the "legal" amount of liquor would pay for the gas while we figured out another way for him to make enough money to pay his share of the apartment rent and have some spending money.

As it was, upon his return to Sanford, John showed his total lack of business sense by "selling the liquor on credit" to a black woman who sold and served bootleg liquor "by the drink" from her home. (She also sold other services but we won't go into that!) Of course, she never came up with the money to pay him. All this affair did was provide us a valuable lesson and some laughs (much later).

Soon after that, I was able to talk the manager of the furniture store into hiring John as another furniture mover. The manager thought it added to the reputation of the store to have a former school teacher and the son of a distinguished State Department official working there. John and I had a good time that summer. I continued to party with my former school teacher friends from Sanford High School and was able to connect John to a few interesting girls.

At the end of the summer, John returned to the "French House" and I continued hauling furniture for a few more weeks. I was getting tired of this job and anxious to find a career. So, I resigned from my job at the store, gave up my apartment, and returned to my parents' house, hoping I would find something I liked and could do. I knew it would be difficult for someone with an English Major and Spanish Minor (who did not want to be a school teacher) to find that satisfying career. But I still believed in miracles.

# Early days of H. H. White family

Jim playing with Dad's pocket watch.

Jim's father and siblings.

**H. H. White family of eight children (Jim is barefoot boy).**

# World War II (1941-1946) and its Effect on H. H. White Family

**Brother Frank, Army.**

**Jim, Navy.**

**Brother Bob, Air Force.**

**Ready for college, 1946.**

With friend/roommate Bob Bright, 1947.

As senior at Catawba, 1950.

With Mary O. Bowyer studying.

# PART 4

# I "Accidentally" Find my Career--Journalism

# CHAPTER 1
## Going Home Again

LEAVING SANFORD AND returning to my parents' home in Kings Mountain appeared uneventful, but like much of my life, I found out later that was not the case. When I entered the relatively new place my parents had bought on Kings Mountain St. in the small town of Kings Mountain, NC Mom was ecstatic and Dad seemed glad to see me. I was especially happy to be able to spend some time at home at this time. While I had been away at college and while teaching school, Mom had suffered two serious strokes and was partially paralyzed on one side. I knew that her time on this earth was limited. This period also allowed me to spend some time with brother Frank, who lived only two blocks away and brother Bob, who lived just a few miles away in Grover, NC.

Although I didn't know it at the time, this would be the longest time in my long life that I would be close to most of my family members. In addition to Frank and Bob mentioned above, three sisters, Isabelle Blackwell, Faye Shillinglaw and Nell Turner, lived in or near the town of Blacksburg less than 10 miles away; oldest brother, Howard, lived in Forest City, NC, less than an hour away; and youngest sister, Edith Turner, lived in Gastonia about 10 miles away.

So, for the first and last times as an adult, I was surrounded by my family. I have many regrets that I let my ambition to succeed take precedence over spending more time with these dear people. All of them are gone now and the only chance I'll ever have to spend time with them again will be in Heaven, provided the Good Lord forgives my many sins and accepts me into that Heavenly Place.

Returning to the memoir, like the rental house in Shelby, the Kings Mountain house, which my Dad had purchased for $1,500, was small. And like the house they had vacated, it also had an oil stove in the living room that provided heat for the entire house which also included two bedrooms, a decent sized eat-in kitchen and an inside bathroom. Dad paid his brother, Uncle Clarence White, to partially open up the wall between the kitchen and living room and this change made a dramatic visual improvement in the space. But the important thing was that, after all these years, they again owned their own home.

As usual, Dad had a large garden at the back of the house which provided most of the needed vegetables. Despite her declining health, Mom continued to can large amounts of fruits and vegetables. However, since Dad had retired by then, he no longer had direct access to the excellent meat available to him (and the family) while he worked as a butcher. However, since he supplemented his Social Security check with income from a part time job as night watchman at a nearby cotton mill, their standard of living stayed about the same. Neither Mom nor Dad required any great luxuries.

After enjoying a couple of days visiting with my parents and other relatives, I began another job search by again heading to big city Charlotte. After arriving there I soon discovered that my trip from Sanford was not uneventful as I thought. As I was walking down one of the main streets in Charlotte I passed a restaurant and taking a quick glance through the window, I thought I saw someone I knew. He also glanced at me, turned away, and then did a double take with disbelief in his eyes. By then I realized the man in the restaurant was a casual friend from Sanford. After his second glance he got up from his seat and ran out the door to greet me with the words: "I thought you were dead!"

I wasn't quick enough on my feet to respond like Mark Twain who once remarked, **"The news of my death was greatly exaggerated**." Instead I asked for an explanation and he urged me to join him inside the restaurant where he would explain his strange statement. After I sat down at his table, he said: "Obviously, you haven't heard the news." He then went on to say that the day I left Sanford, there was a bad wreck on the highway from Sanford heading west, the direction I was driving. He said that the accident caused at least one death and the Sanford radio station reported that: "Jim White, former teacher and tennis team coach at Sanford High School, died earlier today in an automobile accident!"

He said several people including him were shocked at this report but that he had left town soon afterward and never heard a corrected report--if there was one. We talked for a bit longer and I urged him if he ever returned to Sanford to tell the folks that I was alive and well. I haven't seen him or been back to Sanford since that time so I have no idea how the rumor of my death got started or if the truth ever caught up with the erroneous report. After saying goodbye to the friend, I continued my search, filled out some application forms at a private and public Unemployment Office and returned to Kings Mountain.

# CHAPTER 2

## Messick's Soda Shop Revisited and a "Lucky Accident"

THE NEXT DAY I drove to Shelby and went straight to Messick's Soda Shop again hoping to see some old friends. I also remembered another time I needed help and had found it at Messick's in the form of Milton Hornaday, who was instrumental in persuading me to go to college. Was there a chance magic might happen to me at this Soda Shop again? Hardly, but I could still hope.

While sipping my coffee, Doris Dean Allen Smith, wife of my old friend Herman Smith, joined me at my table. This was the first time I had seen her since she and Herman were married. In fact this was the first time I had seen her since the fracas in front of The Shelby Cafe a couple of years previously. As pleased as I was to meet and have coffee with Doris, I had no idea this meeting would have any impact on my future.

Our conversation began like many among old friends. After some chit chat, Doris confided to me that her marriage with Herman wasn't going well. Since I was a friend of both, I kept quiet and let her vent. After detailing concerns about the state of her marriage, Doris asked me what I was doing for a living. I told her about my brief jobs in Sanford but that I was unemployed at the time and looking for a job. I asked her if she had a job, and if so, where. She said she was selling advertising for The Cleveland Times, a twice-weekly newspaper in Shelby. She then told me that she and another young lady, Joyce Johnson, someone I had known in high school, both sold ads for the paper.

She thought for a second and then said that Ed Post, the Editor and Publisher of the Times, had mentioned the possibility of hiring another ad salesman. She asked, "Would you like for me to introduce you to Ed? He's a very nice man who knows everybody in town and if he doesn't have an opening he might have some other ideas for you." I replied that I would indeed like to meet Ed Post and asked Doris when she could make the introduction. I had a resume in my car left over from the previous day's trip to Charlotte, so I was prepared for an immediate appointment. Doris said she was on the way back to the office right then and if I'd give her a lift she would make the introduction immediately.

When we arrived, I reached into the back of the car and handed her the copy of my resume which I suggested she let Mr. Post look at before introducing me. After Mr. Post had read my resume, he summoned Doris and me into his office so Doris could introduce us. After she left, I had about an hour's interview with Ed Post. He turned out to be a terrific gentleman, a graduate of Duke University, with an obviously impressive intellect. He seemed to have a favorable impression of me and offered me a job on the spot. He would start me on a six week trial basis at $35 per week selling (or as it turned out, trying to sell) ads. This of course was considerably less than I had been making as a school teacher but I was willing to take any offer that might open up other opportunities.

Then Ed mentioned another idea: "I note in your resume that you have an interest in sports, that you recently coached tennis, and that you were an English major in college. These are assets that might fit into our needs." He explained that he had been getting requests to add a sports column to the newspaper. He then added: "The facts that you have an interest in and knowledge of sports and are also an English major suggest an interesting possibility. Would you consider writing a weekly column on sports in addition to your advertising work?"

Like the "add on" job of coaching tennis at Sanford High School (although I had no experience doing either) the offer to add sports writing to my new job of selling ads had more appeal than the job I was being hired for. So I readily agreed to give sports writing a try. Mr. Post concluded our meeting by asking if I could start work the next day and I readily agreed. I was on "cloud nine" that afternoon as I drove the approximately 20 minutes from Shelby back to my parents' home in Kings Mountain.

As expected, Mom was excited at my new job prospects. Dad thought I was nuts to take a job at $35 per week after making much more than that as a school teacher. I wasn't as concerned about the amount of the money I would be making as I was about the possibility of getting into a field that could be exciting and rewarding. I also thought it might offer possibilities I had never seriously considered.

I believed it fortuitous that I had just recently completed a successful season as a tennis coach since I knew that Shelby currently had a highly-ranked Senior doubles tennis player by the name of Buck Archer. Buck's doubles partner at the time was Bobby Riggs, once considered the best tennis player in the world. The fact that a town as small as Shelby had produced a player of Mr. Archer's caliber was significant to me. I didn't think this could have happened without some serious tennis interest in this town. This might help provide an audience for my sports column--should I be able to write it.

The question now was would I be able to take advantage of the "lucky accident" of meeting Doris Smith at Messick's Soda Shop and the opportunity this chance meeting had provided me? Only time would tell.

# CHAPTER 3
## My First Newspaper Job Begins

UPON MY ARRIVAL at the Cleveland Times the next morning after our interview, Ed Post introduced me to the newspaper's small staff which included his wife Maggie, Society Editor, and three people in the printing department whose names I cannot remember. Of course I already knew Doris and Joyce.

After the employees went back to work, Ed took me into his office and presented me with a list of prospective advertisers to visit and, hopefully, persuade them to become advertisers of the Cleveland Times. He gave me some ideas to use in promoting the Times, including the fact that this little twice-weekly newspaper had more mentions in the U.S. Code of Federal Register than any other newspaper in North Carolina. That fact was confirmed by Editor & Publisher Magazine. He also set me up with a desk and typewriter that I could use for both my advertising and sports column work.

I started visiting and talking with prospective advertisers that same afternoon and continued throughout the week. But after a full week, I had nothing to show for my sales efforts. I failed to bring in a single new advertiser. Meanwhile, I was getting set up with a photo, format, and title for my "to be" sports column which had already been announced. Another week went by and I still hadn't been able to sell an ad. However, with some excellent suggestions from Ed, I had turned out my first sports column: "Jim White On Sports."

The results for my advertising sales calls remained the same, week after week: no ads sold. But Ed was favorably impressed by my writing and my weekly sports column was getting some favorable attention. Although it was likely that I was a lousy salesperson, I eventually found out there was another reason for my lack of success at selling ads. One of the girls confessed to me that the list Ed had provided me was a "dead list," i.e., none of them had ever bought an ad from the Cleveland Times.

And I found out that I had another handicap: *I didn't wear a dress and therefore could not display a shapely leg!* Doris and Joyce only half jokingly told me that they often dealt with old "lechers" who liked to ogle them while discussing an ad. Both of these women were young, pretty, and curvaceous. They said the more leg they displayed, the larger the ad! That sounds like a joke but stranger things happen in the newspaper world.

At the end of my first six week trial period, Ed called me into his office. I was afraid he was going to give me the "pink slip." However, he said: "Jim, you haven't sold any ads but your column has been drawing lots of praise. I think you're in the wrong end of the business. I think you are a better writer than a salesperson." Then he said, "I've been wanting to devote more time to writing editorials and tending to the newspaper's business interests and have been wanting to turn over the job of News Editor to someone else who could devote full time to that job. Based on the good job you've been doing with your column you might be that person."

Then he asked: "Would you be willing to take the job as News Editor on a six week trial basis with the provision that if things work out for you and the paper, you'll be offered the job on a permanent basis?" This was an opportunity I had been hoping for so I eagerly accepted the offer, again at $35 per week. At the end of this six week trial period there was no doubt in my mind or in Ed's mind that this had been the right decision.

My career in the newspaper world soon began to blossom with the help and encouragement of Ed Post. He was an excellent teacher and was soon confident enough in my ability to give me a chance to interview and write articles about many important and interesting people. One of the first of these was Dr. Franklin P. Graham. Dr. Graham was a nationally recognized scholar. He had been named president of the University of North Carolina at Chapel Hill back in 1930.

He served until 1949 when he was appointed as a U.S. Senator, serving a short term. After his term was up he was appointed as the first president of the Consolidated University of North Carolina, the position he held when I interviewed him. Despite his fame, I found him to be modest, gracious, and patient. I hoped that I did justice to him in my first front page "byline" feature article.

I soon found that the town of Shelby offered a treasure trove of noteworthy dignitaries available for feature articles. Cleveland County was once known as the "Shelby Dynasty" because of its political elites who exerted a powerful influence on North Carolina politics for many years. O. Max Gardner, a Shelby native, started this dynasty when elected as North Carolina Governor and later as a U.S. Senator. Then his brother-in-law, Clyde R. Hoey, another native of Shelby, also served as Governor and was elected later to the U.S. Senate.

It was an incredible feat for a town the size of Shelby to have had two of its citizens elected Governors and U.S. Senators, much less in the same generation. And it was an incredible opportunity for a cub reporter to have access to interview and write about such distinguished officials.

Had he been a selfish type, Ed would have chosen to handle these assignments himself, rather than to trust a fledgling reporter. However, Ed had won so many journalistic honors he needed no such "confidence boosters." As mentioned earlier, he was recognized as the North Carolina journalist having the most editorials reproduced in the Code of Federal Register (CFR). Many journalists would have been thrilled to have one of their writings published in the CFR.

I found that working for a twice-weekly newspaper had its challenges. Weekly newspapers make little effort to be competitive with daily newspapers because they are invariably understaffed and too much time elapses before they can do "follow up" stories, and they usually cannot afford to "chase breaking stories." Their most important function usually is to concentrate on adding depth to the stories already covered by the dailies or choosing to write stories which are of little or no interest to bigger papers. Daily newspapers hate to miss a story but if they do, they have to wait only until the next edition to pick up a missed story.

As a twice weekly paper, we were in somewhat of an awkward position of trying to be somewhat competitive in both of these areas. On the rare occasion we were able to "break" a story, you could almost hear the repercussions across the street at the Shelby Daily Star. Holt McPherson, the editor of the Star, was a fierce competitor and he didn't take kindly to being beaten even once by a lowly twice-weekly newspaper. But occasionally, we got the "scoop" on the Star.

Although personnel from the two newspapers in the same town and city usually kept their distance from each other, there was an exception to this in Shelby. I became fast friends with a Shelby Daily Star reporter by the name of Jim Jolley. Like me, Jim was a farm boy and we had many common interests. We started meeting for coffee almost daily at a pharmacy coffee shop. We shared many wonderful conversations but never violated the trust of our respective newspapers.

A town the size of Shelby was fortunate to have two newspaper editors of the quality of Ed Post and Holt McPherson. Holt was recognized as the youngest editor of a daily newspaper in North Carolina at age 24 when he became editor of the High Point Enterprise in 1930. He also had experience managing newspapers in other larger cities. I've already mentioned some of Ed Post's accomplishments. *Despite his competitive nature, Mr. McPherson came to my aid once when I needed it after some very bad judgment on my part!*

Another handicap for a weekly or twice-weekly paper is that it is economically unfeasible for them to pay for a staff photographer. Often they must depend upon a local studio photographer. This is less than ideal for at least two reasons: (1) studio photographers are rarely if ever experienced in taking the type of candid shots favored by newspapers and (2) studio photographers may not be available when you need them the most. Remember Murphy's Law?

# CHAPTER 4
## Becoming a Reporter/Photographer

BOTH ED AND I were frustrated by this situation and soon after I took the news editor's job, he stopped by my desk and asked: "If I buy a news type camera, such as Crown or Speed Graphic, would you be willing to take a crack at being a reporter/photographer for the paper?" Since I was equally tired of the stilted, posed-look of photos we had been using to illustrate our articles, I said I would be glad to give it a try. I hoped the experience I had gained at Catawba taking candid photos around Catawba College would help speed up the learning process.

My hopes were soon realized. After Ed turned over a new Crown Graphic to me, it became my constant companion. I was able to put to good use the experience I gained in college and I quickly increased my photographic skills. And the larger negatives and forgiving nature of the Crown Graphic made the job easier.

At first we had to take the films to photo studios to get them developed and printed. This was a time consuming step and it meant we were still dependent on outside people. I told Ed I thought I could learn how to develop and print black and white photos--eliminating the need for outside help. Ed found a small empty room in the building and equipped it as a photo studio. Soon I was developing and printing pictures and handing them, with captions, directly to the printing department to appear in the next edition.

Not all of my time was taken up with exciting things such as covering and writing about sports or interviewing and writing stories about interesting people. Some of the less glamorous work that had to be done included writing obituaries, covering dull meetings, and editing community correspondent columns. The latter required close attention. We had such correspondents in nearby small communities such as Fallston, Casar, Lawndale, Patterson Springs and others I don't recall. Ed gave me some special instructions about editing columns written by community correspondents. Since the columns were written by non-professional, untrained people he told me to overlook grammatical errors, unless they were so bad that they were not understandable.

But he warned that I needed to look carefully for information not suitable for printing in a newspaper. I soon saw exactly what he meant! Some of the columns submitted contained incredibly personal information! The correspondents would sometimes include details about illnesses and bodily functions that would be embarrassing to the reader as well as the neighbor or family member referred to in the article. And the possibility of lawsuits hovered over this process. So, in getting these columns ready for printing, I had to remain very alert and keep my editing pencil handy for indiscretions which were fairly frequent. Of course this reading and editing sometimes provided fun reading for the editor!

Although my self confidence as a journalist was improving by the day, I continued to wonder if I was missing something because I had not taken any journalism courses and had not previously written anything for public consumption. However, I gradually began to realize that my twin loves of English grammar and reading were great preparation for a career as a newspaper journalist.

The fact that I started my career with Ed Post was also crucial. He had the knowledge and patience to teach me the basic skills I needed to become a competent reporter. He also taught me the ethics a journalist should live by, e.g., opinions of the writer should be left out of news stories; they belong on the editorial page. *Unfortunately those journalistic ethics seem to have fallen by the wayside with modern journalism but I will be eternally grateful that I learned these and other rules from a great journalist, Ed Post.*

# CHAPTER 5
## Reporting Not All Fun and Games

WRITING FOR A newspaper may sound exciting and romantic as portrayed in the movies. And it can be both of these, since it deals upfront and personal with all aspects of human life and its foibles. But much dull writing is also required if a community newspaper is to be successful. Thus, the small town news editor must attend dozens of meetings, many of which are deadly dull. And such journalists usually have to write most of the copy that goes in the paper, except for the society page which (at least in our case) had its own editor, Ed's wife Maggie Post. Ed wrote all the editorials, supervised all editorial content and worked with the printing department to layout and print the paper.

It is amazing the number of civic organizations that require coverage, even in a small town. Some of these groups schedule night meetings which can mean a very long day for a conscientious reporter. Obituaries must be written and this is usually the job of the news editor of a small newspaper. Larger papers with a staff of reporters usually relegate the "Obits" to less skilled reporters content to do the "drudge" work. After I graduated to larger newspapers I never wrote another "Obit."

An unusual event happened to me one early evening as I was leaving a night meeting where an organization had just completed its election of new officers. As I was getting a "quote" from one of the new officers, someone tapped me on the shoulder and said: "Jim, a beautiful young woman is waiting outside and wants to see you." After getting the quote which would be included in the short article I would write back at the office, I went outside.

At first I didn't recognize the "beautiful young woman" but when she spoke I recognized that it was "Joyce," who I had dated casually a few times years before. She no longer had any resemblance to "My Little Sister." Her first words were: "Hi Jim. My aunt and her boyfriend and I are going to a club in Blacksburg to have dinner and dance. We hope you will go with us?" In response I said that I appreciated the opportunity but that I had to write a story back at the Cleveland Times so it could be set in type the following morning. She said, "We understand but if it's o.k. with you, we'll follow you to the office and wait for you to finish your story and then drive to Blacksburg."

Joyce Cousins (now Poteat), younger sister of Gladys, my first "crush," was now a gorgeous woman that I barely recognized from our earlier friendship. So I didn't hesitate to say I would be happy to go with her to Blacksburg after I finished my story. So, Joyce, her aunt and her aunt's boyfriend waited while I cranked out a short article which I left on the Linotype machine before leaving the office and locking the door. On the way to Blacksburg, I said to Joyce: "I'm surprised to see you. I heard years ago that you were married and had moved out of state." She replied, "I did get married and moved to South Carolina but my husband and I are separated and will soon be divorced."

We had dinner and danced several times before returning to Shelby to drop me off and say our goodbyes. During the time we spent together that evening Joyce had volunteered that she had "never been able to forget me." Naturally I was surprised to hear that. At the same time I hoped I had nothing to do with problems between her and her husband. After all, Joyce and I had no contact at all for around four years and as far as I knew our relationship had no romantic connotations.

When we said goodbye that evening, I didn't expect to ever see Joyce again. She was living in Great Falls, SC, and I had no intention of going to visit a married woman--even if she happened to be legally separated from her husband. However, a week or two later, she appeared at my office and said she was in the process of moving back to Shelby. Within a few days she had rented a room within walking distance of the Cleveland Times.

Although I was attracted to Joyce, I had some guilt feelings that perhaps I had unknowingly been a factor in the trouble with her marriage. However, it seemed pretty arrogant for a formerly very shy young man to think he could have made any lasting impression on her. She must have said that just to try to make me feel good. If so, it had the opposite effect. It made me feel bad. However, despite some apprehension on my part, her move to Shelby began a long relationship to be discussed in more detail later.

# CHAPTER 6
## Life Goes on at Cleveland Times

MEANWHILE, AT THE Cleveland Times, I continued writing my sports column, covering and writing news articles about various civic organizations, interviewing and writing feature articles on interesting people and of course writing obituaries. Also, I covered an occasional exciting story at the courthouse, some involving rape, murder, etc. Interviews with famous people like Dr. Frank Graham, O. Max Gardner, Clyde R. Hoey, and Princess Teeka Chandu Siva also provided enough stimulation to make up for the necessary but dull work that must be done by the news editor of a small newspaper.

How does the name "Princess Teeka Chandu Siva" belong in the same sentence with the great men mentioned above? All were featured in front page feature articles written by me for the Cleveland Times. By way of explanation, the "Princess" arrived in Shelby at the behest (and payment) of a Cleveland County family with a relative dying of cancer. The "Princess," who claimed India as her native land, had proclaimed that she could "cure" cancer.

With no intention of poking fun at either the family or cancer victim herself, a story about the "Princess," who used a snake as a "jump rope" in the process of "curing" cancer, was too good to be ignored. So I wrote a feature article (with photos) about her. Unfortunately, none of The Princess's miraculous "cures" could help the stricken cancer victim and Princess Teeka Chandu Siva, along with her "jumping rope," left town never to be heard from again in Shelby.

*Note: A few years after I left Shelby, Ed Post also left Shelby to accept a position with the United States Information Service (USIS). His job was to establish an English language photo magazine similar to Look Magazine, The Saturday Evening Post, etc. in India. Many years later Ed and I got together for dinner in Washington, DC, and reminisced about our days at the Cleveland Times. Ed mentioned dozens of prominent Shelby officials--some of whom had been featured in the newspaper at that time. My memory failed me on most of them. But when Ed asked me about the mystical Indian woman who had been the subject of a humorous story I had written, I immediately replied: "You mean Princess Teeka Chandu Siva?" My memory is apparently reserved mostly for the weird!* I wrote many more feature articles for the Cleveland times, but none that got the attention of so many people as the one about the "Princess."

Another really fun event that I covered and wrote several feature stories about was the Cleveland County Fair. This was no ordinary "county fair." It so happened that Dr. J. S. (Doc) Dorsey, who was head of the North Carolina State Fair organization that handled county fairs, was a native of Shelby and he saw that we got the best circus acts available. Each year at the Cleveland County Fair, I had many choices for writing entertaining feature articles on entertainers such as Terrell Jacobs, famous lion and tiger trainer; the bearded lady; the snake charmer; the fire eater; the sword swallower; the human cannon ball and others who were part of the Freak Shows.

By the second year at the Cleveland Times I had really grown as a newspaper reporter. Then tragedy came into my personal life. Christmas week, my mother had her third and last stroke. Although she had made almost miraculous recoveries after the first two, we soon knew that she would not be able to recover from this one. On Dec. 20, 1951, she drew her last breath. Dad and I couldn't bear to watch her pass away and went into the next room where I prayed to myself that God would remove her from further suffering.

Dad and I sat there silently with tears streaming down our faces. Brother Frank bravely stayed with Mom until her last breath and actually tried to resuscitate her. It seemed to me that Mom, who had been in poor health for many years, stayed alive until all three of her boys came home from the War and the youngest, that she worried about the most, was fully engaged in a career. Then she gave up the fight and went to be with The Lord.

Mom's funeral was at the Smyrna ARP Church and she was buried next to her father, Robert Hayes Mitchell and her mother, Isabella Elizabeth Morrow. Much of the time between Mother's death and burial remains a blur. I do remember that my cousin, Hayes Mitchell Faulkner, met me at the graveyard and we hugged each other and cried. It was a blessing that I had so much work waiting for me to do back in Shelby to help get my mind off my mother's death.

The heavy work load helped me get through the Christmas holidays without Mom. However, I was never able to enjoy another Christmas season as I had in the past because I could not separate it from my Mother's death. One thing I've been eternally grateful for is that during the last months of her life I was working nearby and able to spend time with her every day.

After Mother's death, I began thinking it was time for me to leave my comfortable "nest" at The Cleveland Times as well as my parents' home. I had been receiving modest raises and my salary was now $45 per week. I was still using my car without any allowance for it. I never asked for a raise because I didn't think the paper could afford to pay me more. Also, I was extremely grateful for the opportunity Ed Post had provided me. And I was so comfortable at the Times I resisted efforts to seek another job. I was never sure whether my continuing to live at home with my Dad helped him to deal with his grief or make it worse. He was a silent man who did not share his emotions and I had no idea whether he wanted me to stay with him or not.

Then, one day in 1952 after I had been at the Times for two full years, I was approached by an out of town man who was planning to start a new weekly newspaper in nearby Kings Mountain. This newspaper would use a new "offset printing" process to replace the old, labor intensive "Linotype" process used by The Cleveland Times and many other newspapers around the country. Linotype operators required specialized training and were well paid in return. The Cleveland Times operator was paid $125 per week, almost as much as the rest of the employees' salaries combined!

Although I had never even heard of the "offset printing" process, the potential publisher convinced me this was the wave of the future. He urged me to jump on board and become Managing Editor of the new newspaper in Kings Mountain. This move seemed like a great opportunity for me. I would be paid a salary of $65 per week and would be responsible for all editorial content in the new paper. Even more important, I would be part of a new, more efficient way to publish, and I would be spared the roundtrip to Shelby each day.

# CHAPTER 7
## Leaving My Comfortable Nest

WITH A QUIVERING heart, I accepted the new newspaper's offer and gave the Cleveland Times a four week notice. Ed asked me to help him find a replacement and I had an immediate name for him. I recommended Les Roark, a dear friend I had known since we were little boys together in Cherokee County. Both Les and I came from share-cropping families and thus had been "dirt poor" as children. Both of us had served in World War II, but Les had not taken advantage of the GI bill to get a college education.

However, I knew he was a well read, self-taught, talented writer. I had read several of the poems he had composed in his head while standing on a ladder painting houses before putting them on paper. I also knew he had aspirations to be a professional writer and that he could obtain the knowledge he needed to be a journalist from Ed Post. I took him to meet Ed who was favorably impressed with him. So, Les took a big salary cut as a house painter to take over my old job at the Cleveland Times.

At the appointed time, I said goodbye to the Cleveland Times and moved into the editor's office at the new Kings Mountain newspaper. My new salary of $65 per week seemed like more than an adequate salary at the time. Meanwhile, Les took over my spot at the Cleveland Times at the usual $35 per week starting salary.

I already knew that initially I would be overworked as the only news person at the new paper. It would be up to me to write and/or edit all the news that appeared in the paper. My job would also include writing editorials which I had never done. I suffered no illusions that I would be the "next Ed Post" as an editorial writer which requires quite different skills from someone who exclusively writes news and features. Of course, I would have access to "boilerplate" articles which I could use to help fill up odd spaces in order to have "balanced" columns and pages but I vowed to myself to keep their use to a minimum.

It didn't take me long to figure out that I was "on my own" as far as editorial decisions regarding the newspaper were concerned. The publisher apparently knew next to nothing about how to put out a newspaper. As far as I could see his interests lay entirely in the process of printing. He seemed totally unaware of the work involved in finding good news sources, interviewing people to gather information, putting this material into news stories, and laying out a newspaper.

And in his job as publisher, he had made few advance provisions for securing advertising and circulation needed to support the paper. To his credit, he had secured some local funding ("spite money") from businesses that disliked the policies of the existing newspaper. He even suggested that I go out and solicit some ads in my "free time." Since I was already working from morning until late at night attempting to handle all the editorial responsibilities, there was no way I could do that.

By working long hours, I succeeded in putting together an issue of the newspaper and began working on the second one. But as I struggled alone to put together the second issue, I realized that I was on a sinking ship. Since we had no circulation or advertising departments, we had few subscribers and even fewer ads. At the end of the second week, I told the publisher that he would need to find another editor. I was willing to work until I could find another job and/or he could find a replacement.

I didn't need to work long. After putting out the second issue, the newspaper closed its doors forever. So, now I was free of this nightmare caused by my ignorance of the business world. I didn't think about or have the knowledge to check the financial status of the "want-to-be" paper. So, now I was unemployed again. My position at the Cleveland Times was already filled but I was committed to finding another job as a news reporter. Hopefully, it would be with a daily rather than weekly or semi-weekly. I knew Ed Post would be more than willing to try to help me because we had parted on very good terms.

However, I didn't think that Ed could be much help even though he would be willing to try. I had never known him to associate closely with other editors or journalists around the state. To my knowledge, he was pretty much a "loner" in the newspaper world outside of Shelby.

# CHAPTER 8
## An Unexpected Ally Leads to a New Job!

THEN I HAD an idea: I made an appointment to see Holt McPherson, editor of the Shelby Daily Star, because I knew he had a record of cultivating friends with other journalists--other than those with whom he competed! At our appointment, he welcomed me into his office like an old friend. I told him about my situation and asked if he had any ideas for me. He immediately picked up the phone and dialed a number. He began talking with Mr. Talbot Patrick, publisher of the Rock Hill (SC) Evening Herald, a high quality daily newspaper. Apparently Holt and Mr. Patrick were long time acquaintances.

I listened as Holt gave Mr. Patrick a glowing endorsement of my skills both as a newsman and news photographer. After he hung up, Holt said Mr. Patrick had a job opening that seemed to fit with my skills as a writer and photographer. He said this job was with the Rock Hill newspaper but would require that I live in the town of York, which was the York County Seat where many of the sources and news stories would be found. He said I should call Mr. Patrick to learn more details about the job, salary, and the like.

Holt gave me the telephone number for the Evening Herald and suggested I call Mr. Patrick right away to make an appointment to visit the newspaper. He even let me use his telephone to make the call. As I recall, after making an appointment with Mr. Patrick, I drove to Rock Hill the next day for an interview with him, Managing Editor Connie Morton, and City Editor/ Editorial writer, Deward Brittain.

These top people at the newspaper told me that the job they needed to fill was one of the most important jobs on the newspaper. It required a "self starter" since there would be no supervisor nearby. And it required someone who could cover and write about a large variety of stories--not just ordinary news such as car wrecks and other accidents, weddings, and deaths but all the things happening in several municipalities and the York County courthouse in the town of York.

Covering the York County courthouse activities sounded like a daunting task for one reporter who would be responsible for everything happening there, including court trials, meetings of the Legislative Delegation, activities at the Sheriff's Office, etc. Also, this reporter would be responsible for news and feature articles for the towns of York and Clover as well as outlying villages of the entire county. In effect, this job entailed covering all the news for The Evening Herald outside of the City of Rock Hill. And, as an add-on, the York reporter was expected to cover sports stories for all the county high schools, except for the two in Rock Hill. This reporter would work directly with the newspaper's Sports Editor on this coverage.

The job paid $80 per week, plus a car allowance of at least $65 per month. Based on Holt McPherson's recommendation, some sample articles I had brought with me, and the interview itself, the Evening Herald offered me the job on the spot. You bet I accepted it immediately. It was a dream come true--working for a daily newspaper with a staff including 10 reporters and two professional news photographers. Although the job requirements seemed pretty heavy for one person, I was assured that in a pinch I would have access to others on the news staff located in Rock Hill.

I wondered aloud how I could cover stories all over the county and get my articles and photos to the Rock Hill office of the newspaper in a timely manner. *Remember there were no computers or cell phones at that time.* Not to worry, they assured me. One of their female employees lived in York and could deliver the articles and photos directly to the editor's desk every morning in time to get them in the afternoon paper.

They told me that the package containing material for the newspaper needed to be left on her porch by 6 a.m. each day to make that day's paper. If something really hot happened after I dropped off the package, I could either drive to Rock Hill to deliver my new material personally, or if time did not permit that, I could dictate my articles to a secretary by telephone. They also said I would be reimbursed for any other expenses incurred while pursuing a story.

As soon as I accepted the job, my editors suggested that I drive to York to meet the man I was replacing. He had planned to leave earlier but the paper had asked him to stay around long enough to meet his replacement and introduce that person to some of the major dependable contacts. The reporter who was leaving introduced me to all the key contacts available at the courthouse. He also gave me a list of other major sources, e.g., school principals, county police, county sheriff's office, various town officials, etc.

I wondered if the reporter I was replacing was leaving on good terms. He assured me that the only reason he was leaving was because he had been offered a reporting job with a Georgia newspaper near his home. He assured me that my job would be demanding but interesting and that he was sure I would like the job. Without my asking, he suggested a convenient place I might want to rent.

He took me to a home right next door to the courthouse where a very nice elderly lady, living in one of York's fine old homes, had converted a former outside kitchen into a small cottage. The cottage would be available as soon as the man I was replacing left, i.e. that afternoon! This turned out to be a real blessing. After meeting the owner and seeing the cottage, I immediately paid a deposit to hold it for me. I went back to Kings Mountain late that afternoon to pack my few belongings. Early the next morning I said goodbye to Dad, drove to York, and moved into the cottage. Moving in was a piece of cake since I had no furniture of my own. Fortunately the place I was moving into was fully furnished, including towels, cooking utensils, and bed linens.

The cottage consisted of one room large enough to include a small kitchenette, bathroom, a sitting area with a table to hold my typewriter and space for a bed. It was clean, private, and extremely close to the action since it was next door to the Courthouse. I was happy to stay there until I bought my first house about a block away several months later.

During my first few hours, I was a little bit lonely, especially in the evenings. After all I didn't know a single person in York and had only briefly met with three people at the Evening Herald newspaper. However, that loneliness didn't last long. News doesn't wait for anyone and within a day or two I was covered up with news stories and meeting people of every description and in various locations.

# CHAPTER 9

## Beginning My New Job

ON MY FIRST full day at work for the Evening Herald, I covered and wrote several news articles that I packaged and dropped off at the Evening Herald employee's front porch late that evening. They were delivered to the paper early that morning and some appeared in the afternoon newspaper with my byline. I was pleased to see my byline in a daily newspaper for the first time. This started a pattern of long but mostly satisfying hours and many late nights when the package was delivered just before the newspaper's employee left for work.

That first week when I was just getting acquainted with the people working in the courthouse, I was immediately faced with the problem of covering court at the same time the Legislative Delegation was in session. I quickly learned to attend one activity for awhile to get the flavor of what was happening and then slip away to do the same thing for the concurrent activity.

I also soon found out who I could depend upon to fill me in on court trials while I attended sessions of the Legislative Delegation. The Clerk of Court and the Assistant Clerk were invaluable in providing me information about what was happening in court. And even some of the judges became valuable resources that would enable me to write stories that made it appear that I was present the entire time. With the Legislative Delegation, I could attend part of a session, leave to cover other stories, and then get a summary of what happened from a Delegate I could trust after the meeting adjourned.

This same juggling act also worked for covering sports. For example I might go to a game in Clover, talk briefly with the coach, get a few pictures of the early plays, then return to York to catch the last half of their game. Then I would call the Clover coach for the final score and a few quotes. Finally, I would write articles and photo captions for both games and put them, along with the unprocessed film, into a package to go directly to the Sports Editor for that afternoon's paper.

Between important activities taking place at the York County Courthouse, I was establishing valuable contacts with other officials in both York and Clover. Since York was larger and many more things were happening there, this town claimed more of my time. But I had to remain available to go anywhere news was happening in the county--except for the City of Rock Hill.

The town of York had an excellent Police Department headed by W.T. (Bill) Ivey who became a major news source and good friend. Chief Ivey was not your small town policeman portrayed by movies and the major media--especially those up North. He was a highly-trained law enforcement officer who took every opportunity to improve his knowledge by attending FBI seminars and staying abreast of local, state, and federal laws.

The County Sheriff was also very helpful as a source. I was informed by "people in the know" that his office had been stripped of much of its power by the Legislative Delegation, i.e., the State Senator and his associates. They had turned over many of the Sheriff's duties to a newly formed county police department. This political move reduced the sheriff's function pretty much to serving papers.

This left the occupant of this office somewhat bitter but he handled his limited duties faithfully and he turned out to be a wonderful news source for me. *I was to learn about and act on some unsavory activities of the county police which will be detailed later.*

# CHAPTER 10

## Politics: Southern Style

ONE OF THE most important things I needed to do in my new reporting job was to learn what I could about the local political landscape. All my sources agreed that the biggest power in the county (and reputedly one of the three most powerful politicians in South Carolina) was a State Senator. I was told I needed to get on the Senator's good side; that he could be a good friend or a fierce enemy.

The fact is the Senator was very conscious of the power of the press and made every effort to get on my good side by inviting me to many social events at his home. I was told that plenty of good food, liquor and other forms of entertainment were available at these events. I never accepted offers to any of these parties knowing that such attendance would compromise my work as a journalist.

This man turned out to be a charming rascal. Although he had little formal education, he was highly intelligent and literate. His grammar was impeccable and as a recent teacher of this subject, I was a good judge of that. In all the time I was around him I never heard him mispronounce or misuse a word. And his vocabulary was extensive.

He was also a bit too conscious of the press. In a crowded room where I was covering a story, he would look around and say, "I see Mr. White of the Evening Herald is with us. I'm sure he will write a good story about..." *Then he would proceed to tell me what I should say in my article! Naturally, I never let him influence the tone or content of any of my writing.*

I was told that the Senator had passed the State bar examination and received his law license without benefit of college. In fact, I was told he did not finish high school but can't confirm that. Obviously, he had great natural intelligence to pass the State test. *(Note: standards for receiving a license to practice law in South Carolina did not require a law degree at that time. I assume that he, along with many other attorneys without formal education but who passed the required test, was "grandfathered").* York County citizens wasted no time in telling me about the Senator's "dark side." *They told me that he had almost killed a man with a pool cue in a bar room fight but I cannot confirm that either. I can confirm that he threatened me personally by telephone on more than one occasion.*

It might seem strange that a man who had only one visible means of support could live lavishly on the $1,500 a year that SC state senators received at that time. Yet he drove fine cars, had frequent big parties and lived like a wealthy man. How do you do that on the low salary paid by the State? It was common knowledge around York County that the Senator bought cheap land and then was instrumental in building nice, hard surface roads through that land. Naturally he could then re-sell the property at higher prices. Again, I never confirmed this personally but it seemed to be common knowledge!

It didn't take me long to realize that I had stepped into a hotbed of raw Southern politics as practiced in South Carolina. So, while I was getting acquainted with needed sources by visiting schools, and county, state and local offices, I kept a wary eye out for political intrigues. Although I avoided any personal entanglements with politicians, instinctively I knew I needed to know as much about them as possible. That proved prophetic as I will explain later.

*On a personal note, while all this was happening my relationship with Joyce continued to grow. Since I had moved away from the Shelby area, Joyce decided to move to Charlotte where her chances of getting a good job were better. Despite her great looks and basic intelligence, the fact that she had only a 9th grade education was a severe handicap in getting work. She moved into the YWCA in Charlotte until she was able to team up with a couple of other girls and move into an apartment. Since she had never learned to drive an automobile, the girls moved to a place close to public transportation.*

Soon after starting my regular "beat" work in York, I often stopped at a popular drug store coffee shop where I often got "tips" about possible stories along with my coffee. Once, a young man sat down on the stool next to me and after awhile, asked: "Are you Jimmy White?" I looked around and saw my old Kings Creek buddy, Bascomb Love! We were both overjoyed at seeing each other for the first time since Blacksburg High School.

It turned out in our "catch up" conversation that both Bascomb and I had served in the Navy. Although both of us went through "boot camp" at Bainbridge, MD, we were there at different times and never had contact while in the Navy. After the war ended, I went to college while Bascomb began a business career. In York, he was owner of a watch repair business in a jewelry store next door to the coffee shop and owned an automobile franchise down the street! He said he had seen my byline in the Evening Herald and wondered if this Jim White could possibly be his old friend from Kings Creek. Apparently he had spotted me enter the coffee shop and thought it might be me despite my changed appearance.

Our meeting allowed us to renew, even expand our friendship. Ironically, our roles had reversed over the years and this seemed to enhance our friendship. I had become more outgoing and he had become more reserved. We had coffee together frequently and he often stopped by my little cottage on his way back to his home and family at Kings Creek. Bascomb was a natural born businessman. In addition to his watch repair business and car dealership, he dabbled in land purchases, etc.

Both Bascomb and I shared a lifelong love of automobiles. Although his knowledge of cars was far superior to mine, he discovered I had one special talent--spotting signs of repaired damage on a car. He began asking me to go with him to take a look at cars he was thinking about buying or taking in on trades. I remember once we were 50 feet away from a car when I said: "Bascomb, that car has been hit on the right front." With a doubting look at me, he crawled under the car and said: "You're right."

If I could arrange my schedule (e.g. on a dull news day) I would occasionally go with him to out-of-town car auctions. This would enable us to spend enjoyable time together while inspecting cars to be auctioned and while he was bidding on a car. If he was the successful bidder, I would drive one of his cars back to York for him. If some news broke while we were gone, I didn't mind staying up all night to write the necessary articles. Sometimes it would be close to 6 a.m. when I dropped the package to be delivered to the Evening Herald. Missing a good night's sleep was a small price to pay for the time spent with a dear friend.

Meanwhile, I was turning out lots of work and making friends in York County. Police Chief Bill Ivey had become one of my best friends as well as news source and "protector." I'll explain the reference to "protector" later. I had also become a close friend and customer of the owner of a small locally owned restaurant. After a few visits there, he would ask me to go back in the kitchen and make my own milk shakes; put together my own burger, etc. Since I was eating most of my meals out, his friendly acceptance of me made me feel almost like I was eating at home.

I also made it a point to get to know the owner/publisher of the Yorkville Enquirer, a weekly newspaper which was one of the earliest newspapers in South Carolina.

I also became close friends with their only reporter, an old seasoned newspaper veteran (at least compared to me). Bill was a highly intelligent man who had many interests but no longer had the energy to pursue them.

One day Bill handed me an obviously very old book saying, "You might find this interesting when you have some spare time." Because I was so busy establishing contacts and writing articles for the paper, I had no time then for pleasure reading. So I thanked him, put the book in my car and later transferred it to my cottage to be perused later when things settled down. I did note that the title made reference to "Ku Klux Klan Trials in Columbia..." but never dreamed such trials would have any relevance to me. *Boy was I wrong and I'll explain that later!*

# CHAPTER 11
## The People of York: New Friends and One Enemy

ANOTHER NEW FRIEND, the Vocational Agriculture teacher at York High School had some advice for me. He said: "Jim, I think you will like it here. The people are very nice. But they're very provincial. Unless your family has a long history in York you will be accepted only so far. Don't expect to be invited to their house for dinner. I've been here for over 20 years and I'm still considered an 'outsider' in York."

*Had I checked my family history, I would have learned that my great-grandfather Andrew Jackson White was one of the early settlers of York County. And another White relative had been a prominent physician in the town of York. I knew none of this at the time and it wouldn't have mattered to me, anyway.*

Two other especially good friends I made soon after my arrival in York were both black men (called Negroes back then). The first was Isaac Wright, owner of Wright's Funeral Home and the second was Jim Williams, owner of a grocery store in the black part of town.

Isaac lived next door to the funeral home he owned, which was very near to the home where I dropped off my daily package for the newspaper. I don't remember exactly how we met but do remember that he invited me to his home soon afterward. After that, when both of us had time, we would have a beer or glass of wine together in his living room and discuss race relations, politics, philosophy, etc. Isaac, or "Fine" as his black friends called him, was highly intelligent and well educated with a Masters Degree from Boston University. He told me that his family's social life was centered around a private club in Charlotte and that I was one of his few close friends in York. Despite that, his funeral home business in York was highly successful.

I met my other black friend, Jim Williams, one day as I was passing his grocery store and stopped by for a cold drink. We conversed that day, made a connection, and I would stop by for a chat any time I was in his neighborhood. Both of these friends became my eyes and ears in the black community. Chief Ivey and the police department also kept me informed of anything they thought might be of interest to me. All of these friends felt free to call me anytime day or night and I was always appreciative of their efforts. Soon my phone was busy with "tips" from my many contacts.

Although I was very happy with the little cottage, I began to feel the need to set up my own darkroom, something I did not have room to do in the cottage. So, when a house with three bedrooms, two baths and three-car detached garage, came on the market at a very reasonable price I bought it. Since I was eligible for a GI Loan, my upfront cost was only about $150 and my monthly mortgage payments were $35 per month.

I used the experience I had gained while working in the Sanford furniture store to furnish the place with good quality used furniture pieces at very little cost. I also purchased black and white photo development equipment and a used "like new" Omega D3 enlarger. I converted the smallest bedroom into a darkroom. Although I still sent most of my film to the newspaper for development, if I had the time I developed the negatives for the paper in my darkroom. This gave me a chance to choose the copy that best illustrated the story.

Soon I was getting non-newspaper requests for photography, especially from school officials. This was a losing proposition financially but a good way to make friends with school teachers and administrators. Since they usually wanted to pay me $1.00 for taking a picture, developing it and delivering the prints, I decided just to donate my services to them. I followed my old Enquirer Reporter Bill's adage: "I'd rather get nothing than damned near nothing" for my work.

However, I was also beginning to get some requests to film weddings and other paying events, and my new darkroom setup made it possible for me to conduct some business on my own. This sideline business was fine with the newspaper. Unexpectedly, one of my first business opportunities came from friend Isaac Wright. He told me that relatives and friends of the dead people at his funeral home frequently asked him to take photos of their bodies in caskets and at funerals.

He explained that black people became very emotional with the loss of a relative or close friend and wanted to preserve their memory in this way. He said he was not trained as a photographer and didn't feel at all comfortable in providing that service. He said he feared that something might go wrong and the family would end up with no photos of their dead loved ones.

Isaac then asked if I would consider providing this service for his funeral business. He had seen my photo caption credits, so he knew I was a competent photographer. I was caught short by his request but I could see he was totally sincere. He went on to explain how this arrangement might work: the grieving person(s) would ask for this service and he would contact me to see if I could be available. If so, I would set the price for taking the pictures, developing, and printing the requested number of prints. He said he would be responsible for collecting the money and paying me.

"If I don't collect the money first, you may never get it" he said, adding, "Once the funeral is over, the emotions will cool and they will no longer be willing to pay for the pictures." He said this had happened to him when he first started in the business until he learned to collect the money in advance. Although I didn't relish the thought of taking pictures of dead bodies, I agreed to give it a try. I felt I was helping out a friend and obtaining some money to help pay for my photographic equipment. I photographed several black funerals and always received my money from Isaac.

I only performed this service at one white funeral. The occasion was for a well-loved minister of a small, fundamentalist church. The minister was well known for driving his new Oldsmobile 88 at extremely high speeds around the county. One day he lost control of the car and died in a one-car accident. I was called by one of the church members and asked to take photos of the dead minister.

Since the church member knew that I had been taking photos at black funerals, I didn't feel I could refuse. Almost everyone in the congregation wanted prints of their deceased minister. Unfortunately, I didn't have Isaac to collect the money up front. And when I arrived at the church with the ordered prints not a single member of the congregation wanted to buy copies. I trash canned the whole batch and never photographed another white funeral.

My career was going extremely well with one exception: the Senator. I never set out to be his adversary. In fact, I was a liberal Democrat at the time and he was State Senator of the same party. However, when something controversial involving the senator occurred (which was pretty often), I had no hesitation in reporting it in the newspaper. Then I began to notice that, though most of my copy went through the editing process and was printed the way I wrote it, any text that reflected badly on the Senator was being altered or deleted from my articles. At first I thought the deletions might have been made because of space limitations. But eventually, I knew they were being altered for political reasons, i.e., to protect the Senator. I knew I had to do something about this matter to get it corrected or I would have to leave the paper.

After much thought, I decided that Mr. Patrick, the publisher, needed to know about this and asked for an appointment with him. I carried a few copies of the articles with notations of changes that had been made. Mr. Patrick thanked me for coming in and "confirming some doubts" he already had about one of his editors. He said: "Jim, you don't need to worry, I'll take care of this problem. I've been suspicious for some time that some of our people have become too political. I want my paper to be as objective as possible." Within two weeks the editor in question was gone and I never experienced any further "political" editing of my copy.

That didn't mean the end of problems with the Senator, however. One day, Police Chief Ivey asked me to come by his office. He closed the door and said: "Jim, I'm concerned about your safety. Several of my officers have picked up rumors that the Senator is very angry at you and has been making threats to do you harm."

The fact was that I had been receiving quite a few "hang up" calls and calls that sounded like the Senator but I could not positively identify him. Then around 2 a.m. one morning the phone rang, and I recognized the alcohol thickened voice of the Senator. He made a direct threat to the effect that I should be careful of my writing or bad things might happen to me. I hung up the phone without responding but was pretty sure that I now knew the source of the "hang ups" and unrecognizable late night calls.

At the end of our discussion, the Chief then reached into a drawer, drew out a pistol and holster and said: "I'm authorizing and advising you to carry this pistol with you so you can defend yourself." I thanked him for his concern but declined the offer. The Chief then added, "O.K., but I'll have my officers drive past your house as often as they can." After that I was pleased to see the number of York police cars that drove slowly past my house at all hours of the night.

I continued to hear rumors about unsavory actions that involved the Senator and the County Police but since I didn't print rumors and couldn't confirm these actions, they didn't appear in the paper. One rumor: the Senator would send county police into black neighborhoods with pockets of one dollar bills to bribe the citizens to vote for him or one of his cronies. The county policemen would actually haul these voters to the polling place in their police cars, according to the rumors. Obviously, if true, which I had no reason to doubt, these actions were clearly illegal.

Later, I received confidential information that some highly placed county police-men were confiscating illegal whiskey, and instead of destroying it or putting it under official lock and key as evidence, were instead selling the whiskey and pocketing the money. I knew this was too serious to deal with on my own, so I again called the publisher Mr. Patrick and asked for a private audience with him.

I told Mr. Patrick what I had heard from a reputable source and he said: "Jim this is serious stuff. I'm calling the State Bureau of Investigation (SBI) and they will handle this from now on. I don't want you to be involved." The SBI did in fact investigate and two of the top county detectives went to jail as a result. Fortunately my name was kept out of this case.

# CHAPTER 12

## Another Good Contact--and Renter

ONE DAY CHIEF Ivey called and asked me to drop by his office to meet someone. When I entered his office, he introduced me to a new highway patrolman just assigned to the York County area. After we chatted a while, the Chief said that the patrolman needed a place to live. Would I be interested in renting him one of my bedrooms? The patrolman said he was willing to pay $20 a month for a private room and bath.

Since the patrolman was clean cut and appeared nice, I didn't need to think long about this! Not only would I have someone to share the rent, I would have a first-hand contact with the South Carolina Highway Patrol who would be an excellent source as well as a protector in my own home. After he moved into my second bed-room, his radio soon became a priceless source of information to me. And I received no further after-midnight threats.

Because he left the radio on full time during the day, I would sometimes hear reports of accidents and be the first to arrive at the scene. Once when this happened, I inadvertently caused pain to someone. I'll never forget that incident. By habit, I grabbed my camera bag and hurried to the location mentioned on the patrolman's radio. With the bag in hand, I ran to the back of a pickup truck in the middle of the road where a man was leaning over the body of a teenage boy. At the sight of me, the man quickly jumped up and ran to me saying: "Thank God you've arrived, Doctor!" I had to tell him that I was no doctor; that the bag he saw was a camera bag.

That was one of the worst feelings I ever suffered as a newspaper reporter. I put my camera bag back in the car without taking a picture. I learned that the man was hauling hay in his pickup truck and his young son wanted to ride on top to hold the hay down. Unfortunately, the hay slid off, along with the boy, whose head hit the hard surface of the road. He was dead before the ambulance arrived. There was no way I could console the father. It still bothers me to see children riding in the back of pickup trucks--a practice too common in the South.

Another unexpected incident occurred while I was in York. One morning before daylight, I was awakened by a call that a small plane had crashed in York County. I dressed quickly, put my camera in the car and headed for the scene. I took pictures, using my flash to try to illuminate the scene, and rushed back to write a brief story about the plane crash. I added the article and the unprocessed film to the package I had already placed on the porch of the Evening Herald employee. Fortunately she had not left or I would have had to make the trip to Rock Hill myself and my other scheduled jobs would be missed.

The story I had written did not contain the name of the pilot, the only person in the plane, since it was not known at that time. The pilot was taken to the little Catholic Hospital in York and pronounced dead there. Understandably, Sister Margaret Mary did not want the name released until the family was notified. But after I learned that the family had been notified, she was still opposed to my using the pilot's name. So, without using her as my source, I called the name in to the news desk and told them to add it to the story I had written.

Sister Margaret Mary was very angry when she saw the name of the pilot published in the Evening Herald that afternoon. She called and chewed me out thoroughly. But Chief Ivey, a good friend of both of us, helped mend my fences with her. I never knew why she opposed use of the pilot's name after the family had been notified. But this did not change my view that she was a fine human being and the little hospital she headed was a big asset to the community.

# CHAPTER 13
## Some Fun Along with Serious Work!

THINGS WERE NOT always as serious as the events above might indicate. One example of combining work with fun: the Sheriff still had authority to break up liquor stills so when he was planning a raid he would call me to see if I could accompany the raiding party. If I had the time I would meet the group at the Sheriff's office where we would get our briefing. Before leaving for the raid, the Sheriff would deputize me and provide me with a pistol. Of course my only authority to use the weapon was to help shoot up the still. I didn't want nor have any part in making arrests.

The raiding party would steal through the woods as quietly as possible until we got close to the still. Sometimes, the bootleggers would hear us and run, leaving their liquor and still behind. That would begin a chase that ended when the still operators were caught and returned to the site of the still. Often the still operators were too drunk from imbibing their own product to run and readily submitted to the arrests. At that point, I would take pictures and gather information for a story to appear in the next day's newspaper. The bootleggers never objected to being photographed or interviewed. Perhaps they were too drunk to object or looked forward to seeing their picture in the paper. Their 15 minutes of fame!

After the chases by deputies (except me) and arrests, interviews, photographs, etc., the culprits had to wait in the police car while we shot up their stills. Our purpose was to disable the stills so they could not be used for future bootlegging purposes; bullet holes also helped get rid of the mash that was working.

I wouldn't tell the next part of the story if the "statute of limitations" had not long ago passed. Before loading up the high proof finished liquor to be used as evidence, the Sheriff would pick out one of the clearest gallon bottles and present it to me. I didn't like the taste of this high powered liquor but a good friend in Charlotte loved it so I would save it until he came for a visit. So, I would end up with a story and pictures for the paper, get to shoot a pistol, and go home with a gallon of good quality but illegal whiskey.

*During this time I was visiting Joyce in Charlotte as often as I could get away from work. With time our relationship was growing stronger and we felt we needed more time together. Eventually, we decided to get engaged and at Bascomb Love's suggestion the two of us drove to Columbia, SC, to purchase a ring from Bascomb's older brother, William Bird Love, who owned a jewelry store there. William Bird sold me a perfect one carat diamond ring at a great price!*

A few weeks later we decided to get married and needed to find a minister to marry us. A Catawba friend studying for the Ministry had said he wanted to perform the ceremony when I was ready to get married. I knew that he was minister at a church in Lexington, NC, so I called him and reminded him of our agreement. He asked me if either of us had ever been married. I told him that Joyce had been married before but was now divorced. He hesitated and then said: "Jim, I hate to tell you this but my Church rules do not permit me to perform a marriage for someone who has been divorced." I was very hurt by this but didn't share this hurt with Joyce for obvious reasons.

Eventually, I located a Charlotte based Christian minister willing to perform the ceremony. However, our romance was beginning to seem like a "star crossed" affair. Earlier, when I told Dad that I was planning to marry Joyce, he replied: "Your mother would be very hurt; she didn't like the fact that you were dating a woman who had been married before." I was surprised by this since my mother had never shown any disapproval of Joyce to me.

These two incidents gave me some forebodings about our future together but things had progressed to the point that I didn't feel I could rethink the situation and risk causing more damage to someone who I knew was already in a frail, emotional state. After we were married, she often cried about pain she felt from her mother's treatment of her and her father. Later, she spent much time in therapy trying to rid herself of the emotional damage she said she had received as a girl. *That will be detailed in a later part of the memoir.*

Incidentally, her father was an extremely nice (but henpecked) man who spent his working life in low level cotton mill jobs and seemed to have no ambition for the finer things in life. As far as I know he never even owned his own automobile. There might have been some psychological significance to Joyce's attraction to me. Her father had red hair and a stocky build. In retrospect, I realize that I looked more like him than I did my own father, who was a tall, rangy man.

# CHAPTER 14

## For Better or for Worse

ONCE I WAS married and Joyce moved into my house, Bascomb didn't feel as comfortable visiting as he did when I was single and living in the cottage, so I made a point to stop by his repair shop more often. We would then go next door for coffee and conversation. He continued to invite me to go to auctions with him when I had the time which was infrequent because of my continually growing workload, which also limited time with my family. However, my fellow WWII veterans, Robert and Frank, each helped make up for this by driving to York occasionally and accompanying me as I raced around the county covering news stories and taking pictures with my trusty Speed Graphic. I thoroughly enjoyed these occasions because it gave us a chance to spend time together as adults--something we had rarely been able to do. And both brothers seemed to get a kick out of my adventurous work life, especially compared to their mundane mill jobs.

One thing that apparently amazed brother Bob was that since I had a PRESS sign on my windshield, I never bothered feeding parking meters. I was told later that he feared I would be ticketed for ignoring these meters. Of course I was aware that almost every lawman in York County knew my vehicle and was not going to give me a ticket.

After I had been at York for a year or more, I was told that Connie Morton, the Managing Editor, was leaving for a public relations job and that the paper was replacing him with a newspaper man from North Carolina. Although I knew I would miss Connie, I had no serious concerns about this management change. Then something happened that seriously alarmed me. I was told that the new editor wanted to spend his first week at the Evening Herald following me around.

I couldn't imagine what I had done to deserve such close scrutiny by the new Managing Editor. He must have heard some unfavorable things about my work! But there was nothing I could do but say I welcomed spending time with the new Editor whose name was Frank Jeter, Jr. I heard from several fellow employees at the paper that he was a highly qualified, experienced newspaper man but I had no personal knowledge of him.

Although I was initially pretty nervous about having my new boss looking over my shoulder every day for a full week, Frank and I got along fine and toward the end of the week I was actually enjoying our time together. I never asked him why he had taken what I thought was a strange approach to getting familiar with a new job.

*I had my best chance to do that several years later when we both ended up as Information Officers in Washington. When we were having lunch together one day at the USDA cafeteria, I finally asked him the question that had been bugging me all those years: "Frank, I've always wondered why you wanted to follow me around the first week you were on the job at the Rock Hill Evening Herald!" He laughed and said: "Jim, I gave a one-month notice to the newspaper I was leaving to take over the job in Rock Hill. So, I asked the Evening Herald to send me daily copies of the paper during that month. I read the paper from cover to cover and marked the best articles. At the end of the month, I tabulated the figures and found that you had written 90% of the "live" news stories appearing in the paper."*

*I must have still looked puzzled because he said: "I wanted to get to know you first since I figured I would have to depend on you in order to put out a good newspaper." "Well, you scared the hell out of me, Frank!" I replied. Incidentally, that week we spent together those many years ago resulted in establishing a friendship that lasted until both of us moved away from Washington and lost contact. I'll mention a favor Frank Jeter, Jr. did for me later in this part!*

# CHAPTER 15
## "The Book" Forces Attention on Race Relations

ALTHOUGH MY SCHEDULE remained tight, I finally got around to taking a closer look at the book that my old Enquirer friend, Bill, had handed me. Although he "lent" me the book he never asked for it back. Apparently he thought that the book had more significance to me than anyone else in York. *In my opinion, he was right.*

I got the shock of my life (up until then) when I read the "Reporters' Note" that preceded the "Introductory Part" of the book that was titled: **"Proceedings in the Ku Klux Klan Trials at Columbia, SC,"** during The United States Circuit Court, November Term, 1871. The "Reporters' Notes" in the book said: "The following pages contain a report of the proceedings before the Circuit Court of the United States vs. Allen Crosby, et al and evidence and arguments in the case of the United States vs. Robert Hayes Mitchell, et al, is strictly a verbatim report of all that occurred..." **Robert Hayes Mitchell was my maternal grandfather!**

The revelation that my grandfather was involved in the KKK stunned me to the point that I had to stop and take a deep breath before proceeding further with the book. Although he had died before I was born, I had heard only positive things about him: that he was a loving husband and father, a pillar of the community and an extremely gentle man. I could not imagine him participating in a conspiracy, committing a crime or belonging to the KKK.

My image of him was formed by the newspaper articles I had read about him as well as family remembrances. I had been told that he loved my grandmother so much that when she died April 15, 1915, Grandfather Mitchell stood over her grave at the cemetery, broke off a cherry tree branch overhead, tossed it on the casket and said: "By the time this cherry blossom blooms, I will be joining you." Prophetically, two weeks later he died and was buried next to her under that cherry tree. That story was told to me by my mother and my oldest sister, Isabel White Blackwell; and the timing of my maternal grandparents' deaths is well documented.

Back to the book about the KKK trial, I had to read through pages of legal arguments about the makeup of the jury, instructions to and qualifications for the Grand Jury, quashing of the indictments, and many lengthy challenges, other legalese and sentencing of some people who had pleaded guilty to some undefined "conspiracy" before I was able to get to the information I was seeking. On page 146, Part III, I finally got to "**The case of Robert Hayes Mitchell, Sylvanus Shearer and Others.**"

Even then I had to wade through many more pages of legal arguments still looking for the crime my grandfather was alleged to have committed. After much more legal wrangling, the U.S. District Attorney, The Hon. D. I. Corbin, and Presiding Judge(s) The Hon. Hugh L. Bond of Maryland, Circuit Judge, and the Hon. George S. Bryan of Charleston, District Judge, decided to separate Robert Hayes Mitchell from the other defendants and try him separately. But this action still did not reveal the nature of the crime.

The legalities continued on with attempts by the prosecution to identify members and leaders of the KKK, as well as wording of the "Obligations" and "Constitution" of the KKK. When asked for reasons for formation of the Klan, witnesses said they were needed for "burnings" and "threats" in their community. When asked to describe the functions of the Klan, witnesses declared their purposes were to "whip" or "kill" those "making threats" and "doing burnings."

Page 171 revealed that "the specific charge against the prisoner (I presume my grandfather) is, that he belonged to a conspiracy to violate the rights secured by the Act of 1870, that is, the right to vote or do anything else that was secured by the Act of 1870." On page 178 it was stated by a witness that the leader of his Klan was John Mitchell. (*Later he was referred to as John W. Mitchell*). I believe that was my grandfather Robert Hayes Mitchell's older brother. Another witness testified that the leader of his Klan was Charles Byers.

Finally, on page 223 of the book, it was revealed that the name of the victim I had been looking for was Jim Williams, Captain of a black militia! Further on that page more details of the story are told by a member of Capt. Williams' company, Andy

Tims, a witness for the prosecution. Under questioning, Tims said that KKK members first came to his door, broke it down, and asked where Jim Williams lived. Some time after he gave the Klan members this information, Andy Tims apparently joined with other black militia members who tracked fresh horse and mule tracks from the Williams house to houses belonging to KKK members. At one of these houses that they knew was occupied by a KKK member, they found a mule which was "muddy and sweating with saddle." Sims said they followed its fresh tracks back and before reaching the Williams house they found him hanging from a tree.

At this point my emotions would not let me continue any further reading of the book. Obviously, my first horrific thoughts were about my friend with that same name. I had to wonder if my grandfather was involved in the murder of his grandfather, or other close relative. I will probably never know the answer to that question. I don't know whether I want to know the answer. I didn't stop visiting Jim Williams' store and talking with him but I was never as comfortable with him as I had been before.

Much time passed before I regained the urge to open up this book. When I did, I began to skim through the many legal arguments presented by both sides until I found the prosecution's closing arguments beginning on page 375 and ending on page 389. The argument by Hon. D. H. Chamberlain, one of the prosecutors, was one of the most touching and eloquent closing arguments I have ever heard uttered in a courtroom. *And as a reporter I have heard many.* A small but especially poetic part of the Prosecutor's closing follows, verbatim:

*Gentlemen of the jury, no eloquence, no ingenuity, no art or power of forensic advocacy, such as will delight and impress you in the arguments of the distinguished counsel who will follow me, will ever efface from minds the ghastly horrors of that night which witnessed those crimes. The bright moon looked down upon a scene never before paralleled in our land.*

*The education, the intelligence, the property of York County, represented by the Ku Klux Klan, had been assembled to execute the purpose of the order, on the person of Jim Williams. Robert Hayes Mitchell is there. Williams is hung; hung by the Ku Klux Klan; hung because he is a Radical; hung in pursuance of the conspiracy whose monstrous nature was written in its constitution, which now receives its conclusive interpretation in the blood of its victim.*

*What American citizen can think of that scene without a shudder and a blush! Why did not the very elements--why did not Nature herself cry those wretches "Halt?" Why did not the stones beneath their feet, and piney boughs that sighed above their heads, bid them "Stop?" I should have thought they would have heard such words as greeted the ears of the terrified Alonzo, when all nature seemed breaking into voice to herald his crime:*

**"Methought the billows spoke and told me of it;**
**The winds did sing it to me; and the thunder--**
**That deep and dreadful organ-pipe--pronounced**
**The name of Prosper; it did bass my trespass."**

*He continued, "no, gentlemen of the jury, the voice of nature, of conscience, of God, fell on deaf ears. The conspiracy passed on; the deed was done; the dreadful secret was hidden by the oath of death. Months pass by. Williams moulders in his grave. Robert Hayes Mitchell walks forth still safe and unpunished. But Justice-- Justice, whom the ancients pictured with the feet of velvet and hands of iron--is on his track, and now, at this moment, holds him in her unrelaxing grasp, and commits him to your just judgment..."*

The Prosecutor closed with, *"Let your verdict be the invincible arm of the Government, striking down the oppressor and lifting up his victim."* At this point, I put down the book again and years passed before I re-opened it and found that my grandfather was found guilty and served 18 months in a federal prison.

Back in York I continued to accept invitations to share a drink and conversation with Isaac Wright. I had noticed, however, that he never accepted my invitations to him, alone or with his family, to visit me. At first I attributed this to his need to remain close to his business. Finally, I asked him directly if there was any reason why he never reciprocated my visits. He smiled, took me by the shoulder, and said: "Jim, my people will accept your visits to my house but your people would not accept a black man paying a social visit to a white person. It's a cultural thing."

He added, "I'm not going to cause you any trouble in this town by visiting you." I protested that I was willing to take that chance but he was having none of that. I had been making assumptions that white southerners' feelings about race had changed a lot since I had grown up in South Carolina in the 30's and early 40's. But then I recalled what happened in New Orleans when we were returning from the War and my black shipmates were refused service at the restaurant where we all planned to have our final meal together.

*Then I was further reminded that the feelings of some Southerners had not changed much during a conversation with the Evening Herald's Circulation Manager. I was driving him back to Rock Hill in my car when we passed The Wright Funeral Home. Isaac was standing outside and I waved to him. My passenger turned to me and said, referring to Isaac, "He's a pretty smart 'darkie' isn't he?" This by a non-educated white man who didn't even own a car about a successful black businessman with a Master's Degree from Boston University and a new Cadillac in his driveway! Perhaps we had not changed as much as I hoped!*

# CHAPTER 16
## Time to Think About "Moving On"

AT AROUND THE two year mark as a Reporter-Photographer for a small city daily newspaper, I began to think that it was time for me to broaden my work experience. I had received two unsolicited offers to assume Managing Editor jobs from two smaller news-papers located in Anderson and Chester, both in South Carolina. I checked both out but declined the offers, thinking those jobs, as pleasant as they might be, would be taking me back where I started. By that time I might be going in the wrong direction.

The offer to head the Chester Reporter did have some appeal. The publisher of the Chester newspaper, as well as the one located in Lancaster (both owned by Col. Elliot White Springs) told me that he was planning to retire in a couple of years and he thought I would be a good prospect to succeed him. I asked one question too many, however. I asked the publisher if Col. Springs ever interfered with the "editorial content" of the pa-pers. He replied: "No, he leaves that up to the editor(s)." Then he hesitated for a moment and added: "He might exert some influence if there is a union issue involved."

My juvenile journalistic ethics immediately kicked in and lowered my interest in the job. In retrospect and with many more years of experience, my feeling may have been quite different. Later, I realized that an owner has (or should have) the right to run his business as he sees fit--especially in the situation as described by the publisher. For example, I knew that Col. Elliott White Springs had been very successful in managing his mills and in providing good jobs to many people for years. And I don't blame him for not wanting his own newspapers to possibly sabotage his efforts to fend off Unions.

Although I checked out the job offers at Chester and Anderson and thought they might be fun and interesting, I decided that taking either of these jobs would mean that I was giving up my dreams of working for the top newspapers in the country. I still wanted to test my competence as a reporter at a higher level and had no re-grets about turning these offers down. Before revealing any thoughts of leaving The Evening Herald, however, I decided to use up some of my vacation time (which had been accumulating because the paper couldn't figure out a way to fill the gap while I was away). In addition to having some time to relax, a vacation would give me a chance to check out some other job possibilities. Joyce and I agreed that a visit to Florida just might be a good place to do both.

Since the Evening Herald management felt that they could not leave all the work I had been doing uncovered for two weeks, they decided to try something new by bringing in an Intern as my substitute while I was on vacation. I agreed to postpone my vacation until they could find a suitable candidate. I would also stay around long enough to brief him and introduce him to my key sources. Ultimately they decided on a senior in journalism at the University of North Carolina.

Soon after I met the young man I was to train as my substitute, I began to have some concerns about him. His self confidence bordered on arrogance. When I would intro-duce him to a contact who invariably offered to be helpful to him he would shrug and say: "I don't expect to have any problem handling this job!" I could see many raised eyebrows at this response from someone who knew nothing about the job he was ex-pected to do. The newspaper editors themselves seemed concerned about the amount of self confidence the young Intern displayed but agreed to let me go with one provi-sion: that I check in with them by telephone every few days. That was fine with me.

So Joyce and I headed for Florida on our first vacation together. Our first stop was in Jacksonville where I had some meetings with the top editors at the Jacksonville Florida Times Union and left some clippings of my work with them. Management at the newspaper said they liked what they saw but didn't have an opening at the moment. At night, we enjoyed the Dog Races which neither of us had seen before. After a day or two we drove on to Orlando.

One of the reasons for going to Orlando next was that I had a contact there. My good friend John Huddleston's parents had retired from the State Department and had settled in Winter Park, a suburb of Orlando. John had called me and invited us to come visit him at his parents' home. Before we headed south, however, John later wrote saying he had re-enlisted in the Army and would not be at Winter Park to greet us. He insisted that his parents still wanted us to come visit them. They knew that he had spent many holidays at my parents' house. Also, they knew that he had spent the summer with me at Sanford after blowing the money sent to him to "study" in Mexico!

Despite John's assurance that his parents wanted us to stay with them I thought it best that we visit them but stay in a motel. After we checked into a motel in Winter Park, I called them and they gave us directions to their house. We had a nice time and had our first opportunity to pick tree ripened grapefruit and oranges from their orchard. The next morning I called the Orlando Sentinel, which I knew to be the largest newspaper in Central Florida, and was immediately able to schedule a meeting with the City Editor, Ned Martin. I took my resume and sample copies of articles for my appointment with him. We had a good meeting and he told me he had a job vacancy, similar to the one I had in Rock Hill. He offered me the job which would entail being a Reporter-Photographer working in a nearby small town as an area correspondent for the Sentinel. I told him I wanted some time to think about the offer, that I wanted to explore some other opportunities while I was in Florida.

Since I had been away from Rock Hill for a few days by that time, I decided to call the Rock Hill newspaper as I had promised. When the editor I was supposed to call came on the line he said: "Jim, you've got to cut your vacation short! That college intern has antagonized everyone in the York area and he has not written a single story we could use since you've been gone." He added that the intern had insulted our contacts to the point that they were sending him all over the county on "false leads." The paper had already sent the guy packing back to Chapel Hill. The experiment of using an intern had failed miserably. So, we cut our "vacation" short and headed back to York/Rock Hill. My contacts welcomed me back and the news resumed coming out of my Royal Manual typewriter.

Although I had not accepted the job offer at the Sentinel, I was pretty confident that they or the Jacksonville paper would make an offer I could accept. I thought the time had come to tell my editors that I had applied for jobs at a couple of newspapers but that I would not leave them in a "lurch." I would help them find a suitable replacement. Soon afterward, I received a call from Ned Martin. He said: "Since I haven't heard back from you about the area correspondent job, I assume you're not too interested in it. I'd like to offer you a job on the City Desk at the Sentinel." This of course was what I had been interested in all along--working in a large newsroom with many reporters!

Ned offered me $65 a week starting pay but when I refused that he said they would pay me the same thing I was making at Rock Hill, i.e. $80 per week. He said this was the highest starting salary they had ever offered anyone. I accepted their offer on condition that I could give my present newspaper a four week notice. They agreed but urged that I come as soon as possible.

Since I already had a good prospect in mind to fill my job, I headed to Shelby to talk to my old boyhood friend, Les Roark. By that time Les had accumulated two years experience under the excellent tutelage of Ed Post and I knew he was ready to move up in the newspaper world. I felt bad about taking Les away from the Cleveland Times but felt he was ready to move on to a better paying, more challenging job. He readily agreed that he needed the change, put in his resignation, and prepared to move to York where the little cottage near the courthouse was vacant and awaiting him.

I mentioned around the courthouse that I would be leaving and that my house would be for sale. The Assistant Clerk of Court immediately made an offer which I accepted. When the owner of the Enquirer heard that I was leaving, he called and asked me to come by his office to talk. I couldn't imagine what he wanted to discuss but went to see him immediately. After we settled down, he said: "Jim, I've been wanting to retire for some time but never had found anyone I trusted to take over my newspaper. I'd like to sell the paper to you; I think you would be the right person to run this paper, which I love." After telling him I appreciated his offer but that I had no money, he replied that I didn't need any money; he would finance me and that I could pay him back in installments. He asked me to give the matter some serious thought and get back to him. I did think about his proposition but decided I really needed to test myself in the competitive world of a large newspaper such as the one in Orlando, FL.

When I left town for the Orlando Sentinel, the Enquirer printed an editorial lauding my ethics and work as an "investigative reporter" which I appreciated very much. Ironically, soon after I agreed to take the job at Orlando, the Jacksonville newspaper I had interviewed with a few weeks before called and made me a firm offer. I felt I had to turn down this offer since I had already made a commitment to the Orlando Sentinel. When it rains it pours. That was one of the old sayings I had heard growing up.

# CHAPTER 17
## New Job and New Challenges

THE MOVE TO Florida is somewhat of a blur to me. As I recall, Joyce and I made a weekend trip to Winter Park to select an apartment there, which was just minutes away from the Sentinel. I pulled a rental trailer packed with our furniture down to Florida arriving the day before I was to report to work. I don't recall who I was able to get to help me unload the furniture but succeeded in getting the furniture into the apartment the same day we arrived.

I was scheduled to start my first shift the next day (Sunday) from 2 until 10 p.m. These would be my regular hours since the Sentinel was a morning paper; I really looked forward to those hours since I considered myself a "night person" at that time. On Sunday afternoon shortly before 2 p.m., I arrived at the newspaper expecting to find someone to give me instructions. When I arrived at the newspaper, however, there was no one there except a woman secretary to answer the telephone.

Unfortunately, this woman had received no instructions regarding what I should do. I was puzzled but knew I wasn't going to spend the next 8 hours sitting around doing nothing. So, I asked the secretary if she could point me to my desk, provide me with a telephone directory and a copy of the Sentinel's "style book." *(Note: all major newspapers and wire services have their own "style books" that their reporters are supposed to follow).*

The secretary didn't seem to know about a "style book" but eventually found one and brought it along with a telephone directory to me. As for the desk I would be using, she told me to "pick any desk" I wanted. So, I selected a desk and spent the next hour or so perusing the "style book." *Most newspapers have at least some peculiar abbreviations and the Sentinel was no exception. I still remember that "Hwy.Ptlm" stood for Highway Patrolman.*

After becoming somewhat familiar with the "Style Book" I thought I should start getting some real work done. So, I began scanning the white and yellow pages of the Orlando telephone directory, and started jotting down telephone numbers for all the hospitals, Police Departments, and Sheriff's offices. Then I began making telephone calls to these offices in Orlando, Winter Park, Cocoa Beach, and other nearby towns and villages, making notes on any newsworthy events.

Using my notes, I then began writing articles for the next morning's paper. I also remembered that I needed to use carbon paper to turn over to the city desk for the next day's afternoon paper. Those reporters could use copies of my stories and update them as the basis for the afternoon paper. I only wished I had been provided something like that to start with in a strange, new situation. I could not imagine turning this sort of situation over to a new reporter, without any kind of instructions. All they knew about me was in a short resume, samples of newspaper articles, and an hour's interview!

At around 8 p.m., I became aware that an older man was standing at the desk giving me an unfriendly stare. I looked up and asked: "Is this your desk?" He nodded "yes" and I apologized and got up to find another desk. I tried to engage the guy in some conversation, but he declined any efforts to communicate with me. Later, I found that he was an "old salt" reporter from a national news service, now defunct. He would not deign to waste his time conversing with an obviously young, wet-behind-the-ears reporter.

A few more reporters trickled in before my shift ended at 10 p.m. None offered to assist me or claimed the desk I was using, so I continued my solitary search for late Sunday news stories. Before leaving I clipped all the articles (plus carbons) into a package and left it on Ned Martin's desk, along with a note telling him I had left them.

The next day upon my 2 p.m. arrival, I found what I expected to find the previous day: a room full of reporters, telephones ringing, and typewriters clacking. I had a brief meeting with City Editor Ned Martin and he apologized for failing to leave any instructions for me. He also complimented me on my ingenuity in dealing with an awkward situation. Then he assigned me to a desk and gave me a list of assignments, including doing a brief article each day about the Tides times for the Coastal towns within the Sentinel's readership area.

Getting the Tides times right for the various towns turned out to be the toughest assignment I ever had as a reporter. I had to add (or subtract) for the various beaches (e.g., the tide information for Cocoa Beach and Jacksonville Beach would always be different). I don't think I ever got them completely right. *Remember, I failed college algebra!*

It didn't take me a full day to realize that morale among the reporters at the Sentinel was not good. I quickly began to get an earful of the discontent--at least from those not afraid to talk. I was informed that the owner/publisher did not want to see reporters talking to each other. His motto, according to those brave enough to talk was "if reporters have time to talk to each other we must have too many reporters." Some of those seen talking together would not be there the next day!

The publisher obviously did not know that a certain amount of interplay between reporters results in more and better stories. Often, good reporters share information helpful to all in a newsroom. But apparently this publisher had his own way of treating his employees. That might explain the reason the Newsroom at the Sentinel had 10 vacant positions (out of 100) when I was there in 1954.

More complaints centered around the salary situation. Some reporters said the paper was heartless; that if the editors knew that you owned your own home, had a family and did not want to leave Florida, your salary would be lower than a comparable reporter who was free to move to another state, i.e., they capitalized on a reporter's individual situation. An example cited was that the Sports Editor, who supervised three or four other sports writers, was trapped and was only being paid $65 per week. I didn't share the fact that my starting salary was $80 per week, not wanting to stir up any more feelings of jealousy or resentment.

By the end of the first week I felt comfortable on the job (except for figuring out the Tides) but I did not see a long-range career at the Sentinel being a part of my future. I was already thinking that if the work situation did not improve, I would stay only for a respectable time, e.g., a year, and then start looking for another job. Perhaps I might again contact the Jacksonville paper which had offered me a job a few days too late.

# CHAPTER 18
## An Unexpected Call and Job Offer

THEN, AS I was nearing the end of the second month, I got an unexpected call one day at the newspaper. The caller was Dr. Frank H. Jeter, head of Extension Service Information, at NC State College (now University) in Raleigh, NC. After introducing himself over the phone, Dr. Jeter told me that his son, Frank Jeter, Jr. had suggested he get in touch with me. Dr. Jeter said he had a vacancy for Assistant Information Specialist at the State Extension Service located on the NC State campus and that his son, Frank Jeter, Jr., my former editor at the Rock Hill Evening Herald, had given me an excellent recommendation for the job.

Dr. Jeter said his son had moved on to another job but that he was able to get in touch with me through my former employer, The Evening Herald. I asked Dr. Jeter what the job required and he replied that it involved several things. One would be writing news and feature articles about various Extension and Experiment Station Service activities and sending them to newspapers throughout the State as well as to magazines and the wire services. Another would be writing a weekly by-lined column for distribution to Extension Service offices. And, most important of all, I would be asked to develop and conduct a state-wide program for training Extension and Home Demonstration Agents in how to improve their communication skills, with emphasis on news and column writing. He said my newspaper career and educational background made me a perfect candidate for the position.

Dr. Jeter said, based on his son Frank Jr.'s high opinion of me, he was prepared to offer me the job, sight unseen. Without asking what the salary was, I accepted the job and prepared to give two weeks' notice--which I thought was adequate in view of the fact I had been there only two months.

However, when I met with Ned Martin, the City Editor, to break the news that I was resigning and giving a two week notice he was not happy. I told him I hoped he would understand; that Raleigh, NC was one of my favorite places and that the opportunity to work at NC State was just too good to pass up. Ned said: "Jim, I'm very disappointed that you're leaving this soon; I won't be able to give you a good recommendation in the future should you ever need one." I replied: "Well, then, Ned, if you feel that way I don't feel obligated to stay here two more weeks." Ned then changed his tone, apologized, and said: "Jim, I'm sorry I said that; I would appreciate it very much if you stay with us for two more weeks. And I'll be happy to give you a good recommendation should you ever need it."

So, I left the Orlando Sentinel on a somewhat friendly note and never regretted that decision. Also, I never needed Ned's recommendation for another job. As a matter of fact, the experience in Orlando ended my career as a direct newspaper journalist, although I continued to work closely with all types of mass media, including newspapers, magazines, radio and television, throughout my long career. And, fortunately for me, the world still seemed to revolve around the written word.

Two weeks later, Joyce and I left the Orlando area pulling another rented trailer loaded with our furniture and headed to one of my favorite cities, Raleigh, NC. I was also entering another phase of my career.

# PART 5

# CAREER CHANGE TO EDUCATIONAL JOURNALISM AND ANOTHER DEGREE

# CHAPTER 1
## Back to North Carolina!

AS JUST MENTIONED, Joyce and I packed up our skimpy furniture and furnishings again and headed north toward Raleigh, NC. Both of us were happy to leave the steamy August heat of Central Florida and return to a state and area we both loved. Soon we were settled in a nice apartment on Hillsborough Street within sight of the building where my office was located. That office would be in old Ricks Hall, the Entomology Building, on the NC State campus.

Since we had a week before I was to report for work, Joyce and I drove back to South Carolina where I dropped Joyce off for a brief visit with her family at Fort Mill while I drove to York to check on how Les Roark was doing and to later visit Dad and a few other close relatives. I had no trouble locating Les and he gave me a briefing on his time with the Evening Herald. He seemed to be fitting into the job and community quite well.

However, he shared a bit of disturbing news with me. He had become fast friends with Senator Lew Wallace and had thoroughly enjoyed parties the Senator had hosted. I thought it was a mistake to become too closely involved with a politician of any kind but soon found that my attitude toward this didn't match Les's. More about that later.

My first visit to Ricks Hall was to meet Dr. Jeter and the rest of the State Extension Service Information staff with whom I would be working. Of course I was anxious to find out what my salary would be. After asking, I was pleased to learn that I would be making $5,000 per year or almost $100 per week! This was a figure I had hoped to reach some day--certainly not only four years out of college! And as a State employee, some good benefits would go along with the job.

Soon after arriving at NC State, I was visited by Ken Griffin, my old suite mate from Catawba. He proudly told me he had reached the $5,000 mark that year for the first time. However, he said he had to hold three jobs to accomplish that goal. These jobs were teaching at the high school level, serving as head coach of the school's basketball and baseball teams, and conducting some sort of delivery business when school was not in session. We were two proud sharecropper boys to be making that kind of money!

Since returning to the Carolinas I had continued to remain in close contact with friend Les Roark. In one of his calls to me, he said that Ed Post had accepted a position with the U.S. State Department and that he (Les) had accepted the Cleveland Times offer to return to Shelby as Managing Editor of the paper. Then, shortly after that, he called to tell me that in a recent election the Senator was defeated! He said that he had heard that many people in York County gave me credit for the Senator's defeat. *I didn't deserve credit for that or seek to get the Senator defeated. All I wanted to do was write the truth and let the voters decide how to vote.*

I wondered what the ex-Senator's reaction would be should we inadvertently bump into each other someday. Would he bop me over the head with a cue stick as he reputedly had done to a political foe or give me a big hug? Since I still had strong ties to the York community, it didn't take me long to find out. At a stopover at this historic little town, I bumped squarely into the former State Senator. He embraced me like an old friend and insisted on buying me a cup of coffee.

We chatted over coffee, and he gave me a full briefing on his activities since his senatorial defeat: he was now engaged in a business venture growing chinchillas (or some such furry animal) and was fully enjoying life. He invited me to stop by his "ranch" anytime I was in York. Neither of us mentioned the word "politics." Didn't I say he was a "charming rascal" at the beginning of my discussion of him? If I had time, I would have taken him up on his invitation to visit. My differences with him were never personal.

# CHAPTER 2
## Starting the New Job

AT THE END of the week Joyce and I returned to Raleigh to start our new life. Early Monday morning I appeared at my office ready to go to work. My appearance at Ricks Hall could not have been more different than my first official visit as an employee of the Orlando Sentinel. I was warmly welcomed by J. C. Brown who would be my immediate supervisor as News Editor of the Information Division for the State Extension Office. I would share an office with J.C. Brown, Helen Jean Anderson (Home economics editor) and a secretary. *A staff that handled publications, headed by Bill Carpenter, was located in a separate office down the hall.*

Also, as indication of his desire to increase the professionalism of his staff, Dr. Jeter had recently hired a highly trained professional TV home economics person, Miss Dorothy Mulder, a graduate of Michigan State University, to join the staff. The news office, publications office, a small radio/TV staff, a staff artist and a staff photographer constituted the main components of the State Extension Information Division.

My first job was to learn details about my new duties from J.C. Brown. These initially turned out to be: (1) serving as editor of the periodical Extension News newsletter; (2) covering and writing articles about various news and feature events involving the State Extension Service and State Experiment Station (which paid part of my salary); and (3) developing and participating in training programs for State Extension and Home Demonstration Agents to better communicate their services to farmers and homemakers.

At the end of the first day, I was very happy about my new job. I had found J.C Brown to be a warm, accepting boss. Although his newspaper experience was limited to time spent at a weekly newspaper, he more than made up for his lack of experience with a brilliant mind. I was initially a bit concerned that J.C. might harbor some resentment that Dr. Jeter had personally handled my hiring based solely on his son's recommendation but that did not appear to be the case. Both Dr. Jeter and J.C. both soon assuaged my concern. They assured me that they had agreed on the need for more professionalism on the staff. So, J.C. and I hit it off right away and this became a learning experience for both of us.

As mentioned, I had always lacked self confidence and this often reflected itself in my reaction to questions asked of me. In the past, when I couldn't immediately come up with the right answer, I would feel guilty. I felt that something must be wrong with me if I didn't know the answer to any question I was asked. *In the classroom I had been so afraid I might give the wrong answer that I would say I didn't know--even if I was pretty sure I knew the answer. This made me rely entirely on written tests to achieve good grades. I knew I would receive no points for oral or class participation.*

J.C. had no such illusion. Despite (or perhaps because of) his high intelligence, he had no trouble saying "I don't know" when asked a question to which he didn't have the answer at his fingertips. After awhile I learned to emulate J.C. and could say "I don't know" without embarrassment or guilt. Despite this new freedom, I still remained very hard on myself and it was a long time before I could comfortably say "I don't know" in a group setting.

The relationship between J.C. Brown and me soon went from boss/subordinate to friends. We both gained from our relationship, with one exception: *J.C. did not tolerate fools gladly and made no bones about it, whereas I was more likely to tolerate stupidity without notable rancor. Although I admired J.C.'s perceived intolerance in one sense, I later found that this hampered my career on one occasion as you shall see later.*

The third professional in our office, Helen Jean Anderson, also possessed great talent and intelligence. And she was a "looker" to boot. *More later about this young lady who became Managing Editor of the nation's best known woman's magazine (The Ladies Home Journal) and an internationally known writer of cookbooks.* So, you can see why I was so thrilled to be working in a setting with talented people who realized the benefit of sharing ideas, compared to the place I had just left where people were so fearful of losing their jobs that they were afraid to talk to each other.

My first assignment at Raleigh was to write a brief article for the Extension Service News about two new employees, Jim White and Dorothy Mulder, both of whom had just been added to the Extension Service staff. Once I settled into the job, I was able to devote more attention to the emotional problems that Joyce had demonstrated almost from the first day we were married. We had frequent heart to heart talks about her situation. Although I had a minor in psychology in college, I knew that I was not equipped to deal with her deep problems on my own. So, I located a psychiatrist who agreed to take on her case and she began weekly sessions with him.

I noted some improvement but she still had frequent crying sessions in the evenings which left me feeling helpless and frustrated. I discussed this with her doctor and he told me that it might take years for her to recover from the damage she suffered as a child. I was willing to do what I could to help her achieve good mental health but her seeming helplessness and needy personality certainly put a crimp in our marriage.

A pleasant surprise occurred one day soon after I was on the job at Ricks Hall. One morning I was told that an electrician was coming to replace some faulty lights and that I might need to move my chair out of the office while this work was done. As I was typing away, the electrician appeared and when I looked up I saw that it was my nephew Blair Turner of Gastonia. We had lost touch for some time but I found out while he was changing some lights that he was now an electrical engineering student at NC State. He was working part-time at the college to help pay his way through college.

I had known that he had worked as an assistant to an electrical contractor from his neighborhood since around the age of 12. He still worked for this company when home on holidays and summers away from school. Now he had grown into a strapping six-footer with no sign of the polio he had contracted as a little boy. I remembered him from that time as a pitiful little boy, unable to walk and expected never to walk again, his little legs appearing like match sticks. We arranged for a small scale "family re-union" after work that day and we became very close over the following years and were re-united again when both of us worked in Washington, DC.

Incredibly, he began his career as an electrician while still in elementary school. He became friends with a neighborhood family whose head of the household was an electrical contractor. The contractor recognized that Blair was an inquisitive, smart, eager-to-learn youngster and began to give him simple electrical jobs to do. By the time he graduated from high school he had the skill and knowledge to wire a house. As a young adult he was using his vacation time in college doing professional quality electrical work for his contractor friend. In addition he was doing work for large companies such as Western Electric. These part time jobs largely paid for his college education. His simple job of changing out lights at NC State provided him money for his food.

As another example of his skill and resourcefulness, when he started college he needed a reliable automobile which his parents could not afford to buy. So, he saved up around $50 to purchase an old worn out Mercury car with a bad engine. Then, with some help from his Dad, he completely rebuilt the engine from scratch. The Mercury faithfully transported him throughout college and even took him and his bride to Washington, DC where his salary at the National Security Agency (NSA) allowed him to purchase a new car.

Throughout his time at NC State he never complained about work, lack of money or anything else, except for one issue: his engineering adviser at the college insisted he concentrate strictly on engineering courses. However, Blair knew that any career required good communication skills. So, somehow, Blair was able to cram in some English courses against his adviser's wishes and this resulted in a rare type of engineer, one who has technical knowledge along with being excellent at communicating the written word.

I'll have more to say about Blair Turner in this memoir. Suffice to say for now that he was one of the most admirable people I've known in my life. He was born to a brilliant father with a drinking problem and a beautiful, clever and resourceful mother--my youngest sister, Edith. He inherited his father's superior brain and expanded on it with a solid education; he was also resourceful like his mother.

# CHAPTER 3
## Newspaper Skills Put to Good Use on New Job

RETURNING TO MY own work situation, in subsequent days, months and years, J.C. Brown made full use of my experience and talent in writing feature articles about interesting farming activities around the State. One of the most important of these events involved the work of a County Agent in Johnston County, NC, one of the poorest NC counties at that time. The agent became aware that many black farmers in that county lost a large percentage of the hams they tried to cure. Instead of ending up with a very desirable product, too many of the hams rotted instead.

Bothered that these farmers were not fully benefiting from their hard work, the agent set about to organize a comprehensive program to train them how to preserve the hams from the pigs they were producing. He began by teaching the farmers the proper way to cure their hams so they did not go bad. As an extra incentive for the hog farmers--and a way to promote the program, he organized an annual "Ham & Egg Show" to be held in Smithfield, NC. This promotional event encouraged the farmers who soon gained the knowledge they needed to produce a great product. And the Ham & Egg Show helped provide a greater market for Johnston County farmers' now excellent pork products.

With assistance from the State Extension Service, the Smithfield Ham & Egg Show became a really popular event. I visited the show each year, accompanied by talented photographer Ralph Mills. The two of us thoroughly enjoyed the smell and taste of the country hams cooking. And we combined our talents to prepare lively, illustrated feature articles about events there. Also we did feature articles and photographs of individual farmers. Our office then sent these articles and photographs to newspapers and magazines around the state. After a few years, the Smithfield (NC) hams were competitive with the better known Smithfield (VA) products.

J. C. also asked me to use my brief (but useful) experience as a public school teacher to help in developing two week training sessions for NC County and Home Demonstration Agents. Communication skills are among the most important assets these agents need in order to carry out their daunting tasks. Since I had written columns and news articles professionally, J. C. wanted me to take the lead in developing a system and conducting workshops to help agents improve their skills in this area. Obviously, since we would be able to offer only two week training sessions, this training had to be kept at an elementary level. *I probably benefited more from this work than the agents themselves because it prepared me for development of future training programs at the national level. But, of course I was not aware of that then.*

In our efforts to promote agriculture in North Carolina, Ralph Mills and I traveled the State of North Carolina extensively, following up on interesting aspects of the State's varied agricultural activities. *Since I followed my usual pattern of failing to keep copies of stories I had written, I have nothing to go on but a fading memory of stories that especially caught my attention. I do remember that I spent few nights away from Raleigh because of my concern for Joyce. This required some very long days.*

One feature article I recall vividly involved a NC farmer who raised bison--not your usual farm animal. While I was getting information for the story from the safety of one of the farmer's jeeps, Ralph Mills was out in the middle of the herd filming close-ups of the animals. Even the farmer, who didn't know Ralph, became very concerned that the bison might become angered by a small human crawling around among them and go on the attack. The jeep in which the farmer and I were riding provided close-up evidence of what an angered bison was capable of doing.

Nevertheless, Ralph stayed within the bison herd until he had all the photos he wanted and then casually walked back to the jeep. The bison looked at him with curiosity but made no attempt to harm him. The assignment was memorable and the article and photos were picked up around the state and nation but I was not anxious to do a sequel for fear of injury to Ralph.

Another feature article that Ralph and I worked on also gained much attention. This article was about a farm owned by famed poet Carl Sandburg who wrote the poem "Chicago" which he described as "The City of Broad Shoulders." The farm called Connemara Farm, still exists in the little town of Flat Rock, south of Asheville, NC. Actually, the article and photos were almost entirely centered around Carl Sandburg's wife, Paula, who had great affection for special breeds of goats. Paula Sandburg gained national prominence as a dairy goat breeder while her husband became a highly successful writer of poetry.

Although my memory is fading about the details of Mrs. Sandburg's goats, Wikipedia reminds me that she called her animals the Chikaming herd, and it included Nubians, Sanens, and Toggenburgs. What interested Mrs. Sandburg most was breeding for high milk production. The operation at Connemara Farm was not the "plaything" of a famous family. In addition to breeding and raising the goats, Mrs. Sandburg ran a commercial dairy. At its peak, the Chikaming herd had about 200 goats, though now the National Park Service, which runs the farm as a National Historic Site keeps it to about fifteen.

These goats are not milked and thus no production records are kept today. During our visit to Connemara Farm and the Sandburg's home, we had extensive discussions with Mrs. Sandburg, who clearly loved her goats. Ralph snapped many photos of Mrs. Sandburg and her beloved animals but neither of us saw evidence of the presence of the famous poet. *Meanwhile, the little town of Flat Rock itself has become equally famous for being the home of the Flat Rock Playhouse, now designated as the "State Theatre of North Carolina."*

J.C Brown also worked it out so that I could use a week of my vacation time each year to cover and promote the North Carolina State Fair for North Carolina and national media outlets. I got paid for this work by the State Fair held in Raleigh. In this case I was working in familiar territory since I had already covered many of the Fair's events at the Cleveland County and York County Fairs. Also, I was already familiar with many of the Fair performers.

Naturally, since I was now on a "first name" basis with famous lion & tiger trainer Terrell Jacobs, his act and life became one of my first feature articles about the Fair. I had also already interviewed and written many articles about other acts, including the "Freak Show" people. Because "Doc" Dorton was still manager of the North Carolina State Fair it boasted the best entertainment available. And as usual the James E. Strates Midway dominated the Fairgrounds.

I remember that singer Julius LaRosa was one of the star attractions during that period of 1954-57. He had recovered from his public firing by Arthur Godfrey and exuded self confidence. He also seemed inordinately attracted to the Miss North Carolina who was also a star attraction that year. I never heard whether their relationship went beyond the Fairgrounds but LaRosa was really attentive to this beautiful young lady. Although it was fun covering the Fair, one incident still stands out in my mind. *And It Was Definitely Not Funny!*

# CHAPTER 4

## A Scary Incident at the State Fair

THE INCIDENT STARTED when a casual friend of mine, who owned a small grocery store, urged that Joyce and I get together with him and his wife the last night of the Fair. He had received complimentary tickets to several rides and thought it might be fun for the four of us to meet at the Fair and use up his tickets. *Of course as a Fair employee, I had access to any tickets I wanted but it seemed important to him to "treat" us.* I mentioned the idea to Joyce and she liked the idea of meeting some new people.

Since only a closing or "wrap up" article remained of my Fair duties that evening, getting away from the "official" Fair Office for a couple of hours was no problem. As planned, the four of us met at a ride that the other couple had been anxious to try. When the friend presented his complimentary tickets to the person handling the ride, he was rudely told that the ride was not accepting complimentary tickets on the final night of the Fair.

This was not a big deal for Joyce and me, but my friend was incensed by the refusal to accommodate us. Despite our urgings to walk away, our friend became belligerent with the carnival worker. I knew this was a big mistake and tried to pull him away but he stubbornly resisted all efforts to leave this ride and find our entertainment somewhere else.

That proved to be a bad mistake. Suddenly, without warning, my friend was surrounded by carnival workers who began hitting him. *(I never heard the "Hey Rube" yell supposedly uttered by Carnies when one of them is in trouble. But they must have received some signal to come help a "fellow Carnie").* My friend who seemed so eager to fight appeared stunned by the sudden change in circumstances and didn't try to defend himself. Fearful he might be seriously injured, I foolishly waded into the group to try to pull him away. Then I suddenly found myself in a vice grip from behind by someone wearing a heavy leather jacket. And I then became a new target unable to defend myself from several blows to the head because I was held so tightly from behind. My little wife Joyce saved me from serious damage when she started screaming at the top of her lungs and trying to get between me and my attackers.

Joyce's loud screams led to a large crowd gathering and the carnival workers rapidly dispersed. To my embarrassment, I found out that I had been held immobile by a large, strong woman! *Could she have been an early transgender?*

Of course, Joyce was stroking me and crying, fearful that I had been badly hurt. After a brief self examination, I found that all I had suffered were a few scratches and bruises. My friend's wife, who had fled from the scene, rejoined us and said: "He's always starting trouble and I just go away until it's over." At that point we said our "permanent" goodbyes. We decided on the spot never to associate with them again. I gained a greater appreciation of Joyce and the courage and love she displayed in defending me.

Sequel: Several people who witnessed the event wanted to call the police but I didn't want that type of publicity--either personally or for the State Fair. However, I thought James Strates needed to know what happened inside his Midway, so we stopped by his tent to tell him what had just happened. Strates immediately reacted positively, asking me if I wanted him to call the police and bring charges against the perpetrators. I told him I didn't want any police action so he then went outside and closed this particular ride down for the rest of that year's Fair.

Early the next morning the Fair and Midway exhibits were loaded up and left the Fairgrounds along with the performers. I filed my final story and returned to my regular job with mixed memories of that year's event.

# CHAPTER 5
## Old Friends Re-Appear in My Life

WITH ALL MY duties at NC State, I had stayed in touch with my good friend Les Roark. Soon after we moved to Raleigh he came for a visit and I introduced him around. At that time he said he still hadn't found a suitable replacement for the News Editor job at the Cleveland Times, and asked me if I had anyone to recommend.

I immediately thought of my suite mate at Catawba, the brilliant Joe Austin. Our other suite mate, Ken Griffin, who had recently visited me in Raleigh, had said that

Joe was currently living in Cleveland, Ohio, and was working in a factory--not exactly the type job I had envisioned for him. I told Les I would try to contact Joe and see if he would be interested in returning south to work for a small newspaper. Les was pleased by my suggestion and said he would hire Joe upon my recommendation.

The Catawba Alumni Office located Joe for me and I called him immediately about the Cleveland Times job. He expressed interest and I gave him Les' phone number and a brief description of what the job entailed. He called Les, came to Shelby, and was soon sitting at my old desk. Later, I called Les and asked how Joe was doing. He said, "Joe is a talented writer, and is very bright, but deadlines seem to make him very nervous."

A month or so later, on one of my assignments to that area, I stopped by the Cleveland Times Office to say hi to Les and Joe. Les was his usual ebullient self, but Joe was sitting at the typewriter with an agonized look on his face. When I got closer, I saw that his shirt was unbuttoned and he had one hand on his heart. Apparently a deadline was approaching and his heart was racing. He simmered down enough in my presence to express appreciation for getting him the job and said he was going back to Cleveland that weekend to close out his affairs there.

Two weeks later, Les called me to say that Joe never returned to Shelby from his visit to Ohio. Apparently his job pushing a "dope wagon" in a Cleveland, OH factory was easier on his heart than working for the Cleveland Times. I continued to maintain a close relationship with Les, however. On one of his visits to Raleigh I introduced him to Jean Anderson and before he left town the two had arranged a date a few weekends later.

On Saturday the weekend of their date, Jean called me at home and frantically said: "Jim I don't know what to do. I made a date with Les Roark for tonight and find that an old boy friend is going to be in town and I promised to go out with him." I said, "Well Jean, I think you better find another suitable date for Les since he is on the way here and expecting to see you." Jean thought for a moment and said: "Do you think Dorothy Mulder would be a suitable replacement?" Since I knew and liked Dorothy, I said: "If you can persuade Dorothy to date Les at this late date, I think that might work."

Jean gave a sigh of relief and said, "I'll go to work on that." She called me later and said she had persuaded Dorothy to go out with Les. He and Dorothy apparently hit it off. Before leaving Raleigh, Les told me he was going to see Dorothy again soon. I was pleased to hear they had a good time on their date but did not see their relationship ever going beyond friendship. Too many differences.

The two certainly did not match up well as far as formal education was concerned. Les had graduated from little Grover, NC High School and said he wasn't even a serious student there. It seems he was interested in agriculture and shop and took no college prep courses (although it's doubtful Grover would have even had such courses at that time). He could have gone to college on the G.I. Bill but had no interest in doing so. Instead, he and several other World War II vets (including my brother Bob) took advantage of the "52-20" Club and, "goofed off" and/or played poker for a year.

On the other hand, Dorothy had advanced college degrees and her work career had been centered around prominent universities, e.g. Wisconsin and Michigan State. Despite his lack of formal education, however, I knew that Les was the equal of almost anyone intellectually. He had the soul of a poet and was well read. The two also had very different upbringings. Les was the son of hardscrabble farm parents and his father died while he was a little boy. He said there were many nights as a child that he went to bed hungry. On the other hand, Dorothy's family operated a successful dairy farm in Holland, Michigan. Her family also placed great value on higher education.

Despite what appeared to me to be irreconcilable differences, the two of them were married a few months later. Dorothy moved to Shelby and began a new career with Cleveland Tech. *So much for my prognostications on man/woman relationships.*

# CHAPTER 6

## Things at NC State Take an Unexpected Turn

MY CAREER AT NC State settled into a busy but rewarding time. The only upsetting thing was the retirement of Dr. Jeter. It was unexpected to me and sad. After all, he had rescued me from an unhappy situation in Florida and offered me a wonderful job in one of my favorite areas. And he was such a solid rock for the entire unit. With just a few exceptions, staff members were now performing more professionally and it was a pleasure to be associated with most of them.

None of us was familiar with his successor O.B. Copeland. My immediate impression was that he was politically astute but not particularly strong in the areas of communication. He turned out to be very likable and pretty much left the office work functions to continue as they did under Dr. Jeter. Then a few months after "Cope" took over management of our group, J. C. Brown called me aside to tell me he had been offered and had accepted a much higher paying job and would be leaving almost immediately.

He said: "You're my obvious successor and I'm going to recommend you for the job. Would you accept it?" I told him I would much prefer that he stay there as my boss, but if he was going to leave I would accept the job if offered to me. Soon afterward, Cope called me into his office, told me that J.C. was leaving and that I was the obvious successor. "Would you accept the job?" he asked. I told him I would take the job if that was his desire. "Then, as of now you're the News Editor of this office," he said, shaking my hand.

That night Joyce and I celebrated my promotion with a bottle of wine. My new, higher salary would permit us to rent a larger, nicer apartment or even a house. So, we talked about that possibility. The next morning I was at the office early, ready to clean out my desk and move to J.C.'s spot. Almost immediately, Cope called me into his office and told me, "Jim, I'm sorry but I have to withdraw your promotion. I'm embarrassed by this but last evening several of the other employees came to my house uninvited and demanded that I withdraw my promotion offer to you. These employees said they have nothing against you personally but J.C. Brown had not shown respect to them while there and they feared you might be the same way since you and J.C. were close friends."

He said he argued with them adding "they offered no good reason why you should not get the job but they were adamant and I finally agreed to withdraw your promotion." He added that since he had been on the job only a short time, he didn't feel strong enough to defend his decision to offer me the job. He also knew that one of the group protesting my promotion was a close family friend of the Extension Director, Cope's boss. I was really dismayed that the head of our department would let himself be bullied in this way. It would never have happened under Dr. Jeter's watch.

I was momentarily very distressed by this sudden change in my fortunes. But then I realized that J.C.'s attitude of "not tolerating fools gladly" actually had an inadvertent detrimental effect on my career. But I had probably shared in that blame. I had not openly shown my contempt for the lack of professionalism on the part of some employees as J.C. had, but my unspoken feelings may have given me away. It was difficult for a professional to completely accept that one of these communications specialists had been a high school driver education instructor with no communications training or experience. And it was common knowledge that two others got their jobs through political pressure. These turned out to be leaders of the group that disputed my promotion.

I soon went from feeling crushed to becoming outraged by this political ploy that cost me the promotion. It was really my first exposure to how politics can affect a career. *I learned much more about that after I went to Washington, DC.* Back in Raleigh, J.C.'s successor turned out to be a nice guy with obvious political connections known to all of us. I never knew (nor cared) whether the group at Cope's house had anything to do with his selection. I was just happy that he was someone I knew and could respect and was professionally competent.

These recent events let me know that my career at NC State would not be a lasting one. But I was determined to make the best of the situation while there. Since I felt no resentment toward my new boss, I immediately set out to help make him successful in the job. I continued to write the newsletter, write feature articles, and take the lead in the County Agent/Home Demonstration training programs. We showed mutual respect for each other and developed a friendly relationship that made my remaining stay in Raleigh bearable.

# CHAPTER 7
## New Opportunities Emerge

A FEW MONTHS after the promotion fiasco, I was asked to represent NC State at a big national meeting of the American Agricultural Editors Association. It was to be held that year at Penn State College, PA. I thought, *"They're trying to make up for that fiasco a few months ago."* I didn't care that guilt may have caused them to offer me this opportunity. I accepted the offer immediately, realizing that this might open some more doors for me. And, boy, did it! Although I did nothing to seek it, while I was there, representatives of three major universities corralled me with offers of graduate assistantships.

The universities of Oklahoma State, Wisconsin, and Illinois all offered me the opportunity to get a Master's Degree with all tuition, fees, etc. paid, plus a livable salary. Of course I would be expected to work part time while there. I told these university representatives that I was interested in their offers but that I could not make a decision until I returned home and talked with my wife.

I was excited about the prospect of new experiences, an advanced degree which I knew would enhance my career in educational journalism, and a change in scenery from my present job situation at Raleigh. I left Penn State for Raleigh with renewed hopes for the future. After arriving back in Raleigh and discussing the new possibilities with Joyce, however, I knew I needed to talk with her counselor before making a decision. As soon as it could be arranged, I met with the psychiatrist and laid out my concerns. Would going to a strange, new place for a year be detrimental to her treatment? If he thought so, I would not accept any of these offers.

The psychiatrist thought for awhile and then said: "Jim, there are several issues we need to discuss. First of all, with you having a college degree and Joyce not even finishing high school there already is a great difference in your respective educations. Once you have a Master's Degree, this difference will be even more pronounced. On the other hand, if you plan to stay in educational work, you really need one or more advanced degrees."

After these observations he cogitated for a few more minutes and said: "Jim, you also have the right to a fruitful life and I feel that if you don't seize this opportunity now, you will become resentful that Joyce's emotional condition kept you from having the career you deserve. It would only be human if you blamed her for holding you back." He then added something that took me aback: "I must be honest with you, Jim. Joyce's problems are so deep-seated that it might take a lifetime for her to overcome them. And I cannot even assure you that she will ever conquer her demons even if you do everything in your power to help her get well."

I was momentarily stunned to hear that Joyce might never get well. I then asked: "Considering these factors, do you have any suggestions for me?" The doctor thought for awhile and said, "I can't tell you what to do, but I will suggest something that might work: if you decide to go, let me know which university you plan to attend and I'll locate a qualified counselor there who could treat Joyce until your return to Raleigh." He then added: "On second thought, a new counselor and new environment just might have a positive effect on her. We can always hope."

After leaving the doctor's office, I knew that I had some important decisions to make and I had to make them soon or the doors would be closed to me. I hurried home to discuss things with Joyce. When I arrived back at our apartment, I gave Joyce the gist of my meeting with her doctor, but obviously omitted any mention of her doctor's concerns about her future prognosis. Her initial reaction was encouraging. She actually seemed thrilled at the prospect of going to a new area, and meeting new people.

With her encouragement, I began to start the process of leaving NC State for a year of graduate work. I told Cope of my wishes and he said he would ask the administration for a sabbatical for me. This came through and I began to make plans that would change my life in ways I never envisioned. I was now at the point I needed to decide which one of the three universities was my first choice and notify it of my decision. Although all the universities offered similar benefits, I immediately leaned toward the University of Illinois.

My degree there would be a Master's Degree in Journalism or Mass Communication. The other two offered degrees that read "Master's Degree in Agricultural Journalism." I didn't like the idea of having a qualifier on my degree. Not that I was ashamed to be working in the agricultural field but I thought this designation might be a limiting factor in my future.

After some more thinking about my choices, I contacted Hadley Read, at the University of Illinois, to tell him I would like to accept his offer if it was still available. Hadley said he had been holding the position for me and that he needed only one thing: a transcript of my college grades. He said that the University of Illinois requires a "B" or better for admittance to its Master's Program. News of that requirement caused me to be suddenly confronted with a possible problem I had never considered! Recalling my nonchalance regarding grades I suddenly wished I had been more studious and not so much into gaining social skills. I need not to have worried. My transcript came through with a solid B+ average.

With my acceptance at Illinois assured, I called to express regrets to Oklahoma State and Wisconsin. Then I had to plan the move to Champaign-Urbana. Hadley Read had told me that my position would make me eligible for Married Student/ Staff housing. We could move into a furnished one-bedroom apartment at a very reasonable price. It was a great blessing not having to move furniture from Raleigh to Urbana. I found a place we could store our furniture and all I needed then was to rent or purchase a small trailer in which to carry our clothing and personal articles.

# CHAPTER 8
## Bound for Illinois

JUST BEFORE THE start of the 1956 fall session, we said goodbye to Raleigh and began the long trek pulling a small trailer through the North Carolina mountains on Highway 74. *Interstate Highway 40 did not exist at that time.* This was quite a challenge since I had little experience driving through mountains and had never pulled a trailer before. It took us two days of driving through North Carolina, Tennessee, Kentucky, and Indiana before reaching Champaign-Urbana, IL, home of the University of Illinois. It was great that we could travel Highway 74 the entire way without worrying that we would get lost.

We located Married Student/Staff housing not far from Hwy. 74 in Urbana and I called Hadley Read from the lobby. He had arranged for a couple of people to help us move into the apartment which was quite nice considering the price we would be paying. The next morning I reported to Hadley's office and he took me to the Registrar's Office where I would be enrolled. I was soon a graduate student at the University of Illinois, a huge campus with about 25,000 students (at that time) compared to little Catawba College with an enrollment of 800 students!

After my admittance was complete and I had purchased my required textbooks, I returned to the State Extension Office where Hadley explained in detail what type work I would be doing on my 20 hour per week job. I had assumed correctly that I would be writing about agricultural topics. But I didn't know until then that I was assigned as Department Editor for the College of Veterinary Medicine. Then he laid a truly scary surprise on me: a significant part of my job would be to prepare and conduct a weekly interview show that would go out over WILL, the National Public Radio (NPR) station located on campus.

The writing part did not bother me since I had been earning my living doing that for several years. But conducting a radio interview that would play all over the Midwest was something I had never done nor anticipated I would ever do. Now, suddenly this sharecropper boy from the South who had always suffered from stage fright would become the voice of The University of Illinois College of Veterinary Medicine over an NPR station!

Fortunately, the graduate student who had handled this job before I arrived was still around and gave me some pointers. He also introduced me to Veterinary Medicine staff members who might be suitable subjects for my interviews. I needed to get to know them on a somewhat personal basis as possible future subjects for the radio programs. And he introduced me to a Veterinary Medicine staff member who was media savvy and would always be willing to suggest story ideas. *That proved to be a mixed blessing!*

After giving Joyce some time to settle down, I gave her a tour of campus, including the Extension Editor's Office, and my office at the School of Veterinary Medicine.

Joyce was impressed with the looks of the campus, as well as my work place(s). And the U of I staff and students who got a look at Joyce were overwhelmed by her beauty! Not to be provincial, but the mid-western, corn-fed girls and women I had seen on the Illinois campus looked positively stodgy in comparison to my slim, leggy little wife. I was suddenly the envy of many of the men on campus! And Joyce was certainly initially enjoying the attention she was getting. She seemed the happiest I had seen her in a long time.

The second week on campus I met with the well respected counselor who had had long distance discussions with Joyce's Raleigh counselor about her case. After the two of us discussed the situation, the Illinois counselor agreed to take Joyce on as a patient. As I recall Joyce was immediately signed up for one or more one-hour sessions per week.

# CHAPTER 9
## Course Selection and Heavy Schedule Begins

SINCE I HAD never taken a course in journalism, I had hoped to take some news writing courses during my year of study. No way, said my adviser. He said such courses would be a total waste of time for someone with my experience. "You probably learned more from your first three months as a working reporter than you would as a journalism major. You'll be concentrating on communication theories here in graduate school."

Since I had been out of college for over six years at that time, I didn't expect things to be easy and they were not. After attending my first classes, I realized that I would be in for a rough year. The subjects were complex and required extensive reading, research, and writing about theories I was just learning about.

I knew that I had to develop some serious study habits if I were to maintain a B average--something required to remain in graduate school. One grade below B and I would no longer be a graduate student. I didn't relish going back to Raleigh after failing graduate school. However, I had to consider that possibility because I knew that many graduate students go home after the first semester. But it was not my style to give up because something is difficult. So, I dug into my studies, spending many hours each day in the library or working in my office at Veterinary Medicine, or (rarely) the apartment.

Meanwhile, since the former graduate assistant had left, I was now completely on my own preparing and disseminating information emanating from the Veterinary Medicine School. Should you think that sounds like easy work, let me assure you that, with the many research efforts alone, this could be a full time job. Merely selecting a Veterinary Scientist or Professor for the next program and working with that person to develop an interesting and educational approach was time consuming.

It was up to me alone to figure out and write down the questions I would ask, and at the very least, provide a narrative outline of the answer for the interviewee. Then the person being interviewed and I would go to the studio for a trial reading and rehearsal of my script. To add to spontaneity, I would encourage the "expert" to ad lib some of the answers as long as he stayed within the time and general confines of my questions and answers.

Some of the "experts" were good at adlibbing while others insisted that the entire script be written out--which really increased my work load. After discussing any needed changes and/or refinements to the script, I would make the introduction and we would then record the 20 minute session to be broadcast over WILL two days later.

I couldn't believe the playback of our first recording session. Although I was conscious of having a Southern accent, I had no idea of how pronounced it was until I heard my own recorded voice played back. My nerves no doubt contributed to the heavy Southern drawl. But we did not have enough time then to work on my accent. So, the broadcast went out "as is" with the words: "This is Jim White of the University of Illinois College of Veterinary Medicine, along with Dr. (so and so). Our program today explains the need to vaccinate your livestock for...*(some current ailment)*."

After a few broadcasts, I learned that several graduate student friends of mine were so entertained at the sound of my voice that they would congregate around the radio when the program was being broadcast in order to enjoy some good laughs at my expense. Learning that I was the subject of their entertainment did not sit well at all with my sensitive nature and this motivated me to lose my pronounced Southern accent. By the end of the semester, I had succeeded to the point that my voice sounded more like a mid-westerner than many of the "experts" I interviewed.

When I returned to the Carolinas, people who didn't know me thought I was a "Yankee." *I saved one of these tapes through numerous moves over the years and after retirement planned to have a "modern" CD made of it. Alas, I haven't found it so far; posterity may just have to live without it!*

I thought I would become adjusted to my heavy schedule and have more time to relax and enjoy college life. But that was not to be. As word got around about my professional journalism background, the College of Veterinary Medicine professors and scientists were taking full advantage of that fact and were steadily adding to my "after hours" work load. My nature made it difficult to say "no" to their requests. And the "media savvy" professor that I had counted on earlier to supply me with leads was relentless in providing suggestions for more and more stories. I could not possibly complete this work in a 20 hour week so I was spending more and more time at the Veterinary Medicine School and less time on my studies.

Fortunately, Hadley Read, who was keeping an eye on the situation, recognized what was happening, and paid a personal visit to Veterinary Medicine to tell them that I was not a full time employee and that I needed to spend less time with them and more time on my grad school work. It had been difficult for me to say "No" and I really appreciated the fact that Hadley interceded on my behalf. I'm sure that was not the first time he had to do that for a graduate assistant.

However, the one thing Hadley couldn't help me with was Joyce. After the euphoria of the new situation had worn off, her "demons" had returned. Although she was going to the counselor and seemed mostly normal during the day, by the time I arrived home in the evening, she would be staring out the window with a glass of wine in one hand and a cigarette in the other. She would temporarily "perk up" with my arrival but would eventually drift back to her childhood problems and she would cry herself to sleep. This became an almost nightly event and it was difficult for me to get a decent night's sleep because of my concern for her versus my need to study.

A couple of times I privately visited Joyce's counselor to discuss Joyce's problems and get advice on how I could best deal with them. At one of these visits the counselor asked me "Who is Billy?" I explained that Billy was a young man from Georgia who was a graduate school classmate and good friend of mine. He was a lonely young man just out of college who attached himself to me. I had brought him to the apartment for meals and we had become confidantes and close friends.

Billy had confided that he had impregnated a young lady back in Georgia and was concerned about what to do. I was sympathetic to his need for an adult shoulder to lean on and provided that shoulder when I really could not spare the time. Joyce also tried to console him when I had other duties and wasn't available for him. He was so grateful for her attention that he wrote a poem about her that she showed me. I thought it was sweet.

# CHAPTER 10
## A Warning I Should Have Heeded?

BECAUSE HER NIGHT time emotional breakdowns continued to worsen, I again visited Joyce's counselor for some advice on what I could do to be helpful. Instead of offering me the advice I sought, she expressed more concern about my friend Billy's relationship with Joyce. She thought that something must be going on because Joyce continued to bring up Billy's name during their counseling sessions. She asked me point blank if I had any concerns that his relationship with Joyce was not as innocent as I thought.

I was somewhat shaken by what appeared to be the counselor's questioning of the relationship of Joyce and Billy. I repeated that I had no concerns at all because Joyce was a tender-hearted person and was just being kind and sympathetic to a lonely, homesick, young man. "Well, Jim, I know as Joyce's counselor that I shouldn't mention this, but I think you should be concerned about this Billy and his attachment to your wife." I still thought the whole idea of something other than friendship between my good friend and my wife was not a possibility. Was the counselor grasping at straws because she had been unable to make progress in dealing with Joyce's problems?

Since I'm not inclined to jealousy, I felt no real concern that something other than need and friendship were involved. I rationalized that their closeness was a benefit for both, believing that Joyce's concern over Billy's problems might help her deal with some of her own. I felt that the fact that Billy had made no other friends on campus contributed to his neediness. He seemed to consider us his family away from Georgia. Was I being naive? Perhaps!

So, things continued on with my heavy work and study schedule and Joyce's nightly emotional binges. My work at Veterinary Medicine had returned more to about 20 hours per week since Hadley's intervention and I had become more comfortable with my weekly radio broadcasts over WILL. There was one memorable recording session I'd like to mention. It happened when I was asking prepared questions and the interviewee of that week was answering them. Then he badly misread the script. His mistake was so funny that we both broke into laughter. I stopped the tape until we could regain our composure. Thinking we were back in control of ourselves, I restarted the interview but at that same point, we both broke into virtually hysterical laughter.

This continued for several more minutes until we were forced to give up our studio time. We agreed to meet the next day to try to resume the recording. Although I was fearful that we might repeat the previous day's fiasco, we finished the interview with no further problems and the program was broadcast the following day.

As the mid-terms approached, Joyce mentioned that it might be best if I drove her back to Raleigh over the Christmas holidays. She thought it would be helpful if she could immediately resume sessions with her original counselor, explaining that she didn't feel she was making much progress with her Illinois counselor. She added that she would find a job to help with the double expenses. I expressed concern about her being alone for the first time in years but she countered this by saying she felt at home in Raleigh and thought returning there to live would help her deal better with her problems.

I still had my doubts about the advisability of Joyce being alone back in Raleigh. After all, since our marriage she had become dependent upon me to deal with any problems we had. However, she continued to promote the idea of returning to Raleigh and I gradually began to believe that this might be the best solution for both of us. I knew that the long, tiring drive from Champaign to Raleigh and back to Urbana would not be easy and could be devastating to my preparation for mid-term finals.

Things had become extremely complicated for me. I knew that once we returned to Raleigh I would need to help her find an apartment and get settled there before I left. Then, when I returned to Illinois alone, I would no longer be eligible for Married Student/Staff Housing and would have to find another place to live. By that time, I would be facing mid-term exams with little or no time to study. Finally, however, I yielded to her insistence about returning to Raleigh and began making plans for the drive. Joyce had already been packing her clothing and toiletries for the trip back.

# CHAPTER 11

## Joyce Goes Back to Raleigh

A FEW DAYS before the mid-terms and the Christmas season, I returned to the apartment one day at lunch time to find Billy and Joyce waiting for me. Billy was the first to speak, "Jim, I'm dropping out of school and going back to Georgia before Christmas." I immediately remembered the cautionary words from Joyce's counselor and wondered if the fact that both Joyce and Billy were leaving Illinois at the same time might be more than a coincidence. Remembering Billy's poem and the counselor's warnings that something may be going on between the two of them, I decided this was the time to face the issue head on.

I asked: "Be honest with me Billy. Does your leaving the University at Christmas have anything to do with the fact that Joyce is also leaving here at that time?" There was momentary silence in the room and then both nodded, yes! I then asked, "Are you two planning to get together after you leave here?" Both again nodded, yes. Then, Billy said "Jim, I'm really sorry about this but Joyce and I love each other!" I asked Joyce if she loved Billy and she said "yes." I had a hard time accepting this betrayal by my wife and someone I had thought to be a close friend.

Then my initial hurt began to change to anger. Turning to Joyce I said: "I can't believe you were planning to cause me all the trouble of moving you back to Raleigh and possibly lose my fellowship so that you could see Billy behind my back!" She shamefacedly nodded and said "Yes, I'm sorry but we were planning to get together in Raleigh after you went back to Illinois."

At this point I said: "I'll save the two of you and me a lot of trouble. Why don't you just go back to Raleigh together; I don't see why I should have to go to all this trouble to deliver you to him!" Both of them apologized to me again and agreed that it made more sense for them to go back together rather than separately. They said that separating before the two of us traveled back to Raleigh together would be easier on all of us—especially me. Billy left to finish his packing and Joyce went to our bedroom to make her final preparations for the trip to Raleigh. Billy soon returned to pick up Joyce and the two of them left the apartment before dark leaving me alone.

I was left behind to grieve. But I couldn't help but be concerned for Joyce's welfare. After all, we had married each other "for better or for worse." As far as I was concerned, this was as "worse" as it could get. However, I also had to deal with personal guilt. I faced the question of whether my personal ambition had caused Joyce to turn to someone other than her husband because I was neglecting her needs. *That concern remained with me for many years but I eventually decided I needed to end this self flagellation. Otherwise this real or perceived guilt or "self pity" might take over my life.*

Later that evening as I tossed and turned in my bed, the telephone rang. It was Joyce. She said, "Jim, I already know I made a terrible mistake by leaving you. I hope

I'll be able to repair that mistake some day." My reply was, "Give me a call when you get to Raleigh to let me know you're safe and we'll talk about possible repairs to our marriage later." Between fits of crying, I got through my midterm exams. I still don't know how I survived that ordeal. But I survived and made B's in all my courses after fearing that I would fail every one of them.

Then I had to face finding a new place to live and move from Married Student/ Staff Housing. One of my graduate school classmates offered me an option which I accepted. He lived in a large basement apartment with an extra small bedroom. He was aware of my grief and offered me consolation which was initially helpful. Then I gradually began to realize that he was offering more consolation than I needed or wanted. Although appreciating his efforts to help me, I was becoming uncomfortable with the relationship he seemed to want.

After living in the basement apartment a couple of weeks, two other classmate friends approached me and asked if I would be interested in joining them in renting and sharing a three bedroom apartment in the nearby town of Champaign. I knew that the three of us had more compatible interests than I had with my present apartment mate and agreed to go with them to see the apartment and a short time later to sign the lease.

It was difficult for me to break the news to the fellow student who had been so kind to me but I knew it needed to be done. He was understandably upset that I was leaving. However, we remained friends the rest of the school year---but at a distance!

# CHAPTER 12
## Adjusting to Life without Joyce

I WAS INITIALLY very lonely for Joyce but gradually began to appreciate the fact that I no longer faced the nightly drama of trying to deal with a lovely but emotionally damaged woman. Having the company of two lively younger men who liked to party and enjoyed good food and drink (as well as chase girls) gradually helped bring me back to the point that I could return to having some fun in my life.

One of my apartment mates was Robert (Bob) Nemcik, whose family came here from Czechoslovakia and lived in a Czech village called Elsie, near East Lansing, Michigan. He was a recent graduate of Michigan State and his journalism specialty was advertising. The other one was Joseph (Joe) Moylan, an Irishman from Chicago's South Side. He had graduated from the University of Illinois the previous year and was working on a regular journalism master's degree. Both young men were Roman Catholics. The mix of cultures and religions we represented was interesting. We became fast friends and never had a serious disagreement.

Joe and Bob also enriched my life experience. As mentioned, Bob Nemcik was from a Czech family and he invited me to go with him to the little town of Elsie to meet his family and enjoy some good ethnic food his family prepared to celebrate the end of Lent. The spread at the Nemcik table was unbelievable to this Southern country boy. I didn't know the name of many of the dishes but remember goose and duck as two of the delicacies I had never before experienced. The Nemcik family also embraced me like a member of the family. That was an enjoyable and memorable occasion for me!

Joe Moylan also took me to meet his Irish family living in South Side Chicago. They also wined and dined me and accepted me with typical Irish warmth. And while we were there Joe introduced me to the elegant London House Restaurant where we enjoyed its fine food, atmosphere, and live jazz (by then my favorite form of music). It featured internationally known jazz artists e.g. Marilyn McPartland. Although I considered the London House out of my league, I soon adjusted to it and continued to visit it at every opportunity over the years when I was in Chicago.

Although my sadness at the loss of Joyce lingered for a long time, these two young "party guys" immediately started urging me to go to parties with them as a way to deal with my grief. The first few times I tried to party were burdensome. But after awhile I was able to get into the party mood and no longer needed urging. One thing that helped: after an alcoholic drink, my Southern drawl would return and I would become the center of attention. Other party-goers treated me like some exotic creature from another land. After awhile I made no effort to control my Southern accent since it was turning out to be an asset at parties on the Illinois campus. I was urged to talk even more than I wanted so they could listen to the soft sounds roll off my tongue. Who would ever have thought that?

I did have to deal with some misconceptions about Southerners. I had to explain that we did not all worship Elvis Presley and we didn't all fit the images of Southerners portrayed by writers such as Erskine Caldwell and William Faulkner. And we were not all racists. Despite having to fight these misconceptions I enjoyed being the center of attention for the first time in my life. And I may have exaggerated the Southern accent on occasion!

The most extreme example of the fascination some northern people had for us strange Southern folks happened one night at a party. During the evening, I received lots of attention from a young Jewish woman from Chicago. She engaged me in conversation at every opportunity. Sometime during the evening, one of the hosts approached me and said that the young lady in question had become ill and needed a ride home; since I was known to have an automobile, would it be too much of a bother to take her to her place a short distance away? I said that I was getting ready to leave anyway because I needed to study, so it would be no trouble for me to drop her off.

We got into my car and started to her place. I noticed she appeared to have made a very quick recovery from her "illness." By the time we got to her place she showed no signs of any illness. Expecting her to get out of the car, instead she pulled me over and gave me a passionate kiss. Surprised, I asked "What was that all about?" She replied "I faked the illness so I could see what it felt like to kiss a Southern man."

Since the kiss was unexpected and I was not especially attracted to the young lady anyway, I fear that my lack of responsiveness may not have been representative of a Southern man's kiss. But she didn't complain. I drove on back to the apartment to study. Although that encounter was not particularly enjoyable I began to make friends with many more desirable girls on campus. That was a bit surprising since the man/woman situation at U of I was so one-sided. *The ratio of men to women on campus was about three men to every woman.*

This ratio scared many of the young men away from the most attractive girls. The fear that they would get turned down caused some to avoid the dating scene. Some very attractive girls told me they sat home dateless on Saturday nights because the boys appeared to be afraid to ask them out. Of course my social confidence level had improved and I no longer shared those fears.

Obviously I was not ready for any serious relationships since I was still married to Joyce and still loved her. However, after overcoming my extreme early shyness I have always enjoyed the company of attractive women. So, I had no hesitation in developing relationships with "friend girls" as opposed to "girlfriends." I didn't try to fool any of these women; I immediately told them I was married but separated. These friendships helped make my stay at Illinois more pleasant.

# CHAPTER 13

## Doing My Duty for Illinois!

APPARENTLY WORD OF my active social life got around campus, leading to another interesting situation. The University had hired a new professor from Belgium and he had just arrived on campus along with his pretty blonde wife and her equally pretty blond sister. The latter had come for a short visit to see the great country she had read and heard about so much. After two days, someone in the University's public relations office decided that the young lady from Europe should not leave the U.S. without dating an American boy. I was asked to be that American boy.

Naturally I agreed to this as my duty to Illinois U. and the USA. A time was set for me to pick up the pretty blond Belgian girl, who as it turned out spoke English with a delightful French accent. Louis Armstrong was performing on campus that evening so the University provided me with two very desirable tickets to Satchmo's concert. After we were seated and waiting for the concert to begin, Michelle peeked around, giggled and said: "My chaperones are sitting two rows back." She described them to me and I was able to discreetly spot them.

We enjoyed the concert and then "just for the heck of it," decided to try to evade the chaperones who were following in their car. We succeeded in evading them easily since they were not familiar with Champaign-Urbana. Then we stopped for coffee and conversation for another hour before I took her back. Later, the family must have decided I was trustworthy and let us go out without chaperones for dinner and conversation. A good friendship resulted and I was really sorry to see her leave the USA to return to Belgium. We exchanged letters for a couple of years but never saw each other again. I hope I was a good ambassador for American manhood.

As mentioned earlier, my drinking experience when I arrived in Illinois was limited. On special occasions, I might have a shot of bourbon diluted with Coca Cola or some other soft drink. Except for the wine I bought for Joyce, I didn't keep alcohol in the apartment at that time. I was still inhibited by my upbringing in a house that did not allow alcohol.

However, when I started going to parties at the University, my drinking habits started to change. If I wanted to partake, I had two choices: martinis or Harvey Wallbangers. I tried a martini and almost gagged on it. I tried a Harvey Wallbanger, which was sweet and tasty. But I was warned by experienced drinkers that this concoction of rum and mixers was treacherous. The inexperienced drinker who consumed more than one of these tasty treats might not be able to get out of bed the next morning!

Since both my apartment mates were martini drinkers who kept tempting me with sips, I gradually became a devotee of martinis which consist of gin and a "whiff" of dry Vermouth plus an olive. *Basically it is alcohol diluted with a small amount of another alcohol.* After some time living with these two fun loving guys, I lost much of my cautious nature. Since we were all on graduate assistantships, we received our monthly stipend on the same day. After putting aside money for rent, we would then head to John's Steak House in nearby Rantoul, Illinois.

After skimping the entire month, we would cut loose at John's. We would start with large martinis, order a bottle of wine which we would consume with our wonderful steak, and finish off with a brandy--usually a French or Greek one. We would head home satiated, almost broke but ready to skimp until the next paycheck arrived. I was no longer the boy who cautioned his friends about drinking and over-spending.

# CHAPTER 14
## An Unexpected Call and a New Career Possibility

SHORTLY BEFORE THE end of the second semester, I received an unexpected call from a high level State Department official asking if I would be interested in a foreign assignment once I had finished the Master's Program at Illinois. His name was Benjamin Birdsall and he was head of the Agricultural Division of the International Agency for Development (AID) post in El Salvador. He said the agency was interested in interviewing me for the job of Agricultural Advisor for that struggling Central American nation.

I told Mr. Birdsall that I would definitely be interested in hearing more about this opportunity and he said, "Would you be able to meet me in Chicago next week?" I told him I would adjust my schedule and meet him. He said "Let's spend as much time as we can so we can get to know each other." We met in Chicago before noon and we had a really enjoyable lunch together. This gave me an excellent chance to learn more about the job for which he was interviewing me. He seemed to already know much about my background: that I grew up on a farm, studied and briefly taught Spanish, and had worked as a newspaper reporter.

He said all of these activities fit well with the job in question. He said it was a real asset that I was fairly articulate in Spanish (at that time) since I would be working to help Spanish speaking farmers improve their farm practices. The day passed quickly as we shopped together, talked, and visited little coffee shops. There was never any lull in conversation and I felt I had known Ben Birdsall for years. Apparently he felt the same way since, as we were saying our goodbyes he volunteered: "Jim, you will be hearing from us when you get back to Raleigh. I'm going to recommend you for the job." I felt that God was really looking out for me as I drove back to Champaign-Urbana.

As the semester ended and I was completing my course work, I began having meetings with Hadley Read about my required thesis. He would be my faculty adviser on the project. We discussed several possibilities. Hadley mentioned an idea that had been near and dear to his heart for a long time. His idea was for a thesis exploring "Factors that influence the treatment of agricultural news that newspapers receive from various sources."

Other graduate students he had discussed this with had shown no interest in the subject. Because of my background as a farm boy and later, a newspaper reporter, this idea was a natural for me. We discussed the approach to the thesis and agreed that my major work would begin with in-depth interviews of selected newspaper editors around the state of Illinois. Hadley had been right on target with me on that approach since he already knew of my distaste for statistics, the major tool used by most graduate students in preparing their theses and/or dissertations.

Hadley helped me make appropriate selections of the newspaper editors I would interview over the summer. Of course, all of this depended upon my passing all the course work. I hit the books especially hard hoping that I would pass my final exams with at least a B in every course. I received B's in all my subjects except one in which I received an A. *Must have over-studied on that one.*

During the summer session, I expected to and did enjoy the in-depth interviews with editors. I felt right at home with them and after we finished with my prepared set of questions, we usually had some time left for personal "newspaperman gossip." Once I had completed all my interviews I began putting my interview notes into some semblance of order while continuing my work at the College of Veterinary Medicine. The real work on the thesis, under the best of circumstances, would require weeks and months of intense effort with few or no distractions. While trying to balance requirements for the thesis with full time work, it took three years of vacation time to complete the thesis, get it accepted, and receive my Master's Degree from Illinois.

*Although three years may seem like an inordinately long time to spend on a thesis, I was the only one of the three grad students sharing the apartment in Champaign to complete the thesis and get my graduate degree. I was startled to learn that a high percentage of people who complete their course work at universities never complete their thesis or dissertation required for a graduate degree.*

It was soon the end of the summer session and end of my assistantship. Time to leave Illinois and head back to Raleigh. Since I had enough space in the car to contain my limited wardrobe and toiletries, I sold the little trailer and this made my drive back much more pleasant.

# CHAPTER 15

## Saying a Bitter-Sweet Goodbye to Illinois

I SAID MY goodbyes to my friends still on campus at the University as well as my two apartment mates, Bob Nemcik and Joe Moylan. I could not have had better friends and apartment mates. They had seen me through one of the roughest times of my life. We vowed to stay in touch and did so for a long time.

Saying goodbye to Hadley Read was especially hard for me as I expressed my gratitude for his support to me both professionally and personally. I don't think I could have survived the stress of the heavy workload and the problems with Joyce, culminating with her leaving with my best friend (or so I had thought) had not Hadley Read been on hand to offer his guidance and friendship. *I've heard he has passed away but I still think of him as one of the finest men I've ever known.*

I had tears in my eyes as I left Champaign-Urbana. I had forged stronger friendships with several people there (including my two apartment mates) than I had in Raleigh--other than the friendship with nephew Blair Turner of course. After several hours of driving, my sadness and pensive mood began to change when I first viewed the beautiful fall foliage of Western North Carolina. I don't believe I have ever seen a more beautiful scene than the one I encountered as I entered this state. Although I had come to appreciate the Midwest during my year there, its flat, dark, almost treeless terrain did not compare favorably with the tree topped rolling hills of the Carolinas.

A few hours later I reached Raleigh. My heart leaped into my throat at the idea of seeing Joyce. Because of the emotions involved, my recall of that first meeting after our long separation is somewhat blurred. During the past few months she had called to tell me that Billy had dropped her off in Raleigh, left immediately, and they had no communication since. She had also told me that she had taken a job as a dance instructor at the Arthur Murray Dance Studio in Raleigh. My first view of her surprised me. She had always been slender but the exercise she was getting as a dancer had made her even more shapely. She was almost gaunt but still beautiful.

Our first meeting was short because I needed: (1) to report to the NC State Extension Office and (2) find a place to live. I don't remember where I spent that first night but the next day I found a small, furnished basement apartment and moved into it. Later, Joyce and I had more serious discussions during which she expressed the hope that we might get back together as a couple sometime in the future. I was non-committal at the time but had growing doubts that I could ever trust her again.

I recalled some things that had happened much earlier that had caused me some pain, but they were not serious enough to cause me to mistrust her. Once after we had been married for a couple of years, with no pressure from me she confessed voluntarily that she had a brief affair after we were engaged and just before we were married. Although we were not married at the time of the affair, her revelation of a brief affair with someone else while we were engaged hurt me deeply. I soon recovered by rationalizing that her unsolicited confession was an effort on her part to be totally honest with me. I had forgiven and almost forgotten it by then. But since it had happened again after we were married, the earlier betrayal became an adverse factor in the issue of trust.

And to be completely honest, I must confess that remembering her psychiatrist's warning that she might never recover from issues of her childhood added to my hesitance in re-establishing our relationship to the point of staying married to her. If I had been a better, more forgiving human being, that last issue might not have been such a serious factor. But it was and I have carried a certain amount of guilt about this the rest of my life. I hope God will forgive me for my selfishness.

True to Ben Birdsall's word, soon after I arrived back in Raleigh, he sent me the paperwork needed for my formal application for the job in El Salvador. I filled out the paperwork and while it was being reviewed by the State Department, I received more instructions from El Salvador, including required vaccinations and other things I would need to bring with me, e.g., a car with manual transmission, certificates of my required vaccination, etc.

# CHAPTER 16
## Graduate School Begins Opening Doors

AS I WAS working on these things I received a call from a Navy recruiter asking me to meet him for lunch. I wondered why the Navy was interested in me but agreed to meet him. It turned out that the Navy recruiter was someone I had met once but had no contact with in years. After some casual conversation, I asked him if he had any particular reason for contacting me. He answered: "Jim, the Navy is badly in need of Information Officers. I've checked on you and learned that you have experience as a newspaper reporter and a Master's Degree in journalism. That's the type of person we're looking for."

He then went on to add that this job would carry the rank of full Commander. I was almost overwhelmed to learn that I might go from a second class petty officer ranking earned in World War II to a Commander. I asked him what I would be required to do to achieve this high rank. He replied: "You will have to pass a test that will take you all day to complete." I said, "I'll never be able to complete that type of test."

The recruiter replied: "I know your academic background and experience and know you will have no trouble passing the test." Then, he said with a wink: "I'll be giving the test." I never knew whether he truly thought I could pass the test with ease or he was going to give me a helping hand. Hopefully it was the former.

I returned to my office with two job offers to consider. Going to graduate school had definitely opened doors for me! The idea of becoming a full Commander in the Navy was nothing I had even dreamed of achieving. On the other hand, working in a foreign country where I could become really fluent in Spanish while living in a strange new culture was also appealing.

The major reservation I had about rejoining the Navy as a high commissioned officer was remembering how I felt when I heard the sound of a gate clanging behind me and knowing I couldn't leave there without someone's permission. That had always been bothersome to me because I cherished my freedom. Perhaps the "locked in" feeling would not be as prominent for a commissioned officer, but I didn't know. In any event, after much thought I called the Navy recruiter and told him I was opting for the foreign assignment but thanked him for the opportunity.

Then I went to work seriously about getting ready to leave for El Salvador. I had received a letter from the State Department personnel office (plus a phone call) officially stating I had been selected for the job at a certain grade. (A level 5 as I recall). Since then I had also received more information from the AID along with an invitation to dinner with the Ambassador. So, I traded my car with automatic transmission for one with manual transmission. And I completed required shots.

When I received my official letter stating that I had been accepted for the job I resigned my position at NC State. I was surprised when Cope arranged for a large raise in pay if I would withdraw my resignation. However, I said my decision to leave was firm and they began to search for a replacement. They asked me to stay on as long as possible and help train my replacement and I agreed to that.

As I continued my preparation for leaving, I received another "Official Authorization to go to El Salvador." I felt this was strange since I had already received an "Official Authorization." Fortunately, I decided to re-read the new authorization more carefully and spotted (in fine print) that the grade level of my job was different. Instead of level 5 it was now shown at level 6, one level higher. *To those unfamiliar with the Foreign Service this would appear to be an improved position. However, Foreign Service jobs are in descending order in importance, as opposed to Civil Service jobs which are in ascending order.*

I couldn't believe the State Department would deliberately change my grade level after I had received a written offer, plus a follow up phone call. It must be a mistake--perhaps a "typo." I immediately called the State Department Personnel Office in Washington, DC and told them that the offer I had just received did not match the offer I had earlier received by letter and telephone call. The personnel office head came on the line and said: "The person who made that first offer was not authorized to start you at that grade. We never start anyone at that level. However, you will be eligible in six months for the next grade." My reaction was immediate: "I don't want to work for an agency that doesn't keep its word. You can find someone else because I won't be going to El Salvador."

As soon as that call ended, I called Ben Birdsall, told him what had just happened, that I appreciated his support, and had looked forward to working with him. Under the new circumstances, however, I would not be joining him in El Salvador. He expressed his sorrow and added that the State Department personnel office had been accused of some improper actions of this type in the past. They would dangle a higher grade until the prospective new employee was strongly committed and then change the grade level at the last minute.

As a matter of principle, I could not let myself be manipulated in this manner, so I rejected appeals from the State Department that I accept the level 6 grade with the promise that within six months I would receive the grade promised. I didn't believe their promise.

# CHAPTER 17
## One Door Closes, Another Opens

THIS LEFT ME in a really uncomfortable situation. My successor had already been hired so after another week I would no longer have a job. The Navy recruiter had left town for "I don't know where." I had traded for a car I didn't really want, i.e., one with a manual transmission I had been advised to buy before coming to El Salvador. I had also jumped through a bunch of other hoops getting ready to go to El Salvador.

At that point I didn't know what to do. Then, before the end of the week I received another call from Washington, DC. This call was from Dr. Bryan Phifer, an official with the U.S. Department of Agriculture. He introduced himself and said: "Jim, I've just heard that you've finished your course work for a Master's Degree at the University of Illinois and that you have had lots of experience as a newspaper reporter. We have a job here at USDA's Federal Extension Service that needs someone with your qualifications. It's available right now and the job is at the GS-12 level." *I didn't know anything about Civil Service GS levels but assumed that level would be satisfactory.*

I told Dr. Phifer, "I've just turned down a Foreign Service job and I'm available now if you need me." He replied: "I hope you will catch the first plane you can tomorrow and meet me on the 5th floor of USDA's South Building at 12th and Independence Ave." I breathed a sigh of relief and said "Thank you, Lord," under my breath. I climbed aboard a plane bound for DC early the next day and caught a cab to the USDA South Building. My life was about to head in a completely new and exciting direction.

# PART 6

# The Move to the Nation's Capital as Federal Information Officer

# CHAPTER 1
## Meeting My New Boss and Fellow Employees

I ARRIVED AT the South Building, USDA, in early afternoon the fall of 1958 and got my first real view of the beautiful city of Washington, DC. Entering the huge USDA South Building, I found my way to an elevator and rode to the 5th or 6th floor, where the Federal Extension Service Information Office was located. I was quickly escorted to Dr. Bryan Phifer's office and he came around his desk to greet me like we were old friends. I immediately liked and felt comfortable around him.

After chatting for awhile, he took me around to meet the head of the Extension Information office and various staff members. One of these, a tall, friendly guy by the name of Ed Roche immediately asked me if I had any thoughts about where I would live. I didn't of course and asked for his advice. Ed said: "There's a wonderful boarding house at DuPont Circle where many of the new professionals stay for a few weeks or months until they find a more permanent place. I stayed there my first few months."

Ed then wrote down the address, phone number and person to call to get further information about price, meals served, accommodations, and how to apply to stay there. I thought this was extremely thoughtful and pocketed the information with my thanks.

After briefly meeting with the staff, we went back to Dr. Phifer's office where he said: "Jim, you have the job but you will need to complete some paperwork required to make you an official Civil Servant." I filled out the papers and handed them to Bryan, who checked them and said: "That looks fine. My wife and I hope you will have dinner with us tonight. You can ride home with me after work."

I gladly accepted the invitation since I didn't know a single restaurant in Washington and had no transportation except taxicabs. After we arrived at his house in Arlington, his wife greeted us and then kiddingly chided Bryan for not getting a hair trim so he would look more presentable for our first meeting. Bryan responded that he also was embarrassed that his hair looked so "ragged" but that he simply did not have time that day to get a trim.

Although later I thought this was a really dumb move on my part, I volunteered to give him a hair trim. Without asking any questions about my hair cutting qualifications, Bryan hustled around and found a sharp pair of scissors and a comb. I gave him a hair trim at his kitchen table. He was pleased with the results and I breathed a sigh of a relief that I had not messed up the hair of my new boss. *After I got to know him better, I found out he liked to save a few bucks!*

Strangely, I do not remember where I spent that night but after a delicious home cooked dinner and lots of conversation, Bryan delivered me to the place I was staying. I caught an early flight back to Raleigh the next morning and began to make my final plans to move to Washington.

Although I had been seeing Joyce occasionally, mostly at the Arthur Murray Studio, I had made sure there was no physical contact other than occasionally dancing with her at the studio. *Several of the dance instructors rented a large house conveniently located next door to the studio. Joyce's new living/career arrangement somewhat relieved my concern for her. She was earning her own livelihood, had developed friendships, and seemed to be taking care of herself without my assistance. Her dancing had improved tremendously to the point that she was being invited to New York to appear on the Arthur Murray TV Show!*

Since I had never had dance lessons, I was surprised when the owner of the studio approached me, complimented me on my dancing, and asked me if I would be interested in becoming a dance instructor of "free style" dancing. Since I just followed what the music told me to do, this seemed like an "oxymoron" to me. I didn't think I could teach dancing that is completely instinctive. I was somewhat flattered by his offer but immediately declined it. I was happy with my present career track.

Despite still caring deeply for her, I was becoming more certain as time went by that it would be a mistake to continue marriage to Joyce. Although I had not been able to completely "cut the string" with her, I felt that the physical distance between us after my move to Washington would make it easier for both of us to make a final separation. *The physical distance would ensure that we would not continue to accidentally bump into each other and re-open wounds. Each time this had happened, it caused some heartbreak and sadness for both of us. The fact that I still had strong feelings for her did not overcome the issues that caused our parting.*

A week after accepting the job as an Information Specialist for the Federal Extension Service (FES), I packed my car for the move to DC. When I found the boarding house at DuPont Circle, it was just as Ed Roche described. I was assigned a large room with private bath, enjoyed breakfast and dinner served family style, and found the room and board extremely reasonable in cost and convenience for the Washington, DC area.

# CHAPTER 2

## Starting the New Job!

MY FIRST DAY at work consisted primarily of discussions with Bryan Phifer about what he envisioned for me. He had a whole list of things he had been compiling but had never had the time or people to get them done. Like in Raleigh, I would be responsible for preparing the Extension Newsletter, except this would be at the Federal level. It would be signed by the Extension Director of Information.

Bryan had envisioned that my experience as a newspaper man as well as my educational background would be helpful to him in fulfilling some longtime objectives for the division. These objectives involved preparing booklets on news writing, column writing, and public relations; preparing material for two-week communications short courses FES would conduct at State Land Grant Colleges around the nation; and writing an "Occupational Brief" explaining the Extension Service, how it was formed and its major missions. And of course I was subject to the old "other duties as assigned" clause!

All three major projects had been on Bryan's "wish list" for a long time. I was determined not to spare any effort in helping him achieve these objectives. I was more than a little bit surprised that no one had written a brochure (Brief) about the Extension Service explaining its functions as well as the functions of the State/Federal Extension Service offices.

Bryan wanted me to start writing content for the news and column writing publications right away. I didn't have to start from scratch in this endeavor because I had already put some of this information together while working at NC State. And with additional thought and effort, much of this information could serve a dual purpose: basic information for publications and as aids for training sessions. Of course the information would need to be formatted to suit the needs of each.

I began working to put the information together my first week on the job. But almost immediately, I had to put this task on hold while I took on a more urgent task of preparing the Extension Service section for the 1959 Annual Agricultural Yearbook. Bryan had failed to mention that in his list of major projects although it would be an important yearly chore. *And it became my first "other duties as assigned."*

Gathering and writing Extension's annual contribution to the Yearbook turned out to be a greater chore than I expected. My duties were to interview various Federal Extension specialists (mostly scientists & economists) and develop information that had consensus approval. This was vital since the Yearbook would explain and even establish agency policy in several areas. Since I had met many of these people and found them friendly and courteous, I didn't anticipate any serious problems. That assumption turned out to be completely wrong. When I completed an interview, I would first put my notes into the proper form and get approval of the draft from the author.

I would then circulate this draft to the other Extension staff experts. *That's when trouble would start.* After their critical reviews and numerous suggestions for change, one or more of the other experts would complain: "That guy doesn't know what he's talking about." *And these people were supposedly close friends who ate and had coffee together! Needless to say, I had to go back and forth rewriting sections trying to get consensus until I was losing patience and becoming sick of the job. I never before realized how argumentative economists could be!*

Finally, I got agreement enough to finish the section and submit the package to the editors of the Yearbook. In succeeding years I gained enough confidence that I did not allow myself to get "jerked around" in compiling information for the Yearbook. FYI, once the Yearbook is published, copies are widely distributed around the country. Members of Congress each year order thousands of copies which they make available to their constituents.

After finally finishing this frustrating job, I was able to return to my number one priority: working on the News Writing and Column Writing handbooks. The information contained in these publications would provide "stand alone" information for FES personnel at the Federal, state and local levels. And I was counting on the fact that they would provide me with background information I could use for training sessions and as "hand out" information to leave with class members. However, this euphoria didn't last long. I soon found that the "other duties as assigned" usually had a higher priority than my regular duties. *More about these later.*

# CHAPTER 3
## I Discover a Fine Place for Jazz!

ON A PERSONAL note, in addition to finding a nice, convenient place to stay, I soon found a nearby wonderful place to listen to jazz. And it was within sight of the boarding house near DuPont Circle. The little hole-in-wall bar, called "Charlie's Cafe Lounge," soon became my regular hangout in the evenings. The modern jazz music was provided by the Eddie Phyfe Trio consisting of Eddie Phyfe, drums, Wilbur Little, bass, and Tee Carson, piano. They were all accomplished musicians but Tee Carson was a sensational pianist.

*Note: It has been my experience that musicians quickly recognize and respond to people who understand and appreciate their music. So after just a few visits to Charlie's, Tee Carson would sit with me and talk while taking his break. As a result, Tee and I soon became fast friends. Over the years he often invited me to his home for parties, where Bill Mayhew, (a popular Washington disc jockey) and I were usually the only white people there.*

When I first met him, Tee had just returned from two year-long tours as pianist for first singer Pearl Bailey and second jazz singer Ella Fitzgerald. *The latter was my favorite jazz singer. In her long recording career, she sold millions of her albums and won numerous Grammy awards, as well as Presidential awards from Presidents Ronald Reagan and George H. W. Bush. Like most musicians, Tee Carson had needed a regular job to support his family. His friend, Bobby Kennedy (brother to President Jack Kennedy), got him a job with the U.S. Marshals Service. Kennedy also used his considerable influence in Washington to get Tee "leaves of absence" to tour with Pearl, Ella and other famous musicians.*

Tee soon left Charlie's Cafe Lounge and formed his own trio with himself, Wilbur Little on bass, and Bertell Knox on drums. They became the backup to internationally known jazz and classical guitarist, Charlie Byrd, at the Showboat Lounge, partially owned by Byrd. I never became a close personal friend of Byrd but admired his talent. (When Wilbur Little left for New York City, he was replaced by Keter Betts, once described by a famous musical periodical as the "most sought after bassist for studio work in the world.")

Charlie Byrd was also given much credit for introducing a new type of music, the Bossa Nova, from Brazil to the U.S., shortly after he did a concert tour of that South American nation. Antonio Carlos Jobim, a Brazilian composer, pianist, songwriter, arranger and singer was credited with advancing this type of music internationally. Jobim, with the help of important American artists such as Byrd, merged it with jazz in the 1960s to create a new sound with remarkably popular success.

Byrd and Jobim were aided in making this "new music" popular in the U.S. by Felix Grant of Washington Radio Station, WMAL. Grant was one of the most well known, knowledgeable, and popular jazz music disc jockeys in that part of the country for many years. Felix Grant was also known for supporting local musicians. He was highly impressed with this new form of jazz music and promoted it heavily on his popular late night music program by featuring Charlie Byrd and his playing and recording of several Bossa Nova songs written by Jobim and brought back from Brazil by Byrd.

As a fine guitarist, Byrd was an ideal person to introduce the Bossa Nova to U.S. music lovers. The reason? Byrd was equally adept at playing classical music and jazz. Since the classical guitar with its nylon strings was the instrument of choice in playing Jobim's Bossa Nova music, Byrd didn't need to switch guitars after playing a solo classical set and then gradually shifting to a modern jazz or Bossa Nova number.

*I'm honored to have personally witnessed the dramatic change from classical to jazz on many occasions by Charlie Byrd. To set the stage, Byrd's first set would begin on a darkened stage playing alone with the spotlight trained on him. Then, as the classical music set was nearing its end, the Tee Carson Trio members would slip back into their seats. Byrd would gradually shift from classical to jazz and the Trio would softly join in with Byrd's guitar. As the lights gradually became brighter all of the musicians would increase tempo and volume and the entire group would soon be fully engaged in a Bossa Nova jazz set.*

*This transition from classical to jazz at the Showboat Lounge was unique in my experience as a listener. It still amazes and thrills me when I recollect the scene. Before long I was really feeding my hunger for live jazz music which had languished since I had left Illinois and the many jazz clubs in Chicago. These clubs were not easily reached from Raleigh--not known as a jazz town. In addition to the Showboat Lounge, Washington boasted The Bohemian Caverns and several other DC night clubs which offered good modern jazz when I arrived there. Soon I rarely spent an evening alone reading or listening to my Hi Fi set.*

# CHAPTER 4

## Finding Another Place to Live

ALTHOUGH THE BOARDING house had been a great place to stay for a short time, after a few months it was time to start looking for a more permanent place to live. I had become friends with a young man by the name of George Turner from Long Island, New York. He was staying at the same boarding house and was also ready to move to something more permanent. We decided to team up and locate an apartment we could share.

After much looking, George and I agreed that a small apartment building located just across the river in the small town of Anacostia, MD was convenient and inexpensive enough for us to afford. *(At that time Anacostia was so safe you could walk around the neighborhood at midnight with no concern for safety; a few years later, if you drove through the town even in daylight you were warned to roll up your windows, lock the doors, and run a red light rather than to stop at a traffic signal.)*

George and I became even closer friends as apartment mates. We began attending parties and social events together. Both of us were new to the big city of Washington, DC, and were ready for some excitement. And as I had hoped, this new lifestyle gave me more emotional separation from Joyce. Although still not close to thinking about a serious relationship, I was getting more interested in meeting people of the opposite sex. George, a recent graduate of the University of Delaware, now had a job and some money and he, too, was ready to start having an active social life.

As it was at the University of Illinois, my apartment mate and I were from different cultural and religious backgrounds. And again, we enjoyed our differences. George was a devout Catholic who was primarily interested in meeting women of the same faith. I was Protestant and hoped to meet fellow Protestants. *Since I wasn't attached to a church at that time, the religious issue wasn't as important to me as it was to George. Also, I knew that most Catholic women would shy away from me because I was divorced.* So, it made sense for me to try to find eligible Protestant girls although I wasn't interested in a serious romantic relationship at that time.

It was interesting that at large parties, where quite a few attractive women were available, George would invariably end up spending most of his time with a Protestant woman. On the other hand, most of the time I would end up attracted to a Catholic woman. We never figured out why this happened but it occurred again and again. George eventually got engaged (and after a long courtship) married a Protestant girl he met at one of these parties, while I eventually became engaged and married to a Catholic woman. *But that was much later.*

# CHAPTER 5
## Learning About Washington, DC

BACK TO MORE mundane matters, although I never lived far from the USDA building, finding a parking place after getting there by car was a continuing problem. Parking in the South Building parking lots were reserved for car pools or officials at much higher levels than my GS-12. That left on-street parking or "car pooling" for the majority of us. If you were lucky enough to find parking space on the street, there was a two hour parking limit which meant you had to watch the time and rush to try to find another parking space to avoid being ticketed. That was stressful and difficult to maintain as a dedicated public servant. Public transportation had not been reliable since the city took it over from Roy Chalk who had operated the system efficiently. Eventually I was forced by reality to join a carpool--something I had resisted because of the loss of independence and privacy.

*I discovered one especially strange custom in Washington. Before coming to the nation's capital I had rarely, if ever, been asked to reveal how much money I was making. It was considered discourteous to ask this type of personal question. In this city of Federal employees, however, one of the first questions people ask is: "What grade are you?" If you answer, the person immediately knows what your salary is--except for the steps in grade raises for longevity.*

It didn't take me long to find out that starting a Federal Government job at the GS-12 level was unusual--unless you had political clout. Most people told me they started at the GS-5 or GS-7 level. My relatively high starting grade made me feel even better about my move to Washington and my new job. However, I would soon realize that I was "low man on the totem pole" among the professionals at FES.

At work I shared an office with a very nice woman, Frances Clingerman, as well as a young secretary who worked for the two of us. Since I had brought my faithful Royal manual typewriter with me, I continued my practice of writing first drafts on my own typewriter and passing them on to the secretary for final typing.

*I was not good at and did not like dictating to a secretary. I did my best thinking through my fingers! However, every time a government efficiency expert came around, I had to fight to keep my typewriter. The expert always tried to take it away, insisting that it was more efficient to dictate my writing directly to the secretary. This might generally be true but it was not for me. The fact is I could still type faster than most of the secretaries! And I was far from being facile at dictating. So I continued using the system that was most efficient for me. Despite periodic attempts to take it away, the old Royal followed me the rest of my Civil Service career and after.*

In addition to the time consuming work of preparing Extension's part for the Yearbook, other assignments kept cutting into the time and effort I needed to finish the work I had begun my first week on the job. For example, during my first year on the job, I was asked to be involved with the Community Development and Rural

Development programs that were becoming popular around the U.S. My boss Bryan Phifer picked up on this trend and asked me to start looking for a good example of a State Community Development Project. He said that if I could locate such an example and turn it into an attractive brochure, this might be useful in extolling the success of USDA and Extension's community development work.

Since I had most recently been employed by NC State and knew that state best, I called friends there and requested suggestions for a suitable project. My friends talked with the North Carolina Community Development people who decided that Watauga County would be most suitable for such a project. This county was nestled within majestic mountains criss-crossed with beautiful mountain streams--scenery to "die for." At that time, however, Watauga County, which included the then tiny village of Blowing Rock, was undeveloped and dirt poor.

The town of Boone was also located in Watauga County and had a very good college called Appalachian State Teachers College (now Appalachian State University). In the mid 1950's, the county lacked golf courses, ski slopes and antique malls needed to be a tourist attraction. And it needed guidance, financing, and publicity that could be provided by the Federal government.

After selecting this North Carolina county, I then asked my NC State Extension friends for another favor. Would they allow me to have Ralph Mills, their fine photographer, for several days to make the photographs to be used to illustrate the proposed brochure? They agreed to do that as long as Ralph was identified on the brochure as an NC State Extension Service employee. Naturally I agreed to that.

The leaves were in full glory that early fall day when I picked Ralph up in Raleigh and the two of us headed toward the mountains. We arrived at Blowing Rock and met with the Community Development Team, which included a USDA representative and top local town and county officials. At the time, the major project underway with partial federal funding under the aegis of Community Development was an 18 hole golf course. The Development Team thought that the new golf course would become the centerpiece for turning the county into a tourist attraction.

Ralph and I spent two or three days in the Blowing Rock/Boone area while I conducted interviews and Ralph took black and white and color photographs of the people and scenery to be included in the brochure. Then I dropped Ralph off at NC State and returned to Washington, DC to write up my interview notes for brochure text.

A few days later I received many beautiful photos that Ralph Mills had taken of people and scenes in Watauga County. I selected the photos I thought best illustrated the text I had written and put together a draft of the brochure which I then took to the professionals of USDA's large Information Division which would do the layout and put the final touches to the brochure.

Once the brochure received all the proper approvals, I took it to GPO under the title "The Watauga County Story." Apparently some high officials at USDA were so impressed with the draft copy of the brochure that they got high priority for the printing at GPO. In a short time the brochure was printed and sent to relevant people around the agency. At that point I lost all control of the product.

The next thing I heard (through the grapevine) was that the brochure text and photos would be used in a visual/oral version. Neither Ralph Mills nor I were asked to participate in this expansion of "The Watauga County Story" nor were we given any credit for doing the initial work of putting the brochure together. Although not invited to the showing, friends alerted me to the time and place it would be presented to the highest level of USDA officials. I sat in the back of the room while someone I didn't even know took credit for this information piece without even acknowledging my writing or Ralph Mills' photography. I made no fuss about this but felt betrayed that people who did none of the work on the brochure got credit for it. This reinforced my growing belief that politics affected almost everything in Washington, DC.

Returning to my regular work at FES I found my duties demanding but not as exciting as my recent trip to North Carolina. I resumed working on preparing training material for anticipated training sessions around the country. Although I had had experience and training in news and column writing, Bryan introduced me to other resources with which I had no experience.

One of these was the research Dr. Rudolph Flesch had done on measuring "readability." Dr. Flesch had written a book on the Flesch Formula to improve and measure writing skills. This concept was a revolutionary idea to me and turned out to be extremely useful as a structure for developing training material.

I had always followed the newspaperman's credo "if it's interesting to me it will be interesting to the reader." Of course that worked fine for working reporters and editors. *Too many wrong decisions about what is interesting reading, and you were out of a job or relegated to writing obituaries.* But this new approach by Flesch offered valuable guidance for non-professional, occasional writers such as Farm and Home Demonstration Agents with whom I would be working.

*The Flesch "Reading Ease Formula" is described as "a simple approach to access the grade-level of the reader. It's also one of the few accurate measures that can be relied on to produce reliable results. It has become a standard readability formula used by many U.S. government agencies, including the U.S. Department of Defense." (And of course USDA in my case). In conclusion, the Flesch Reading Ease Formula "emphasizes that the best text should contain shorter sentences, paragraphs and words."*

The best thing about the Flesch Formula as far as I was concerned was that I could use it as a tool for measuring improvement in writing during my training sessions. It could serve as an objective measuring method rather than just my own judgment of what constituted "good" or "bad" writing. I could present information to the class early, give the class some writing assignments, and then work with them to use the Flesch Formula on "readability" to see how their writing stacked up. If time permitted, I could do a "before" and "after" approach to writing assignments.

# CHAPTER 6
## Two Year Separation Approaches

*SOMETIME DURING THIS period, the two year separation from Joyce had been reached and we could get divorced "without cause." By then, I had decided that it would be best for both of us to dissolve the marriage, thinking that it was too damaged to be repaired. However, I thought it might be more gentlemanly and less hurtful to her reputation if she were allowed to file for the divorce. So, I offered to pay for everything and let her get the divorce if she preferred. She said she simply couldn't do it but she would not object if that was what I wanted.*

I called my old boss and friend, J. C. Brown in Raleigh, and asked him if he would be a witness to the two-year separation. He agreed to testify and the divorce was granted. I was emotionally shaken by the experience to the extent that I could not stop by and say goodbye to Joyce in person. So, I left Raleigh as a free but emotionally stricken man. My eyes were bloodshot when I arrived back in Washington and I went straight to my apartment to grieve. Later that night I called Joyce to tell her that we were no longer married and we both broke down before finishing our conversation.

Although I remained sad that my marriage to Joyce had ended in divorce, my many job responsibilities and other activities gradually helped relieve some of the guilt and sadness I was feeling. However, I continued to care for her and to be concerned about her welfare. *Even now, tears come to my eyes when I think of this beautiful, sweet little woman beset by demons which were not of her own choosing but that she could not control.*

Back to my working life: after completing preliminary drafts for publications on news and column writing, I was put to the test when a major Land Grant University sent the first formal request to the FES Information Office to send me to teach a two-week course on those subjects for County and Home Demonstration Agents. The surprising thing to me was that the first request came from Clemson University in my home state of South Carolina.

I was now faced with the urgent job of putting together enough acceptable training material to teach this course, since Clemson wanted me down there and ready to teach within the next two weeks. The short time to get materials ready for conducting the first FES Information Office training program of this type made things pretty hectic for me. I wanted to be fully prepared for our first venture of this type. I definitely did not want to fall on my face in my home state by not being prepared.

By working non-stop and receiving some guidance from Bryan, as I neared the end of the second week, I felt reasonably well prepared. I had assembled lots of information from my own journalism background, the draft publications, and Rudolph Flesch's book. Now, I could spend my remaining time reproducing copies for "handouts" and establishing a workable format for the two week session. I reasoned that if the prepared program fell apart, I could use all those years as an active newspaper reporter to "fake" my way through.

I felt good about the fact that this training session offered me a "hands on" opportunity to test the draft publications to see how well they worked in real life before putting them in final form as publications which might be around for many years. Nevertheless, this assignment in my home state was one of the most nerve wracking jobs I had faced in a long time. I would be completely on my own with no guidance from Bryan. And I had to overcome my normal stage fright by meeting the problem head on.

*Personal Note: my dread of facing a large group of strangers was somewhat relieved by the fact that this assignment would provide me a chance to visit friends and relatives in both Carolinas. With my busy schedule and the distance involved, I had neglected my family much too long.*

# CHAPTER 7

## Back in My Home State

ON THE WAY to Clemson, I stopped in Grover, NC to spend a night and day with Brother Bob and his wife, Lena. I arrived at Clemson late Sunday afternoon with my car loaded down with visual and written teaching aids. Early Monday morning, I was getting acquainted with the State Extension Editor (Jim Copeland, brother of O.B., my former boss at NC State) who had requested my presence at Clemson, when his phone rang and he told me that the call was from another Clemson staffer down the hall who wanted to meet me. He agreed to lead me to this person's office after we finished our discussion.

As we were walking down the hall to the appointment, he volunteered that the person wanting to talk with me was S.C. Stribling, who wrote a weekly farm column for Clemson that went out to newspapers around the State. I remembered Mr. Stribling's name from my days at the Rock Hill Evening Herald. He was well recognized around the state as "Strib." And he had achieved both a state and national reputation for the quality of his columns.

I shook hands with Mr. Stribling and he asked me to sit down. As soon as we were seated he said: "Jim, I noticed from your bio that you were born in Cherokee County and that made me especially interested in meeting you." He continued, "When I graduated from Clemson, the State Extension Director told me he was assigning me to the county with the lowest income and lowest literacy rate in the state of South Carolina. *Our state then ranked last in the nation in those categories, even lower than Mississippi. And the county that ranked lowest in South Carolina was Cherokee.*"

*By the end of his first statement I began remembering my experience as a 10-11 year old at Kings Creek Elementary School when a young assistant county agent visited our school with the purpose of starting a 4-H Club at our school.*

My first question to Mr. Stribling was: "Did you visit Kings Creek School in the mid-thirties with the idea of starting a 4-H Club?" He thought for a moment and then said: "Yes, I do recall coming to Kings Creek Elementary School my first week on the job." I said: "What happened to you, Strib? Why didn't you come back?" He began to turn red and hastened to explain: "Jim, as soon as I arrived in Gaffney, I met a young school teacher who had just graduated from Winthrop College. After that I was so in love I didn't know what I was doing for awhile. I've felt bad about my failure to start that 4-H Club at Kings Creek ever since!"

*My reaction was to laugh and say: "Not to worry, Strib. None of us at the Kings Creek School could afford a decent project anyway and we certainly were not going to be competitive with any other 4-H Club in the area much less the state. My own project consisted of some highly bred biddies, most of which died from a disease they caught from our yard chickens. Most of the kids didn't even bother starting a project!"*

Both of us were amazed at the coincidence of meeting again after all these years. We had a long conversation about Cherokee County, its assets and drawbacks. I left his office pleased about our conversation and for receiving the answer to a long ago question. I was also hoping that my reaction to his early failure might relieve any guilt Strib might still have about never returning to finish his job.

But, as I was walking away, I wondered why I was being asked to teach column writing to County Farm and Home Demonstration agents at a State University with perhaps the best Farm Column Writer in the country. That person was of course S.C. Stribling! Must have been a case of "No prophet is acceptable in his home town."

With the help of the wonderfully cooperative and supportive Farm and Demonstration Agents at Clemson, I soon overcame much of my stage fright and actually found myself enjoying the sessions at Clemson. Hopefully the agents learned enough to make their time and my trip there worthwhile. I'll always remember them and Clemson, which offers its delicious "homemade" ice cream and blue cheese served in the cafeteria. Students and guests could eat all they wanted of these treats! And the training experience did in fact help me improve the final versions of the publications I was working on.

# CHAPTER 8

## A Long Awaited Chance to Meet a New Friend

THE LAST WEEKEND on the way back to Washington, I stopped off in Blacksburg to spend the night at my sister Nell Turner's house. This stopover also offered me the chance to meet with other family members residing in the Blacksburg area. It also turned out to be especially rewarding for another reason. My niece by marriage, Carolyn Turner, finally had a chance to introduce me to a very special young lady friend of hers--Anita Jones of nearby Gaffney. Carolyn had wanted to introduce us since my breakup with Joyce but this had been difficult to do since the two of us were rarely at the same place at the same time.

Carolyn was not trying to "fix us up" romantically but thought we would enjoy each other's company because of mutual interests. She had told me that Anita was currently working as a newspaper reporter. Coincidentally, when we met, I learned that Anita was a reporter for my former employer, The Rock Hill Evening Herald. As already mentioned in this Memoir, I had worked as a reporter there from 1952-1954.

Anita, daughter of prominent parents in Gaffney (L.D. and Louise Jones) turned out to be a bright, talented, and attractive young woman. She was valedictorian of her classes at both Gaffney High School and Winthrop College in Rock Hill. Winthrop was a highly rated small women's college at that time. *I later learned that Anita also had a Master's Degree in Journalism from Northwestern University but she never mentioned that to me. Anita obviously inherited good genes for intelligence! Her only sibling, younger sister, Nancy, earned a PhD. and became a college professor.*

The two of us hit it off right away and began seeing each other when I was in the area. Our greatest fun was going to The Evening Herald office at night and reading each other's articles. *Mine were on microfiche.* That may seem like a strange date to a non-newspaper person but it was perfectly natural for us; it allowed us to get to know each other better and to share experiences. We also visited my nephew, Dan Turner, and his wife, Carolyn, in Charlotte, NC, where they moved after Dan secured a job with Duke Power Company (now Duke Energy).

Distance kept our relationship from developing beyond friendship and that distance soon became even greater. Anita called to tell me she had accepted a job at a large newspaper in southern Florida. I knew we would likely not see each other often (certainly not often enough to establish a serious relationship) but I was pleased and proud that she was moving up in the newspaper world. I later read in Editor & Publisher (a trade magazine) that she had become the first woman Editor of a major American newspaper, The Palm Beach (FL) Post!

*(To my surprise several years after she moved to Florida, Anita called to say she wanted to come visit me in Washington. I met her at Washington Regional Airport (now Reagan). I was surprised to see how her looks had changed. She had grown from an extremely slender young woman (built more like a pre-teenager) to a shapely woman. But the story of that meeting and future events will be related in a later chapter. That story turned out to be both poignant and tragic).*

Back at USDA, after my Clemson experience, I made final revisions to the publication on "News Writing" and it was ready to be published and distributed. Because Dr. Phifer had been so helpful, I suggested that his name be added as co-author of the publication. He was pleased to see his name along with mine on the finished product which went out to all State Extension Offices around the nation. *(In the early 2,000's*

*I happened to be in a County Agent's office and he pulled out a well worn copy of the news writing brochure from his desk drawer. He said FES had never sent out revised versions of any of my publications).*

I then went back to finish work on the two other publications: the one on "Column Writing" and the other on "How's Your Public Relations," and a few months later they were published under my name alone. *If you're wondering what took so long to get these brochures published, you've never dealt with the Government Printing Office (GPO)!*

Joyce called me occasionally and on one of these occasions she said she was fed up with the pressure the Arthur Murray Studio put on instructors to sell "lifetime memberships" to people who had no sense of rhythm and never would be good dancers--except with an instructor--and had resigned her job as a dance instructor.

*(Note: I fully understood her feelings when I recalled the experience of a newspaper reporter friend of mine. He paid for many lessons with a pretty, young dance instructor at that same studio. He became very fond of her and assumed she was fond of him. She finally convinced him to purchase the very expensive "lifetime membership" by persuading him: (1) he had the potential to become a great dancer and (2) as a "lifetime" member he would be able to dance with her any time he cared to schedule her.*

*He had told me that as soon as he paid for the lifetime membership he was assigned an older, unattractive instructor that he intensely disliked. And he was never again allowed to dance with the pretty young thing. He stopped going to the studio, losing a large chunk of his money. I wondered (aloud) if he might sue to get some of his money back. Joyce told me that Arthur Murray management boasted that they had never lost a case when one of their lifetime member clients sued to try to get some or all of their money back. She said their contracts had been tested many times in court without a loss).*

Joyce said that she had a new job as a "Pixie Pinup" photographer for the J.C. Penney chain. I was amazed at that for two reasons: (1) she had never shown any interest in photography and (2) she didn't know how to drive a car. I knew that "Pixie Pinup" photographers traveled extensively. When I asked her how she would get from city to city since she could not drive, she said she had taken driving lessons and had received her driver's license. She had also been given some specific "Pixie Pinup" photography training by J.C. Penney. So, she was ready to hit the road.

# CHAPTER 9
## More Travel to Conduct Training

NOT LONG AFTER the Clemson experience, Bryan received additional requests that I conduct two more training sessions. The requests came from Auburn University and Oklahoma State University. Getting ready for these two out-of-town sessions helped get my mind off the divorce and concern for Joyce and on a more positive track. I had to lick my wounds and get ready for two new slightly different training sessions.

Since I had cut my teeth on preparing for and conducting the training sessions at Clemson, preparation for the next one was easier and less stressful. Soon I was on the plane bound for Alabama. Bob Chesnutt, Alabama State Extension Editor, met my plane on Saturday afternoon. I arrived early because Bob wanted to spend some time discussing plans for the next two weeks. Bob had one serious change he wanted to make in the schedule.

For convenience of out-of-town farm and home agents, Bob suggested we hold two sessions of one week each at two different locations. We would spend one week in one part of the State with about half of the Farm and Home Agents attending. The next week we would go to another part of the state to accommodate the remaining group. I agreed with his idea of conducting shorter sessions with fewer people per class so I spent Sunday condensing my material to one-week sessions. Bob and I traveled to the first location Sunday afternoon ready to start our first session the following morning. The thing I liked the most about the new, smaller group plan was that it allowed greater interaction between instructor and students.

Bob and I would go back to our motel each night to discuss the next day's session, enjoy some libations, and then go to dinner at a place recommended by the local class members. We became close friends and ate some good Southern food in the process.

For the two weekends I was in Alabama, Bob had placed me in an old, dilapidated, but clean hotel in the center of the town of Auburn. Bob also introduced me to the owner of the hotel. I got to know him quite well over my two weekend stays. The hotel owner was an interesting fellow and each evening I was there he invited me to join him for drinks, snacks, and conversation. During those conversations, he told me how he acquired the hotel back during the height of the Great Depression.

The hotel owner said that one of his uncles was an inventor at the time automobiles were just becoming available to the general public. One handicap of these early models was they had to be started by using a special hand "crank" to start the engine. This required strength and could be dangerous if you didn't quickly remove the crank when the engine started turning over. A broken arm was not that unusual for those doing the cranking of early automobiles.

The hotel owner's uncle supposedly solved this problem by inventing a switch that would start the car electronically from inside the car and sold it to one of the "big three" automakers. He said his uncle was offered a large amount of cash or an interest in the company to obtain patents for the switch. The uncle chose the large amount of cash and when he died during the depression, left his nephew $50,000 as his share. *Imagine inheriting this amount of money in the middle of the Great Depression!*

This sharecropper boy listened in awe as the recipient described what he did with this fortune *when my family and many others were virtually penniless.* He said he spent $25,000 of the money the first six months on fancy cars, travel, and having fun. Then, realizing that at this pace he would soon be broke, he invested most of the remaining money in two grocery stores. They went broke. He then invested what was left in the old hotel we were occupying at that moment. "My mortgage is greater than the hotel is worth today," he said shaking his head. *I'm sure that situation changed as Auburn University and the town of Auburn grew--provided he held on to the property.*

After returning from Auburn, between routine work I began getting ready for the Oklahoma State training at Stillwater, home of Oklahoma State University. The Oklahoma State Extension Editor wanted me to conduct classes for a full two week session to a selected group of county farm and home demonstration agents. And the session would be held on campus. By that time I had continued to refine the material and getting ready was not nearly as much of a chore. Also I was not suffering as much from stage fright by that time. The classes were well received and I received many compliments as I was driven to the Stillwater Airport by Oklahoma State officials.

Then once I was dropped off at the airport, strange things started to happen. I had boarded the flight for Washington and was sitting in a window seat when I saw that my bag was being transported back to the airport rather than being loaded onto the plane. I immediately summoned a flight attendant who made some quick calls and got my bag carried back. This time I watched closely to ensure that it was being put into the plane's baggage compartment.

Relieved that my bag would be going with me on the same plane, I fastened my seat belt for takeoff. Then the plane was suddenly delayed again. *Naturally it was because of me.* FBI agents boarded the plane and headed straight for my seat. They asked for my identification and then called the University Extension Service office I had just left. I could hear that they were discussing and (to my relief) confirming my identification.

I asked one of the agents what this was all about and he said that a man described as having red hair had robbed a bank at a nearby town. The agent added that soon after they were notified about the bank robbery they received a call that a red-haired man of similar description was seen at the Stillwater Airport. They had rushed to the airport hoping to apprehend the bank robber before his plane took off.

Satisfied that I wasn't the criminal they were looking for, the FBI agents left the plane and we were finally able to take off. The only repercussion: the merciless teasing I got from the Oklahoma Extension people who had verified that I had been conducting a training session when the crime was committed! They never let me forget the incident!

# CHAPTER 10

## A Move to Virginia

AS TIME WENT by, George and I reached the conclusion that it was time to move out of Anacostia. George wanted to be closer to his fiancée and I wanted to move to a new apartment in Arlington, Virginia, where I would be closer to work and where more of my close friends lived. George and I remained good friends although we did not see as much of each other after our move.

During the time I was living in Anacostia, however, I had become friends with a fellow former Navy man by the name of Dave Griffith. Educated as an engineer, he had a high level job with the Navy Hydrographic Office near Andrews Air Force Base in Maryland and did much international travel for the Navy. Dave Griffith had been a commissioned officer in the Navy during World War II and thus had privileges at the Navy Yard Officer's Club in Washington. Soon after our meeting, he invited me to Sunday Brunch at this facility. That brunch offering was something to behold. Lobster tails and other delicacies were available in unlimited amounts at Sunday brunch! I never turned down an invitation to accompany him for brunch.

The two of us became regular party goers together and often went on double dates. Also, while I was living in Anacostia, Dave had introduced me to a young lady who lived nearby. We dated a few times and became good friends. *I later introduced her to a good friend who worked for the USDA Foreign Agriculture Service. They fell in love and were married. Later, after they completed a tour of duty in Italy and bought a house in Arlington, I attended many social events at the home of Buck and Nancy Pritchard. At one of their dinners, I met a fellow guest, Murray Chotiner, who had attained national fame! (More about him later).*

Back to my friendship with Dave, each year, he invited me to an annual Navy Hydrographic Office party at which time a new Miss Navy Hydrographic "beauty queen" was crowned. He said these parties were great fun. But I always had other plans and declined his invitations to this event. He also often mentioned a beautiful woman who worked at Navy Hydrographic. Suspecting he had a crush on this woman I asked him why he didn't ask her out. He said he had asked her out but that she wouldn't go out with him because she was Catholic and he was divorced. *(This story also continues later!)*

Dave and I joined the first Vic Tanney gym near Alexandria, Virginia, and began working out together. *Since boot camp days, I had always done 50 push-ups nightly before going to sleep. Sick or tired it made no difference: 50 push-ups at bed time was my routine. Now, I thought it was time I increased my physical capabilities beyond push-ups. At Vic Tanney's, in addition to regular weight lifting and other bodybuilding exercises, the instructor introduced me to a new (and much more difficult way) to do push-ups.*

*These were called "dips" and involve pushing your body up between parallel bars until the arms are straight; then repeating the process of letting the body down and pushing it back up. At first I could not do even one of these "dips." But I kept working at it until it became easy. Then, to increase the difficulty, I had an attendant fasten 25 pounds of weight to my ankles. Eventually the 25 pounds became easy and I had the extra weight increased to 50 pounds. At first I could do only a few of these but soon worked up to two full sets of 12 "dips." One day I decided to do another set. Suddenly, my right shoulder made a loud "popping" sound heard around the gym accompanied by my screams of pain.*

As usual, I had foolishly overdone the exercising. I had ruined my rotator cuff and was never again able to do a single push-up (even from the waist) and suffered shoulder pain for the next 50+ years. *(Unlike character actor Jack Palance, I was never able to do a one arm push-up). Once I had coffee with him and asked him about this feat and he said there was a trick to it. (He never explained the nature of the "trick" to me).*

*Finally in my eighties, a fine surgeon at Ortho Carolina in Charlotte, NC repaired the shoulder by using a reverse transplant. He had to use a different muscle to lift my arm since the rotator cuff was unusable. My shoulder which caused me great pain for around 50 years is now free of pain. But, now in my nineties, I no longer feel the need to do push-ups.*

# CHAPTER 11
## An Office Problem and Another Lesson Learned

AFTER ABOUT A year at Extension, our office began having serious problems with our secretary. She was having difficulty in her marriage and this problem carried over to the office. Frances Clingerman and I talked with each other and with the secretary who told us she had become the "family breadwinner" because her husband had lost his job and had been unable to find work.

She said her husband had applied for a job with the DC Police Department but had flunked the psychological test. (She revealed that he was a racist and had wanted to be a policeman so he could "beat up niggers!") Thank God the Police Department gave him a psychological test which he flunked. Otherwise he might have made it to the force! Sympathetic to her problems, we tried to work with her. Despite the best efforts and patience of Mrs. Clingerman and me, her work continued to deteriorate. And when we caught her in some lies that caused embarrassment to the Office, we knew she must go.

Since Mrs. Clingerman was so soft hearted, she wanted me to initiate the personnel action to get the secretary transferred or relieved of her job. So, I agreed to be the "bad guy." When the secretary was notified of the action being taken against her and saw my name as the complainant, she told personnel that I had tried to fondle her in the office. To tell the truth, I was doubly insulted by her charge since: (1) I found her extremely unattractive physically and (2) my own ethical standards kept me from even dating, much less becoming physically involved with a fellow employee.

Despite not having any sort of physical contact with this young woman, I was suddenly in trouble. However, when Mrs. Clingerman learned of this charge, she immediately went to the personnel office and told them that the secretary had made up this story about me; that I had never been anything but a gentleman around the secretary. I gave a big sigh of relief when personnel promptly dropped the charge against me. I was eternally grateful that Mrs. Clingerman acted so promptly and strongly to get my name cleared. *I was also glad that she was one of the people who never left her desk during working hours to take a coffee break!*

This was my introduction to how hard it is to discipline or get rid of an incompetent Federal employee--especially a minority. This problem also educated me to the fact that in almost any action taken by a male supervisor against a female employee, it was pretty well standard practice to charge the male with sexual harassment or racism, or both. Although we eventually succeeded in ousting this employee, the story doesn't end there.

One day as the administrative procedures to remove the secretary were ending, the secretary's burly husband paid a visit to our office and threatened to do physical harm to me if I didn't re-instate his wife. *This was prior to 9-11 and anyone had free access to Federal Buildings.* Although he probably outweighed me by 40 pounds, I didn't take kindly to his threats and started around my desk toward him. Before I could reach him, Ed Roche and two other employees restrained me while Mrs. Clingerman called security. They escorted the husband out of the building and he never returned as far as I knew. That was the last we heard from the fired secretary and her husband. My hope is that the husband got a job but not as a policeman.

I was still a bit apprehensive when Personnel sent us a new secretary. However, my concerns were soon just a distant memory after we got to know our new secretary, Sarah Webster. She turned out to be a totally different type of person from the one who caused us (especially me) such problems. Sarah was not only attractive and personable, she was modest, completely truthful, honest, diligent and efficient. We only had to show her something one time and she took care of it from then on.

Although we became social as well as work friends, our relationship remained strictly platonic. I did try (unsuccessfully) to "fix her up" with some of my younger friends. However, at a party held by either Larry Mark or me (or both of us) she met one of our mutual friends, Silvio Capponi, who later became her husband. *I'm still in email contact with her and her husband 55 years later. Although friends all these years, until recently Sarah still called me "Mr. White," out of respect for our office relationship.*

# CHAPTER 12
## On the Road to Morocco--Maybe!

WHILE AT FES, I was again contacted by the U.S. State Department about another overseas job. This time they tempted me with an assignment to Morocco, again as an Agricultural Adviser with the Agency for International Development (AID). Since I had become friends with a native of that country while at NC State and he had regaled me with stories of his exotic country, I was intrigued with this possibility. Without waiting for paperwork to be completed, I was having visions of Casablanca, Tangier and, of course, "The Casbah." *In my imagination, I could hear Sam playing the piano and singing "As Time Goes By" in Rick's Bar Americain!*

Although wary that they might be up to their old "bait and switch" action they had pulled on me with their earlier offer, I nevertheless decided to give the State Department's new offer some consideration. The job would be in Rabat but would involve travel all over Morocco. Since the Moroccans spoke French, the State Department planned to send me to their vaunted "French School" located just across the Potomac River in Arlington, Virginia, before traveling overseas.

*On my own, I called the Peugeot factory in France, and found I could fly to Paris, purchase a Peugeot 404 from one of their dealers at a discounted price, drive through Spain to Gibraltar, take the ferry from there to Casablanca and then drive on to Rabat. Or perhaps I would arrive a day early and visit Rick's Bar in Casablanca before driving on to Rabat!*

I had selected the Peugeot as my choice because of its many awards for reliability and ruggedness. My friend from Morocco had warned me that the mechanics in Morocco were not that great, so reliability was all important. As appealing as this assignment sounded, before enrolling in the French School I forced the issue of my salary. The personnel people again tried the "bait and switch."

So I told them I was no longer interested. I remembered the old refrain, "Fool me once, shame on you--fool me twice shame on me!" I had not sold my car or resigned my job this time. That ended my ill-fated flirtations with the State Department.

# CHAPTER 13
## Time to Explain Extension to the World

AS ALREADY EXPERIENCED with the Yearbook, I had other time consuming assignments that cut into the time and efforts of my regular job. One of these was writing Occupational Briefs number 92 which described the work of USDA's Extension Service. These "Briefs" are illustrated publications that are disseminated by Science Research Associates, Inc. and represent "America's Job Fields." The subject of this particular publication was "Agricultural and Home Economics Extension Workers" with the notation that this Brief "represents original research." I was listed as the author.

I began the text with:

*"A school, nationwide but without a classroom, a teacher who comes to your home or gives you directions by telephone, no armload of books, no homework assignments! Sound unreal? Well, it isn't. It's a unique educational system operating in every state, with an enrollment of 12.5 million families.*

*The school is the Cooperative Extension Service; the student, anyone with an agricultural or home economics problem; the teacher, the agricultural or home economics extension worker. This worker may be one of several people: the county agricultural agent, also known as Extension agent, or farm adviser; the home demonstration agent or home adviser; the 4-H Club agent; or an assistant to any one of these."*

*The brief (mentioned above) explains that the Cooperative Extension Service was established in 1914 (by the Smith-Lever Act) as a joint educational project along with the State land-grant college system (created by The Morrill Land-Grant College Act of 1862).*

*This combination proved to be a perfect complement to each other. State Extension Service Offices, State Extension Directors and various Extension Specialists, e.g., agronomy, livestock, marketing, agricultural economics, home economics, horticulture, and entomology are normally located at our Land-Grant Colleges and Universities. State Extension Service offices and Specialists are sources of guidance and information for County Extension Agents, Home Demonstration Agents, and 4-H Club Agents in all states.*

*Note: The Morrill Act provided grants of land to states to finance the establishment of colleges specializing in "agriculture and the mechanic arts." Some states sold the land to establish new schools; other states gave the money to existing state or private colleges to create schools of agriculture and mechanic arts. These became known as "A&M" colleges, e.g., Texas A&M. Military training was required from the start for all land-grant schools and this led to the establishment of the Reserve Officers Training Corps. This educational program led to future Army, Navy, and Air Force officers.*

*The Cooperative Extension Service was designed to teach agriculture, home economics, and related subjects to the public (primarily farm people) in each state. CES performed especially great service during the depression, providing assistance to make it through this difficult period when many people did not have enough to eat. Extension helped ensure that sufficient food was produced and distributed to those who needed it the most. They also assisted with loans for small landowners and helped deal with the educational needs of rural youth.*

*Duties of Extension people in modern times have been expanding and agents are being called upon more and more to help nonfarm families. They are becoming increasingly involved in providing advice on gardening, landscaping, and food safety and quality, as well as more advanced across the spectrum issues such as pest management, sustainable agriculture, waste management and revitalizing rural America.*

# CHAPTER 14
## A Sudden Change at the Top

I WAS WELL into my second year at FES when we got the news that our Director of Information was retiring. Since he had been a supportive and knowledgeable boss, all of us regretted seeing him leave. Except for the FES newsletter which went out under his name, I had not had a great deal of direct contact with him. He depended on Bryan Phifer, his second in command, to handle the details of much of our work. But I had great respect for his professionalism and management skills.

His replacement, for some strange reason (at least to me) was a Dairy

Specialist--not a trained and experienced Communications Specialist we had ex-pected. *Politics just might have entered the picture somewhere in this selection--not unusual for Washington, DC.* The new boss's name was Elmer Winner. He was an affable man and I expected no trouble with him. *It turned out that my optimism was not warranted in this case.*

The first sign that trouble lay ahead was when I wrote a draft of the FES Newsletter and submitted it to Mr. Winner for his review and o.k. He rejected it outright and asked me to rewrite it. This surprised me since his predecessor, a professional jour-nalist, had always reviewed and approved my drafts, usually without change and with complimentary comments.

With total rejection of my first draft, I discovered that Mr. Winner's idea of com-munication was quite different from mine and that of the former director. I thought (and the previous director agreed) that the newsletter should be readable and inter-esting. Winner favored a style of writing that was long winded, used lots of big words, and was full of technical jargon.

After several attempts I realized that I would not be able to please him, so I sug-gested that Ed Roche might be a better choice to reflect his style. Ed had been in the bureaucracy longer than I and spoke the jargon better. He turned out to be a good choice and I escaped that chore.

# CHAPTER 15

## A Busy Last Year at FES

WITHOUT THE BURDEN of writing the newsletter, I went on a roll. Soon, I com-pleted another Extension Service section for the 1960 USDA Yearbook. This section was less painful since I had learned how to deal better with the economists. I was no longer in awe of them and refused to allow them to have me running back and forth from specialist to specialist. I told them to iron out their differences with each other until they reached agreement. That allowed me time to put the finishing touches on the Public Relations publication, the final one of the trio Dr. Phifer had envisioned.

In addition to my other duties, Dr. Phifer told me to be prepared to handle two especially significant events occurring in Washington DC during that year. These events, both involving national news coverage, were the "Annual National 4-H Conference" and the highly publicized "1960 White House Council on Children and Youth." Both of these involved the White House.

The first big event was the "National 4-H Convention" held the summer of 1959 while children were out of school. The highlight of this Conference, as far as news coverage was concerned was an event held at the White House. I took a USDA staff photographer with me to get photos of the 4-H Club attendees who were meeting the President in the Rose Garden. President Eisenhower circulated around and shook hands with everyone and allowed photographers to take pictures of him with the 4-H members. *(The staff photographer and I watched from a distance, since our job was selecting the best camera shots to be used later).*

As the White House event began, I was interviewing the State 4-H Representatives individually and making notes for articles about each one. By making this my top priority, I was able to complete my interviews and write feature articles about each state's 4-H representative. I then sent the articles and photos (with captions) to their state newspapers and magazines. As a result, the 4-H Club Convention received huge coverage both within their own states and nationally. The 4-H officials said they had not had this type of coverage at previous conventions.

The second, and even bigger event, was President Eisenhower's "1960 White House Conference on Children and Youth." Although I did not realize the significance of my involvement at first, the opportunity to participate in it came about in an unusual way. I was told that the Federal personnel offices had scoured the personnel records of government information types to see who, if any, had actual newspaper experience and could help publicize the event. I was one of the few Federal employees selected.

I didn't know quite what to expect when told I would be writing articles for this big affair. When I reached the Sheraton Park Hotel and saw the Conference newsroom I was suitably impressed. There must have been 50 or more desks set up, each with a telephone and typewriter. Someone (I don't remember who) gave us a short briefing on what was expected of us. We were told that Federal, State, and local officials as well as other designated people would provide us with information relevant to the Conference. It would be our job to quickly prepare newspaper type articles from this raw information.

The briefer said we would receive most of the information by telephone but could expect an occasional visitor with information. When the briefing was concluded, I was escorted to my desk which contained a telephone and manual typewriter (that's what we all used back then!). I immediately noticed something different about my typewriter: it was equipped with a roll of newsprint paper instead of sheets of typing paper. This was reminiscent of my days as a "real" reporter.

Using rolls of newsprint paper was designed to save time. When a story was finished, it was torn from the roll and taken to an editor without the person doing the typing having to remove a completed sheet and insert a fresh one. And to ensure that the reporter wouldn't have to stop typing to tear off the writing and take it to the editor, each of us was provided a personal "runner" to do this for us. All we had to do was formulate an article, type it, and hold up a hand to summon the runner who would tear off the article and "run" it to an editor. Once I was settled at my desk, the phone started ringing and I was furiously taking notes. When I got a break from the phone calls, I began writing the stories and at the end of each, I would hold up my hand and the "runner" would be at my desk within seconds, to tear off the story and take it to an editor. This continued throughout each day except for an occasional break.

At the first break in this marathon of writing, I met my "neighbors" who had been following the same routine. On my left the reporter introduced himself as working for "WashPost", i.e. The Washington Post. The person to my right said he worked for "The Times." Even this country boy knew without asking that he meant The New York Times. I looked around and didn't see a single person I recognized and deduced that few if any of the Federal Information people had made the cut.

When the conference ended, I was told that I more than held my own in competition with the "big city" newspaper reporters. I was especially grateful for the fast typing speed I had gained in the U.S. Navy's Yeoman School as well as for the experience I had received in the newsroom at the Orlando Sentinel, where I sometimes wrote as many as 50 stories in one 8 hour session.

*On a personal note, I became good friends with my "runner," Miss Pam Templeton, a recent graduate of Fairleigh Dickinson University in New Jersey. We began seeing each other and she invited me to accompany her to Florham Park, NJ, to spend a weekend at her parents' home. They took us to dinner at Jack Dempsey's Restaurant in Manhattan, and later to a Broadway show. Although no serious romance developed for the two of us, Pam and I remained in contact for many years.*

After the conference, I learned that President Eisenhower's 1960 White House conference had some lasting effects. One of these was establishing the Council of National Organizations for Children and Youth (NCCY), a national coordinating council serving some 400 individual youth and children service providers and State Committees for Children and Youth. This committee within the national council, serves as an information clearinghouse, and acts as liaison between federal agencies and regional and state child-service providers.

A big concern of the NCCY was the glaring lack of literacy among many of the nation's youth. As a result of this concern, remedial reading programs were established for young teens who greatly needed to improve their reading skills. This effort has involved cooperation between independent agencies, e.g. The U.S. Department of Labor's Manpower Administration, local schools, and social workers. *(Imagine the literacy problems we would have today without this program!)*

Although I didn't learn this until later, the 1960 conference attracted more than 7,000 participants, drawn from every state and territory in the U.S. *I was so busy gathering information and typing I had no idea that so many people participated.*

# CHAPTER 16

## The Beginning of the End at FES

AS I WAS still feeling the glow of success from the second big conference, I was summoned to Elmer Winner's office. I foolishly thought he was going to tell me he was putting me in for a GS-13 so that I would have the same grade as the other professionals in the office. Indeed, he began by praising me for my good work saying my recent work at both the 4-H Club Conference and the 1960 White House Council on Children and Youth was "exceptional."

Then, he told me that although he was happy with the quality and quantity of my work, he was dissatisfied with my work habits. I asked him what the problem was with my work habits and he said, "I see you taking lots of coffee breaks." He mentioned other professionals who never took a break and sat at their desks all day long. I was stunned to hear this criticism since no supervisor had ever criticized my work habits.

I replied: "Elmer, when I'm at my desk I think hard and work hard and produce lots of copy. However, with this hard thinking and effort I need to get away from my desk a few minutes to refresh my brain. That's why I need to take a couple of coffee breaks a day." I started to add, "Some of those folks you mention, who never take a break from their desks also don't seem to produce much. None of these 'desk bound people' you seem to admire has conducted any training, produced any publications, written anything for the Agriculture Yearbook, covered any National Conferences or done anything else of substance that I'm aware of."

Thankfully, I did not say anything of the sort. *But I recalled that Ed Roche and I had chuckled over the fact that one of those he mentioned was responsible for a monthly newsletter to inform State and Federal specialists about various aspects of his area of expertise. Ed had a copy of a letter this specialist wrote to state and federal officials apologizing for not sending out a single newsletter the previous year! To make up for this failure, he promised to write and send out 18 newsletters the following year.*

*After that year ended again without a newsletter, his next letter began: "It has been 13 months since I last contacted you . . ." Ed and I laughed so hard I could hardly say, "I guess he'll promise them 24 newsletters the coming year!"*

Before leaving Winner's office, I decided to face my future prospects head on and asked: "Will my work habits affect my chances of promotion?" He dodged that direct question and replied instead: "Jim, I admit that most of the work you do is top notch and at the GS-13 level but some of your assignments are at the GS-12 level; therefore, I can't promise you a promotion at this time."

Since by then I had spent almost three years with the Federal Extension Service and now had a boss who didn't approve of my work habits, I knew that my career aspirations there were thin and none. It was obvious that Winner preferred people who sat at their desks all day and produced little of value to a high producer who left his desk a couple of times a day for a cup of coffee. It reminded me of the publisher back at the Orlando (FL) Sentinel who had a similar view. It was time to look elsewhere.

It was late 1960 when I left Winner's office. Instead of going back to my desk I continued on down the hall to the Agricultural Research Service (ARS) office where several friends worked. I told them I was interested in changing jobs and one of them took me to the office of the Director of Information at ARS, Bob Rathbone.

I told Bob I was interested in leaving Extension and asked if he had any openings. He told me they had no GS-13 vacancies, but they would like to have me if I would take a lateral transfer as a GS-12. I immediately accepted the offer and by the end of the year I had parted company with FES. *Although the general rule in government is never to accept a lateral, I broke that rule twice—both times it worked to my advantage.* As I was becoming familiar with my new job requirements at ARS, friends at the FES office invited me back to meet my successor and I went to his office to wish him luck. I found he was a really likable black man. After some small talk, he volunteered: "Jim, I know you got a raw deal here. When you left, they divided your job into two positions: one a GS-13, which they gave me, and a GS-12 for a younger person with little experience." After apologizing again for the way I was treated he added: "Since they wanted a minority in here, I thought I would be as good as anyone else." *I was pleased they selected a quality minority person and I did not begrudge him the position.*

*The fact that the agency now had two people to do the work I was doing alone spoke volumes of how the political (and political correctness) game in Washington was played--even back in the 60's. However, again this seeming setback in my career turned out to be a blessing in disguise.*

# CHAPTER 17

## A Fresh Start in an Exciting New Job

AT ARS, I was assigned to an elite group of Information Officers who provided support for a variety of Federal/State Cooperative Programs. My assignment was with Plant Pest Control (PPC), with headquarters in Hyattsville, Maryland. This agency had responsibility for dealing with foreign pest invaders--with the goal of eradicating them before they could become established in the U.S. or in a new area of the country if efforts to eradicate them failed.

PPC turned out to be the one agency in USDA with the most controversial Federal-State Cooperative Programs. And the most controversial of the 21 programs under PPC's purview was the Imported Fire Ant Program (IFA). That was the one that needed my urgent attention. *Lucky me!* Other programs assigned to me included: The Gypsy Moth, Grasshopper, Pink Boll Worm, Boll Weevil, Golden Nematode, and approximately 15 other foreign pests already present or that would come along later (e.g., the Mediterranean Fruit Fly).

Val Weyl was Branch Chief of the group I was assigned to which included several Public Information Officers, plus a talented artist, Bob Fones; radio and radio/TV specialist Vince Marcley, plus several other support personnel. Although I was already familiar with some of the media I needed to use because of my work as a news reporter, the radio work I did at the University of Illinois and publications I prepared at FES, I realized quickly that I had much more to learn.

I was grateful that ARS had competent professionals to assist me in preparing exhibits, posters, and (especially) movies since I had little or no experience with these type media. Since it was up to each Information Officer to develop his own information program that included all forms of communication, this offered me a great opportunity to enhance my qualifications. Thank goodness I inherited a movie about the Imported Fire Ant to start with, along with some outdated publications about this pest. And the main USDA Information Office had professionally trained movie script editors, photographers and other ex-Hollywood types to assist us with any additional materials we might need.

Other Information Officers who operated on the front lines, included the following:

**Ken Goodrich**, who handled the screwworm information program. This program not only involved cooperation with several border states and the Federal Government, but also Mexico. Ken and his family eventually moved to Mexico City for five years so he could be in daily contact with Mexican officials involved in the program to eradicate or control this destructive enemy of cattle. Through USDA efforts, the screwworm was confined to an area around Mission, Texas, but was a potential threat to the entire cattle industry in the USA. It was already a major problem for cattle in Mexico.

**Larry Mark,** who arrived about a month after I did, was initially assigned to preparing and conducting information efforts dealing exclusively with swine brucellosis. Later after serious outbreaks of hog cholera, this program also became his responsibility. He had to deal with outbreaks throughout the nation but especially in midwest states where swine, soybeans and corn were the principal crops.

**Mike Bay,** who was primarily responsible for the cattle brucellosis information program; Mike had earlier been responsible for handling both the cattle and swine brucellosis program until Larry joined the group.

**George Beshore**, who handled information for the Plant Pest Quarantine (PPQ) program. If you've traveled across country or overseas, you have probably been involved with PPQ inspectors looking for illegal plant or animal products. Many of the promotional and/or informational pieces used in airports, ports, and some state inspection stations were probably initially prepared by George. He also developed a stylized bug symbol used to signify Plant Quarantine for many years.

All of the "front line" Information Officers had had professional experience with either or both newspapers and magazines and other media. And when not traveling, we were encouraged to take coffee breaks together and exchange ideas. We would not only solve the problems of the world but help each other solve work related problems.

# CHAPTER 18

## A New Fun Place to Live

SINCE LARRY MARK had just arrived in the DC area and was temporarily staying with his sister, he needed a more permanent place to stay. I had been thinking about moving to a more "active" apartment complex, so we discussed moving to the same location. We were both single and shared common interests, e.g. attending parties, meeting girls, dancing and listening to jazz music. After some discussion and looking, we decided on Arlington Towers, an "extremely active" singles complex which had earned the title: "Northern Virginia's Peyton Place."

Both of us ended up in the "Jefferson" building, with Larry selecting an apartment on the 7th floor while I selected one on the 10th floor. Another single male friend of ours, Bill Tarpening, younger than either of us, moved into another Arlington Towers building and soon became a regular partier with us. Bill provided entertainment at our parties by singing and playing the guitar. Unfortunately, he was just learning to play the guitar and had a limited repertoire. His favorite song was: "99 Beers On The Wall." *Boy, did that get the party going! Ugh!*

Arlington Towers was not only a good place to have fun, its location was ideal for nearby entertainment and work. It was a football field length from Key Bridge, which led directly to Georgetown, with its plentiful supply of fine restaurants and bars. It was also in sight of Memorial Bridge which led to the National Mall where much free entertainment was usually available. Some of the most inspiring entertainment we enjoyed on or around the Mall, included performances by the National Symphony Orchestra, as well as components of the U.S. Navy, Air Force, Marine and Army bands.

Our location near the Mall, offered us easy access to other events, such as the Smithsonian Folklife Festival, A Capitol Fourth Concert, and a Fireworks Display held on the Mall. There was rarely a time when good entertainment was not available free to the public. Memorial Bridge also led to various Federal buildings including: the USDA South Building (where Larry and I worked), the USDA Administration Building, the U.S. Treasury Building, the Energy Department's Forestal Building, and the Smithsonian Museum of Natural History which was only a block away from the South Building. Continuing straight down Independence Ave. just a few more blocks, you could see the U.S. Senate, U.S. House, and U.S. Supreme Court buildings.

The Washington Monument is visible from the northwest side of the South Building. There were many interesting places, including great seafood restaurants, e.g. The Flagship, Hogates, et al, on the Wharf, within walking distance of our workplace when our busy schedules permitted.

During the early period at ARS, realizing that Larry Mark and I shared a love of music, especially jazz, I had taken him to the Showboat Lounge to listen to and meet Tee Carson and his Trio. Tee had recently told me that he had become physically exhausted by playing at the Showboat Lounge until after midnight, getting to bed at around 2 a.m.

and then having to wake up at 6 a.m. to go to his regular job as a U. S. Marshal. His doctor told him he had to either give up playing music or his regular job--that his body couldn't continue to function with the little amount of sleep he was getting.

Tee's exhaustion was very visible to me the night Larry and I visited. However, nothing seemed to affect his fine piano playing. Tee later told me he had discussed his health situation with Charlie Byrd, and Charlie advised him to give up his day job; that he would give him enough work so that he wouldn't need to work as a U.S. Marshal. Tee's new job at a higher salary would involve more hours playing, plus becoming the regular Master of Ceremonies (MC) at Showboat.

Besides being a great musician, it turned out that Tee was a natural as the MC; he had a silken voice, a cool, easy manner with guests, and a highly sophisticated knowledge of music. Broadly intelligent, he had studied performance music at a major university while also studying engineering. *He even worked as a professional engineer for a short time after graduating from college! But the love of music won him over.*

The change suggested by Byrd seemed to be mutually beneficial to both Tee and the Showboat Lounge. Tee's health rapidly improved and he was doing a great job playing the piano and being MC. Then, just before Christmas that year Tee called me at the office in a panic saying that Byrd had found a cheaper piano player and had let him go. I was angered by hearing this and felt Tee had been betrayed. But I felt help-less to do anything for him since I did not have a single business connection with the music industry. *As I recall, since he had resigned instead of taking leave, Tee could not immediately get his old job back although he did eventually return to work as a U.S. Marshal and retained the job despite many leaves of absence until he retired.*

By a stroke of good luck, however, friend Larry Mark had recently mentioned to me that he had heard that Webber's Char House, a popular eating place within walking distance of Arlington Towers, was considering opening up a music room in its walkout basement. Although I had eaten at the Char House, I had never met the owner, Bill Webber. After work that day I drove to the Char House and asked to meet him. I told Webber that I had heard a rumor that he might be opening a music room. He said he was considering the idea but hadn't made a final decision.

I volunteered that if he decided to open up a music room, I had the perfect musi-cian for him and that I thought the area would support a high quality music room. I then gave him a brief oral resume of my musician friend, mentioning his contacts and musical and MC talents.

Bill Webber gave me his card and asked me to tell Tee to get in touch with him. I gave Tee the card and the two of them got together soon afterward. Tee was playing "cocktail" music at the Char House by Christmas.

*Oh, by the way, I had failed to tell Webber that Tee was black because I never thought of him in racial terms with one exception which I'll explain. It was well known that Tee was considerably more affluent than his black neighbors. He had a music recording studio with valuable recording equipment. Thus, despite his best efforts to secure his home, he was often the victim of burglaries. He was also concerned about the safety of his young son, Donald, and his wife, Jan.*

*Fed up with the situation, Tee decided he would like to move to a suburban neighborhood, i.e., a "white" neighborhood in northern Virginia. However, when he tried to submit applications he had not been successful. We both knew the reason for that. This was before "fair housing" laws were fully in effect and some parts of Virginia still practiced segregation. I was offended that a person of his quality was being kept from living in a nice, safe neighborhood because of his skin color. So, I offered to be an intermediary for him. We looked at some nice, new developments together but Tee ultimately decided to stay where he was. I got the feeling that one reason he backed out was because he was fearful that I might suffer some adverse reactions for helping him.*

Before long, business was so good at the Char House music room, that Bill Webber allowed Tee to bring his full Trio to work there. The Trio at the time consisted of Tee, drummer Bertell Knox, and bassist Wilbur Little. Then Wilbur moved to New York and was replaced by Keter Betts. There was no loss of quality with that exchange. Keter had played with some of the top bands in the country. I once read that he was one of the most "sought after bass players in the country" as a recording studio bass player.

# CHAPTER 19

## Great Jazz Only a Short Walk Away!

THE CHAR HOUSE music room became a regular night time hangout for me, Larry and other friends who appreciated live jazz by world class musicians. Tee once told me that he originally planned to stay there for no more than a year but remained for three years adding, "It was one of the most pleasant gigs I've ever played."

I asked him once if the fact that he was playing nightly in the state of Virginia, where segregation was still prevalent, had ever caused him a problem. He replied: "Only once in three years; one night a guy who had had too much to drink asked Bill Webber why that 'nigger' was sitting at a table with white folks." Bill Webber said: "Because he was invited to sit with them." He said Webber then told the man, "You're no longer welcome in this music room."

Back at work, the new job gave me an opportunity to travel extensively and to meet many high level officials at both the State and Federal levels. And most importantly, it was providing me a chance to improve my communication skills in a variety of ways. Also, soon after my arrival at ARS, I was asked to take a non-work assignment to represent ARS on a committee to plan the annual weekend party for all the information people at USDA.

*All that is, but female employees!* I had never attended this event precisely because of what I had heard about it. Not only were females not allowed, friends had told me the annual party consisted of "adult only" entertainment, plus lots of drinking, card playing and cigar smoking. As busy as I was, I accepted the assignment, hoping to make some changes.

At our first planning meeting, I voiced my objection to a "males only" party. I then expressed the opinion that the "adult only" type of entertainment was not appropriate for our group. After a good bit of discussion (and a few heated arguments), a majority of the committee voted to try a different kind of annual "get together." I finally got the majority to agree to a new set of rules and a one year trial of a dinner-dance at one of the better restaurant/night clubs in DC.

The new rules stated that "all" information employees and their dates, wives or husbands would be invited to attend. That dinner-dance celebration went over so well that as far as I know USDA never again had a "males only" annual party. Although a few people voiced their disapproval of the changes, most agreed that it was past time to change to a non-discriminatory celebration with some class. Not being a "joiner" anyway, I then dropped off the planning committee. Mission accomplished.

When we were not traveling, PPC Information Officers used the time to prepare new information materials or to revise old materials about the pest programs assigned to us. Of course, we always had to be prepared for emergencies when a dangerous new foreign pest was discovered in the country (or a new area of the country). At any moment, depending on our assignment, we were expected to jump on a plane and go wherever we were needed to provide public information about the pest, its dangers, and treatment programs which (in my case) often involved airplanes spraying dangerous pesticides over fields, houses, towns and cities.

Once on the scene, I would usually be asked to serve as spokesperson for the State and Federal governments before and during the treatment period. Many government officials tried to find a hiding place when it came to dealing with the public and media regarding controversial programs. *I must have been naive or dumb to accept these assignments that my cohorts managed to avoid!*

As already mentioned, my most demanding and controversial program by far was the Imported Fire Ant (IFA) eradication program. This large red ant, a native of Argentina, entered the U.S. from a ship anchored in the Port of Mobile, Alabama. It apparently came ashore when baggage was unloaded. Since they had no "natural" enemies here, they quickly established a colony in the Mobile area and gradually began spreading throughout the southeastern states. As the ant colonies grew, they adapted faster to different climates and spread more rapidly. By the time I was assigned to this program, the ants were already established in Alabama, Louisiana, Mississippi and Georgia and were reaching into the Carolinas.

The IFA is sometimes confused with the smaller and much less fearsome native fire ant. The IFA stings and bites are much more serious and their mounds are sometimes several feet higher than the mounds built by their smaller cousins. The IFA mounds can cause major problems to livestock, farm equipment, planting and harvesting work. The ants' stings and bites can be extremely dangerous to people and livestock when the mounds are disturbed. IFA stings cause large welts and people who are allergic to them can die from multiple stings if not hospitalized in time. There are also documented cases of livestock dying from imported fire ant stings when they stumbled and fell into a fire ant mound.

# CHAPTER 20
## My battle with Rachel Carson and "Silent Spring"

ALTHOUGH I WASN'T aware of her when I started my new job, I soon became very familiar with one name: Rachel Carson of "Silent Spring" fame. I quickly found out that she was bitterly opposed to all the USDA/State programs using powerful chemicals sprayed from the air. But the imported fire ant was her favorite target. *Wasn't I lucky!*

Wikipedia, in discussing this subject says, "...By 1959, the USDA's Agricultural Research Service responded to the criticism by Carson and others with a public service film, "Fire Ants on Trial"; Carson called the movie 'flagrant propaganda' that ignored the dangers that spraying pesticides posed to humans and wildlife." That spring, Carson wrote a letter, published in The Washington Post, that attributed the recent decline in bird populations--in her words the "silencing of birds"-- to pesticide overuse.

"Flagrant propaganda" or not, the fact that the film **"Fire Ants On Trial"** had already been produced saved me much time and effort. It was an excellent film and I made good use of it. However, you can see that with this one program, I had stepped into a big mess on my exciting new job. When her book "Silent Spring" was published in September 1962, criticism of our spray program reached a fever pitch. *And it was my job to calm the waters!*

I felt that Ms. Carson was highly exaggerating the effect of our spray programs. Others more immediately involved as decision makers in our pest control programs were outraged at her charges and decided that the incidents cited by Ms. Carson needed to be investigated. They asked and I agreed to be part of the "investigative team." Our team investigated many of the incidents described by Ms. Carson in her book and found that they were either exaggerated or in some cases, made up completely. I wrote up the results of our investigation but cooler heads made the decision that our findings might just stir up more trouble and were never published. *Sorry, I didn't keep a copy!*

That was not quite the end of the story for me, however. Progressive Farmer Magazine, one of the top farm publications in the country, apparently heard about our investigation and requested that USDA send me to the Mississippi Delta to write a feature article for their magazine reflecting the pesticide/wildlife situation there. I was given the assignment with the provisions that neither I nor the USDA would be identified as the source of the article.

I traveled to the town of Greenville, MS, near the majestic Mississippi River. This area was one of the top agriculture producing areas in the nation. If widespread losses of birds and other wildlife occurred because of the heavy use of pesticides, it should be in the Mississippi Delta. Of course I didn't find any such thing. Blackbirds and starlings sometimes darkened the skies over the fields. And when we drove around the countryside, we saw and heard song birds in abundance. Deer were so numerous that they constituted a pest. I gathered first hand information and headed back to my office to write the article.

My lead to the story was: "Spring is not 'silent' in the Mississippi Delta!" I went on to describe the heavy pesticide uses in the Delta and the abundant wildlife there. Progressive Farmer used the article and photographs supplied by a Greenville photographer without change. Shortly afterward, they sent me a check for several hundred dollars. I returned the check, explaining that I couldn't personally accept money for writing the article since I was a government employee.

*The magazine was allowed to pay the government for my travel and other expenses, however. And as an expression of their gratitude to me, they sent me a copy of several books they had recently published including The Progressive Farmer's "Southern Cookbook." This wonderful cookbook featured "Southern Food Ways." Although my copy is coming apart because of use and years, it is still a cherished part of my collection of cookbooks.*

Back to our investigation, although we determined that the incidents described by Ms. Carson were largely nonexistent, something good came about from the bad publicity generated by our spray programs. The Agricultural Research Service decided to design a monitoring program that would provide objective information about the effects of pesticide use. The monitoring program began at five locations--two in Arkansas and three in Mississippi. One of the study areas was the Mississippi Delta--where I wrote the earlier feature article for Progressive Farmer. Later I returned to the Delta to prepare a "Picture Story" describing the monitoring program with text and photos. The title was "Teamwork On The Delta," with the subheading of "ARS scientists study the impact of pesticides on the environment."

Giving myself permission to "steal" my own words, I wrote: "The heavily farmed Mississippi River Delta is being studied by the U.S. Department of Agriculture to learn more about residues resulting from normal agricultural use of pesticides. By recording the pesticides used in a representative area, and chemically analyzing samples of soil, water, crops, livestock, and wildlife taken from those areas, researchers hope to determine the rate of accumulation or depletion of residues."

I went on to describe how the "field team" gathered samples of soil, water, sediment, crops and certain land and water animals to be studied by a laboratory in Gulfport, MS, where they were chemically analyzed for pesticide content. The "Picture Story" was printed on slick paper and consisted of 10 pages with over 20 illustrations and carried the notation that "magazines and newspapers may obtain glossy prints of these photographs in any size up to 8X10." Others could purchase these prints at very reasonable rates. *Surprisingly, I found an original copy of the text.*

# CHAPTER 21
## Don't Throw Me into that Briar Patch!

IF YOU'VE READ this far, you know that I inherited some extremely sensitive and difficult programs most of which were located in the South. Decisions about the Imported Fire Ant Program, along with several other foreign pests were made at the USDA Southern Regional Office in Gulfport, Mississippi, with approval and guidance from Federal PPC headquarters in Hyattsville, MD. The Director of the Regional Office, Mr. William (Bill) Fancher, wanted me to visit his headquarters at least once each month to discuss priorities since I could not be at all the places I was needed at once.

Many people dreaded having to visit this extremely sleepy little village often. Since gambling casinos had not yet arrived, Gulfport at that time was one of the dullest places around. When I started going there, I had one place to stay: an old run-down hotel and one decent eating place--if you happened to like deep fried seafood.

People who had visited Gulfport probably wondered why I didn't complain about being asked to spend so much time there. Why, like Brer Rabbit, did I not say: "Don't throw me into that briar patch"? The reason? Because the sleepy little town of Gulfport is located about one hour away from the great, fun-loving city of New Orleans, Louisiana--one of my favorite cities in the USA. Flights from Washington DC to Gulfport required a stop at New Orleans! You get the picture.

Since the IFA was spreading rapidly throughout the South, many of my early assignments involved that pest. Once a decision was made by Mr. Fancher as to the area to be treated, my job was to go to the town or city in advance of the treatment program and prepare to put the best face possible on the treatment. This could be difficult in view of the fact that we were going to use low flying planes to spray highly toxic chemicals over towns and cities, ponds and lakes, livestock, pets, and even field workers who couldn't find shelter quickly enough--despite my public warnings.

And again, I had Rachel Carson to thank for some of that problem. Because of her crusade against DDT, we could no longer use that relatively safe chemical and were therefore forced to use two much more dangerous chemicals: Heptachlor or Chlordane. *I and most program officials considered DDT, which was widely used directly on the bodies of soldiers with no ill effect during World War II, much safer than the ones we were forced to use because of Rachel Carson's antipathy toward DDT.*

*So, I had no choice except to defend the use of these more toxic chemicals. I prayed we would come up with a safer alternative. This finally happened with the development of Mirex, a product that contained an attractant with a minute amount of a non-contact killing agent much less toxic than the two we had been using. Mirex was a wonderful chemical against the Imported Fire Ant for several reasons:*

(1) *Since the product included an ant attractant it did not require 100% coverage to be effective. It was designed to attract the worker ants which would take it back to the mound and feed it to the queen and babies killing them and thus, in a short time, ending that mound's existence.*

(2) *Only a tiny amount (1/10<sup></sup> of an ounce per acre) of the killing agent was required. Also, the active ingredient in Mirex was not highly toxic to humans, pets, or wildlife.*

(3) *It was environmentally friendly, i.e., it left little residue.*

Until the arrival of Mirex, however, I did the best I could to defend the use of heptachlor and chlordane applied at relatively high doses. And the fact is there were no documented cases of damage to wildlife, livestock, or humans from these applications.

*I soon developed a routine that worked for me. As soon as I arrived in a town to be treated, I met with State and Federal control officials to discuss strategy. Then I would visit with town officials, newspaper offices, and radio and/or TV stations to give them a personal briefing about the treatment program. I would try to re-assure them by emphasizing all the safety precautions taken to ensure the safety of people, pets, and farm animals. Then I would leave written material, including a schedule for treatments over a particular area and how I could be reached.*

Aside from the chemical agent itself, I was often concerned by the application mechanism, i.e., the condition of the aircraft being used to release the spray from the air. Sometimes the planes were so decrepit looking that I feared they might come apart and crash right into a city. Since the government usually accepted the "low bid" contract, this sometimes resulted in less than stellar planes being provided by the contractor. There was nothing I could personally do to get this corrected but sometimes my call to Washington resulted in a brief treatment delay while a better plane was flown to the site. Also, sometimes a plane wouldn't be able to take off and USDA officials could demand a plane in better condition. Fortunately no planes ever crashed on my watch.

During my visits to the print media, I would almost always be asked to personally write the articles that would appear in newspapers and magazines. And I had to be prepared to appear in person on radio and television stations to explain the treatment program. This made me grateful for the experience I gained as a newspaper reporter and as a graduate student required to produce a weekly radio program while at the University of Illinois.

As for the program itself, although our stated purpose was to eradicate this pest with our spray programs, seasoned pest control experts would privately express their doubts to me about this possibility. So, if I couldn't fully justify the concept of eradication in my own mind, I could rationalize the idea that, at the very least, we were slowing their rate of spread and reducing their numbers.

Before spraying actually started, I would get on the USDA "spotter plane" and we would ride around the spray area making notations of lakes, ponds and other sensitive areas to alert the spray plane pilots of places to avoid as best they could.

Despite this preliminary work, too often one of the planes would get careless or lost and spray a pond or lake, killing the fish. It was then up to me to try to placate the people affected by the accident.

# CHAPTER 22
## This Time I had Help Creating Catastrophe!

I WAS USUALLY the only Information Officer to handle a particular job but I remember one occasion when I was accompanied by the State of Georgia's Agriculture Commissioner's public relations man, Jack Gilchrist. The next area we were going to spray for Imported Fire Ants included the city of Columbus, Georgia. Jack was a friend of the Mayor of Columbus and thought he could ease tension about the treatment program if he went with me to personally brief his friend, the Mayor.

The meeting was cordial and the Mayor expressed only one major concern: a beautiful large lake at the edge of the city. He said this lake was the pride of the Columbus community and had just been freshly stocked with fish. We assured the Mayor that we would make every effort to ensure that the spray planes stayed well away from the lake. In fact we assured him this area would be treated by hand.

You can guess what happened! Although the pilots were shown the lake on the map and warned not to fly close to it, one pilot got lost on his way back to the airport and dumped his full load of hydrocarbon pesticide which the wind carried over the lake. The next morning, dead fish dotted the surface of the lake. Jack and I immediately headed for the Mayor's office to apologize but the Mayor was inconsolable. We were glad to get out of that town. Although that incident at Columbus, GA was hard to forget, my frequent trips to Gulfport (and New Orleans) helped me live with that and other mistakes.

Since I was unattached, I soon developed a routine that most men would envy. At my request, our secretary would make my airplane reservation to New Orleans for late Friday afternoon with an "open" return. She would also make my "late arrival" reservation at the Roosevelt Hotel. I would bring my packed suitcase to the office that morning and at the end of the work day, I would take a cab to the airport and board a plane. This allowed me to spend the weekend at one of my favorite cities. When I arrived at the Roosevelt, I would check in, take my bags to the room, and then come back down to the Sazerac Lounge where I would sample their three trademark libations: *The Sazerac Cocktail, Ramos Gin Fizz, and Bayou Swizzle*. Then I would go back to my room to shower and dress for a night on the town.

# CHAPTER 23
## My Weekends in "The Big Easy"

MY NIGHTS WOULD usually consist of dinner at one of the city's fine restaurants (Commander's Palace was my favorite) and then find a place to dance or to enjoy live music. I often tried to catch Pete Fountain at his place but never succeeded because he was always on tour. I was able to catch Al Hirt in town occasionally. But even without the big stars, there were many places to enjoy good live music in New Orleans. Preservation Hall was just one of many such places. Pat O'Brien's never failed to entertain with live music and their famous "Hurricane" drink. *(As tasty as they are, don't have more than one of these if you expect to walk back to your hotel unassisted).*

The rest of the weekend I would enjoy Cafe Du Monde for its cafe au lait and beignets and many fine restaurants, including Felix's Oyster Bar, Brennan's, TuJaque's, Galatoire's and Antoine's and many others, all within walking distance of the Roosevelt. *And even the known "tourist trap" restaurants in New Orleans serve great food!* And there was always Royal Street barely a block from Bourbon Street and the French Quarter. Royal Street is famous for its wonderful antique shops and fine art galleries. The street is a shopping and dining mecca along with its street vendors, musicians, and artists. You never know what surprises you might run into on this busy street

A dinner jazz cruise aboard the Steamboat Natchez was also a great way to spend an evening listening to music and dancing. It was easy to meet people on those cruises and I usually found good dance partners. I dated a few ladies I had met and danced with on evening cruises. One of these was a beautiful young lady, a native of Honduras. I once attended a dance with her where all the attendees but me appeared to be Hispanic. I thought I could dance most popular Hispanic dances, e.g., the rumba, mambo, cha cha cha, and meringue until I saw the native Latinos dance them. *Seeing them dance caused me to leave the dance floor and watch.*

*After an enjoyable weekend, early Monday morning I would take a rental car to Gulfport to start my work week. Sometimes I would return to Washington before taking my next out-of-town trip to "put out a fire." At other times, I would need to leave from Gulfport directly to another town or state to deal with problems there. Although I usually packed for one full week, sometimes my job demands kept me away for as long as a month.*

One such emergency trip occurred when I was spending a week in Mississippi working on the pink bollworm program. A heavy outbreak of this pest had flared up and was causing heavy damage to that state's large cotton crop in the Delta area. As I was finishing up there and making plans to return home for the weekend, I received an urgent phone call from Plant Pest Control officials at Hyattsville saying that an outbreak of the dreaded Mediterranean Fruit Fly (Medfly) had just been discovered in the Miami/Fort Lauderdale area of Florida.

# CHAPTER 24

## An Emergency Trip to Miami

BEFORE I GOT off the telephone, the top PPC people at Hyattsville urged me to drop everything and catch the first available flight to South Florida. Mississippi State officials took me to their office at the State Capital in Jackson so I could make flight arrangements. There, I scheduled a flight and obtained a motel room for later that evening after I arrived in Miami. And, equally important, I was able to obtain an old brochure on the Medfly from Mississippi officials. Although the brochure was prepared in 1950 when the Medfly last invaded the U.S., it was a life saver to me. I knew nothing about this citrus pest except I had heard it could devastate Florida's valuable citrus crop if not stopped immediately. With information provided by PPC Headquarters in Maryland, I re-wrote the publication during the flight and sent the revised version to Washington for a quick reprinting before going to bed that evening. *This time the GPO proved they could act quickly when motivated and I received copies of the revised brochure in the matter of a few short days.*

I was on the scene at Opa-locka Airport, headquarters for the Medfly Eradication Program, by 6 a.m. the next morning and for the next three weeks. The program manager took me to a desk and told me that all telephone calls from the media, public officials, and the general public would be routed through me. He said he did not want to risk different people providing different answers. This was a bit of a shock to me since I had assumed I would just be handling the media. I mentioned that I was not familiar with the Medfly, and that I had just become aware of this pest the day before I arrived. The manager was adamant, however. "I want us to have one voice and that voice will be yours," he stated emphatically.

This meant I had to "get up to speed" in a hurry. The mixture of Malathion and soy base was touted as being very safe for humans and other mammals and that became my mantra. Safety was a major concern since we would be applying the Medfly killing agent over the cities of Miami, Miami Beach, and Fort Lauderdale on a seven-day cycle. The treatment mixture had one drawback: it could cause great damage to the paint on General Motors cars. If washed off fairly quickly it would not cause problems for Ford and Chrysler vehicles. (Note: There were not enough foreign made cars in the U.S. at that time to be concerned about them).

So, I began every day at 6 a.m. by studying the spray map and discussing the schedule (and any special anticipated problems) with the manager. After that I began calling all the local newspapers, radio and TV stations to give them that day's schedule for spraying and to emphasize any needed precautions to protect their automobiles and "clothes washings" from the spray. *Incredibly, even as late as 1960 some people were still putting their freshly washed linens and clothing on clothes lines to dry!*

Another important job was to keep in close contact with all the automobile dealers in the area to make sure they were aware that the Malathion mixture could cause heavy paint pitting for General Motors automobiles (Cadillacs especially) but could be washed off without damaging the paint of Ford and Chrysler products if done quickly enough, i.e. within a day. Dealers who handled all makes of cars were advised to cover them to avoid having to wash the "nasty" stuff off their cars before the hot July sun made it more difficult to remove. I also made sure the dealers had the telephone number where I could be reached so I could provide them with the up-to-date schedules of spraying in their particular area.

We had one catastrophe caused by the Malathion while I was on the job at Miami. The largest Cadillac dealer called me to find out when the next spraying would occur. I told him that his spray was five days away. Imagine my horror when he called me the following day around noon to tell me that 20 brand new Cadillacs which had arrived the previous day and were parked outside the dealership uncovered had been sprayed with our chemical. I told him I would call him right back and went to investigate what happened. The manager and I queried all the spray pilots and found that one of them, on the way back to the airport at daybreak, spotted a line of ornamental trees and finished unloading his tank of chemical mix on them. He did not notice the line of shiny, new Cadillacs parked behind the row of trees. I called the dealer back to give him all the information I had, apologized profusely, and assured him I would contact the proper officials in Washington who would handle the problem. After returning to DC, I learned that USDA paid thousands of dollars to get the new Cadillacs repainted.

A few days after my return, the manager who had been in charge of the Medfly program called to thank me for my help. He said that figures showed that the calls I had handled over the three week period averaged over 300 calls per day! And that did not include the outgoing calls I made to the media, car dealers and other special groups. Of course I could not have done that without (1) working from 6 a.m. until 6 p.m. daily and (2) had not the manager brought me a sandwich to eat at lunch while I continued to handle incoming calls. I was also proud of the fact that of all the abusive calls I received (mostly from Miami Beach), I had hung up on only one caller, a woman who said she hoped our planes would crash.

*One thing that made my time and efforts bearable: one of the people I met at the Opa-locka Airport had a large experimental mango orchard and he would bring me some mangoes of different species on a daily basis. I would take them to my hotel room and stuff myself with these delicacies each night before going to bed. One thing that allowed us to be away for long periods of time was that the government supplied our group with credit cards to use while we were on the road. Access to these funds gave us the flexibility we needed to do our jobs! And, unlike some reported abuses by today's Federal workers, I never knew anyone to use the government credit cards for personal or illegal use.*

# CHAPTER 25

## A Party that Changed My Life!

SOON AFTER MY Medfly experience, Dave Griffith again invited me to the annual Navy Hydrographic Office party. This time I had no conflicts and accepted the invitation. He said we would be seated at a large table with our dates, plus two other couples. After we were seated with Dave on one end of the table and I at the other, I looked around the room and spotted a dark eyed, dark haired beauty. She was by far the most beautiful woman in the room of 200 or more people. And she was staring right back at me. I was wondering how I could meet her!

Then, as women often do, all the females at our table left to "powder their noses." As soon as they were out of sight, I saw the woman I had been staring at leave her table, come to the table where Dave was sitting and start whispering into his ear. I hurried to that end of the table to introduce myself to her. We chatted briefly until our dates were seen coming back to the table. I got her name: Gwen Hazleton, but didn't ask for her telephone number knowing that I could get the number from Dave when I would be able to write it down.

The climax of the evening came when the MC announced that it was time to transfer the reigning Beauty Queen's crown to her successor. It turned out that Gwen Hazleton was the reigning queen. I may be prejudiced but I didn't think her successor even came close to meeting Gwen's standards.

After dropping off my date, and returning to Arlington Towers, I called Dave at his house and asked: "What was Gwen whispering in your ear?" Dave responded: "She asked me, who is your red headed friend?" Without hesitation I said: "Dave, I need to get her telephone number from you." He replied: "Jim, you would be wasting your time. You're divorced and she is Roman Catholic. She won't go out with a divorced man. I've tried to date her several times." I persisted, however, and he reluctantly gave me her phone number.

I was up early the next morning but knew it was too early to call Gwen. After several cups of coffee and a light breakfast I called her at about 10 a.m. She had just returned from early mass. I asked her if I could pick her up at about 1 p.m. so we could drive down to Waldorf, Maryland. She readily agreed and gave me directions to the home she shared with her mother. Why Waldorf MD? At that time, Waldorf was a "wide open" town with legal gambling, alcohol and live entertainment, even on Sunday.

Gwen and I had a good time and I told her I was leaving the next morning on a week-long business trip to California but would call her as soon as I returned a week later. *I would be meeting with California Department of Food and Agriculture (CDFA) officials but had already arranged for a Saturday night stay in San Francisco so I wouldn't get back to Washington until late the following Sunday.*

That Saturday night in San Francisco was memorable. I knew that singer Carmen McRae was performing at "Jazz At The Black Hawk," one of my favorite jazz music rooms that featured top flight jazz musicians. I thought it would be nice to have a companion to share this anticipated fine entertainment. Having a drink at the bar just before leaving for the Black Hawk I met a lovely young woman who had just arrived from Los Angeles. We chatted for awhile, I found out she was also a music lover and invited her to go with me to the Black Hawk.

When we arrived at the jazz club, the Vince Guaraldi Trio (who I had never heard of before) was playing backup to the famous Ms. McRae. Although I enjoyed the singing of Carmen McRae I was more impressed with the music of Vince Guaraldi and his trio and we stayed on for his second set before leaving. *Vince Guaraldi, whose piano playing was reminiscent of the great Dave Brubeck, later gained fame as the epitome of West Coast jazz. He also became popular with non-jazz fans for his composition and playing of "A Charlie Brown Christmas." Unfortunately he passed away at age 47.*

After I returned to Washington, I called Gwen and we went on our second date. I thought it was time to find out if we might have a future together so I told her that I was recently divorced and hoped that this would not disqualify me for the future. She said it wouldn't disqualify me. When I mentioned Dave's comment about her not dating a divorced man, she said that wasn't the real reason she wouldn't date Dave. I didn't pursue that issue further. However, the fact that Gwen was dating me ultimately did adversely affect my friendship with Dave.

On one of my early dates with Gwen I brought her to a party at Arlington Towers. (I believe it was at Bill Tarpening's apartment). Larry Mark was also there with a girl he had just started dating. During the evening, the fire alarm went off. Gwen looked puzzled when no one reacted. She asked: "Aren't we supposed to leave the building or something?" I replied: "No one pays any attention to those things!" The party continued without pause.

# CHAPTER 26
## I Need and Get an Assistant

MANY INTERESTING THINGS besides the Imported Fire Ant program kept me busy at the job. I suppose that my method of operating in the field must have favorably impressed my Branch Chief. For example, when I returned from a field trip, I would type up a detailed analysis of the problem I encountered and how I handled it. And I would bring back copies of my work.

The other information officers would usually hand him a page with a couple of written paragraphs and give him a short oral briefing. I felt my method was a learning experience for me, for him, and for future new employees. In any event when we had an unusual situation that required quick action, Val would invariably ask me to handle it. Since I was being overwhelmed with work, Val finally decided that the job was too much for one person and asked me to look for an assistant.

I knew that finding someone who could do the job independently would not be easy. A fellow staff member gave me a lead on a magazine writer. I reviewed examples of his work and found them to be first class. So, with my friend's recommendation and excellent samples of his work, I felt comfortable enough to invite him for a personal interview. In our interview, he seemed competent, likable, and personable. So, I asked Personnel to put him on the payroll. I soon regretted that decision.

When he joined our group, I assigned him some writing tasks that would have been handled easily by any competent writer. However, I was shocked at his ineptitude. His writing was full of grammatical and spelling errors. And he seemed to understand little about context. I had to assume that the samples he submitted with his application were either prepared by someone else or that they had been heavily edited and possibly even rewritten by someone more capable. We also assumed that the glowing letter of recommendation from his previous employer was a ploy to help them get rid of him.

There was no way we would be able to send him out on a job alone and there was no one in the office with the time and capability of reworking his submissions to make the work acceptable. So, in consultation with Supervisor Weyl, we decided that, as painful as it was, I needed to let him go before the end of the 90 day trial period. *Fortunately for me, Federal employees are hired on a trial basis for the first three months.*

After more searching and interviewing, I finally found someone I was confident would be able to represent our office. This was put to the test soon after the new person was hired. With some "in house" training and one exploratory trip together, the two of us headed to Dallas, Texas for an IFA treatment program which would involve spraying the city and its surrounding area. This was a highly sensitive program because of the size of the city. My new assistant followed me around as we met program officials, city and county officials, and the media. He observed my appearance on two of the Dallas TV stations.

Then, as we were getting settled in for the spraying to begin, PPC Headquarters called to say that there was a new outbreak of the Mediterranean Fruit Fly in Brownsville, Texas, and neighboring areas in Mexico. They said I needed to leave Dallas in the hands of my new assistant and head to Brownsville. I regretted leaving the new man alone so soon but since he had recently left the Military as an Air Force Officer, I felt that he would know how to handle himself adequately with telephone assistance from our Branch Chief.

# CHAPTER 27
## The Spokesman on Medfly in Texas

WHEN I ARRIVED in Brownsville, TX and met with the Official in Charge, I found out I was the only person there who had any experience with the Medfly program. So, I was asked to be spokesman for the duration--handling all public contact with town officials, the media, automobile dealers, etc. As expected, I described the program in detail, making my usual assurances of safety--with of course the exception of possible damage to GM cars accidentally sprayed.

Also, as usual, I was asked to write the articles for the newspapers and this time they insisted on using my byline above the articles. I called the agency to see if this was allowed and got an o.k. There was one complicating factor from my previous experience. This time we not only would be spraying over U.S. cities but would also spray over parts of a foreign country, Mexico, which meant I had to coordinate the spray schedule with Mexican officials. In fact, the city of Matamoros, Mexico, was almost in the center of the area outlined for spraying. Any previous capability I had with the Spanish language had left me long ago, so communication was sometimes dicey.

The accessibility of Matamoros from Brownsville, however, did offer some nice after hours diversion. The latter was enhanced by Mr. Douglas MacEachern, head of the Texas State Pest Control Office located in San Antonio. He was a Clemson graduate and a fellow South Carolinian by birth. We had met several years ago and had become long time friends.

Mr. MacEachern was considerably older than I, but his advanced age did not slow him down. In fact, it was hard for me to keep up with him. After spraying had stopped for the day and I had contacted local media with spray schedules for the next day, he would usually suggest we take a cab to Mexico. Since he was very familiar with Mexican towns along the U.S.-Mexican border, Mr. MacEachern knew the best (and safest) places to get good Tex-Mex food.

After getting our fill of excellent food, we would often hail a cab to "Boys Town" (the red light district) where brothels offered good libations and entertainment. *NO and definitely NO*, despite enticements by the pretty girls, neither of us ever went into the back room with any of them. But we enjoyed the Margaritas, the music, and the free entertainment. One night when Doug and I were in one of the "Boys Town" establishments, I became aware that a Caucasian man across the room was staring at me.

I ignored the man until he walked over to our table and asked me: "Did you go to Catawba College?" I responded "yes" and he re-introduced himself to me. By then I recognized him as someone I had known at Catawba. After we had a brief reunion he asked me if I had been on television the past few days. I told him that I had been on TV several times, that I was acting as spokesperson for the Medfly Program then in progress in the area around Brownsville and Matamoros. He said he had seen someone who looked familiar on TV but wasn't sure whether it was his old Catawba friend or the Governor of Texas, John White. *I could understand his confusion. Many local people had expressed the same problem. In addition to the same last name, the Governor had reddish brown hair and other similar physical attributes.*

When I asked my Catawba friend how he happened to be in Matamoros, he replied that he and his family had been touring Mexico for some time in their RV. He said they were on their way back to North Carolina and parked the RV in a park outside of Brownsville. He said his family was tired so he had left them at the RV park and had driven back for one last evening in Mexico. We said our goodbyes and I haven't seen him since.

After about three weeks I was able to return to Washington. This time I brought back with me copies of articles and other related information about my work on the Medfly Spray Program from beginning to end. I then organized the information into a report that could serve as a guide for future programs (for me or another Information Officer) should this pest again invade the U.S. I had already been caught short twice and had to "wing it." *That was the last Medfly program that I worked on. My career had changed when the Medfly later invaded California.*

# CHAPTER 28
## A Change of Pace--Making Movies!

WHEN I COULD get away from the IFA and Medfly programs, I devoted as much time as possible to preparing information material on the less controversial pests. Some of the more interesting endeavors took me into an area in which I had absolutely no experience, e.g., movie making. Branch Chief Val Weyl and I decided that movies about the gypsy moth program in New England, and the grasshopper program in the West were needed. And ready or not, it was my job to write the scripts and in the end supervise the making of these movies. I would write the first draft of a movie script, making sure to include all the essential information we needed to convey.

Once Branch Chief Weyl and I were satisfied that all the important points had been covered, I would confer with our staff TV/Movie person (Vince Marcley) and consider his suggestions for improvement. After that, I would go to USDA's main in-formation office where the former professional movie writers would offer their input. *Most outsiders would never suspect that USDA's information staff would contain people who had actually worked on Hollywood productions. But many of them had that experience. Their reasons for leaving Hollywood to work at USDA? Most said that they were tired of the "feast or famine" aspects of professional film making in Hollywood. They were happy with a steady salary at a lower rate.*

The first movie I worked on involved the Gypsy Moth program in the northeastern states. This foreign pest was devastating forests in Massachusetts, Vermont, and Maine and threatening damage to nearby state forests. It would eat the leaves to the point that the trees would die. And they became terrible pests in public parks, school yards, and even people's back yards. As larvae (or ugly worms), millions of these disgusting creatures would climb all over picnic tables, chairs and buildings. *These were guests no picnicker would welcome.*

I wrote a script describing the damage to forests and neighborhoods being done by this voracious pest, followed by a detailed description of what the cooperative Federal-State program was doing to eradicate or at least contain this pest. Then the script went through the usual editing and review process and was finally deemed ready for filming to start. At that point I got in touch with State officials from the affected states and asked them to help us select the best sites to film gypsy moth damage in their states.

Our office then made motel/hotel room reservations for me, Vince Marcley, and a movie/still photographer. State officials located a helicopter and pilot for us to use while we were filming in New England. As I recall, Vermont was the first state we visited.

After a night out dining in a fine restaurant and discussing our anticipated first day's shooting, we headed to our motel and then went to our respective rooms to get a good night's sleep so we would be rested for the busy day ahead. Alas, a good night's sleep was not in the cards for me. After putting on my pajamas and getting into bed I was just about to doze off when I felt something that felt like a bite. Thinking that the tension of what lay ahead in a few hours might have caused my imagination to go into overdrive, I again tried to go to sleep. This time there were multiple bites and I knew that I wasn't imagining them.

I flipped off the bed covers and turned on the light and could see fleas jumping about. I got out of bed almost as fast and called the desk. A motel desk clerk arrived promptly and confirmed that my bed had a flea infestation. While being moved to another room, the motel representative said that the previous occupants of that room had obviously violated the motel's "no pets" policy. Although the new room appeared to be free of fleas, I did not have a comfortable night fearing that some fleas could have hidden in my suitcase or clothing and would attack me at any moment.

Filming started the next day. Following suggestions from the film photographer, the pilot had removed the glass panel at the front of the helicopter. The pilot, photographer, and I sat in the front of the helicopter. We had nothing obscuring us from viewing the trees, camp and park lands infested by large numbers of gypsy moths at the larval stage. As film director, it was my job to give instructions to the pilot of areas to be filmed. *I made quite sure that my seat belt was tightened properly since there was nothing but open space in front of the three of us.*

After returning to the ground, we visited as many of the areas filmed from the air as we could find, and the still photographer made close-ups of the infestations. Vince Marcley served as on-the-scene narrator. At the end of these sessions nothing more was required of me until after the experts put together a "rough cut" of the filmed material and script. *I did not receive any type of award for this movie but it served its purpose.*

I followed a similar routine in making the grasshopper movie. The terrain was very different however. All the filming was done around the area of Cheyenne, Wyoming. I spent about three days in that dry, arid countryside. One time while we were driving to a location for some ground filming, I was startled when the local official driving us said: "Look at that crazy Indian!" I looked and saw two dark skinned people having sex on the side of the road. I guess they "couldn't wait!"

# CHAPTER 29
## Things Get Serious--Romantically

BACK TO PERSONAL matters, things were now getting serious with Gwen and me. After dating each other exclusively for a few months, we began discussing the topic of marriage. I asked Gwen to marry me and she said yes, but that she would feel better if we could get approval from the Roman Catholic Church. She assured me, however, that if we could not get that approval she would marry me in a civil ceremony. At that point we became engaged to be married and began seeing each other nightly, when I was in town.

Once a strange thing happened to me when I was returning to Arlington Towers at around 2 a.m. after dropping Gwen off at her mother's house. I entered the basement of the Jefferson Building from the parking lot, pushed the button for the elevator, and waited while it descended. The elevator door opened and I entered expecting to be alone. However, I had company: a young woman wrapped only in a throw rug. I asked: "What happened to you?" She responded, "I went outside my door to get something and threw the rug around me so I wouldn't have to get dressed. The door closed behind me and I was locked out of my room. Will you let me use your phone to call the desk to get my door unlocked?"

Since she smelled of alcohol, I was reluctant to let her use my apartment telephone but finally relented. That proved to be a mistake. I opened the door for her, she entered and promptly threw down her throw rug cover and said: "Whew, let's party!" I told her I wasn't interested in a party; I wanted her to call the desk and get her apartment door opened. I handed her the phone and she pretended to make a call but I could see she was faking. I then realized I was dealing with an inebriated naked woman (who may be lying about her situation), and that I had to get her out of my apartment as soon as possible. I thought a cold shower might sober her up so I told her to get into the shower, dry off, put on an extra bathrobe I owned and then leave my apartment. She took the shower and put on the bathrobe I had placed by the shower door. However, she refused to leave and wanted me to give her a drink. Finally I felt I had no option except to forcibly remove her. So, I opened the door and pushed her out. Before I could get my door completely closed, she said: "I'll scream 'rape'" and I said, "Go ahead and do it. No one will believe you!" After the door closed, she shouted, "How can I get your bathrobe back to you?" I shouted back, "Keep it!"

I thought this little episode was ended but when Larry Mark and I took a coffee break the next day, he said: "Jim, you won't believe what I saw this morning. When I was coming in the front door of the Jefferson Building, a woman who appeared to be wearing nothing but a brown bathrobe was leaving!" I said "You should have seen her before I gave her my extra bathrobe." I told him the rest of the story and we both got a good laugh out of it.

# CHAPTER 30
## Old Friend Anita Jones Comes for a Visit

SOON AFTER I became engaged to Gwen, I received a call from Anita Jones in Florida. She said she was coming to Washington and asked if I would be able to meet her at National Airport at a certain date and time. I checked my schedule and then told her I would meet her at the airport on that day and time. I assumed that she had a stopover in DC on the way to or from some other city. Of course, I told Gwen that evening about the upcoming meeting and she had no concerns.

At the pre-determined time, I met Anita at the front of one of the lounges. I would not have recognized her except for her charming southern drawl which I still remembered. She no longer looked like the very slender young lady I had dated four short years ago. Her figure had filled out and she was dressed like a New York model. When we settled down for coffee and conversation, she told me this was no stopover on the way to somewhere. She said she made the trip specifically to see if our relationship might be revived. She explained that she was being pressured to get married by a guy she was dating. I listened as Anita expressed doubts about her pursuer.

She added that the man was foreman of the composing room at the Palm Beach Post (where she was editor), had a high school education, and although he was intelligent and exciting to be around, she was concerned that he was too "rough around the edges." And she was concerned that he was putting too much pressure on her to marry him.

At that point I told her that I had just become engaged and thus there was no future for the two of us, but that I was still very fond of her and that Bob Spearman, the guy she mentioned, did not seem like a good match for her. We chatted for a couple of hours and then said goodbye as she boarded her plane back to Florida.

*Note: for sake of continuity, I will now finish my story about Anita Jones.* After our parting at the airport, I heard nothing more from Anita, but my niece Carolyn Turner called to inform me that Anita got married soon after she visited me in Virginia. I hoped that Anita did not marry the man she told me about. But I later found out that she had in fact married this man, Robert Spearman.

Years went by with no more news about Anita. Then one day Carolyn called to ask me if I had heard about what had happened to Anita. I said "no" and she said, "Anita was murdered by someone her husband hired to kill her." I was stunned and saddened by this news. Carolyn couldn't provide me with any details of Anita's murder so I was left to wonder what happened.

Several years later, after I returned to Upstate South Carolina, I had a chance to meet and talk with Anita's sister, Nancy Jones, who told me the whole story. She invited me to the Jones family home in Gaffney where she handed me a large box of newspaper and magazine articles about Anita's murder and the trial at which her husband was convicted and sentenced to life in prison.

Nancy wanted me to read all the material in the box hoping that I might write a book about Anita from the standpoint of an old boyfriend. I read the information and returned it to Nancy telling her that although her idea was very promising, my health was very bad at the time and I did not want to spend my last years writing something that difficult. I remember that the box contained many detailed articles about Anita's death and also a copy of a small book called "Gun For Hire" the story of "The Soldier of Fortune Killings."

Anita's murder and her husband's trial and conviction were the major part of the book but several unsuccessful attempts to kill several other people, plus one other successful murder, were interspersed with the story of Anita and her husband's fate. Robert Spearman did not take his lifetime prison sentence lightly. He tried to pay a "fellow prisoner" about to be paroled $50,000 to kill both the prosecutor and lead detective responsible for his conviction. The "fellow prisoner" turned out to be an undercover officer. Shortly after that failure Spearman offered another man $50,000 to fly a helicopter into the jail's outside prisoner exercise area and then fly him to a small airport where he (Spearman) would steal a plane and fly to a South American country where he couldn't be found. This plot was foiled because the "helicopter pilot" was also an undercover agent. Soon after that, Spearman was found hanging by his neck in his cell. That ended the story of this evil man except for occasional presentations on TV's Forensic Files.

Prosecutors who eventually rounded up all the "murder for hire" gang called them "The gang that couldn't shoot straight" for their many misses. However, unfortunately one of their few successes resulted in the brutal death of Anita Jones.

*Sadly, her sister never got over Anita's murder. Nancy Jones told me she had a nervous breakdown over what happened to her sister, gave up her career as a college professor, and had never recovered. I later learned Nancy passed away at an early age. I've often wondered what would have happened if I had not met and become engaged to Gwen just before Anita visited me in 1972; no one will ever know.*

# CHAPTER 31

## Complications Result in Civil Ceremony

BACK TO REAL time, the fact that Gwen was willing to marry me with or without her church's permission further assured me that she truly loved me. And this act of love made me that much more eager to find a way we could get married in her church. We both knew that my willingness to have any children born to us be raised as Catholic would have a powerful influence on the Catholic Church's ultimate decision on whether we could have a Catholic wedding.

We met with her priest and he assured us he would do everything he could to marry us in his church. His first question was: "Did a pastor marry you or were you married by a magistrate in a civil ceremony?" *Had Joyce and I been married by a magistrate, I would not have been considered married in the eyes of the Catholic Church.* However, I had to say that a pastor performed the ceremony. He then said he would consult with higher authority to try to find a way around the rule. We heard from him occasionally with progress (or non-progress) reports and additional questions.

Although my ex-wife, Joyce, had not called me in several weeks, I was fearful she might call me at an inappropriate time, e.g., when Gwen was at my apartment. So I thought it was time I let Joyce know that I was engaged to be married. I called the last number I had for her but after many tries, couldn't make contact. Finally, I called her sister and she would not tell me how I could get in touch with Joyce. Not knowing what else to do, I told her the reason I wanted to get in touch with her sister.

That proved to be a terrible mistake! A few days later I received a letter with a Pennsylvania post mark. I opened it and found a letter from Joyce that I will never forget. Joyce's letter began: "Jim you certainly picked a good time to send me word of your engagement to be married. I'm currently in a mental institution in Pennsylvania where I'm trying to recover from a nervous breakdown I suffered some time ago." She went on to berate me for being so hard-hearted using language that almost tore my heart out.

I called Gwen and asked if I could come to her house right away and share a letter I had received. Recognizing the urgency in my voice, she told me to come over as soon as I could get there. I was still teary eyed when I handed the letter to her. She read the letter and immediately took me in her arms to console me. Because she realized how shaken I was, she insisted I spend the night and sleep on the couch in the house she shared with her mother. I'll never forget the tenderness and compassion Gwen showed me that night.

*I've never completely forgiven myself for the pain I caused Joyce while she was trying to recover from a mental breakdown. We've never seen each other or talked since that time. However, a reporter friend, Miles Hughey, who had worked for the Charlotte Observer told me he had bumped into a very pretty young woman while visiting a fellow reporter who lived in the same apartment building where apparently Joyce also lived.*

*The woman was wearing a Belk's Store badge with the name Joyce White on it. Miles innocently said, "I have a friend by the name of Jim White who works for the Department of Agriculture in Washington, DC. Would you by any chance be related to him?" Joyce said: "I was married to that S.O.B. at one time!"* Hearing that reaction made me feel better because in my mind her sorrow had turned to anger, which I thought might be a healthier emotion since it would help her transfer her anger and guilt from herself to me.

Returning to the year 1962, after several months of waiting for clearance from the Catholic Church, Gwen and I decided to go ahead and get married by a magistrate in a civil ceremony. That was on Sept. 29, 1962. We both took a week's vacation and went on our honeymoon to a resort in the Pocono Mountains in Pennsylvania. Incidentally, we were told that the magistrate who married us had officiated at the divorce of Jackie Kennedy Onassis' mother from her father, John "Black Jack" Bouvier, supposedly because of his love of drinking, gambling, and womanizing.

The reason this was interesting to us was that almost everyone who saw Gwen thought that she looked like President John Kennedy's wife, Jacqueline "Jackie" Bouvier Kennedy. And people were about equally divided in saying I looked like Jack Kennedy or Richard Nixon.

Our honeymoon was wonderfully romantic with one comic twist. A New York couple on their one-year anniversary apparently couldn't stand to be alone with just the two of them. Although we liked this couple, we did not choose to spend all of our time with them. However, they failed to take hints and pursued us relentlessly. We finally made a game of finding new ways to avoid them so we could spend time alone.

When we returned from our honeymoon we spent our first few weeks of married life in my apartment at Arlington Towers. *Shortly before I met Gwen, I had made a down payment on a high rise condominium. The condo was under development in a redevelopment area within sight of the Potomac River waterfront and the present Environmental Protection Agency Headquarters on M Street, S.W. Washington.* Work on the condo was completed shortly and we moved into it as our first real residence together.

# CHAPTER 32
## Luxurious Condo has Serious Problem

ALTHOUGH THE CONDO was luxurious, the surrounding area was still undeveloped. I wasn't concerned about this as a single man when I made my down payment. That changed after I was married and we moved into the condo. My concern was based on the fact that once she resumed work Gwen would be walking to and from her car and our building about 100 feet away. This situation became acute for me when I saw some unsavory looking characters walking through the condo's parking lot.

Our condo was on the 7th floor and I would go out on the balcony to watch for her car to arrive in the condo parking lot. I would keep an attentive eye on her as she made her way to the elevator on the first floor. However, what could I do if she were confronted by someone walking through the parking lot? If I jumped from the balcony to try to come to her aid I would at the very least break my legs; if I took the elevator I might be too late. What a quandary!

My state of mind over Gwen's safety worsened when, after about three months, we found out that she was pregnant. Now, in my vivid imagination, two precious lives might be at risk. There was no way my sensitive nervous system could deal with this fear on a daily basis. So, we immediately began looking for a house in Maryland, close to where Gwen worked. *However, our financial situation was even worse than Bill and Hillary Clinton's situation when they left the White House!*

My profligate lifestyle up until that point had left me with no savings account and an inexpensive car with a lien on it. Gwen was in a similar situation. We had already agreed she would resign her job as soon as our child was born. Since we were determined to buy our first home in a safe neighborhood, our plan was for Gwen to withdraw her Civil Service retirement money and I would sell my condo. We hoped that those two actions might provide enough money for a down payment on a decent house. We didn't think we would end up with enough money to allow us to buy a really nice house in a prime location.

Then fate took a favorable turn. We discovered that the developer of a small, up-scale subdivision near the Navy Hydrographic Office had gone broke and was selling a few nice brick homes at heavily discounted prices. The only drawback was that some of the finish work was not completed and none of the landscaping had been done on the available houses. Nonetheless, we decided to make a "low ball" offer for one of these houses and the offer was accepted. We would worry about the finishing later. The house was already livable so we moved in well before Mitch was born.

# CHAPTER 33
## Becoming "Mr. Harry Homeowner" Not Easy

UP UNTIL THAT point I had no skills related to home ownership. I didn't own a hammer, saw, screwdriver, or pair of pliers. *I hate to admit that when I moved into my apartment at Arlington Towers, a girlfriend brought over tools and installed draperies for me! But that was the past and this was the present and I needed to learn how to do some "home improvement" in a hurry. Gwen came to my rescue by buying me an excellent "Harry Homeowner Book" with "how to do carpentry, electrical and plumbing work."*

That book became my guide for finishing the trim work and making some substantial improvements to this house. With some added advice from knowledgeable friends, I removed parts of a load bearing wall in the "step down" living room and installed small "headers" to support the weight on each side of the steps. I was then able to create a built-in china cabinet in the dining room (which was too narrow for a large china cupboard) and on the living room side installed built-in cabinetry for the TV and stereo equipment.

I was too dumb to understand that an amateur wood worker should not be tinkering with a load bearing wall or trying to create such a complicated set of cabinetry as his first home improvement project. I even moved electrical wires without flipping the electric breakers to "off," i.e., I handled them "live" because I didn't know the location of the breaker box. But I had "beginner's luck" and both the house and I survived despite my ignorance.

The home improvement book remained at my side for years as I progressed from a total ignoramus to someone not afraid to take on the job of total restoration of houses as my skills improved. *Eventually, restoration of old houses became my favorite hobby!*

As the end of Gwen's pregnancy neared, we checked with her priest and when he saw that she was in late term for child bearing, he smiled and said: "I've got good news for you. I've just heard from my Superior and expect to get approval for me to marry you in the Church any day now." A few days later he called to set a date with us for the Catholic Church ceremony.

We were married for the second time in a small room of the Catholic Church Gwen attended; it was NOT in the sanctuary and only her immediate family attended but the ceremony enabled Gwen to remain in good standing with her church. She would be able to extend her perfect attendance as a member. I had helped her in this effort by always locating in advance a Catholic Church where she could attend Mass when we traveled out of town.

About two weeks before our child was due, Gwen and I hosted a small cocktail party for a few friends knowing it might be our last party for awhile. Both of us had a drink or two before our guests left. *At that time, prospective mothers were warned about the possible danger of smoking to an unborn infant so Gwen had stopped smoking as soon as her pregnancy was known. However, warnings of possible damage to a fetus by drinking alcohol were not widely known in 1963 so she had continued social drinking.*

Shortly after all the party-goers had left, Gwen's water broke and thus began a wild scramble to call the doctor and get ready to drive to Sibley Hospital in Washington where the doctor would meet us. We arrived at Sibley shortly before midnight and Gwen was admitted. I sat holding her hand for the next two hours. Then, suddenly my quiet little wife gave a scream like I had never heard before. A nurse and doctor came running to her bedside and gave her an injection. I needed little urging to leave the room. *Thank God back then husbands were not invited to watch the birthing process.*

At around 2 a.m., Sept. 16, 1963, the doctor came to the area where prospective fathers were waiting and told me that I was the parent of a healthy little boy. And I do mean little. Perhaps because he was slightly premature and his mother was small (113 lbs.) he weighed less than 7 pounds. Consequently, we were told that our new baby boy would have to stay in the hospital longer than average. He might be kept there for a week or more rather than the usual 3 days. Infants at that time were kept in the hospital until they weighed at least 7 pounds and they usually lost a few ounces of weight initially.

Anxious to see Gwen and my new baby boy, Mitchell Eugene White, I was told to wait a few minutes while the nurses ministered to the mother and child. I was taken to see Gwen first and found her smiling and radiant. The first thing she said to me was: "Let's have another baby soon." I couldn't believe she could think that way so soon after that terrible scream caused by the pain of childbirth. That must be something a man is not supposed to understand.

I was then taken to the nursery where I could look through a big glass window and spot my son being "cleaned up." He had a head of dark black hair and the loudest voice in the nursery. Apparently he had been born hungry and was letting the world know about it. Soon, a nurse appeared with his first bottle and he quickly calmed down. *Unfortunately for Mitch, he was born at a time when "breast feeding" was not popular and Gwen tended to follow trends. So he was not breast fed.*

On my daily visits to the hospital after work, I could sit with Gwen but could only visit Mitch through that large window. I had no trouble finding him in that crowded nursery. If I did not immediately spot that mass of black hair, all I had to do was listen for the loudest voice and it would be Mitch.

Sibley Hospital was strict about protecting a newborn baby from infection and I don't recall being able to touch him until shortly before we left the hospital three days later. Contrary to the doctor's prediction that he would lose some of his birth weight initially, Mitch had started gaining weight immediately and reached the "magic" 7 pounds before the day when he would be eligible to leave. So we left the hospital at the usual time for a newborn.

# CHAPTER 34

## Becoming a Father for the First *(and only)* Time

I'LL NEVER FORGET the pride (mixed with fear) I had while holding Mitch for the first time and carrying him to the car where I placed him in his mother's arms. *That was before infants were required to be strapped into special safety car seats.* While still an infant, Mitch was "christened" into the Roman Catholic Church by the priest who married us. Only Gwen's mother, aunt, and a couple of her cousins were there to see the ceremony.

Gwen and I quickly settled into the routine of being suburban parents. I cherished every moment I could spend with my little family and began transferring as many of the out-of-town trips as possible to my assistant, King Lovinger. When I was forced to travel more than a couple of days, Mitch would not recognize me when I returned. I found this heart breaking. He would look at me with the expression on his face of: "Who is this stranger wanting to hold me?"

Mitch continued to grow and before the year was over, he was in the 90+ percentile for size. His doctor predicted he would be at least 6 feet tall and possibly could reach the height of 6 foot 4 inches. *He reached that height before age 18.*

Despite having generally good health, Mitch had two health problems that bothered him as well as his mother and me. The first was that he had frequent ear infections which required visits to his pediatrician and prescriptions for antibiotics. *At least his overly-protective father required that he be taken to the doctor.* Gwen, correctly, thought that Mitch's body should be given a chance to develop some resistance to ailments before seeing the doctor but I was too nervous to go along with that thinking.

The second was that when he was about three weeks old, Mitch began to have a painful stomach problem diagnosed as colic. Thus began a long search for a formula that would not cause severe pain to his stomach. We tried every formula known to the medical profession but none of them relieved his stomach pain. *Many people think that breast feeding might have prevented this stomach ailment.*

After many sleepless nights, we finally found something to relieve Mitch's stomach pain. The solution was to drape him across my chest at bed time. Whether it was the steady pressure from my chest or the rhythm of my heartbeat against his little heart, we never knew. All we knew was that it worked and that was a nightly procedure until he was around nine months old and the colic cleared up. *Mitch and I have always been very close and have wondered if those months of "bonding" chest-to-chest might have helped engender that closeness.*

Our family gradually settled into a pleasant routine. Gwen seemed to enjoy her "stay-at-home-mom" life and doted on her little boy, who looked so much like her with his curly black hair, big blue eyes, and beautiful features that caused people to say, "He's too pretty to be a boy." By the time he was three years old he would show his hurt over this description and we urged people not to say how "pretty" he was in his presence.

Despite his development into a large, strong boy for his age, Mitch was slow to walk and we made no effort to hasten his walking. We had heard that the brain of a child benefited from protracted crawling, that it was bad for a child's brain to be coerced into walking early. Finally, when he was 13 months old, things changed suddenly. We were visited by a couple who had a very small girl, age 3. Naturally the little girl was running all over the house. Mitch watched her walking and running and began taking his first steps without assistance from anyone. By the time our visitors left, Mitch was walking like he had been doing this for months! Seeing that little girl walking was all the inspiration he needed.

One thing we liked about our neighborhood was that there were several children only slightly older than Mitch. We had thought it would be wonderful when Mitch was able to walk and play with these youngsters. Unfortunately, this didn't work out as well as we had hoped. The two houses nearest to us each had three or four children. The parents of these children were much younger than we and much more casual about supervising their little ones.

We were located just below a steep knoll on the street running in front of our houses. Although there was a 25 mph sign for our neighborhood, many drivers paid no attention to this and would roar over the knoll and have to "screech" to a stop because of small children standing in the street. Then the children would casually move out of the way but return to the street as soon as the car passed. This didn't seem to alarm our neighbors; they would mildly warn their children not to play in the street but as soon as the parent or parents turned their backs, the children were back playing in the street.

It appeared to us that because these neighbor parents had more than one child and were young enough to produce more, they could afford to lose one! But we couldn't! We started dreading the moment when Mitch was old enough to go outside to play with the other children. When that time came, we cautioned him not to play in the street and then watched to see that he obeyed. He was an obedient child and we didn't need to caution him many times before he got the message. Then it saddened us to see him standing alone by the side of the street while his friends played in the middle of or on the other side of the street.

Gradually, our concern over this and the fact that Prince Georges County where we lived was beginning to have some crime problems caused Gwen and me to decide that our best solution might be to move. Since Gwen was no longer working, our main reason to remain in that neighborhood was gone. After much discussion and some looking we decided that the State of Virginia offered us the best options.

# CHAPTER 35
## Looking for a Safer Place to Rear a Child

IN OUR FIRST search, we found an available attractive property that we could afford in the Great Falls area of Northern Virginia. It was on a one-acre lot with 5 contiguous acres at a really good price. The owner offered to hold the property for us until we sold our house in Maryland. *We knew this was a great investment; years later we learned that one acre lots in that area were going for a quarter of a million dollars.*

But there was a problem with the house that defied solution; the house was built in sections by the owner with his own hands after work and weekends. He built the middle section first. Then he added sections on each side but the final result was that the front line was noticeably crooked. *Obviously he did not use a builder's transit or even run a string across the front of the house to ensure that it was straight.*

Since the construction was concrete block I could not figure a way to straighten the house. I even brought an experienced contractor to give me advice and he advised me to tear down the two side sections and rebuild them--a mammoth job. The crooked line explained why the owner, a physician from the Philippines had not been able to sell his property for a reasonable price. And for that same reason, Gwen and I passed on the house and began looking elsewhere.

After much looking we found a wonderful 5 acre building lot on Clifton Road, only about a mile from the picturesque town of Clifton. This little village had once been a bustling town with an upscale hotel, which served people who wanted to get away from the heat of Washington, DC. It had a railroad station, general store, restaurant, and other amenities. Not to mention wonderful Victorian houses, mostly of the cottage variety. Then, over the ensuing years the town deteriorated until it was inhabited primarily by hippies and the homeless.

Clifton was saved by a visionary real estate broker who bought up the houses, kicked out the riff raff, and completed a few restoration projects on his own. Once the town was deemed safe, buyers began purchasing the restored homes. Other more daring people then began buying the rundown and abandoned properties to restore for themselves. By the time we bought the lot outside of town in the late 60's, Clifton was once again a very desirable little Victorian village which drew thousands of visitors on "Clifton Day." The town also became the center of upscale subdivisions which consisted of large homes placed on 5 acre lots.

After we bought our lot we began considering house plans and contractors to build a custom house where Mitch would be able to enjoy the countryside in a safe environment. After settling on a house plan and selecting a contractor, we rented a house in a Springfield, VA, development for several months until our house reached "move-in" condition. We could not afford to pay the contractor to completely finish the trim work or landscape the property. It remained my job to finish the trim work on evenings and weekends. Gwen turned out to be an excellent painter and landscaper--two areas I was totally lacking in expertise and had no desire to learn.

One of the first visitors after our move in and completion of the custom house was Tee Carson, my musician friend. I tried to interest him in buying the lot right next to ours and having a nice custom house built on it but he had decided to stay where he was in DC. He brought Mitch a small piano and promised he would come give Mitch lessons on our full size piano after Mitch was a little older. (*Unfortunately, future events kept those lessons from happening. However, Mitch still has the little piano 45 years later*).

On another visit, Tee brought his wife Jan and their infant son, Donald, with him. This created an interesting situation for Mitch, who had never seen a black baby close up. When he first looked at young Donald's dark skin, his eyes opened wide with wonder but within minutes he was down on the floor playing with him. On another occasion, Tee brought Keter Betts, the great bassist, with him and we enjoyed showing them our new home and area.

After three years at the Char House, Tee and his Trio were offered a long term engagement at the prestigious Shoreham Hotel. The trio played regularly in the Marquis

Lounge and also served as opening act for big name entertainers in the Blue Room. These included Sammy Davis, Jr., Lena Horne, Pearl Bailey and Robert Goulet. Tee also worked with and became personal friends with many other famous musicians such as Billie Holiday, Ahmad Jamal, Roger Williams, Matt Dennis, Art Tatum, Count Basie and Oscar Peterson.

Tee invited me for jam sessions at his home with Art Tatum, Count Basie and Oscar Peterson but by that time I was too busy to accept these invitations. He also called to invite me to join him and a wonderful guitarist by the name of Herb Ellis for a game of golf but I couldn't get away from work that day. *Missed opportunities!*

Although family and work reduced the time I had for music and time spent with Tee, he always remembered one of my favorite jazz tunes (Satin Doll). Whenever I entered an establishment where he and the band were performing, he would immediately play that tune to acknowledge my presence. It happened every time I went to hear him play at the Showboat lounge and the Shoreham's Marquis Lounge or Blue Room.

Once, when Tee and his Trio were playing at the great jazz venue, The Village Vanguard, in New York City, I thought I would surprise him. I had not known I would be in New York until the last minute and had no opportunity to tell Tee I would be there. When I entered the Vanguard, he was playing the piano with his back to the door and no mirror to spot my entrance. The place was crowded with jazz music lovers. Somehow, he sensed my presence because the very next number was "Satin Doll"!

Being a good looking man with suave manners and superb talent, Tee attracted "groupies" of all colors. But to my knowledge, he never took advantage of this. However, I eventually learned of marital troubles in the Carson household and Tee left Washington, DC suddenly for San Francisco without even saying goodbye. By that time, we had lost touch and I never knew the details of what happened--except what I read in the Washington Post. And it wasn't pretty.

At this point I want to leave chronological order again and finish The Tee Carson Story as far as I know it. Some years later, I was in San Francisco for a few days on business and stayed in the St. Charles Hotel. Thinking I might be able to regain contact with Tee, I called every Carson in the telephone directory with the first name of Tee or Tecumseh. None was my old friend from Washington, DC. Still later, I found that Tee had an outstanding musical career in the Bay Area and continued his U.S. Marshal's career until retirement age.

Tee became well known in the area for his musicality, playing at San Francisco's Cypress Club as well as the posh New Orleans room of the famous Fairmont Hotel, which overlooks the city. He also had a popular weekly radio show on KCSM, an all-jazz station in nearby San Mateo. He gained even greater fame when he took over the piano for the Count Basie Band when the Count's health deteriorated. Tee traveled with the Basie Band for many years as pianist (and sometimes leader) of the band until Basie's death in 1984. After Basie died Tee became band leader as well as pianist of the Basie Band, traveling all over the U.S., Europe, Japan and South America. A chain smoker, Tee contracted lung cancer and after a long battle with this dreaded disease passed away in the year 2000.

*Sadly, I found out that the night I made so many calls trying to re-establish contact with Tee, he was playing at the Fairmont Hotel just up the hill from where I was staying. It saddens me that I never had a chance to say goodbye to him. I'm left to wonder if he played "Satin Doll" the evening I was trying to call him.*

*On another bittersweet note: In the early 2000's Mitch attended a concert in Washington and had a chance to re-introduce himself to Keter Betts after he put away his bass following the concert and was free to chat. Mitch said one of the first things Keter asked was: "How is your Dad?" Mitch said Keter also mentioned coming to our house in Clifton with Tee. Keter Betts also passed away shortly after Mitch chatted with him.*

# CHAPTER 36

## Back to Chronology in Clifton

BACK TO CHRONOLOGY, at ages 3 and 4 Mitch was an extremely active child. That activity resulted in one unhappy event! One day when his mother turned her back for a moment, young Mitch climbed into our newly purchased (almost new) Chrysler Newport sedan, pulled the transmission lever out of park and the car began going downhill backwards. Its back bumper struck a small tree, glanced off and then hit a large tree which brought it to a stop with a severely bent bumper. Gwen recalled that when she heard the crash she ran to the car, and saw Mitch crouching on the floor beneath the dash. She said his first words were: "Mama, it was an accident!" He has always been a good talker!

With no children his age within walking distance, Gwen made every effort to find playmates for him, either transporting him to their houses or picking them up and transporting them to our house. A sociable child from birth, he needed no encouragement in his mother's quest to get him "socialized."

When he reached the age of 5, Mitch began playing "T Ball" as his first organized sport. He had become friends with another little boy named Joe Presta who lived in a five-acre neighborhood not far from us. Joe's father was Frank Presta, an attorney who was interested in (and knowledgeable of) sports and who could get away from his office to provide transportation and to introduce his son and mine to organized sports.

It seemed only a short time later that Mitch was in the first grade at Clifton Elementary School. His mother and I both shed some tears the first time he boarded the school bus alone for school. Soon Joe and Mitch had progressed to Little League baseball where Frank Presta was an active youth coach. This was convenient for all concerned, since Frank could easily transport two of his team members to practice and games. As it turned out, with the aid of his coach, Mitch became skilled both as pitcher and shortstop.

It was about this time, we realized that we had a very athletic son. He entered a Boy Scout Olympics and won top prize in almost all events of his age group. Furthermore, he was asked to compete in a race with the winner of the older group and they finished in a tie. Since neither his mother nor I could ever run a lick, we wondered: "Where did this speed come from?"

When he was nine, we joined Chantilly Country Club so that Mitch could take tennis lessons from the Club's excellent pro. After finishing his first course of lessons, he showed no great interest in the sport and instead concentrated on Little League Baseball and fishing. At the age of 10 playing in the 12 year age group, he led his team in hitting with an average of over 400 and struck out only once the entire season. He led his team in fielding, making only two errors all season.

The fielding errors came on one play when he tried to field a ball that would have been a sure hit against any other shortstop in his league. He dove and stopped the ball; then made a hurried throw that went over the first baseman's head. Thus, two errors on one play. Although his team won easily with Mitch getting base hits every time at bat, Mitch was unhappy with his performance. After the game his coach said "Mitch won the game with his bat." But Mitch was inconsolable because he had made those errors.

I was beginning to have visions of "major league ballplayer" but Mitch never played baseball after that season. The reason? Soccer had just arrived in Northern Virginia and Mitch loved the action of this sport as soon as he tried his hand (uh, feet) at it. He said he never really liked baseball that much because the players "stood around so much." So, it was soccer for the next three years. His second season he made the "All Star" team and was asked to join the "traveling squad."

# CHAPTER 37
## Tennis becomes Mitch's game

AT AGE 13, Mitch decided he wanted to play both tennis and soccer. He won the Chantilly Country Club tennis championship and his old tennis coach advised me to enroll him in the U. S. Tennis Association (USTA) Junior Tennis program. Because I had been so busy with my career, I was unfamiliar with this program but followed the tennis coach's advice and enrolled him at age 13 in USTA Tennis in the "14 and under" age group. I was caught completely by surprise by the high level of tennis played by these youngsters.

Expecting Mitch to hold his own in USTA tennis was unrealistic but after he didn't win a single game his first two matches (both of which happened to be against nationally ranked USTA youngsters) I knew he needed more serious training and practice against better players to be competitive. Also, we quickly learned that it was very difficult to combine two sports as demanding as tennis and soccer. After some family discussions, Mitch decided to drop soccer and concentrate on tennis.

After Mitch began participating in USTA tennis, we found that being two-weeks premature was costly in terms of rankings and morale. The reason: USTA Junior Tennis year begins on Oct. 1. Had he been born as scheduled, he would have had another year with this age group. However, since Mitch would be 14 on Sept. 16 instead of early October, he would have to enter the "16 and under" group for his next match which meant he would be even more over-matched! And it would make it much more difficult for him to get a high ranking in USTA Junior Tennis.

A high regional and national ranking is helpful in several ways. For one, a high ranking gives these players a better chance of getting tennis scholarships as well as better tournament "seedings." A high seeding may get a player a "bye" in the first round of a tournament. At the very least higher seeded players don't have to compete against other highly seeded players in the early matches.

Although we knew it would be very expensive, Gwen and I decided to help even the odds for Mitch by placing him with the best junior coaches in the Washington, DC area. Several high quality coaches held what was called "drill groups" of the best junior players in the Washington, Maryland and Virginia area. We hoped this high level coaching and competition might give Mitch a chance to catch up. When he had "try outs" with the first such "drill group" Mitch finished last in the group and was assigned to compete on court no. 6, i.e., the last court. The best players competed on court no. 1.

As the season wore on, Mitch began to work his way up the ladder and at the end had progressed to the point he was playing on court no. 1. The same pattern continued the next two seasons as we sought and found higher talented drill groups and coaches. Competing against higher level players turned out to be very helpful in raising the level of Mitch's game. His game began to blossom and he began winning matches even though he was still handicapped by being younger and less experienced than most of the other junior tournament players.

Meanwhile, he had graduated from elementary school and entered Robinson High School (one of the largest high schools in the DC area). He tried out and made the school tennis team at no. 6 position his freshman year. He won all his matches except one where he felt his opponent was "greasing" him (the term used in tennis for cheating). He became so upset at the cheating that his game deserted him. He was part of the no. 3 doubles team that went undefeated. And he won the "most valuable player" (MVP) award for the year.

That summer, Mitch worked extremely hard at his game and made steady improvement. The no.1 player all four years at Robinson had graduated and it was assumed that the no. 2 player for the past three years and a senior would move up to no. 1. I hoped that Mitch would move up to no. 4 or perhaps no. 3.

However, on the first day of practice, the coach asked the players to take to the court where they thought they belonged. Much to my surprise Mitch walked confidently to court 1, where the expected no. 1 player was waiting. After their warm up, the coach told the two of them to play a 10-game match to determine who would be the top player for the team. Mitch won a close 10-8 match. The older player challenged him to a rematch the following day and Mitch won that match easily and became the no. 1 player at Robinson until he graduated. He won the MVP award all four years and was declared no. 1 in the entire district his senior year.

At age 17, Mitch played his first Men's Tournament at Devil's Reach Racquet club in Occoquan, Va. After a struggle with a seeded player he won his first match. Then he easily won his following matches and suddenly he was matched in the quarter finals against the no. 1 player from the University of Maryland. We were congratulating him on getting this far in the tournament but expected him to lose badly in what we thought would be his last match in the tournament. But he beat this highly regarded player in straight sets. I don't remember who he beat in the semi-finals but he lost in the finals to a former All American Tennis Player from Duke University.

I had overheard someone ask the former Duke player how he would play this "youngster." The seasoned Duke ex-great said: "It would be suicide for me to get into a hitting match with this kid. I'll give him nothing but soft balls and hope he'll 'overhit' them into the net or blast them against the back stop." That's exactly what happened. Mitch didn't see a hard hit ball the whole match. Nothing but well placed "dinks" came from the racquet of the more experienced player.

# CHAPTER 38
## Gwen Gets Part Time Job

AFTER MITCH HAD reached the point that he no longer needed (nor wanted) 24 hour per day care, Gwen decided to get a part-time job. She had developed a knowledge and liking for houses and decided she might enjoy working in the housing industry. So, she enrolled in the Northern Virginia Real Estate Course, and took and passed the test. Shortly after that, she passed the State test for real estate agents and took a job with one of the smaller real estate agencies.

She listed a friend's house for sale in Springfield and guided the process through to closing. *After that I became her prime sales target. I soon found out that she had fallen in love with one of the remaining unrestored Victorian cottages in the town of Clifton. So, soon after shepherding her first listing to completion, she presented me with a "Contract to Purchase" this cottage which had been condemned by Fairfax County for the past 10 years.*

At the time, I had just finished the first phase of our custom house. However, I still had the full unfinished walk out basement with 9 foot ceiling to finish, plus I had planned on enclosing the large garage into a large family room as my next project.

After that I planned to build a large detached garage. I had paid the original contractor to "rough in" plumbing, heating, and electrical to make it easier to convert the garage into the family room. For that reason, I had never had garage doors installed. After again explaining the long range plans to Gwen I declined to sign the "Contract to Purchase" paper.

With some help from a friend whose basement I had helped finish, I went to work on our basement. I even built a brick retaining wall at the back of the basement ground floor entrance so that a level walkway could be laid. I knew nothing about laying brick but fortunately a contractor friend stopped by and showed me how to ensure a straight line and how to break a brick so that the bricks would line up properly. Although the job was not perfect, it was "passable."

As I neared completion of this phase, Gwen brought me another "Contract to Purchase" for that same Victorian cottage in Clifton. I again declined to sign the contract but she must have sensed that my resolve was weakening because as I was completing the basement she returned with a third version of the "Contract to Purchase." This time she told me that this would be a "family project" with the three of us: Jim, Gwen and Mitch all participating in the work. This third approach worked and I signed the Contract. This began a six-year project which will be detailed in PART 7.

Despite my preoccupation with restoration work, I had not neglected my demanding job for the Federal Government. Restoration work was done after hours, weekends, and vacation time. Also, the Pesticide Regulation Division (PRD) of ARS formally requested my help dealing with public relations problems caused by their inability to meet their deadlines.

PRD was over a year behind in the registration process and companies were growing vociferous in complaining about the delays. *(The companies cannot market their products until the registration process has been completed.)* Most of my work was with the Director of PRD, Dr. Harry Hays and Assistant Director Harold Alford, who had a special interest in and appreciation of effective communications.

This change in job function cut my travel demands dramatically which gave me more time with my family and the restoration project. Although the new work with PRD was not nearly as exciting as traveling to strange places to "put out fires" for the Plant Pest Control Division it turned out to be a good trade off for that time in my life. And it had a tremendous impact on my future as a Federal Government employee, though I did not know that at the time.

Throughout this time, my career had been stuck at the GS 12 level. I had one hopeful development but that did not turn out as expected. Our Director Bob Rathbone's assistant was retiring and that opened up a GS 13 (with a possible GS 14 later) for someone in our office. I didn't apply for the job but soon the "scuttlebutt" was that Rathbone had narrowed the field down to me and the head of the Publications Unit. Since the latter was so highly respected by everyone (including me) I assumed he would be selected.

Then this highly-qualified individual decided he no longer wanted to live and work in the Washington area, and left for a State field job. This apparently left me as the only candidate. Everyone on the staff began congratulating me, wanting to take me to lunch, etc. They were even already planning a celebratory luncheon for me. I tried to quash all this since no formal announcement of my "promotion" had been made.

To everyone's shock and surprise, another employee was announced as the new Assistant Director. Although I liked this person as a friend, he had seemed to be the least likely of the entire group to be selected for this job. *Perhaps all of us could be faulted for not paying attention to the fact that this employee's wife worked in a high position at the White House! I was given the PO PO Award job of Assistant to Branch Chief Val Weyl. (Note: in Washington lingo the PO PO Award signifies: pissed on and passed over!)*

However, along with this job I was promoted to a GS-13. As welcome as this promotion was, it did not assuage my feeling of being passed over for a job that I and the entire staff thought I was best qualified to do.

Shortly after that a friend, Dennis Avery, formerly with USDA's Foreign Agriculture Service but then with USDA's Agricultural Stabilization and Conservation Service (ASCS), called and asked me to have lunch with him. *Note: for the novice, ASCS is considered the "political arm" of USDA and receives and spends a huge percentage of USDA's budget. As an indication of the "power" residing in this agency, Kenneth Frick, Administrator of ASCS, had his own Federal Government limousine and driver! I've been told that ASCS Administrators are the only officials below cabinet level who receive such perks!*

Congress had just passed a revision of the 1970 Agricultural Act that needed to be implemented. Earl Butz, a Department Head at Purdue University was the new Agriculture Secretary and he was serious about changing USDA's philosophy toward the agricultural industry of this country. This 3-year farm bill gave Secretary Butz broad authority to make these changes by replacing some of the more restrictive and mandatory features of the previous law. It replaced some acreage allotments, planting restrictions, and marketing quotas with voluntary annual cropland set-asides. The law also adopted annual payment limitations. There were many other changes in the law that needed to be implemented.

The major factor was the change in philosophy promoted by Secretary Butz. Instead of the Government managing major areas of this hugely important industry, Secretary Butz thought that farmers themselves and the "Market" should be making more of the decisions rather than having them made by Washington bureaucrats. He hoped to eventually get rid of the large subsidies doled out to farmers (sometimes for **not** growing a crop). Butz called this new philosophy the "Market Oriented" approach.

ASCS's Information Division was given responsibility for providing guidance for this new approach to all aspects of the farming industry as well as Federal, State and local officials. In many cases, ASCS information people not only disseminated policy but actually formulated policy with their newspaper and magazine articles, policy papers, and speeches prepared for delivery by "higher ups."

My friend, Dennis Avery, had been named Assistant Director of ASCS's Information Division, because of his economics/journalism background. He was also known to share Earl Butz's philosophy. The Division Director was William Cummings, a retired Military Officer, who had no real background for the job. Fortunately Cummings was intelligent enough to recognize this deficiency and allowed Dennis Avery a free hand in finding, hiring, educating, and managing the division personnel. Cummings served as a pleasant figurehead while Dennis ran the shop.

# CHAPTER 39
## A New Job with New Challenges

DENNIS AVERY HAD problems getting ASCS Information Division people (all hired by previous Democratic administrations) to accept the new approach advocated by Secretary Butz and the revised Agricultural Act. I had known Dennis socially since my days in FES. Thus he was aware that after being exposed to the Democrats' way of governing, I had changed my registration from Democrat to Republican a few years previously.

He assumed, correctly, that I would have no trouble understanding and promoting the agency's new policies since they coincided with my own thinking. Most of the existing information people were career civil service who remained loyal to the policies of previous administrations with which they were familiar. However, under Civil Service rules they could not easily be replaced.

Dennis wanted to start the process of replacing some of those not willing to follow the new policies by hiring me at the GS-13 level. Although this was another lateral move, I was excited about being offered an opportunity to help implement policies more to my liking. Also, I thought it wouldn't hurt me to learn something about politics in the government. I had seen firsthand how difficult it was to move up the career ladder by hard work alone. And, finally, I still had some ill feelings about the recent personnel actions which had caused me embarrassment.

After my paperwork was transferred from ARS to ASCS, I moved across the street to the USDA Administration Building. Bill Cummings took me to meet Claude Greene, a North Carolina politician, who was the new Director for the Southeast Area ASCS. Although I would continue to be part of the ASCS Information Division, Greene would be my de facto boss in the field. Cummings thought that I would be a perfect pick for the Southeast Area job since I was born and raised on farms in South Carolina, had worked at NC State and spent all but one year of my working life in the Carolinas.

He couldn't have been more wrong about me being the perfect pick for this job. As soon as we sat down, Claude Greene immediately went on the attack. "I see from your resume that you're a journalist and have a graduate degree from the University of Illinois. That's impressive but what makes you think you can relate to Southern farmers?" Without giving me a chance to respond, he continued to aggressively attack my credentials for understanding or being able to help introduce new policies to Southern farmers. Cummings bravely tried to interrupt Greene long enough to give him a more accurate picture of my background but Greene was wound up and refused to listen.

As soon as he finished lambasting my credentials, he ushered Bill Cummings and me out of his office and into the hallway. On the way back to the Information Office, Bill Cummings tried to re-assure me that this was just Greene's personality; that I would get along fine with him as soon as we got to know each other. I looked at Cummings with disbelief and said: "You've got to be kidding, Bill. I'm not going to work for that S.O.B!" We walked the rest of the way to the office in silence.

A few minutes later, Cummings came back into the office and said: "Jim, I've just found out that the Southwest Information Officer position is still open and I'd like to take you over to meet J. P. Jones, Director of the Southwest Area ASCS, tomorrow. I've already sent your resume to his office. *(It should be noted that Area Director jobs at ASCS are all filled by appointees of the party in power.)*

The conversation with Mr. J. P. Jones could not have gone better. He had taken the trouble to really read my resume and learn about my background. After we talked for awhile he told me he would be "honored" if I would accept the position of Information Officer for the Southwest Area. Of course I accepted. My only regret about the change was that I would be required to be away from family for longer periods of time because of the distance to the Southwest Area states. They ran from Arkansas to Hawaii!

I learned that J.P. Jones had been Chairman of the Texas Farmers and Ranchers for the Nixon organization. But you wouldn't know that by his attitude and modest demeanor. He was honest and straightforward with me from the first to the last of our relationship. And he demonstrated his trust in me by telling state and federal people under him that I was fully in charge of all public relations and information issues involving ASCS in the Southwestern States.

From a personal standpoint, J.P. Jones was also an interesting person. He owned his own airplane and invited me to travel with him on his private plane when it was convenient for me. I soon found he was an accomplished pilot and his little French Bellanca plane was aerial aviation's equivalent to a "hot rod." It could cruise at 200 mph and had a top speed of more than that. It also had an electronic retractable landing gear--unusual for a plane of that size.

# CHAPTER 40

## A French Plane becomes My New Way to Travel

ALTHOUGH I HAD traveled millions of miles by commercial airlines, flying long distances by private airplane was a new experience. Although it made me a bit nervous, traveling with J.P. made sense in many ways. It gave us more time to get to know each other and it made sense logistically since we would always be able to reach our destination at the same time. The first trip we made together was for a meeting in Albuquerque, New Mexico. The purpose was to acquaint local officials with the policies of the new Agricultural Act.

I had prepared J.P.'s presentation to the group and was also available to answer questions. *(Note: J.P. Jones was a newcomer to speaking about policy matters. He was not as familiar as I was with regulations and policies of the new Agricultural Act which would affect the ASCS and its personnel).* I had a big advantage over J.P. because Dennis Avery had scheduled long training sessions to explain the intricacies of the new Act to Area Information Officers. *The fact was that Dennis knew more about this new Act than most of his superiors. And, as a friend of Carroll Brunthaver, Secretary Butz's assistant, Dennis actually formulated many of the policies to be implemented.*

At the end of the day-long session, J.P. and I were invited to go out to dinner at a fine Mexican restaurant with a group of top state and county officials. *This was my introduction to "New Mexico style" food and found it to be quite different from the "Tex Mex" food with which I was familiar. I quickly developed a liking for this style over the more prevalent "Tex Mex" style popular in most of the U.S.*

This dinner also gave me a chance to learn more about J.P. and his air exploits. Things I didn't know to ask! During dinner, one of the wives asked: "J.P., did you file a flight plan with the FAA before leaving the Washington DC area?" J.P. rather shamefacedly admitted that he had not filed a flight plan.

The lady then added to his discomfort by asking, "Did you know (and she named an individual)?" J.P. said yes, that he knew him. She then said, "He was flying to Nevada a month ago and never arrived." She added: "We checked to see if he filed a flight plan to help locate him and found out that he had not. Assuming his plane crashed, officials have been looking for him for a month but no one has been able to find him or his plane! I thought you needed to know that, J.P. We don't want to lose you." *(I didn't want to lose either of us!)*

That conversation caught my attention big time and I never flew with him again without first asking: "J. P., did you file a flight plan?" Since we were heading to another location the next day, I made sure that J.P. filed a flight plan before we left Albuquerque for our ultimate destination, Nevada.

After leaving the next morning the weather became very rough and the fog was dense. After awhile, J.P. said "We've got to land at the closest airport we can find." I think we were still in New Mexico but may have entered Colorado. In any event, from what I could see through the dense fog, the area appeared to be sparsely popu-lated. Before landing J.P. said, "Jim, you watch for towers and trees on the right and I'll watch for anything ahead and to the left." *That became our standard procedure when taking off and landing!*

This time we landed at what turned out to be a deserted airfield. We sat in the plane for only a few minutes before a station wagon arrived from the nearby small town to pick us up. The driver told us that the bad weather and fog were supposed to continue until late the next day and that we wouldn't be able to fly for at least 24 hours. He then dropped us off at a hotel where we registered as "Jim Jones" and "Jim White." The desk clerk gave us a funny look but provided us keys to two rooms. J.P. used the telephone in his room to reschedule our meeting and we went to dinner at an old fashioned family type restaurant.

The next day we drank coffee and talked until the fog lifted enough for us to take off for our next stop which we expected to be in Nevada. We never made it to Nevada that trip although we made every effort to do so. We headed west and flew over Bryce Canyon--rather we flew to about the middle of this huge can-yon. Then, although the plane's speedometer (air speed indicator or ASI) showed we were flying 200 MPH, I watched a spot on the floor of the canyon and we didn't travel past that spot for the next two hours. The headwinds were keeping us from making any appreciable forward progress, despite what the speedometer indicated.

Finally, as darkness was approaching J. P. turned the plane left (or south) and we were able to make headway toward a small airport located deep in the mountains of Utah. As we approached the short runway, J. P. urged me to be especially watchful because we had to fly through a narrow path of tall trees to land. Later that evening, he also volunteered that he was very near sighted. This information didn't do any-thing for my nerves.

In the morning, J. P. decided that the weather would not permit us to continue westward so he decided to fly south to Texas where he would spend the weekend at his home. I returned to Washington DC on a commercial flight. That trip may sound like a terrible waste of time but it had one lasting benefit. During the time we spent together, J. P. and I developed a friendship and trust that might have taken months to develop otherwise.

# CHAPTER 41

## A Last Memorable Trip in the Bellanca

J.P. AND I made several more business trips together in the little Bellanca plane but our last one was most memorable. We started from Manassas (about 15 minutes from my home in Clifton) where he parked his plane at a private airport. Our first stop was again in Albuquerque where we had another meeting scheduled. As we were starting the landing process, I noticed that a gauge was showing "very low battery."

Before we left the Albuquerque airport for our meeting, J.P. asked the airport mechanic to charge the battery. I had thought he would ask the mechanic to see what was causing the low battery light to come on. But I didn't argue with him figuring he knew more about airplanes than I did.

We finished our meeting, spent the night in Albuquerque and headed to our next meeting which was in Salt Lake City, Utah. Before we were halfway to Salt Lake City I noticed the battery was creeping into the danger zone. J. P. said not to worry, he would turn off everything using power and we would make it to our next stop without a problem.

When we approached Salt Lake City Airport and started to land, the battery indicator was fully in the danger zone. It also took some extra effort for J.P. to lower the wheels for landing. This time I was sure that J.P. would request the airport mechanical service to do a complete check on what was causing the battery to go down. But he again just asked them to charge his battery. I urged him to get the mechanics to fix what was wrong but he said that since he was heading back to his home in Texas for the weekend he would get his own mechanic to take care of any problem with the plane. Since I was flying commercial back to DC anyway, I didn't argue with him too much.

We finished our business and said our goodbyes, and made plans to get together the following Monday morning. I flew to Washington National and got home Friday evening. Monday morning came, I went to J.P.'s office, but he was not there to greet me. He called my office later that morning and said: "Jim I won't see you for a couple of days; I had to crash land my plane in a cotton field near my home in Texas! I wasn't hurt but my plane is a mess. I'm taking a commercial flight back to Washington in a couple of days and will tell you all about it then."

When J.P. returned to DC, we spent time together while he told this story: Soon after he took off for Texas the "danger-low battery light" came on and he turned off all the navigation equipment, radio, etc., retrieved a flashlight and a map and kept on flying toward Texas in the dark. He used the flashlight to look at the map and used city lights to guide him back home. When he tried to land at his local airport, he could not get the landing wheels down. Fearing what might happen if he did a "belly landing" on concrete, he chose to land on a nearby cotton field. He walked away with just a few scratches but his plane suffered serious damage.

He then said: "Jim, we'll have to fly commercial while I get my plane fixed." I agreed and added: "J. P., I have a wife and small child so I have already decided to fly commercial from now on." He said he understood and I continued to work with him while I was with ASCS. And I never had a more pleasant working relationship than I had with J. P. Jones.

He once told me that he had a hard time believing how much the speeches I wrote for him "sounded just like me"! I told him it was my job to make speeches sound like the speaker--not the writer.

# CHAPTER 42

## A Speech and Another Person to Remember

ALTHOUGH NOT AS exciting as flying around the Southwest with J.P. Jones, a particularly humorous work-related thing happened while I was carrying out another duty at ASCS. *One of the jobs of the Information Division was to prepare speeches for Headquarters ASCS officials (from Deputy Assistant Secretaries all the way up to Secretary Butz).* On the occasion in question, I was assigned to write Deputy Assistant Secretary George Hansen's final speech before he left USDA to return to Idaho to try to regain his old Congressional seat in his home state. Mr. Hansen was a physically impressive, handsome man, 6 ft., 6 inches tall. He was also incredibly naive for Washington, DC political types.

All of us dreaded writing Mr. Hansen's speeches. He wanted every speech to sound like a 4th of July speech. Nothing was too maudlin for him. Just for the heck of it, I decided I would fill the speech with every hackneyed phrase I knew--thinking that this was one speech even George would reject or at least ask me to tone down.

I tried it out on fellow information types and they thought it was hilarious. I turned the speech over to George and waited for his reaction. He absolutely loved it and didn't ask for a single change.

Later, as his resignation was imminent, all of us information officers were invited to visit him in his office to say goodbye and wish him good luck in his Congressional campaign. When I entered his office he grabbed my hand, put his arm around my shoulder, and began reciting passages from the speech I had written for him. I felt like a total heel.

After regaining his Congressional seat, George ran into lots of trouble. First, he was charged and convicted for violating a campaign regulation requiring the disclosure of financial contributions. *None of us who knew him believed he was guilty. We thought someone on his staff must have misled him.* In fact, the federal judge who sentenced him to two months in prison later changed his mind and only made him pay a small fine saying Mr. Hansen's failure to comply with the law was "not evil" but "stupid." We could believe that!

Trouble continued to haunt George Hansen. He was convicted in 1984 of "violating the 1978 Ethics in Government Act, for failing to disclose a large sum in personal loans and other acts." He served six months in prison in 1986, paid a large fine and was released on parole. Then the following year he went to jail for another six months for violating his parole. He appealed these latest convictions all the way to the U.S. Supreme Court which ruled in his favor, vacated his convictions, and ordered that his fine be returned to him. Members of the Court apparently believed his contention that the government was "pursuing a vendetta against him" for his "opposition to federal intrusion into all our lives." Those of us who knew him, regardless of political affiliation, believed the Supreme Court was right in their decision.

George went to prison again for 40 months in the 1990's for another financial transgression. He was convicted of defrauding two Idaho banks and 200 individuals in an investment scheme. Hansen protested that the people willingly gave him the money and about 100 of them came to his defense with affidavits saying he was right. The judge took these affidavits into consideration and gave him another light sentence.

But George Hansen probably gained his greatest public fame by making an unauthorized visit to Tehran in 1979 after Iranian student terrorists overran the U.S. Embassy there and took dozens of hostages. His purpose was to try to get the hostages released. Despite two visits to Tehran, however, Hansen failed to get any hostages released. But George got great TV coverage for his vigorous attempts. He died at age 83 in Pocatello, Idaho. But he will be remembered by many of us who worked with him as "one of our most unforgettable characters."

# CHAPTER 43
## Another Memorable Character

DURING THIS SAME period, I met another unusual character, also heavily involved in politics. This happened when Gwen and I were having dinner at the home of Buck and Nancy Pritchard, the couple I had introduced to each other several years previously. As mentioned earlier, the memorable character's name was Murray Chotiner, who was a fellow guest at the dinner party. As we shook hands, I said, "You're not THE Murray Chotiner are you?" He smiled and said "I'm afraid so."

Because Chotiner was given credit for much of the political success of President Richard Nixon, I was excited about meeting him and seized the opportunity to spend time with him. Since I appeared to be the only person at the party with knowledge of and interest in Murray, I'm afraid I monopolized his time that night. And he was more than willing to talk with me about his role in President Nixon's political career. We ended up alone in a corner of the house for much of the evening and he invited me to ask him questions.

I asked him first about how he met the future President. Chotiner told me that the "Nixon Story" actually began before he met Nixon, when he and a group of fellow public relations friends discussed the possibility of taking a completely unknown person and seeing how far they could advance him (or her) in the political world. After doing some research they came up with the name of Richard Nixon, who had served in the Navy and had a law degree from Duke University.

Since the public relations gurus were located in California it made sense to start with someone in that state and Nixon lived and practiced law in Whittier, CA at the time. Murray said that Nixon seemed to be the perfect candidate for this experiment. He was highly intelligent, ambitious, had the right scholastic background, was a veteran of World War II, was living nearby, and had never run for public office. *And the potential candidate had to agree to let the public relations people prepare him and run the campaign without interference from the candidate. The candidate had to agree not to say or do anything without their approval. He said Nixon agreed to all these terms and became the candidate for congress.*

With the help of Chotiner as his chief adviser, Nixon ran and was elected to the U.S. Congress as a Republican on his first try. Helen Gahagan Douglas, who will forever be linked with Nixon, was also elected to the U.S. Congress as a California Democrat at the same time. For those who did not follow politics at that time, let me explain that Mr. Nixon and Mrs. Douglas were polar opposites on the political scale. Nixon was a conservative with strong anti-communist tendencies while Mrs. Douglas, a former famed Hollywood actress (who married fellow actor Melvyn Douglas) was not only liberal but was well known for her socialistic leanings.

In fact her Democrat opponent in her 1950 Senate primary race, Manchester Boddy, the owner and publisher of the Los Angeles Daily News referred to her as "the Pink Lady," declaring publicly that she was "pink right down to her underwear." *I'm not sure how husband Melvyn Douglas felt about that revealing statement!*

In our conversation about the 1950 Senate race between Nixon and Douglas, Murray said he and Nixon merely took full advantage of the ammunition supplied them by her Democrat primary opponent. Without any trace of shame, he said he had thousands of leaflets **printed in pink** and sent them to Democrat voters with derogatory information about Mrs. Douglas.

*Nixon won the election easily with 59 percent of the vote. As a result of the tactics used against Mrs. Douglas, however, Nixon gained the name "Tricky Dick" that stuck with him until his death.*

Murray regaled me with other stories about Nixon and the campaigns he had managed for the President. He said Nixon won every election where he (Murray) had been allowed to run the campaign. The elections Nixon lost were managed by others. He explained that as Nixon grew in stature, he surrounded himself with "classier" advisers and moved Murray to a background position.

At the moment, he had a small office in the Executive Office Building, rather than the White House, where the President and his more impressive appearing advisers held forth. *To be perfectly honest, Murray Chotiner was not particularly physically impressive, i.e. he would never be mistaken as a "movie star." To me he appeared modest and soft spoken--not the rough and ready, aggressive person one would expect for someone with his "bare knuckle" approach to politics.*

When the night ended, Murray handed me his card with private number and said, "Jim, if you ever need my help call that number and say 'Mr. Chotiner wants to talk to me' and I'll pick up the phone."

I never expected to need his help but circumstances changed that. One day I received a call from former Catawba College Head Basketball Coach Earl Ruth, who had been elected as a U.S. Congressman from North Carolina. Congressman Ruth asked me if I could have lunch with him at the House dining room. I was somewhat surprised at that since I had seen him only a few times since I graduated from Catawba. He volunteered that he remembered and was impressed by my activities at Catawba and thought I was quite intelligent. We agreed on a time I would meet him at his office from where we would go together to the dining room.

As we were eating lunch, Congressman Ruth told me that one of his top staff members had a drinking problem and asked if I could recommend someone to take the job. The Congressman *made it clear I was his first choice as the person he wanted to hire. Since his re-election campaign was imminent, he needed me right away.* I told him I would need to think about it and get back to him soon.

*I must admit that this possibility piqued my interest since I had always been intrigued by the "behind the scenes" aspects of politics. I had just recently written a speech for a Virginia Republican politician.* I went back to my office and asked an administrative supervisor if I could get a short leave of absence to work for a Congressman and then return to my present job. I knew this had been done in the past but he said this "would not be possible at this time."

This led me to think that perhaps I should talk to Murray Chotiner about this problem and gave him a call. I got through his screener by saying "Mr. Chotiner wants to talk to me." He immediately picked up the phone and I explained the situation to him. He said, "That's not a problem for me to get that done. But, Jim, I know you have a good Federal career going and you should know that if you do this, when you go back to work as a Civil Service employee you will always be regarded as a "political type" rather than a regular employee. Think about these implications and call me back before I intervene."

After thinking about it and talking with Gwen, I decided that I did not want to put a cloud over my Civil Service career. So, I called Murray to tell him I was going to follow his advice and "stay put" with my present job. I then arranged another meeting with Congressman Ruth to give him my decision. At the same time I gave him a typed out "re-election plan of action" I had prepared immediately after our first meeting in Washington. I don't know whether my plan was helpful to him or not, but Congressman Ruth was re-elected for two more terms before losing on his fourth election try.

After losing the election, Congressman Ruth received a presidential appointment as Governor of American Samoa from 1975-1976. He died August 15, 1989 in Salisbury, NC the home of Catawba College where he had coached.

I never saw or conversed with Murray Chotiner again but read in the Washington Post that he was in an automobile accident resulting in a broken leg and was being treated at Washington Hospital Center. Two weeks later, I read that Murray had appeared to be recovering from the broken leg but the evening before he was to be discharged "he started to gasp uncontrollably."

X-rays revealed a blood clot near the lung and treatment was unsuccessful. He died of pulmonary embolism at the hospital. What a sad, premature ending for such a vital, strong-willed individual like Murray Chotiner.

# CHAPTER 44

## A Sudden Turn in My Career

THINGS SETTLED INTO a routine with me at USDA. I was happy in my GS-13 grade which was the highest grade I had earlier hoped to achieve. Then my career took another turn. One morning as I arrived at the USDA parking garage, I was approached by Harold Alford, who I had worked with while on the special temporary assignment for the Pesticide Registration Division. As mentioned earlier, Harold was Assistant Director of that division under Dr. Harry Hays and I had worked closely with him.

Although I had a pleasant, productive time at PRD and had developed a close relationship with Dr. Hays, I had one fairly serious problem while there. PRD had made a costly mistake that could have serious repercussions if publicly divulged. I knew that there was no way this mistake would not eventually be made public. I immediately recommended to Dr. Hays that we get on top of the situation ourselves before it was "leaked" to the media. If or when that happened, we would have no control over how the event was portrayed to the public. If we revealed the mistake, apologized for it, and let the public know we were taking steps to prevent this from happening again in the future, the public would be more forgiving.

Dr. Hays was adamantly opposed to this approach. He wanted to continue trying to hide PRD's mistake believing strongly that it would never be revealed to the public. I then discussed the matter with my Information Director, who in turn went to the head of USDA's Main Information Division to get his thinking on this. Both agreed that it would be a mistake to continue this "cover up" and I was told to write the story regardless of Dr. Hays' protests.

I wrote the story honestly but put the "best face" on it I could and the story went out. I delivered an information copy personally to Dr. Hays. He exploded when he read the story. He called me a "traitor" and said our friendship was ended. My Information Director paid a personal visit to Dr. Hays trying to patch things up by telling him that I had no choice in the matter--that the entire agency's integrity was at stake and that the mistake would eventually be found out, along with attempts to cover it up. But Dr. Hays was not swayed by that reasoning. Sadly, he never forgave me and our friendship was lost forever.

Although I did not discuss this matter with Harold Alford, I felt that he agreed with my position. Sometime later, I read that Dr. Hays had resigned as Director of PRD. At about the same time it was also announced that this Division was being transferred to the newly-formed U.S. Environmental Protection Agency (EPA). However, I knew nothing about the effect of this pending move upon the rest of the PRD personnel until later.

Thus, I had no inkling of what Harold had in mind when he approached me and asked if I could spare a few minutes while he briefed me on the new situation involving the transfer of PRD from USDA to EPA. He told me that he had been named "interim" Director of PRD and that the agency would remain in the USDA South Building for now.

*(Note: EPA was initiated by President Nixon who accompanied his statement establishing the EPA with a Re-organization Plan dated July 9, 1970. Nixon informed Congress that he wanted to put together the new agency from parts of three federal Departments, plus various Bureaus, Administrations, Councils, and assorted other offices).*

*The Interior Department would turn over the Federal Water Quality Administration, and its pesticides research work. The Department of Health, Education, and Welfare (HEW) would turn over the National Air Pollution Control Administration as well as its pesticide functions. The Food and Drug Administration (FDA) would turn over its pesticides research, and the Bureaus of Solid Waste Management, Water Hygiene, and (portions of) the Bureau of Radiological Health.*

*The U.S Department of Agriculture would lose the pesticides registration program, a mammoth job handled by the Agricultural Research Service, as well as specified activities of the Atomic Energy Commission and the Federal Radiation Council. The Council on Environmental Quality's ecological research would also be transferred to EPA. By combining USDA's pesticides registration and monitoring function with the pesticides programs being transferred from HEW and Interior, the new agency would be given controlling power over the introduction of pesticides of various kinds into the environment.*

# CHAPTER 45
## The Possibility of a Career Change?

SINCE THE ARS Registration work had to continue without any pause, it was one of the last units to be physically moved to the EPA facility. Meanwhile, Harold Alford told me he was re-organizing PRD to deal with the problem of moving pesticide registrations through the system in a timely manner.

In our brief encounter at the USDA parking lot Harold said: "Jim, I want you to be an important part of our new organization. I know we don't have time to discuss details right now but I need to know if you would be interested in coming to work with me. I can give you a GS-14 to start." Naturally I told him I would be interested in the job. I continued on to my ASCS office and didn't think too much about the possibility mentioned by Harold. To my surprise, about two weeks later, Harold called and said: "Jim would you be able to come to my office to take a look at the Position Description (PD) I've been working on?" I told him I would be right over.

When I entered Alford's office, he shook my hand and then handed me a copy of the PD for the job and told me to make any changes I thought needed to be made. I read the PD and found it perfectly fit my background; I don't recall making a single change. Harold said: "If you agree, I'll take this to personnel and you'll be hearing from them soon." I expected a long wait. Personnel usually took its time with these types of matters.

After returning to my office, I met with Dennis Avery and Bill Cummings to tell them about the offer I had received. Much to my surprise, Cummings immediately began to make serious efforts to try to keep me at ASCS. He provided me with a copy of a two-page single spaced paper he had written and sent to top ASCS officials and the personnel office detailing my contributions to the agency and requesting they "secure an exception to the freeze on promotions" and immediately upgrade my position to a GS-14. *Although Dennis and I never discussed this unusual effort by ASCS to promote me, I suspect he might have had something to do with it.*

Although I appreciated the effort to keep me at ASCS, I was already sure that my future work career lay with EPA. The matter became a moot point when a few days later personnel called me to say that the transfer had been completed and I should report to Harold Alford who was now my supervisor. I said goodbye to Dennis Avery, Bill Cummings and my other friends at ASCS as well as to Area Director J. P. Jones and headed back to USDA's South Building.

*At my last session with J. P. he had confided something to me I never breathed to anyone--until now. J. P. told me that he had been informed by his staff that Administrator Kenneth Frick's own large California farm had been found "out of compliance." J. P. said that it was a serious violation but that he felt sure that the violation was not deliberate. He said he had scheduled a face-to-face session with Administrator Frick to discuss the problem with him. That was the last time I saw J. P. Jones in person though we talked by telephone several times.*

In one of our conversations, J. P. told me that his meeting with Administrator Kenneth Frick did not go well. In fact, the administrator had fired him from his job as Southwest Area Director over the "non-compliance" issue. However, J. P. assured me that he had enough political clout of his own to protect his career with ASCS. He said he had just accepted a good job at the Texas State ASCS Office.

He added that despite the sudden ending of his Southwest Area Director job he had enjoyed his time there and his close work with me. With both our busy new schedules, our only contact after that was by telephone. It must have been fate that J. P. and I both left our positions with the ASCS Southwest Area within a week of each other.

# CHAPTER 46
## A Different Type of Information Work

MY FIRST DAY at the PRD main office was an "eye opener" for me. Although I knew in general the nature of the work I was going to be doing, I didn't know the details. I found that Harold had completely re-organized the main office where he was now the Director. He explained that he had been spending too much of his time dealing with details and he had come up with a new system that would allow him more time to deal with the really serious issues, e.g., clearing up the "log jam" of registration applications.

He explained that the new system would revolve around three people: himself, Charles Smith and me. Harold would be in the center of the office with his private secretary. Smith would occupy the cubicle to the right of Alford and I would occupy the cubicle to the left. Smith and I would share a secretary and Alford's secretary would help out when needed and available. Smith would handle scientific matters and I would handle any matters that involved public information or public relations.

All written material coming to the office would be checked initially by Alford's secretary who would decide whether it should go on Smith's desk or mine. Once we received the material, we were to review the document and (1) write one paragraph summarizing the problem and (2) write a suggested solution, not to exceed one page. Alford would then read each summary and either use it "as is" or return it to either Smith or me with suggestions he thought should be included, expanded upon, or excluded. He was not a "nit picker" and usually accepted the suggestions Smith and I passed along to him.

*An interesting side note: As a child, Harold Alford had a learning disability--something like dyslexia. Despite that, he had received a Master's Degree from Auburn University, and was widely known as the top authority on U.S. pesticide laws and history in the world. The only remaining sign of his learning disability was that it would take him several minutes to read one page--something I could do in seconds back then. There was another big difference in our approach however. When Harold finally finished reading the page he could repeat it back word for word. I could come up with a summary but could not repeat verbatim a single line I had just read. Mr. Alford is the only person I've ever known who had a truly photographic memory. He had turned his disability into an advantage, becoming the top expert in his field. And he also was one of the best managers I ever knew.*

The system developed by Harold Alford was a dramatic success. Within a few months, using the system Alford had put into place, PRD had completely eliminated the 1½ year "back up" of registrations which had plagued PRD for years. The agency was now current in the handling of registrations for the first time in memory. Alford's system worked like a well-oiled machine until the registration and other USDA pesticide activities were finally turned over to EPA and we were all moved from the USDA South Building to 401 M Street S.W., location of the rapidly growing U.S. Environmental Protection Agency.

This translocation and combining of elements from many governmental groups brought many changes to all of us as well as the functions affecting pesticides in the U.S. Some of these changes were good and some very bad. These will be discussed in PART 7 to follow.

PART 7

# My Career Takes Another Turn: Working with USDA, EPA, & DOE

# CHAPTER 1
## Changes in FIFRA Bring Many Agencies Together!

I'M NOW AT the great Environmental Protection Agency and ready to help them save the world --or at least some of the environment in which we live!

Before going further, I need to explain how the agency was formed and how I was expected to fit into this labyrinth of groups coming from other Federal agencies. Let's begin by explaining that shortly after the formation of the EPA, the U.S. Congress in 1972 made many important revisions of the law affecting pesticides, i.e., **The Federal Insecticide, Fungicide and Rodenticide Act** (known as **FIFRA**). Changes in FIFRA coincided with the transition of most pesticide regulatory functions from **USDA's Pesticide Regulations Division (PRD)** to EPA. Functions and people from other agencies and groups involved with pesticides, e.g., **HEW's Public Health Service,** were suddenly transferred to EPA.

Amendments to FIFRA were largely responsible for bringing me and many others to EPA. It contained extensive changes designed to provide greater protection to pesticide users, the public, animals, and the environment. The new or revised functions that affected me most directly were Section 4(a) & 4(b), Section 5, Section 18 and Section 24. All these provisions were assigned to the newly-formed EPA Operations Division where I was placed within the Office of Pesticide Programs (OPP). Ultimately, management of all of these functions became my responsibility.

**A brief explanation of each of these functions follows**:

**Section 4 (a)** required development of standards (regulations) to be required for applicators of "Restricted Use" pesticides, i.e., pesticides considered particularly hazardous to humans and the environment; **Section 4 (b)** required development of regulations whereby each state would develop a plan (with approval by EPA) for carrying out training and certification of pesticide applicators in their state. "General Use" pesticides could still be applied without any special training or certification.

**Section 5** allowed manufacturers of pesticides to field test their products under development with Experimental Use Permits (EUPs) issued by EPA with designated provision to ensure safety.

**Section 18** gave the EPA authority to allow State and Federal agencies to permit the use of an unregistered pesticide in a specific area under the Emergency Exemption Rule of FIFRA, again with specified procedures to be followed.

**Section 24(c)** authorized EPA to allow states to register a new pesticide for general use, or a federally-registered product for an additional use, if there is both a demonstrated "special local need," if the state met certain conditions.

At the end of Part 6, I discussed the system that Director Alford had put into place and which had successfully solved the problem of the huge backlog of pesticide registrations which had plagued PRD for many years. We had hoped that EPA would recognize this success story and keep that system and personnel in place. But as so often happens, re-organization often occurs during changes. Pesticides Regulation Division became Office of Pesticide Programs (OPP), with several divisions being placed under the umbrella of OPP.

To the shock and horror of many of us, Harold Alford was removed from his position as Director of PRD as we were moved from South Building, USDA, to the new EPA headquarters building on Maine Ave. in Southwest Washington. He was moved basically into an empty office with none of the important duties he had handled so well when serving as Acting Director, PRD. *(This is an old governmental trick to remove any semblance of authority for previously highly-placed officials who have career status and cannot easily be fired. The good ones always find jobs elsewhere and leave willingly).*

One of the hurtful things to Harold was that some of the people he had helped the most turned their backs on him after he was removed from his position as Director. I happened to be with him when two of these ingrates feared to be seen riding with him on the same elevator. They pretended to change their mind and went another direction! Although Harold knew they did this out of fear for their jobs, their rejection was still painful to him.

I tried to help make up for this by arranging for the two of us to walk down the center aisle together and sit at the same table at the big American Association of Pest Control Officials (AAPCO ) Annual Dinner. Heavy hitters of the chemical industry are members of AAPCO and, along with top government officials involved with pesticides, attend this fancy dinner. Harold and I waited until almost everyone was seated and then walked slowly side-by-side to our table near the front of the room. No one in the crowd could miss the statement we were making. Harold really appreciated that public gesture of friendship.

*P.S. Not surprisingly, as soon as the state of California found out Harold Alford had been "re-assigned" they made him an offer to work in a cooperative State/Federal program, first in Sacramento with the California Department of Food and Agriculture and later at the University of California, Davis. These were highly sought after jobs, with very good pay, and the chance to receive another retirement--this one from the state of California.*

# CHAPTER 2
## A New Job in a New Agency

AS MENTIONED ABOVE, I was placed in the newly-established Operations Division with the title of Federal/States Relations Officer. My regular duties were defined as primary contact with headquarters EPA, Regional EPA Pesticide Offices, and State Pesticide Regulatory Offices. I also initially wrote the OPP Newsletter.

Soon after transferring to EPA, I was told I had been selected to be a member of a group of EPA officials invited to spend a week in Hawaii evaluating the effects of EPA regulations upon the agricultural practices of this "tropical paradise." (I suspect Alford had a hand in my receiving this high visibility assignment!)

The trip was financed and organized by associations representing Hawaii's two major crops: pineapple and sugar cane. Top officials of these two powerful organizations, along with Hawaii's state officials, planned the entire week for us including trips to experimental farms and processing plants where we interacted with Hawaiian agricultural scientists and growers. And of course they had planned our meals and evening entertainment. The latter two functions featured wonderful food and entertainment representative of the varied social and ethnic groups in Hawaii's rich culture.

Although I initially wondered how I would fit into and contribute to this heavily scientific activity, I soon found my role: acting as intermediary between scientists of the home state and those representing the EPA. I made notes of various EPA pesticide regulations which were not applicable to Hawaii's environment and included these in my report of the trip to the appropriate OPP officials at EPA.

*One such example I recall: a requirement that registration tests be done using a species of shrimp not found anywhere in the Hawaiian Islands! That test was then changed to a species that was available. There were other examples I don't recall of requirements that could not be done for various valid reasons.*

We had a busy week touring the Islands of Oahu, Maui, and the Big Island of Hawaii which was our final stop. As we were getting ready to leave there, our hosts made time for us to purchase tree or vine ripened fruit to take home with us. A pineapple lover, I bought two large cases of this prime fruit. Then I began wondering how I would get these large crates, along with my luggage, through customs and onto the plane. Not to worry! Our hosts transported us and our fruit and baggage right past customs and the plant and animal health inspectors (APHIS) who normally check all passengers for illegal fruit and animal products. *Of course, I had worked with that latter group while employed at USDA and was not likely to be "hassled" but it was nice to be escorted directly to the plane.*

This trip also introduced me to a memorable character by the name of Dr. Jake Mackensie, EPA Region IX Pesticide Chief. Organizationally, Hawaii, Guam, American Samoa and some other South Pacific Islands are included as part of Region IX. Jake, a Scotsman with a delightful Scottish "brogue," turned out to be the "life of the party" at the evening events. And he became a close associate and friend of mine for my remaining years at EPA. Much more about him later.

My title remained the same for awhile but my duties changed quickly. I was asked to serve as the "Chairperson of the Sub-Committee" to develop "draft Standards for Pesticide Applicator Certification" to meet the requirements of Section 4 (a) of amended FIFRA. *To my surprise, I saw my name listed as "Chairperson" of this committee in an early 1973 issue of the Federal Register. I never expected to see my name prominently displayed in this important document.*

The new duties required me to assemble a group of representative Regional EPA and State Pesticide Regulatory officials to begin work on these new standards. I was given leeway in selecting participants but was told to restrict the total number to 10. *Incidentally, I suspect Harold Alford, who still carried "clout" because of his outstanding career in pesticide regulations, also had something to do with my being named to head the Subgroup on Certification Standards.* This was another "high visibility" job and I can think of no other plausible reason that I got this assignment since I was new to EPA with little scientific expertise. Harold never mentioned this to me but then he would not have wanted any credit in my auspicious start with EPA.

With this new title, I faced the difficult choice of selecting members of the Certification Sub-Committee. Naturally, representatives of the EPA Regional Offices and State Pesticide Regulatory Offices would make up most of the Sub-Committee. The choice of who was selected could be controversial, as will be described later. Although not members of the Sub-Committee, I would ask representatives of many outside organizations to participate by providing input and suggestions throughout various stages of the process. These groups would include various pesticide applicator and chemical industry representatives as well as environmental groups.

Since there were 10 EPA Regional Offices, each with a Pesticide Branch Chief, plus 50+ states and territories, each with Pesticide Regulatory functions, I was immediately faced with a big political problem. The question: How do I select 10 people from a group of more than 60 without offending someone or several someones? The answer: I couldn't. But with the advice of two existing members of the Sub-Committee I would do the best I could.

# CHAPTER 3
## My Initial Members were Life Savers

THE TWO PEOPLE already selected to be a part of my Subgroup were: Dr. Burton R. (Bob) Evans, who had been transferred from the Public Health Service (PHS) of Health, Education and Welfare (HEW) to the Operations Division of EPA, and Ivan Dodson, Pesticide Branch Chief of EPA Region VIII, located in Denver, CO. Although now an official member of the Operations Division of OPP, Dr. Evans would remain located in Chamblee, GA. Ivan Dodson would keep his Regional Branch Chief status as his primary job but would assist the Sub-Committee on an "as needed" basis when my schedule and his could be reconciled.

By virtue of his education, experience and availability, Dr. Evans was a life-saver to me right from the start. He had a PhD in Entomology and for many years served as a Commissioned Officer for the Public Health Service (PHS) which turned over Bob and much of its work involving pesticides to EPA.

Since my degrees in English and Journalism and background in newspaper writing and Public Information work provided me with little to no scientific credibility, Dr. Evans' credentials helped make up for my lack. *The little scientific knowledge I had acquired came from my work with PPC and the short time I worked with Harold Alford's unit. Those experiences turned out to be valuable in my varied functions at EPA.* However, that was not generally known at the time so it's easy to see how someone with Bob's background was essential--especially in the beginning stages of the Certifications Sub-Committee.

It pains me to admit that initially I had difficulty even pronouncing the names of some pesticides we were considering developing safety and environmental standards around. But, with Bob's help I eventually overcame that problem. However, I never pretended to be an expert in this field and was not too proud to admit it. From the beginning, I knew that even if Harold Alford gave me a boost, I still had to pass muster if I were to survive or advance with EPA. I suspect the agency knew my background was in writing and that I had only a superficial knowledge of pesticides. However, I had a few other assets that turned out to be valuable to the effort.

These attributes were: (1) I knew and was friends with many of the state officials who would be responsible for actually carrying out the provisions of the Certification Program, (2) my journalism background assured that any proposed regulations the Subcommittee came up with would be understandable (often not the case with government writing) and (3) since I had been with the Federal Government, I had established a reputation for meeting deadlines—not a characteristic common to Federal Government employees.

Along with the responsibilities EPA had placed upon my shoulders, the agency gave me the authority to consult with any of the experts at EPA. It turned out that Bob Evans and Ivan Dodson were the only experts I needed in the beginning. The two of them kept me out of serious trouble. Later, I did take advantage of and use the knowledge of other experts at EPA.

Bob deserves full credit for the initial writing but I soon began to get a better feel for contributing to the content as well as managing the project. It was also a great asset that Bob already had a good idea of what needed to be included in the "general" standards, i.e., rules that would apply to all applicators, regardless of their particular specialty or specialties. In the beginning I didn't know enough about the law or subject matter to begin writing the first draft but Bob Evans did and I let him take the lead.

Ivan Dodson was an invaluable member of the Sub-Committee in various ways. Not only was he knowledgeable about pesticides, he offered policy guidance and suggestions for other Regional representatives to be added. Ivan was blessed with high intelligence and an unmatched sense of humor. Regardless of how serious a situation appeared, Ivan could find some humor in it. He soon became a close personal friend as well as supporter of our activities. I was so fortunate to have two very competent people with such different types of personalities and skills. We soon reached a complete level of trust without a single conflict or serious disagreement.

The first two meetings Bob Evans and I had were quite interesting to say the least. I went to Chamblee, Georgia, where Bob was located, for our first meeting. I was immediately impressed with his knowledge, modesty and pleasant personality. There was just one problem: he was smoking a "stinking" cigar the whole time I was there. I have always been highly sensitive to tobacco smoke but since I was in his space, I suffered in silence. Then he came to visit me at my office in Washington. As soon as he sat down, he lit up a cigar. I promptly said "Put out that damned cigar!" He looked shocked but promptly put out the cigar.

We got along fine after that and we've had many laughs over the years about our first and second meetings. Bob loved to tell that story. *You need to remember that the anti-tobacco crusade had not reached its peak in the early 70's. Even my bosses gave me questioning looks when I put up a "no smoking" sign in my office at EPA. And in the early days, EPA employees themselves smoked anywhere they wanted —including the EPA Building elevators and snack shop!* Despite our "rocky" start, Bob and I soon became fast friends. When he came to Washington Gwen and I would often invite him to stay at our home.

# CHAPTER 4

## A Six Year Project from Beginning to End

RETURNING TO ANOTHER subject, closing on the abandoned and condemned Victorian cottage in the little village of Clifton, VA, began a six-year project during which I saw little of Gwen and Mitch except for late evening and a few minutes each Saturday when they stopped by the cottage on their way to shop. To avoid frequent interruptions in the narrative, I will complete this story below.

I knew that before any substantial work could be done, I would need a building permit. And I knew that I would need a professionally drawn blueprint before the county would consider letting me remove the "condemned" label and issue me a building permit. Since most of the houses in Clifton had been labeled as "condemned" before the town's revival, I sought the help of a young architect (Jim) who had been active in restoration of several houses in Clifton including his own home.

After looking at the job, the architect saw a major problem: because I wanted to add an addition to the kitchen at the back of the house, a "variance" would be required. The reason? The house itself was already too close to the side street but could be "grandfathered" if no changes were made to the exterior walls. However, any change that resulted in any part of the house being closer to the street would not be allowed without a "variance." The kitchen addition would result in further encroachment. Aggravating the situation was the fact that the back of the house was "angled" toward the street.

Jim prepared a beautiful blueprint and went with me to the county department handling building permits and other issues. After looking at the blueprint and discussing all the issues with Jim and me, the official issued a variance and signed a building permit which I immediately stapled to the front door, replacing the "condemned" sign. The architect also told the county official that he would be available to consult with me on an "as needed" basis and this helped me become designated as "homeowner general contractor" for the restoration and addition.

The main advantage of the latter designation is that it not only allowed me to do as much work as I could but would also let me hire sub-contractors who could do the masonry work, electrical and plumbing, drywall hanging and finishing, floor installation and finishing, etc. That cut out much of the "middle man" costs for sub-contractors. However, I was still required to get all the necessary inspections.

As soon as I stapled the building permit to the front of the house, I unloaded my tools and went to work. I began by setting up "saw horses" which would provide me a solid surface for removing nails from the old Victorian trim I was going to remove and recycle. Most of the trim would be beautiful after the many coats of paint were removed, holes were filled, and fresh coats of primer and finish coats of paint were applied. But I was a long way from that stage.

The toughest part of this job initially turned out to be removing all the old plaster and lath from the interior walls and ceilings. I would pull the nails and save the trim for later re-installation. But it would be my unpleasant job to carry all the old plaster, lath, appliances, etc. from the house to the county landfill. This would have to be done to enable the installation of new electrical, plumbing and heating/air conditioning systems. After all this was "roughed in" and insulation added, drywall would be used to cover the walls and ceilings.

I began by removing all the trim, pulling the nails, and stripping the many layers of paint which had been covering the trim for around 100 years. This was the easy part. Then I began removing the old plaster and lath and hauling it to the dump. It was tough enough removing the old plaster and lath from the downstairs, shoveling it into my pickup, transporting it to the county dump several miles away, and then shoveling it off the truck.

Then things got even harder when I moved to the stairway and second floor. Clever devil that I am, I built a chute from plywood that allowed me to transfer this waste material through windows to the ground below. Unfortunately, the rough terrain around the house did not allow me to park the truck underneath the windows to catch the material. So it was back to using the shovel to load the chute which would carry the waste to the ground below where it would again be shoveled onto the pickup for transport to the landfill to be shoveled off there.

*If you watch HGTV remodeling shows, you've likely seen several strong men remove old plaster and lath, place it into a large container which can be loaded, picked up and hauled away never to be seen again. Oh how I wish I would have had access to that system (pictured on TV).*

Once I got all the old plaster and wooden strips removed from the interior and unloaded at the landfill, I got another shock. With the walls and ceiling now open I could see that the ceiling joists and wall studs were not uniform in size. These wood studs and ceiling joists were installed before "dimension" lumber was available. Some of the wall studs measured a true two inches thick by 4 inches wide, while others might be 1½ inches by 3½ inches. The ceiling joists differed in size by as much as two inches. When the house was built, these differences were compensated by the plasterers using more plaster on the smaller dimension lumber and less plaster on the larger.

Since I would be using drywall instead of plaster (a dying art even back then) I was left with the job of adding "shims" to the smaller wall studs and ceiling joists with the appropriate size to match up with the existing studs and joists. This was especially difficult for me because I didn't initially own or know how to use a table saw to rip a large piece of wood into shims. I corrected that omission by purchasing a used Sears table saw and learning how to use it without losing any limbs.

While doing the demolition work, I realized that the small kitchen, which had been added after the main house was built, needed more space added to it or to be removed and replaced with a better constructed and larger kitchen. So, it made sense to me that while the excavation work was being done that the footing and foundation be made large enough to support a two-story addition which would include a new, larger kitchen on the first floor and a master bedroom and bath on the second floor. It also made sense while doing all this work to include a partial basement.

So, I called in an excavation contractor and instructed him on the work that needed to be done. I was trying to get this work completed before winter set in because the entire structure at the back of the house was at risk as a result of the shoddy work done by adding the kitchen at a later date than the house.

The contractor had completed the main excavation and was digging trenches for the foundation footings when his machine broke. He removed the broken part and told me he would have to order a new part which might take several days to obtain and install. The several days stretched into weeks. I knew that it would be difficult to get a new contractor to come in and complete the job so I had no choice except to wait.

# CHAPTER 5

## Disaster Strikes!

THEN CATASTROPHE STRUCK. The Washington DC area had its earliest major snowfall in history. The excavated hole was filled with snow. Once the snow began melting, I borrowed a large pump from a contractor friend and began trying to pump water, snow and mud out of the hole. Each time I got this mess out more rain or snow would fall.

Meanwhile, well dressed Gwen and Mitch would stop by the cottage every Saturday morning on their way to shopping. I would usually be standing in water and covered with mud. The "family project" had quickly turned into "Jim's project."

Because of the continuing rain and snow, the old 4x4 posts holding up the kitchen kept moving and sinking deeper into the mud. Thus, I would have to continually sledge hammer the posts back into place using thicker shims to keep them tight. Otherwise, the posts would fall down into the water--followed by the old kitchen! Note: although I had decided to dispose of the old kitchen eventually rather than add on to it, I did not relish the idea of removing it from a huge mud hole!

As for the pump I was using to try to stay ahead of the snow and rain, I had been warned not to let the top of the pump (where the electrical connector was located) touch the water. If that happened while I was standing in the water, I could be electrocuted. So, I had been very careful to keep that part of the pump clear of the water. However, one day, when the water was especially high, I began sliding in the mud while I frantically tried to keep the top of the pump clear of the water! Fortunately I was standing near one of the posts supporting the old kitchen and fell backward into the post which stopped my sliding into the water taking the pump with me. Because the post stopped my slide into the water, I received only a slight electrical shock.

This situation did not leave me unscathed, however. The used post which stopped my fall contained rows of old rusty nail heads about an inch apart. These old, worn nail heads slashed through the back of my shirt and continued on into the skin on my back.

Although painful, this was a small price to pay for keeping both me and the electrical pump from being submerged in the water, which could have been fatal. When I arrived home, Gwen cleaned, treated and bandaged the wounds. Fortunately I had just had a tetanus shot so there was no "lock jaw" problem. At that point, I decided it was too risky and too futile to keep using the pump to remove water and mud. I unplugged the pump, lifted it from the water, and returned it to its owner.

The rain and snow continued and one day after work when I made my daily visit to check the cottage, I found that the old kitchen had fallen into the water, taking with it the entire back foundation wall of the main house! With no rear foundation to provide support, the floor joists holding up the parlor and dining room were already beginning to sag. This made me fearful that we would lose the entire house. *I probably felt worse than the Tom Hanks character in the movie called "The Money Pit"!*

We did not have the money to hire a professional company to come rescue the house, but I had an idea of how to save it myself. Fortunately I had recently purchased four used "railroad" jacks that I thought I might need to level the floors. My idea was to buy enough treated 2x8 lumber to construct a large (doubled layer) beam that would extend from one side of the house to the other. Although it would take several people to get such a large beam in place, I could carry single pieces under the house and then fasten them together with nails and glue to form a large beam that would eventually support the rear section of the house.

At that point, with the help of one other strong person, we could use the jacks to lift the beam up, get rid of the sag, and support the back of the house until spring came and we could finish the job properly. As an extra precaution, I also used concrete block piers to support each beam in case the jacks slipped.

When I mentioned this idea to a friend, Evan Hale, who was Assistant to Agriculture Secretary Earl Butz, he said: "Jim, as you know, my family is still in Walnut Grove, CA. Secretary Butz is out of town this weekend and I have nothing urgent to do. If you would like, I will be happy to come to your house and help you with this job." I was surprised by Evan's offer but immediately accepted it. I invited him to spend the weekend with us while we got the job done. Gwen provided excellent meals and we turned that dirty, difficult job into a pleasant weekend. It was extra special that a "super grade" like Evan Hale didn't mind getting his hands dirty. Soon after that, Evan was offered a job he "couldn't refuse" back in Walnut Grove and we lost touch but I remained grateful for his help.

Spring finally came and the hole dried up, making it possible to remove the remains of the old kitchen. The contractor was then able to finish his work of digging and pouring footings, so that my brick mason could build four new foundation walls. Once the new foundation was completed, I hired a young man to help me install the sill plates, floor joists and plywood sheathing for the floor of the new addition. I was really pleased when we finished the subfloor of the addition. With a little bit of "jacking" and use of a few "shims" the old floor was made perfectly level with the adjoining new floor.

Now it was time to tackle the job of building the walls for the new addition. Trying to reduce the amount of cutting with the hand saw I was still using, I carefully measured the wall heights needed so that the new floors and ceilings would match up with the old 9 foot walls.

To my pleasant surprise, I found that if I used double floor and triple ceiling plates, plus "non pre-cut" 2X4's, I could match up floors and ceilings of old and new 9 foot high walls with very few cuts. Note: Non pre-cut studs come several inches longer--just right for matching up with the existing walls as long as I used extra top and bottom plates! Pre-cut studs are shorter so that by using traditional single bottom and double top plates the result is an 8-foot wall rather than the taller walls I needed to match up with existing house studs!

After all this was done I could begin construction of the two-floor addition, i.e., the new, larger kitchen and half bath downstairs and the master bedroom, bath, and walk-in closet upstairs. In addition I needed to frame for a second full bath upstairs to serve the two existing guest bedrooms.

Since I was still not comfortable with using a power circular saw, I constructed the first floor walls using my weird system of double bottom plates and triple top plates--all interlocked at the corners. After I finished framing out the first floor addition, I called for the required inspection. The county building inspector looked at what I had done and started laughing. He said, "I've never in my life seen this type of construction. But the way you've interlocked all these top and bottom plates, the wall is certainly strong, so you can continue on the way you're going."

By the time I started the second floor, however, I had developed enough skill and confidence to use a power circular saw. This was absolutely essential because of the many short cuts as well as cuts for door and window headers. With increased ease of making cuts, I abandoned my "weird" construction methods and used traditional building methods to construct the second floor walls and ceiling joists. Despite my new skill with a power saw, it was still laborious and time consuming to build all those walls by myself. And of course I had to get help in lifting and nailing the walls to the floor and together at the corners.

Finally, I had installed the addition's exterior 1/2 inch plywood sheathing, passed all my needed inspections, and called for delivery of the factory-made roof trusses. It goes without saying that doing a solid, professional looking job of connecting the two roof lines is a job rarely undertaken by a novice like me. In my case, I didn't know enough not to decide to try to do this myself. In my defense, however, I did spend considerable time perusing the USDA Forestry Service's construction manuals and picking the brains of builder friends before I got to that point! And I cannot overstate how tough and dangerous this job could be for someone who had never done this before--or even seen it done. And I could not expect anything but some physical help from my inexperienced assistant who had even less knowledge than I. Consequently, I made many mistakes that had to be corrected.

The first big mistake came early, when I failed to specify that the trusses be lifted onto the top floor walls so that all I would have to do was stand them upright and see that they were properly spaced before fastening them to the top plates. I allowed the trusses to be placed on the ground. Because of my ignorance, it was now up to me and my young, inexperienced helper to lift those heavy trusses many feet off the ground and to place them in position on the top plates.

Somehow, by using ropes and pulleys we got the trusses up and lying flat on the top plates. I had measured the space between the trusses for a 16 inch-on-center installation. I provided each of us with a tape measure and we began spacing and fastening the trusses. *(Another stupid mistake! I should have cut two pieces of wood as spacers or should have marked in advance where the trusses should be nailed to the top plates)*. As it happened, the first few trusses were spaced closely enough that the edge of the plywood roof sheathing lined up almost perfectly with the trusses. But as we neared the half way mark, the trusses on my assistant's side were off center enough that I had to start measuring and cutting the plywood sheathing to fit what was obviously unevenly spaced roof trusses.

I went to my young assistant's side to see what was happening. He admitted that in the beginning he had carefully measured the space between the ceiling joists. But as we went along he decided that he could space the trusses close enough "by eye." Since we had already compensated and permanently nailed down all the sheathing on my side and about half of the sheathing on his side, it made sense to continue on in that manner. In addition to the time this extra work took, I was left with many pieces of plywood which were unusable. But on a positive note, none of my mistakes were visible to the naked eye.

As mentioned earlier, the roof sheathing part of a renovation job can be really scary and dangerous. In our case, these factors were magnified because one side of the new addition was so close to the street below. Things were proceeding slowly but as I was cutting a piece of plywood to fit closely against the existing slanted roof, I failed to notice that sawdust from the circular saw had accumulated on the nailed down section of the new roof. Suddenly I began sliding down the roof toward the paved street which was 40 or more feet below. Before going over the edge, I was able to grab a roof vent, which fortunately, the plumber had just installed. Holding on to the vent with both hands, I was forced to let go of my recently purchased circular saw which smashed into the street below.

The vent pipe no doubt saved my life. I spent the next few minutes regaining my senses, then spent more time trying to clear away the sawdust so I could re-gain my footing. Finally, my young assistant securely fastened one end of a rope and let out the rest of it so I could wrap it around my waist and tie it securely. With my helper's assistance, I was then able to pull myself back to the one opening not yet covered. I then let myself down on a step ladder to the second floor and went to the street to retrieve what was left of my circular saw and let my heart return to its normal beat.

Expecting the saw to be completely useless, I was pleasantly surprised that, though it was bent, I could straighten it out enough to continue using it to complete this job. *That made me a believer of the quality of Sears Craftsman tools.* I finally got the roof's last opening covered and used our 24 foot ladder to get back down to the ground. Then I called for the roofer who re-roofed the entire house. The roof looked original and it never leaked while I lived in the Clifton area.

# CHAPTER 6
## Time for the Pros to Take Over

WITH THE HOUSE now under roof, I knew it was time to turn much of the rest of the work over to specialists who do this type of work all the time. I knew that certain functions of house building or restoration are best handled by profession-als. So I hired professional electricians, plumbers, heating and air, and drywall people to do their thing. However, because of my perfectionist nature, I wanted to install the moldings myself. Although some of the original Victorian trim had been salvaged for re-installation, much more was needed for the addition and to replace old trim too damaged to use. I had been looking for additional "old" Victorian trim for some time.

As I was about to give up on finding matching trim, I spotted a newspaper ad saying that a Victorian cottage in Maryland was going to be torn down and that it contained salvageable trim, windows, doors, etc. However, there was a serious problem. By the time I was able to get in touch with the owner, he told me that the wrecking ball was coming in two days.

In describing the trim, the owner revealed that it included the top "bullet" corner blocks and the thicker, bottom "plinths." This of course sounded identical to the trim on our house. *(Note to those unfamiliar with Victorian trim: corner blocks at the top of a door or window and plinth blocks at the bottom of door trim add authenticity and "fanciness" to a Victorian cottage).* Another important feature is that using corner blocks and plinths eliminates much of the need to "miter" corners--something difficult to do in an old house that has "settled" or is otherwise out of "plumb."

Since it was too late to make the trip that afternoon, I arranged for Mitch and me to meet the owner the following morning. This meant that if the trim was suitable, I would have only one day to drive to Maryland, take down the trim without damage, pull out the nails, and load everything on my truck. (The nails had to be pulled immediately in order to get all the trim and some doors in my pickup; time wouldn't permit us to make two trips to Maryland the same day).

We could not believe our good luck when we arrived at the Maryland house, looked inside and saw that the trim and doors were as I had hoped: identical to that of the Clifton house. I immediately paid the owner what he asked for the material and went outside to bring our removal tools from the truck. Mitch was strong enough by then to give me a hand in loading and unloading. But I knew I would have to do all the removal and nail pulling so I went to work.

By working steadily and going without lunch, we were able to get all that precious trim removed, nails pulled, and the trim and doors loaded on the truck. Then we transported it back to Virginia and stored it safely in the cottage--all in the same day. However, this came at a price. All that stooping to pull out the nails caused my back to go out. With only moderate pain, I could install door and window trim and baseboard, but trying to install the shoe mold on my knees caused excruciating pain.

Mitch volunteered to give this a try. Although I still needed to do the cutting, with some lessons on how to pre-drill, hammer in a small finish nail, and use a "nail set," 12-year-old Mitch finished installing the shoe mold! It looked like the work of a master carpenter in the proud eyes of his father.

At this point, the house was now safe and the restoration effort was far enough along that we could spend some "fun time" together as a family. Some people might not consider this "fun time" since it involved finding some fancy exterior trim appropriate to a Victorian cottage. We had exhausted the possibilities of finding such trim in the DC area and had driven to a large architectural antique salvage yard in Richmond, VA hoping to find some unusual Victorian items to "dress up" the front of our little cottage. We didn't find anything worthwhile there but had an enjoyable day together.

Then, I read (or heard) about wonderful architectural antiques available in New England. So, we decided to take a short vacation to Boston with stops along the way. We thought that this trip would provide us a rare chance to enjoy the scenery, eat some fresh New England seafood, and, hopefully, find some fancy Victorian items for the exterior of the cottage. In high spirits, we set out for Boston, Massachusetts, in our large Ford station wagon. We thoroughly enjoyed eating lobster and sightseeing in Boston.

Although we didn't find any architectural antiques that suited our house there, we got a lead about a large salvage yard in Hyannis Port, Mass., so that became our next destination. I was amazed at the amount of fine interior and exterior Victorian house parts for sale at this salvage yard. Before starting for home, we purchased several rare Victorian house parts. The most important of these items were two fancy matching large porch corbels. These were in perfect shape and were just the right size to support the roof of the small front porch I planned to build as soon as the brick mason built the brick porch floor, steps, and short walkway to the street. I had held off building the porch floor until I knew the size of the roof. We now had the desired corbels and got them for a steal--only $75 each for the two!

On the way back to Virginia, we spent a night in Fall River, Mass. *(That was before Fall River native Emeril Lagasse became famous)*. We went to a local Irish family-style restaurant recommended by local people for dinner. When we arrived, the restaurant dining room was almost completely filled with Irish "regulars" who were enjoying dinner and having a great time. The owner initially claimed there was no room for us. However, with my red hair, I must have looked Irish enough that some of the "regulars" told the owner they would "make room for us." The restaurant owner then seated us and we enjoyed the companionship of the "regulars" as well as great, small "chicken" lobsters at $1.00 each!

As soon as we arrived back in Virginia, I called a bricklayer and he helped me to (1) temporarily fasten the corbels to the front of the house and (2) outline the area for a small brick entry porch to complement the corbels. The front of the house looked smashing once the brick had been laid, the mortar dried, and the small roof was permanently installed, supported by those wonderful corbels.

Over the six-year period I had spent on this project, I had to do much of the work alone or with young Mitch's help. However, as the finishing time came, that changed. Gwen did all the painting for the house's interior and it was superior to the painting of any professional house painter. She could paint walls, ceilings, and trim without spilling a drop of paint on the floor (or getting any on herself). And in that period Mitch had changed from a little boy to a robust, athletic pre-teen and as mentioned above could help me with the trim work.

Finally our Victorian cottage was move-in ready (and also ready for showing as it turned out). As we were finishing the final coat of exterior paint (a Victorian yellow with white trim color selected by my artist wife), representatives of the annual "Show of Homes" for Fairfax County appeared and wanted to view the house. After looking it over inside and out, the "Show of Homes" representatives asked if we would permit them to use our house as the No. 1 house for that year's "Show of Homes" event to be held in and around Clifton. Naturally we agreed.

They also wanted to use an image of our house on the cover of the "Show of

Homes" brochure. We were thrilled that those years of work were being recognized. Gwen volunteered to do the artwork for the brochure cover. On Show day, people were lined up for blocks away to view the house, inside and out.

Shortly after the "Show of Homes," we moved from our contemporary style home into our newly-restored cottage in town. At that time we had three large Alaskan Malamute dogs. We had a fence installed around the property to allow our three dogs freedom to get their exercise. And I had personally built "dog runs" to keep them separate for their meal time.

Although they were closely related (mother, daughter and son) the "girls" became aggressive over the food bowls. We were fearful our 130 pound male (Blackie) would not get sufficient food because his much smaller female relatives would not let him near his own food bowl. Talk about chivalry! It was alive and well in our "dog world," at least with Blackie.

Although the little house was beautiful and comfortable, the Malamutes caused us a problem right from the start. The Norfolk-Southern Railway runs right through the middle of Clifton, and always gives townspeople plenty of warning with their loud train whistles. This train sound set off the Malamutes with their "wolf howls" long before the trains arrived and continued for some time after the trains were out of town. In case you're not familiar with them, Malamutes are noted for being the closest relative to their ancestor--the wolf. In fact, Malamutes often play the part of "timber wolves" in movies. Their bark sounds more like a wolf than a dog, and their "wolf howl" is loud and eerie. Imagine hearing those howls every time a train passes by.

To make a long story short, we could find no way to restrain the Malamutes from howling and ultimately we knew we had a choice of either moving back to our "modern" house, or doing another restoration (away from close neighbors and railroad tracks) and moving to it. Since our tastes had changed since we built the modern house, we chose the latter option.

After some looking, I found a small abandoned farm house on a beautiful wooded five acre lot for sale in a new development of five acre lots. I liked the lot and little farm house but there was one serious problem: a clause in the sales contract for this lot required demolition of the little 1,000 sq. ft. farm house. The developer thought the farm house was beyond restoration and had discounted the lot by $3,000 to help pay for the required demolition.

I talked with the owner about the lot and began trying to convince him that the little farm house was worth saving. But he feared that it had deteriorated to the point that restoration was out of the question. I asked him if he would consider letting me restore the old house if I presented him with an architect's blueprint demonstrating how I would add a large addition in keeping with the looks of the little farm house that would meet the subdivision standards. And I assured him that I would restore the old house to "better than new" condition. He accepted a deposit to hold the lot until I could present him with blueprints of my restoration plan.

Soon afterward, I met with Jim, our young architect friend and we went to look at the property together. At that time I described what I wanted to do, starting with a new foundation large enough to support the little house as well as an attached three-car garage on one side and a three-level, 4,000 square foot addition on the other side. When completed, I also wanted the garage to include a large overhead artist studio in which Gwen could do her artwork. The studio would contain skylights to her specifications and would be completed in the same style as the rest of the house. Note: the old house had 9' ceilings so we had to be careful to make all the additional floors line up with these.

I wanted the studio accessible from both the old and new house by stairways with access to a hallway connecting both buildings at the second floor level. Entry to the ground level floor of both houses could be reached by separate front entrances with almost identical front doors. Also, entry to the rear of each house from the garage could be reached through the restored old house or through a new enclosed back porch addition to the old house.

A large deck would be built behind the new main structure and connected to the new back porch serving the farm house. As a final touch, a greenhouse would surround the large chimney at the first floor level with entrances from each side of the great room chimney. The greenhouse would add balance to the property as well as provide solar heat when the doors were left open.

The entire new foundation would be built beginning about 30 feet back from the front lot line. When completed it would support the little farm house, a three car garage on the left, and the large three level addition on the right. Once the foundation was completed, house movers would lift the little farm house, move it back and place it on its new foundation between where the garage and new addition would be built.

The architect friend did a great job of drawing the blueprint to be presented to the developer as well as to Fairfax County building officials (provided the developer agreed to accept my plan). When I showed and explained the blueprint for the completed house, the developer was extremely pleased. It turned out that he had a sentimental attachment to the little house but assumed that no one would want to go to that much trouble and expense to preserve it. At that point, he revised the purchase agreement giving me permission to keep and restore the farm house as long as I followed the plan shown on the blueprint. And he let me retain the $3,000 meant for demolition.

Of course work on this project would not begin for some time. For one thing, I could not take time off from my demanding job to do much of the work myself. Since we already had mortgages on two houses, we didn't want to take on another mortgage to provide funds to hire professionals to do the work. As luck would have it, this was the period of the terrible housing market recession of the late 1970's that continued into the 1980's. We had tried to sell our modern house on five acres but received no offers because of the recession. So the new project had to be put on the back burner. More about that later.

# CHAPTER 7
## Enough Fun--Back to the Subject of Work

THROUGHOUT THE PERIOD described above I was working on the draft standards, making numerous calls and getting advice from people about the remaining make-up of the Sub-Committee. I knew that I needed Regional EPA and state officials so that all areas of the U.S. would be represented. I also knew I needed suggestions from Regional offices to guide me in selecting appropriate and reasonably representative state officials for the Sub-Committee. *It goes without saying that I had to have a state official representing California which was/is the largest producer of agricultural products in the nation.*

Ultimately, I completed filling the committee with either a State or Regional official to represent all areas of the country. That was the best I could do since I was limited to 10 people selected from 10 Regional EPA Offices and 50 plus states and territories. Fortunately I was also able to receive advice and support from Errette Deck, head of pesticide regulatory affairs for the state of Oregon and Jake Mackensie, Branch Chief for Region IX, San Francisco. Although not officially members of my sub-committee, they worked closely with me on an ad hoc basis.

Because of the importance of agriculture in California, I often needed to visit that state while working on the standards--both the Regional Office in San Francisco and California Department of Food and Agriculture (CDFA) in Sacramento. An interesting paradox existed in that state. California was the leading producer of agricultural products in the nation and thus a leading user of chemical pesticides. At the same time, California also led the nation in the number and influence of environmental groups. Since I had to deal closely with these issues, I was a frequent visitor to Sacramento and San Francisco.

Although I had many interesting experiences in California, San Francisco provided some of the most memorable personal ones--enhanced by the wonders of this city, plus my friendship with Jake. We had become friends since our earlier meeting in Hawaii. He was also a frequent visitor to HQ/EPA. Gwen and I sometimes invited Jake to spend nights at our house in Clifton when he was called to Washington. And Jake often invited me to spend nights at his house in Petaluma or apartment in the city.

As a result of our time together, Jake knew of my appreciation for historic buildings. When it was my turn to visit San Francisco on business, he knew I would want to take full advantage of this city's great food, entertainment, and architecture. *(Note: if you are an old house aficionado like I am, you've probably heard of San Francisco's "painted ladies," a term used to describe that city's many Victorian houses painted in three or more colors that emphasize their fancy architectural details).*

When I didn't plan to stay at his home, Jake found me a place to stay that met all my expectations, i.e., was reasonably priced, convenient to the EPA Regional office, and comfortable and pleasing to my taste. He could not have found a more perfect place for me to stay than the Raphael Hotel. It was described at that time as San Francisco's "elegant little hotel." It had been recently remodeled when I made my first visit there. It was beautifully restored with Victorian trim and was convenient to all the landmarks I wanted to enjoy such as Union Square, Chinatown, Nob Hill, and of course, Fisherman's Wharf.

The Raphael was within walking distance of places to enjoy good music including the "Purple Onion," "The Hungry Eye," and my favorite, "Jazz At The Blackhawk." The Raphael was located on 386 Geary Street in downtown San Francisco. On my first stay at the Raphael, while awaiting the elevator to my room, I looked around the small but beautiful lobby and spotted the hotel's cocktail lounge about 20 feet away. I also saw a sign for a well-known breakfast place adjacent to the hotel. After showering and dressing for my night "on the town" I stopped by the lounge and was pleased to see that plentiful, upscale snacks were available.

And when I sat down at the bar, I found that the "house brands" for alcoholic beverages included: Beefeaters Gin, Jack Daniels Bourbon, and Johnny Walker Scotch. I looked no further since a martini made with Beefeater Gin had become my favorite adult beverage. After enjoying a martini and snacks, I wasn't very hungry so I strolled leisurely up Castro Street--then noted for its "painted ladies" but later as the center of the "Gay" community!

Upon reaching Chinatown, I browsed its shops and then caught the cable car down the hill to Fisherman's Wharf for a fresh seafood dinner. Jake had prepared me with a list of best restaurants, i.e., those catering to locals, versus "tourist traps." For seafood at Fisherman's Wharf, he recommended Pier 39 Restaurant. While this fine restaurant expertly prepares your fresh seafood meal, you can experience views of the Golden Gate Bridge, ships passing by, sea lions hanging around the wharf and the island/prison of Alcatraz (*the first U.S owned property I saw upon returning from World War II*). After dinner, I walked back to the main wharf to catch the trolley at the "turn around." The trolley would drop me off in front of the Raphael. From there, if not too tired from "jet lag," I would walk to one of my music places to listen to live jazz. That became my regular routine when I traveled to San Francisco alone.

On one memorable visit to San Francisco, Jake invited me to dinner at the downtown apartment he shared with his wife. He was just getting ready to put steaks on the grill for the three of us when the phone rang and we heard his wife say: "You're at the airport? Come on to the apartment. Jake is putting steaks on the grill and he'll put one on for you." Jake's wife re-appeared and said: "Mary is stopping by for a visit with us before she goes to see Emily Harris, who says she is getting very homesick." My first thought was that this "homesick" woman might be Emmylou Harris, then a popular American singer and songwriter who sometimes performed in San Francisco. However, Jake quickly disabused me of that thought. He explained: "This Emily Harris is in jail and gets very lonely if her friend and attorney, Mary, doesn't come to visit her often." Seeing the questioning look on my face, Jake explained, "Emily is the wife of Bill Harris. I'm sure you've heard of them!" I asked if he was referring to "the" Bill and Emily Harris who kidnapped

Patty Hearst, (granddaughter of Randolph Hearst, newspaper and publishing magnate who built the famous "Hearst Castle," one of California's landmark estates). Jake said, "Yes, that Emily."

*Although I had read about the kidnapping of Patty Hearst by radical members of the Symbionese Liberation Army (SLA), the urban guerrilla group, I certainly didn't expect to be having dinner with one of the defense attorneys!*

The steaks were good and the conversation lively that evening. Naturally the conversation soon turned to Patty Hearst and Bill and Emily Harris. Mary immediately began trying to defend the SLA and justify the kidnapping on the basis that the U.S was a racist and unfair nation; and that rich people (e.g. the Hearsts) shared a large part of the blame for this condition. I countered immediately that there was no excuse for kidnapping--that everyone deserved protection from predators regardless of race or financial status.

Jake quickly took my side of the discussion which pleased me greatly. *(Since Jake had resided in the "leftist" city of San Francisco for some time, I would not have been too surprised had he been silent or even agreed with the Harris' attorney!)*. For those who have forgotten or never knew of the infamous Hearst kidnapping, here is a brief summary of that incident.

At the time of her abduction by SLA, Patty Hearst was a sophomore studying history and art in college and living with her fiancé in San Francisco. Reputedly, after she was taken to SLA headquarters, members terrified her with machine gun fire and beat her unconscious. I later read that after that horrific treatment, the SLA began the process of "brainwashing" her into becoming a part of their "urban guerrilla group" which touted the philosophy that black convicts were victims of a "rotten and racist" American society. The SLA leader was an African American by the name of Donald DeFreeze, an escaped convict. The SLA financed its radical activities by burglarizing homes and robbing banks.

According to her testimony when she herself was on trial later for bank robbery, Patty claimed she was blindfolded, her hands were tied behind her back and she was placed in a closet for a week, during which time the SLA leader repeatedly threatened her with death if she did not join them. She was let out for meals and, still blindfolded, was urged to join in the political discussions. Although still kept in the closet, her blindfold was eventually removed and she was given a flashlight and ordered to read SLA political tracts. After several weeks of confinement, she said "The SLA leader told me that the War Council was thinking about whether to kill me if I didn't join them and that I better start thinking about that as a possibility."

In court, Hearst said "I accommodated my thoughts to coincide with theirs." Thus, when SLA leaders asked for her decision she told them she "wanted to stay and fight with the SLA." At that point, the blindfold was removed permanently, allowing her to see her captors for the first time. After this she was given daily lessons on her duties, especially weapons drills. A woman SLA member told Hearst that the others thought she should know what sexual freedom was like in the unit. Then she was raped by some of the male members.

On April 3, 1974, two months after she was abducted she made an audiotape saying that she had joined the SLA and assumed the name "Tania." Using that name, she actually participated in SLA activities including a bank robbery where she was photographed with an M-1 carbine *(the same type weapon I carried in the Pacific)*.

SLA leaders tried to use the Hearst kidnapping as a means of getting two SLA members in jail for murder released in exchange for releasing Patty. They believed that the Hearsts had sufficient influence to achieve this exchange. When this ploy failed, the SLA demanded that the Hearst family distribute $70 million worth of food to needy persons in California. That also failed to happen. However, Patty's father eventually did arrange for donation of $2 million worth of food to be given to the poor of the Bay Area.

Meanwhile, Patty Hearst continued to participate in SLA's radical and illegal activities but soon afterward police surrounded the SLA main base and six SLA members inside died in the resulting gunfight. Although it was originally feared that Patty Hearst had been killed in the shootout, she and William and Emily Harris escaped and were now the only survivors of the SLA unit.

In September 1975, Hearst was arrested in a San Francisco apartment. At the time of her arrest she weighed only 87 pounds and tests showed she had suffered a loss of 18 IQ points from her ordeal. Also, she suffered huge gaps in her memory regarding her pre-Tania life. Many people were sympathetic to Patty's plight and a court-appointed doctor and authority on brainwashing stated after a 15-hour interview with Hearst that she was a "classic case" of coercive persuasion or "brainwashing." After some weeks Hearst repudiated her SLA allegiance.

Later, she changed attorneys to F. Lee Bailey *(the same one I followed as speaker at Las Vegas, to be described later)*. Details of the trial are too complex and too long to detail here. However, on March 20, 1976, Patty Hearst was convicted of bank robbery and using a firearm in a felony. She was given the maximum sentence: possible 35 years imprisonment which was later reduced to 7 years. President Bill Clinton granted her a pardon on January 20, 2001 and she was free of her nightmare. P.S. Two months after her release from prison, Hearst married former policeman Bernard Shaw, who was part of a team of bodyguards protecting her while she was out on bail. The marriage lasted until his death in 2013.

Back to more mundane work matters, since we had completed selection of the Sub-Committee members it was time to put them to work. With Bob Evans doing much of the early writing, we had come up with the first draft of general standards from which applicators of Restricted Use Pesticides would be tested. The early draft of the general standards required commercial applicators to know such things as: the most common features of pests, how they develop, and kinds of damage they do; methods that can be used to control pests and how to combine these methods for the best results; how pesticides work; why reading pesticide labels is essential; how to use pesticides so they will not harm you, others, or the environment; how to choose, use, and care for equipment; and the Federal laws that apply to the things applicators do on the job.

Private Applicators (mainly farmers) were treated differently. The law and regulations prohibited the Federal or State governments from requiring farmers to pass a written test. However, this didn't stop several state agricultural commissioners from publicly claiming that EPA was going to disregard that provision and require farmers to pass a written test! More about that later.

The draft standards offered states a variety of methods to deal with certification of farmers to ensure that they could show that he (or she) possesses a practical knowledge of the pest problems and pest control practices associated with a farm's agricultural operations, as well as proper storage, use, handling and disposal of the pesticides and containers, and related legal responsibility. States were also allowed leeway in how the competency of farmers attempting to meet certification standards could be determined.

# CHAPTER 8
## Gathering Input and Meeting a Future Boss

MY OFFICE DISTRIBUTED these draft standards first to members of the Sub-Committee and asked for their input. After they reviewed the draft, they began organizing meetings with their constituents and requests for one of us to attend these meetings began pouring in. Since this was now my primary job and Bob had other duties at Chamblee, most of the travel and speaking burden fell on me.

We used the draft guidelines to gather input from various groups representing agriculture, commercial pest control applicators, chemical industries, environmental groups, and state and Federal agencies involved with pesticides. I also began receiving invitations to speak at Association Meetings of groups involved with all aspects of chemicals and pesticides use and storage. By that time I was up to speed on content of the standards as well as the history and legislative authority behind the revisions of FIFRA.

Although I never reached the point that I regarded public speaking as "fun" I gradually became more comfortable with the practice. Most of these speaking engagements were for the purpose of disseminating information and answering questions about the certification program. In most cases, I wasn't there to entertain. I of course was on familiar ground with these topics since I was heavily involved in their development.

However, I recall a speaking engagement in Raleigh, NC, where I was asked to be the after-dinner speaker at a large dinner meeting arranged by the NC Agriculture Commissioner. Knowing that the audience was expecting a modicum of entertainment, I had added several jokes to my speech. I thought I was doing pretty well at both functions since the crowd was attentive and laughing at my jokes. I was starting to feel relaxed when I looked up and saw my old boyhood friend and fellow journalist, Les Roark of Shelby, NC. He was standing in the door grinning at me. Momentarily addled at his presence, I soon regained my composure and finished to applause.

After the meeting ended, Les and I got together and reminisced about the times we were both tenant farm boys in Cherokee County, SC. By this time my career was blossoming and so was Les's. At that point Les had left the field of journalism and was serving as personnel director for U.S. Senator Robert Morgan. He later served in that same capacity for Senator Terry Sanford. Still later, he was appointed Deputy Attorney General for the state of North Carolina. His success without ever attending college was amazing to me!

The most nerve wracking of my public speaking appearances, however, occurred at a Conference of Aerial Applicators held in Las Vegas. The after dinner speaker there was F. Lee Bailey, famous lawyer, pilot and raconteur. (As mentioned above, he was also Patty Hearst's second attorney). Bailey had the audience "eating out of his hand" with his stories. He was wildly applauded after his speech by the approximately 1,500 people present.

Although I wasn't scheduled to speak until the following morning at the breakfast meeting, attendees were still chuckling over the dynamic Bailey's performance when I arrived for my speech that morning. Sensing I was very nervous, Billy Buffalo of North Carolina brought me an alcoholic drink from a nearby bar. That helped calm me down before I had to climb to the podium. I managed to get through my speech but knew it was "deadly dull" compared to Bailey's.

Days later, at a meeting of USDA and state officials in the USDA South Building where I again spoke about proposed new certification standards, I met Dr. John Osmun for the first time. As head of the Entomology Department at Purdue University, Dr. Osmun was already a legend in both the entomology and education worlds. I was very impressed with his knowledge of and interest in our program. He offered several helpful suggestions and I incorporated them into the draft proposal. *I wondered why no one had suggested him to be a member of my Sub-Committee but of course he did not fit either of the categories I had to select from!*

Then, shortly after that first meeting, I learned that Dr. Osmun had been chosen to head up the Operations Division of the Office of Pesticide Programs (OPP) at EPA. I welcomed him warmly as my boss and felt that EPA was fortunate to have a person of Dr. Osmun's qualifications. After all, Section 4 of FIFRA, involved education in the use of pesticides and he was recognized as an expert in both education and pesticide use. I felt very lucky to have him as a boss and a shoulder to lean on.

And as "icing on the cake" I found out that Dr. Osmun was a long-time personal friend of Agriculture Secretary Earl Butz. Both had been at Purdue University in West Lafayette, IN. Obviously, it was a real asset to us to have a highly-respected, high level EPA official with connections at the very top of the Agriculture Department. The importance of pesticides in agriculture and the effects of pesticides regulation on the agricultural industry cannot be over-stated.

Besides these obvious assets, Dr. John Osmun was one of the most personable individuals it has been my good fortune to meet. He immediately validated the work that Bob Evans and I were doing and added his own great knowledge to our efforts--without ever being presumptuous or "pushy." And he took over the top job in the Operations Division with even stronger convictions than any of us that it was vital for the nation's quality of life to preserve as many of the essential uses of pesticides as possible, while implementing strong educational and training programs to ensure that especially toxic pesticides could be used safely.

It was helpful that I, Dr. Osmun and Dr. Evans (along with Ivan Dodson) shared the belief that Standards for Certification had to be reasonable and acceptable to the states, which would bear major responsibility for implementing the educational and regulatory functions of Section 4. For that reason, we knew that state officials needed to be heavily involved from the start in developing standards that they could live with and yet meet our goal of ensuring safe use of pesticides. *We deliberately made the standards general enough that a state could add its own touches because of their own unique circumstances.* At the time, we thought we were on solid ground with our approach. When we were satisfied that the standards were sound and acceptable to us as well as state officials, we requested a meeting with EPA's Review Board which had the power to approve or disapprove all regulations before they were submitted and entered into the Code of Federal Register (CFR).

# CHAPTER 9
## Meeting with Review Board; A Bad Scene!

DR. OSMUN AND I met with the Review Board (which consisted primarily of EPA scientists, attorneys, and those dealing with political issues) and provided each with a copy of the proposed standards. Dr. Osmun made a brief introduction of the draft standards and I provided a description of the procedures the Sub-Committee followed, emphasizing our efforts to work closely with the states and other groups and individuals affected by the proposed new regulations.

Much to our chagrin, the group began to tear our Standards as written apart. And, shockingly, they attacked our basic approach of involving others (especially state officials) in the process of developing the Standards. *(This despite congressional sentiments expressed in the earlier CFR of the need to involve others)*. The reviewers, especially the attorneys, said that state officials should not have played any role at all in developing the Standards--even though they would be expected to carry out the mandates of Section 4 (a) and (b).

We knew at this point that we were in for a big fight since the group disagreed with our basic premise (and Congress' expressed wishes) that those who would be most affected by a law should be involved it its development. *At that point the vast difference in philosophy between us and the "hard liners" of EPA became obvious.* Dr. Osmun, who had long been a state official, was especially incensed by the provincial attitudes expressed by the reviewers.

However, tempers eventually cooled and we reluctantly agreed to try some other approaches which we hoped would gain Review Board approval while still being acceptable to state officials and other affected groups. The most significant change we agreed to make was to spell out the various Commercial Applicator categories and subcategories and write specific standards for each of these groups. We also agreed to write more detailed standards states would have to follow in certifying Private Applicators (Farmers).

Dr. Osmun and I headed back to our office to "nurse our wounds," and reflect on how to proceed next. It was obvious our agreement with the Review Board required much more work and travel for us. We both dreaded going back to the state officials with details of the compromises we had to make to get even conditional approval by the Review Board. That fear was justified. Many state officials were already furious about the specificity forced upon them. They were especially upset that they were being required to carry out an expensive Federal program with very little funding by the Federal Government. Now, in their view, EPA bureaucrats were telling them exactly how they were to conduct these costly programs!

Our greatest fear was that if even one state was pushed too far and refused to carry out a Certification program (which some had threatened to do) it would then be the responsibility of EPA to conduct the certification program, which it clearly was not equipped to do. If enough states decided not to cooperate in the Certification Program the entire system might be abandoned. In that case the door would be opened for the extreme environmentalists to get more, vitally needed, pesticides banned.

Many of us were aware of the number of people who had died or otherwise been incapacitated by the loss of DDT which was by far the most effective, least expensive and safest way of controlling mosquitoes that cause malaria around the world. Misinformation about the public health impacts of DDT spread by Rachel Carson and other environmental activists caused public officials in other nations to reduce or even ban its use in some places. With reduced use of DDT, malaria rates skyrocketed worldwide by the 1990s after having reached historic lows in the 1960s while DDT was in use. For example, in Sri Lanka, which stopped using DDT in 1964, cases rose from a low of 17 to about 500,000 by 1969!

After much discussion, Dr. Osmun, Dr. Evans and I went to work feverishly utilizing our own knowledge, plus resources used in our previous effort to identify various categories. Our goal was to make the Certification program the epitome of State/Federal cooperation--within the constraints placed upon us by the Review Board.

Dr. Osmun, with his vast and deep knowledge of pesticide use, took the lead in beginning to define the categories needed. He identified 10 different major categories and a few sub groups. With help from Dr. Evans and Dr. Osmun, I began developing a draft which included suggested specific standards for each of the major and sub-categories. And we followed the same course in beginning to add more detailed requirements states should follow in granting private applicator certification.

Once overcoming the angst we had suffered from the Review Board's criticism, we began to see that some of the Board's suggested ideas had merit. So, within a relatively short time we had prepared another draft outline reflecting the Review Board's requirements but retaining as much of the original document as we thought we could get away with. After circulating the drafts internally, we asked for another meeting with the Review Board and presented our plans for the revised (and hopefully final) draft. It included most of the changes demanded by the Board. This time the Review Board approved what we had done without any further suggestions.

With that approval, we began disseminating the revised draft to our outside sources, including recognized national and international experts, for their input. But we knew that our biggest problem lay ahead, i.e., getting state officials to accept the changes made to our original documents. Without that acceptance, the program was dead in the water.

# CHAPTER 10
## I Go Looking for Cooperation

BY THIS TIME I had become the "Primary Spokesperson" for the Certification standards. Thus it was my job to explain the new draft version to all concerned groups and gain acceptance to the new approach from those groups most affected by the changes and to incorporate their suggestions and ideas when appropriate. I was almost overwhelmed by requests to attend meetings with groups and explain the current status of the revised standards.

In addition I had to use every tool in my toolbox trying to "sell" the new approach to state officials and other groups to be affected by the Certification program. Despite our best efforts to re-assure them, some states remained outraged that the EPA had insisted on tightening the standards and had taken away many of the states' prerogatives allowed in the earlier draft.

Dr. Osmun and I had many discussions about what we could do to relieve the tension that had built up between state officials and EPA. I mentioned that it might be helpful to add someone with state experience to our staff. At the time, Dr. Osmun and I were the only people in the Ops Division with official state experience. And it was obvious that with full implementation of the various provisions of amended FIFRA, we would need additional staffing to handle these responsibilities anyway. Therefore I suggested: "Why don't we try to hire someone working in a State Pesticide Regulatory Office and add that person to our staff? This might relieve some of the tension and add more legitimacy to our efforts." Dr. Osmun jumped at this suggestion and said, "Jim, that's a good idea. I'd like you to find us the best state person available and convince him to come to Washington." I started looking for and talking to state people around the country. Unfortunately, most of the ones that seemed promising did not want to face the hassle of living and working in DC.

Finally, on a business trip to California, I decided to talk with John Hillis, head of the California Dept. of Food and Agriculture (CDFA), to get his reaction to my advice. Because John had been so helpful to us, I wasn't about to go over his head to talk to one of his employees without his permission. I told him about the problems we were having and that we hoped to help reduce this problem by hiring a state person--someone the state people might better relate to.

Then I told John that after looking around and talking to many state employees, I had found none who suited our needs and/or wanted to work in Washington. I then said that I was most favorably impressed with one of his own employees, Paul Levingston. But I quickly told John that I would not consider talking with Paul without his permission. After thinking about the situation for a few minutes, John said: "Jim, I would hate to lose Paul but if you think he might help save the certification program, I would not stand in your way if you want to interview him about the job." John then called Paul at his office and told him that "Jim White of Washington would like to stop by your office for a few minutes." Paul said he would be glad to visit with me.

After a casual conversation with Paul, I told him that I had his boss's permission to make him a job offer. I then told him that I would like for him to be my assistant at EPA and that this job would be an excellent way for him to broaden his experience in a hurry by working with State Regulatory officials around the nation. I knew he was ambitious and I told him that Federal government experience would be a big boost to his career. *On a personal level, I know that he was legally separated from his wife with no hope of reconciliation (for reasons I can't discuss). And I told him that being in a new environment might lessen the pain he was feeling about the loss of his family.*

When he showed interest in my offer, I told him we would finance an exploratory visit for him to get a firsthand look at the situation. He thought this was a good idea and after getting an o.k. from John Hillis, I immediately asked to use Paul's phone to make a call to my office and make arrangements for Paul's trip.

Paul arrived in Washington a week or two later and after introducing him around, I made him a firm offer of the job at a nice raise in salary. In addition to exposing him to the work that needed to be done, we "wined and dined" him during his exploratory visit. He flew back to California to consider our offer and soon called to say he would take the job on a trial basis. This acceptance worked well for both of us since Federal employment is based on a 90 day "trial basis."

A couple of weeks later, Paul drove his car across country to EPA HQ. With our assistance, he found temporary housing in nearby Alexandria, Virginia, and arrived at the Operations Division ready to go to work. He worked closely with me during the trial period and caught on to things quickly. I was happy with him and his work performance and he seemed happy with us. Then it was time for him to return to California to cut his ties with CDFA and take care of other personal and business matters. We arranged it so that this would be a "business trip" so he wouldn't have to pay the fare out of pocket. He was to be gone a week.

The week ended and Paul returned to DC, but only to say "goodbye." Paul immediately asked for a "closed door" meeting with me to explain the reasons he had changed his mind about accepting our offer. He said that when he was getting ready to leave DC for California the week before, he was walking toward his car carrying his briefcase and a bag of candy for his little daughter (who he hoped to see during his visit). He had parked his car as close as he could to the HQ building so he could drive his car directly to the airport.

As he neared his car, three black teenagers surrounded him with the intent to rob him--and perhaps do him greater harm. Mild looking but quite athletic (he was a runner on his university track team) Paul surprised the young hoodlums by breaking away and beginning to run. He ran past his car the first time knowing that by the time he unlocked the door his pursuers would be on him. So, he circled several blocks and kept running until he had gained enough lead that he could get into his car and speed away before his "would be robbers" could catch up with him.

Paul then said, "Jim, I'm sorry to disappoint you but I can't live this way. I'm going back to Sacramento to work and live." I didn't really blame him after that potentially dangerous experience. Soon he called to tell me he was back at his desk at CDFA. I was never able to find an appropriate replacement for him. So, Osmun and I remained the only members of the Operations Division with state experience.

# CHAPTER 11
## Severe Problems with Many States

SINCE WE HAD put our hearts and souls into the certification program, we were dismayed that resistance to any State/Federal program involving the EPA had flared up again and was now threatening our Certification Program. Anger against the agency was strong all across the nation but especially bitter in the Southern and Rocky Mountain states. I was determined to pursue any avenue available to convince the state people that the Certification Program was the only avenue left for them to preserve many pesticide uses.

Note: I had close enough contact with the environmental community and EPA to know that their preferred course of action was actually to ban the use of pesticides. They didn't believe (as we did) that pesticides could be used safely with proper training. I knew personally that some EPA program people would meet with environmental groups to provide them with inside confidential information, and to encourage them to sue EPA as a means of strengthening the hands of EPA "anti-chemical" employees--who were plentiful even back then. Believe you me, it got much worse after Osmun and White left the agency!

As a result of Rocky Mountain officials' renewed opposition to EPA mandates, Ivan Dodson, Region VIII Pesticide Chief and charter member of my Sub-Committee, sent an urgent request that I make a two-week swing with him through the Rocky Mountain States to try to quell the growing discontent there. *It should be noted that these states have historically prided themselves on their independence. Some state officials also had problems with one of the top Regional officials. (In fact, one state official had made a public threat to "kick the butt" of that EPA official. And he mentioned him by name).*

When I arrived in Denver, Ivan had made arrangements for us to meet with state and county officials as well as chemical and related industries in all the states in EPA Region VIII. I made presentations at all of these locations, stressing the point that developing and implementing effective safety standards was the only means left to preserve many vital pesticide uses. Both Ivan and I then answered questions (sometimes for hours at a time) about new regulations affecting pesticides. At all these meetings, the audience seemed appreciative and we were thankful that no one threatened to "kick our butts!"

Ivan and I ended our last meeting in Helena, Montana, an old mining town. Although it was the capital of that state, Helena had fewer than 20,000 residents at that time. It literally looked like an "old cow town" portrayed in the movies and the fact that its main street was named "Last Chance Gulch" was appropriate. On the last night of our trip, Ivan and I left our hotel rooms in Helena to find a little excitement to celebrate what we thought was a successful series of meetings. We walked down the main street and the most interesting place we saw was a bar with a large poolroom filled with locals—most of them wearing western clothing.

Hoping we didn't look too much like "city slickers" we bought beers and went to watch the action around the pool table. Soon we were asked to join in and had a good time playing pool and chatting with the locals. When we left the bar to walk back to our hotel, a Helena police car followed us back. We waved goodbye to the police but were left wondering why we received an escort.

After I returned to Washington, Ivan called to tell me our trip had achieved its purpose, that tempers had cooled considerably and he no longer thought any of the states in Region VIII were "going to jump ship." I was grateful to hear that. My next outing "to quell the savage beasts" was a visit to some southern states, many of which, like the Rocky Mountain states, also opposed any type of Federally-imposed standards. This tour worked out well since I had already received an "all expenses paid" trip to Mississippi paid for by Redd Pest Control Company.

Redd wanted me to spend three days with Mississippi Pest Control Applicators explaining and answering questions about the new law and proposed regulations. This seemed like an excellent idea since I needed to firm up the resolve of several southern state officials—some of which I could visit on the way to Mississippi.

Because I had been away from my family so much in recent months, I decided to take Gwen and little Mitch with me at my own expense. Mitch was then around four years old and my frequent travel was worrisome to me since I was missing so much of his early growth. *(Later I asked him if he recalled those early days and he said he mostly remembered me as a man who left our house early on Mondays with a suitcase and returned late Fridays for the weekend. He remembered our trip to New Orleans and an incident in a motel swimming pool, as explained later).* I hoped that the trip with him and his mother would allow me to make up a bit for my long absences.

As we began the trip our first stop was Richmond, VA, where I met briefly (and productively) with Harry Rust, Arthur Hart and other Virginia State Pest Control officials. The next stop was Raleigh, NC where we stopped for the night in a motel just blocks from the State Capitol--the site of my early morning meeting with Billy Buffalo and his pest control staff.

Gwen and Mitch relaxed in our room while I went to my meeting at the State House in Raleigh. By 11 a.m. I was back at the motel and passing through the lobby on the way to our room to pick up Gwen and Mitch to continue on south. On the way to our room, I passed some public telephone booths. As I continued toward our room, I had a "nagging feeling" that a man in one of the booths resembled one of my apartment mates at the University of Illinois. Common sense told me it couldn't be him; that my old friend lived in Chicago, his hometown. And all I'd seen was a partial profile since his back was to the door of the booth. However, the brief view of the man in the telephone booth kept tugging at me, and I decided I had to go back to make sure it wasn't Joe Moylan, my apartment mate at Illinois University.

When I returned to the phone booth I saw that in fact it was Joe! We had a brief reunion and I learned that he had moved south, was an official with The Council of State Governments, and was based in Atlanta, GA. I went back to the room and brought Gwen and Mitch to the lobby to meet my old grad school apartment mate. Soon duty called and Joe and I both needed to continue south. We promised to stay in touch but as so often happens, time passed and we lost touch again.

*Recently, while writing this memoir, I decided to try to locate both Joe and our other apartment mate, Bob Nemcik. I wanted to thank them for their kindness to me after my painful separation from Joyce in Illinois. With the help of the Internet, I finally tracked down both of them. I located Bob, who was in bad physical health at his home in Indianapolis, IN. Although he was very weak and couldn't talk long, Bob's wife said my call made him smile for the first time in ages. Soon afterward, she called to tell me he had passed away.*

*I eventually located Joe's home address and phone number in a suburb of Atlanta. His wife answered the phone and I introduced myself to her and asked if Joe was home. She told me that Joe had passed away three years previously. I said that I had wanted to thank Joe for his many kindnesses when we were at Illinois together and she responded: "Joe was kind to everyone and he would not have expected any thanks for being that way. But I thank you for making this call." Although I had not been able to say "goodbye" to either of them, I was glad I made the effort. The next time we'll see each other will be in Heaven—if I make it there.*

Continuing on to Mississippi, the meeting set up by Redd Pest Control in Jackson, MS went extremely well. Everyone at the meeting needed and wanted information about how the new law and regulations would affect them. They were a very receptive audience and I received many questions during and after the workshops. A great deal of my "after hours" time, which I had hoped to spend with Gwen and Mitch, was taken up with small groups wanting to "pick my brain." A fellow speaker (a clinical psychologist) pulled me aside and said: "Jim, it looks as if everyone here wants a piece of you!" I considered that a compliment.

# CHAPTER 12
## A Chance to Show Off My "Old Haunts"

AFTER THE MEETING concluded, Gwen, Mitch and I took the "long way home" by stopping for two nights in New Orleans at a motel just outside the city, arriving late on Friday. We stayed close to our motel that night and rested. During the next morning, we roamed the streets of New Orleans until Mitch was tired. Then we went back to the motel to spend time at the swimming pool. We got a scare when Mitch followed a new (and older) friend too far into the deeper water.

When I rushed to get to him, he was standing in water over his head but was holding his breath and seemed completely calm. This changed when I, in a panic, scooped him out of the water. That scared him and he began crying. I regretted that my abrupt action scared him but his crying let me know he was o.k. Soon afterward, I thought we had enough excitement for one day and we went inside the motel to rest.

Gwen and I had been able to get a "certified baby sitter" recommended by the motel for that night so the two of us left Mitch in her care while we visited some of my "old haunts" back when I was single. I took her to the Roosevelt Hotel where she could sample their "trademark" drinks at the Sazerac Lounge. While there I also showed her the magnificent Blue Room as well as the Fountain Lounge where Peter Toma still played music for dancing. We then had dinner at Commander's Palace, my favorite eating place in New Orleans.

Later, we dropped by Preservation Hall for a short time to listen to New Orleans jazz by the "ancient," mostly gray-haired musicians. Our final stop that night was at Pat O'Brien's to listen to music and enjoy one of O'Brien's famous "Hurricane" drinks before heading back to our motel. Sunday morning we got up for "early mass" at the famed St. Louis Cathedral, the oldest Cathedral in North America. It was founded as a Catholic Parish in 1720 along the banks of the Mississippi River in New Orleans. It is one of the notable landmarks of the city and overlooks Jackson Square where General Andrew Jackson sits on his bronze horse.

Usually I remained outside while Gwen took Mitch to Catholic mass but I didn't want to miss the opportunity to see the inside of this beautiful landmark with its triple steeples. So, I made an exception this time and stayed inside through mass. After leaving the Cathedral, we began our return trip to Clifton, VA. We arrived home late the following evening and I enjoyed a few hours sleep before I got up to drive to Springfield, VA to meet my carpool.

A few days later I received a letter with a check from Richard Redd thanking me for my participation at their big conference. Richard said the check was to cover expenses for Gwen and Mitch, but of course I returned the check uncashed. Government employee rules!

Although we kept our word and the final draft of the Standards included some of the changes insisted on by the Review Board, we stuck to our guns on a few important points. First of all, we did not make any changes that conflicted with the actual FIFRA law. For example, despite the desire of many within EPA to require that private applicators (farmers) pass some type of written test in order to be certified, the final draft that appeared in the CFR specified that Private Applicators (Farmers) WOULD NOT be required to pass any type of "written exam" to be certified. In addition, we insisted on retaining the "General Standards" as written, supplemented by "Specific Standards" strongly suggested by the Board and reflecting the broad spectrum of pesticide uses.

The one thing we rejected outright from our earlier meeting with the Review Board was their insistence that our basic approach of soliciting input from those individuals and organizations most affected by our revised standards was wrong. We refused to bend on that, believing that our approach was philosophically correct and that it was the only way we could expect any cooperation from those affected by the regulations--especially the states.

*Ironically, after our approach of seeking input from others was emphasized in the final version printed in the CFR, the EPA Administration later issued a policy paper stating that the issuance of all future EPA regulations should include involvement of those most affected by those regulations--especially those involving the states. So our approach was fully vindicated. P.S. EPA later offered me the job of reviewing draft regulations to ensure that this policy was followed but I declined their offer.*

# CHAPTER 13
## My Office had an "Open Door" Policy for All

TRAVEL WAS ALMOST always exciting but time at my office was never dull either. On most mornings I wasn't traveling, representatives of the "Big Three" pest control companies were either waiting or arrived soon after I sat down at my desk. The "Big Three" pest control companies and their representatives were: Orkin (Bob Russell), Western (Dick Sameth), and Terminix (Charley Hramada). I soon grew to know Bob, Dick and Charley well. They were there to try to get information about the present status of the Standards (Regulations) for Certification of Applicators. Naturally their primary interest was in protecting their applicators.

I maintained a good relationship with the "Big Three" representatives despite their being very suspicious of EPA as were most companies and individuals involved with the use of pesticides. I needed to retain as much good will as possible from this important industry. However, I knew that their visits were not strictly out of friendship. Their purpose was to try to get the certification requirements eased as much as possible for their companies' economic interests. Since I was aware of the reason for their frequent visits, I kept some distance by declining to let them treat me to lunch. I knew that a few pest control companies were unscrupulous and were known for such activities as: (1) diluting active ingredients to the point that the applications were ineffective or short lived thus necessitating frequent re-applications, (2) misusing a chemical not registered for a particular use (e.g., applying chlordane to the interior of a house), and (3) hiring untrained persons off the street, giving them a couple of hours of training, and then providing them fancy uniforms before sending them out as "trained" professional applicators. So, for several reasons I was careful not to get too close to them.

*Once, after I retired from EPA, one such "professional" rang my doorbell and offered me a "special deal" for a treatment of my Blacksburg house. I knew it did not need treating but I decided to listen to his "spiel" and ask him a few simple questions. His "spiel" was unconvincing and he couldn't answer any of the questions I asked. It was evident that he had little or no training. He didn't even know the name of the chemical he was going to apply. The only thing professional about him was the fancy uniform. The Certification Standards were designed to combat these and other unsavory aspects of the industry.*

Back at EPA, often after the pest control representatives left, I would be visited by one or more representatives of environmental groups. They were at my office for the opposite reason from the pest control representatives--they wanted to make sure that the standards were very tough, in fact unrealistically tough. These visitors represented organizations such as The Environmental Defense Fund, Natural Resources Defense Council, Friends of the Earth, and the Sierra Club, plus other lesser known groups. Although I had serious reservations about some environmental groups and their activities, I was always respectful, noted their concerns, and made sure they were invited to all public meetings on the subject of Pesticide Certification Standards.

Another frequent visitor (who became both a business and social friend) was Ron Grandon, who was editor of a newsletter devoted to pesticides and environmental issues. As fellow writers, we had an immediate connection. After I found I could trust his discretion, I would sometimes give him a "scoop" which he greatly appreciated. He never violated anything I ever said to him in confidence.

*(Note: I need to leave chronology to complete an interesting personal story about Ron Grandon).* As our friendship grew, Ron confided to me that he wanted to travel the world to gain the knowledge he needed to write his "Great American Novel." Toward that end, he was constructing a hand-made boat to transport him on international travel overseas. I thought all of this was just a "pipe dream" that most writers have at some time in their lives.

Then one day when Ron visited my office he told me that his boat was now "seaworthy." He had resigned his job, and was ready to start his voyage. He said two friends were going to accompany him on the first leg of this journey. He was going to drop them off somewhere on a Caribbean island and then continue on to "God knows where."

I was aghast that he was actually going to do this and warned: "Ron, you're crazy; that home-made boat may come apart and all of you may be swimming for your lives!" He laughed at this warning, gave me a "good bye" handshake, and left my office with a jaunty salute. I was fearful that would be the last time I would ever see him alive. My concern for Ron turned out to be prophetic. A few days after the three of them left, Ron's girlfriend called to inform me that "Ron's boat went down somewhere around the Bermuda Triangle." I was fearful that my prediction had come true! She said that after the boat sank, "Ron and his buddies were swimming in the ocean when a U.S. atomic submarine spotted them, surfaced, and brought the three of them on board."

Since the submarine was headed to Scotland, that's where they dropped Ron and the others off, she added. When I asked where Ron was, she replied that she didn't know; that the other two men had left Scotland by plane and were now back in the U.S., but that Ron was continuing on by himself. I was not able to get any further word about him. I assumed I would never see him again.

About 18 months later, a strange man, very thin and with skin so dark I wasn't sure of his ethnicity, appeared at my office door. This startled me since strangers rarely visited my office without an appointment or at least a telephone call. I asked what I could do for him and he grinned, walked to my desk and said: "I'm Ron Grandon, Jim." I was speechless for a moment because the man standing in front of my desk did not resemble the Ron Grandon I had known. The one I had known had average skin color and was several pounds overweight. This man was gaunt, with hollowed out eyes, and really, really dark brown skin.

When I finally grasped that this in fact was my old friend, Ron Grandon, I asked him to have a seat and tell me what he had been doing. He gave me details of the "nightmare" at sea and being rescued by the atomic sub. After the sub left them off in Scotland, he said goodbye to his two companions and set off alone on his journey through Europe, parts of the Middle East, and Africa. He said he traveled at first by public transportation until he ran out of money. After that he walked and hitch-hiked and "lived off the land."

I asked him about his book and he handed me a manuscript to read. He said he had sent the manuscript to several publishers but so far had received nothing but rejections. I asked him what he planned to do to make a living and he said he had rejoined his old newsletter staff as assistant editor, working under his former assistant and would continue working on his manuscript. I took Ron's manuscript home with me and read it; I found it highly entertaining and interesting--but then I was probably prejudiced.

With his changed status Ron no longer had reason to visit me on a regular basis and we gradually lost touch with each other. I hope he eventually got his book published. Wherever he is, those close to him will never be bored with his company.

# CHAPTER 14

## Another "Redhead" Joins Operations Division

EARLY IN HIS tenure, Dr. Osmun called a meeting of the Operations Division to inform us that he had just hired a distinguished PhD entomologist by the name of Dr. Fred Whittemore to be his assistant director. He told us that Dr. Whittemore had just retired from the Food and Agriculture Office (FAO) of the United Nations after spending 9 years in Rome, Italy. Osmun said he met Dr. Whittemore when both attended graduate school at Boston University and that Whittemore had served in the Army during World War II as a Public Health Officer ending up as a full Colonel.

Several in our group wondered why we needed an "old codger" who had already retired from two careers but soon changed their minds. Fred Whittemore was already in his late 60's when he arrived at EPA but he was far from finished as a contributor to society. In fact, his work schedule exceeded that of many of the younger employees. Fred had a heart problem and sometimes had to slip a nitroglycerin pill under his tongue to deal with it. *In addition he also kept a bottle of vodka in his desk drawer and claimed that a drink of vodka did the same thing as the pill. I administered the vodka a few times when he was out of pills and urgently needed something for his heart!*

Dr. Whittemore also had red hair (now graying) and his close friends still called him **"Big Red,"** the name he gained as a sprinter on the track team at Boston University. Since I still had quite a bit of red hair at the time, I became known as **"Little Red"** around the agency even though I was quite a bit taller than Fred. With his advancing age and heart condition, Fred was realistic about his inability to defend himself while walking the dangerous areas surrounding the EPA HQ building. Thus, he asked me to accompany him on occasional trips to the nearby bank or other businesses near EPA. I was happy to act as his "bodyguard."

*As an indication that his concern about safety was warranted, a female secretary was stabbed to death while sitting at her desk in the EPA HQ building. The killer stole her purse. I left the agency before learning details except that the killer was a black man from the neighborhood.*

Fred also wanted me to go to lunch with him when we were both in town and could leave the office for a longer lunch. He would drive us to "The Flagship" or "Hogates" in his brand new Jaguar. As pleasant as it was, lunch with Fred created a problem for me. Because Fred was accustomed to having Italian wine with his meals while in Rome, he continued this custom. Although his favorite wine was cheap in Italy, a bottle of his preferred wine was over $40 in the DC area, pretty pricey back in the 70's. He also insisted I share the wine with him.

Although he wanted to pay for the bottle of wine himself, this went against my principles and I insisted on paying half. Since paying for my lunch and half of the wine exceeded my entire weekly lunch "allowance," I felt I had to begin turning down his invitations for lunch. I could not afford the time or cost.

It didn't take long for the staff to realize that the Operations Division had a real "jewel" in Dr. Fred Whittemore. Because of knowledge acquired while dealing with the military bureaucracy, he was more adept than the rest of us at dealing with our agency bureaucrats. The fact is that both Osmun and I had problems holding our tempers when dealing with EPA attorneys and other bureaucrats. We viewed these people as obstacles who stood on the sidelines "throwing rocks" while we desperately tried to fulfill the demands made upon us. They never seemed to produce anything themselves. Fred Whittemore was hardened to such "rocks" and easily deflected them.

Soon after Fred arrived at EPA, his old office at FAO contacted him and asked him to recommend someone from EPA to attend a large international conference in Rome to discuss in detail the history of the development of pesticides and their regulations. Knowing that Harold Alford was the top expert on this subject, Fred recommended Harold as the U.S. representative. When EPA heard that Harold was Fred's selection they directed him to select someone else. He refused to do so and no one from the EPA attended the conference.

Because of this and other strong stands on principles, Fred soon gained the name "The Neanderthal" within the agency. And Fred wore that description proudly. (More about my relationship with "Big Red" in a different setting later).

Meanwhile, as for the revised standards, with the help of Drs. Osmun, Evans and Whittemore the revised Section 4 (a) standards were submitted for publication in the Code of Federal Register. My name was listed as the primary contact. And despite all the delays encountered, these regulations were ahead of the Congressional deadline for publication!

Throughout the long process, I had been receiving praise within and outside the agency for my work in bringing together people with diverse interests, and achieving workable compromises. With just a few exceptions, the Standards were considered quite acceptable by all parties. Note: the only consistent dissenter I heard about during the standard developing process was a Region V Pesticide Director. Also, a couple of state officials kept repeating, erroneously, that we were going to require a written exam for Private Applicators (i.e., farmers) despite facts to the contrary.

As I was writing the Introduction to the Standards before submitting the package to the Federal Register, Dr. Osmun had called me into his office to tell me that in recognition for my achievement in getting the standards ready for publication while handling my duties as acting branch chief, he was putting together a new job for me that would be at the GS-15 level. I was surprised and happy about this and could hardly wait to share this good news with Gwen. The extra money could help speed up the restoration work; and it might even result in a slight raise of my usual dollar a day lunch allowance!

Coincidentally, the following week Dr. Osmun and I were heading to Chicago to participate in a large meeting. The first part and centerpiece of the meeting was discussion of the process and completion of the Section 4 (a) Standards. I would be among the speakers the afternoon of our arrival and Dr. Osmun would wind up that part of the meeting the next morning before I returned to Washington. My busy schedule would not allow me to stay for the entire meeting. Osmun would stay to participate in discussion of other issues. Therefore, we would not leave together. That turned out to be a "blessing" for me.

# CHAPTER 15

## A "Dinner too Far" in Chicago

AFTER THE AFTERNOON meeting was over, the major participants and attendees were invited to dinner at a nice restaurant. In addition to all Pesticide Division Directors and other upper echelon officials at EPA, the dinner would include the head of the Office of Pesticides, Deputy Assistant Administrator of EPA, Ed Johnson, and other EPA dignitaries including the Region V Assistant Regional Administrator, who was hosting the meeting.

I approached the dinner still feeling the glow of being rewarded with a grade level I never expected to reach. That glow didn't last long. Before the dinner was half finished, the Assistant Regional Administrator was complaining in a voice loud enough for me to hear, that Region V had been "left out" of the decision making for the Certification Program. Specifically, he claimed that I had made a bad decision in selecting the state official to represent Region V. He said I did this "on my own" without consulting the Regional Pesticide Office. I kept quiet for awhile but when I heard him make this claim directly to DAA Johnson, I finally snapped.

My response was totally inappropriate, to state it mildly. Instead of smiling and gently correcting him, as I should have done, I did just the opposite. I called him some very unflattering names and despite the efforts of old friend Charles Smith (an associate when our boss was Harold Alford) to calm me down, I invited the official to go outside the restaurant where we could settle the issue. The official promptly shut up and didn't make the situation worse. Thank God he showed more sense than I by not accepting my invitation.

The dinner was finally over and all of us went back to our rooms. The following morning I went back for the final session on Section 4 (a) which Dr. Osmun was scheduled to wind up. Needless to say, he did not greet me warmly. I had just taken my seat to listen when someone tapped me on the shoulder and whispered: "The Assistant Regional Administrator would like to speak to you in his office." I followed the person to the office, prepared to be berated for my behavior the previous evening.

Instead of berating me, this official grabbed my hand to shake it and said: "Jim, I owe you an apology. I called a meeting of my staff early this morning to discuss the matter of whether you had solicited our input in selecting a state official to represent Region V during the development of the standards. They told me you had been totally cooperative with them during the entire process, including the selection of this particular state official in question. They said you discussed various other options of who might represent our region and that they fully supported your first choice."

After saying this, the official apologized again and added: "Jim, if I can ever be of assistance to you, please call on me." My head was swimming when I returned to the meeting. When it was over I just had time to head for the airport and back to Washington. I did not regret the fact that I had no chance to discuss the matter with my boss, Dr. Osmun.

Needless to say, my good feelings about the promotion were dashed. As soon as I returned home, I told Gwen, "I hope you didn't spend any of that additional money I was to receive for my promotion." I then explained what had happened and said I was sure that when we saw each other again on Monday morning, Dr. Osmun would tell me that he had withdrawn the paperwork for my GS-15.

Come Monday morning, that's exactly what happened. Dr. Osmun didn't bother to explain why he had withdrawn my promotion papers and I knew better than to ask him. Perhaps I should have been crushed by this but I wasn't. For one thing, I had never expected to reach that level in the first place. And I wasn't sure I was ready for another promotion since I had already had two within the past five years. In addition, EPA had given me cash awards and two extra "time in grade" raises which had increased my salary considerably.

Strangely, although I was expecting to remain embarrassed for a long time because of my boorish behavior in Chicago, I quickly found out that my personal status at EPA had gone through the roof. It seems that this "cold eyed" Irishman official had offended other EPA people and they were very pleased that someone had reacted as I did.

One such example was John Ritch, a retired Navy captain, who had taken over as Director of Pesticide Registration at EPA. He was at the same table in Chicago when I confronted the official who had bad mouthed me. After we arrived back at EPA HQ, he couldn't wait to tell me how much he admired me for standing up for myself. I was surprised at Ritch's reaction. He knew I was a great friend and supporter of Harold Alford, his predecessor. Until that time, Ritch had not been overly friendly with me. After the "Chicago incident" he became such a fan that I had to "shoosh" him when we met because he wanted to tell everyone in hearing distance about it.

A short footnote to this story: This Regional Assistant Administrator was later promoted to Assistant to DAA Ed Johnson and was assigned to the Washington office. My office was one of first places he visited after his move to DC. He tapped at my door, asked if he could come in and greeted me with a big smile and warm hand shake. We chatted for awhile and he repeated his offer to call him if I ever needed his help. I appreciated this and gradually came to realize that he was being completely sincere. He was always among the first to greet me in a crowded room.

# CHAPTER 16

## Time for a "Breather"?

AFTER SECTION 4 (a) of FIFRA Standards were published in the Federal Register I thought I might have a little time to catch my breath, spend more time on my regular duties, and deal with a health problem. The latter involved a succession of urinary tract infections I had been having. With antibiotic treatment, the infection would clear up briefly but would soon recur, requiring more antibiotic treatments. Both Gwen and I were concerned about this but my Internist did not seem to think the problem was serious.

My respite from the pressure of getting the Pesticide Standards published was brief. Within days, I was told my next assignment was to develop regulations for Section 4 (b) of revised FIFRA, rules that states would be required to follow in conducting certification programs in their states. I had no idea that I would be responsible for this part of Section 4 because of its many legal implications. But apparently the fact that I had been the only subcommittee chairperson to meet the Congressional deadline had been the deciding factor in my selection to handle this set of regulations.

Although the subject matter was different, I was able to utilize many of the same resources to prepare this new and different set of regulations. However, I relied heavily on the advice and counsel of Lowell Miller, OPP'S top attorney. He was the most knowledgeable attorney at EPA on the "legislative history" of pesticide regulations in general. He also had detailed knowledge of "Congressional Intent" utilized in revising FIFRA. I had to become a quick study on these issues in order to do my job. (It also turned out that ultimately I needed more and different legal advice! But that's another story).

While I had been concentrating on getting the Standards published, Dr. Osmun had set up a new branch, called **The Liaison and Training Branch** and named me as Acting Branch Chief. The new position added more responsibilities e.g., all training activities involving the Certification Program. This added to my responsibilities but also provided me with more authority to hire people. I was able to bring in two new employees: George Beshore and Alvin Chock, two very competent people I already knew.

I met both Beshore and Chock when I was with (ARS) USDA. George was a fellow Information Officer in our group. I knew him to be a creative and productive writer. Although I hadn't worked directly with Chock, I knew that he had a brilliant mind and energy to match. I gave both of them promotions and their presence allowed me to devote more of my time to my regular and expanded responsibilities. I even had some time to spend on less demanding but important programs including implementation of Sections 5, 18, and 24 (c). Of course I would still devote most of my time to developing Section 4 (b), standards that states would be required to follow in order to set up systems for certifying applicators in their state.

George Beshore took full responsibility for writing and producing the newsletter and writing any relevant news stories affecting OPP. Al Chock became my "go to" person to help me deal with technical matters. With the help of several other highly intelligent and highly competent individuals added to my new branch, e.g., Walt Waldrop, Jim Boland, and Andy Caraker, the branch was really shaping up.

With help from Drs. John Osmun, Fred Whittemore and Bob Evans, we put together a working draft of State Plan requirements. Dr. Whittemore and I then set up a travel schedule to devote six full weeks of visiting all areas of the U.S. to solicit input. Dr. Evans couldn't go with us, so our "travel team" consisted of Dr. Whittemore, me, and Sue Schmaltz, the Division Secretary. Dr. Whittemore and I would conduct the meetings and lead discussions. The three of us would all make notes of significant comments and suggestions for changes from attendees. Then, after the meetings ended, Fred, Sue and I would confer and agree on any changes needed as a result of input received at that week's meetings. Sue would take our revised draft and make fresh copies for distribution at meetings the following week.

Each Monday morning the three of us would meet at the office and leave on an early flight. Then we would return to the office late Friday; we repeated this routine weekly for six straight weeks. This system was grueling but productive. We accomplished a great deal in a relatively short time. Dr. Whittemore and I disagreed on one point. Reflecting his long-time military background, Dr. Whittemore insisted the meeting be strictly controlled with every session devoted to the working draft at hand. I wanted more "open" meetings where attendees would be encouraged to introduce new, original ideas that might be superior to the ones contained in our present draft. After I stated my disagreement with the "rigid" approach, Dr. Whittemore convinced me that his uncompromising, "stick to the draft" approach was the way to ensure that we meet our deadline. As a result, at the end of the six weeks of travel, we had an "acceptable draft" although it did not contain as much original thinking as I had hoped.

After circulating the final draft inside and outside the agency we soon deemed it ready to take to the Review Board. That's when I really appreciated having Fred as part of our team. His familiarity in dealing with bureaucrats made it easy for us to deal with the Review Board and this time our product sailed right through that process. Our State Plan Draft was ready for some final "tweaking" before being submitted to the Federal Register. After I wrote the Introduction it would appear in the CFR.

# CHAPTER 17

## My Job Continues to Grow

WHILE WE WERE on the road, Dr. Osmun again reorganized the branch I was serving as Acting Branch Chief. It became the **Regional Support and Certification Branch.** I would continue to serve as Acting Branch Chief of the new branch which would become the contact for all Regional Pesticide Activities, and would manage the Certification and Training, as well as to review and officially approve or disapprove State Certifications Plans when they were submitted. I would be the "approving official" until selection of a "permanent" branch chief. At that time, I would drop back to "assistant branch chief."

In addition to being responsible for all aspects of **Section 4 (a&b),** this branch would be responsible for (1) **Section 5** which allows manufacturers to field test their products under development; (2) **Section 18** which allows State and Federal agencies to permit the use of an unregistered pesticide in a specific area under the Emergency Exemption rule of FIFRA when exercised properly; and (3) **Section 24(c)** which allows states to register a new pesticide for general use or a federally registered product for an additional use, if states met certain conditions.

Full implementation of these programs meant that about 90 percent of the Operation Division's work would be handled by this one branch. The remaining 10 percent would involve policy development and miscellaneous other activities such as interaction with Congress and other EPA political matters.

While naming me as acting branch chief for the Regional Support and Certification Branch, Dr. Osmun urged me to apply for the job of permanent branch chief. That job would be at the GS-15 level. Although flattered by his suggestion, I felt that the tremendous responsibilities of this position might be better handled by someone with a scientific background, e.g., someone with a PhD in an agricultural science area such as Entomology or Agronomy.

I told him I would be happy to stay at the GS-14 level and work closely with anyone he selected for the branch chief job. The fact was that I felt insecure about heading up a large national program for a prominent federal agency. I sometimes found myself wondering: *"What am I doing managing a science-based program with world-wide implications?"*

Although Dr. Osmun agreed to try to find someone whose background was better suited to this highly demanding position, he had one unusual provision: "I'm going to insist that you interview anyone I send you. And you must either approve or disapprove of that individual before I put him or her into that job." This seemed like a strange arrangement but since I would be working under that person I agreed to conduct the "final" interviews, make an appropriate assessment of their capabilities, and pass this information along to Dr. Osmun for his decision. Thus began a parade of highly educated candidates (all with PhD's in a scientific field) through my office.

Although this will certainly sound self-serving, I wasn't satisfied that any one of these people was up to the job. So, I finally told Dr. Osmun, "I think I'm best suited to do this job." He smiled and said, "I hoped you would come to that conclusion." So, that's how I became a GS-15 Branch Chief, supervising 14 professionals (one being an attorney and three being PhD scientists), some clerical employees and several consultants.

At Dr. Fred Whittemore's suggestion, I soon added another highly rated person (female) to my staff. Fred was politically astute and learned that Lois French, wife of one of DC's top industry lobbyists, had been hired by EPA but had been placed in a "dead end" job. She was seeking a more responsible, more demanding job in the agency. Fred approached me one day and said: "Jim, we're top heavy with men and need to add at least one competent professional woman." This was the period when pressure was just beginning to push federal agencies to hire more professional women in government.

Fred then explained, "Rather than waiting and having someone forced upon us, I think it would be a good idea to hire a woman we know is a competent professional. With the responsibilities of revised FIFRA that have been assigned to your branch, I know you could use some more help." At his suggestion, I met with Lois French, was impressed with her and quickly asked personnel to re-assign her to my staff. It turned out that Fred's evaluation of Lois might have been understated.

Not only was she highly intelligent and competent, Lois also "knew where the bodies were buried" in the agency and in DC. Having someone on staff with "insider" knowledge was a terrific asset to someone like me who was not politically connected. Lois and her husband "partied" with people such as Sen. John Warner and his wife, actress Elizabeth Taylor. It was not long before I made her Assistant Branch Chief and put her in charge of the office when I had to travel or needed to handle special assignments (which came up much quicker than I expected).

# CHAPTER 18
## An Unexpected Problem Looms

WHILE I WAS beginning the process of submitting the "Regulations for Submission of State Plans" for publication in the CFR someone asked me: "How will your State Plan Regulations affect Indian reservations?" I was speechless! It had not occurred to me, or anyone else who had reviewed them, to consider the effect of these regulations upon American Indian reservations. I had completely forgotten that Indian reservations are treated like separate entities within the states where they are located. In fact, some are treated like separate nations within the U.S.

In the rush to meet the Congressional deadline, I had neglected to consider this issue and no one had mentioned it to me until that point. If I had gone ahead with getting the Regulations published in the Federal Register, someone would have eventually noticed this omission and since my name was again listed as contact person, I would have been the one in trouble. So, I put an immediate stop to the publication in the CFR.

What to do? One thing I knew was that I needed to talk to someone who knew more about the Indian Nation than I. Through my resources, I found the name of an attorney by the name of Leigh Price who had been heavily involved in legal matters involving Indian tribes. He also had close Indian friends in Congress and the Bureau of Indian Affairs. When I learned of his background, I thought he might be the answer to my problem. I quickly called him and invited him to visit my office to discuss a very important matter involving the Indian Nation.

Leigh Price soon came to my office and I filled him in about the problem we were facing. At the end of our discussion, I knew he was the person I needed to help me deal with this problem. I asked him if he would be interested in a job with EPA and he said: "Yes, but not on a permanent basis. I'll be glad to help solve this problem for the Agency and for the Indian Nation." I quickly wrote a request to personnel explaining why Attorney Price was urgently needed; that we could not proceed with publishing the State Plan Regulations until the "Indian problem" was resolved.

With help from "higher ups" Leigh Price was quickly reporting to me as a staff member with one responsibility: dealing with the Indian problem related to the Certification Standards as well as "State Plan Regulations." I began the process by asking him to study all the relevant material and then give me his preliminary analyses of whether we could apply these standards to Indian reservations and if so, how.

His preliminary analysis showed me how some tribes and reservations could be treated much like states while others with different treaties had to be handled differently. I asked him to proceed with a plan to "solve the Indian issues related to our regulations." Leigh began digging deeply into the Certification Standards and State Plan Regulations. Soon he became familiar enough with both sets of regulations to begin making recommendations on how they could be adapted for application to various Indian tribes and reservations. His knowledge of how the different tribes and reservations operated was invaluable in writing a plan to accomplish this.

Because of Leigh's expertise we soon had what I thought was a satisfactory system of dealing with the Indian tribes and reservations and I added a new section to the State Plan Regulations. I did not send this section out for wide-spread review but sent it only to affected states. As I recall, I got few suggestions from the affected states or from the Review Board which took a final look at the entire package. So I wrote a new introduction and prepared the final (official) version of FIFRA Section 4(b) Regulations for publication in the Federal Register. It was published soon after and received no adverse reactions.

# CHAPTER 19
## Goodbye Dr. Osmun and Hello "Wild Bill"

I BARELY HAD time to celebrate the above momentous occasion before Dr. Osmun announced that his "leave of absence" was up and that he was leaving EPA and returning to the Entomology Department at Purdue University in West Lafayette, IN. It was a sad day for me when I had to say goodbye to someone who had become my mentor and friend. When I was advised I could add consultants to assist my Branch, my first selection was Dr. Osmun. Lest you think this was an "agreed upon" arrangement, be assured that this was not a case of "quid pro quo." I hired the best people available to work as my consultants. In addition to Dr. Osmun, I added Dr. Bob Evans and Dr. Jerry Weekman of North Carolina State University to the list of consultants.

Dr. Osmun's successor was retired Marine Lt. Col. William Holmberg, a giant of a man at 6 ft. 5 inches in height and a rawboned 230 pounds. When I shook hands with him, I noted that his wrists were twice the size of mine. A brief resume extracted from various sources on the Internet follows:

*Bill Holmberg graduated from the U.S. Naval Academy, and holds advanced degrees in Personnel Administration, Soviet Affairs and the Russian Language. While on active duty, Bill served in the Cold and Korean Wars. He commanded platoons, companies, a battalion landing team and a Marine Barracks. As a 2nd Lieutenant serving in Korea, he received The Navy Cross for "extraordinary heroism in connection with military operations against an armed enemy of the United Nations while serving in action against enemy aggressor forces in the Republic of Korea on 13 June 1952."*

Note: Although those of us who knew Bill did not consider him an overly modest man, we must have been wrong since he never mentioned receiving The Navy Cross and other awards for heroism to any of us who worked with him at EPA! And he never posted a single military award on his desk or office walls. Holmberg was an Aide to two Chiefs of Naval Operations, one of whom was Admiral Thomas Hinman Moorer, admiral and naval aviator in the U.S. Navy. Admiral Moorer later served as Chief of Naval Operations from 1967 to 1970 and as Chairman of the Joint Chiefs of Staff from 1970 to 1974.

Obviously, our new director was a well connected Washington, DC power player. Known as "Wild Bill" Holmberg by the military, he showed a definite streak of "wildness" as a civilian Civil Service employee. The first thing he did upon his arrival at EPA was try to fire many of the employees he inherited at the Operations Division. Obviously he was unaware of how difficult it was to fire Civil Service employees. Despite his best efforts, he was unable to fire any of the employees outright. The best he could do was to scare a few into taking early retirements.

Dr. Whittemore and I, along with Division Secretary Sue Schmaltz had no such problem with Holmberg. In fact, he went out of his way to make the three of us feel needed. Later on I learned the reason. One day Bill showed me a list of Ops. Division employees with "stars" by three names: Whittemore, White, and Schmaltz. I assume he must have asked someone to do an evaluation of the Operations Division Staff because he was planning to "clean house" of "dead wood" employees.

Holmberg asked Dr. Whittemore to continue on as assistant director. Holmberg obviously had great respect for Dr. Whittemore's knowledge and background. After all, both had been high level military officers during war time. Mr. Holmberg then announced he was going to move almost all the rest of the division personnel, including training, into my already "top heavy" branch.

The two retired military officers worked well together, with Holmberg coming up with ideas by the dozen and the more pragmatic Whittemore shooting most of them down. Soon after the change in directors of the Operations Division, the EPA personnel office notified Dr. Whittemore that he had reached "mandatory" Civil Service retirement age and had to retire. Suddenly "Big Red" was gone and "Little Red" was moved into the office next to director Holmberg.

The experience of being next door to Wild Bill Holmberg was something I will never forget. With new ideas springing from Holmberg's inventive brain daily and sometimes more often, I would hear loud banging on the wall that separated our two offices. That was my signal to drop what I was doing and appear immediately in Holmberg's office.

Then I had to listen to Bill's latest idea to "save the world." The majority of the ideas were interesting but had nothing to do with the mission of the Operations Division. In fact many were completely outside of EPA's area of responsibility, not just with our division. It was my duty to tell him that although a particular idea might be great, that it had no application for us. Usually Bill readily accepted my judgment on his ideas; but occasionally he would be so much "in love" with an idea that we would get into a vociferous argument about it. Things would cool down eventually and he would usually end up grudgingly agreeing with me.

I recognized that Holmberg was using me as a "sounding board" and he would have lost confidence in me quickly if I agreed with him just because he was my boss. It didn't take long for Bill Holmberg and me to realize that we had widely different opinions about the chemical/pesticide industry and environmental matters. With some exceptions, I admired the people providing the money needed for research as well as those producing and applying the chemicals that enabled Americans to enjoy the quantity and quality of food unheard of in many parts of the world. Also, with some exceptions, I generally appreciated the work of the national, state, and local officials that regulated this great industry which allowed us to become "the world's breadbasket."

On the other hand, Bill related more to environmental groups, most of which opposed the use of chemicals and had a jaundiced view of those producing the chemicals, those applying them, and state officials who were regulating them. Bill was highly attuned to those promoting organic farming and reducing reliance on chemicals and fossil fuels. Although I appreciated the concept of organic farming, I knew that from a practical standpoint, organic farming was not then, and may never be, capable of producing the high quality and quantity of food and other agricultural products expected and needed by our citizens. *Much progress in organic farming has been made in recent years and I have been gradually revising my earlier opinion.*

There was no doubt that Bill was far out in front of anyone I knew in his appreciation of alternate fuels and organic farming. He was also the first person I heard use the term "fuel cell" which as I write is just now reaching the point that a Japanese auto maker is starting to market a car which operates on fuel cells. Not only was he closely allied with environmental groups, he had friends in Hollywood who embraced environmental issues. One of Bill's closest Hollywood friends and a fellow environmental activist, was actor Eddie Albert (Green Acres, etc.). Eddie called Bill often. (Sometimes too often). Sometimes when Eddie called, Bill would tell the secretary "I don't have time to talk with Eddie; transfer the call to Jim." Since Eddie Albert and I had little in common, my role was mostly to listen while Eddie talked. Later, when Bill had time to listen, I would relay Eddie's message to him.

# CHAPTER 20
## A "Green Acres Day" with Eddie and "Flower Children"

SOMETIME IN EARLY April of the late 1970's Bill gave me an assignment that I'll never forget. He banged on the wall and I went to his office. He said: "Jim, I know you're not a great supporter of Earth Day *(held every year on April 22 since 1970)* but I need you to do me a favor that day." Since I knew I had no choice in the matter, I asked "What does that favor entail?" He replied: "Eddie is flying in from Hollywood for Earth Day and wants me to escort him around. I can't do it and want you to entertain him for that day."

So, Eddie Albert and I spent the day walking around the National Mall, mixing with the hippies and flower children attending Earth Day. I did my best to pretend I was interested. Eddie was enthralled by the whole celebration but frequently mused: "Wonder where Bill is today; I had so looked forward to seeing him." *I was wondering the same thing.*

This might be the time to tell a funny story involving Eddie Albert and a new employee of mine by the name of Richard Moorer. Holmberg didn't ask me before hiring Richard. He just brought him to my office, introduced him and said "Richard is a new member of your staff." *If you suspect that Richard was related to Holmberg's former boss, Admiral Thomas Hinman Moorer, you are right. Richard, my new employee, was Admiral Moorer's son.* Richard turned out to be a "classy" young man who never used his famous father to get ahead, (other than his original hire which was probably Bill Holmberg's idea anyway). Modest almost to a fault, he never discussed his privileged family background and he never hesitated to do what I (or Holmberg) asked him to do. He probably should have refused one assignment that Holmberg gave him while I was out of town. This incident also involved actor Eddie Albert, who was visiting DC and staying at the home of a U.S. Congressman. The morning Eddie was leaving the Congressman's home to return to California, Washington media outlets loudly "outed" this Congressman as being "gay."

Eddie apparently panicked over the situation. Apparently, he did not want the world to know that he was spending nights at the home of a gay Congressman. (That was during the good old days when being a "homosexual" definitely was not considered an asset). Eddie had his bags packed and was ready to leave the front door when he spotted members of the press gathered on the sidewalk outside. In desperation, Eddie climbed the tall fence surrounding the Congressman's house. On the other side of the fence he found himself on the grounds of the Australian Embassy. From there, he called his good friend Bill Holmberg to come or send someone to rescue him and his baggage.

So Bill sent Richard Moorer by taxi to the Congressman's home with instructions to go inside the Congressman's house, bring out Eddie Albert's two packed suitcases sitting by the front door, put them into the taxi, pick up Eddie from the Australian Embassy and bring him and his baggage back to the EPA. Once there, Bill would take Eddie to the airport. I was told that the press photographers waiting outside took lots of pictures of Richard as he hurried to the Congressman's house and returned to the cab. Eddie hurried to the cab which drove him and Richard to the EPA.

*Apparently the press did not recognize Richard and thus did not use his name in the photos that appeared later in the Washington media outlets. I suspect that Admiral Moorer would not have been happy had his son been identified in the photos.*

# CHAPTER 21
## Bill and Chemical Industry: Not Simpatico

ALTHOUGH REPRESENTATIVES OF the chemical industry did not know Bill Holmberg until he came to EPA, they soon decided he was not their friend. He was far too involved with the environmental movement for their taste. And I could tell that they were becoming more wary of me because of my close association with Bill. Then, by a wild coincidence, something happened that put me back in good standing with them.

Shortly after "Earth Day," Bill called me into his office to discuss some new ideas involving environmental issues that intrigued him. At this time I don't recall specifics of these ideas but I immediately saw that the ideas were completely out of EPA's area of responsibility. And even worse, he wanted to use taxpayer money to help fund these activities. Without arguing the merits of the ideas, I voiced my strong objections to spending EPA's (taxpayer) money to finance activities not related to EPA's responsibilities.

In response, Bill told me that he didn't have the time then to discuss the matter fully since he had to go to a meeting. He added that after the meeting he was going away for a weekend at the beach, something I had been encouraging him to do. I knew he needed some rest and recreation to help him maintain some semblance of sanity. So, he asked me to write down my thinking about the matter so he could read it at his leisure. He said, "I'll take it with me and read it at the beach." I was sorry to hear that he was taking work along with him on his short vacation. However, I went back to my typewriter and wrote a three-page memo explaining point-by-point my objections to his new ideas. I signed and clipped the pages together and placed them on his office chair and left to meet my car pool.

The following Monday when he returned to our office, Bill made no further mention of the ideas. I assumed that he had accepted my arguments against the ideas and had abandoned them. This was the usual pattern. A couple of weeks went by and I had almost forgotten the matter when an industry representative dropped by my office. After a brief conversation, he reached into his briefcase and brought out some water stained pieces of paper and handed them to me. When I looked at them I recognized that they were the pages I had prepared for Bill stating my adverse reactions to his ideas. I asked, "Where in the heck did you come across these?"

He replied, "Two weekends ago I was at the beach and saw Bill Holmberg farther down the beach. He was sitting and reading a stack of papers so I didn't disturb him. He put some of the papers down and a gust of wind came along and sent the papers flying everywhere." The industry man could hardly contain his laughter while he described the scene of Big Bill running around the beach trying to retrieve his papers.

The chemical rep added, "Bill left before I did and when I walked past where he had been sitting, I spotted some sheets of paper he apparently had missed finding. They were lying right at the water's edge as you can see by the water stains." He added, "I decided I would see if I could rescue those papers, dry them out and then bring them back to Bill's office. After they dried, my curiosity got the better of me and I couldn't stop myself from reading them. After I had read them, I didn't dare return them to Bill," he said. "But I can assure you that other members of our industry know about this and now consider you a good friend of our industry."

That's how my standing with the chemical industry was restored. But I admit I felt a little like I was being a traitor to my boss, although I had nothing to do with industry reps being able to read my written words that pleased them.

# CHAPTER 22
## A Rare Federal Employee "Workaholic"

LT. COL. HOLMBERG was one of the few "workaholics" I encountered as a federal government employee. I knew plenty who were diligent employees but because most depended upon carpools to get to and from work, their hours were usually limited to eight hour days. I of course depended on carpools and was similarly limited but made up for this by eating a small lunch at my desk while continuing to work. Also, in urgent situations, I took work home with me. I also paid no attention to hours worked when I traveled for the government. I was too anxious to return home to be with Mitch and Gwen to spend a weekend away from home unless absolutely necessary.

Holmberg had his own individual parking permit and didn't have to worry about delaying a carpool. He often spent up to 20 hours per day on the job. Soon after he arrived at EPA, he went outside of normal channels and hired a group of employees who worked the "night shift" with him. Although I strongly suspect this was a violation of Civil Service rules, he paid no attention to that fact, and as far as I know, never suffered any consequences for it--except for his family life and his health.

From a distance he was an extremely impressive physical specimen. Up close, however, you could see the blood shot eyes and exhaustion from lack of sleep. His work life obviously interfered with his family life. I was aware of that because at every tax season, his wife Mary would call me at the office (obviously in tears) and tell me that Bill wouldn't take the time to look at and sign their joint income tax return. She begged me to prod him about this. I went as far as I felt I could to get him to take the time to review and sign the return. I don't know how effective I was in doing this but as far as I know, the IRS never went after him or his wife.

However, I felt sorry for Mary, who had to get the tax return information together, take it to an accountant, and then attempt to get Bill to stand still long enough to check and sign the return before the deadline. As long as we worked together at EPA this was a yearly event. I learned that she died of cancer after I retired from the agency.

Just as I was getting settled into handling my new duties, I was notified (along with other employees recently promoted to GS-14 and GS-15 positions) that I needed to be prepared for a Desk Audit of my position to ensure that I was properly qualified for the job. I was not unduly alarmed to learn about the Desk Audit but I didn't take it lightly either. I didn't want to lose a GS-15 twice!

So, I got out a copy of my GS-15 Position Description (PD) and made a list of the major requirements for this particular position. (Fortunately, by this time I had learned to save some copies of my work, something I regrettably failed to do as a newspaper reporter). With some thought and attention to detail, I matched up all the PD requirements with examples of my work. The person doing the audit pulled out his own copy of the PD and began asking me questions about each requirement. After a brief discussion of each job requirement, I would hand him marked examples of my work that corresponded with the requirement.

This went on for less than an hour before the Desk Auditor grinned and said: "Jim, you've really got your S - - T together. We don't need to continue this because you obviously have the job well in hand. I'm obliged to spend a couple of hours here but let's just have coffee and talk about something interesting, like fishing or sports." We spent another hour in casual conversation, shook hands, and the desk audit was over.

My GS-15 was secure and I was now fully conscious that I was managing a national program that affects the lives of millions of people. Then, soon after the desk audit I received notice that I had been selected to attend an expensive Executive Management Training Seminar that, once completed, would put me in line for a "Super Grade," a GS-16 or higher. I chose not to take advantage of this opportunity because I had invested so much of my energy in helping to save a program I cared so much about (the Certification program). Nevertheless, I began receiving (but ignoring) openings for positions at the GS-16 level.

*This situation reminded me that during my senior year in high school we were asked to write down our ambitions for the future after graduation. I still have that record of my goals in life on an old school paper saved by my Mom. I came across the original copy of it recently in gathering material for this Memoir. I listed my future ambitions at that time as: (1) filling station attendant or (2) carpenter's helper. (Obviously my ambitions had grown considerably since then).*

# CHAPTER 23
## Problem: No System for Classifying RUP's

AFTER THE PUBLICATION of the latest regulations in the Federal Register, I again thought I might have a "breather." However, I was almost immediately faced with an old problem, actually aggravated by our recent successes. Briefly stated, the Certification Process required three things: (1) A set of Certification Standards, (2) An approved State Certification Plan, and (3) A system for classifying highly-toxic or environmentally hazardous pesticides for "Restricted Use," i.e. for use only by a Certified Applicator. I had been given the responsibility for completing the first two of this trio and had met the Congressional deadlines for their completion.

However, No. 3, a system for classifying pesticides for Restricted Use, had missed its Congressional deadline and had no immediate prospects for future viability. Because the classification program had not been done, there was not a single "Restricted Use Product" (RUP) available for use by Certified Applicators. This failure rendered the entire process moot.

This situation was embarrassing to the Agency and hazardous to the future of the Pesticide Applicator Certification Program. Because of the failure of the Agency to complete its work, resistance to the whole issue of Certification of Applicators and requirements that states submit plans for certifying applicators had re-emerged and was growing. Those state people responsible for conducting certification programs as well as those seeking certification could not believe that after all the work they had gone through to get ready for certification, that EPA had been unable to develop a classification system for pesticides. The leader of this resistance as usual was Tommy Ervin, Agriculture Commissioner (and potential candidate for Governor) of the state of Georgia.

Of these issues, I didn't see how I could do anything to speed up the process for classifying pesticides since I had no responsibilities and little knowledge or experience in that area. And coincidentally, my own personal health issue was becoming more bothersome. I was just finishing up my latest round of antibiotics which I hoped might help resolve my health problem.

After much thought, an idea occurred to me that might temporarily ease the long, drawn out resistance the agency had encountered from Commissioner Ervin and buy some time. Hopefully, the plan, if successful, would give the agency enough additional time to solve the classification problem.

*The idea sounds so devious now that I hesitate to take credit for it. My idea involved (in fact depended on) my old friend Jack Gilchrist, Commissioner Ervin's public relations man. The plan (if I could get approval to conduct it) was to devise a "win-win" situation for both the certification program and Commissioner Ervin. I had heard from knowledgeable sources that Ervin was considering running for governor and might welcome some positive publicity even if it involved his pet "whipping boy"--EPA and its Pesticide Applicator Certification Program.*

The plan I dreamed up had three parts: (1) to convince Jack Gilchrist that the certification program was essential for preserving the use of vital pesticides needed in the state of Georgia and the nation, (2) to urge him to convince his boss that he had already received the maximum benefit from his highly publicized opposition to the program, and (3) to show Jack (and the Commissioner) how it would be beneficial for the state and nation for the Commissioner to change his position from opposing the Certification Program to actually supporting it.

Number three of course was the trickiest part of the plan. I hoped to accomplish this by: (a) getting a series of articles published in the Atlanta media giving Commissioner Ervin credit for forcing EPA to make its requirements "more reasonable" (especially for farmers) and (b) giving the state of Georgia the honor of becoming the first state in the nation to have an approved State Pesticide Applicator Certification plan. Obviously there were some hurdles to overcome before any of these ambitious goals could be attained.

First, I had to get EPA's approval. I thought my plan was "crazy" enough that Director Holmberg would like it! As I anticipated, he loved the plan! But the question remained: would he be able to get the required approval of "higher ups" at EPA? If we got that approval, I, as creator of the plan, would then have the unenviable job of contacting Charlie Frommer, head of the New York agency responsible for Environmental Affairs, and try to get his blessings.

*Charlie, who had been a long-time supporter and friend of mine and the Certification Program, was already prepared to submit a State Certification Plan as soon as I gave him the word. Charlie badly wanted his state to be the first in the U.S. to have an approved State Plan and he and his state certainly deserved that honor. I felt like a heel asking him to hold back on his submission. Charlie wasn't happy about it but after hearing about the problems the agency was having and my plan for dealing with it, he reluctantly agreed to delay his submission, providing I could get all the tricky elements described above to work. I swore him and Bill Holmberg to secrecy.*

# CHAPTER 24

## Crazy Idea Leads to "Secret" Trip to Atlanta

AS A REFLECTION of the desperate situation of the entire certification program, I was soon given the Agency's approval to proceed. My first move to implement the plan was to call Jack Gilchrist to ask him to meet secretly with me in Atlanta. Jack readily agreed and said he would pick me up at the airport the following Friday and we would spend the weekend at his cabin on a large lake outside of Atlanta.

After arriving at his cabin, we had a drink together and I began laying out the philosophy and need for saving the endangered certification program. Since we had worked closely together on other State-Federal Cooperative Programs, we already had a good, trusting relationship and he was receptive to my concerns that we might lose this program.

I saved details of my plan until the next day when we were going to spend most of the day in his boat fishing. Within a few hours of talking and fishing, Jack was onboard with the idea and was optimistic that he could talk the Commissioner into going along with it. Fortunately, I had packed so that I could spend the entire week in Atlanta if necessary. So I asked Jack to make reservations for me at a hotel close to his office for the following night and week. I didn't want to intrude on his hospitality beyond the weekend and also needed to be able to spend private time with Dr. Bob Evans to discuss actually writing the Georgia State Plan, using our newly published regulations as guidelines.

Of course everything depended upon Jack being able to convince the Commissioner to go along with the plan. I had already called Bob Evans to alert him that I might need his help with a "top secret" mission in Atlanta and he was in "standby" mode. Early Monday morning, I met Jack in his office to start work while he went to meet with Commissioner Ervin. Confident that Jack would be successful, I used his typewriter to begin writing the series of articles. Within a few minutes Jack returned with the Commissioner's "thumbs up" for our plan. I called Dr. Evans to come to Jack's office where I briefed him on my plan to "buy time" until the classification problem could be solved and asked him to start writing a Georgia State Certification plan.

I began the series with an article reiterating the Commissioner's original objections to EPA's Applicator Certification Program but ended on a positive note that EPA was giving serious attention to his concerns. Succeeding articles became more and more positive until I could state that the Commissioner was now convinced that EPA had reacted to his strong objections by removing certain unacceptable provisions involving requirements for Private Applicators, i.e. farmers. And I quoted him as saying that he was now ready to support the program.

Within a few days I had completed the series and they were appearing in the Atlanta media (obviously not with my byline.) Before the end of the week, Dr. Bob Evans had completed Georgia's State Plan for Pesticide Applicator Certification.

Commissioner Ervin signed it, and I then signed the submission for EPA under my own authority. I then wrote the final article that Georgia's State Certification had been submitted and approved by EPA.

Before I headed back to Washington, headlines in Georgia newspapers were announcing that "Georgia Is First State in the Nation to have an Approved Pesticide Applicator Certification Plan."

I had one unpleasant duty to perform before I left Atlanta. That was to inform the Region IV, EPA Regional Office of what had happened. Because of possible leaks (or even worse: active opposition) I had thought it too risky to inform the Regional Office in advance about the plan. Bob Evans and I went together to the office of pesticides for Region IV where we laid all of our cards on the table. I apologized profusely for not giving the Regional Office advance notice of our intrusion into Region IV. The top pesticide official listened intently and voiced no objections to what had been done. After we left the office, Bob said: "Jim, I think they took that very well, don't you?" I replied, "Yeah, it appeared that way. But I suspect I'll catch hell from Region IV when I get back to Washington."

I didn't know what to expect when I returned to Headquarters EPA. Director Holmberg was waiting for me with a non-committal expression on his face. He congratulated me for carrying out the plan and then grinned broadly and said: "Guess what! The Region IV Administrator called the EPA Administrator and demanded that Jim White be fired!" He then added: "I went upstairs and explained what and why we did things the way we did. I suspect you will be rewarded rather than punished for what you accomplished." *And I later did receive another award--that made no mention of my foray into Georgia.*

Feeling that Jack Gilchrist deserved further reward for his work on behalf of the Certification Program, Holmberg then used his clout with the military to have Jack (a Marine Reservist) be given a place of honor in a large parade celebrating the Marine Corps. A few weeks later Jack, (*who I believe was a lowly Lieutenant when on active duty during WWII*), called to tell us that he rode upfront in the parade, along with Marine Colonels and Generals. *Jack said that he really enjoyed being in the parade and associating with these senior officers.*

# CHAPTER 25
## A Real Physical Checkup Could Possibly Be Bad News

WHEN THE EUPHORIA of the "Georgia Plan" wore off, I was forced to give more consideration to my health problems. When I reached the GS-15 level I had become eligible for free health exams performed at EPA. Although an exam was not mandatory, I was urged to report to EPA's health office so they could add my name to the list of those eligible for free annual checkups. Since my regular doctor had been unable to solve my urinary tract problem, I also thought it might be a good idea to get another opinion so I made an appointment to see the EPA doctor.

After giving blood and urine samples, I spent some time with the agency physician who seemed quite troubled when I described my urinary tract system problems and the recurring treatments with antibiotics prescribed by my Internist. The EPA doctor made extensive notes about my situation and placed them in a large folder with my name on it. Before I left, he advised me to get my doctor to check my prostate for possible prostate cancer.

He also suggested that my doctor refer me to a urologist. Since I had recently been treated for another recurrence of a urinary tract infection, I was due a "follow up" visit to my Internist a short time later. At that time I told him what the EPA doctor had advised. He replied that the antibiotic he had prescribed had cleared up the infection and that I was "o.k." He did not check my prostate or refer me to a urologist. After I arrived home I told Gwen that Dr. Kay said that my urinary tract infection was again "cleared up" but that I still did not "feel o.k." Gwen had been growing increasingly concerned about my health and said, "I've been describing your problems to a nurse friend of mine and she thinks you should see a urologist right away." I replied that the EPA doctor had also advised me that I should see one and asked: "Did your nurse friend mention the name of a doctor she recommends?" Gwen replied: "Yes, she recommended Dr. Patrick Carroll, who is qualified both as a urologist and oncologist. She said she would be happy to make an appointment for you."

A short time later, I went to see Dr. Carroll who examined my prostate gland digitally and then said: "Jim I don't like the feel of your prostate. I need to get a biopsy done and sent to the lab." Since I was going to Denver on a business trip for EPA in a few days, I asked if it would be o.k. for me to make my trip. He said that the trip should not be a problem for me and that by the time I returned he would have received results of the biopsy.

The meeting in Denver went well. Dr. Osmun was there as a consultant and I told him of my health concerns. He tried to cheer me up but I could tell he was also concerned. As it turned out his concerns (and mine) were justified. As soon as I returned from Denver, I called Dr. Carroll's office and his nurse said the doctor wanted to see me right away. Since the nurse didn't tell me the results of the test, I was immediately suspicious that Dr. Carroll had bad news for me. When Gwen and I entered Dr. Carroll's office the next day, he rose to greet us and didn't beat around the bush. "Jim, I have some good news and bad news for you. The bad news is that the biopsy revealed that you have prostate cancer; the good news is that I think we caught this cancer in time before it spread."

He then explained his recommended treatment: a surgical procedure to remove the part of the prostate gland containing the cancer tumor, followed by a series of 38 radiation treatments, plus chemotherapy in the form of daily pills to reduce the supply of male hormones which drives prostate cancer. He hoped this would help prevent or reduce the chances of the spread of cancer to other parts of the body while killing off the prostate cancer cells.

I was momentarily shocked by the news that I had "Big C"--the most fearsome ailment I could imagine. Gwen and I embraced and shared a few tears before settling down with Dr. Carroll to schedule the surgery--which he would perform at Fairfax County Hospital. The doctor said he would arrange for the follow up radiation treatments to be done at this same hospital after I healed from the surgery.

The radiation would be performed five days a week. I requested an early morning radiation treatment schedule so I could go directly from the hospital to EPA. I was able to get an underground parking sticker for the duration of the treatments but would rejoin my carpool as soon as my condition allowed.

My staff members were upset when they learned that I had cancer. I told them optimistically that I was going to "beat Big C" and that I was asking Lois French to be Acting Branch Chief when I was unavailable for health or other reasons. All of them volunteered that they would work harder than ever to try to make up for my absences.

But first I had to get through the prostate surgery. While waiting for that day, I did some research on prostate cancer as well as on Dr. Patrick Carroll. Research on prostate cancer revealed that my symptoms were "text book" signs of the presence of prostate cancer which left me wondering why my Internist had not checked or had me checked for this cancer. A close friend's slightly out-of-date Physician's Desk Reference (PDR) left little doubt that my symptoms indicated a strong possibility of the presence of prostate cancer. Apparently this doctor had not bothered to check his PDR!

My research on Dr. Carroll showed that he had an excellent reputation both as a urologist, surgeon and oncologist. I found it especially interesting that as a surgeon he was recognized for being the first surgeon to successfully re-attach a severed penis. *The man with the attached penis later fathered a child!* Although I didn't expect the latter to happen to me, I strangely found some comfort in Dr. Carroll's historic accomplishment.

Because of my relatively young age, Dr. Carroll was especially concerned by two things: (1) that my sexual life would be adversely affected by the cancer itself as well as the surgery and radiation treatments to combat the cancer and (2) that prostate cancer in young men is more likely to spread quickly and is therefore more deadly. I was in my early to mid-fifties when I first contracted prostate cancer so I was at great risk. At this point, although I obviously wanted to protect my sexual capability, my major concern then was staying alive.

If the cancer had already metastasized (i.e., spread from its original site) my chances for survival back in 1976-78 were slim at best. Dr. Carroll told me that he was only going to remove the half of my prostate containing the tumor with the hope that this procedure would cause less damage to my sexual capability than removal of the entire prostate.

There was nothing he could do about damage already caused by the delay in diagnosis and the damage to occur as a result of the upcoming surgery and radiation. *(At that time radiation was not nearly as precise as today's treatment)*. The surgery went well according to Dr. Carroll. And he expressed hope that he had removed all of the tumor, and that he had caught the cancer before it spread outside the prostate gland. Also, Dr. Carroll had succeeded in placing me with a new Internal Medicine doctor by the name of Dr. Ed Gallagher.

I no longer had faith in my doctor because of his failure to (1) diagnose my cancer for a period of at least two years or (2) send me to a urologist who would have noted that my symptoms matched up precisely with symptoms of prostate cancer. Despite his high position and reputation at a local hospital, I was never going to put my care in his hands again. I was pleased to now have two very nice Irish physicians taking care of my health needs.

After I had healed from the surgery, I began my radiation treatments. Other than the helpless feeling of being entombed in a small space, the early treatments were not as bad as expected. As a matter of fact, although I was about two hours late for work each morning, I continued to put in a rigorous though shortened work day at EPA. After the fourth week of radiation treatment, however, things changed dramatically for the worse. The effects of the treatments became more acute. About halfway through the treatment, the radiation had burned my rear end to the extent that a large cyst appeared. Dr. Carroll temporarily halted the radiation and recommended several sitz baths daily. This did not work and I was sent to Fairfax Hospital to have the cyst removed surgically.

A strange thing happened at the hospital shortly after I was assigned what was supposed to be a private, "non smoking" room to await surgery. Gwen was sitting beside me knitting when suddenly there was a commotion in the hallway and an injured young man was wheeled into my room on a stretcher. He had suffered a bullet wound while in a fight, we were told. And several very rough looking individuals came into the room with him. I was told that the man he was fighting was also hospitalized in another part of the hospital.

I wasn't happy about having another patient in what was supposed to be a "private room." This rough-neck group was certainly not what I expected and I could see that Gwen was also very uncomfortable. Then things got worse as friends of the injured man began lighting up cigarettes in my "non smoking" room. And they were loudly discussing the fight. As I quietly pushed the button to summon the nurse, I picked up a pair of scissors from Gwen's sewing basket. When the nurse entered the room I told her in an assertive voice to "get these people out of my room immediately."

She informed me that no room was available but that one was being prepared for the injured man momentarily and she told the smokers to extinguish their cigarettes and stop the loud conversation. Otherwise, all of them would be removed from the room immediately to wait in the hallway. To their credit, they did as she asked and apologized to Gwen and me for their disruption and for lighting up without our permission. Within minutes they were gone and I returned the scissors to Gwen.

It's doubtful I could have provided much defense from an attack with the scissors but that was the only weapon at my disposal. I never heard what happened to the men injured in the fight and didn't really care. My surgery was done the following morning and I was told it went well and I immediately felt more comfortable. Dr. Carroll gave me two weeks to recover before radiation was resumed. This delay caused me to require more treatments than originally planned, however, and that impacted upon my future chances for treatment.

My remaining treatment after radiation was chemotherapy given to me in the form of female hormone pills. I began taking them daily but I soon realized that my breasts were growing and I seemed to be losing my male physical attributes. Unwilling to let this humiliating treatment continue, I flushed the remaining pills down the commode and never had the prescription refilled. At this point in late 1977, I began to realize that my doctors had few other treatment options to battle this deadly cancer.

Also, Gwen was becoming increasingly withdrawn and unable to discuss my cancer with me. Since Mitch was at the critical teenage years, I didn't think it fair to have in-depth discussions of my deteriorating condition with him. So, I faced a lonely battle.

# CHAPTER 26
## Need to Keep Working

DESPITE WANTING TO spend more of my remaining time with my family and restoration project, I still needed to continue working for as long as my health permitted. Gwen had resigned her job years ago to be able to spend time raising our son and most of our money was invested in three real estate properties with three mortgages. Since the area was in the midst of a recession, our financial situation could quickly become precarious if I had to stop working. Our finances were fine if I could continue working; I had reached the top salary for a federal employee. (With a few exceptions federal employees could not make more than a Congressman's salary and I had reached that point by dint of my GS-15, plus cash awards and other awards of "steps" in grade).

In case my condition continued to worsen I needed to know my options for continuing to support my family. Realistically, since I had only 20 years as a federal government employee and was in my mid-fifties, I was a long way from the combination of age and years of service required to reach the magic number of 80 for "full" retirement. And I feared I would have to be on my "death bed" before I could receive a "Disability Retirement." In any case, even if possible, early retirement would result in a heavy reduction in my pay. *Retirement pay in the government is based on grade level and time served.* Although my grade level was high, my time served was dismally low, only 22 years including my military and post office employment time.

So, retirement in any form was not a good option as long as I could keep working.

I did think I might be able to slow down a bit, since I had been successful in getting both of my major responsibilities, Certification Standards and State Plan Regulations, completed and entered into the Federal Register before their deadlines. Slowing down a bit was not for me, however. Soon after my radiation was completed and I was back at work full time, I was summoned to the office of Deputy Assistant Administrator (DAA) for the Office of Pesticides (OPP) Ed Johnson.

Ed greeted me warmly and then said: "Jim, I congratulate you on getting your sections of FIFRA completed within the deadlines and published in the Federal Register. However, that still leaves us with a serious problem. The folks I assigned to develop a system for classifying pesticides for Restricted or General Use have worked for five years and have failed to come up with a workable system. That means we have not been able to classify a single chemical for Restricted Use. So, although some states are submitting their plans for certification and already have some applicators certified, we have no way to classify anything for Restricted Use. You of course know that this situation places our agency in a terribly embarrassing situation. And even worse, this failure threatens the success of the entire Section 4 regulatory program of Amended FIFRA."

*Of course, I had known the success of my efforts in Georgia were only a "stop gap" measure to "buy time" to get the classification system in place. And of course I had long been aware of the problems caused by the failure of the people assigned to come up with a workable system, but I had no idea what I could do about it.*

When I asked the DAA what he had in mind to deal with the problem, he grinned and said: "I'm thinking about establishing a Classification Task Force consisting of top scientists in the Agency. I've been trying to decide who will head this Task Force, you or Dr. Bill Wells." I couldn't believe I was part of that equation and said: "Ed, you must be kidding. I'm a journalist, not a scientist, and this is a highly scientific project. Also, as you know I'm fighting cancer. Furthermore, I know that Dr. Wells, who has a PhD in one of the hard sciences, really wants a chance to take on a high profile project like this. Please give this assignment to him."

As he was leaving Ed said "I realize your concerns, Jim, and I'll give the matter more thought and then decide which way to go." We then said our goodbyes and I went back to my office thinking, "He's got to give this job to Dr. Wells!"

# CHAPTER 27
## Cancer or Not, I have a New Assignment

THE NEXT DAY, Ed poked his head into my office, then sat down in front of me, and said: "Jim, I've given the matter of who should head up the Classification Task Force lots of thought and I've made up my mind to ask you to be that person." Before I could react,

Ed said: "Jim, you've been the only person in OPP to meet the deadlines for our Revised FIFRA Regulations and I really need you to complete this final piece of the Applicator Certification puzzle. If you'll agree to accept the assignment, I'll place any of our scientists at EPA at your disposal.

"Your duty will be to select the members of the Task Force, work with them to figure out a classification system, and have the Task Force classify at least a few of the most dangerous chemicals for Restricted Use. I've already set up a separate office for you with a private secretary. Let me know if you need anyone or anything else. It will be your baby if you accept the assignment. I won't let anyone second guess you."

I was overwhelmed this was happening but replied: "Ed, I'm flattered that you have that much faith in me and I'll do the best I can to justify that faith. But I need a promise from you that if my cancer gets so bad I can't function, you'll sign my disability retirement papers so I can spend my remaining days with my family." Ed smiled and said, "It's a deal. All you have to say is that you need to retire and I'll get the paperwork done and sign it."

My first thoughts were: "Before my cancer gets worse, I've got to come up with a system that will quickly result in getting a few chemicals classified for Restricted Use." After some thought, I figured that the first thing I needed to do was compile my own list of chemicals which I knew to be highly toxic. Then the Task Force would have something concrete to start with. Also, I obviously needed someone I knew and trusted to handle routine matters involving the Task Force, as well as to advise me on technical and scientific matters.

I considered several people but finally settled on Walt Waldrop, one of my own staffers. I knew that Walt had advanced degrees in the hard sciences, and thus was knowledgeable about chemicals. Also, I knew him to be a very steady and responsible employee with good communications skills. Walt was ready to try something new and immediately began helping me compile the list of potential chemicals to be submitted to the Task Force for their input. He was also helpful in advising me on selecting appropriate agency scientists to serve on the Classification Task Force.

This move, along with appointing Lois French to be acting Branch Chief for the duration of my special assignment, freed up the time I needed to make good decisions on various key matters, including selection of the Task Force members, the list of chemicals I would submit to them, and how I could best use their expertise. I could not afford to make mistakes in these choices. The fact that I had a person of Lois French's talents to keep our office functioning was a real blessing to me. When Walt and I had agreed on our selection of Task Force members and list of chemicals, I called everyone together, gave them a brief introduction of our goals, and gave them a copy of our suggested list. I then asked them to study each chemical and provide reasons why it should remain on or be taken off of the list.

At that time I also scheduled regular meetings of the Task Force to discuss various chemicals and find consensus on which chemical should stay or be dropped from our list. *Each member would also have the opportunity to add chemicals that might be better candidates than the ones on the list that Walt and I had put together.*

My goal was to classify a limited number (20-25) of active ingredients for "Restricted Use" from the larger list Walt and I had assembled along with any added by Task Force members. Note: Even a "limited number of active ingredients" can result in many products and thousands of use patterns, clearly enough to start fully implementing the Certification Program. That's why we needed to be highly selective in the chemicals we chose. Not enough uses for a chemical would not meet our goal, while too many uses for a particular chemical could cause our proposed system to quickly bog down.

Note to those not that familiar with pesticide regulations: We had to consider the two major ways a pesticide can be harmful to individuals or the environment: (1) exposure to a highly-toxic chemical that can cause immediate harm, or even death, and (2) long term, low level exposure from pesticide residues found in food, air, water, soil, etc. which may eventually cause serious harm to humans and the environment.

For reasons of expediency, I asked the Classification Task Force to concentrate on the first issue, i.e., chemicals which are so toxic that a single drop may be fatal. We didn't have time then to address the second issue which is long range, i.e., chemicals that may take a very long time (or perhaps forever) to cause harm to humans or to be recognized as an "environmental hazard." From a public relations standpoint which was an important element of this process, we knew that it would be easier to get public support for restricting the use of a chemical that can kill quickly as opposed to a chemical that "may or may not" be determined to be an "environmental hazard" many years later.

When completed, the Classification Task Force consisted of the top toxicologists at EPA (one of whom had been in charge at Hazleton Lab), prominent chemists, and other top scientists in related fields at EPA. I asked them to evaluate the list that Walt and I had compiled, along with their own selections so that the most acutely dangerous chemicals would be included in the first group of Restricted Use Chemicals. After the Classification Task Force members had agreed on which chemicals should be on this list, I began gathering input from affected groups (obviously many of these were the same groups and people I had used in my earlier efforts to get regulations passed).

As expected, some of the companies objected to their chemicals being on the list and I recorded these objections. Also, it was no surprise that the environmental groups and some individuals were unhappy that we had not included more chemicals thought to be environmentally hazardous. For example, I had a call from one of EPA's Congressional Liaison people (who incidentally was the husband of a lady who headed up one of the environmental groups) urging me to add Chlordane to the list of potential RUP products. I listened to him respectfully but made no commitment.

Anyone familiar with this chemical knew that the only time it had caused any immediate problems to humans or animals was when it was misused. The only case of that kind I knew about occurred in Georgia where a large well known pest control company applied Chlordane to the interior of a house. As I recall, the people could not live in their house until the contamination was removed. This of course was a clear misuse of a wonderful chemical which was registered only for underground use. My reasoning was that the Certification program would help prevent such misuse of this chemical. And I knew from USDA's experimental work that use of Chlordane was by far the safest and most effective treatment for termites when used as directed. History has borne that out. So, I wasn't about to put it on that list!

After receiving input from interested individuals and groups regarding the makeup of the draft list of chemicals, I called a meeting of the Task Force to evaluate suggestions for changes needed, and members then revised the list accordingly. When this task was completed, I sent the draft out for final public scrutiny. I quickly received another call from Congressional Liaison and this time the caller was less than polite. He got right to the point by saying: "Jim, apparently you didn't understand me when I asked you to put Chlordane on the list. I was giving you an order." I replied just as quickly, "I understood you the first time; the fact is I don't work for or take orders from you!" He never called me again which let me know Ed Johnson was living up to his promise of protecting my back.

I personally talked with several company representatives who were upset because one or more of their chemicals was on EPA's list of potential RUPs. I explained to them that in putting their product on our list we were actually trying to "save" their chemical. I explained that some top officials at EPA, closely associated with environmental groups, actually preferred that these chemicals be banned rather than "Restricted." Usually they understood my point and removed their objections to their chemical being on the list.

Soon, with these limited goals, we began receiving strong support for our system from within and outside the Agency. So, I began preparing the Introduction, discussion of the RUP System and list of potential Restricted Use Pesticides for submission to and printing in the Federal Register.

# CHAPTER 28
## Horse was Already Out of the Barn Re Cancer

SOON AFTER I began this work I got some unsettling news from my oncologist about my cancer. After examining my latest bone scans, Dr. Carroll reached the conclusion that "the horse must have been already out of the barn" when he began treating me. Dr. Carroll explained that my recent scans showed that the cancer was spreading rapidly. And my PSA number was also going up. *Normal PSA's are from below zero to about three, depending on several factors. Mine was now above 30 and climbing steadily, eventually exceeding 65.*

I thought it was time to give DAA Ed Johnson an update on Task Force progress as well as my health situation. I told him that the Task Force had finished its work on a system to classify the 22 most important (and dangerous) chemical compounds representing thousands of use patterns. And I told him that the system the Task Force had put in place was operating smoothly. He was happy about that. (I learned much later that the simple system developed by the Task Force was utilized by EPA /OPP for many years while they were developing more sophisticated classification systems).

Then I informed Ed of my most recent tests, showing my cancer was spreading rapidly along with my rising PSA. He said, "If you need me to, I'll ask Personnel to start the paperwork for your disability retirement. And incidentally, Jim, I've already put you in for a Bronze Medal for the progress you've made in establishing a system for Classifying Chemicals for Restricted Use. But that award won't come through until after you retire."

This was sometime in August, as I recall. Personnel soon called and said they could have my retirement paperwork completed by September but that it would benefit me financially if I could delay my retirement until October. I agreed to the later date, and continued to put together the information needed for the Introduction to the Code of Federal Register. Then I began the process of turning the Classification System project over to Walt Waldrop and turning over my branch activities to Lois French, as Acting Branch Chief. *Soon after I left she was named permanent chief of that branch.*

As word leaked out that I was about to retire, I received a most interesting call from EPA Region IX. The call was from Bob Kuykendall, who had succeeded Jake McKensie as Regional Pesticide Chief, when Jake was moved up in the organization. Bob had an interesting proposition for me. After congratulating me on my upcoming retirement, he said, "Jim, as you know, Region IX includes Hawaii and a number of territories in the South Pacific, including Guam and American Samoa. The fact is that we don't currently have a way to adequately serve them. We've just received permission to hire someone to represent us in this vast area. We have special dispensation to offer you that job on a consulting basis. You and your family would live on Guam or American Samoa and you would travel by water or air as you see fit or as needed to the other South Pacific Islands."

"Wait a minute, Bob," I exclaimed. "You may not have heard that I'm retiring from EPA Headquarters because of cancer that is rapidly spreading. As exciting as this job sounds, and I'm flattered that you're offering it to me, I would not be able to accept it." Bob said he was aware that I had been fighting cancer but didn't realize it was that serious. He added, "I thought that living and working in an environment as nice as that might help you beat the cancer. Obviously you would be a great choice for this job because of your general knowledge of pesticides and dealing with pest problems gained in your careers at USDA and EPA, as well as your demonstrated skills at communicating that knowledge."

Although I was 99 per cent sure that it made no sense for me to take this job, I decided to discuss it with Gwen and Mitch before making a final decision. So, I said to Bob: "Let me talk with my family and I'll call you back with my decision in a few days." That evening I talked with Gwen and Mitch about my offer of this exotic job. We discussed the "pros" (additional salary, exciting job in exotic part of the world, and climate that would allow Mitch to play tennis year round) and "cons" (question of health care should cancer continue to worsen, the long distance from family, and how to deal with our real estate properties).

Gwen, Mitch, and I had fun discussing the possibility of making such a drastic change in our lives but ultimately decided that the "cons," especially the cancer problem, outweighed the "pros" and we made the decision to remain state-side. I called Bob, thanked him for offering me this opportunity, and wished him luck in finding the right person for the job.

# CHAPTER 29

## A Chance to Say Goodbye to Friends and Associates

IT TRICKLED OUT that on my last day at EPA, my friends at EPA, USDA, and some State and Regional offices, were planning a big "surprise" party for me at the Flagship Restaurant on Maine Ave., in Washington, DC. The theme was "Jim White Is Hanging It Up." *Most of my friends and associates knew that my favorite hobby had become restoring old houses. So, they designed posters, etc. with a drawing showing me dressed in a carpenter's apron with a hammer clutched in my hand.* George Beshore (then at EPA) and Larry Mark (still at USDA) took the lead in planning the party, assisted by my secretary.

On party day, around 250 people from around the country attended and I felt so blessed by this demonstration of friendship. Harold Alford and John Hillis were there from California. John Osmun came from Indiana. Officials from many other states around the nation were also there. Larry and George also read some of the letters from people who could not attend, including one from old childhood friend Les Roark.

Larry and George kept the proceedings light by reading humorous recitations of my life as a single man in Washington with a preference for beautiful women. Harold Alford, my old boss and good friend, read a letter written by hand while on the plane from Sacramento to Washington, DC. His beautiful expression of friendship as he wrote it follows in its entirety:

> *"Of all the misadventures I have taken part in, recruiting Jim White into the Pesticides Regulation Division was one of the most rewarding and enduring.*
>
> *Needless to say, the Pesticides Regulation Division, OPP, and EPA have not been the same since Jim joined us in 1971. His enthusiasm, sincerity, and integrity have been an inspiration to all of us.*
>
> *The proper mix of good humor and fiery temper has added the right amount of excitement and surely no one has been bored in his presence,*

*His ability to write as if each word was joined with little gold safety pins is unique in the regulatory paper mill and serves as an example for those inspiring young people who are willing to learn.*

*Jim, on behalf of all your co-workers, I would like to present to you a plaque for '22 years of distinguished and dedicated service,' along with my wishes for you:*

*May your retirement be long and happy,*

*May your winters be warmed by friendly sun,*

*And your summers cooled by gentle breeze.*

*May your harvests be bountiful and your flocks feed on the greenest of pastures."*

*Signed: Harold G. Alford*

I've saved and re-read this handwritten note several times since I retired from the federal government in October, 1978. I was helped along the way in my career by so many people, including Dr. Bryan Phifer, who gave me my start in Washington; my supervisor Val Weyl at ARS, who helped give me the courage to "troubleshoot" potentially disastrous situations around the nation; Dennis Avery, who guided me through the political world of USDA/ASCS and remains a close friend; Harold Alford, who was instrumental in helping me transition from Information to Management; Dr. John Osmun, a friend and supporter both at EPA and afterward.

I also want to express my gratitude to EPA, an agency far to the left of me politically and philosophically but which never let these differences interfere with my career. The agencies and the people mentioned above, as well as others, helped inspire this "sharecropper boy" to more career success and a more fulfilling life than he had a right to expect. Many of these friends have now passed away. The "sharecropper boy" had to leave this familiar world for the fight of his life. My friends could no longer help me. From now on it was up to me, with help from the Lord, to fight this battle.

# PART 8

# THE REAL BATTLE BEGINS WITH THE BIG "C"

# CHAPTER 1
## Relaxing Followed by a Brief Look Back

I SPENT MY first few days after retiring enjoying the euphoria from the fine retirement lunch and relaxing from the pressures I had experienced during my time at EPA. During this time I also reflected on my career, which I probably took too seriously. Although my jobs had all been stressful, they also gave me wonderful opportunities for growth and a career that far exceeded my expectations. *Remember, my goals as a senior in high school, i.e. carpenter's helper or gas station attendant? Becoming manager of a national program for a major Federal Agency never entered my mind!*

My thoughts still lingered upon my last assignment at EPA, i.e., serving as chairman of a Task Force to develop a pesticide classification system while still serving as manager of the Pesticide Applicator Certification program. All of this while fighting cancer. In my opinion, the remarkable thing about my EPA experience was that I could have easily been pigeon-holed into "dead end" jobs. After all, my conservative views did not match up at all with the liberal views and actions of the majority of EPA employees and the Agency. *I never made any attempt to hide my views; however, I never flaunted them.*

Luck had been on my side with my first big assignment at EPA. That of course was being asked to serve as Chairperson of the Sub-Committee to develop draft standards for the Certification of Pesticide Applicators Certification Program which I quickly became passionate about. I did not have to "fake" any of the enthusiasm I had for this program since I sincerely believed it would save lives while at the same time preserving vital uses of pesticides needed to protect our way of life. It is rare that a person gets the opportunity to spend most of the last seven years of his career working on a program he sincerely believes in and loves.

# CHAPTER 2
## Looking Ahead

ACTUALLY, I DIDN'T dare look too far ahead because of uncertainty about my health. However, I knew I needed to concentrate on: (1) battling cancer with all my strength and will power, (2) getting started on what I thought might be my last "building project" and (3) trying to ensure that my family would be provided for after I was gone. I was kicking myself pretty hard over those issues.

Although I really enjoyed my jobs in Washington, the demands on me had kept me "stressed out." Now the nature of the stress had changed to fear that cancer would totally incapacitate or take me, and fear we would not be able to come up with enough money to finish the building/renovation project. These fears were intertwined, i.e., if I were unable to finish this large building project before I died, it would create additional hardship for Gwen and Mitch and leave them in a very vulnerable situation--financial and otherwise.

*Not to sound overly noble, my biggest concern at that time was what would happen to Gwen and Mitch should I pass away before getting our financial situation in order. Gwen had not worked outside the home since before Mitch was born and I was concerned about her ability to resume her career after the long absence from the work market. I was particularly concerned that Mitch might not have the resources to attend college.*

Regarding No. 1 above, I was beginning to regret that I didn't take a more active role in getting myself checked for prostate cancer earlier, before it had a chance to begin spreading beyond the prostate gland. Unfortunately, at that time I was still naive enough to believe that having one of the top Internal Medicine physicians around would provide all the protection I needed. Because of having too much faith in the medical profession, I disregarded warnings from an EPA friend who had warned me that the urinary tract infections I had experienced (and had been treated for) the last two years were indicators of the possibility of prostate cancer. He got this information from his "out of date" Physicians' Desk Reference (PDR). Surely my Internist had an updated PDR!

As for 2 and 3 above, I was very critical of my own judgment in allowing our financial situation to become so fragile that my early death could spell disaster to my little family's financial resources. As already mentioned, our two nice homes both had mortgages that required large monthly payments. Also, we had used a "line of credit" to purchase an expensive 5 acre lot with a "falling down" old house on it.

Debts incurred with the two earlier houses inhibited what I could do about the new house additions and rehab efforts. I spent many sleepless nights trying to figure a way out of this situation. There was plenty of blame to spread around. First was Gwen's insistence on buying the Victorian cottage and my willingness to sign the contract for that property. I rightfully blamed myself as "head of the household" in not showing stronger leadership in all these matters.

But sitting around blaming myself and others would not achieve anything positive. In preparation for what my future might hold, I began reading relevant books and other material on how to deal with death. Among these was a groundbreaking book "On Death and Dying" published in 1969 by Dr. Elizabeth Kubler-Ross, MD. While facing my own possible demise, I gained knowledge and some comfort by reading and learning about Dr. Kubler-Ross's theory regarding the 5 phases of grieving experienced when people learn that they or someone they love is dying or has died. The phases she described are: (l) Denial (2) Anger (3) Bargaining (4) Depression, and (5) Acceptance. (More details about how I dealt with these phases later.)

Although this reading was comforting, I also instinctively knew that "staying busy" at something I liked doing was the best way for me to combat depression caused by cancer. And I was now responsible for completing the big project of moving and restoring the little farm house and adding a 4,000 square foot addition. Although the recent experience of restoring the Victorian cottage in town may have adversely affected my health, I had learned a lot from the successful restoration. The knowledge I had gained during that time would certainly be helpful to me in completing the present even larger project. And it was apparent to me that working on this project would help take my mind off cancer.

Despite my appearance of normality, I was terribly concerned about what might happen to Mitch if (or when) cancer took me away. Would he be able to attend college? My best hope was that he would win a college tennis scholarship. Even if Gwen were able to resume her career, I didn't know if her salary and my survivor's annuity would be enough to pay for Mitch's college education. As a result of my fears for the future of Mitch and his mother, I began putting more pressure upon Mitch to concentrate on his tennis--since a tennis scholarship might be the only avenue left for him to get a college education. It soon became obvious to me that he resented the pressure I was putting on him to practice and concentrate more on tennis. But as his father, I felt his future was worth risking some alienation from him.

*In my defense, his mother and I had sacrificed a lot in order to allow him to pursue this expensive sport. We had spent money we could barely afford to join a country club solely for the purpose of providing him access to tennis courts and an excellent tennis coach. Later, as he improved, we took the advice of his country club tennis coach to get him enrolled in the U. S. Tennis Association (USTA) tennis program for young players. Once involved, we were amazed at the high quality of these players. Mitch had the bad fortune of having to play his first two matches against nationally ranked players and did not win a single game against either of them.*

*That experience was an eye opener for Gwen and me. We realized then that if he were to be competitive with these players, we needed to turn him over to the best coaches we could find by enrolling him in the high-level tennis "drill groups" involving the best young tennis players in the Mid Atlantic area. Eventually, through these drill groups, he received coaching from such accomplished players and coaches as Graham Stillwell, who had been on the English Davis Cup team and was once ranked No. 10 in the world; Gene Russo, a fine professional player and coach from Australia; and Skip Bishop, a local player who was then on the professional tour.*

*Finally, he joined Jack Schore's drill group. Schore was recognized for coaching many top winning players, including Dan Goldie, who was NCAA Champion from Stanford, following John McEnroe, the previous winner. With all these drill groups, Mitch started in the last court but gradually worked his way up to the No. 1 court as his game continued to improve.*

*We had no regrets about the money we spent on Mitch's tennis and he had exceeded our expectations. His first serve was timed at 130 mph with a wooden racquet. This was second only to Roscoe Tanner's serve at the time. (Note: with modern composition racquets and livelier balls, many of today's top players serve at speeds exceeding 130 mph).*

But tennis is such a competitive sport! Despite our efforts to provide Mitch with the best tools available, we could not afford to send him to combination school/tennis facilities such as Nick Bollettieri's Tennis Academy located near Bradenton, FL. Still, Mitch's natural athletic ability and work ethic (and my pushing?) enabled him to continue raising the level of his game.

# CHAPTER 3
## Title IX and Its Effect on Tennis Programs.

CONTINUING THE STORY of Mitch's tennis, I was feeling pretty confident that Mitch would be able to go to college on a tennis scholarship. I was aware that Congress had signed Title IX into law with its requirement to "equalize public spending for female athletes," as one of its primary provisions. But with his achievements in tennis, excellence in the classroom, and flawless character, I didn't think this law would seriously affect his chances for a scholarship. Boy, was I wrong. Over the years since Title IX had passed, colleges and universities had received continuing pressure from Title IX advocates to allot more money for girls' sports, which meant reducing and sometimes eliminating funds for boys' "minor" sports.

Since Title IX went into effect, great strides have been made in women's athletics. However, this progress was costly to many men's athletic programs. Figures showed that more than 400 men's athletic teams were eliminated as a result of universities needing to become compliant with the new law. The sports most affected were low revenue Olympic sports such as wrestling, swimming, track and field, and tennis.

Unfortunatley, in 1981 when Mitch graduated from high school, the money for tennis scholarship funds for boys had just about dried up. Mitch was getting lots of offers from colleges, but few included athletic scholarships for tennis. We were aware that Virginia Commonwealth University (VCU) located in Richmond, VA was making a serious effort to become one of the top "tennis schools" in the country. Their No. 1 player had graduated and was now playing on the pro tennis circuit. VCU's coach wanted Mitch to play for his team, but said that because of Title IX, he had no scholarship money to offer.

However, later that summer, learning that many top college players (including VCU's No. 1 & 2 players) were participating in a tournament at Devil's Reach Racquet Club in nearby Occoquan, VA, we entered Mitch in that tournament, hoping that if he were successful against top college players his scholarship chances might improve. Mitch played well in the tournament right from the start and soon he was matched in the quarter finals against the University of Maryland's top tennis player. Thinking this would be the end of the tournament for Mitch, we were amazed when he beat the UM player in straight sets.

Matched in the semi-finals against VCU's top player, he prevailed again. Although he had to struggle, he beat VCU's No. 2 player in the finals. A few days later, the VCU coach called and said he had found enough money to offer Mitch a half scholarship immediately and would try to get him a full scholarship later. Mitch accepted this offer and headed off to Richmond that fall. (More about that later).

# CHAPTER 4
## Worry, Worry, Toil and Trouble

MEANWHILE, ALTHOUGH FEELING better and regaining some strength, I was still having trouble sleeping nights, running the dwindling money situation over and over in my mind like a bad movie. We were having trouble paying our three mortgages, plus living expenses, and trying to get the large construction project started. We knew that when heavy construction began, our meager savings would disappear at a fast rate.

I was also becoming increasingly concerned about our marital situation, as my cancer was taking its toll upon Gwen as she continued to distance herself from me. I suspected that my physical deterioration was the cause. And of course my concern about what the future held regarding my cancer and our financial situation no doubt made me more difficult to live with. Both of us knew that the financial situation would be helped considerably if we could sell just one of our properties. But we had little hope that in the midst of the housing slump, either of our properties would sell.

Other people we knew were even more adversely affected by the housing recession than we were! One such example was a nearby neighbor couple who were close friends of ours. Although still young, the husband owned a successful commercial electrical company, i.e., he provided electrical work primarily for large commercial buildings.

The neighbors, Travis and Suzi Worsham and their three girls, Ginny, Sherry, and Sarah, had been living in their large "in town" restored home before the building crisis. After seeing our beautiful, spacious lot, they decided to buy a five-acre lot near us in the same subdivision, "Redlac Estates." (Calder spelled backward). They also took an option on the lot between us which, when activated, would allow them space to keep a couple of their prize "polo ponies" close by.

***Yes, I said "polo ponies" in the State of Virginia!*** *Their ponies were specially bred "Thoroughbreds" with many of the same characteristics as regular Thoroughbreds but with shorter legs. Although still fast, their shorter legs increased their quickness which is more important in polo than pure speed needed for "flat racing."* Travis and Suzi already owned a "polo farm" with restored farm house and barns, on acreage just outside the town of Manassas, VA, where they kept their 10 polo ponies. They had paid thousands of dollars each for the ponies purchased in South America (Argentina, as I recall).

*Gwen and I spent some wonderful times watching polo matches from the porch of the Worsham's farm house. The matches were followed by "party time" with all types of catered food and beverages. Guests included riders, relatives and friends. In our opinion, the Worsham family had the finest things money could buy. In addition to the polo farm and ponies, their custom built home on five acres near us was so outstanding that it was featured in a national magazine almost as soon as it was finished.*

As I recall, they found and bought the weathered tobacco barn wood used for exterior siding in New England and Travis hauled it back to Virginia in one of their horse trailers. In addition, the aged wood was used for "accent" in some interior areas. The house when completed looked as if it had been built 100 years ago but had been preserved in "like new" condition. Suzi, well known for her skills as decorator and designer, handled most of the decorating personally.

Although the housing recession hurt many people around the nation, because of the nature of their business, the recession hit Travis and Suzi harder than most. Soon, the national real estate market collapse put them in an untenable situation. We sadly watched as our friends began losing their expensive automobiles, polo ponies, and finally, their beautiful custom home near us. Just before loss of the house, Travis had almost completed an outside brick structure when he ran out of brick. I had some leftover brick that matched the project he was working on and offered them to him. He rejected my offer, saying, "Jim, I can't even pay as much as $50 for them and I will not accept them as a gift."

*I would like to complete the inspiring story of how our friends, the Worshams, dealt with adversity:* Not willing to sit idly by and moan about their bad luck, Travis had an idea that eventually led to a "fine dining" restaurant that attracted customers from all around the Northern Virginia area. Suzi said Travis had built several restaurants in the DC area and had the "know how" to equip the kitchen, etc. She added: "I was actually afraid to do the restaurant but Travis said we needed the cash flow and that I was a good cook and business person."

Travis' faith in his pretty blonde wife, Suzi (who at one time was an understudy for movie actress Tuesday Weld) was soon fully justified. At that time Clifton was on a fairly busy road that led from Springfield to Centerville and Manassas, VA, but there was no place on the road to get a good meal. After studying the situation, the Worshams decided to rent one of the large, vacant buildings in Clifton and open up a restaurant. They named the place "Heart in Hand" reflecting Suzi's insecurity about opening a restaurant without experience as a restaurant owner.

Initially the restaurant served just Suzi's homemade soup and sandwiches and was open only for lunch. However, soon after the restaurant opened, many local people as well as those passing through town were stopping at the restaurant to enjoy Suzi's wonderful soup and sandwiches. As their business grew, they gradually expanded the menu and also began offering dinner once or twice a week. The restaurant's reputation spread rapidly and it became a successful business, open for both lunch and dinner and with a full course menu.

*After I left the area, I received a newspaper clipping which pictured First Lady Nancy Reagan and national syndicated newspaper columnist George Will leaving the "Heart in Hand" together. Mrs. Reagan was quoted as saying that the "Heart in Hand" was one of her very favorite restaurants in the Washington, DC, area.*

This is a success story I like to tell since it represents the entrepreneurial spirit of America so well. *I was told that Travis was able to restart his successful electrical contracting business after the recession eased.*

# CHAPTER 5
## Time to Start Work on Major Project

AFTER A FEW days enjoying my retirement, I knew I needed to start serious work on the big project. Obviously, with the high cost of construction, it wouldn't take long for our savings to be eaten up. This meant that I was going to have to watch expenses very carefully and do as much of the work myself as possible. Realistically, I knew I needed a good carpenter to help me. I finally found just the man I needed (named Roger). He was young enough to have plenty of energy but experienced enough to follow a complicated blueprint.

This meant that he could accurately "lay out" the "footprint" of the project. I didn't dare trust my limited experience to do that job because it would affect the project from beginning to end. *(I remembered a friend of mine--a successful businessman--who did his own lay-out and his expensive new house ended up out of square by three inches. He could never completely hide this defect).*

And perhaps even more importantly, Roger understood the situation we were in and was willing to work with us to adjust his schedule (when possible) to accommodate my health and money problems. After all, his profession was one of the hardest hit by the recession and carpenters were in need of work. *Roger and I mutually agreed that when he had the opportunity for a steady job at higher pay, he would take that job but come back to assist me when that job ran out. This turned out to be a "win-win" situation for both of us.*

Roger and I began by placing stakes in the ground to define the new area that needed to be excavated. And he used a builder's transit and blueprint to ensure the accuracy of the lay out. Unfortunately, we soon found out that the excavator had knocked down some of the stakes used to define where the footings and foundation walls would go and apparently "guessed" where the right side of the addition would be located. We discovered this error only after we started precisely measuring and framing for the "footings" of the foundation walls. This was a critical error since the new foundation would have to support the three car garage, the little farm house, and the 4,000 square foot addition.

At the same time we also discovered that the excavator had not left space for the large fireplace chimney! Alas, that meant we couldn't complete framing for anything until much more excavation was done. The chimney alone needed to serve three large fireplaces: in the basement, the main floor "great room," and the third level master bedroom suite. Also, the chimney at the main floor level would be used as a "heat sink" for the greenhouse which would surround the large chimney at that level. Doors to the right and left of the chimney would allow entry to the greenhouse from the great room. Thus the footing for this chimney base had to be unusually large. Fortunately, the excavator soon returned and enlarged this area so we could finish framing for everything, including the chimney.

# CHAPTER 6
## Little Farm House Claims Attention

MEANWHILE, IN ANY "down time" (e.g. when Roger had a better paying job else-where) I was working to stabilize the little farm house for its eventual move onto its new foundation--when completed. As mentioned earlier, the old house had to be moved back or torn down because it was too close to the cul-de-sac. That was part of the purchase agreement. Although I did not know the extent of termite and water damage to the farm house, from past experience I anticipated there were unseen prob-lems with this abandoned 100 plus-year-old house. I thought I had gained enough experience to handle most of this work myself and thus save money. However, I quickly discovered that getting the house ready to move would be more difficult than I had thought.

When I tried to take a closer look at the house's underpinnings, I found out that the crawl space was so limited I could crawl no more than a few feet to inspect for damage. To get a better look, I obtained a "Boy Scout" shovel and used it to dig a channel large enough for me to crawl from one end of the house to the other. After inspecting the underpinnings of the house, my worst fears were confirmed. I found that all the floor joists had suffered severe termite and water damage. They were sag-ging and obviously required strengthening before the move. In its present condition the house would collapse upon itself when lifted by movers. Although faced with a time consuming and difficult job, my experience with restoring the Clifton Victorian cottage had become quite handy.

I knew that the best way to strengthen the damaged joists was to "sister" (or fas-ten) a new joist to the old one. The first thing I did after more digging with the Boy Scout shovel to gain more space to work, was to purchase enough new, treated 2X8's (cut to size) to be used as "sister" joists. After placing each in position near the dam-aged joist, I used my old "railroad jacks" (those from the Clifton cottage restoration) to lift and level the old sagging joist. I then placed cement blocks underneath to keep the old joist temporarily level while I applied glue liberally to the sides of both the old and new joists.

After that I used the jacks to lift the new "sister" joist so the glued sides would be "side by side" and level with each other. At that point, I drilled holes through both joists so they could be joined together permanently by long bolts. Once the bolts were installed and tightened, the glue had dried, and double joist hangers were installed, the combined joists would be stronger than the original joist.

*This process required fast work to ensure that the old and new joists were level with each other and fastened with the long bolts before the glue had time to dry. Because of these complications, it took me almost a full day to complete the strengthening of one joist.* I finally had all the damaged joists strengthened and the little farm house was ready to be moved onto its new foundation when it was completed.

After the excavator had corrected his error, Roger and I finished framing for the rest of the footings. At that point, I called for the concrete trucks to come pour the footings. Once the concrete had dried and the framing had been moved out of the way, brick masons went to work building the new masonry foundation walls. After this work was completed and had time to set, Roger and I installed the treated sill plates to support the old house as well as the new addition. The foundation walls and sill plates had to be extra wide because I was using 2X6 wall studs to hold thicker insulation to increase the house's energy efficiency.

# CHAPTER 7
## Moving Day for the Little Farm House

MEANWHILE, I HAD located a house moving outfit and contracted with them to move the little farm house onto the new foundation about 30 feet back from the entry road. And you can bet that this time I allowed plenty of crawl space so that electricians, plumbers or any other construction people could do their work underneath--without the need of a Boy Scout shovel! Some friends, neighbors, the developer, and Roger and I, were present as the house movers slowly lifted and then moved the little house 30 feet and lowered it onto its new, level foundation.

There was an audible "squawk" as the house settled and was level. The back door, which we had never been able to close because the house was so unlevel, closed and locked shut on its own! The key to the back door had been lost long ago so we had to remove and replace the door lock to get the door open again. But it was joyful to see the little house level and plumb---perhaps for the first time in nearly one hundred years!

Within another day or two, trucks from Manassas Lumber Co. arrived and unloaded material we needed to begin installing the floor joists, the subfloor, and studs for the first floor. The new additions would surround the little farm house on three sides with only the front showing. We began by framing for the three car garage with the art studio for Gwen above and to the left of the old house before framing for the back porch to be added to it. The next major framing would be for the three story addition to the right of the old house. A large deck to be added later would join the old house's new back porch and would continue around the side of the house to support the greenhouse which would be the last part of the project to be completed.

The full walkout basement underneath the addition would have room dividers, a fireplace and "roughed in" plumbing, electrical, and AC/Heating ductwork for later finishing. There were numerous details that helped take my mind off my troubles. For example, I had to make sure that the electrical "breaker" box and heating and air conditioning systems would be over-sized to accommodate the large addition, as well as the little farm house and the soon-to-be artist studio over the three car garage.

In addition, I had to ensure that the septic field was large enough to accommodate at least five full and two half baths which would eventually be installed. This would include plumbing for a master bath and another bath for the two guest bedrooms on the second floor of the addition; a full bathroom for the farm house which had never had an inside bath; a future bath for the basement; a half bath to be located near the kitchen on the main floor and another half bath for the art studio.

The master bath on the second floor of the addition would have a separate shower and tub, a bidet, double sink and large linen closet with an adjacent large walk-in closet. *I rebuilt and painted the old two-hole "outdoor john" and turned it into an attractive and interesting "potting shed" for Gwen who liked to garden.*

As you can see, this was a pretty complex project for someone with my limited experience and who was fighting cancer. I was enjoying brief "remissions" and was able to work alongside Roger during these times. On the occasional days when I didn't have the physical stamina for this demanding work, I would spend time in bed but try to muster enough energy to stop by the project to confer with Roger and discuss any problems that might have popped up. My close personal involvement in the project appeared to be beneficial to me physically, mentally and emotionally, so I tried to stay as involved as my health would permit.

# CHAPTER 8
## Visits to a "Head Doctor"

AS MY CANCER continued to spread, my urologist/oncologist, Dr. Patrick Carroll, scheduled an appointment for me with a psychiatrist. He said doctors who deal with cancer patients had found that such patients needed psychiatric counseling to help them deal with the fears and depression associated with this dreaded disease. I visited the psychiatrist Dr. Carroll had referred me to and found him extraordinarily helpful. He began our first session by asking me to describe my cancer experience thus far. I told him about my long time symptoms and the treatments I had received from my doctor over a two year period before my diagnosis.

He was appalled when, after hearing my symptoms, I told him that the doctor kept prescribing antibiotics for urinary tract infections but had not checked my prostate. I told him my wife's nurse friend had made my appointment with a urologist/oncologist after my own doctor said he could find nothing wrong and dismissed me. At that point the psychiatrist became indignant and said: "That doctor was going to let you die!"

After we finished our discussion of my cancer experience thus far, the doctor wanted to know how I was dealing with the fears and depression which affect most cancer patients. I told him I was dealing with these problems by (1) reading books and other materials on death and dying (specifically Dr. Elizabeth Kubler-Ross's book) and (2) staying busy with a major house moving and restoration project. The psychiatrist was favorably impressed with my approach and state of mind and suggested I continue on the same path. After one more session, the doctor dismissed me saying, "Jim, I think you're dealing with this disease as well you can. I don't have any advice except to keep on with what you're doing. You don't need to waste your time coming to my office unless you feel a need to talk with me."

As I was leaving, however, he said: "I really need to talk with your wife because the mate of someone with cancer often has a bigger problem dealing with the disease than the patient." I agreed with the doctor about that point. It had become obvious to me that my cancer was taking a terrible toll on Gwen. She had changed from a happy person to a sad one. She had become increasingly withdrawn as my cancer worsened.

The thing that hurt me the most was that she was becoming less and less affectionate and was avoiding close personal contact with me--something I had always needed and especially needed then. From the start, she had been reluctant to discuss my cancer, which I badly needed to talk about. When I would attempt to discuss the subject with her she would utter something like: "I could die in a car accident tomorrow." So I stopped trying to talk with her about my disease!

*As an extreme example of her refusal to be open about my health problem, her family members later told me that they never had any idea that I had Stage 4 cancer and was not expected to live more than a few months. They said they got the impression from Gwen that I had just some sort of recurring stomach upset!*

As further evidence of her withdrawal from me, she began avoiding kissing me on the lips and moved away when I tried to be close to her. And probably even worse, she seemed to be depending more and more upon alcohol to help her cope. Meanwhile, I had pretty much lost my taste for alcohol during my cancer fight.

# CHAPTER 9
## Diet Preferences Change

MY DIET PREFERENCES had always been based on red meat such as prime ribs and porterhouse steaks--prime grade being my favorite. Now my body began to crave cruciferous veggies such as broccoli, cauliflower, cabbage, kale, and spinach--foods I had never especially liked. And I'm taking time off from my busy schedule to drive to Manassas almost every day to stuff myself on these foods at the Golden Corral salad bar.

I did not understand why my food preferences had changed so much after all these years. I was unaware that a "Select Senate Committee" headed by Senator George McGovern was studying nutrition research which led to the development of guidelines to combat leading killer conditions such as heart disease and cancer. The guidelines had concluded that we should eat more fruit, vegetables, and whole grains, the foods I was now craving. I no longer wanted red meat, one of the foods the McGovern committee said we should reduce or avoid consuming.

Although completely unaware of the McGovern committee and its guidelines at the time, my body was telling me much the same thing. And I was listening to my body's demands. I later learned that the veggies I was craving (particularly crucifers) contain cancer-fighting properties. Broccoli especially is known to have a sizable amount of a particularly potent compound that boosts the body's protective enzymes and rids the body of cancer-causing chemicals. *Unlike President George H.W. Bush, I now found broccoli tasty!*

Even my breakfast preferences had changed dramatically. An ideal breakfast for me had always been eggs with sausage, bacon, or ham. On special occasions I would have steak and eggs for breakfast. Now, I was craving old fashioned oatmeal for breakfast and getting up early before Gwen and Mitch awoke to cook it. The funny thing is that the awful pain I had suffered earlier had not returned and I was spending more time working and less time in bed. Furthermore, I had not seen or talked with a doctor about my cancer in more than two years. (More details about that later).

# CHAPTER 10
## Relationship Continues to Suffer

DESPITE THE GOOD news on the health front, our marital and social life was steadily heading downward. For awhile, friends continued to invite us to their homes for parties. But when we tried to reciprocate, Gwen would often drink too much and food would not be served until time for the guests to leave. This was embarrassing to me and Mitch.

Eventually, Gwen made a particularly hurtful suggestion: that the two of us might rest better if I moved to a guest bedroom. I did not like the idea at all because I feared it would result in our growing even further apart. I knew that her reason lacked credibility because I was the one with frequent bouts of insomnia, while she never appeared to have any problem sleeping. Despite my forebodings, however, I acceded to her wishes and moved to a guest room.

As I feared, this change did in fact increase the emotional distance between us. Grasping at any straw, I decided to tell Gwen about the doctor's statement that mates of cancer patients often suffer as much or more than the patients and thus needed to talk to a professional about this. As I feared, she didn't appreciate this and snapped back, "I will never reveal my inner thoughts to a psychiatrist or anyone else." Soon after that, her doctor found that she was suffering from severe hypertension.

Perhaps I was being delusional, but I felt that Gwen's hypertension was being exaggerated by her practice of hiding her grief, but we were never able to mutually discuss things like that and of course she wouldn't talk to a counselor. In any event, her doctor put her on a "beta blocker" to try to get her blood pressure back to normal. I regretted that she was put on this particular drug since I had been told it had serious side effects. In Gwen's case, her personality immediately began to change for the worse. Although this medicine had been effective at treating her hypertension, she was going from an agreeable happy person under normal circumstances to a quarrelsome and openly unhappy person.

I had not only read that this beta blocker could cause serious personality changes, but I had some personal knowledge of it. One of my own sisters, ordinarily a very loving person, had told me that soon after her doctor prescribed this product for her high blood pressure, she began having awful thoughts about her extremely nice husband. She said that when it reached the point that she had thoughts hoping he would die, she called her doctor and told him of this. The doctor immediately changed her medication to another product and her personality quickly returned to normal.

Because Gwen's personality had changed so drastically since she was put on this beta blocker, I suspected it might at least be partially responsible for her change in personality. I knew she would reject any suggestion of mine that her medicine was having any adverse effect on her so I didn't know what to do. Then I had an idea. Since she still had half a bottle of these pills, I poured some of them down the drain so that I could talk to her doctor when I got a refill for her. I soon met with the doctor and explained Gwen's change in personality to him. I pleaded with him to change her to another medication. However, he refused my urging because the medicine he had prescribed had proven effective at controlling her hypertension--apparently his only objective at that time.

Unable to do anything about her changed attitude toward me and Mitch, I became more and more fearful about our family's future together. My greatest fear was that she no longer loved me. Since she would not discuss such things with me personally, I began writing her letters expressing my great love for her and my hopes that we would be able to rebuild our loving relationship. After reading my letters, she finally told me that my instincts were right--she no longer loved me.

Although I had feared the worst, hearing it from her personally sent my hopes for the future tumbling. It was hard to accept the fact that in a few short years, she had gone from wanting to sit on my lap to not wanting to be in the same room with me. And it was especially hard for me to believe because we had once been known as the most loving married couple in our community.

*Incidentally, although Gwen's change in attitude toward me was by far the most hurtful, I also noticed changes by others. Many people I considered friends had begun distancing themselves from me after my cancer diagnosis. I was not too surprised that some of the industry people quietly began cutting their ties with me. I had always suspected that their friendliness (and desires to take me to lunch) had been enhanced by my position at EPA.*

But I was very disappointed that some fellow employees and other people I had thought were genuine friends began avoiding me. Did they think my disease might be contagious or did they just not know how to act around a cancer victim? Other cancer victims have told me that this sort of "distancing" also happened to them. In one case with me, however, the reverse happened. An industry rep went out of his way to make sure our friendship remained strong and it actually grew stronger after he learned about my cancer. After I left EPA, he continued to call me frequently and even drove through the heavy traffic from DC to Virginia to visit me personally. A fellow employee, Jesse Clark, also remained a close friend and confidante. I was pleased that a few industry people and fellow employees took the time to send me "goodbye and get well" cards and letters.

Back to the project: despite several problems that came up, Roger and I were making good progress on the house. We had quickly developed a completely trusting relationship. When I wasn't around because of illness, he kept his own time card and at the end of the week I paid him without any question or doubts about his honesty.

# CHAPTER 11
## God Comes Back into My life

SINCE MY MAJOR worry was leaving Gwen and Mitch with an unfinished major project and other debts, I began seriously working on my prayers that God would allow me the time I needed to get our financial affairs in order. Doesn't that remind you of *"There are no atheists in fox holes"*? I'm ashamed to admit that since I had moved away from my home church in Blacksburg, SC, many years earlier, I had attended church only sporadically. Praying was not big on my agenda. My alienation from organized religion had begun in college and continued afterwards.

The only prayer I remembered was one I learned as a child. It began with the words: "Now I Lay Me Down To Sleep." I hoped that the Lord would understand and forgive my lack of experience in this area so I began my new religious experience repeating that simple childhood prayer (silently) at bedtime. After awhile, as I gained some confidence, I began talking with Christ on a more personal basis, telling Him of my fears and concerns and asking Him for forgiveness. With this new personal revelation, I no longer felt the need to utter a memorized or rote prayer--and was soon talking to Christ/ God on a fairly regular basis. I still did not dare ask God to save me from the cancer because I didn't think I deserved that help after all those years of neglecting Him.

As I feared, the lack of money soon became an even bigger detriment to working on the project than my health. It was rapidly reaching the point that we had virtually run out of construction money and were having difficulty paying the mortgages and taking care of our own living expenses. Gwen and I agreed that we would not let our dire financial situation affect Mitch's life as long as we could prevent it. His tennis skills were improving rapidly and we realized that unless our financial circumstances improved, a tennis scholarship might be his only way to get a college education. So, we continued to tighten the notches on our belts and could only employ Roger occasionally, and he had to supplement his pay elsewhere.

Gwen and I decided that we must find a way to increase our income or lose everything. Since neither of us had experience in looking for and applying for a job (fortunately job offers had almost always come to us) we decided to get advice from some close friends about the best way to find work. We were pleased that they were more than willing to offer their suggestions. They mentioned such possibilities as: (1) Gwen getting a job in a fine woman's clothing or art supply store and (2) I could use the experience I had gained in house restoration to get a job at Lowe's or another home improvement store in Fairfax.

# CHAPTER 12
## Serious Job Hunting Begins

AFTER LISTENING TO these suggestions, Gwen and I went home to consider them. After thinking and talking about it, we decided that we had the experience and knowledge to enable us to find something better than minimum wage jobs. Gwen decided to test the water first by calling her former office, which had changed its name from the Navy Hydrographic Office to the Navy Oceanographic Office. She immediately got an encouraging "maybe" about rejoining her old office with the promise of a call back within a few days. The next week she was offered her old job back with a raise. Her job was "drawing official ocean floor maps" to benefit ocean navigation around the world.

I decided I would start by calling my former boss, Bill Holmberg, who had transferred from EPA to the Department of Energy (DOE) since I had retired. I did not plan to ask Holmberg for a job. First of all, I knew he was fully aware of my cancer problem and assumed he would not want to hire me for that reason alone. And the truth was that we had quite a few serious disagreements about policy when I worked for him at EPA. However, since Bill was a "Washington insider," I hoped to get some ideas from him. With his fertile brain, I hoped he might have some good ideas of where I might find some appropriate part time work.

However, to my great surprise when I called Bill Holmberg to explain our situation and ask him if he had any ideas of where I might get some part-time work, his response was immediate: "Can you start work this afternoon?" I told him it was a little too late for that afternoon but that I could meet him at the Forestal Building the following morning. He didn't tell me what he had in mind but I knew that anything involving Bill Holmberg would be interesting.

When I was directed to Holmberg's office the next day, a well dressed man was sitting across from him. Bill introduced him to me as a top personnel officer for Computer Science Corporation (CSC) a large IT company. Bill then explained that CSC had several contracts with DOE, one of which was "to develop a plan for State/Federal Alcohol Fuels production and marketing." He said that he (Bill) was in charge of energy development for DOE and that developing such a program was one of his many responsibilities.

Bill said: "Jim, we desperately need someone to develop a system for alcohol fuels similar to the State/Federal Plan for Certification of Applicators of Restricted Use Pesticides that you developed at EPA." Then he shocked me further by saying: "I hope you will be the person we hire to develop that system." He said that the CSC officer sitting across from him was actually there to offer me a job doing just that--starting that day!

I immediately said that I appreciated the offer but that I knew nothing about alcohol fuels except that it was called "Gasohol" and that I didn't see how I could be of any help to him. And I reminded him of my cancer. Bill responded by saying, "Jim, we don't need an expert on alcohol fuels to do this work. I need someone who knows how to develop a workable system involving Federal, State and local resources." He added: "You can learn all you need to know about alcohol fuels from this stack of material I gathered up yesterday afternoon for you to read. By next week you will know enough to start developing a process similar to the one you did at EPA. Of course, I'm aware that you're fighting cancer but so far it does not appear to have affected your brain and that's what I need from you right now."

Seeing my skepticism, he commented: "I recall that you were the first project manager at EPA to develop a successful program under Amended FIFRA. In fact you were the only one who met the law's deadline. I also know that you were a journalist, not a pesticide specialist, and that this didn't seem to handicap you from doing the job of a pesticide specialist. In fact, being a first rate journalist may have been an asset. I think you're especially well suited for this job because you're already friends with many of the State Agriculture Department people who will be in charge of the alcohol fuels program in their states. You worked with them while you were at both USDA and EPA and they trust you."

He continued: "Remember, Jim, I got to know a lot about you when you were working for me at EPA. During that time you were responsible for publication of both Standards for Certified Applicator and Guidelines for State Plans to carry out the program. I was also there when Assistant Administrator Ed Johnson called a meeting of the three of us in his office. At that time, he said he wanted you to head up the Pesticide Classification Task Force to develop a system of classifying pesticides into 'general' and 'restricted use.' Of course that was a highly scientific process and you successfully completed that job."

Bill concluded his little speech by declaring, "Ed Johnson wanted you for that job knowing that you had cancer and lacked a scientific background. Despite those factors you successfully completed that job before retiring and it's still being used by EPA at this time." Before I could ask any more questions or say "yes" or "no," Bill turned to the CSC representative and said, "Jim will tell you what he expects in the way of a starting salary."

Although I had not had a chance to discuss the job or salary with Bill privately, I had had the foresight to check with Civil Service and found that under Federal Retirement rules I could earn up to $30,000 a year without impacting my disability retirement. So I said, "If I take the job I would like to start at $30,000 per year."

The CSC personnel man gulped and said "I don't think we've ever started anyone that high." Bill said, "Well, he's worth that and more." The CSC man then said "I'll put his papers in at that rate starting today, and hope that I can get corporate approval." Then he asked: "Jim, can you come by our office in Virginia tomorrow so we can complete the paperwork and get your picture taken for your CSC ID badge?"

My head swimming, I thought the decision to accept the job offer had already pretty much been made and that approval would come through at the figure I wanted. So, I told him I would be there the following day and got directions to the CSC office. The next morning, after signing some papers and getting my photo taken, I left the CSC office in Virginia with my new photo ID showing I was a bona fide CSC employee assigned to the Department of Energy. *(When the remission ended and I eventually became too sick to continue work at CSC they allowed me to keep the badge and I still have it).*

# CHAPTER 13
## The Start of New Careers?

WHEN I REACHED the Forestal Building I used my CSC badge to gain entry into the building. After I reached Bill Holmberg's office, I spent the rest of the morning with him while he filled me in on what had been going on with alcohol fuels, and the roles of DOE, The Bureau of Alcohol, Tobacco, and Firearms (BATF), and CSC. He explained that over a year ago CSC, under its contract with DOE, had assigned some of their own people to develop a National/State/Federal System for alcohol fuels.

Bill added: "They had a full year to work out a system for this program but failed to produce anything I could use." He explained that this was why he was so pleased and acted so quickly when I called him about a job. As for BATF, he said this agency would help with the Federal laws affecting production and sale of alcohol.

After lunch I set up my old manual typewriter and other supplies in an office next door to Bill's. I returned to his office and asked him if he had any further advice and/or guidance for me. He handed me the package he had assembled the previous afternoon and said, "After you read this material you will know enough about the subject to get started writing. I'm putting this program in your hands starting today. I'm delegating full authority and responsibility to you for developing a workable system."

Before ushering me from his office he concluded: "You already know what to do, so just get started and I'll back you up on whatever you come up with. CSC will provide you with administrative, clerical, and printing help if and when you need it." *Note: this was before personal computers were common and I had to depend upon one huge (Wang) machine that CSC used for word processing and printing. A "trained computer expert" at CSC would handle all my printing needs.*

I spent the rest of that day familiarizing myself with the material Bill gave me but I didn't wait long to begin drafting an analysis of the problems I anticipated and a suggested basic approach for solving them. Using my work at EPA as a framework, I also began putting down some suggested guidelines that states could follow. As Bill had anticipated, it was soon obvious that my experience at EPA would be the asset Bill expected. It would let me quickly begin to build a similar workable program for alcohol fuels.

However, I needed to make one significant change from the EPA system. Since most lead agency state officials responsible for this program were employees of their State Departments of Agriculture they would not be as familiar with alcohol fuels as they were with pesticides. Because of that deficiency I knew they would need more "hands on" assistance for this new effort to help solve our growing energy problem. Therefore, I suggested we begin with two pilot states with which I would work on an intensive basis. In my analysis, I wrote: "DOE will provide the pilot states with guidelines and some grant money as well as 'hands on' technical assistance. We will expand the program state-by-state as states gear up to develop their own knowledge and competency." *I had quickly discovered that states had not made progress trying to operate with their own limited resources and without any written guidance from DOE.*

Note: in the material I received from Bill Holmberg were letters from some very recognizable state officials including: Bill Clinton, Governor of Arkansas and later U.S. President; Lamar Alexander, Governor of Tennessee and later U.S. Senator from that state; and John D. Rockefeller, Governor of West Virginia. These and other lesser known governors wrote letters to DOE agreeing to establish contacts for a State/Federal Alcohol Fuels Program. But with the exception of South Carolina and South Dakota, none of the other states had yet done so. For that reason I selected those two states to be my pilot group. *I was encouraged that these two states had at least taken the initiative to designate a specific person to work on the program.*

With my decision to select South Carolina and South Dakota as the pilot states, I began some more serious thinking and writing and two days later submitted my first written material about alcohol fuels to Bill. I had found several real and potential problems and offered possible solutions for dealing with them. I also provided some suggested preliminary guidelines for states to follow in order to be certified by DOE. I waited while he read the information I had prepared and without changing a word, he said "o.k.," and then asked his secretary to "make copies of that document and send them to all DOE Department Heads." He then returned my original copy and said: "Go with what you're doing and I'll back you all the way." Those were reassuring words to a novice to this new program.

Meanwhile, Gwen had rejoined her old Navy Oceanographic Office meaning that we were both now gainfully employed and would soon be able to easily pay our bills and employ Roger for longer time periods. My primary goals then (besides fighting cancer) were to get the mammoth building project finished and work hard to justify Bill Holmberg's faith in hiring me for this important job.

# CHAPTER 14

## Representing DOE in Columbia, SC

BY COINCIDENCE, JUST days after I became a consultant to DOE, I learned that the Energy Department had been asked to send a representative to attend a state Energy Conference to be held in Columbia, SC the following week. The conference had been arranged by the SC Governor's Office and Bill told me I would need to go as DOE's representative. This was pretty scary to someone who had been on the job less than a full week at that time but I took this as a vote of confidence and asked the office secretary to make plans for me to head to Columbia.

When my plane landed in Columbia, Bob Stein, the young man assigned to the fledgling SC alcohol fuels program, met my plane and immediately took me to Governor Richard Riley's office for a short meeting. My first impression of Governor Riley was that he was pale and frail but his handshake belied that description. His grip felt like it belonged to a "log cutter." My hand was sore the rest of the day! Since I had spent little time in South Carolina except to visit family, I was not at all familiar with the Governor.

However, Bob supplied me some biographical material about Gov. Riley and a brief excerpt follows:

*As Governor of South Carolina, Richard Riley spearheaded a comprehensive and highly successful reform of that state's school system, an endeavor that most informed observers at the time considered to be an impossible task. But Riley had accomplished this by bringing together a coalition of groups, including business people, educators, and parents. The Business Round Table called him, "a star and a pioneer in reform."*

Governor Riley was pleased when I informed him that I had selected his state to receive some grant money. After we left the Governor's office, Bob and I went to his own office where we discussed his role in the plan I was developing. Also, I asked him if he knew what, if anything, I would be expected to do at the meeting the following day. *He showed me the program which listed me as one of the principal speakers!* Luckily, I had brought the analysis and potential guidelines I had prepared for Bill Holmberg and I began thinking about how I could use this information as the basis of my presentation.

The next morning, Bob picked me up at my hotel and the two of us went to the Energy Conference. When it was my time to speak, I pulled out the material I had submitted to Bill and began describing my analysis of potential problems and suggestions for dealing with these problems. I also touched on my plans for including individuals and groups in the process of developing state plans for alcohol fuels.

This information turned out to be a big hit with the attendees so I was really happy that I had brought it with me—with no idea initially that I would need to use it.

In the question period after my speech, most of the questions were centered around my future plans for including state and local officials, industry, and others in the alcohol fuels program. I had no problems answering these questions since I had spent much of my time since taking the job thinking about these types of questions. Fortunately, no one asked me any technical questions! *I still shiver when I think what I would have done if I had not put this stuff in my briefcase before leaving DC.*

As the meeting was breaking up, two members of the audience approached me and one said: "You're not Jim White!" This startled me and I replied: "I always thought I was." It turned out that the two people before me were employees of Duke Power Co. (now Duke Energy). After getting a quick look at the program and spotting the name "Jim White" they had assumed that their own Duke Power Vice-President Jim White would appear on the stage. *Coincidentally, the Jim White they were referring to was my first cousin formerly of Shelby, NC, where I, as well as other family members and Shelby residents, always called him "Jay."* It turned out that the Duke Power employees knew their V.P. mainly by reputation within the company.

They had seen him in pictures and at a distance but had no personal contact with him. However, they had noticed significant physical difference between the two of us. For example, their "Jim White," who had also once been a redhead, was now almost completely bald with a fringe of white hair while I still had a full head of red hair. They accepted my word that I was Jay's first cousin. They also said their Jim was known as "Big Daddy" to the engineering staff he headed.

*At a White family reunion a few months later, I asked Jay when and why he had become "Jim" rather than "Jay" White. He explained that immediately upon graduation from NC State he was hired by Duke Power Co. The editor of the Duke Power in-house newsletter had written: "Let's Welcome New Employee, Jim White." My cousin then explained, "Because I was a brand new employee, I didn't have the nerve to correct the editor." So he became "Jim White" as far as Duke Power was concerned. Obviously the name worked well for him since he retired as the No. 2 man of this giant corporation.*

# CHAPTER 15

## A Visit to the Second "Pilot" State

BACK IN DC, Bill read my trip report and also heard that the meeting in Columbia went well. He then suggested that I schedule a trip to Pierre, South Dakota's capital, to meet the person assigned to alcohol fuels and look the situation over there. This contact's name was Vern Brakke. Vern met my plane and immediately took me to meet SD Governor Bill Janklow. Like Gov. Riley of SC I was totally unfamiliar with Gov. Janklow but it was no surprise that this Governor was equally pleased to learn that DOE was giving his state a special grant to help get their Alcohol Fuels Program started.

As far as I could tell, that was the only similarity the two governors shared. Gov. Janklow proved to be another "unforgettable" character among the many I encountered during my career. For one thing, when I met him in his office, the first thing I noticed was that he was wearing a "six shooter" on his hip. *I suspect he was the only governor in the nation to be dressed like the "Lone Ranger," complete with cowboy boots, holster and a real, loaded pistol. His cowboy hat was on the hat rack.* This attire and pistol were not as unexpected as you might think when you learn something about Bill Janklow's unusual background (*excerpted from Wikipedia below*):

*Bill Janklow was born in Chicago, Illinois. Following a series of scrapes with the law, young Janklow was ordered by a judge to either join the military or attend reform school. Janklow dropped out of high school and joined the U.S. Marine Corps, serving from 1956 to 1959. Upon his return he attended and graduated (in 1964) from the University of South Dakota. He went on to earn a J.D at that university's School of Law two years later. Janklow served as Legal Services lawyer for six years on the Rosebud Indian Reservation, advancing to director of the program. In 1973, he received his first political appointment as the Chief Prosecutor of South Dakota and quickly earned a reputation as a top trial lawyer. He served as South Dakota's attorney general from 1975 to 1979 and was first elected governor in 1978. He was easily re-elected in 1982 with 70.9 percent of the vote, the highest percentage won by a gubernatorial candidate in the state's history.*

*At the end of his second term, Janklow revealed that he had nearly resigned after a book and magazine article, both published in 1983, repeated an old rape allegation against him. Three federal investigations determined that the allegation--that he had raped a teenage girl in 1968 on the Rosebud Indian Reservation--was untrue. But controversy followed Janklow his entire life as further noted below!*

*On August 16, 2003, while serving as a U.S. Congressman, Janklow was involved in a fatal traffic collision while driving his car. He failed to stop at a stop sign, accidentally killing a motorcyclist. The accident occurred at a rural intersection near Trent, SD and Janklow himself suffered a broken hand and bleeding on the brain as a result of the accident. After an investigation, Janklow was arraigned and was convicted by a jury of second-degree manslaughter. A few days later, he resigned his seat in Congress, and was sentenced to spend 100 days in jail.*

Back to the matter at hand, Vern Brakke drove me to visit various state offices expected to participate in the South Dakota alcohol fuels program, and we were greeted with enthusiasm everywhere we went. *Regrettably, although we were near them, we did not have enough time to tour the famous tourist attractions such as the Black Hills and Mount Rushmore where the sculptures of George Washington, Thomas Jefferson, Theodore Roosevelt, and Abraham Lincoln are located.* Unfortunately, that was the story of my career while working for USDA, EPA and DOE. My work took me to all U.S. states (except Alaska) but I never got to act like a tourist!

# CHAPTER 16

## Our Cup "Runneth Over!"

SOON AFTER THAT trip, because of our "new careers," Gwen and I had been able to replenish our construction account and Roger returned to work on the house almost full time. Then "our cup runneth over." Our nearly new custom built "contemporary" house on five acres on the outskirts of Clifton sold. We were especially pleased about this for several reasons: (1) we received more cash to be added to our construction fund, (2) it allowed us to "pay off" one of our mortgages, and (3) it removed some of the pain we had suffered when a couple we had considered friends had rented our modern house at a low monthly rental and betrayed our trust by "trashing" it.

By way of explaining the latter: we had been friends with this couple for years. They were in the process of building a new custom home but sold their house before the new house was completed. They desperately needed a place to live until their new house was "move in ready." There was nothing suitable to rent in our area and the closest subdivisions with houses to rent would require them to sign at least a one year lease.

*Others had approached us about renting the house but we had refused to do so for fear of damage by renters who smoked, had small children and/or pets, or appeared "careless." After all, our house was in pristine condition and the floors were covered in the most expensive white wool carpet we could find. (Note: High quality wool carpet was a preferred floor treatment at that time).*

However, when our friends called us and explained their predicament and asked about renting our house, we thought that could be a "win-win" situation for both parties. After all we knew them and their well behaved children. And we knew they didn't smoke and had only one pet--an outside cat. Our friends vowed to turn our house back over to us in as immaculate condition as it was when they moved in. We felt so good about the situation we rented the house to them at a ridiculously low price for the time they needed and with no contract that held them to a lease.

A few months later, the wife called to tell me that their new house was nearing completion and that they would be moving out at the end of the month. As we were about to say goodbye, I heard her shout to one of the children: "Get that cat out of here!" When I heard this, I thought I should stop by to take a look at our soon-to-be-vacant house. When I stopped by later, the first thing I saw upon entering was a young puppy running around on that expensive white carpet. Obviously, the puppy was not "house trained" since I could easily see many dark spots on the previously "like new" carpet.

In looking around I could not miss noticing that one of the large double glazed glass windows was broken. The wife quickly said, "The carpet, along with the rest of the house, will be spotless when we move out." When I pointed out the broken window, she said: "Don't worry about that; we've already ordered the replacement for the window. It will be installed before we leave." She then volunteered the name of the place in Manassas where they had placed the order for the window and its installation.

After our "friends" vacated the house, Gwen and I went to check on things and found that the dark spots were still present on the white wall-to-wall carpet. Suspecting the worst by this time, we noted that the broken window had not been replaced as promised. We both knew by then that our "friends" had betrayed our trust.

We first drove to Manassas where the wife had told me they had paid to replace the glass. You guessed it! When we talked to the manager, he said that our "friends" had ordered the new window but had not paid for it or for the cost of installation. It cost us several hundred dollars to pay for the new window plus installation costs. Then we addressed the issue of pet damage to our expensive new carpet. First, we purchased the best carpet cleaner we could find and tried to clean the spots but were unsuccessful. We then hired professional carpet cleaners and they lessened the stains but they were unable to completely remove the dark spots.

After all the trouble and expense they had caused us, our "former" friends had the gall to request return of their security deposit. Needless to say, they did not get it and we were no longer friends.

# CHAPTER 17
## Standards Get Preliminary Approval

BACK AT DOE, things were progressing well. I now had a DOE preliminary "approved" version of "Standards for Production and Marketing of Alcohol Fuels." I had also completed writing a set of related guidelines to assist states in putting together an official

"State Plan." After sending them out to all states, my two "pilot" states immediately requested my help in developing their own specific State Plans for Submission to DOE. And I was happy to oblige. I spent a day or two at each state helping them with their plans which I brought back to DOE for approval, and Bill signed them. In addition, while I had been traveling, Mississippi Agriculture Commissioner Jim Buck Ross had called Bill Holmberg and told him to "tell Jim White to get his butt down here to Jackson and help us put together a State Plan for Alcohol Fuels!" Since I knew Jim Buck personally, I wasn't offended by his salty language and put that state down as the next state to visit.

After visits to assist these three states, I received another urgent request to travel. As a result of being a Pilot State already "certified" to develop an alcohol fuels program, South Dakota was holding a big one-day, state-wide "Alcohol Fuels Public Forum." Invitations had gone out to hundreds of South Dakotans to attend the Forum, along with Federal and State officials and the media. The event was to be held in Sioux City.

Bill Holmberg told me I would be DOE's representative at the Sioux City event and would need to contact South Dakota Congressman Tom Daschle's office for details about the Forum. Daschle was to be one of two principal speakers at the event. And, you guessed it. I was to be the other. I called Congressman Daschle's office and was told that the Congressman would like for me to meet him at Dulles Airport the morning of the Forum which was just a few days away.

When I asked Daschle's office for some idea of what the Congressman planned to say (so our presentations would be reasonably compatible) they had nothing specific to offer but said the Congressman would probably build his speech around a new publication based on Alcohol Fuels Research, assuming the publication was available before we left. They said they expected copies of this document momentarily and that they would send me a copy as soon as they arrived from the Government Printing Office (GPO).

With no confidence that GPO would deliver the publication in time for me to study it, I reviewed my trusty "standards" and "guidelines," put them in my briefcase and prepared to "wing it." My lack of trust in GPO was confirmed when the GPO delivered copies to the Congressman's office as he was getting ready to leave for the airport to attend the Sioux City meeting. That's when I knew that the two of us were in trouble.

Since I had never met Congressman Daschle, I asked his Executive Assistant how I would recognize him. I asked: "Should one of us be wearing a red carnation?" His office laughingly told me: "A red carnation won't be necessary. You'll recognize him easily. He'll be standing right at the counter of the airline you will be traveling on; he will be the man dressed in a dark suit looking like a teenage boy dressed up for the prom!"

The description was apt and I had no trouble spotting the youthful looking Congressman. After we were seated and the "fasten seat belt" sign was off, Daschle reached into his briefcase and lifted out two copies of a large (two-inch thick) document. He handed one of these to me. Seeing my questioning look, Rep. Daschle explained: "This document just came off the press from GPO. I've had no chance to look at it until now. This contains the information you and I are supposed to discuss at the Forum."

He then added that plans were for the two of us to be on the stage together, with each of us to make short introductory remarks and then refer to the large document to discuss the data contained therein. He added: "We had better start reading this document. As thick as it is, the best we'll be able to do before we land is skim it." So, we both began "skimming" our copies. After an hour or so of "skimming" this technical information, I turned to the Congressman and said, "Tom, this document is too technical to get anything out of it in the time we have."

He agreed and we began to discuss the mechanics of how we would handle this difficult situation. We agreed on the format: we would perform as the "Tom and Jim Show." After each of us made our short introductory remarks, we would stand side-by-side at the podium to answer questions--supposedly based on the document that neither we nor they had had a chance to study.

When a member of the audience or media asked a question, if one of us had some idea of a sensible answer, he would begin the response and the other would chime in at will. If neither of us had any idea of how to answer the specific question, we would obfuscate until one of us could think of a reply. I could always change the discussion to DOE's alcohol fuels analyses and plans for involving relevant state and local people and groups in conducting the program. *I can assure you I made full use of that avenue.*

After these decisions, we relaxed and spent the rest of the flight getting to know each other. We shared talk about our backgrounds, family, and likes and dislikes. We were comfortable with each other by the time we arrived at Sioux City. At the Forum site, we were amazed at the number of people waiting to hear us speak. There must have been 2,000 people there, including members of the press, broadcast stations, and others. All of them were waiting for us to enlighten them on alcohol fuels! Although neither of us felt competent to answer any complex question, we had a slight advantage. We had a chance to scan part of the document while the audience's first view of it was when we held it up.

Fortunately for us, since Forum attendees were not familiar with the technical publication, we had virtually no technical questions to deal with. Most of the questions were general enough that either of us could give a reasonable response. Of the few technical questions we received, we gave our best "guesstimates." No one in the audience knew enough to question our "guesstimate" or ask a follow up question.

Thus, the "Tom and Jim Show" survived the event. Neither of us had any ego involvement in the program and we were just happy to get off stage. Speaking of the "blind leading the blind," this could best be described as the "dumb" leading the "dumber." After the event was over, Congressman Daschle and I went to the hotel lounge for a cocktail. We wanted to celebrate the fact that we had been able to "fake things" well enough that we were applauded at the end (rather than stoned).

I whispered to Tom that my answer to a rare technical question had been off by three zeroes, i.e. instead of the answer being billions it should have been trillions. Tom laughed and whispered back: "No one knew the difference." *The only way I knew of my mistake was that I had sneaked a peek at the document we brought with us.*

Tom Daschle made a very favorable impression on me at that time. He appeared to be a modest, sincere and friendly person--not at all like a self-centered, self-important politician. Volunteering that I was a registered Republican, I remember saying: "Tom, if you ever run for President, I might just vote for you." And I meant it then. Shortly after I arrived back to the DC area, I received a hand-written note from Daschle dated September 29, 1980, that read:

*Dear Jim,*

*I want to take a moment to personally thank you for coming to Sioux Falls last Friday. I appreciated it very much. We had numerous compliments on the meeting and particularly on the report. I hope that you thought it was worth your while.*

*It was a special pleasure to visit with you on the way out, Jim. I hope that young son continues to do well. He is obviously a source of great pride to you.*

*Again, my sincere thanks. Your presence was a real help to us.*
*Sincerely,*
*Tom Daschle*

*(Note: he must have been laughing while writing this!)*

As most of you readers probably know, the Tom Daschle I knew briefly back then, changed dramatically over the years. After becoming one of South Dakota's two U.S. Senators, Daschle gradually became a highly partisan politician. This characteristic probably helped him become Majority Leader of the Senate but it changed him from the modest, sincere human being that I might vote for to be my President. It's a shame what "Capitol Fever" can do to a person's character.

Back at DOE, after reviews from state officials and the BATF, I got final approval for the "Standards" and "Guidelines" that states were advised to use in implementing their Alcohol Fuels Program. Since this program was emanating from a new Department and did not have a Congressionally passed law requiring this step, I was not required to have the "Standards" and "Guidelines" published in the Federal Register before sending them to the states. All I needed was Bill's final approval which he gave immediately.

# CHAPTER 18
## Cancer Problem Worsens Drastically

SOON AFTER THE above mentioned success, I received some really bad news about my cancer! My temporary remission had expired and I now had Stage 4 cancer. Even worse, scans showed that it was now present throughout my body--including my bones and brain. I was told that no further treatment was available for me. Wanting a second opinion on my condition, I requested that the Lombardi Cancer Center at Georgetown University review my case. All of my recent scans, X-rays, and other test results were sent to Georgetown for review.

After the Lombardi Cancer Center doctors finished their review, I visited the Center to get what I hoped would be "good news." It was not to be. Their doctors-scientists told me that after studying all the medical material sent to them, they concurred with my doctors' findings that the cancer had metastasized to the point that they had no further treatment to recommend. That was devastating news to me.

With an early death apparently my only choice, I began pressuring my oncologist Dr. Carroll to tell me how long I had to live. He resisted for some time but I insisted that I needed this information in order to better prepare for Gwen's and Mitch's economic survival. Finally, he said: "Jim, only God knows how much time you have left; as a doctor I can only project that you may have as much as a few months to a year." (Later, he told me: "I didn't really think you had more than three more months to live!" *I was grateful for his lie!*)

Soon the pain was so bad that I was taking a powerful pain killer (Demerol) every two hours with little relief. I was spending much more time in hospitals. The only positive thing for the hospital stays was that they gave me access to morphine--the only thing that gave me temporary relief from the pain.

I also remember that I began receiving visits from close friends wanting to say their "last goodbyes" to me. One of these was EPA Deputy Administrator and Head of the Office of Pesticides Ed Johnson, who spent several hours one late afternoon and early evening with me. Another was old friend Dennis Avery, who had left USDA and now worked for the State Department. He spent several hours with me although I never knew he was there until he told me later. Still another faithful friend, Dr. Fred Whittemore (Big Red), who had been Bill Holmberg's assistant at EPA, stopped by almost daily during my long stays in the hospital. *After being retired from EPA because of age, Fred had received special Congressional dispensation to resume his career at the U.S. State Department. During that time, our friendship grew even closer.*

*We began a routine where Fred would stop by my hospital room on his way home from work. When he entered, he would give me a quick peek at a small silver flask hidden in his jacket pocket. This was my signal to ring for the nurse and ask her for some iced soft drinks or juice (i.e., setups). He would then surreptitiously mix two drinks and hand one to me. We would spend a pleasant hour or two talking. He might have two drinks during his visit and I would sip on one, rarely finishing it. Although I had stopped drinking alcohol early in my illness, I thoroughly enjoyed the companionship with "Big Red" and thought that I had reached the point that whether I drank a bit of alcohol or not no longer mattered. I was dying!*

Meanwhile my unstoppable pain continued except for the morphine I received in hospital visits. Some time back, Dr. Carroll had told me that the only way he might be able to relieve my pain was to perform a special surgery that I knew would further diminish my libido and adversely affect my sex life. The latter had already been reduced from damage caused by the prostate cancer and the heavy radiation I had received in attempting to stop the cancer spread.

*It should be emphasized that radiation of the prostate gland area was much less controlled back then than today's radiation treatments. As already noted, I had more than one serious health problem caused by radiation. Today's prostate cancer treatments have fewer side effects and are vastly superior to earlier treatments. There are now a variety of prostate cancer treatments not available when my cancer was active. One of these treatments known to work well in at least some cases is only slightly invasive. It involves "seeding" around the prostate gland to kill cancer cells. Two of my nephews became free of prostate cancer after this treatment.*

In my own case, since the treatments described above were not then available, I had few alternatives to the surgery suggested by my oncologist. In addition to the physical and libido damage caused by the surgery recommended by my oncologist, he had informed me that unfortunately, studies had shown that, although it could reduce pain, it would not extend the life of people who received it. When he mentioned this possibility to me, I had vehemently said, "No thanks. I prefer to die rather than have that humiliating surgery which does not even give me a chance to live longer."

On the job front, Bill Holmberg had kept me on the payroll during this period and continued to bring work for me to do at my hospital bed. He always stayed for a chat. As much as I appreciated his effort to be supportive, I finally had to tell Bill that I was no longer able to continue working. I had to devote what little energy I had to fighting cancer.

*I'll always appreciate Bill's efforts to keep me employed. I felt really bad that I could no longer help him with the alcohol fuels program. My conscience was somewhat assuaged by the fact that I had been able to develop the "system" that Holmberg had wanted and needed to promulgate the program. I had essentially gotten the alcohol fuels program off to a good start with officially approved "Standards" and "Guidelines" and several approved State Plan submissions based on those publications. My system was now DOE's policy.*

Ironically, soon after that, the Administration changed and the alcohol fuels program was put on the back burner where it languished for years. I was told that Reagan Administration officials met with Bill Holmberg and told him that he would be able to retain his position at DOE, if he would be more cooperative, i.e., if he would let up on his efforts to push for alternative fuels--at least until they could be proven to work and be reasonably cost effective.

I was told that Bill's response to this offer was to tell them "where to stick it!" He then resigned his position, walked out of the Forestal Building, and went to work with one or more environmental groups. As I write this memoir, an internet search reveals that he is currently heading "The American Council on Renewable Energy."

In retrospect I'm not overly proud of my success in helping to get the alcohol fuels program functioning. At the time, I was sold on the program because Bill and the literature he provided me presented convincing arguments that an alcohol fuels program would help solve our energy problem, be beneficial to the environment by reducing $CO_2$, and serve as a financial boon to small farmers. Bill truly believed in the program. He was convinced that individual farmers would be able to set up legal "stills" and sell alcohol, thus improving their deteriorating financial situations. I never thought his view of helping individual farmers produce alcohol that could be made into "gasohol" was realistic. However, I believed that farm communities might be able to set up cooperatives that could provide farmers assistance in producing and marketing alcohol.

I now believe that the whole alcohol fuels situation was a "pipe dream" by big hearted but impractical people. In my opinion, history has proved that. The program has not resulted in cleaner air and has been of little assistance to small farmers--the people ostensibly to be helped. Instead it has become a political football largely benefiting large corn farmers and very large companies, e.g., Arthur Daniels Midland. On the negative side, it caused a rise in food prices for American consumers, resulted in making gasoline more costly, and (in the opinion of many) gasohol is not as good as 100 per cent gasoline.

# CHAPTER 19

## The "Right-To-Die" Issue Comes to the Forefront

*DURING THIS PERIOD, I continued to be given "bone scans," with each new one worse than the previous, i.e., the scan showed more black dots. These scans looked like a dart board used for 20 years in a saloon. When I saw these black dots had crept into my brain, I said "that's enough" and refused to take any more bone scans.*

Since my doctors had given up on me, I stopped going to them and decided I would die in dignity on my own. *Or as much dignity as someone fighting "terminal" cancer can muster.* I had been talking with an old friend (who shall go unnamed) who believed that it was "cruel and inhuman punishment" to force people to endure dying in great pain with tubes inserted into their bodies. *I'd already witnessed that indignity up close and personal.* This old friend was a member of the Hemlock Society which believed in the right-to-die concept and was working to get state laws passed that would make that legal. (*Note: I believe that Oregon was the only state in which the Hemlock Society and its supporters were successful*).

After watching several friends and one relative die horrible deaths from prostate cancer, I began to look more favorably on the right-to-die concept. What bothered me the most was the fact that after a certain point, these cancer patients were helpless to do anything to end the pain. I began thinking that if I wanted to use that option I had best obtain the materials I needed while I was still able to get and use them. So, using information supplied by my friend, I put together a packet of materials that could end my life painlessly when I was ready and able to go.

I'm not about to reveal the formula, which involved a three-stage process. But after the pain progressed to the point that the only painkiller that would give me any relief was morphine, I decided it was time to conclude my life as painlessly as possible, while I was still able to do so. Of course, I fully realized that this was a violation of Christian religious principles. But unbearable pain can overcome many principles. *Note: If you have never had cancer that has spread to the bones you have no right to judge me or anyone else if they decide to end the pain!*

So when the pain became so intense that I might soon be helplessly strapped to a hospital bed and connected to various tubes, I decided to try to end the pain. On two separate occasions, late at night after Gwen was sound asleep, I completed the first two stages. As I prepared for the third stage after which I would go to sleep and never wake up, the same event stopped me. Both times, Mitch came home unexpectedly, forcing me to stop the process--although he was not aware of it at the time. After the second such incident, I decided that God might be telling me that it was not my time to go and decided to begin doing everything in my power to stay alive.

During this time I also made two other life changing decisions: (1) to talk to an attorney friend about the possibility of instituting a medical malpractice suit against the doctor for his failure to give me a simple digital prostate test that might have revealed my cancer quickly enough for my treatment to be effective and (2) to agree to have the surgery recommended by my oncologist--something I had said I would rather die than have done to me.

As for No. (1) above, I had always had serious objections to malpractice suits because of my faith in doctors and the medical profession. But intense pain over a long period of time can change a person's long held beliefs. I thought my doctor needed to feel some pain of his own for what he was costing me and my family. So, my attorney friend and I discussed the possibility of filing a malpractice suit and he felt so strongly about the negligence of the doctor that he offered to represent me on a contingency basis using his own funds.

He assured me that he felt we had an "iron clad" case because my doctor had ignored my obvious prostate cancer symptoms over a two year period. He said my case was strengthened by (a) the fact that the EPA doctor had immediately suspected prostate cancer and written that on my medical records and (b) the psychiatrist's reaction when I related my symptoms to him and his exclamation, "That doctor was going to let you die!" I immediately felt some relief that perhaps a favorable verdict in this case would permit Gwen and Mitch to have a reasonably comfortable life after I was gone.

Extreme pain was the major cause of my changed attitude about No. (2) above. I called Dr. Carroll and told him I could no longer endure the pain and would accept the surgery he had recommended. At that point, the pain had made me willing to accept any kind of surgery, including removal of my arms, legs. or any other part of my body to relieve the pain.

Before putting me to sleep to perform this surgery, Dr. Carroll assured me that no one would know that I had undergone the surgery unless I told them. However, wanting to be honest, he could not guarantee that the surgery would stop all the pain. *And he reiterated the fact that medical science regrettably did not show that this surgery would prolong life.* However, it would probably make the remaining time less painful. When I awoke from the surgery, much of the pain was gone and I felt no different as a man.

During the recovery period, I did much thinking of how I would spend the remaining time I had to live. One thing was confirmed--God had not been ready for me to die immediately as was the fate of many younger men who contract prostate cancer. I also reached the conclusion that further extension of my life would not involve just medical science. Instead, should it happen, I knew it would be based on my own efforts and God's wishes.

Soon after my recovery from the latest surgery, my attorney asked me to come to his office to meet an associate who had offered to help my attorney pursue our malpractice case. This attorney apparently had more experience in such cases and after being briefed by my attorney and me, he agreed we had an "air tight" case. He made one immediate suggestion: that we obtain a copy of the EPA doctor's notes regarding the fact that my symptoms suggested a strong possibility that I had prostate cancer.

I asked: "Do you want me to go to EPA to obtain these notes or would you prefer that an attorney legally obtain them." They discussed this for a few moments and said, "We think it would be better for one of us to obtain a copy of your file and bring it to the office so it would be in our custody the entire time." I then gave them instructions about who and where they should go to obtain my medical records and left their office.

A few weeks later, my original attorney called and said: "Jim, we went to the office you sent us to and we talked to the clerk there who searched but could not find your medical records." I then replied that I would go there personally and get a copy. The next day I went to the Employee Records Office, talked with the person in charge, and she took me to the large file cabinet which contained all the medical records of employees whose names started with the letter "W." She pulled the proper drawer out for me and I immediately saw a folder with the name: James H. White at the top.

I opened the folder, looked and there was nothing in it! It was completely empty! Not even a reference to my visit! And the doctor who had examined me was no longer with the agency and they did not know how to reach him. Then the supervisor asked around the office if anyone had any idea of what could have happened to my medical records. No one did. I reported this immediately to my attorney who was as puzzled as I but who replied: "Well, we have plenty of evidence of neglect without that piece of paper."

Shortly after that, I was notified that I was scheduled for a Legal Deposition where I would be questioned by the Defendant's Attorney. When I entered the room, I saw several people who I assumed were attorneys, a person who would record the deposition, and the doctor I was suing.

This was the first time I had seen him since he had dismissed me with the words: "You must be o.k. I can't find anything wrong with you." He would not look me directly in the eye.

The doctor's attorney began asking me to describe my symptoms, the doctor's treatment and if I had had any interaction with other doctors about my illness. I gave him straightforward answers, including the fact that the EPA doctor who conducted my physical, after hearing my symptoms, had immediately said he suspected I had prostate cancer and advised me to get my prostate checked as soon as possible. I also told him that the psychiatrist I had seen at the request of my oncologist had said, after hearing my symptoms: "That doctor was going to let you die."

At that point, my former doctor showed some emotions for the first and only time; he winced and stared at the floor for a moment. The defendant's attorney ignored my discussion with the psychiatrist but zeroed in on the EPA doctor and his advice to me. He asked, "Do you have any kind of paper or any proof, other than your word, that your EPA doctor advised you to get your prostate checked?" I replied: "I saw him make detailed notations of our conversation and place these notes in my medical records file." I then added: "My attorneys and I have gone to EPA to secure a copy of those records; we found my medical record folder but the file was empty. We have no idea who removed them from the file. Do you?"

He failed to answer and the deposition ended shortly after that. The two attorneys and I had a meeting in my attorney's office later that day. The attorneys agreed that the deposition went well and that our case was still very solid--despite that empty medical record file. The attorneys told me that such cases often take many months or even years, but that they would move it along as quickly as possible.

# CHAPTER 20
## My Personal Search for Cancer Cure Begins

SOON AFTER THE deposition, I began a personal investigation that I hoped might extend my life. I started by contacting a medical doctor friend who had connections with a government agency, the National Institute of Health (NIH). My doctor friend had told me earlier that he was doing research for NIH including evaluating various experimental cancer drugs. This interested me and I mentioned my willingness to be a "guinea pig." My doctor friend then said he would try to get me into an experimental cancer drug program with which he was involved. This held out some hope for me.

That hope was dashed when my doctor friend told me that the NIH scientists who received and reviewed my medical records determined that the amount of radiation I had received precluded my participation in their programs. In their opinion, I would not survive the dangerous experimental drugs being tested.

Grasping at straws, I began researching drugs available in other countries, especially Mexico. I was aware that U.S. cancer patients were crossing the border to gain access to drugs being used there but not approved for use in this country. At the time I was searching for any alternative treatments of my cancer. I had heard and read about Laetrile. This product, which is found naturally in several fruits and vegetables (but especially in apricot pits), was not legal in the U.S. but was readily available in Mexico. *Some U.S. celebrities (including Steve McQueen) were crossing the border for treatment with Laetrile and lauding its cancer fighting ability.*

About that time (1980), I also learned that the National Cancer Institute (NCI) had begun a study to evaluate the use of Laetrile in cancer patients. That gave me some hope but then I learned that the NCI study had found that Laetrile was ineffective and they had discontinued the research. However NCI did report that some patients "felt better" while taking Laetrile and some doctors expressed the opinion that Laetrile was effective in controlling cancer pain. Some cancer patients also reported that cannabis (marijuana) was useful in relieving cancer pain.

Remembering the agony I had suffered until the latest surgery and fearful that this pain would return, I began to think that a trip to Mexico might be worthwhile for me to investigate alternative cancer treatments in that country. Perhaps I could buy some Laetrile and/or marijuana while there and slip it back over the border! Then, in an unbelievable coincidence, an old and dear friend (Bob Cross) from college days called and said: "Jim, I'm making a trip to Mexico and wonder if you would like to go with me?" He then told me that he had recently retired from his job as controller of a large, regional trucking company and wanted to spend several weeks in Mexico exploring possible places where he might retire.

I told Bob about my cancer that seemed to be in remission at the time and that I would discuss such a trip with Gwen and call him back. When I mentioned a possible trip to Mexico to Gwen, she was enthusiastic about the idea. *(In fact I thought she was a bit too enthusiastic about this idea!)* Seriously though, both of us thought the trip might relieve our family stress. I immediately got back in touch with Bob (who lived in Charlotte, NC) to tell him that I was eager to go to Mexico with him. We began making plans to meet at the home of my sister, Nell White Turner, who lived just outside Blacksburg, SC. I would arrive at my sister's house the day before, spend the night there, and be ready to leave when Bob arrived.

Before leaving Virginia, however, I called two old friends from USDA days to tell them about my trip. The first was Mike Bay, who had retired from USDA and was now living in Brownsville, Texas, which is on the border with Mexico. The second was Ken Goodrich, who was USDA's Information Officer for the joint U.S./Mexico screwworm program. He was currently living in Mexico and working out of the U.S. Embassy in Mexico City. This could be an important stopover since he was traveling extensively in that country. I had been a close associate of both Mike and Ken while serving as Information Officer for USDA APHIS.

When I told Mike that my friend Bob and I would be passing Brownsville on our way to Vera Cruz, he urged us to stop by the house he shared with his wife, Betty. He said they owned a condo in Mexico and that we might have an opportunity to stay in their condo and check on it for them. He said the condo was on the Pacific

Ocean in the village of Puerto Vallarta. *This town was just becoming a tourist attraction because the movie, "Night of the Iguana," starring Elizabeth Taylor and Richard Burton was filmed there.*

Mike explained that Betty's mother was quite old and infirm and that her fragile condition prevented them from visiting and checking on the condo as often as they would like. Since Bob and I had already planned to stop overnight at a motel in Brownsville before crossing the border, a visit with Mike and Betty Bay seemed like a great idea. We felt they could help guide our trip and give us some useful information about Mexico. And it would give us a chance to talk about the possibility of visiting their condo. *At that time our plans did not include a visit to the Pacific Ocean, but then plans can change.*

When I called to tell Ken Goodrich we planned to visit Mexico City, he made me promise to call him as soon as we arrived in that capital city. He also said he wanted us to stay with him and his wife, Beverly, and two sons, who lived in the suburbs of Mexico City. He said they were always happy to have American visitors.

# CHAPTER 21

## Mexico--Here We Come!

BOB ARRIVED AT Sister Nell's house just after daybreak and I moved my trip belongings, including medicines, into Bob's almost new van which he had equipped with a single bed. The neat thing about this bed was that we could alternate driving with one of us resting on the bed or even dozing while the other drove. Soon we said goodbye to my relatives and we headed south, following a map prepared for Bob by AAA. The map showed that the trip to the Mexican border should take about 20 hours with one overnight stop. By alternating driving, we arrived at our motel in Brownsville well before dark the second day and called the Bays, who invited us to dinner and gave us directions to their house.

Betty had prepared a terrific Tex-Mex dinner for us and then the two of them began urging us to change our itinerary to include Puerto Vallarta. They explained that after they retired, they purchased two condominiums, one for them, and one for Betty's mother. But after moving there, the mother's health began declining rapidly and they needed to return to the U.S. for her medical care. They sold one condo and purchased homes on the U.S. side of the border in Brownsville, TX. They kept the second condo for investment purposes and as a vacation home.

They said that because of Betty's mother's continuing severe health problems, they had not visited their remaining Mexican condo in a long time, and that they would really appreciate it if we added that town to our itinerary. They said that since "The Night of The Iguana," Puerto Vallarta had become a popular place to visit and that we could have an enjoyable (and free) stay there as long as we wanted.

They hoped we would inspect their condo and if we found anything wrong let them know ASAP so that they could have the problem corrected. After some further thinking and discussion, Bob and I decided to change our itinerary to include Puerto Vallarta-- even though it added many miles to our trip. The Bays then gave us a key to the condo along with directions to it. Since we planned to re-enter the U.S. at a different American city, they asked me to mail the keys to them after I returned home. They also asked me to call them with a report on our visit to Mexico, and especially, Puerto Vallarta.

Once we entered Mexico and the border town of Matamoros the next morning, we found that almost everyone we encountered could speak passable English. After we entered "the real Mexico," we quickly found we were on our own in the language department. The farther we went, the harder it was to find anyone who could speak any English. I had foolishly thought that, when I began listening to Spanish on Mexican radio stations, the Spanish language I had taught at Sanford, NC, high school some 30 years ago would quickly return.

Nothing could have been further from the truth. After a day of intense listening and attempting to converse in Spanish with any Mexican we met, very little of that long buried Spanish had emerged from my memory bank! When we arrived at our first night's stopover in Mexico, I did not even remember how to order our room. And the clerks there spoke no English. I shamefacedly retrieved the English/Spanish dictionary I had brought with me and used it to find the Spanish words to order a place to spend the night.

With help from the dictionary I finally came up with: "Quiero una habitación de usted hotel para dos." A pitiful and ungrammatical first attempt! *A simple "Quiero cuarto," had I remembered, would have done it!* With further information from the dictionary, I was finally able to secure a suite for us that had separate bedrooms. Needless to say, the English/Spanish Dictionary became my companion for much of the rest of the trip. After a month, some of the long-hidden Spanish language did begin to emerge from my memory and I did not have to rely on the dictionary as much.

Our next stop was at the beautiful seaside city of Vera Cruz, which I had visited while a member of the Naval Reserve. As mentioned earlier, Vera Cruz is famous for its fresh seafood and we eagerly partook of that. *We, of course, had been warned not to drink the water (unless boiled) and not to eat fresh raw vegetables, i.e., don't order a salad with your meal.* Most of the time, we observed those food/liquid rules religiously. We had brought along a portable water boiler to use in our suite or room each night. However, before leaving Vera Cruz, one night at a restaurant I ordered an iced drink with my meal, forgetting that the infamous "tourista" bacteria could (and did) survive in ice.

Bob was protecting himself by drinking straight tequila by the water glass full! A few days later, we left Vera Cruz heading in the direction of Mexico City but stopping and sightseeing at small historic villages designated by AAA. Bob continued drinking straight tequila and remained in seeming good health. On the other hand, I occasionally had an iced drink with my meal. Each day my stomach became more and more "queasy." I attributed this to the food we had been eating and the odor of feces that now seemed to follow us everywhere we went.

Before going to Mexico we were aware that many of their farmers used human feces as fertilizer but we did not expect the smell to be omnipresent. We even began dreading to go into what appeared to be nice restaurants because we knew the smell would penetrate walls and kill our appetites. The scent was not bad in border towns and larger cities where tourists tend to congregate. But Bob and I had wanted to get to know the "real" Mexico and ordinary Mexicans, so we avoided most large cities and border towns. And paid a price for it!

# CHAPTER 22
## "Tourista" Grabs Hold of Me

BY THE TIME we arrived at the capital city, I was in terrible shape. We stopped at a business location within the city and found a clerk who spoke some English. When he saw the condition I was in he asked if he could help me. I told him I needed to speak to a friend at the American Embassy. He volunteered to make the call for me. After dialing and getting a response, he handed the phone to me and I asked for Ken Goodrich. Ken picked up the call quickly and said: "Jim, I'll check out of the office right now and come get you. The two of you can follow me to my house. Bev is expecting you."

I replied: "Ken, I'm going to die and I don't want to complicate your life by dying in your home. Can you make reservations for us somewhere close to where we are now?" *(I asked the clerk to give him the address we were calling from)*. Ken replied that I probably had the "tourista" or "Montezuma's revenge" as some call it, but that I would not likely die from it--although I might want to.

He added: "After a night's sleep, you'll feel much better. Actually, you're in luck about finding a place to stay tonight; if you look across the street you will see a nice, small hotel that our Embassy uses to place guests. I'll call them now and make reservations for you and your friend. And we'll be able to get you a nice discount. Call me tomorrow as you get ready to check out and you'll be ready to enjoy a stay at our house."

I thanked him and the young Mexican man who had assisted us and we drove across the street to the hotel where Ken had reserved a suite for us. The suite had a kitchen and two bedrooms and two baths. However, the person sleeping in the second bedroom had to come back through the first bedroom to get to the second bath. Although it was not yet dark, I immediately went to bed in the first bedroom. Bob left to get a light supper for himself while I remained in bed. Even the thought of food made me nauseous. When Bob returned and finished freshening up in his bath room, he went to his bedroom. I did not expect to see him again until morning.

With the condition I was in, I slept fitfully and became aware that Bob was walking through my bedroom to his bathroom. Since he usually slept through the night, I suspected something was wrong and asked if he was also getting the "tourista." But he replied that his stomach was fine but he was "seeing things," e.g. "strange patterns and shapes" every time he tried to sleep. *Google says this is known as a "visual hallucination." For example, "you might see insects crawling on your hand or on the face of someone you know. Or brightly colored spots or shapes." Once, when I was running a high fever, I saw "newsprint" on the walls and ceiling of my bedroom. Shades of my old newspaper career???*

By the next morning, my stomach was much better and I was ready to again start enjoying Mexico. After awakening, Bob was no longer "seeing things" and was also ready to go. At mid morning I called Ken to tell him, "I am back among the living. Is your offer to put us up still good?" When he said "yes" I told him that we could entertain ourselves until he got off from work. He said: "I won't wait until quitting time. I'll be at your hotel before check-out time and you guys can then follow me home."

As I recall, the Goodrich family lived in a large, comfortable home enclosed by a tall wall. As an indication of the life Americans can live in third world countries such as Mexico, they had a house maid and yard man. We were glad to be with friends who spoke English and our hosts were happy to have visitors from "back home."

During our conversation that evening, I brought Ken and Bev up to date on my health situation and told them I wanted to obtain some marijuana and alternative medicines, such as Laetrile, while in Mexico. They, of course, were well aware that both of these products were illegal in the U.S. but were legal and easily available in Mexico. Ken said, "I would have no problem getting you marijuana right here but it may be easier to get the Laetrile along the border, where alternative medicine doctors are treating Americans with cancer."

With a grin, he added: "If we go outside to our fenced back yard, you may be able to pick your own marijuana from a 'wild' plant growing back there." His smile made me suspect that the back yard marijuana plant may not have been completely "wild." After all, one of the Goodrich's sons was a rock musician and might be familiar with "weed." Also, the native yard man could have put in a few "wild plants." I didn't try to pin Ken down on such matters.

During our stay, Ken also cleared up the issue of Bob's "strange visions" he suffered the night we arrived in Mexico City. When Bob told Ken about his "visions," Ken laughed and asked, "Have you been drinking lots of tequila?" Bob sheepishly admitted that he had been drinking straight tequila every night. Ken then explained that although tequila is not regarded as a "true hallucinogenic drug," it can sometimes make a novice drinker "see things" if they drink too much of it. With that information, Bob cut down on his tequila consumption and no longer "saw things" when trying to sleep.

Ken had traveled Mexican roads extensively and he re-enforced the need to be cautious of both Mexican "policia" and "banditos" while on Mexican highways. Before we left, Ken took us to a bank to obtain lots of small bills with which to pay "Mordita" (Spanish for bribe) to policemen who might stop our car for any or no reason. He said that the policia would usually accept a small amount of cash and let you go. Otherwise, you might end up in a Mexican jail--something to avoid if possible. After discussions of the practices of the Mexican policia, I decided it might not be smart to carry marijuana in our van while traveling around Mexico.

In addition, I had begun to have doubts about the advisability of carrying any illegal items into the U.S. in my friend's van. I certainly didn't want to cause him any trouble and carrying illegal drugs could conceivably cause his new van to be confiscated. This whole issue required more serious thought.

After spending a couple of enjoyable days and nights with the Goodrich family we prepared to start our journey toward Guadalajara, one of the cities we most wanted to visit. Ken perused our AAA travel itinerary and agreed that AAA had provided us with a good travel guide. When we told him we were changing our itinerary slightly to include Puerto Vallarta, he made appropriate changes to our map.

Ken had a couple of parting warnings: (1) do not travel at night because of possible attacks by "banditos" or running into livestock which often run loose in Mexico, and (2) be aware that there is no direct route from Guadalajara to Puerto Vallarta. "Be sure to take the long mountain highway route up (north) and then down on the other side following the Pacific Ocean to Puerto Vallarta."

# CHAPTER 23

## Deeper into Mexico

WE SAID OUR goodbyes to the Goodrich family and began "meandering" south, stopping at the many historic sites outside of Mexico City. Some of these towns included Puebla, Querétaro, Morelia, Guanajuato, and Cuernavaca. All of these places were charming and well worth visiting. However, since we wanted to see as much as we could in the shortest time, we concentrated on some things we had already determined would be our high priority. First of all we wanted to visit the pyramids built by the Mayan people who had once lived in southern Mexico, Guatemala, Honduras, El Salvador and Belize. Since the pyramids of Mexico are concentrated in and around Chichen Itza, that was one of our first and longest stops.

The pyramids (built starting nearly 3,000 years ago) are among the most popular tourist attractions of Mexico and Central America. We learned that there are two major types of pyramids: one used for sacrificial rituals and the other for sacred ceremonies. We also learned that some of the Mayan pyramids rising above the jungle were built to serve as landmarks. In addition to the pyramids, we found the ruins of Chichen Itza itself both interesting and educational.

Then we moved on to an extremely attractive city, Merida, which is located near Chichen Itza. We stayed one or two nights at Merida, known as the White City. *(No, the White City was not related to my family name!)* It got its name because (1) its streets and sidewalks are cleaned twice every day and (2) limestone was used to construct most of the city's buildings, giving them a clean white look. Merida is renowned for its elegant hotels and amenities along with its concerts, festivals, parades, and celebrations. Bob and I checked into one of these hotels which had a huge open courtyard used for various celebrations.

Our first night there, an impressive wedding ceremony was underway. And we soon got a firsthand look at a huge Mexican wedding and celebration. We stood on our balcony watching as hundreds of people dressed in formal attire watched and/ or participated in the wedding celebration. There seemed to be more than enough food and drink for everyone there. A large band provided music for listening and dancing. The attendees soon became aware that two "gringos" were watching them from above and began waving to us. We might have tried to join them if we had been better dressed.

Considered one of the safest major cities in Mexico (reflected by its low crime rate) Merida ranks high as a center of diverse culture and rich history. Its beauty includes ornate colonial architecture, (including the oldest cathedral in the Americas) and abundant ancient Mayan ruins that dot the countryside. It also has a welcoming attitude toward tourists and has great food and entertainment. These are just a few features that help explain why Merida is such a joy to visit.

After a couple of days and nights in Merida, we left that beautiful city (regretfully) and resumed our trip heading south toward Guadalajara--one of the major stops on our itinerary. This large city is known for its hospitality, beauty, cuisine, and culture. It is also especially noted for its welcoming of Norte Americanos, as reflected by the large American colony located there. In addition to the above, we had two specific reasons for visiting Guadalajara. They were (1) to explore the city as a possible retirement area, and (2) to check out the small home that old Washington, DC friend, Jesse Clark, had already purchased with the intention of retiring there some day.

*The truth be told, before I contracted cancer I had discussed with Gwen the idea of retiring to Mexico once Mitch had completed college but the cancer had changed our retirement plans considerably.* However, Bob and I spent several days exploring Guadalajara and its surroundings, especially several suburbs where American expatriates seemed to be in the majority. And using directions supplied by Jesse Clark, we finally located the small house he had purchased. The house had little appeal that we could see. It was located in a less desirable part of town and was "squeezed" into a small space between two run down houses.

Knowing Jesse, it was apparent to me that he had not seen the house or area in person and I suspect he bought the house just to "get his foot" into Mexico's door. No doubt he would not be happy to reside in this house long term.

Unfortunately, one late afternoon we overlooked Ken's warning not to ride around Mexico after dark. We had explored some small villages outside of Guadalajara and suddenly realized that it was getting dark and we were lost. After some wrong turns, we finally found ourselves back in the city but didn't know which way to go. Bob spotted two policemen ahead and stopped the car near them. I got out to ask if they would direct us to our hotel. In Spanish, I gave them the name of our hotel and asked them how we could get there.

The policemen did not appear eager to help these "gringos" but one of them finally pointed in the direction we were headed and in rapid Spanish gave me directions. All I could follow was the word "direcha" which means to the "right." I told Bob what I thought the policeman had told us and he turned right at the next intersection. We drove a long ways without finding our hotel.

Then I began to think that I might have misheard the policeman. Perhaps he had said "directo" which means straight ahead. We retraced our drive and this time went straight ahead—this time right to our hotel. After more sightseeing in and around Guadalajara (during daylight hours!) for several days, Bob and I thought it was time to leave this beautiful city and continue our journey. Early one morning and following the map, we headed west toward Puerto Vallarta. We spent considerable time that night discussing the route we planned to take.

# CHAPTER 24
## Heading for Puerto Vallarta--or Not!

WE REMEMBERED KEN'S warning not to take what appeared to be a direct route across the country--despite what the map showed. When we left Guadalajara, we still had not made the final decision and were still wondering if we could escape that long trip up and down the mountain. After an hour or so driving on a nice four lane paved road out of Guadalajara, we spotted a sign pointing to the right to a two lane road up the mountain. Bob slowed down and paused while we decided whether to take the mountain road or continue following the nice four lane road straight ahead toward Puerto Vallarta.

We thought that the direct route might have been completed since Ken was in that part of Mexico and continued on past the sign. After all, the current map we were looking at clearly showed what looked to be a road going all the way to the Pacific Ocean. So, after Bob had driven past the sign to the mountain highway we made the decision to keep going on that nice, straight road.

We continued straight ahead on this highway for several hours until we entered a very modern looking small town and sailed right through town on its wide, well maintained street. Then, just as we were congratulating ourselves on disregarding Ken's advice, the road ended abruptly. Dead End! Not a single lane continued west.

We turned the car around and began trying to find someone who spoke English and who might show us the direct way to Puerto Vallarta. We talked with several Mexicans and with a combination of their "broken" English and my "broken" Spanish, we eventually learned that the road which appeared to continue on toward the Pacific was just a trail that could only be traveled by donkey or on foot. Since we didn't care to exercise either of those options, we knew that the only course left for us was to: (1) go back the way we had come, almost to Guadalajara and take that dreaded mountain road or (2) go all the way back to Guadalajara, spend another night there, and get a fresh start the next day.

After more discussion and still in a "daredevil" mood, we decided to take a chance on driving in darkness and dodging bandits, burros, cattle and other animals as well as people we might encounter on the mountain road. We had the foresight to fill the van up with gas before proceeding so we wouldn't be stranded in the dark on the side of a mountain. It was my job to watch for anything (or people) in the road while Bob paid full attention to driving that narrow mountain road. It was a scary ride and Bob had to make several sudden stops to avoid hitting animals or people but at around 10 p.m. we arrived in Puerto Vallarta. Then we began looking for Mike and Betty Bay's condo.

Within a half hour, we found their condo building and took the elevator to their floor following directions from the envelope which also contained the key to the condo. After finding the right door number, I first tried to open the door with the key but failed. We then took turns trying to get the condo door to open. We didn't bother ringing the doorbell since no one was occupying the condo. Or so we thought! Then, as we stood in front of the door, to our great surprise, the door was suddenly opened by a partially clad Mexican man who appeared to be as surprised as we were.

In good English, the Mexican man quickly began explaining that he was an attorney for the condo development and that he was checking on the condo. His story didn't make sense. Why would a condo attorney be checking an owner's condo with clothing askew at 10 p.m.? Then his story fell completely apart when another scared looking man (also not fully dressed) appeared at the door. This man was also quite noticeably effeminate.

Both began apologizing profusely for being in "our" condo. We gradually realized that they were a pair of homosexuals who feared they might be in serious trouble because they had no right to be in this condo at night. Thinking that the best defense is a good offense, we boldly told them to finish dressing and "get out of our condo." They got out in a hurry, apologizing as they fled toward the elevator.

We were lucky we arrived when we did because neither bed had yet been disturbed. Bob and I were both very tired after the long day driving on narrow mountain roads, the last hundred or so miles in the dark! So, we wasted little time discussing the day's events and headed to our separate bedrooms. However, before I went to sleep, I did wander around the condo a bit and thought it strange that none of the family pictures placed around the condo showed Mike or Betty Bay. Must have been some of their favorite relatives pictured. Then I went to sleep.

The next morning, Bob and I figured out how to use the coffee maker and spent an hour or so drinking coffee and talking about our experiences the previous day. We chuckled about the frantic manner in which the two obviously gay men finished dressing and fled down the hallway. We still wondered why the key Mike gave us didn't work and figured we might need to visit the condo office to ask for another key.

Then a thought began to form in my mind. Asking Bob to stay inside the condo (so we wouldn't get locked out), I went outside and made a final try to open our door with the key Mike had provided. Still no luck! Asking Bob to keep the door open, I walked across the hall and tried the key in the door to that condo, which opened easily. I did a quick look inside and saw a plaque with the words: "Mi Casa Es Su Casa" signed "Mike and Betty Bay." I also spotted several pictures of Mike and Betty on the walls of that condo.

This confirmed what I had begun to suspect: Mike had given us the correct key but had mistakenly written down the door number to what had once been their second condo. *Which of course had been sold to someone not presently occupying it*. We quickly moved all our belongings across the hall to the condo the Bays still owned. Luckily we had left the door to the second condo open so we could return to straighten it up and to leave a brief note to the real owners explaining what had happened.

We spent a few pleasant days and nights in the Bay's luxurious condo. While sight-seeing one day, we went to the dock to see the Princess Line's Cruise Ship (known as "The Love Boat") arrive in port. The disembarkation looked just like TV's version of the then popular ABC show "The Love Boat," a continuing TV series about Princess Line's cruise ship, and some of its crew and passengers. You may remember: Ted Lange, as Isaac the Bartender; Bernie Kopell, as Doc; Fred Grandy, as Gopher; Lauren Tewes, as Julie the Cruise Director; and Gavin MacLeod, as Ship Captain Stubing.

The only crew member visible to us that day was the ship's real "cruise direc-tor" who stood at the top of the gang plank helping passengers disembark with her skirt blowing in the wind just like Julie's at every disembarkation in the TV show. *Note: although Fred Grandy played the part of "slow thinking" Gopher, this part did not reflect the real Fred Grandy who was a Harvard graduate, a four term U.S. Congressman from Iowa, CEO of the large charitable organization, Goodwill, and finally a star on radio station WMAL, Washington DC.*

Other than watching the "The Love Boat" come and go, we rested up from our many days en route, browsed and enjoyed good food and drink at this suddenly popular tourist attraction. We also explored the small towns and villages near Puerto Vallarta but always returned to the condo well before nightfall. *(There were no prob-lems with the condo to report to Mike and Betty, but we shared some laughs about the mix up of key and condo). From my personal standpoint, the stay at the condo gave me a chance to get some restful sleep for a change.*

By way of explaining that last comment, although Bob and I had been friends for many years, we had never spent a single night in the same facility. On this trip, I discovered that he snored loudly and continually while sleeping. (I suspect the easy availability of cheap alcohol might have worsened this problem). When we were able to get accommodations with two bedrooms, things were not so bad sleep-wise for me. But sometimes when darkness was approaching and we were caught in a small town where we had to share one room with two beds, I was in serious trouble.

In these cases, Bob was always the first to go to sleep at which time the loud snor-ing began and sleep became impossible for me. Often, my desire for some peaceful sleep forced me to go outside and spend the night in the van. I was told that this was extremely dangerous; that Mexican bandits were always on the lookout for American vehicles to break into. Although their purpose was to steal, if occupants were inside the vehicle, they would most likely be attacked, robbed or even killed. Because of Mexico's strict gun laws, I didn't dare bring my pistol with me on the trip so I was essentially defenseless when sleeping in the van. But sleep deprivation caused me to take chances I would not ordinarily take.

# CHAPTER 25
## Thinking of Home

AFTER A LITTLE over a month exploring Mexico, Bob and I agreed we had enjoyed about all of Mexico we could stand. Both of us had become acutely sensitive to the stench of human feces that permeated the air almost everywhere we went. *So after some discussion, the two of us decided to cut our expected 6 week tour short by about a week. By that time, neither of us had any remaining interest in retiring to Mexico. And I had decided not to risk buying and transporting illegal marijuana or Laetrile into the U.S.*

But we still had a long drive back to the U.S. with several large, steep mountains standing in our way. If you've never traveled across the interior of Mexico in a vehicle, you probably cannot grasp just how difficult it can be. I'm talking about the high mountains you must cross from southwest heading northeast to the Texas border. First of all, mountain roads in Mexico are extremely rough and narrow, hardly wide enough for two vehicles to pass each other. These roads also must accommodate humans on foot, in wagons, trucks, buses, etc. Then you have to deal with wildlife and livestock.

Adding to travelers' discomfort are the scenes of cars, buses and trucks which have gone down the side of a mountain. It's really sad to see the number of religious artifacts (usually crosses and flowers) placed along the side of mountain roads as memorials to relatives and friends who failed to survive trips up or down the mountainside. These pathetic memorials, along with lack of guard rails, do not inspire confidence in those who have to travel Mexico's mountain roads.

Finally, after a couple more days, we breathed a huge sigh of relief when we were past that last mountain and crossing the border to U.S. soil! When we arrived safely in the town of Laredo, Texas, we headed for the first McDonald's we could find. Neither of us were fans of these fast food places but the thought of a clean restaurant which smelled of burgers and fries (with no hint of human feces) had both of us drooling. *Incidentally, we had passed through Nuevo Laredo, the last place we could legally buy marijuana and Laetrile, without even slowing down.*

After eating some "Big Macs," drinking some water that did not require boiling, and being able to take some deep breaths, inhaling clean air, we decided to head to our respective homes with no further overnight stops. I drove the entire night across

Texas and several other states while Bob slept (and snored). He awoke in time to finish the drive the next day to Sister Nell's house. I spent the night with Nell and Clayburn Turner and Bob continued on to his home in Charlotte.

# CHAPTER 26

## Back Home in Old Virginia

WHEN I RETURNED home to Virginia, I was excited to see Gwen and (later) Mitch. However, Gwen had some bad news for me. Old and dear friend, Dr. Fred Whittemore (Big Red) had passed away at his desk at the State Department while I was in Mexico. Although Gwen and I had talked a few times (when I could find a public telephone that worked, which was infrequent) she did not want to break this sad news to me by telephone. I appreciated the fact that she represented us at Fred's funeral. And his wife, who knew how close Fred and I had been, asked Gwen to take several of Fred's shirts (bought just before his death) home to me.

I treasured those shirts, wearing them for years, but never putting one on without thinking of my good friend now gone. I shed quite a few tears for his absence. Knowing he is with God helped lessen the pain of his loss but few days go by that I don't remember him--especially as I get older.

Some good news upon my return was seeing the progress Roger had made in finishing the exterior of the addition, along with interior walls. Together, we began building the large deck on the back of the addition, along with an enclosed porch on the back of the little farm house. We also completed framing for the studio over the 3-car garage. This required some extra time because of the three skylights Gwen wanted placed precisely to give her proper lighting for her painting.

Then I began helping Roger install the special roof sheathing required for metal roofing which would extend across the entire project, including garage, old farm house, and new addition. Then I called the specialists in metal roofing to cover the project and soon the house was "dried in" i.e., protected from the weather so that installations for drywall, trim, flooring, etc. could begin.

During the entire reconstruction and construction period, I had been looking for appropriate material that would match the look we wanted to achieve. Some people described it as Georgian style. One day we had found a large, beautifully carved front door with leaded glass in an antique shop in Woodbridge, VA. Both Gwen and I thought it was perfect for the main house. However, we hesitated to buy it, knowing it would be difficult if not impossible to find a smaller door to match or complement this door. Then we remembered that several weeks earlier, Laws Auction in Manassas, VA had planned to auction off a smaller, but very similar door.

Although we both thought this door would be perfect for the front entrance to the farm house, we did not even attend the auction because of the same fear that kept us from buying this door. We thought that there was only a small chance that the door we saw at Laws Auction might somehow still be available. But there was that possibility and we might be lucky.

I asked the antique shop owner if she would hold the large door for a couple of hours while we drove to Manassas to see if by chance the beautiful, smaller door had not sold or if it had sold, try to get the name of the buyer and see if he would sell it to us for a profit. *At that point, we would have paid almost any price to have these two doors which would be perfect for the front of our new home.*

The antique shop owner was perfectly willing to hold the door for us. I gave her a small, non-refundable deposit and Gwen and I began the drive to Manassas. Although normally a very careful driver, I threw caution to the wind and we violated all speed laws as we raced to Manassas. As soon as we arrived, I located owner Sonny Laws and told him our story. Sonny grinned and said: "Jim, a guy bought that door, gave us a deposit, and told us he had to go home for the rest of the money. We held it for him more than the required time but he never came back. We're going to put it in our next auction."

Since we had been good customers of Laws Auction for years, we asked Sonny if he would consider selling it to us now, rather than put it in the auction again. He agreed to sell it to us at the same price it brought at the previous auction. We loaded this door in our station wagon, took it to the building site and immediately drove back to the antique shop to finish paying for the larger door and to transport it back to Blue Dan Lane. When we placed the two doors side-by-side, they were an almost perfect match--except for size. We could not believe our good fortune.

# CHAPTER 27

## Search for Architectural Antiques Continues

SOON AFTER THAT success, I read a newspaper ad saying an old "ice house" was being torn down and that it contained lots of old "heart pine" wood that could be salvaged. I immediately thought I might be able to get enough old pine to use as flooring for the addition. Hopefully, it would match or complement the heart pine floors in the little farm house. We had already gone to a large salvage yard in Richmond, VA, hoping to find appropriate flooring material. The Richmond salvage place had no old flooring that came close in looks to our existing flooring.

The Richmond salvage company did have flooring material from large beams salvaged from old mill buildings being torn down. After it had been re-sawn and planed it was beautiful, but it was very expensive and we didn't think it would match up well with the existing floors. We decided to hold out for authentic, aged, heart pine flooring--if it could be found. Then, we decided to take a look at the old ice house about to be torn down. I knew that when ice houses were being built, heart pine was inexpensive and readily available. I had nothing to lose except a couple of hours of my time, and money for gasoline.

A couple of days later, I was in my pickup heading toward Edinburg, VA which is a little over an hour away just off I-81. I soon located the old ice house facing demolition and went inside to check it out. Although the old floors were in pretty rough shape, a good sanding might make it compatible with the existing floors which could use some sanding and finishing themselves. Then I looked up and saw that the builder had used two layers of the same tongue and groove flooring materials for wall sheathing. Since this wall covering had never been walked on, it was in perfect condition, though over 100 years old.

Needless to say, I immediately purchased more than enough of the material to use as finish flooring for both levels of the 4,000 square foot addition. Of course I knew Mitch and I faced some hard work in removing the material from the walls, pulling the nails, and then hauling it back to the job to be installed. I also knew I would need to make several trips in my ¾ ton pickup to make sure I had all the material I needed, plus about one third more. I paid the representative to hold the material for a few days since I needed to bring more tools (and Mitch) to help with this job.

Before leaving the area, I spotted an antique shop and decided to go do a little browsing while I was close by. Inside the antique shop, I immediately saw two large, matching antique fireplace mantels made from old heart pine. I thought these would be perfect for the new great room and master bedroom suite fireplaces. I purchased and loaded the mantels on the pickup to take home with me. This trip had certainly proved productive.

As another stroke of good luck, I remembered seeing a supply of wider heart pine planks (without tongue and groove) at the old ice house. I stopped back there and selected enough of this material to make a third mantel for the basement level. Since I had the tools and know-how to make a matching basement mantel from this material, I was ecstatic about that day's activities. *Note: By that time I was owner of an old model Sears Roebuck table saw which enabled me to make precise cuts. It also had its own attached planer which was useful in finer detail work.*

Then, God continued to shine His light on me. Wondering how I would find enough vintage trim to make the addition to the little farm house appear authentic, I spotted a small notice in a Washington area paper stating that Linton Hall, a very old private Catholic school in Bristow, VA was going to be demolished that summer and replaced with a new building. That was certainly worth exploring.

*A brief history of Linton Hall: its land was once part of the Linton's Ford plantation in Bristow, VA. It was owned by the Linton family since the 18th century. In 1894, Sarah Linton converted to Catholicism and became a Benedictine nun, and donated the property to the Roman Catholic Church. She asked that the property be used to establish schools for poor girls and boys. Linton Hall Military School was founded in 1922; however, in 1989, the school ended its military and boarding school status and became coeducational. Before I saw it personally, it had already been renamed Linton Hall School many years earlier.*

Although no mention was made in the ad as to whether or not any material from the old building could be salvaged, I decided it was worth a trip to see. Soon afterward, Mitch and I headed to Bristow where we located the school building as well as the Benedictine nun in charge of the project to demolish and rebuild. When I asked if we could look inside the building she said she was glad to show us. When I asked about the possibility of salvaging parts from the building, she said this question had not been considered but she was open to suggestions; that they could certainly use the money.

After a tour of the building, I wrote down a list of items that I wanted to salvage for use in our project at Redlac Estates. Among these were: (1) enough beautifully carved vintage window and door trim to finish our large house; (2) enough 150 year old handmade wainscoting to accommodate our formal dining room; (3) a wide 10 foot plus tall staircase ending with a fancy, circular bottom landing; and (4) enough solid 6-panel interior doors in the right sizes I needed for our house. Although we probably salvaged many other items, e.g. light fixtures, they escape my memory.

The nun in charge (don't remember her name) was happy that parts of the old building would be saved and re-used but had no idea of what to charge me. After getting prices from Manassas Lumber for new material, I shared these prices with her. She was very pleased to accept my offer. *The fact is, I would never have found anything really "comparable" to these architectural antiques at a lumber yard or trim shop.*

The two things that stand out in my mind the most were: (1) the wonderful wainscoting and (2) the beautiful, over-sized staircase. I would never have been able to find those items new and it would have cost a small fortune to have the material copied in a millworks shop. And my visits to various architectural salvage yards never resulted in "finds" such as these.

# CHAPTER 28
## After Successful Search--Finishing Begins

I KNEW THAT it might be difficult to make some of these items fit our house's walls but had enough faith in Roger's skills that I was reasonably sure he could solve any problem of retrofitting if and where needed. I tackled the wainscoting myself. My major problem was that the wainscoting had been handmade by carpenters to fit several smaller rooms which were part of a structure built 150 years previously. They were enclosed within the newer Linton Hall built around 1922.

Thus there was a variety of lengths and widths of the wainscoting which complicated getting a perfect fit for four different walls all the same height, in our "soon to be" formal dining room. The first thing I did to make these disparate vertical strips fit was to cut all of them to the same length. To compensate for the slightly smaller height, I used a taller baseboard. Then I began "sorting" and "lining up" the custom made sections to see how close a fit I could obtain. After moving the sections around several times and making small adjustments I was satisfied enough to tack the sections in place. This allowed me to make any final changes needed before I began fastening them to the wall permanently.

Ultimately, I tacked them into place four times and took them down four times before I was satisfied with the fit on the fifth try. The last piece of wainscoting left me with a one inch space in one corner. I was able to hide this "less than perfect" fit by sawing and then gluing a one inch piece to this panel. The table saw and planer really came in handy in making precise cuts here. Once I glued the two pieces together and painted everything, no one could spot the difference.

I knew that installing the oversize staircase was way beyond my capability, so all decisions on that job were left to Roger. He enlarged the opening enough to accommodate the extra width and adjusted the risers to shorten the staircase slightly. But, since Mitch and I had had to disassemble the staircase to get it out of Linton Hall and then into the house, this process had made things easier for Roger. By removing the same small amount from each riser, when he re-assembled the staircase he was able to get an exact fit for each floor. And the large, fancy, circular bottom landing looked as if it had been custom made for the house. Fortunately, the architect's plan had called for a 10 foot wide hallway so there was plenty of room for the circular landing.

Hanging the Linton Hall doors was simple for Roger. He made door frames from new wood to fit all the interior doors and they went into place like "pre hung" doors. For the sake of energy efficiency, I bought high quality new, double insulated windows appropriate for a Georgian style house and Roger quickly installed them.

After that, a drywall crew installed and finished the walls and ceilings and a flooring contractor installed the beautiful, wide heart pine flooring salvaged from the old ice house. As soon as this was finished, Roger began installing the interior door and window trim we had removed from Linton Hall. *Note: While awaiting installation of the trim, I had built a large vat out of marine plywood and had dipped the trim into this vat filled with water and Red Devil Lye. After soaking in the vat a few hours, the lye/water bath loosened and removed much of the old paint. Any remaining paint was easy to scrape off. After thoroughly cleaning the trim, I patched and sanded any areas that needed it. Finally, after it dried and a new coat of good primer had been applied, the trim looked almost like new and was ready for Roger to install.*

**A word of caution: although Red Devil Lye is effective at stripping old paint from wood, it can be quite dangerous and persons doing this should wear protective clothing, mask, safety glasses and waterproof gloves.**

The finishing work went fast and efficiently with a crew hanging and finishing all the drywall in a few days, followed by another crew installing the floors which would be sanded after most of the work was done. Electricians, plumbers, and heating and air conditioning crews finished their work. I was able to get a good deal on solid cherry wood kitchen and bath cabinets by paying cash and Roger handled the installation. Everything was soon in working order and the house passed final inspection.

In the final stages, as Roger finished with a room, Gwen and I painted it. *Gwen was far better at painting than I and deserves most if not all the credit for the beautiful finished job.* As soon as an area was painted and dried, we began moving furniture into it. We were anxious to move to our new house and away from the railroad tracks that were now far enough away that no one would have to listen to the "wolf howls" of our Alaskan Malamutes when a train passed through town. During odd moments, I had built new dog runs for our three Malamutes along with new houses for each of them. Blue Dan Lane was getting ready for us and the Mals.

# CHAPTER 29
## Time to Complete the Move

I DON'T REMEMBER the exact time but after everything was installed and painting was completed, we made the final move to Redlac Estates. Soon after we were settled, I moved the table saw and other tools into the old farm house so restoration there could be completed. Much of the restoration had been done concurrently with work on the addition. The old trim and plaster had been removed from the walls and ceilings so that the electricians, plumbers. HVAC, et al, had completed "roughing in" these installations while working on the new addition. The same was true of drywall and other work.

We had saved the old, existing trim from the farm house so that Roger and I could re-use it to keep the Victorian cottage look in that part of the house. Fortunately, I had saved some left over Victorian trim from the Clifton cottage restoration which matched the farm house trim perfectly, i.e., with identical square "bullet" corners and floor plinths. Combining all the Victorian cottage trim, we had enough Victorian trim to complete the old house and replace any that was badly damaged. *(Note: I had given this trim the same treatment as that removed from Linton Hall).*

Because of the square "bullet" corners and floor plinths, installation of the Victorian trim went very fast and soon all that was left to be done was to repair and refinish the old, narrow heart pine flooring. Some of the flooring was badly damaged with big gouges in several places. I decided I was best suited to do this job. Professional floor installers and refinishers rarely have the patience or desire to do this work.

Although I had done little refinishing of floors, I had observed lots of this work and an old retired carpenter had shown me how to cut out and replace damaged pieces of tongue and groove flooring without the repair being obvious. *(Ironically, over the years I had to teach this to some professional carpenters unfamiliar with this process. Because of the time and patience required, many carpenters don't want to learn how to do this, preferring to replace an entire board or even section with new boards and try to stain it to match the old!)*

Some of the damage to the floor could be sanded out so I didn't bother with that. When the damage was too deep I began cutting out and replacing these areas. Fortunately, all the stairway needed was sanding and refinishing. Once I was satisfied with the floor repairs, I went to a rental place in Manassas and rented the necessary large floor and hand sanders needed. With some last minute advice from the rental outfit I brought everything back to the house and began sanding.

It probably took me many more days to refinish the floors and stairway than a professional but doing it myself allowed me to preserve much more of the original house material and it was worth the extra time and effort. With more professional advice, I learned that I could greatly speed up the refinishing process by using expensive, wide roller covers--much like painters use. The "low gloss" finish and several light applications with fine sanding in between gave the floors a beautiful soft glow that I wanted to achieve.

# CHAPTER 30
## Improved Health and New Hope

MEANWHILE, ON THE physical health front my health seemed to be improving steadily. My body was still craving and I was eating mostly healthy cancer fighting food by then and feeling much stronger. I had regained some of the weight I had lost from the cancer and people began commenting about my improved, healthier appearance. Some time back I had put away the crutches I had been using. And Gwen and I had stopped looking for an antique wheel chair--which we had thought would eventually be necessary.

Even with this improvement, I had no illusions that I would ever be able to say I was "cured of cancer." Although my improved physical condition was probably just a "remission," I was grateful that I was now completely free of pain and living a more normal life. Of course, I was sad that my relationship with Gwen had remained cold and distant and that I was still relegated to a guest bedroom. But I still loved Gwen and hoped that someday there might be a chance for reconciliation. Also, my relationship with Mitch, which was never bad, was improving daily. I enjoyed going to his tennis matches and did my best to refrain from "wincing" when he missed or made a bad shot. I really enjoyed watching him practice and play. This time we spent together resulted in a "bonding" that might never have occurred.

Time passed and my health continued to improve. Once when I was driving from Manassas to Fairfax, I saw a familiar figure standing by a car parked on the side of the road. It was old friend Dennis Avery, with whom I worked at ASCS, USDA. (Earlier in this memoir, I mentioned that Dennis had visited me in the hospital but that I had no memory of his visit.) When I pulled behind his car to offer assistance, he almost fainted. The first thing he said was: "Jim, I thought you had died. I said my 'goodbye' to you in the hospital when you didn't seem to recognize me. I never returned because my emotions couldn't stand to see you slowly dying. That's why I never visited or called again." After that chance meeting on Veteran's Highway, Dennis and I rekindled our friendship and it remains firm to this day.

On another day, my old friend from EPA, Jesse Clark, who had remained close and supportive of me throughout the cancer ordeal stopped by for a visit. As he was getting ready to leave, he presented me with a book called "Recalled By Life" by Dr. Anthony Sattilaro, MD. Jesse said: "Jim, you may want to read this book. It's the story of a doctor who tells of his recovery from cancer--the same type and stage as yours." He said that the book described how Dr. Sattilaro had changed his diet and lifestyle and credited these changes to his recovery. Jesse added: "I've seen a big change in your health since you changed your diet from mainly red meat to more fruits and vegetables."

Although I was skeptical that the book would have any relevance to me, I was pleased that Jesse was still demonstrating his friendship by buying, reading and bringing the book to me. So, as soon as he left, although still skeptical, I began reading it. First of all, I was impressed to learn that Dr. Sattilaro had practiced traditional medicine for 25 years and had reached the position of chief executive officer of a large metropolitan hospital in Philadelphia. No quack here!

A brief summary from the book:

*The story of Dr. Sattilaro's battle and ultimate victory over one of the most dreaded diseases in America began in late May 1978, with a physical examination. After the tests were done, the radiologist telephoned him to say there was something abnormal in the test results. His X-rays revealed a large tumor in his left side; there was infiltration of cancer in the skull, the right shoulder, the backbones and sternum. Tests had shown cancer of the genital region although the oncologists weren't sure if the prostate or the testicles or both were infected. The prognosis was that he had about 18 months to live.*

*The following week, Sattilaro admitted himself to Methodist Hospital and surgeons performed a biopsy of the prostate, a surgery similar to mine. In addition they opened his chest and removed a rib which was also cancerous. The surgeons determined that his cancer had spread to other parts of the body and decided he needed further surgery which meant he had his third operation in three weeks. The doctors had hoped that with all this surgery his cancer would go into remission. After waiting six weeks, however, his condition was not improving and the doctors decided that treatment would have to continue. Because of continuing pain, his doctors prescribed heavy dosage of several painkillers hoping to give him some relief.*

Wow, I thought. This guy had been in worse shape than I. Although my scans revealed the spread of cancer throughout my bones and into my brain, and our treatment had been similar (i.e. a trans rectal biopsy of the prostate), radiation, additional surgery too gruesome to describe, and female hormone (which I soon flushed down the drain), my pain had lessened since the surgeries while his apparently had not.

I was anxious to find out what remarkable treatment the doctor had found that allowed him to use the words, "Recalled By Life" as the title of his book so I continued reading. I learned that the doctor had found out from lay people (not part of the medical profession) that cancer could be cured by religiously following an eating plan called the "macrobiotics diet." With lots of doubt about the viability of such a diet in curing cancer, the doctor received detailed instruction in the macrobiotic way of life by its proponents. *At that point Sattilaro said to himself, "What the hell, I've got nothing to lose; I'm going to die anyway, so I might as well give the diet a try."* Within ten days to two weeks after beginning the diet prepared for him, Sattilaro said the majority of the pain had disappeared and he stopped the pain medication.

Meanwhile, his colleagues at the hospital were dubious or outright critical of this strange new approach for dealing with cancer. Dr. Sattilaro himself said he had periodic doubts about whether he was doing the right thing because of his long training in traditional medicine. *However, when he remained true to his diet his condition became stabilized, he regained his normal weight and "felt better than he had in years." In fact, he felt so well he decided to have bone scans and other tests done. When results of the bone scans and other tests came back he was completely free of cancer!*

Reading this book gave me the courage to begin thinking that perhaps my diet (somewhat similar to Dr. Sattilaro's) and my improving physical condition might mean that I had a chance to beat cancer. Therefore, I called my primary care doctor and asked him if he would set up a bone scan for me. *Since we had not seen each other in a long time, he was surprised to hear my voice, assuming I had died.* He quickly agreed to get me an appointment at the hospital where a bone scan could be performed. He asked me to come by his office and pick up the prescription and take it to the hospital. He seemed quite surprised at my ruddy complexion and my overall improved appearance. As I left, he said he would call me in a couple of days to give me results of the scan.

I waited a full week and did not receive a call from the doctor. Meanwhile, I was beginning to wish that I had just "left well enough alone." I reasoned that the doctor had not called because he didn't want to give me the "bad news." Finally, I called his office and his nurse said: *"The doctor wants to see you."* My heart sank. *It's rarely good news when the "doctor wants to see you." But I agreed to come to his office the following morning.*

When I entered the doctor's office, he came around his desk, took both of my hands and said: *"It's gone!" I thought he was saying that the bone scan somehow got lost and I asked: "The bone scan?" "No," he replied, "The cancer--it's gone!" I then asked: "Why did you wait so long to tell me?" He said, "I've been studying medical history for the past few days trying to figure out how to explain this to you. I can't find a single case where a patient has survived prostate cancer as advanced as yours!" I replied with a smart ass question: "Why didn't you just call and say, 'It's gone'?"*

My head was swimming when I left his office. I headed straight home to call Gwen at work to give her the good news and suggest we go out that evening and celebrate. She sounded reserved but happy and early that evening we were sitting in our favorite restaurant, to toast my recovery. *After about an hour of idle chatting, I broached the subject I had to bring up. I told her I hoped she would agree to work with me in making an effort to revive our relationship. Instead, as I feared, she said: "Jim, I need space and now that you've recovered, this is the best time for me to go away on my own."*

Although distressed by Gwen's abrupt refusal to even consider reconciliation, I tried to be understanding. I appreciated the fact she had stuck with me throughout the toughest part of my cancer ordeal. I also knew she had to make the break quickly while I was cancer free. *After all, this probably was just a remission and she would have to face a recurrence in the future if she stayed with me.*

Knowing that she had been a good mother to Mitch, I then asked: "Don't you want to keep our son in your life?" Without hesitation she said, "I don't want anyone in my life. I want to be alone." I said: "I still love you Gwen, but I won't try to force someone who doesn't love me to live with me the rest of my life. However, I'm not going to immediately leave the home I've worked so hard on and move into a small apartment somewhere." Then she suggested we live in the same house but maintain our separate lives from each other, i.e., to continue the relationship we had had since soon after the cancer diagnosis.

Because of my deep feelings for her, I knew this arrangement wouldn't work for me very long but perhaps I could stand it while I figured out what to do should my cancer remission be long term (I didn't dare use the word "cure"). I needed time to plan whatever life I had left without Gwen. Despite my sadness and emotional distress about the future of our little family, I drove us back to our beautiful new home and to our separate bedrooms where I cried quietly for hours. Despite what had happened, I was still concerned about what the future would hold for Gwen and Mitch. In fact, my concern may have been even greater since I might not be available to help should they need me immediately or urgently.

The next day I called my lawyer to give him the good news of my apparent recovery and to inquire about the progress of the malpractice lawsuit. At the very least, if my case was settled favorably, my family would be taken care of financially. When he answered the phone, I told him that tests had just shown that I was now free of cancer. He said he was happy for me and asked if this was a remission or cure. I told him *only The Lord could answer that question.* Then I asked him how the lawsuit was progressing. He hesitated and said, "Jim, I need to have a meeting with my co-counsel to discuss progress of the case and I'll call you back with a status report within a week or two."

As promised, the attorney soon called me back to brief me on the case. He said, "Jim, I must tell you that my co-counsel and I have agreed that we should drop the case." I asked him, "Why are you dropping it? A few months ago you said we had an 'air tight' case."

*The attorney replied: "You didn't die, Jim."*

PART 9

STARTING LIFE ANEW, CANCER FREE, AND
AN INVITATION FROM PURDUE UNIVERSITY

# CHAPTER 1
## Adjusting to a New Situation

I SPENT SEVERAL days just trying to adjust to my new situation. Naturally, I was extremely happy to be free of cancer but sad that I had lost the woman I had loved (and still loved) for all those years. I had also just learned that my failure to die had possibly cost my wife and son a financially secure life. Selfish me! Despite these factors, I had no way of knowing whether or not my cancer would return. Was it just a temporary remission?

As my remission continued and my health kept improving, I began giving serious thought to what I was going to do the rest of my life. I was too young to retire, but I didn't want to resume a career at either USDA or EPA, feeling that the stress I had encountered in those two jobs might have contributed to my cancer. And the job at DOE had evaporated with the change in administration. Whatever my future work turned out to be, I didn't want it to be stressful enough to be dangerous to my health. But I knew that I had to start getting busy doing something useful since I was only in my middle fifties.

Because of my love of houses (plus some knowledge I'd accumulated), I finally decided that I might give real estate a try. I knew such a career could be rewarding (but also frustrating and demanding). At the very least, it would "get me out of the house" and help distract me from my present situation. Remembering Gwen's experience, I contacted the Northern Virginia Association of Realtors (NVAR), located in Vienna, VA, about half an hour from our home. They offered a two week course to prepare potential agents for the Virginia real estate test, which was widely known to be very difficult. In fact, I was told that about two thirds of the people flunked it the first time they took it and some never passed it!

I drove to Vienna and signed up for the course and learned that the next session would start in a few weeks. Officials there told me that the course was very intense. They said that although it would cover only two whole weeks, plus three weekends, it was comparable to an entire college course. They told me to expect to receive advance study material a week or more before the start of the course. When I received this material, I skimmed through it and put it aside for later study. Unfortunately, I didn't pick it up again until I was ready to head to Vienna for the first class beginning at 8 a.m. the following Monday.

The classroom was full--mostly of young to middle age people. I spotted what I thought were retired military types known in the DC area as "telephone Colonels." (Note: these are Lt. Colonels where the Lt. is omitted when the office clerk answers the phone). These officers are often a victim of the "up or out" system of the military, meaning if you don't make "full" Colonel within a certain time you are "out," i.e., forced to retire. This is not meant to denigrate them; they're often highly intelligent people who are victims of a harsh system. *You can see quite a few of them doing a great job as analysts for Fox News!*

After about an hour's lecture based on the study material (which I had not studied), the instructor stopped instruction and passed out test questions (timed for 20 minutes as I recall). I didn't get a single test question right. Then, the instructor resumed the teaching for another hour before stopping and passing out another test. I also flunked that one. By the end of the day, I had taken eight tests and flunked all of them! If I had a tail, it would have been between my legs! These failures really got my attention, however. Although I never kept count, I didn't think my total number of "F's" in my entire life had totaled as many as I received in that one day! Before dismissing the class, the instructor passed out a large volume of study material which he suggested we give full attention to before arriving for class the next day. *I paid close attention this time! As soon as I got home, I began studying the next day's lesson and didn't stop (except to eat) until 10 p.m. that evening.* I got up early the next day, fixed and ate my oatmeal, and headed for Vienna. I had spotted a fast food restaurant within sight of NVAR that looked like a good place to get coffee, study, and then walk half a block to the NVAR facility. That became my routine for the rest of my class work at NVAR.

This dedication and routine soon began to pay off. By the second week, I became the "go to" person for other members of the class who wanted to get my views on things discussed in class. And I was making perfect test scores every day before the end of the first week. That weekend was also spent continuously studying. I had gone from "F's" that first day to wanting to be the first person to make a perfect score on the State test. Also, because of my fear of flunking the math part of the State test, I paid for several sessions with a private math tutor.

As testimony of the success of my recent study habits and good grades, the head instructor called me aside and asked me to take "mental notes" at the State exam and then sit down soon after the test and transcribe the significant areas covered by the test. He asked me as a favor to pass along these notes to NVAR so that special emphasis could be placed on those significant areas for succeeding students who would be preparing for the State test. He also asked me to try to remember the "trick" questions famous for "tripping up" those taking the tests.

The test was easier than I expected. In fact, because of my special work with the math tutor, I was actually disappointed that the math questions had not been more challenging. I breezed through the timed test, easily finishing before time expired. My confidence was soaring when I turned in my work to the test monitor.

I met with the NVAR instructors soon afterward to pass along my notes and discuss the test with them--still hoping I had achieved that perfect score. Soon afterward I was notified that I made a very high mark on the test but the record of no one getting a perfect score on the test still remained. ***Darn those trick questions!***

Despite my less than perfect test results, I received calls from several of the top real estate agencies wanting me to come to work for them. After some thought, I decided to go with one of the largest real estate agencies in our area at that time (early 1983). The real estate agency asked me to stop by their Fairfax office to see the space they had assigned me and to pick up my business cards which had already been printed. I looked forward to starting to work with them very soon.

# CHAPTER 2

## Intervention from Heaven?

THEN GOD MUST have decided to take another hand in my future. Over that weekend, the phone rang, and Gwen said: "Jim, it's Dr. John Osmun calling from Indiana." I was pleased to hear from Dr. Osmun, who had been my boss at EPA while he was on sabbatical from his job as head of the Entomology Department at Purdue University, West Lafayette, IN. The first thing John said was: "Jim, I just heard about your recovery from cancer and your friends and I around the country are happy for you." After some chit chat, he suddenly asked me: "Now that you're well, how would you like to 'unretire' and come to work for Purdue University?" I was so surprised I was speechless for a moment and then asked, "What would I be doing at Purdue?"

Dr. Osmun replied: "Purdue has come up with a system of computerizing pesticide chemical brands and uses for each product made from a particular chemical. We're going online soon and thought you would be the right person to help us launch this program, starting in the U.S. but eventually expanding to provide this computerized information around the world. We would like you to be our User Services Manager and No. 2 man working with Dr. Richard Collier, inventor and Director of the system called National Pesticide Information Retrieval System, or NPIRS as we refer to it."

I thought it was strange that someone who had never touched a computer, and did all his writing with an old black Royal manual typewriter, was being offered this important job which obviously would require some knowledge of computers. I immediately made that point to Dr. Osmun. He replied: "Jim, we have plenty of people who are computer experts but none has the knowledge of the subject matter and the writing ability and background you have."

Dr. Osmun continued, "We can teach you how to use a computer. And you have another big asset--knowing and being friends with most of the State pest control officials who will be involved in implementing NPIRS. These officials largely comprise our 'pilot' group and will constitute our first members." He then added, "Initially, you can write the documentation and training materials needed for startup on your old manual typewriter and we'll have someone put it on the computer system. Before long, you will know how to use the computer well enough that you won't need this extra step. Also, that knowledge will allow you to begin giving demonstrations of the system around the country. Dick Collier, who invented NPIRS, will personally make sure of that."

Dr. Osmun then asked: "Would you like to make a trip out to Indiana to check out the situation in person before you make a decision? If you want to take a first-hand look and meet the people you would be working with, we will send you a round trip ticket and find a place for you to stay while you're here." Anticipating a concern that had immediately entered my mind, he said: "If you're wondering if Dr. Collier also wants you, please be assured that he has heard you speak at national meetings and is enthusiastic about the idea of having you come to work for us."

This last statement was extremely important to me; I didn't want to step into a situation where my immediate boss-to-be had been pressured to take me because I was good friends with a "mover and shaker" like Dr. John Osmun. After Dr. Osmun hung up, it took me awhile to absorb the information I had just received. I was astounded that a person working in the Indiana State Chemist's Office had solved a problem that had defied solution by professionals in that field for so many years.

After all, I had been at USDA when that agency spent millions of dollars hiring information technology (IT) companies which tried but failed to develop a program for computerizing pesticide label and usage information. Then, I was at EPA when it spent more millions trying to do the same thing. Efforts by both of these Federal Agencies and their IT companies failed largely because of the huge amount of information involved that needed to be computerized. Most of the basic chemicals had hundreds of products (brands) and thousands of different uses!

How then did Dr. Richard Collier (who I found out later had no computer training) succeed where all these highly-trained professional IT companies failed? You had to know Dr. Collier and see his brilliant mind in action to understand. I later learned he had many and varied talents in other fields.

# CHAPTER 3
## A Trip to Check Out the Purdue Situation

I WENT BY the real estate office that following Monday morning to pick up my business cards and look at the office. However, I felt obligated to inform this company about my Purdue offer and tell them that I wanted to postpone any actual presence on the job there until I had made a decision on whether or not I would be moving to Indiana. Then I called Dr. Osmun and asked him to plan an early trip for me to West Lafayette. Among other things, I needed to make absolutely sure that Dr. Collier really wanted me for this job or whether he was acceding to Dr. Osmun's wishes.

After all, John and I had become close friends while I worked for him and, conversely, while he served as one of my consultants when I became Chief of the Pesticide Certification Program. I knew how persuasive Dr. Osmun could be. I also wanted to make sure I was "up to the job" before putting Dr. Osmun, Dr. Collier, and other fine people at Purdue University in an awkward position. I needed this assurance before giving them even a tentative O.K. to proceed with the hiring process.

When I arrived in West Lafayette, I found that John and wife, Dottie, had arranged a party for me at their home and that Dick and Linda Collier, along with other prominent Purdue people, would be there. It turned out to be a pleasant outside "pig picking," a common way to celebrate in Indiana--a state famous for growing corn, soybeans, and hogs.

*While the party was underway, Dr. Osmun got me aside and told me that as soon as I was settled in at Purdue, he wanted my advice about installing a very old, but still functional, very large windmill in his back yard. He said he had tried to do this once with a large group of his strongest male students but they were unable to get this heavy, unwieldy thing upright and in the ground. After looking this situation over I did not wait to respond: "John, this job is too difficult and dangerous for amateurs without proper equipment to handle. I recommend that you call a professional company with the right kind of heavy equipment to do the job." He took my advice and the large windmill was installed in a short time at moderate cost and injury to no one.*

During this pleasant visit, Dr. Collier assured me personally that offering me the job was as much his idea as Dr. Osmun's. After getting a better idea of the demands of the job, and my ability to handle them, I accepted his job offer verbally. My recent experience with the real estate training and passing the state test made this acceptance easier, giving me confidence that I still had the ability to learn new things, and that I was capable of handling the job.

The assurance that I would receive help in learning how to use a computer from some very bright people also made it easier for me to say "yes" to the job. I felt there would be less stress on me at a university than in the "pressure cooker" of Washington, DC. As expected, Dick told me that "University Protocol" dictated that he go through a certain hiring protocol before I could be officially hired. But he anticipated no serious problems. He said this process could take several weeks because of the "red tape" involved in hiring someone for this job.

He confirmed my suspicion that his office had received many applications for the job and that he was required to sort through and evaluate all of them in order to be able to defend his decision to hire me. What he didn't tell me, and I suspect may not have known himself, was that at least two people on the staff were disappointed that they were not selected for this job. I quickly sensed that there was resentment that they had hired an "outsider," especially one who didn't know how to use a computer. I was happy that I had received my master's degree since Dr. Collier confirmed that because of its location within an academic institution, the position required at least a master's degree. Although as far as I could tell the advanced degree from the University of Illinois had little to do with my job performance, it certainly had been helpful to me as demonstrated by this situation.

Although I never asked about salary, Dr. Collier was aware that I had retired from EPA on a Medical Retirement. So, he simply asked me how much I could make without interfering with my Federal retirement. When I returned home, I again checked with Civil Service to find out that amount and called to inform Dr. Collier of that figure which became my starting salary. Before I began work at Purdue, Dr. Collier informed me that I would also be eligible for all staff benefits, including health insurance, counseling, retirement, and discounted tuition for any of my children who attended Purdue. As a Federal retiree, I never expected to need these benefits but they actually became very useful to me.

# CHAPTER 4
## The Start of My New Life

THE DECISION TO accept the position at Purdue and thus move to Indiana was the beginning of the end of my life with Gwen after 20 plus years of marriage. But it certainly did not end my love for her and the hope that someday she might change her mind about her decision not to consider reconciling. My hope of reconciliation had been diminished a lot by remembering what happened when the Roman Catholic Church removed some of its restrictions which Gwen had followed religiously since she was a child.

*One day Gwen surprised me by saying she was "leaving the Church." When I asked why, she said simply, "The Catholic Church lied to me all these years about what is a sin and what isn't." So, this woman who had prided herself on never missing Mass walked away and never entered the Catholic Church again to my knowledge. When she told me of this decision, a chill went down my spine. I thought: "If I ever seriously disappoint her she might walk away from me the same way she did the Church!" Talk about prophecy.*

When I returned home from Indiana and told Gwen I was taking the position at Purdue, I also said I would be extremely happy if she would go there with me. Not surprisingly she refused that offer. I had arranged a separate meeting with Mitch to fill him in on our situation, i.e., that his mother and I were separating and I would be moving to Indiana. After hearing this, Mitch immediately said that it would be better for me to leave the house and my memories behind and get a new start away from Clifton. Mitch often impressed me with the depth and maturity of his thinking. I don't think I would have survived cancer and my loss of Gwen without his love and support.

*To my everlasting regret, all of these recent family issues probably had a damaging effect on Mitch. He had always been a happy, well-adjusted child. Now his obvious distress caused by my cancer, as well as his mother's inability to deal with it, was beginning to show. Although perhaps it was not noticeable to others, I was aware that the situation was deeply affecting his outlook toward life. It left him with scars that I know lasted for years. And I have guilt about that to this day. As a reflection of this change in all our lives, his attitude changed more to the concept: "Eat, drink, and be merry, for tomorrow we may die." Note: the Internet describes this phrase as a "conflation of two biblical sayings, Ecclesiastes 8:15 and Isaiah 22:13." Ecclesiastes said: "Then I commended mirth, because a man hath no better thing under the sun, than to eat, and to drink, and to be merry." The Isaiah reference said: "Let us eat and drink; for tomorrow we shall die." I feared that this attitude might make a permanent difference in his approach to life.*

One reason for my concern about Mitch was the fact that instead of going to classes at VCU, he was spending his daylight hours hitting with a professional nationally ranked tennis player who was taking a break from the tour. And he was spending much of his night time managing a rock band! Obviously college no longer appeared that important to him. Consequently, he dropped out of school at the end of the first semester with nothing but "F's" and "incompletes" to show for his time at VCU.

This attitude was vastly different from the youngster I had known who had always been a faithful and diligent student without needing parental pressure. Gwen and I had always been the envy of friends and neighbors in the Clifton area because of Mitch's exemplary behavior over the years. Alcohol and drugs were beginning to become a problem with many of the young people in this affluent community but Mitch could not be persuaded to stray from the "straight and narrow" path while he was part of a happy, functional family.

After leaving Richmond and returning to the DC area, Mitch moved out of our home and began sharing an apartment with a friend and helping him start a small trucking business-- similar to today's "Two Men and a Truck" company. However, he remained active in USTA tennis and continued to invite me to his tennis matches so we were able to spend quality time together.

# CHAPTER 5

## Goodbye to My Real Estate Career

ALL OF THIS was happening in the spring and early summer of 1983. As soon as I returned from Indiana, I went by the Fairfax office of the real estate company to tell them my plans had changed. As much as I appreciated their offer, the Purdue job was too good to pass up. They were very understanding and our parting was amicable.

Although we still had a small amount of interior finishing work (mainly installing and finishing drywall in the greenhouse), since I would soon be leaving for Indiana, we went ahead and signed a listing putting the Blue Dan Lane house on the market. We gave the listing to the real estate company I had planned to join. As it always seemed to happen to us, when we needed to sell a house, real estate was experiencing another "down market." We received lots of interest but no solid offers at that time.

In early July, I got a call from Purdue saying that all the paperwork had been completed for my position, and they would very much like for me to be there and on the job by August 1. They said that the deadline for NPIRS to be online was just six weeks away. Over the telephone, Dr. Collier told me that my first priority after unpacking was to complete a large and detailed "NPIRS Users Guide." He said other high priority projects included planning and preparing training material for the 12-member "pilot" group, plus other potential members around the country. I would also need to design and write the first issue of NPIRS News, a newsletter for clients and potential clients, and begin working on a comprehensive Marketing Plan for NPIRS.

Obviously, I would need to hit the ground running once I arrived at Purdue University! Dr. Collier also added that he had already scheduled me to meet with our "pilot" group (A total of 12 mostly state officials) to discuss marketing plans for the system. And he said I would need to travel to Washington, DC to give a demonstration of NPIRS to potential international members.

*Although I looked forward to meeting with the pilot group to discuss things I was familiar with, I was especially nervous about handling my first demonstration of NPIRS. Obviously, I would have to learn enough about computers to go online and conduct searches for strangers who may or may not speak English. At that point I had never even turned on a computer, much less hooked its components together, along with a large monitor that I was told projected the results of searches. The only positive thing I could think of was that the event would be held at the USDA Administration Building where I had once worked. Someone there might be available to give me a hand. I could always hope!*

The deadline for arriving at Purdue meant I had less than a month to wind down my affairs in Virginia and say goodbye to Mitch and Gwen. I had managed to have a "heart to heart" conversation with Gwen about my leaving. For the last time, I asked her to reconsider her decision to "go it alone," to at least leave the door open for a reconciliation someday. She again rejected my suggestion.

After hearing that firm rejection, I said I did not want the two of us "left hanging" forever and that if there was no chance she would ever consider the possibility of reconciliation, I wanted us to have legal separation papers prepared and signed before I left. I thought I would heal faster if some of the strings of our marriage were severed. I did not want to be like "the dog that has its tail cut off an inch at a time." Gwen agreed with me about this issue. Since we did not expect our parting to be confrontational, she agreed we could share an attorney to draw up the paperwork.

*Now, a bit of background about the handling of our finances. Because I had traveled so much during our marriage, I had turned over almost all of our banking and financial affairs to Gwen soon after we were married. This happened after I returned from several trips to learn that Gwen had kept no records of checks she had written or money she had spent. After we had to pay penalties for several overdrawn checks at the bank, I told her she needed to take responsibility for paying our bills and to make sure that we didn't overspend.*

She did a great job of controlling our spending the rest of our marriage and I don't recall ever questioning her decisions on that matter, even though I had some embarrassing moments (described later) because she was dead set against letting me have a personal credit card or checkbook. There was one bank book and she controlled that.

In the Separation Agreement, I agreed to let her continue to receive my Federal retirement money to help with household expenses and to pay for the small amount of refinishing needed for the interior of the greenhouse, or for any other work that needed to be done to help sell the house. *I had already arranged with a contractor who would do the greenhouse job as soon as he was able to work it into his schedule.*

Our agreement also specified that there would be no alimony, since she had resumed her career some time back. However, I had included a provision in the agreement that Gwen could have any or all of our furnishings she needed or wanted for her recently purchased townhouse at Reston, VA. Later, after the house at Blue Dan Lane was sold, proceeds from the sale would be evenly divided between us. Any remaining furniture would be auctioned by Laws Auction and the proceeds evenly divided.

Finally, a provision in the agreement stated that when the Blue Dan Lane house was sold and proceeds divided, my retirement pay would be redirected to me. This meant that at that point she would be completely on her own. She was not happy about that provision but I was adamant that if she wanted her freedom that much, she needed to become self sufficient. Because the distance involved made it difficult and expensive for me to transport large furniture items, I asked only that a few personal items (that would not fit in my little Subaru station wagon) would be turned over to Mitch who would transport them to me on subsequent visits to Indiana.

The attorney sent us the paperwork for the legal separation the day before I was to leave for Indiana. All we needed to do was read it, sign it before a notary public, send it back to him and the legal process of ending our 20 plus years of marriage would begin.

# CHAPTER 6

## Our Last Night Together

ON MY LAST night at Blue Dan Lane, Gwen and I went to our separate bedrooms for what I knew would be a sleepless night for me. As soon I lay down, the tears started silently. Some time before morning, Gwen unexpectedly came to my bedroom, got under the covers with me and quietly said: "Jim, I want you to know how sorry I am for the way I've been treating you." I was touched by that and said, "Gwen, are you sure you want to go through with this?" She replied, "Yes, Jim, I still need my space."

Early the next morning, I finished packing and loading personal items into the Subaru station wagon. Gwen then called a neighbor, a notary, to come witness our signatures on the legal separation paperwork. Both of us controlled our emotions pretty well through the first page of signing; then both of us began sobbing. This was the only time I ever saw her cry. The neighbor, visibly shaken, said: "Are you sure you want to go through with this?" Gwen nodded, and through her tears, could only utter "space." We finished signing the paperwork, I kissed her on the cheek, got into the Subaru, and drove away from Blue Dan Lane. I didn't look back. I had already said my goodbye to Mitch, not wanting him to witness my emotional parting with his mother.

After leaving Clifton, I drove west on I-66 to I-81 and headed north toward Hwy. 70 which goes east and west through parts of Pennsylvania, Ohio and Indiana. I struggled (unsuccessfully) to control my tears. The trip was an absolute nightmare to me. Wishing that I had died with the cancer, rather than to go through this painful parting with Gwen, I often had to fight the urge to end my misery by simply letting the little Subaru go over the side of a mountain. But apparently God was still not ready for that and I successfully fought the urge to end things quickly. Finally, with darkness coming and my tears making it difficult for me to see to drive, I stopped for the night at a small motel near Dayton, Ohio.

Fearful that the motel would not register me as a guest because of my tearful, red-stained eyes I remained in the car for quite awhile trying to regain my composure. Finally, I gave up, went inside where a kind, helpful lady recognized my grief and with few questions assigned me a room for the night. I paid in cash, having only one check (which Gwen handed me along with a small amount of cash as I left) and no credit card, as mentioned above.

*Note: I had carried a U.S. Government Credit Card for much of the time I worked for USDA so I never encountered any money problems when traveling for them. I was not issued a government credit card at EPA, so Gwen always handed me some cash as I was leaving on trips for that agency. I had not carried a checkbook with me since early in our marriage after I turned our financial affairs over to Gwen. She was not overly generous with the cash.*

Below are a couple of humorous incidents resulting from this arrangement. At least they're humorous to me now although not too much fun at the time. Once when I was in Canada with one of EPA's top scientists (who also failed to bring a credit card or checkbook with him), after a fine but expensive dinner the final evening, we ran into trouble the next morning when we started to check out from our hotel. It turned out that both of us were slightly short of the money we needed to pay our bills.

We went to the lobby to try to figure out what to do. So there we sat, two well dressed professional men counting our pocket change trying to come up with enough money to pay our hotel bills. We made it with a single dime to spare. Fortunately we were able to travel to the airport in the hotel's free limo. I held on to that dime like it was gold, knowing it would allow me to call my secretary and ask her to bring enough money down to street level to pay the cab driver transporting us from the airport to USDA's South Building. Boy, were we happy when we saw her standing in front of our office building with enough money to pay the cab driver!

On another occasion, when I was traveling alone on an official trip to Tennessee, Gwen handed me a $20 bill as I left the house. Although I had a round trip ticket to Tennessee and back, I still had to pay $5 for a cab to Washington National and back which would use half of the money she gave me. Then I flew to a large city in Tennessee but had to pay $7 to take a bus to the meeting location (which had no airport). The rest of my money went to pay for one night's stay in a motel. That left me nothing for meals or the return trip.

Fortunately, the meeting provided a good meal so I didn't go to bed hungry. My dilemma: How was I going to get back to my home or office with no money, no credit card and no check? Fortunately, I bumped into a fellow USDA employee who lent me $20 to get me back to Washington. Obviously, things were a lot cheaper back then but not so cheap that I could make and return from a trip like that for $20! These two incidents illustrate what a good job Gwen did in seeing that we never overdrew our bank account again. When I was to be in the office, she either packed a sandwich for me or handed me a single dollar with which to buy my lunch. *Once when someone asked me how much I made, I replied, "Five dollars a week!"*

Back to the impending trip to Indiana, although I had a troubled night with little sleep, I had regained enough emotional control the following morning to leave Dayton and continue on toward Indiana. I passed through Indianapolis, got on busy I-65, which goes all the way to Chicago, and finally reached Lafayette, IN. I stopped at a pay phone there and called John Osmun to tell him I was nearby and in a few minutes would be crossing the Wabash River into West Lafayette. I gave him my destination: a nice apartment complex with a beautiful location overlooking the historic Wabash River on the West Lafayette side.

# CHAPTER 7
## A Rude Arrival to Indiana

WHEN I REACHED the apartment complex which I thought would be my future home, I followed the sign to the Office, filled out my check for the deposit and first month's rent and then asked to be taken to my apartment. I was dead tired and wanted to go straight to bed, looking forward to going to sleep to the peaceful sounds of the Wabash River. Alas, after the office person got the key and escorted me to my apartment, I got a big shock. I didn't need to go outside my apartment to hear and see plenty of water. My apartment was flooded and pumps were attempting to remove the water. Then I knew I had been "taken."

Having been assured over the telephone that I would be placed in one of their "prime" apartments, it turned out that I had just used my only check for the worst apartment in the complex. It was below ground level and was obviously subject to flooding.

The Office lady attempted to assure me that flooding was infrequent, only occurring when the river was unusually high. Since the Wabash was not especially high when I had passed over it, I didn't buy her story. Knowing that my nervous system would not stand the stress of wondering when my apartment would be flooded again, I asked to be shown another apartment--one above ground level. She told me this was the only apartment available. I said I was leaving and asked for my money back for the check which I had just written to them. They refused to do that but returned my check which was now usable only at that apartment complex. Fortunately, I didn't tear up the check until later.

So, I was now in a strange city with no usable check or credit card, and only a little grocery and lunch money--not even enough to pay a deposit at another apartment complex. So, I called Dr. Osmun, told him that the apartment I had rented was not habitable, and asked if he could recommend another place for me. He gave the name, directions and phone number of a place he could recommend.

I was too embarrassed to tell him about my ridiculous financial situation at that time and headed to the second apartment complex. When I arrived there I asked for the complex manager, introduced myself, and related my story about leaving Virginia the day before with one blank check and just enough cash to last me until my first Purdue check. I told her about the flooding incident at the other apartment complex, and showed her my ruined check. I gave her Dr. John Osmun's telephone number so he could verify my honesty and trustworthiness.

This manager turned out to be an "angel" who looked at my check and accepted my story without even calling Dr. Osmun. There was one remaining problem: unlike the first apartment this one was unfurnished and I had no furniture with me. The manager said she would lend me one of the complex's roll away beds until I got some furniture. So, I slept on the roll away bed that night and went to Entomology Hall the following morning, ready to go to work.

# CHAPTER 8

## First Day on the Job at Purdue

AFTER SPENDING SOME time getting briefed about my job from Drs. Collier and Osmun, I got up enough nerve to tell them my predicament. Both of them immediately went into action. Dr. Collier said he would get me an advance on my first month's salary and Dr. Osmun said he could lend me furniture in storage to get by until I could buy my own. Osmun explained that he had some rental units and that his stored furniture was for one of these. He added that the present renter of that unit wanted to use his own furniture. So he (Osmun) had stored the rental furniture in his attic and basement.

Later that day, Dr. Osmun assembled several of his students, who loaded the furniture on a truck, and moved it into my apartment. That night I slept on a real bed and had enough other furniture to be reasonably comfortable. The place wasn't like my large 6 bedroom 4½ bath home furnished with antique Persian rugs and period furniture, but it was dry and not subject to flooding since it was on high ground.

My advance Purdue pay check arrived within the week and my money troubles were over. I quickly opened up an account with the Purdue Credit Union, and paid the deposit and first month's rent for my apartment. I also had money left over, some temporary checks, and my own checkbook was on the way. In retrospect, all of the confusion and chaos caused by lack of proper planning brought on by a crumbling marriage and health situation might have been a blessing in disguise. With everything that was happening to me, I had less time to grieve over the loss of Gwen.

Then my hectic work schedule took over and forced me to concentrate on that. The few nights I was alone in my apartment were still very difficult. But the Colliers and Osmuns limited my time alone by frequently asking me to their homes for dinner and conversation. They did not allow me too many lonely moments during those first days and weeks--and I'll be forever grateful to them for that.

At work, I had inherited some informational material written by a PhD scientist who had assisted NPIRS while on a sabbatical from another major mid-west university. Of course it was not written in terms that would be understandable to the average person. Again, I was very grateful for the experiences I had gained as a newspaper reporter, information officer, and writer of regulations and manager of a major pesticide program at EPA. Those experiences had prepared me to put a large amount of technical information into understandable English for people--many of whom were as unfamiliar with doing computer searches as I was at the time.

Also, fortunately for me, Dr. Collier was always ready to help when I was having trouble understanding some of the technical information involving computer technology. And surprising only to those who did not know him, he was also a talented writer.

Meanwhile, I was becoming increasingly sensitive to the stares of disbelief (bordering on contempt) I was receiving from fellow staffers who shook their heads when they saw me typing away on the old black typewriter I had brought with me. However, I was already asking computer users around campus about more "user friendly" computers than the IBM computers still on the desks of NPIRS staffers. They were using the DOS language which required memorizing huge numbers of keywords.

Finally, the research paid off when I learned that Apple Computers was ready to put its new computer (the Macintosh) on the market. The Macintosh would use simple icons rather than hundreds of "keywords" needed for searching. I was one of the first to order a "Mac," which would soon revolutionize computer usage around the nation.

That little Mac literally changed my outlook on life. I quickly changed from a skeptic to an advocate of computers. I was soon able to use it for my word processing and logging on to the Internet to do searches of EPA's huge data base by way of NPIRS. Of course in 1983, we were still using the old, slow, dial-up telephone system to log on--nothing like today's high speed networks. But slow as it was to get online compared to today's world, it seemed like magic at the time because it was now easy to obtain huge amounts of accurate information at one's desk.

It didn't take me long to find out that although I was warmly welcomed by Dr. Collier and other top officials, some of the staff members were not so pleased. I learned that one staff member in particular was offended that an outsider with no computer experience had been given the job he had wanted. Unfortunately (for me) he had been one of the staff members assigned to help guide me through the early stages. I immediately saw that he missed no opportunity to make things difficult for me. And he often left little caustic notes obviously meant to belittle me.

I tried my best to get along with him. However, at one of the early staff meetings where I was presiding, he openly tried to embarrass me by boldly asking me what I would do once I finished the "User's Guide." It didn't take a genius to see he was implying that my usefulness would end with the completion of that one piece of work. I decided not to let this situation fester by (later and privately) telling him to "get off my back or else..."

Also, I soon learned that another person who had done some preliminary work for NPIRS also resented me and made that obvious just before my first big meeting when someone asked a question about my user training program. I told him I had just started developing that program but would call him later when I was better prepared to answer his question. The person mentioned above did not like my response and told me that as soon as the meeting started I should sit down while he conducted the meeting.

Since I had already done some serious thinking and writing about what I needed to discuss with the group, I wasn't about to miss this opportunity to get input from them. I politely told him I was prepared to handle the meeting myself. After my introduction I remained at the podium while he reluctantly took his seat. Later, at break time, I heard him "bad mouthing" me to one of the attendees. Our relationship remained frosty after that but I got the input I needed to continue developing a comprehensive training program.

# CHAPTER 9
## Getting Comfortable with the Situation

MY EARLIER CONCERN that my selection for the job might be resented was now confirmed. But by that time, I was already getting comfortable with the job, realizing that my background in writing, planning and conducting information programs around the nation was a real asset. And my familiarity with the EPA pesticide information data base and many of the people who assembled it were "frosting on the cake." I no longer felt I had to apologize or explain my selection, regardless of the obvious jealousy shown by those who had been passed over for the job.

That does not mean that I did not have some nervous moments. The worst came at my first demonstration held in the USDA Administration Building in Washington, DC. This happend within my first two weeks on the job and before I received my Macintosh. This meant I had to memorize some essential keywords in order to do a search on the PC. Just as difficult, I had to learn how to hook up the computer with its large transmitting unit in order to begin a demonstration. I was fortunate to find a USDA employee friend who could show me the "log on" process for the DC area. This allowed me to go "online" and be ready to demonstrate the system before potential members began arriving.

Within a few minutes, people from a variety of nations were lined up to watch the demonstration and make special requests for searches. Many of these international people had limited ability to make their requests in English but somehow we managed to communicate well enough for me to figure out the searches they wanted me to do. I was weary but pleased that I survived this first and most difficult demonstration. Several USDA friends heard that I was there and stopped by for brief visits to say Hi. I didn't think I was emotionally ready to interact with Gwen or Mitch so didn't let them know I was in town.

The work situation continued to improve as I became more familiar with the NPIRS system. Getting information together for the newsletter sped up my own knowledge of the system and better prepared me to pass this knowledge on to users. Then things improved even faster after I received my Mac and got some "hands on" training to use it from Dick Collier. I began using my own computer to write the monthly newsletter, and replacing my old manual typewriter made it faster and much easier to make needed changes to the NPIRS User's Guide as the system grew. I occasionally needed help with technical matters and Dr. Collier was always more than willing to help me. But those occasions became less frequent and I was now pretty much on my own as I went around the country conducting demonstrations of NPIRS.

*Note: although they were not funny at the time, I can now laugh at some of the crazy things that happened to me. Once when I was giving a demonstration at Indiana University (I.U.) at Bloomington, I was provided a large, modern room in which to do my demonstration. I.U. personnel also helped with the setup, covering up the large window walls which provided so much light that the picture from the transmitter could not be seen.*

*After the windows were covered, I logged on and did a quick search on the computer. I then asked the transmitter operator to turn the machine on. "It's on," he said. Then I realized that the room, being modern, had large areas of glass at the ceilings. This meant that there was no way to further darken the room. It was too late to move to another location, so I had to look at my small computer screen and describe what was on the screen. Since this large group represented some of the top educators at I.U. you can understand my embarrassment at this pathetic demonstration.*

*Although members of this group appeared to be very understanding of my predicament, I'm sure that once I left (and knowing the competitive nature of these two schools) I could imagine them saying: "Those Purdue people can't get anything right!" That was pretty much my feeling at the time.*

Despite this embarrassing setback, demonstrations of the new data base system were increasing at a fast pace and my time and presence was much in demand. The knowledge of the pesticide data base gained by working at EPA proved to be invaluable to me in conducting and teaching others how to conduct searches to obtain the huge amount of information now available.

# CHAPTER 10
## Time Alone Still a Problem

BACK TO NON-WORK time, although spending much social time with the Colliers and Osmuns, I still dreaded spending time alone. I still grieved over the loss of Gwen and the inability to spend time with Mitch. Therefore, I decided it might be helpful for me to use one of my staff benefits (counseling) available through Purdue's Psychological Counseling program. This was when I met the head of this group, Dr. Donald Hartsough, who became a personal friend and confidante during our counseling sessions. Although I had done much reading on the subject of "Grief Resolution," personalized professional interaction helped speed up the healing process for me.

Back when medical science practitioners assumed I was going to die, you may recall that I made heavy use of planning and physically working on the large restoration and addition project as therapy for dealing with my cancer prognosis. In addition, reading the material contained in a book "On Death and Dying" by Dr. Elizabeth Kubler-Ross, MD also helped me deal with my current situation. While facing my own eminent demise, I had gained some understanding of myself by reading about Dr. Kubler-Ross's theory of the five phases of grieving experienced when people learn that they or someone they love has died or is dying. After learning more about these phases and my apparent recovery from the Stage 4 cancer, I was now learning that many of the same rules applied to dealing with the end of a long term relationship with someone you love. In a revision of her book, I found that Dr. Kubler-Ross and many other professionals believe that the end of a long relationship is much like experiencing death.

*In fact, while driving from Virginia to Indiana I thought that loss of Gwen was harder to accept than death itself. Death can be relatively quick compared to the ending of a 20 plus year marriage and loss of someone you love and assumed would be with you until the end of your life. With Dr. Hartsough's help, I was beginning to understand that Dr. Kubler-Ross' stages of grieving also applied to the ending of a formerly loving and long relationship such as mine. The final stage (acceptance) was the most difficult for me but I was beginning to achieve it with Dr. Hartsough's help. And when I finally found myself attracted to another woman, this signaled that my relationship with Gwen was beginning to end and that I might someday have a chance for a happy life with someone else.*

# CHAPTER 11
## Need to Develop Outside Interests

ALTHOUGH DR. HARTSOUGH helped me to begin facing life without Gwen and accept less time with Mitch, he also advised me to develop other interests to help keep my mind off my losses and be more at peace with myself. During my marriage to Gwen, we had spent much enjoyable time learning about and buying antiques (when we could afford them). And little Mitch always went with us and found other youngsters to play with. As a family, we attended many auctions and did lots of "antiquing" together. While I was just learning to fully appreciate the beauty of antiques and collectibles, Gwen was already an expert at identifying and finding these treasures.

As a measure of her ability in the latter, she was able to look at a Persian rug and see how many knots per inch it had. *(Note: A major factor in determining the value of a hand woven oriental rug is the number of "knots." The more the better!)* She also became expert in determining the country of origin of the hand woven rugs as well as their type. While we were still together, dealer friends often brought antique Persian rugs for Gwen to identify the thread count, country of origin, and type. With her artistic eyes, she could quickly tell just by looking whether the rug was from Persia (and which area), Pakistan, Turkestan or Afghanistan; and whether it was Hamadan, Tabriz, Kerman, Isfahan, Nain or Qum as well as others. She could tell just by looking at a rug, the number of knots, weaving techniques used, and materials and patterns. Often friends would ask her to accompany them to see a rug before they purchased it.

Although not in the same class as Gwen, I had gained some rudimentary knowledge as well as appreciation of antiques and collectibles--including Oriental rugs. Now that Gwen was no longer my partner in this hobby, I realized I needed to become more personally educated about these things if I were ever able to fully enjoy them again. By asking around, I found that a well known collector (Virgil Scowden of Crawfordsville, IN) was offering a series of night classes on those subjects.

I immediately signed up for his classes, which were held in the Lafayette area where his brother, Francis Scowden, owned an extremely nice antique store. As indication of his reputation, Virgil was known for supplying antiques to Hollywood stars with Indiana connections. When not traveling out of town, I rarely missed one of Virgil's classes. After I got to know him on a personal basis, he invited me to his "museums" located in or around Crawfordsville. One was in a restored former church building, others were in restored buildings such as: The Old Stone House, The Old School House, The Old Barn, etc.

Ironically, I had always wanted to restore and live in one of these same type buildings but the opportunity never presented itself. *Recently I used the Internet to try to find Virgil and thank him for his kindnesses to me but found that he had passed away. A common occurrence to me these days since I seem to be outliving many of my friends.*

To enhance my knowledge and weekend enjoyment, I also began attending auctions within a 50 mile radius of Lafayette/West Lafayette. These auctions, especially farm and estate auctions, often offered a treasure trove of antiques and collectibles. (Note: unlike the farms I was familiar with in the Carolinas, many Indiana farm auctions involved farm families with acres running into the thousands. Unlike the "subsistence" farmers with whom I was familiar, many of these Indiana farm owners were quite wealthy--as reflected by the quality of the items to be auctioned). Attendees at these auctions often had the opportunity to bid on antique Oriental rugs so valuable that rug dealers from Chicago and beyond flocked to Indiana to bid on them.

Auctions also gave me a chance to meet and make friends with many people outside of the Purdue U. circle. I became long-time friends of John and Martha Ervin of Shelbyville at one such auction. With their advice, I bought my first hand-made Jacquard coverlet made and signed by a Pennsylvania weaver. This was the start of a collection of mine that reached about 40 such highly-prized coverlets. The Ervins, who owned more than 200 highly valuable coverlets, were experts in the antiques world and had a knack for anticipating collectibles that might become valuable in the future.

Many of their most prized antique coverlets were featured in the book "Indiana Coverlet Weavers and Their Coverlets." Some of these coverlets were given to them before they became collectible and ended up as museum quality pieces. The same might be said for their wonderful collection of "coin silver."

# CHAPTER 12

## With Help from Friends I Begin to Hold Up "Bid Card"

AS I RECALL, I had attended quite a few auctions before I dared hold up my "bid card." In fact, I recall that it was only with some coaching from John and Martha Ervin that led to my first auction purchase of the Pennsylvania coverlet. Once I broke the ice, however, I began bidding on things to make my apartment (and later my house) more livable.

Meanwhile, I was finding my position on the Purdue staff more and more enjoyable as time went by. Since I could set my own hours, I asked for and received a key to the Entomology Building. This allowed me access to the Entomology Building and its "coffee break" room an hour or more before department staffers arrived. After making coffee for everyone, I would take a cup of my own to the NPIRS office on the second floor where I would have time uninterrupted by telephone calls or visitors dropping by. I could get lots of work done in a short time.

This freedom to work on my own was much more pleasant and productive than following a schedule imposed upon me in previous jobs in Washington, DC. I no longer had the need to meet carpools or to be "deskbound" for eight-hour days as I did while working for the government. It took me less than 20 minutes to drive from my apartment, and parking spaces were not a problem. This free time offered me a perfect opportunity to write the NPIRS News.

Often, by conferring with Dick Collier at the end of the day and getting his suggestions on items to go in the newsletter, I would sometimes be able to knock out a draft of the monthly edition which he could review before leaving the office that day. With a fresh look the following morning and inclusion of Dick's suggested additions or changes, I could have the newsletter ready to go with hard copies going out to all members and potential members the next day.

Although the actual writing of the newsletter was fairly easy for me because of my previous journalism career, I knew that it would be worthless if people didn't read it. So I spent much more time thinking about its readability, jotting down humorous ideas as they occurred to me, and devising ways to include many names of people, including staff and NPIRS members around the country (and later, the world). I soon found out that this early effort to make the newsletter "readable" as well as informational really paid off.

The NPIRS News soon became one of the most useful tools in NPIRS's informational and marketing arsenal. We began getting calls, letters and emails from those receiving NPIRS News saying they were not only reading it but looked forward to receiving it each month. Some suggested that I should send out the newsletter more frequently, but I chose to ignore those suggestions, knowing that it was better to leave people "wanting more" than "wanting less."

Then when I had been at Purdue about a year, our office was told to prepare for a review of all aspects of our work by an outside group. We were told that the study group's findings and recommendations could have a great impact on the future funding of our organization. We received a stern warning from Purdue that we should take this study seriously! And we did, fearing that our funding by USDA, EPA, and Purdue would end before we had a chance to become self sufficient.

Remembering my GS-15 Position Description (PD) experience at EPA, I finished my comprehensive marketing plan ahead of time and appended examples for each aspect of my Purdue PD, including training materials and training sessions. I also included copies of NPIRS News as examples of our printed marketing materials.

After putting everything in proper order with short narratives to explain each aspect of the plan, I turned the packet over to Dick Collier, who incorporated it into his overall presentation to the study group. After some time studying our operation, and reading the material we gave them, the group submitted their report to Purdue. It was more than 90 percent favorable with a few recommendations for improvement that we found useful. They singled out the marketing plan for special praise and said that the newsletter represented an especially compelling piece of marketing that others should emulate. I was pleased by this since I also considered the newsletter a major contributor to our effectiveness.

Incidentally, I also used the newsletter as a management tool in a manner never acknowledged until years later. It involved the management style of my boss, Dick Collier, not only one of the smartest but one of the nicest human beings I ever encountered. After observing the dynamics of our office for some time, I was bothered that some of our top programmers and systems analysts were taking advantage of our good natured boss.

The problem? These programmers and analysts regularly missed their deadlines for completing their assignments. This reflected badly on NPIRS and our director. The employees too often had "one more test" that "absolutely must be made" before something they had promised to complete could be released to members. Our good natured boss didn't seem to have it in him to chastise the employees for their failures. This was putting both him and our organization at risk. So I decided to give him a hand by insisting we include firm deadlines in NPIRS articles announcing the introduction, progress reports and completion schedules of new programs being developed to improve the system.

These public deadlines meant that a systems analyst or programmer who failed to meet a deadline no longer had a place to hide. The miscreant now had me, Dr. Collier and the entire membership to deal with. "I need to do one more test" would no longer be acceptable because the "NPIRS world" would not be willing to accept this feeble excuse too many times. Although there was an occasional failure initially, this management procedure resulted in more jobs being completed on time. Of course my popularity with the staff went down as a result but I felt that the increased ability to meet deadlines was worth it. I wasn't engaged in a popularity contest anyway.

Neither Dick nor I had ever discussed this informal managerial arrangement until long after we had both left NPIRS. Finally, one afternoon years later when we were having a drink together, I asked Dick what he thought of this managerial use of the newsletter. "You mean that was deliberate, Jim?" he asked. I replied, "Yes, Dick. After I observed your management style for a few months I realized that the analysts and programmers were taking advantage of your good nature. For example, you would ask them to estimate the time they needed to have a new program ready to release. But at deadline time their response too often would be, 'We need to do further testing before we can release it.' "

I then said: "Dick, I witnessed this scenario over and over. Knowing that it would be difficult for you to change your 'good guy personality' I wondered how I could help with this problem. I finally realized that I could make NPIRS News into a management tool for your use. I would announce to the "NPIRS world" that we were developing a new "app," describe its usefulness, and set a firm deadline for the release of the new application. By understanding the usefulness of the new application, members anxiously awaited its release. I insisted and you agreed that no last minute excuses would be allowed.

"If the staff failed to meet its deadline, I would urge you to release the application 'as is.' As you know this would accomplish several things including: (1) embarrassing the programmer/analyst who failed to meet the deadline (thus making that person less likely to repeat this mistake), (2) let me become the 'bad guy,' taking some of the pressure off you, and (3) if everything else failed, we would actually involve the users in solving program problems--a system followed by some large I.T. companies."

Dick looked at me and said: "I owe you an apology, Jim. I never realized that you were deliberately sparing me from being the 'bad guy' and taking on that role yourself!" I replied: "Dick you don't owe me an apology. Although I did not relish this role, I thought it was better for me to risk being disliked by some staffers than you. At that stage, NPIRS could not survive without you. In any event, the plan worked so well that all of us benefited. That's all that mattered. As you surely recall, our membership grew from 12 to over 600 during that six-year period we worked together."

# CHAPTER 13
## Traveling with Dick Collier

RETURNING TO "REAL time," Dick Collier and I made many trips together for big events which required both of us to be present. Several of these were to Washington, DC, where two of our major sources of funding were located, i.e., USDA and EPA. During most of those trips, we had many memorable moments usually (but not always) of a humorous nature.

Once after we made a major presentation to USDA, we were in the process of loading the Purdue van with our equipment when disaster struck. I was carrying an armload of equipment including expensive modems. As I was starting down about 15 steps made of granite, I was bumped by a USDA employee in a hurry to leave the building. I was knocked off balance and tried (unsuccessfully) to regain my balance but gained speed with every step. Finally, I went into "free fall" with equipment going in all directions.

My momentum took me completely across the wide sidewalk and I landed at the steps of a bus loading passengers at the front of the USDA South Building. When Dick arrived for another load of equipment, he saw a large crowd gathered around a prone figure. That would be me. Fortunately one of the people waiting to get on the bus was an MD and he checked to see if I had any broken bones. He said, "You were fortunate that you fell relatively flat or you would have broken wrists or arms. As it is, you do not appear to have broken bones but you will be extremely sore for a few days."

After picking up the equipment, some of which was broken, we began our trip back to West Lafayette. Since I was still in pain from the fall, Dick did all the driving. On the way, we were running low on gas and stopped at the only gas station we had been able to find for many miles. It was very crowded and vehicles were lined up several car lengths waiting for available gas pumps. We spent several long minutes waiting in line for a vehicle with a very large tank to finish pumping. As we started to this now available pump, a car driving very fast wheeled in from the road and beat us to the pump.

My usually mild mannered boss was incensed by this driver's reckless and thoughtless behavior. He opened up his door, stood on the van's running board and shouted: "You sorry so-and-so, we've been waiting a long time for that pump!" Since Dick Collier was already a very large man, he must have looked like a giant, standing on that running board. The driver of the car took one look at this huge looking, angry man and immediately gunned his automobile back onto the road. His tail lights were the last we saw of him. I forgot all about my pain momentarily and after Dick refilled the gas tank of the van, we laughed our way back to Purdue. I went to see my doctor the next morning and he kept me off my feet a day or two and also insisted I wear some prescription compression stockings several days to deal with the swelling in my legs.

On another trip, this time to Mississippi State University for a big conference, we were driving on a narrow two lane road shortly after dark within a half hour of our motel near campus. Both of us were dead tired from the long drive from Indiana and were looking forward to going to bed as soon as we arrived and unpacked. I looked down and then up as we approached a car with only one headlight working. From my angle, the one headlight seemed to be coming straight at us. I shouted, "Watch out Dick!" Momentarily stunned by my shout, Dick almost took us into the ditch. After he got the vehicle under control, we both began laughing hysterically and had to fight to control ourselves even after we reached our motel. It seemed that something eventful often happened when we traveled together. However, because of our limited staff I had to travel alone most of the time I was working at Purdue.

Although I kept no records, from memory I recall conducting workshops on NPIRS at USDA and EPA in Washington; at West Chester, and Pittsburg, PA; at Winston Salem and Raleigh, NC; at Clemson University, SC; at Minneapolis, and St. Paul, MN; at Davis and Sacramento, CA; Hot Springs, AK and Reno, NV. The latter workshop was part of an annual meeting that I was required to attend. Since my birthday is May 10, I spent every birthday at Reno for six years.

# CHAPTER 14
## Owning My Own Home Again Beckons

AS THE END of my year's apartment lease approached, I decided that I now liked the state of Indiana enough to start thinking about a more permanent living arrangement there. That meant buying my own house. Since the town of Lafayette was just across the Wabash River from West Lafayette and Purdue and was noted for its beautiful turn of the century homes, that's where I began looking. Before long I found a "dream house" in the historic district of Lafayette. The original sales brochure for this house described it as being as a "Frank Lloyd Wright designed" house but this designation had been marked out as "unable to prove." Despite this lack of proof, however, the home had many earmarks of Frank Lloyd Wright's "Prairie Style" designs.

Some examples that suggested this noted architect's work: (1) The window wall adjacent to the front stairway was entirely encased with beautiful stained glass windows, (2) the "parlor" or living room fireplace was surrounded by custom made walnut cabinets, (3) the built-in dining room cabinetry (china closet, buffet, etc.) along with the wainscoting were custom made of cherry wood, and the rest of the downstairs was finished with walnut trim. Not the type of trim you see today at Home Depot or Lowe's!

Another unusual feature: the ceiling lights in the foyer, first floor hallway, parlor and dining room were furnished with tiny inset bulbs spaced inches apart. This was something I had not ever seen--before or since. The effect was dramatic. *The only drawback was finding light bulbs of the size and wattage needed to replace burned out bulbs. Although the exact match was no longer available, I was able to find good substitutes, a similar bulb of 5 watts which I was able to order from a specialty light company. They were not available in your local hardware store or Walmart.*

As my lease expired, I moved to my large, historic house at 630 Ferry St. in Lafayette. I immediately began fast-walking from house to my office and back home which soon helped me get into good physical shape. My second Christmas there I invited the Osmuns, Colliers, and a few other friends to my house for a party. Although not a "sit down" dinner, I provided plenty of food and drink for the occasion. In addition to hot dogs and burgers, I had used my "power of persuasion" to purchase some fine barbecue, and various Greek and Chinese dishes from my favorite ethnic restaurants. I served everything "buffet style." The only thing I cooked, other than the burgers, was chili cooked in a crock pot.

As a pretty good "partier" in Washington, DC, I had purchased and studied a "Bartender's Guide" back then and still remembered how to make a variety of alcoholic drinks--some of them quite exotic. Then I had honed my skills by being the designated "bartender" at many governmental functions. So, I was able to fill almost any drink request emanating from my Purdue friends. Dr. Osmun, who was already in his 70's had such a good time at my parties he almost always stood on his head to defy his age!

Although my house was in relatively good shape for its age, I saw many areas for improvement. One of the most urgent involved an outside stairway which in the recent past had been the entry place for burglars. In fact, one of these had attacked a lady living in a second floor apartment of the house. Although the stairs themselves were solid, there was no way to keep potential thieves from climbing the stairs, hiding out of sight at the top, and breaking in at their leisure. Since I had neither the time nor inclination to attempt this job on my own, I began searching for a good carpenter.

Luckily, I found a "master" carpenter living just off campus. His name was Bill Hartje, son of a mechanical engineer professor at Purdue. Bill turned out to be such a blessing that I've thanked God many times for bringing him into my life.

Within a week, Bill (with me serving as his helper) had completely enclosed the lighted stairway and installed a steel door at the bottom. When he finished painting the addition, it looked as if it were original to the house. This stairway would no longer be a hiding place for potential burglars. And since we did not need to pour concrete, I wasn't required to get a building permit. This was the beginning of a great working relationship and friendship that continues to this day. (More about that later).

Another problem I discovered after moving into the house was that the dishwasher didn't work. When the inspector and I tried it out during the inspection tour, it turned on and sounded normal. However, later I found it would not wash dishes and had not washed dishes for a long time. I called an appliance repairman and this was my introduction to a real "Mr. Fixit" who (I eventually found out) could handle any electrical or plumbing job. Although I was expecting to pay for purchase and installation of a new dishwasher, Charles Head said, "Mr. White, I can fix this dishwasher for you in a few minutes if you'll wait for me to get a new part for it. It's a very expensive and good quality dishwasher with a minor problem."

After I paid for the part and Charles installed it, I had to force him to take a few dollars for his work. And this was the beginning of a long friendship with him. It wasn't long before I needed him again. At the first freeze (and we had an unusually early and harsh winter for the second year in a row) my water line in the kitchen froze. Charles looked under the sink and said, "Jim, this water line was not installed properly. It was installed on an outside wall with no insulation to protect it from freezing." He then suggested two ways to fix the problem. The first one was to take out the kitchen cabinets on that wall, install the water line properly, and then re-install the kitchen cabinets.

Obviously, this would be a time consuming and expensive proposition. The second option was to install a special light that was temperature controlled near the pipe in question. This light would come on and warm the pipe enough to keep it from freezing when the temperature dropped to a certain level. Charles advised me to select the second option since he had used this method in similar cases and never had a failure. I told him to go with this option. He finished the job within a short time and the pipe never again froze while I was there.

The experience with the frozen pipe and dishwasher let me know that my new friend could handle both electrical and plumbing problems as well as appliance repair. When I called Charles to install a new light switch (or outlet) for me, he uncovered another problem. In the course of this work, Charles discovered that the electrical system was hooked together with the old "knob and tube" system. This did not meet modern code and if it became overheated could set the house on fire. So, at my request Charles went through the entire house removing the old knob and tubing and replacing it with new, grounded outlet boxes.

# CHAPTER 15

## Friendly Pressure to Develop Social Life

MEANWHILE, MY COUNSELOR (and friends) were suggesting that I should add some dating to my social life. They set me up with a few "blind dates" but they proved unsatisfactory. I had also gone to some "Parents Without Partners" (PWP) events and had danced and chatted with a few lonely women. However, I unfairly compared them to Gwen and did not feel the slightest attraction to any ladies I had met. And even worse, I was missing my son, Mitch, terribly. He had made two trips to see me in Indiana but these brief stays made me even sadder when he had to go. I would have to fight back the tears when he left.

Then one evening Mitch called me and said: "Dad, I think I've matured enough now to return to college. Would you mind if I came to Indiana and enrolled at Purdue?" Needless to say I not only didn't mind, but was thrilled at this prospect and told him so. Mitch then said: "Dad, to keep down expenses I would be glad to stay with you in your house." I appreciated that thought but told him he might get more of a feeling of college life if he lived on campus with people his own age.

I also warned him: "Mitch, you know that I'm overly-protective of you and can never go to sleep until I know you're home and safely in bed! This might drive both of us crazy. So, if you agree, I'll check about getting you student housing." Although he didn't say so, I knew he was relieved that I wouldn't be around all the time to look over his shoulder. He ended the conversation about housing with the words, "I'll leave that up to you, Dad."

The next day, I began the process of getting Mitch enrolled at Purdue. I was really pleased at the large discount I received for his tuition, fees, and books because I was a staff member. I sent him a list of required and elective courses available to him for his freshman year. He decided that he wanted to be in the marketing field and made his plans to arrive in Indiana a week or two before the school year began. His mother had not offered to help with his expenses and I never requested any help from her.

Both John Osmun and Dick Collier were fully aware that Mitch was an excellent tennis player and John asked me if I wanted him to contact the Purdue athletic director and head tennis coach about the possibility of Mitch playing tennis for Purdue. Naturally, I said yes. But when John talked with the head tennis coach, he received a cool reception. The coach said he had never heard of Mitch White and doubted he would be good enough to make the tennis squad much less the team. However, after some pressure from John, he reluctantly agreed to take a look at Mitch once he arrived on campus.

The day after Mitch arrived in town I took him to meet the head coach at the Purdue tennis complex. Mitch had injured his right (or serving) shoulder during a tournament just before leaving for Indiana, so I was hoping the coach would give him a few days to recover from the injury before watching him hit. However, when we arrived at the courts, the coach had already arranged a one set match between Mitch and Purdue's no. 1 player.

Obviously, he planned to get rid of this pretender with some clout at Purdue right away. My heart sank when I saw what the coach was doing. But despite not having his usual powerful first serve, Mitch beat the Purdue team's no.1 player 6-1. Things were looking bright, tennis-wise for Mitch. The coach was now forced to take him seriously. And because he was on the tennis team, he was allowed to have a car on campus--a feature reserved for members of athletic teams and perhaps a few other organized groups. He was practicing with the team and fully expecting to play at the no.1 position.

# CHAPTER 16
## The NCAA Rears Its Ugly Head

UNFORTUNATELY, WHAT APPEARED to be an ideal situation for Mitch didn't last long. As the fall tennis season approached, the NCAA suddenly became involved. We had not tried to hide the fact that Mitch had attended VCU on a partial tennis scholarship and that he had dropped out of school after the first semester with no transferrable college credits.

Under ordinary circumstances this would not have been a problem. However, the NCAA had now become involved and said under their rules Mitch's eligibility to play for Purdue was under question. The NCAA said he could have entered Purdue as a true freshman and been eligible to play for Purdue immediately except for the fact he had entered VCU on a tennis scholarship.

In the report at the end of the investigation, the NCAA ruled that Mitch could remain on the team but could not play in matches until he reached a certain grade point average (gpa). When we reviewed the NCAA ruling, we found that Mitch's "F's" and "incompletes" had followed him from VCU. Under the NCAA rules, Mitch would be required to make straight "A's" on all his Purdue courses in order to regain his eligibility to play his senior year. Meanwhile, he could sit on the bench for three years while players with less talent would be playing.

Mitch initially decided to stay on the team while he worked toward getting "straight A's" so he could play on the team for one year. However, the tennis coach made a decision that caused Mitch to change his mind. The coach told Mitch that he would only be allowed to practice against the weaker players. The reason? He didn't want to risk the loss of morale when Mitch beat his top players on a regular basis. Knowing that playing against the weaker players would only weaken his own game, Mitch then left the team.

So, for the next three years to maintain some tennis fitness as well as earn some money, Mitch worked as assistant to the head coach at the area's only indoor tennis complex in Lafayette. Although this kept him in good physical shape, he gradually lost his "tennis shape." However, the money he earned did help improve his lifestyle.

Back to my "relationship" with Gwen, any hopes of maintaining a friendship with her were dashed the first time we were together since I left that fateful morning before the ink on our legal separation papers had dried. Seeing her came at the suggestion of Dick Collier when we were preparing to head for the Washington, DC area to conduct a workshop. Dick, who knew I still loved Gwen and was somewhat of a romantic himself, said: "Jim, while we're in Washington why don't we invite Gwen to have dinner with us?" I called Gwen and she said she would like to have dinner with me and my boss.

The night of our dinner together, we picked Gwen up at her Reston, VA townhouse. But instead of taking a seat near the front with us, she went all the way to the back of the Purdue van and sat there alone. At dinner, she made sure to sit as far away from me as possible and when we finished dinner and prepared to take her to her townhouse, she again took her seat all the way at the back. Dick urged her to come sit near us at the front of the van, but she insisted on going to the back row.

My only question (to myself) was "Why did she even agree to go to dinner with us if she could not stand to be near me?"

# CHAPTER 17

## Gwen Comes to Town

THE NEXT TIME we saw each other happened a few months after Mitch came to Purdue. One day Mitch said: "Dad, would you mind if I invited Mom to come out to Indiana for a visit?" I told him it was fine with me. I said that she could either use one of my spare bedrooms or that I could get her a room on campus at the motel operated by Purdue's Hotel and Motel school. It was available to guests of Purdue staff members at a reasonable price--which I would be glad to arrange and pay for.

She expressed a preference for the latter arrangement and (as I recall) arranged a flight to Indianapolis where Mitch met her plane. Although she spent most of her two day stay with Mitch, Gwen asked if I would mind taking her around to visit area antique malls. I took her to Lafayette area antique stores and malls, as well as to nearby small town malls, e.g., Crawfordsville and Flora. While in Crawfordsville, I also got friend Virgil Scowden to open up a couple of his museums for Gwen to tour.

Gwen seemed to enjoy her visit to Lafayette and thought Mitch had made a good choice in attending Purdue. But she gave no indication that she and I had once been married. It hurt me when we said goodbye again but nothing like that painful parting several months earlier.

My last major heartbreak involving Gwen occurred that following Christmas. This celebration of our Christ's birth has always been a bittersweet time for me because my dear Mother had her first stroke on Christmas Day of 1953. The following year she had her second stroke the day before Christmas. The year after that she had her third and final stroke and passed away during that Christmas season. Since then I have had a very difficult time having a joyful Christmas.

Then, on Christmas eve of 1985 as I was starting to prepare food for my party with the Osmuns, Colliers, and a couple of other friends, the postman rang my doorbell and asked me to sign for a registered letter. It contained **the final divorce papers for Gwendolyn and James H. White!** This brought back tears and memories but I was able to regain enough control of my emotions for me to sign the paperwork and return it to the post office before they closed.

Although I thought the timing for such an occasion could not have been worse, it might have been to my advantage since a few hours later I was surrounded by loving friends who arrived at my Christmas Eve party and helped me through this ordeal. I had no one else in mind at the time, but the Christmas Eve receipt of the divorce papers forced me to realize that I finally must "let Gwen go." And on the advice of Counselor Hartsough and other close friends, I knew I should at least start considering the possibility of having a relationship with another woman. I didn't expect that to be easy.

Because I had always been extremely aware of the role of physical attractiveness in man/woman relationships, I decided it was time to get more serious about my own physical appearance and fitness. Soon after arriving at Purdue, I had joined a fitness club and started working out. *Much of this time was spent "rehabbing" my right hip joint which had largely been eaten away by the cancer and intense radiation of that area. At one point, I was using crutches and Gwen was looking for an antique wheelchair that would not clash with other antiques in our house.*

So, my initial time was spent working hard on adduction and abduction machines at the health club with the hope of rebuilding that damaged hip joint. Soon, any trace of a limp was gone and the right hip seemed almost as strong as the left one. That allowed me to begin working on my overall fitness and appearance. Then, the move to my house in Lafayette opened up another avenue to improve my fitness. The distance from home to office was 1.6 miles each way--just the right distance to walk each morning and afternoon.

At first, I walked at a fairly leisurely pace but soon began trying to reduce my time. After awhile, rain or shine, I was getting from home to office and back in around 15 minutes each way. *I fast marched in place while at stop lights so I wouldn't lose the "burn."* As a result of my concentrated efforts, my body shape gradually changed so much that I had to start accumulating a completely new wardrobe. Although my body was becoming trim and athletic looking (especially for my age) my "up and down" weights while fighting cancer had resulted in loose skin on and around my face. *At times the cancer had made me look bloated and at other times I appeared emaciated. When the rest of my body returned to normal size, my skin did not shrink back to its normal size.*

Finally, my doctor said the only way I could get rid of this excess skin was by surgery. He recommended a reputable cosmetic surgeon who said, "I can take 20 years off your age by removing that loose skin." I took a few days vacation time after the surgeon removed the worst of the sagging skin. He stressed that this should be considered part of my rehabilitation from cancer rather than a "face lift," and he said that no one would know about it unless I told them.

When my face healed and I went back to my office, people did a "double take" and said: "Jim, you're really looking young. What did you do on your vacation to improve your looks so much?" I just smiled and thanked them for their compliments. After another few months, I was really happy that I had worked hard to regain some semblance of the person I had been before cancer.

# CHAPTER 18

## A Barbershop Moment and a Sweet Baritone

SOMETHING TOTALLY UNEXPECTED happened soon afterward when Dick and Linda Collier invited me to accompany them to the Long Theatre which was within walking distance of my house. The occasion was the annual performance of women "barbershop singing groups" in Central Indiana. Although I wasn't aware of it, this was a big deal for lovers of barbershop music (of which I was not one at the time). Not only would the best local barbershop women singers perform, but a "professional," highly ranked female barbershop quartet would perform during intermission. All participants would attend a big party after the show.

The first half of the program was enjoyable, but then Dick whispered, "Jim, you're in for a real treat during intermission when The Audio Express of Chicago performs. I've seen and heard these girls before at various barbershop events. They are rated No. 3 in the world of women barbershop singers. You will quickly notice the difference between this group and our local groups."

Dick was certainly right. When The Audio Express "beauties" danced onto Long Theatre stage, the audience immediately quieted down and watched and listened intently to this group of beautiful and talented women. It was obvious that they were in a different class from the local ladies--not only by their voices but also their choreography. Even a novice like me could see and appreciate the artistry of their performance.

As The Audio Express was beginning to wind down their performance, I leaned over and whispered "Dick, I think I'm beginning to fall in love." He wasn't sure whether or not I was kidding, but said, "Who with, Jim?" I replied, "The baritone." He grinned and said: "Why don't you attend the cast party with us and meet her?"I had planned to walk back to my home after the concert ended but did not want to miss the opportunity to meet this lovely lady, so I quickly decided to attend the party with the Colliers. That did not turn out to be very productive because most of the men there also wanted to meet Cathie Grube, by far the most physically appealing of her very good looking quartet.

Dick introduced me as a good friend and staff member at Purdue. Because of the crowd around her, all I got was a very brief "Hello, I'm glad to meet you," a friendly handshake and a smile. No chance at all for an extended conversation. I wasn't even sure she would remember who I was. Before leaving, I decided to purchase a copy of their vinyl record, "Our First Hello." Alas, the album had sold out by the time I waded through the crowd to buy a copy.

Seeing my disappointment, the lead singer who was handling the album sales said, "Give me your name and address and I'll mail you a copy. You can send me a check after you receive it." However, I wanted to pay her in advance. She handed me her card with address and telephone number. I waited for the record to arrive but it didn't show up. So, I wrote the lead singer that I had not received my copy of the album and still wanted one. And I added: "I was really impressed by your baritone, Cathie Grube. Do you think she would be offended if I wrote to her since we had no opportunity to talk at the party?"

Within a few days, I received a copy of the album, along with a note apologizing for the slowness in sending it, followed with: "By the way, Cathie recently broke up with her boyfriend and would be happy to correspond with you. I've included her address and phone number below. By the way, she does remember the 'Purdue professor with red hair' who spoke with her at the cast party." This began a frequent exchange of letters, photos, and telephone calls. After awhile, we talked or wrote to each other on an almost daily basis. Finally we decided it was time for us to get to know each other in person.

Cathie thought it might be difficult for me to find her apartment in Elmhurst, a suburb of Chicago, and suggested that Merrillville, IN would be an easy drive for both of us. Although small in size, this town was/is noted for its entertainment. Championship fights were held there as well as headliners such as Tom Jones. *Purdue staffers were regular visitors there--even driving to events held there in the dead of winter when I thought it absolutely crazy to venture out on icy I-65.*

# CHAPTER 19
## A Long Awaited Meeting

AS WE MADE final plans to meet in person, I learned that Tom Jones would be performing in Merrillville that same weekend. I already knew that he was one of Cathie's favorite performers so I immediately called to reserve tickets. That turned out to be a good move since it was a "sold out" performance.

Then we addressed the problem of our actual meeting. Since we had only seen each other once several months before, we didn't want any embarrassing mishaps. We agreed to meet at an easy-to-find restaurant, Bob Evans, in Merrillville. As usual, I arrived early but found a waiting line about the length of a football field. How would we find each other in that crowd? Well, fortunately I had the foresight to bring along the Audio Express album which had a photo of Cathie on the front cover. I walked around the line waiting to enter the restaurant, located the manager on duty, showed her Cathie's picture and asked her if she would escort Cathie into the restaurant and to my table. The manager liked the idea of escorting a "celebrity" into the restaurant and as I was sipping on my second cup of coffee, she arrived with Cathie at her side. Cathie was surprised but pleased to see her album on my table.

We enjoyed a leisurely brunch and discussed plans for the day. It turned out that Cathie was also an "antiques lover" so we spent the next several hours visiting nearby antique stores and malls. During this time, we exchanged "life stories" and got to know each other better.

Cathie's story: she had moved from Peoria, IL to Chicago and became a member of the Chicago Audio Express. This women's quartet won a "Johnny Mann Contest" and as a result they received an all expenses paid USO trip to various countries around the world. They also became rated no. 3 nationally in the competitive world of women barbershop quartets. She was currently working three jobs to help pay for expensive clothing, as well as for singing and choreography lessons. *Until that time I had no idea that highly ranked barbershop quartets paid for professional training!*

In any event, we attended the Tom Jones concert and enjoyed it thoroughly. If you've ever attended one of his concerts you probably know that it is customary for women to throw room keys, bras and other personal items up on the stage. This was a new one on me. After hearing Cathie scream and whistle at his performance, I was fearful that she might start disrobing and throwing personal articles on stage as some other women were doing. Perhaps realizing that I was a conservative Southern boy she refrained from going that far and I breathed a sigh of relief.

We saw each other in an "off and on" relationship for almost two years. During that time I had begun having more doubts that this relationship could last. With our very large difference in age, educational level, and other factors, the chance of a permanent relationship between the two of us was probably not going to happen. Another detriment to long range plans: I suspected that she still had strong feelings for her ex-boyfriend. She had told me that during one of our several breakups, she had seen him again briefly. Although hearing this was hurtful to me, I appreciated her honesty. Her beauty, personality, and talent lessened my concern about the future. I was really enjoying the moment.

At the time, (as shallow as it sounds and was) I was enjoying the fact that I was spending lots of quality time with this beautiful, talented and fun woman. *When she walked into any room, men turned and stared at her. That was quite an ego builder for me, an aging cancer survivor who had recently lost the woman he had loved for many years.* In retrospect, I think both of us were using each other. I think she appreciated the fact that I had a pretty high position at Purdue University. That was somewhat confirmed when she described me as that "red haired Purdue Professor." And, in my case, I obviously used her to help take my mind off Gwen and rebuild my own sense of worth.

While we were still together, I even had a chance to "show her off" to Virginia friends, during one of our "on" periods. This happened soon after The Audio Express had just returned from a competition in Hawaii. Dick Collier and I were going to Washington DC on a business trip and I invited Cathie to go with us. When she agreed, I arranged for her to meet us at Chicago's O'Hare Airport so the three of us could proceed on to Washington together. At the conclusion of our business, Dick returned to Indiana and we prepared to have a fun weekend together with close friends Gerry and Connie Newland of Fairfax.

Coincidentally, "Clifton Day," an annual event in the town where Gwen and I had lived, was to be held the following day. We planned to attend that, along with the Newlands. *"Clifton Day" regularly attracts around 10,000 people to this little village of less than 100 people*. The following day the four of us strolled the streets of Clifton meeting many old friends of Gwen and me in earlier, happier times.

While there, I had a chance to show Cathie the little Victorian cottage I had restored in the village, along with the large 5-acre project on Blue Dan Lane, and the modern home on 5 acres just outside the village. Mitch joined us for this tour and remained with us for dinner while the Newlands headed back to their home. We had a fine meal at the "Heart and Hand Restaurant" and the owners, Suzi and Travis Worsham, invited us to their home for after dinner drinks.

I had wondered what reaction I would receive when I introduced Cathie to old friends, many of whom had said sorrowful goodbyes to me before I left for Indiana. As far as I could tell, these friends seemed genuinely pleased that I was still cancer free, well, and enjoying a new relationship. Cathie seemed pleased at meeting some of my old friends and seeing the homes I had restored.

During this time I had also received some assurance that we might have a future together when she mentioned the possibility that she might move to Lafayette so we wouldn't have to travel such a distance to see each other. Apparently her mention of that appeared to be the beginning of the end for the two of us.

One Saturday, soon after we returned to the Midwest, Cathie drove to Lafayette for what I thought was a weekend. Instead, she said that when she mentioned to other members of the Audio Express her intention to move to Lafayette to be nearer to me, they reacted very negatively saying her move would result in the end of the Audio Express. They had even brought her old boyfriend back into her life. I had one question for her, "Do you still love him?" When she replied in the affirmative, that ended our "off and on" relationship and she returned to Chicago never to return.

# CHAPTER 20
## A Temporary Hurt but Many Benefits Gained

THE FINAL MEETING that day was very hurtful to me and I knew it would take some time for me to recover. I would miss Cathie's presence in my life and the fun we had shared but I knew it was best that our "off and on" relationship was now permanently "off." With some more reflection I also realized that my relationship with Cathie had helped me finally reach the "Acceptance" level in my relationship with Gwen. It took some time but eventually I knew that Cathie's decision was best for both of us. It let her return to her pursuit of a musical career and it let me return to a realistic life bolstered by the knowledge that I could love again. *However, it took several years and a move back to my home area to finalize that last point.*

Since we did not remain in communication I don't know how things turned out for Cathie. I hope she was able to re-establish a firm and lasting relationship with her old boyfriend. And I hope she gained the fame she seemed to need. As for me, in addition to learning I could love again, I still had a great circle of friends, auctions to attend, a challenging job, and Boiler Maker sporting events to enjoy. And, most important of all, I was still free of cancer.

Then a few weeks later to my surprise (and of my friends) I found myself attracted to a much more stable lady who was also closer to my age. This occurred when Lafayette friends I had antiqued with many times said to me: "Jim, we have a friend we would like for you to meet. She is a pretty, blond-haired widow by the name of Jo Ann Miller. We think the two of you would like each other because you have a lot in common." They then proceeded to tell me that their friend had owned her own fine dining restaurant and antique mall, and was a lover of music and dancing. They explained that she had to give up the restaurant and mall after her mother and son became so ill that she needed to devote her time to caring for them.

When I asked why they suddenly wanted to introduce me to someone, my friends said: "First of all, Jim, we never thought you were ready for a new relationship but that seems to have changed recently. In addition, the lady we want you to meet was not available until now. Her mother, who had Lou Gehrig's disease, has passed away. And her son, who had been burned by hot asphalt over about 80 percent of his body, has been discharged from the Indianapolis Burn Center."

They added that Jo Ann's husband died several years ago, and they thought she also was now ready to resume a relationship. They said that Jo Ann still loved the food service business but no longer wanted the pressure of owning her own restaurant and mall. However, when *The Cracker Barrel Old Country Restaurant* announced plans to open a new restaurant just off I-65, a mile or so out of the town of Lafayette, Jo Ann Miller was the first person to apply for a job and the first person hired by the company.

Her first job with Cracker Barrel was to train servers and kitchen help. When the training was nearing completion, she was also asked to assist in decorating the restaurant and acting as "floor manager" when that person was unavailable. Once those jobs were completed she returned to her regular job as lead hostess but continued to act as floor manager when needed. My friends offered to give me Jo Ann's telephone number or else take me to the Cracker Barrel and introduce us. Still a little skeptical about being "fixed up" I thanked them but said I would prefer to have a good breakfast at the restaurant and meet her on my own. When I went for that breakfast, a pretty blonde lady greeted me and said she would escort me to a table.

From the description my friends had given me, I suspected that my escort was Jo Ann Miller. About halfway to my table, she whispered: "Hi Jim." Obviously she recognized me from descriptions given by our mutual friends. I had a leisurely breakfast and lingered over coffee until the crowd thinned out and Jo Ann came and joined me for a few minutes at my table. During our conversation, she said that she recently sold her home in nearby Flora, where she had owned and managed "Jo Ann's Restaurant and Antiques." She now lived in an apartment in Lafayette not far from my home. Before we parted I got her telephone number and the hours she worked and promised to call her soon.

Before calling her about a date, however, I had coffee with old friend John Osmun and asked him if he was familiar with Jo Ann and her restaurant. He immediately said that he knew her well and that Purdue professors who wanted to impress out-of-town guests would drive them to Flora to treat them to a meal at Jo Ann's restaurant. "It was a classy place and Jo Ann is a classy lady," he concluded. With John's ringing endorsement, I didn't waste time calling Jo Ann for a date. As I recall, we attended an auction together on our first date.

During the next months (actually years) we became great friends and developed a strong relationship. Over time, I also became close to her four sons: Tim, the eldest, who was a successful architect and businessman; Tom, who was involved in the family's construction business and was horribly burned when hot asphalt exploded and put him into the Indianapolis Burn Center for almost a year; Terry (whose movie star good looks attracted girls like a magnet) worked at various jobs and was a drummer in a rock band; and youngest son, Troy, an artist who drew house plans complete with landscaping, was also a drummer in another rock band.

I could not have received better treatment than I received from these four young men. They treated me almost like I was their father. Not only were they always respectful and considerate of me, they were there when I needed them. For example, once I ran into an unexpected snow storm while traveling from South Carolina to Indiana on treacherous and mountainous Hwy. 75. As I neared Corbin, Kentucky, most of the cars on the road had slowed down, as had I, but we kept going through the heavy snowfall.

Planning to stop at the next motel and resume my trip after the snowfall stopped and the road was cleared, things went out of control about five miles from my destination, The Red Roof Inn. A speeding car raced past me, then hit its brakes when it had to swerve into the "slow" lane to avoid running into the back of another vehicle. I was forced to hit my brakes to avoid hitting the car now in my lane.

Hitting my brakes to avoid a collision caused my top heavy mini-van to slide out of control and into a guard rail. The collision with the guard rail then caused my van to ricochet across the divided highway into a ditch separating the north and southbound lanes. A large truck traveling in the "fast" lane barely missed my "out-of-control" vehicle.

Landing into the ditch between the divided lanes brought my van to a sudden stop and the engine died. I sat there shaking for a few minutes trying to regain my composure before seeing if I could restart the engine. Surprisingly, the engine started immediately. Knowing I could not extricate the van by trying to immediately climb the steep hill to get back on the highway, I put it into gear and headed north still in the ditch. Eventually I gained enough speed to climb the hill and get back into the northbound lane.

Still shaken by the experience, I moved across to the slow lane and turned right at the first exit and found a gas station still operating. To my good fortune, the operator on duty was a mechanic who put my van up on the lift to check its damage. After a few minutes, he lowered the lift and said: "Your van has suffered more damage than I can fix now but I think it is drivable for a short distance. However, I would head to a repair shop tomorrow before going too far."

After hearing this, I got back on I-75 and drove to the motel arriving there around 10:30 p.m. I decided it was too late to call Jo Ann. But I called her from the motel early the next morning and reported what had happened and why I was still in Kentucky. She told me to stay put at the motel until she could check with her sons (all of whom were good mechanics).

In less than an hour, Jo Ann called me at the motel and said that she talked with her boys and that Terry and Troy insisted they were coming to Kentucky to check on me and the condition of my van. She said they were fearful that the van might have an undetected problem, e.g., an oil or water leak, that could cause more serious damage if driven a relatively long distance. After the boys arrived and gave the van a thorough checking, they found that although there was a great deal of damage to the vehicle, further driving of the van would not be detrimental. Their plan was for one of them to drive the van back to Lafayette while the other brother would follow behind in his car. *They also thought my nerves had suffered enough from the snow storm and accident, and that it was risky for me to drive that distance. So I rode in the rear car.* When we reached Lafayette, they took the van straight to a body shop and dropped me off at my house. *(More about Jo Ann and her wonderful family later).*

# CHAPTER 21

## Settling into a Comfortable Routine

MEANWHILE, BACK AT Purdue I continued to settle comfortably into my job. With the aid of my new computer and assistance when needed from an understanding boss, I could not have asked for a better, more suitable job than the one I now had. I found it hard to believe that after five years of retirement and literally fighting for my life, I now found myself in such a desirable situation. The Lord was continuing to bless me!

For the next few years I enjoyed this nice routine. My job allowed me to travel, make new friends and strengthen friendships with people I had known at USDA and EPA. My job offered much satisfaction and some very nice fringe benefits. One of these was the Annual NPIRS conference which I was responsible for scheduling and planning. An important aspect, in addition to selecting and scheduling speakers, was the need to ensure that the setting was attractive, adequate for our purposes, and inexpensive enough to ensure we would attract many NPIRS members. *(The inexpensive factor was especially important to Federal and State employees whose per diem precluded them from attending events held at the more expensive facilities).*

A well attended conference was especially important because it gave us a chance to meet many new members in person, as well as to discuss and receive input from users regarding present and future system needs. Also, since we always conducted training sessions at the conference, this offered us the chance to train a relatively large group at one time, much more efficient than the "one-on-one" training I offered daily by telephone, email, or visits to my office.

Of course a favorite part of my job as conference planner was that it gave me a valid excuse to visit possible sites and decide which one would be the best location for that year's conference. That meant I visited the nicest facilities (hotels) in the most desirable cities, e.g. Las Vegas and Reno, NV; San Francisco, CA; Atlanta, GA; New Orleans, LA; San Antonio, TX, etc. In the course of these exploratory visits, I was "wined and dined" and often given the "Presidential Suite" while I was evaluating the facility.

NPIRS was growing and expanding, both in this country and internationally each year I was there as User Services Manager. It had grown numerically from 12 members (mostly State officials) to a membership of 600, which was also now much more varied. Users included a variety of State and Federal agencies, chemical and pesticide manufacturing companies, environmental groups, various agricultural groups, and representatives of several foreign countries.

By the mid-eighties, we had more than a dozen overseas members. The latter turned out to be a mixed blessing. Although we welcomed them warmly, service to them was difficult because of language and time differences. I personally regretted that I could not provide the same quick and easy user services that I could for our U.S. members. I dealt with the time difference as best I could by arranging to be available during non-work hours. *Actually, I also extended this service to the State of Hawaii because of the time difference there.* I also let our "far away" customers know that I would provide personal "one on one" training if they could arrange for international travel to Indiana. Some felt it was worth the trouble and expense to send personal representatives to Purdue for this training.

Two of the most memorable representatives from distant lands were those from Japan and Australia. First, I arranged my schedule so that I could devote full time to them. I spent time teaching them how to access the tremendous amount of pesticide and chemical information available to them from their keyboard. This was a particularly difficult problem for my Japanese visitor. He spoke some English but had little experience with computers or chemical uses and searches. It turned out that he was a top executive for the chemical company that employed thousands of workers. In retrospect, in my opinion his company should have sent someone with more "work" rather than "executive" experience. Despite his lack of aptitude for accessing a huge data base by computer, I admired his attitude. He tried hard to learn our system and I worked especially hard trying to teach him how to use it.

I soon realized that I faced an impossible task but I went to great lengths not to show it. I'm not sure he left feeling that our time together was worth all the time and expense of the trip but he was extremely gracious in expressing his gratitude to me. After he returned home, he sent me a beautiful oriental vase.

The story was very different for a visitor from Australia. As is usually the case with Aussies, we had no difficulty communicating with each other. And he had the background and aptitude that made it easy for him to get the hang of accessing the NPIRS database. This gave me more time to ensure that he learned more about the U.S. and had a good chance to get to know and appreciate the U.S. and its people while here.

The last was easy to do with the Aussie since I quickly discerned that he appreciated good looking people of the opposite sex. So, after our first training session ended, I took him to the Purdue girls volleyball team match. (That was the only organized sport available at the time). This proved to be a good choice. He admired the athletic talents (and shapeliness) of the girls so much that he asked me to take him to their practice session the following day after we finished work.

In addition to teaching them as much subject matter as possible, I wanted to give our international visitors a taste of "middle America" while they were in the U.S. Thus, I opened up my home to them and also drove them around the Midwest in the limited time we had.

The huge acreage Indiana farmers put into production each year was "mind blowing" to those living in countries like Japan where much of the work is done by hand on very small plots. In fact, this South Carolina farm boy whose family had to exist on a five-acre cotton allotment was awed by the number of Indiana farmers who used huge mechanized equipment to farm acreage that went into the thousands!

# CHAPTER 22

## An Unexpected Friendship

PERHAPS THE MOST unusual and interesting friendship I made while at Purdue was with someone I never met in person. His name was Evan Hunter, perhaps best known by that name as author of the book "The Blackboard Jungle." However, he might be even better known under his pseudonym, Ed McBain, author of the "87th Precinct" series which chronicled beat cops, forensic detectives, and other precinct members as they solved murders, rapes, and other human miseries. How did I get to know Hunter/McBain? He called me by telephone and introduced himself and gave me the brief background information (above) before explaining that, as Ed McBain, he was writing a murder mystery involving the killing of someone by poisoning and needed some information about poisons used around the home.

When I asked how he happened to call me he said he first called FDA, which referred him to EPA which in turn suggested he call "Jim White at Purdue University." He didn't understand (and neither did I) why EPA couldn't or wouldn't provide him with the information he needed but I was pleased about the referral. After a brief discussion, Evan explained that the murder product needed to be something readily available to homeowners. I knew that several home products used as mice/rat killers contained nicotine as their active ingredient. These products could be found in homes at that time (May 1986).

While keeping him "on hold" I did a quick search on NPIRS which yielded official information on several household products containing nicotine and their uses. I read some of this information aloud to him on the telephone. He was pleased at what he heard and asked if I could print this out and send it to him at Norwalk, CT, one of his two homes. He offered to pay for this material but I told him we wouldn't charge him anything. However, I told him I hoped he would give me permission to mention his call to me and his book in NPIRS News. He was glad to oblige.

I sent him the material and we exchanged several telephone calls and then I didn't hear from him for awhile. However, the following month I received a letter from him thanking me for my help and explaining that he was responding "tardily because I was in London promoting my latest book there." He added that he "enjoyed the mention of me in NPIRS News." Mr. Hunter (or McBain) ended his letter to me by saying that he would send me "an autographed copy when the novel--titled POISON, by the way--is published early next year."

Not hearing from the author for almost a year, I finally sent him a short note to that effect. Then, I received a letter dated March 17, 1987, from Evan that began: "Dear Jim: You have no idea how hard I've been trying to find you. When your letter arrived, I threw up my hands and cheered!" He then went on to describe his "sad saga." He said that when he left his Florida home in Sarasota in 1986, he shipped a box containing all his research and correspondence on POISON to his home in Connecticut.

After the book was published on Feb. 27, he asked his secretary to "dig your letters out of the file, the intention being to send you a copy of the book, as promised. The box had disappeared!" He went on to describe the efforts he made to find me and the box and added: "It vanished. Poof! A bigger mystery than the one in the book...So here you are and am I glad to hear from you! I like to keep my promises." Evan had enclosed a copy of POISON with the inscription, dated 3/16/87: "To Jim White--with much appreciation for your poisonous insights! Best Wishes, Evan (Ed McBain) Hunter."

We exchanged telephone calls for awhile and Evan invited me to visit him if I was ever near his homes in Norwalk, CT or Sarasota, FL but that never happened and we eventually lost touch. During the time we were in communication, he confided that he used different names to distinguish his different writing styles. For his "serious stuff" e.g. "The Blackboard Jungle," he used the name Evan Hunter. He used Ed McBain primarily for his 87th Precinct novels and said that writing this series was easy and very lucrative for him. But he didn't consider these books "serious literature" even though much of the world greatly appreciated the 87th Precinct. He also used other pseudonyms in other types of writing.

*In 2005, I spotted a news article in the Washington Post with the headline: "Novelist Hunter Dead at 78." The long article chronicled Hunter/McBain as one of the most prolific writers of his time. Although we never met in person I felt like I had lost a friend.*

# CHAPTER 23
## Thinking About a Lifestyle Change with Better Climate

BACK AT PURDUE, despite the sense of accomplishment I had regarding the success of NPIRS and my adjustment to living life without Gwen, I was beginning to think it was time for a serious change. Despite having an enjoyable, challenging job, I didn't want to spend the rest of my life in that cold Indiana climate. After about three years, I began to suggest to Dick Collier that I was ready for my last retirement and that he should start looking for a replacement for me.

At the end of each year after that, Dick and I would sit down and talk about the future. Each time he would tell me he had not been able to find a suitable replacement for me and ask me to agree to stay another year. During this time, however, I was thinking hard about where I wanted to spend my last days and I was experiencing a desire to head back South. In fact, much earlier while Gwen and I were still together, I had made some trips looking at possible retirement areas along coastal Highway 17 from Virginia to Savannah, Georgia. Two coastal cities in South Carolina, Beaufort and Charleston, were most appealing to me.

On one of these trips, I found an outstanding buy in the beautiful little town of

Beaufort, SC. It was a very run down house but it was located on "The Point," the most desirable and expensive area in this historic town. "The Point" has provided the back-drop for many famous movies including "The Big Chill" starring Tom Berenger, Glenn Close, Jeff Goldblum, William Hurt, and Kevin Kline. This popular movie was filmed about three blocks from the little house I was considering buying. It was shot at the same antebellum house (known locally as The Castle) also used as a location for the film "The Great Santini."

I was amazed that no one had snapped up this little house because I knew that despite its run down condition, it was the buy of a lifetime at $12,000. I called Gwen and she said, "Buy it!" Before signing the final papers, however, I looked at one more property owned by famous author Truman Capote's aunt Marie Rudisill, later known as the "Fruitcake Lady." She certainly lived up to that name in the short time I knew her. Marie found out somehow that I was looking for a house to restore in Beaufort and caught up with me at the North Street house. I had no idea who she was but she quickly informed me that she was Truman Capote's aunt and that she and her sister had more or less raised him.

I had my doubts about this story but was convinced when she showed me the manuscript of a book she was writing about her nephew to be titled "CAPOTE." When I told her I was also a writer who someday wanted to write a book, she urged me to read and comment on her manuscript. My schedule would not al-low me to read the entire manuscript but I did read a chapter or two and found it interesting.

Now, why did she want to meet me? She owned a house she had been restoring but ran into some problems and decided to sell it. She thought I might be a potential buyer. I agreed to follow her to look at the property. *(She was living in an RV parked behind the house with a man I assumed to be her husband).* When we started into the partially restored house, she told me it would be a little difficult for me to see the interior of the house. She explained that this was because one of her two Doberman pinscher dogs had just had a litter of puppies and the mother and puppies were stay-ing in the kitchen of the house.

As mentioned earlier I've always been afraid of dogs. I had no desire to meet up with a Doberman pinscher and certainly not one with young pups. With urging from Marie, I reluctantly went inside the house and peeked into the kitchen. I was greeted by a low growl from the Dobe and never ventured near the kitchen again. And be-cause there was no door to the kitchen I was fearful that too much exploration of any part of the house's interior might make the mother Dobe feel threatened. After a very quick tour of the house, I decided that a graceful exit might be best rather than risk a desperate dash for the door in case the Dobe mother felt I had overstayed my welcome. I said my goodbye to Marie and never saw her again.

How did she get the name "The Fruitcake Lady"? Although I didn't know this at the time, an Internet search in connection with this Memoir revealed that her book, **Fruitcake** (published by Hill Street Press) led to an invitation to be a guest on The Tonight Show back in 2000. During her first visit she showed host Jay Leno and guest

Mel Gibson how to make fruitcakes. This led to several more appearances on The Tonight Show in which she instructed host Jay Leno and other guests in the preparation of other baked desserts. And it led to the name "The Fruitcake Lady."

For those interested, Truman Capote's 1966 book "In Cold Blood" details the 1959 murders of four members of the Herbert Clutter family in the small farming community of Holcomb, Kansas. Before the killers were captured, Capote traveled to Kansas to gather personalized information with which to write about the crime. He was accompanied by his childhood friend and fellow author, Harper Lee, author of the book, "To Kill A Mockingbird." When finally published, "In Cold Blood" was an instant success, and today is one of the biggest-selling true crime books in publishing history.

Then it was back to the North Street property followed by a visit to the real estate listing office and when I left Beaufort, Gwen and I were the owners of a very desirable property on "The Point!"

As related earlier, my life plans changed drastically after Gwen decided to end our marriage. This had not changed my desire to restore the Beaufort property but delayed any prospect for starting this project in the immediate future. However, soon after I arrived at Purdue, I began getting calls from an official Historic Beaufort restoration group (don't recall the name) demanding that I start restoration of the property immediately. I didn't understand the rush since the property had been in disrepair for many years before I bought it.

A telephone call to a Beaufort friend cleared up the mystery. The official calling me was not only part of the town's restoration group; she was a real estate agent with a client who very badly wanted to buy the property. Since my life had changed so much, I decided I did not want to fight this battle from far away Indiana. So, the next time the agent called me I said: "I'll sell the property for $20,000 cash. Send me a contract and a check for $20,000. I won't consider a counter offer."

I had my money within a few days and sent half of it to Gwen. Later I learned that the little house had received a very bad restoration and was sold for over $300,000. The second time it was sold, still not restored to my standards, it sold for over $600,000. With a proper restoration, I suspect it would now be worth over a million dollars. Despite giving up this house on "The Point" I had not given up on the idea of some day buying and restoring a historic property along the South Carolina coast. And, I was thinking it was about time for a "real retirement."

# CHAPTER 24
## More Pressure to Find a Replacement

THE MORE I thought about returning to the South, the more pressure I was putting on Dick Collier to find a replacement for me. Although I had no firm plans of where I would retire, I felt strongly that it would be in the South--hopefully on the Carolina coastline.

On my earlier trips years ago, I had visited the beautiful city of Charleston, SC several times and thought it might also be a great retirement place. So I planned a trip there to see if it held any possibilities for me. On the way down, I stopped to visit Catawba College friends living in Columbia, SC. Not only would it be nice to renew my friendship with him and his wife, also a Catawba classmate, they might have some useful ideas for me. This thinking proved to be prophetic when I learned the husband was Area Legal Council for Housing and Urban Development (HUD).

The following day I continued on to Charleston, where I secured the services of the former head of the Charleston Area Board of Realtors. I asked him to show me historic properties that I might be able to purchase and restore. The only interesting available property he found for me was a carriage house behind a historic home. The carriage house listing price was already out of my price range at $350,000, with the provision that the buyer would need about that same amount to bring it up to "code."

Needless to say that told me Charleston was too rich for my blood. Even if I had that kind of money, I wouldn't pay it for a carriage house. Thoroughly disillusioned about the prospect of buying and restoring a house in Charleston, I headed back to Indiana--again stopping off at my friend's house in Columbia. After I had told him the story of my visit to Charleston he had some possible suggestions for me.

He told me that HUD had several foreclosures in South Carolina, including a townhouse in Mount Pleasant, just across the river from Charleston. He added: "If you're interested, this property might offer several possibilities to you: (1) it would make a nice vacation home, (2) it would be a good investment, and (3) it's near enough to Charleston that you could do your own looking and might find a restorable property you can afford at some future time."

This caught my interest, especially when I saw that the townhouse was located close to Shem Creek (a wonderful place to enjoy fresh seafood). He had a floor plan for the property which showed a living room, kitchen and powder room on the first floor and two bedrooms and full bath on the second floor.

By the time I left Columbia, I was interested enough to ask my friend to draw up the paperwork needed for me to be a potential purchaser of the townhouse. He informed me that I would have to bid for the property against other potential buyers--mostly investors. So I left a low bid hoping I might "luck out." In a short time I received notice that my bid was accepted and I was now owner of a townhouse across the river from Charleston at my bid price of $65,000!

Although I couldn't imagine spending the rest of my life in that townhouse it certainly was a good buy and it had lots of potential as my friend had mentioned. Over the following months, I made several short visits in my van to keep an eye on the property and deliver furniture I had purchased in Indiana. Then a special and unanticipated use of the townhouse popped up. When I told Mitch I was planning to leave Indiana for Charleston, SC within a year or two, he said: "Dad, as much as I would like to complete my degree at Purdue, I haven't given up on my desire to see if I could make it on the professional tennis circuit. If I'm going to do that, I need to give it a try before it's too late; with your approval I'd like to leave Purdue at the end of this semester." He added: "The longer I work as a tennis instructor, the less chance I'll have to succeed on the pro circuit. I can get my degree later at Purdue or transfer my credits to a school closer than Indiana."

Of course I knew that playing "pitty pat" tennis with amateurs was detrimental to Mitch's game but I had selfishly wanted to hold him close to me since he was the most precious thing left from my former life. Then he added the clincher: "Dad, if you agree, I think Charleston would be a great place for me to use as a base while I get in shape for the tour. If I could stay at your townhouse, I could look after it for you, and spend time with you when you take a vacation there."

As much as I wanted him to get his college degree *(at the end of the semester he would be less than a school year away from his undergraduate degree)* I didn't want to further hamper his chance to fulfill his childhood dream. And the idea of being able to spend time with him in Charleston was certainly appealing. So, I said: "Mitch, that seems like a workable plan to me. While you complete this semester, I'll do some checking for you at the Charleston Tennis Club which is less than a mile from my townhouse." Mitch replied: "Dad, I'd really appreciate that. If you have a chance to talk to the head pro there, please ask him if he would work with me to help get me in shape for the pro circuit."

Soon after that I took a few days vacation time and drove to my townhouse. The following morning I visited the Creekside Tennis Club (which it is now called) and asked to see the head pro. After a few minutes, an athletic looking middle aged man dressed in tennis attire appeared. He introduced himself as Richard Shy, head of the club's tennis program. After he learned I had just driven down from Lafayette, IN, he said: "I was the head pro at the Lafayette Tennis Club until I took this job a couple of years ago." I said, "Then you may have known my son, Mitch White, who works there." He chuckled and said: "I hired Mitch and he worked for me a couple of years before I left for this job. He is a fine player and instructor."

When I explained why I was visiting the club, Shy said he would be happy to help Mitch get ready for the circuit. He said: "I'll give Mitch free court time and round up the best players I can find as his practice partners. This area has some excellent tennis players, many of whom have been on the pro circuit, and they would love to hit with someone of Mitch's talent."

*Shortly after leaving Purdue, Mitch moved into my townhouse at Mt. Pleasant and entered his first big tournament, beating the #1 player from Clemson in the finals of that tournament. Later that year, Mitch began competing with tour players around the U.S. Mitch played Todd Martin once and lost in two tie breakers after leading in both sets. Although playing well on the circuit Mitch was struggling mentally and physically. He told me later that he never fully reached the competitive edge he had at age 19. Apparently, the long layoff from highly competitive tennis had been more destructive to his game than expected. Also, sometimes playing up to three matches a day on concrete had caused his old knee problems to worsen.*

*Things reached the point that doctors advised him that damage to his knees had become so bad that very serious knee surgery would be required if he continued playing tennis at that high level.* By then, Mitch had reached age 26 and the type of knee surgery he needed could keep him off the circuit for as much as two years. That meant he would not be able to resume competitive tennis until age 28. At that age, serve and volley players were usually near the end of their careers. *Knee surgery has now advanced to the point that present day athletes can recover much quicker and resume their careers.*

Mitch left the tour and returned to Charleston to begin developing a tennis teaching and coaching business in and around the Charleston area, including clubs at Sullivan's Island, Wild Dunes and Isle of Palms (and others I can't recall). He soon had a bustling career teaching and coaching. *I still cherish a large color photo of him demonstrating his volleying form in an article that appeared in the Charleston News & Courier newspaper after he left the tour.*

Meanwhile, back at Purdue, Dick Collier had found a possible replacement for me. But in a weak moment I agreed to stay another year to serve as my replacement's tutor and to work with Dick in developing a marketing program for a highly technical program involving the effect of space travel on various materials. As I recall, the work was associated with NASA. *Purdue had long been active in the aerospace program and training of astronauts.* Things went well with the new assignment with Dick Collier but not so well as a tutor for my replacement.

Before we could develop a marketing plan for the aerospace program, the two of us had to develop an understanding of the relationship between Purdue and various elements of the space program. The nature of the program and technical issues were easier for Dick Collier since he had a PhD in Biochemistry. My primary job was largely to gather input from the various entities involved in the program. This required me to visit with representatives of various aerospace companies such as Lockheed Martin, Northrop Grumman, and McDonnell Douglas.

As a result of the changed assignment, Dick and I moved from Entomology Hall to the aerospace building just off campus. This made it easier to interact with space management and engineers but lessened our ability to personally know how things were progressing at NPIRS. The thing that bothered me the most was that during the year we were gone, not a single NPIRS News, our major marketing tool, had been written.

# CHAPTER 25

## A Nasty Surprise!

ON SEPTEMBER 22, 1989, I got a nasty surprise. National news outlets began reporting that Hurricane Hugo was approaching the SC coastline toward Charleston, SC. I began trying to call Mitch to urge him to lock up the townhouse and leave town before Hurricane Hugo struck. I had no luck reaching him. That evening a broadcast station weatherman reported that Hurricane Hugo had made landfall just outside

Charleston at Sullivan's Island. He described it as a Category 4 storm with estimated maximum winds of 135-140 mph. I was still calling the Mt. Pleasant townhouse hoping to be able to reach Mitch but getting no response.

At midnight, I lay in bed listening to a Charleston radio station. I'll never forget what sounded like the roar of freight trains from a reporter's open mike. Needless to say, I got little sleep that night and still remember the horrible sounds made by Hugo. Before morning I heard the news that Hugo had produced tremendous wind and storm surge damage along the coast and even produced hurricane force wind gusts several hundred miles inland into both Carolinas. I later learned that Hugo produced the highest storm tide heights ever recorded along the U.S. east coast. Hugo was described as the strongest storm to strike the U.S. in the last 20 years and was the nation's costliest hurricane on record in terms of monetary losses ($7 billion in damage). It is estimated that there were 49 deaths directly related to the storm, most of which occurred in the U.S., Puerto Rico, and the U.S. Virgin Islands.

The next morning, I was about to get in my van and head to Mt. Pleasant to check on Mitch and my townhouse. Anticipating my action, Mitch called to tell me to stay in Indiana while he handled the situation at Mt. Pleasant. He said that in anticipation of the damage, he had left the area the day before for safety reasons as well as to purchase flashlights, batteries, etc. to help deal with the aftermath of the hurricane. He said he would call and give me a damage report later that day after getting a firsthand look at the situation. After arriving back at Mt. Pleasant, Mitch called to report that, despite heavy damage to homes in the surrounding area, my townhouse was virtually untouched. Because of the damage all around, he asked me to wait a few days before coming down from Indiana.

Naturally I was happy to learn that my son and townhouse were both safe. However, I had already planned to attend a family reunion to be held at a church near Gastonia, NC. So I headed south toward Gastonia, where I would spend the night with my Sister Edith and her husband, Frank Ford. We would go together to the reunion the next day.

When I arrived in Gastonia, I was astounded by the hurricane damage that far inland from the hurricane site. I had to pick my way around large fallen trees to reach my sister's house. When I finally arrived there, I found that the electricity was off and trees had fallen all around their house. Fortunately, none had hit the house itself although broken tree limbs cluttered the yard. Realizing nothing could be done at that time, we spent the evening with light from Frank's antique Aladdin kerosene lamps. The following morning my Sister Edith cooked our reunion food on Frank's propane gas cooker on the carport.

Then we drove to the family reunion for an enjoyable time with relatives. After contacting Mitch when we returned home, he provided me with more details about Hugo's damage and told me that the only damage to the townhouse was that all the screens had been ripped off by the high winds. Otherwise, the townhouse appeared to be untouched although some nearby houses had been completely demolished. It looked as if God had continued to look out for me!

A day or so later, I drove on to Mt. Pleasant and spent a few days with Mitch while he checked out the condition of courts in the Charleston area. Unfortunately, most of the tennis courts were unusable and it would be many months before the courts would be repaired to the point that he could resume his teaching/coaching career there.

# CHAPTER 26
## Some Major Decisions to Make

AT THAT POINT both Mitch and I had decisions to make: Mitch immediately decided to return to his home area of Washington, DC, where he was well known and could make a good living teaching and coaching. I decided that I did not want to own property subject to hurricanes and listed my townhouse for sale with a real estate agent before returning to Indiana to finish my final weeks at Purdue.

Dick and I had completed our work on the space program and returned to Entomology Hall. Both Dick and I were disappointed in the lack of progress made by my replacement. Although he proved knowledgeable at solving computer hardware problems, he was unable or unwilling to produce much in the areas of educational and training materials--the most vital part of this job. Sadly, he had not completed a single edition of NPIRS News since I had been away. While spending my "tutoring" effort with him, I had emphasized the importance of revising or writing new training and education materials (including the newsletter) needed to keep users up to date on changes and improvements to the system.

I had also urged him to produce some "drafts" that I could critique and help him get into shape to send out but it never happened. He would respond by saying "Jim, it takes me two weeks to write something you can knock out in a couple of hours." I suspected that he thought if he held out long enough, I might "knock out" one or more issues but I didn't think this would help him address the problem. So, he continued to work in the area he was comfortable with, i.e. solving computer hardware problems for users. I left the problem for Dick Collier to solve.

Back to a decision on my retirement location, I had approached this more on where I did NOT want to retire. The Washington DC area was out because of the painful memories of my leaving there in 1983. The Carolina coast had lost some of its attraction because of Hugo which had led me to sell my potential retirement property in Charleston.

I had never considered retiring to my home area of Blacksburg, SC. I still had memories of my sharecropping days: hoeing and picking cotton, living without electricity, running water or inside bathrooms and other inconveniences I had experienced as a boy. In addition, only a few close relatives and one friend, Les Roark, were still alive and living nearby. In fact, only two sisters and I were left from the eight siblings born to Haskell and Macie White.

However, as the end of my stay at Purdue was imminent, I decided it was time I paid a visit back to the Carolinas to visit my two living sisters, Nell Turner; who lived near Blacksburg, which I considered my "home town" and my other sister, Edith Ford, who lived in nearby Gastonia, NC. My two other sisters, Faye and Isabel, had passed years earlier. A long time before, I had lost my three brothers: Howard, Robert and Frank. So I had few pleasant memories tugging at my heart-strings to return "home."

I did have quite a few surviving nephews and nieces but since I had been away from my home area for so long, I had little connection to them. I had not even seen Brother Howard's youngest daughter, Dianne, and youngest son, Boyce, since they were youngsters. I was sadly reminded that I missed funerals for three of my siblings because I was traveling on my jobs and could not be reached in time to attend.

This visit to Blacksburg quickly began to change my thinking. I had a very pleas-ant visit with several surviving members of my family. Then a call from my niece Sue Perry to my sister Nell added an unexpected element in favor of returning to my home area. In the course of her call, Sue asked Sister Nell to "tell Uncle Jim that the old 'Cash Mansion' is for sale and that he should go take a look at it while he is nearby."

When Nell relayed Sue's message, I replied that I had no idea where this house was located. As a matter of fact, I didn't know such a place existed in this little back-ward town. Sister Nell's son, Dan, who was visiting me at his mother's house at the time, quickly said "Uncle Jim, if you'll wait for me to go across the road to get my car, I'll take you there." I replied that my van was parked in the driveway and that we could go in it if he would show me the way.

When we arrived at the Cash place, one of the first things I saw was that the front door was standing wide open. After we checked and found no one was there, we toured the three levels of the house: first floor, second floor and attic. We would also have checked out the small basement and crawl space but there was a sign on the basement door saying: **"Danger, do not enter; basement is flooded with water."**

That warning was certainly bad news but I was impressed by the space, tall ceil-ings, heart pine floors, floor plan and "grand appearance" of the house. Damage to the house was obvious without even close inspection. Water damage from a leaky roof was apparent as well as termite damage. An 8X10 foot piece of plywood at the entrance kept unwary visitors from falling through the floor into the crawl space.

My nephew Dan said he had heard that since no one had been willing to even make an offer on the place, it would be bulldozed to the ground and buried in the near future. As someone who appreciated grand old houses, I didn't like the sound of that. And, I could not leave the front door unlocked for fear that vandals might burn the house to the ground. I told Dan (now deceased) that I wanted to lock the front door before we left. A quick look at the door lock showed that the door and house had sunk so much that the door's latch and strike plate no longer met. The solution: remove the strike plate and either enlarge or make another hole in the jamb so that the latch and strike plate would meet.

Dan suggested we return to his home to get a screwdriver, chisel and hammer to do the job. I told him that I always carried some tools in my van and that on the way south I had stopped at a flea market and bought an old wooden handle screwdriver sharpened to the point that it could be used as both a screwdriver and chisel. I always carried one of my hammers with me in the van's toolbox. That might be all the tools we needed.

I brought the tools into the house and removed the strike plate using the old tool as a screwdriver. Then I used my hammer and the old sharpened tool to extend the hole so that the latch and strike plate would match up. We then pulled the door closed, and heard a satisfying click as the door locked.

As we were getting into the van to leave, I jotted down the name and phone number of the real estate agent from the "For Sale" sign and drove back to my sister's house. By that time, I had begun to feel an emotional attachment to the house and had a hard time getting my mind off of it. I couldn't help but think that unless I acted quickly the house might be bulldozed to the ground. So, I used my sister's phone to call the listing agent. Before hanging up I made an offer on the house and the three acres on which it sat and left my Indiana phone number with him.

I left Sister Nell's home early the next morning and headed back to Indiana. Late that evening the Gaffney real estate agent called and said the Cash family had accepted my offer. That call set in motion a complete change in my plans and lifestyle. The next day I met with Dick Collier and told him that I had purchased a large "falling down" old house in my home town and that I would need to leave Purdue soon to begin work on restoring the property. Dick told me he understood my situation but invited me to continue tutoring my replacement as long as I could spare the time. I agreed to do so. My last days at Purdue will be described at the end of this Part.

*While I was still in contact with NPIRS, not a single newsletter had gone out from the User Services office since I left. The last time I heard from my "replacement," he called to tell me he had left Purdue and taken a job somewhere in Georgia. Hopefully the new position was better suited to his ability and desires. Soon after that, Dr. Collier called to say he had resigned from Purdue and taken a job in private industry with headquarters in Valdosta, Georgia. So this was no longer the NPIRS I had known and loved.*

# CHAPTER 27
## An Impending Visit South--My New Home?

SOON AFTER THAT I persuaded my Indiana master carpenter and friend, Bill Hartje, to follow me to Blacksburg for the two of us to get a better idea of what needed to be done to the old house I now owned. I planned for us to stay a week to give the project a thorough "going over" in respect to what would be needed to bring the old house back to its potential as an example of beautiful Greek Revival styling.

Since we did not expect to begin any serious work on the house during this visit, Bill did not bring his heavy tools with him. Primarily, we wanted to ensure that the electrical system of the house would be safe for us to stay there during our visit and after we left. I had told Bill that Dan and I had checked the fuse box and found that it had only three large fuses for the entire house. In addition, we had seen loose wires hanging all over the place. We had not seen a modern breaker box or breaker in the house!

The first thing Bill did after we arrived at the Cash house was to check the electrical system. He was appalled at what he found. "Jim, I don't see how this house is still standing. It should have burned down long ago." Then, he shut off the power to the fuse box and began pulling out wires. As he tore them out, I loaded them into a large trash can. He even discovered drop cords stapled to shoe molding. They went into the trash can also.

When Bill finished removing all the dangerous wiring, he said: "Let's go to Lowe's and buy enough new #12 wiring so that we can have safe power for all three floors." (We had not yet dared go into the basement because of standing water). But he made the power cord for the first level long enough that we could safely explore the crawl space which appeared to be dry. *It was easy to access the crawl space through the large hole covered with the sheet of plywood!*

By the time Bill had finished his work of ensuring that we had safe power at all three floors, it was time to get supper at the downtown Bantam Chef and figure out how we would sleep. I don't recall how I happened to possess them but I had brought two roll away beds and bed linens from Lafayette. Bill carried his bed upstairs where he had access to a private bathroom with old clawfoot tub. Surprisingly, we still had running water. I moved my bed into the kitchen near a first floor bathroom containing the second clawfoot tub. Both of us took cold baths that night since there was no working hot water heater. Each of us had old but working floor lamps which had been left in the house.

That night as I lay in my bed trying to go to sleep, I eventually began thinking that I was not alone in the room. I reached up, yanked on the pull chain of the floor lamp and saw mice scurrying to get out of sight! Since it was too late to find a mouse trap, I spent the rest of the night hoping I would not have company in bed. The following morning, after breakfast at a local restaurant, we went to the local hardware store to purchase mouse traps and began to set them throughout the house.

Then we began a room by room inspection of the house. When we got to a second floor front bedroom, I placed a ladder against the outside wall and took a couple of steps up the ladder. (I don't recall the reason why). As I took the second step up the ladder the wall moved outward. Needless to say I got down from the ladder in a hurry. That was our most obvious clue that the house had serious structural problems and we set out to identify them as best we could.

We stripped the "weak" front wall of its plaster and lath down to the bare studs and saw that there was space between the top plate of the wall and the attic above--which this wall was supposed to be supporting! We were not sure what was holding up the front of the attic but we feared the house might come tumbling down at any moment! This finding let us know that we needed to look closer at the supporting sill from the crawl space.

We were happy that Bill had made the first floor electric cord long enough that it could extend through the large opening into the crawl space. That ensured that we could have good light to inspect the foundation wall. And all we had to do to gain access to the crawl space was to remove the large piece of plywood at the entrance and drop down into the hole.

Once we entered the crawl space, it didn't take long to discover that the entire large front outer sill (made of several long pieces of lumber at least 10X10 inches thick) appeared to be rotten. We felt it needed to be replaced as soon as possible to keep the entire front wall of the house from collapsing. Upon making this discovery, I called Dick Collier, informed him of the dire situation, and he said: "Stay down there until you feel it's safe to leave the house."

Bill and I agreed that we needed to remove the old rotten sill and replace it with new treated wood before we could safely leave the house. But this decision left us with some tough questions: (1) how do we remove that big, rotten sill? (Bill had not brought his chain saw and the largest tool he had to work with was a reciprocating saw--much too small to cut through this huge piece of solid wood; (2) even if we found a way to remove this large support sill, where would we find a piece of lumber that size? and (3) if we found a beam that size, how would we get it to the location and put it into place with the limited space and manpower available to us?

We left the crawl space and went back to the first floor to cogitate on the matter. As I sat near the front wall where the baseboard had been removed and part of the sill was visible, I picked up a screwdriver and pecked at the sill in question. Suddenly my screwdriver went into empty space. The visible section of the sill had collapsed. We went back into the crawl space and saw a pile of dust where the sill had been.

That finding was key to removing the large sill. On close inspection, we could see that the remainder of the sill was hollow and consisted of only a thin outer shell. That led to the question "What's holding up this house?" But we were cheered by the fact that all we needed to remove the entire sill was some simple hand tools. Soon all we had left were piles of dust that we scooped into trash cans along with a few pieces of rotten wood. We emptied all of this in the woods behind the house.

After more discussion, we decided that the best way to solve the remaining problem was to fabricate the large sill in layers and sections of treated lumber that the two of us could lift and tap into place. So we figured out the length and number of 2X10's needed to replicate the large sill. We also decided to assemble the treated wood into shorter sections that we could "lock together." This would make them easier to handle and stronger. We would use screws and glue to hold them together for extra strength.

The next day we went to Gaffney Lumber where I established a contractor's account, and bought our needed supplies which were delivered the following day. Later that day we began assembling all the sections and after they had time for the glue to dry, had begun tapping them into place. Although I had not expected to use them, I had brought along the old "handy dandy" railroad jacks I had retained from Clifton days. Obviously they would not be able to jack up an entire wall, but the railroad jacks made it easier for us to lift small areas and tap in sections as we built them. We assured the strength of the completed beam by overlapping the layers of each section and then using full length pieces for the front and back. By the time we finished we had the equivalent of an extremely large treated support beam.

While we were learning more about the difficulties I would face in restoring this large house, I reached the conclusion that, other than planning, this restoration job was too big for me to handle. There was simply too much damage throughout. And close inspection had also revealed that the original contractor had concentrated only on making the house look beautiful and impressive from the street.

Bill and I discovered that in many areas of the house (e.g., large French door and window openings) which should have had 2X12 doubled headers to support the upstairs floor or floors had 2X4 headers! Obviously these supports had to be replaced to meet today's standards. So, while I was in town, I talked with several contractors, two of whom seemed interested in working for me. I got prices from each and ended up selecting as contractor a former brick mason from Ohio, who now lived in Blacksburg.

Finding out just how much work and expense were involved should have started me thinking more about what I would do with the property, once it was restored to "better than new condition." I knew my bank account would be empty by the time that occurred. However, my emotions still ruled my brain and my thinking centered around saving this old house rather than "What will I do with it once it is restored." I left the solution to that problem to be figured out later.

*I still chuckle over the fact that until word got around that I was native to the region, I was described as a "rich Yankee," dumb enough to buy and spend lots of money restoring an old mansion that should be torn down.*

Before leaving Blacksburg, I signed a contract with the contractor, who took the job on a "cost per hour" basis. He said he would keep an accurate record of hours per phase (beginning with removal of the old plaster and lath, electrical and plumbing rough in, etc., etc.) We would follow the same payment plan for both interior and exterior work. I would inspect the quality of each phase before paying him. *(And as an extra attraction, he offered me the use of his vacant garage apartment when I came to check on things). Since I would not be around to order lumber, nails, etc., I authorized Gaffney Lumber Co. to permit the contractor to use my account for supplies needed for my project. I would pay them directly for these purchases.*

Bill and I headed back to Indiana, feeling good about what we had accomplished. Both of us felt that I had made the right decision in turning this project over to professionals. Some of the structural work was way beyond my capacity; and because of the distance, Bill Hartje would not always be available to help me. (The need for professionals to do the heavy work was confirmed later when I learned that the contractor had been forced to rent jacks of 100-300 ton capacity for some phases of leveling the house; sometimes it was necessary to lift all three floors of the house at the same time!)

# CHAPTER 28
## Plan to Leave Purdue on Hold

WHEN I RETURNED to Indiana, Dick Collier began urging me to stay around a bit longer before I submitted my resignation. This agreement came with the acknowledgment that I would make frequent trips to Blacksburg to check progress and pay the contractor for each phase of his work. So far I had been quite pleased at the quality, quantity, and charges for the work. As my time for leaving Purdue approached, I decided to write one final issue of NPIRS News, mainly because Dick wanted to personally announce my retirement and make sure this notice was laudatory. Modesty prevents me from including the high praise I received from him for my contributions to the National Pesticide Information Retrieval System.

The notice of my retirement elicited an unexpected event: the offer of a high paying job (by my standards) that I could do on my own schedule from my home in Blacksburg. A brief explanation follows: One of our NPIRS members owned a consulting business that provided services to companies dealing with the registration of pesticides with EPA. This member, whom I had dealt with for several years, had mentioned several times over the years that he wanted to talk to me about a job once I left Purdue.

Although flattered that he wanted to talk to me about another retirement job, I had not given this matter serious thought. Now, I realized that he was completely serious and I had to devote time and thought to it. In his preliminary offer he said he would let me: (1) set my own salary per hour or per day; and (2) work as much or as little as I desired. He said his company would procure and set up all necessary equipment, e.g., computer, printers, etc. in an office for me in Blacksburg.

When I mentioned the possibility of having an office for this work in my future home, he approved of that idea. His only requirement was that I visit Washington, DC, once a month to confer with him, pick up new assignments and to visit EPA. The latter was to ensure that my contacts there remained current!

Although not committing myself to anything, I told him I would require at least $100 per hour for my time. He said he considered that reasonable--that he would charge the client double or triple that amount. I asked him why he was offering me this high paying job since he might be better served by hiring a pesticide specialist.

He replied, "Jim, we don't need a chemical expert for this job. I know you worked with the pesticide registration division at USDA and EPA serving as Director Harold Alford's right hand man when he was in charge of that Division. Also, when you moved into the Operations Division at EPA serving as a branch chief you worked even closer with chemical industry people who trust you.

"You have worked with the people currently handling the pesticide registration process, and I'm sure they would be more than willing to assist you when needed. Finally, you've spent the past several years teaching people from this country and around the world how to access EPA's data through NPIRS. In fact you've even taught many EPA employees how to access their own data base using the NPIRS computerized system! All you would need to do in the job I'm offering is to: (1) find out the uses a company wants to register; (2) use our membership with NPIRS to search the EPA data base; (3) put together the registration packet in the format required by EPA; and (4) turn this packet over to my company which would submit the package to EPA and bill the company."

Sensing that I was still skeptical, the consultant urged me to swing by his DC office and have lunch and a one-on-one discussion with him the next time I headed south. He told me how to reach his downtown DC office so I could check out the situation personally. I agreed to do that and we agreed on a date and time suitable for both of us.

A few weeks later on the way to Blacksburg we had our meeting at his office. As I entered the city where I had spent 25 years, I got lost because of the many changes to DC. When I finally found his office location, I began attempting to find a place to park. All of the parking garages nearby had the "full" sign displayed which meant I had to find "off street" parking. I found such a space about 20 blocks from his office and walked back for our meeting. We had a cold sandwich from a machine, had our meeting, and I told him I needed more time to think about my decision. I made the long trek back to my van, hoping it would be intact, and headed south.

On the way to Blacksburg, I continued to mull over the situation. I liked the idea of the work (and the money) but did not like the idea of having to return to DC each month and face all the hassle I had just encountered. By the time I arrived in Blacksburg, I had made a tentative decision not to take the job.

Since I was so busy dealing with the old Cash mansion, I forgot to call the consulting firm with my decision. After a couple of months, the firm's owner called and said: "Jim, since I haven't heard from you, I assume you aren't too interested in my offer." I apologized for my delay in calling him and replied: "You're right. After getting a taste of the hassle of that big city during my visit to your office, I could not see myself jumping back into that swamp. I really do appreciate your generous offer and wish you the best in the future."

I was flattered that Purdue folks gave me a big "going away" party the last week I was there. It was attended by NPIRS and other Entomology Department members. After the party, I was ready to head south for good. My retirement date was October 1, 1989 but I commuted back and forth from Indiana to South Carolina for some time while my house in Blacksburg was reaching the point that I could "camp out" there. It also gave me some extra time to work with my replacement who was having some difficulty with the required writing.

The fact is that reconstruction of the Cash house needed more time than we anticipated and it was not yet quite ready for guests. However, it did have hot running water with which I could take a bath! This left me with one remaining problem: selling my house at 630 Ferry Street, Lafayette. Within days, I sold it to a young couple who had been admiring it from the street for some time.

I was happy about the sale until later when I passed by the house and saw that the couple had "bastardized" this beautiful example of Frank Lloyd Wright's style of architecture by placing huge concrete lions (or tigers) on each side of the steps leading up to the front porch. My only hope is that this couple will someday grow to fully appreciate the natural beauty of this Prairie Style house and remove those garish embellishments.

My good feelings for South Carolina began returning soon after I made the decision to "save" that old house on Pine Street. But this time I wouldn't be returning as a "sharecropper boy." I would be going back as a man in his mid 60's who had enjoyed several challenging and rewarding careers.

*Post Script: The appreciation I received as I was retiring from Purdue notwithstanding, I'm certain I received more than I contributed to this great university. I will never be able to repay Purdue people (especially John Osmun and Dick Collier) for their kindnesses to me. At the height of my despair over the disintegration of my family, they sought me out, offered me a wonderful, challenging job, and gave me a graceful way to leave my former home and life. And they took me to their bosom while I went through the healing process. Thank you from the bottom of my heart, Purdue University and its people.*

# Work Career Begins 1950

First job after college was teaching English and Spanish at Sanford, NC. An added job was to establish and coach boy's and girl's tennis teams. As shown below, we were getting courts ready for season. The photo was taken by one of Rock Hill Evening Herald's news photographers.

## Sanford High Netters Prepare For Court Season

Members of Sanford high's first tennis team are shown above conditioning courts for the beginning of practice. Coach Jim White of the newly organized Sanford high tennis teams looks on as Delma Moser (left) and Billy Heins push a roller over the city's tennis courts prior to the first work-out. (Sanford Herald Photo.)

## *Sanford High Net Team To Play Greensboro, Burlington*

### White Says Lengthy Drills Will Have To Start Soon

Jim White, Sanford high school tennis coach stated this morning that so far he has been able to schedule only four matches for the new Sanford high tennis squad, and none of those matches will include the girls team.

White stated that the boys team will have two matches with Greensboro and two with Burlington during April. He also said that tentative matches with the Southern Pines team are being arranged.

The Sanford high coach stated that he is eager to schedule the Southern Pines team because if the Moore county school enters competition it will enter a girls as well as a boys team.

White says that he has contacted over 15 other schools in the state seeking matches for

Raleigh, Durham, Goldsboro, and Fayetteville.

Members of the Sanford teams hope to get practice into full swing this week if weather permits. The courts have not yet been fully conditioned for play but it is hoped that more work can be done on them in the very near future.

No one has definitely been assigned a place on either of the squads as yet, White stated. Before the first match White plans to set a play-off to determine the members of the varsity squad. The Sanford high coach revealed that from time to time during the season, it will be possible for any member of the squad to challenge for one of the varsity positions and a play-off will be arranged.

The Schedule of matches for the Sanford team to date is as follows:

April 5—Greensboro at Sanford.

As newspaper reporter, 1952.

Jim as newspaper reporter.

**Jim at USDA.**

# After Marriage to Gwen in 1962 and
# Birth of Mitch the Following Year

**Holding Mitch as toddler.**

**EPA retirement party w second wife Gwen (Mitch's mom)
and colleague Fred Whittimore.**

**Jim and Assistant Administrator Ed Johnson at Office of Pesticide Programs, EPA.**

**Jim at State Department.**

**Jim in his office at Purdue.**

**Mitch at Purdue with Jo Ann's sons Terry and Troy.**

**Purdue with colleagues Dick Collier (on left) and John Osmun (on right).**

**Purdue retirement party.**

# PART 10

## ANATOMY OF AN OLD HOUSE RESTORATION

# CHAPTER 1
## Finding a Function and Bringing an Old House Back to Life

*THE FORMAT OF this Memoir changed during its writing. Originally, details of the restoration effort were meant to be included in sequence with the stories being told. However, in Part 10, this approach would result in frequent changes of the story line as I went back and forth between Indiana and South Carolina while the restoration was proceeding. So, to make things simpler, the decision was made to complete the entire story of the restoration and landscaping effort in this part of the Memoir.*

The renovation of the Cash house which eventually became the highly acclaimed White House Inn did not begin with the work that Bill Hartje and I did on our first trip to Blacksburg after my purchase of the property. Our work then was to stabilize the house so that it would not fall before decisions could be made regarding the renovation and future of the property.

After some study of the severe damage already done to the house over the years, it soon became obvious that much expensive work was needed to save this old house, built around the turn of the century. The question of what I would do with this extremely large house once restored, then forced its way through the morass of emotions I felt for it. In other words, reality had reared its ugly face. Realizing that restoration of the property would eat up most of my savings, I began devoting serious thought about what to do with this restored beauty. After all, it had been vacant for years with no serious interest shown by potential purchasers.

As a single man, it was obviously larger than I needed for a residence and no one was beating my door down to discuss its use as a business. I had some discussions with a person interested in making it into a funeral home but he indicated that some fairly extensive architectural changes would be required for this use and this did not appeal to me. Also, Blacksburg already had a successful funeral home in town.

After much thought and suggestions by friends, I finally concluded that the only thing that would justify spending this much money, time and effort, was to turn this potentially beautiful old building into an upscale bed and breakfast. The decision to buy it and spend so much time and expense restoring this old house had already resulted in questions about my sanity. When people heard that I was thinking of turning the Cash house into an upscale bed and breakfast in Blacksburg, the question of my sanity was no longer in doubt. I was definitely nuts!

There was more than a grain of truth in this thinking. According to the townspeople and others, no sane person would consider spending that kind of money on property that should be torn down. Unfortunately, some of my own relatives shared that opinion. Knowledgeable local real estate people said I would never get my money out of this place. One fine lady, a real estate broker *(who later became my wife)*, said she had been reluctant to "show" the house because of its terrible condition.

There were sound reasons for the opinion that opening a B&B in what many people considered an old, sleepy town was idiotic. After all, Blacksburg was not what people in the B&B world refer to as an "end destination." It was definitely not a tourist attraction like Charleston or Beaufort. Not many local people could be expected to spend their hard earned money to stay at a fancy place. This meant I must depend on "out-town-people" passing through to make this into a viable business proposition.

But I had an idea: make the B&B I envisioned into its own "tourist attraction." It certainly had the looks on the outside to attract guests. And after years of collecting fine furniture and furnishings, I had most of what was needed to create an interior that matched the view from the street.

Realistically, it probably did not make financial sense to try to accomplish this. However, in my non-realistic thinking, "logic" had gone down the drain! The beautiful old house deserved to be saved and it was up to this "dumb rich Yankee" (as I was first known) who didn't know better to do it. Neither logic nor financial sense mattered at that point. Emotions had taken over. I was so much in love with this old "white elephant," that nothing would stop me from trying to make it into the elegant "White House Inn Bed & Breakfast."

# CHAPTER 2
## Some Vital Requirements for B&B

THE DECISION TO make the building into an elegant B&B had not changed the restoration plan to make the building stronger and better than it had ever been by "gutting it" and correcting everything that needed it. However, making it into a B&B added some additional expense factors. From personal experience, I knew that a successful bed and breakfast required, at a minimum, private bathrooms, good sized closets, an unusually appealing "honeymoon suite," a large functional kitchen, and a large, attractive common area where guests could gather. If the house were brought back to its original "as is" state, it would lack many of these amenities.

Since it was apparent that the house required being gutted to the bare studs, I knew that this was the time to add any of the required amenities. This extra work further affirmed the need to turn the major work over to a qualified contractor. Obviously, this restoration job was beyond my capability to do myself, even with help from Bill Hartje. So I began outlining in general the work that must be done along with the order of work. I would need to provide a list of these duties to any potential contractors:

(1) Take down all the existing trim (door, window and baseboard), remove the nails, and store the boards for possible future use in some way other than trim, and remove all the old plaster and lath and dispose of it.

(2) Once the house interior walls and ceiling are fully exposed, begin identifying and correcting structural problems caused by: (a) faulty construction by the original contractor and (b) damage caused by neglect, water, and termite infestations.

(3) Find and install suitable decorative trim necessary to make the interior into a true Greek Revival mansion not attainable with its original simple plank trim. Otherwise, it would remain only a beautiful house when viewed from "the street."

Before the start of No. (1), however, it was fairly easy for the practiced eye to spot that water and termites had caused damage to sills, studs, flooring, windows, and doors. And many examples of aesthetic and other problems were readily apparent. For example, a 4X8 sheet of plywood kept anyone from falling through a large hole in the wide hallway at the front entrance. Also, there was a large, raised hump in the floor a few feet past the entrance.

All of the fireplaces also had problems. For both safety and aesthetic reasons I needed to have a professional chimney specialist check out and repair all the fireplaces as well as the chimneys themselves. It did not require an expert to see that there was only one authentic style fireplace mantel in the house and it was in the living room. The other five fireplace mantels were of totally inappropriate style: brick with a piece of wood, simulating a mantel, on top. Therefore, one of the first things I did was to contract with a Millworks shop in Shelby, NC to reproduce five replicas of the mantel in the living room. The company came to Blacksburg to photograph the original mantel and to measure all the other five fireplace openings. They needed the measurements and pictures to make mantels to match the one in the living room.

Gutting the entire house to bare studs and ceiling joists revealed just how badly flawed the original construction was. It was now easy to spot just how undersized all the load bearing headers were. Although this was a problem throughout the house the situation was worse on the first floor because of the wide openings for French doors, window walls, etc. The fact was that all of these large openings should have been constructed with doubled 2X12's sandwiched with plywood to support the weight of the upper floors.

However, with everything revealed, we could see that the original contractor had used only two 2X4's placed on top of each other! It was remarkable that some of the walls had not collapsed. No inspector worth his salt would have approved the shoddy work now visible. This meant that on the first floor alone, the headers for three sets of French doors, a window wall, and the front door entryway all needed to be replaced with new headers of the proper size and strength.

Fortunately, the French doors had been taken down and saved when sagging made them unworkable. Otherwise, they would probably have been damaged beyond repair and lost to posterity. Because of undersized headers in the window walls, the windows were not operational.

I had hoped to be able to restore and reuse the windows, mainly because they contained beautiful old wavy glass which is now highly sought after by house restorers. I hired two retired carpenters to attempt to remove and save the old glass for insertion into new or restored window frames. Unfortunately, despite their best efforts to save the glass, it was so fragile that much of it broke during the removal process. I ended up installing new matching, insulated windows that closely resembled the original ones.

Several areas of the house obviously needed to be redone for a variety of reasons, some because of bad design, and others for faulty original construction. One very poor design feature was an outside door in the dining room's west wall. This door led to the porte cochere that was being used as a one-car carport. This misplaced door eliminated the one wall suitable for a large serving buffet vital for a properly functioning B&B dining room.

For a variety of reasons none of the other three walls could be used for that purpose. For example: large French doors leading from the hallway into the dining room did not leave space for a buffet; large windows took up most of the space of the front wall and a large framed door opening from the butler's pantry made that wall unsuitable for placement of a serving buffet. Thus, the simplest and best solution to the misplaced door was to remove it completely and enclose the opening. That's what we did. *Why would anyone want to enter the house through the dining room?* In any event, since much of the siding would be replaced, removing the entry door and closing off that wall created the simplest and best solution.

# CHAPTER 3
## Solving Some Other Design and Structural Problems

STRUCTURAL WEAKNESSES INVOLVING the sun parlor and second floor balcony created more complicated and expensive problems. Addressing the sun parlor first, it appeared to have been added later and its structural integrity was pitifully inadequate. The structure had a weak framework of undersized studs (2X2's) with single pane glass to let light inside. We spent some time trying to decide if it made sense to replace the single glaze glass with a better, stronger insulated glass or completely rebuild the room. Since the structure itself was so fragile, we decided that the best course was to remove and discard this glass (much of it already broken), and rebuild the wall with the proper number and size of studs.

After the new framing was completed, insulated glass windows were then installed. The reconstruction allowed for a set of large double windows at each end and for several windows equally spaced on the long outside wall. When the contractor completed this rebuilding process, the sun parlor was structurally sound and beautiful with the exterior siding and windows matching that of the main house.

In addition, this work made it possible to install insulation along with new electrical wiring, plumbing, heating and air conditioning systems, and telephone, intercom and TV cable wiring. With its many windows, it still functioned as a sun parlor but contained all the necessary modern features. It also provided attractive space for small parties and "over-flow" breakfast guests. Its beauty was further enhanced when my collection of antique stained glass bought at Indiana auctions graced the windows.

Once the sun parlor re-construction was complete, I asked the contractor to see what was needed to strengthen the balcony. It was so shaky that I had placed a lock on the door to keep anyone from walking out on it! Since I planned to offer the Inn as a site for weddings, it was vital to make the balcony safe for newlyweds to walk upon and wave to the crowd below. It would be the perfect place for a bride to toss her bouquet to other women below who might aspire to be a future bride.

When the contractor completed his examination of the structure, he confirmed that, incredibly, the balcony was fastened to the main house with nails! I had suspected this but couldn't verify it until the exterior siding, ceiling, and wall plaster were removed so that the method of construction was visible. Since the present surface fastening system could not be made safe, the best solution to this problem was to "cantilever" the support structure once demolition had been completed in that area of the house.

Of course any reasonably knowledgeable person would realize that cantilevering of the balcony should have been done when the building was erected. Correcting this problem would require running long support beams underneath the balcony and into the main house for several feet. Then these beams would need to be bolted to the floor joists supporting the upper floor. After this work was completed, the balcony floor was strong enough to support as many people as could crowd into the space.

Back to aesthetic things, although the problem of poor design of the dining room was solved, a very ugly element still remained. It was damage to the floor on the side where the badly placed door had been. It was obvious that the door we had removed had been leaking rainwater for years, causing noticeable damage to that area of the heart pine floor. Now that the dining room was beginning to shape up, except for this ugly floor, I decided to tackle this aesthetic problem on my own while the contractor continued major demolition and reconstruction.

It made sense that I do this job because: (1) the work is tedious and time consuming (thus expensive to have a contractor do it), and (2) I had quite a lot of experience in replacing damaged tongue and groove flooring. In fact, as mentioned earlier, over the years I needed to show several professional carpenters the best way to do this!

I began by removing all of the flooring in the room and then re-installing the "usable" old flooring as far as it would go, starting on the "entrance" (most visible) side of the room and proceeding toward the back wall. When I finished installing the "usable" flooring, I was left with an unfloored strip of about six feet wide by twenty feet long. Fortunately, much of this floor area would not be noticeably visible because the oriental carpet, banquet table, and large buffet would hide most of that part of the floor. This meant that a slight difference in the flooring would not be noticeable.

Since I had been unable to find flooring that matched the original, I decided to use newer flooring and stain it as close as possible to the original. So, I made another trip to Gaffney Lumber with a sample piece of old flooring and asked them to find me the closest match they had on hand. They agreed to do this and invited me to accompany them on a trip to all their storage buildings.

After checking several storage buildings, we finally "hit the jackpot" in one building where we found a small supply of relatively old pine flooring. Apparently it was available from many years ago because the supply was limited; but I thought, rightly, that there was enough of it to complete my 6X20 foot job. Although not an exact match (it was not quite as thick as the original), it was close enough to "fool the eye," so I bought all of this flooring as well as a variety of stains.

I then rented the lumber company's manual floor nailing machine, loaded it onto my pickup and took it back to Blacksburg. After installing the new flooring, I experimented with several different stains and finally settled on one that turned out to be a very close match. In fact, once the stain dried, it was difficult for anyone to know where the old flooring stopped and the new began except for the slight difference in height. I took care of this difference by instructing the floor finishers to stop sanding at the edge of the new flooring to ensure that the floor would be perfectly level.

# CHAPTER 4
## A Water Problem that Must be Solved

AFTER TAKING CARE of the dining room floor, I realized that it was time to hire someone to correct the water problem which had contributed so much to the damage of the house over the years. In addition to direct damage caused by the water itself, this situation was an invitation to termites which thrive under moist conditions. Much of our work would ultimately be in vain if we didn't correct the water problems.

I suspected that the major cause of this problem was bad drainage, so I contacted a local man with grading equipment to correct the grade around the property. This allowed the rainwater to be carried around, rather than toward the property. I had personally observed during a rainstorm that rainwater was running directly under the house at the front. I suspected that was the reason the partial basement was flooded with water.

After grading was completed, the water pumped from the basement, and the deteriorated drain pipe unstopped and replaced, much of the water problem was solved. But I could see that the slight remaining water problem was being caused by sinking of the front porch which rested on a concrete base. It did not require a transit to see that the porch was sloped toward the house rather than away. In a hard, blowing rain, water could still enter the front of the house creating moist conditions in the crawl space.

But stopping that small source of water invasion had to wait until the contractor completed the most urgent interior re-construction work and could turn his attention to the exterior where the greatest need was replacing the front patio/porch entirely so that rainwater would be directed away from the house. While accomplishing this, we would clear dirt from around the large Greek Revival columns so we could see what was holding them up. Once all this work was completed, the brick mason would install a brick cover over the porch and the front patio. This work would also allow the contractor to construct and install new porch railings and the restored balusters and post caps--all of which had fallen or been taken down many years ago.

Soon after grading was done and the existing water was pumped out, the basement dried up completely and I could safely remove the "danger" sign from the entrance to the basement stairway. Once the basement surface was completely dry, it was possible to see that a large amount of mud and debris had been carried by the rainwater into the basement over the years. I hired a couple of laborers to clean up this mess and they came back and asked: "Did you know there was a cement floor underneath all that dirt and trash?" I replied that I had no idea of that but asked them to go ahead and remove any remaining dirt and sweep the floor.

After that, Pop Martin, my brick mason friend, came and repaired the masonry walls and added an entrance and necessary steps making it easy to enter the crawl space from the basement. Once we could use the basement to gain easy access to the crawl space, I knew it was time to correct the hole in the floor at the entrance to the first floor, so Bill Hartje and I drove to Blacksburg to take care of that and several other problems. Taking this action would not require the contractor to stop what he was doing.

I had spent much time and thought about the best way repair that hole in the floor and knew that the repair must be done carefully and precisely because its location just inside the front entry way offered the first view of the interior of the house, i.e., it set the stage for the rest of the house. The fact is, I did not trust anyone but Bill Hartje with his skill and careful workmanship, to do this job. Although we would jointly make decisions on what needed to be done, I would be his "helper" in correcting this "eyesore."

Bill and I first considered trying to patch the floor hoping to hide the defect. However, the number of replacement patches and lack of matching flooring for this critical area caused us to reject that approach. We discussed taking up and replacing the entire floor of the wide and long hallway. However, this would be very expensive and the large French door openings to the living and dining rooms would make it almost impossible to hide the difference in flooring of the hall and other two areas.

Finally, I told Bill that I thought our best solution would be to come up with a fix that emphasized the difference rather than trying to hide it. After much discussion, we agreed that designing a beautiful wall-to-wall "inset" to be installed at the entrance was the best alternative. We then began the process of developing an inset that would require taking up the entire floor at the entrance and replacing it with an inset that we planned to create. This began a "trial and error" approach, eventually resulting in a design utilizing three different sizes and species of wood. The final design would consist of a wide outer border of antique heart pine, a small border of black walnut, and a center of tongue and groove (T&G) maple floor boards. Fortunately, I already had enough black walnut, wide heart pine boards, and antique maple flooring left over from previous renovations. Having this material readily available saved us the expense and time of finding and buying it from specialty stores. It also allowed us to experiment with various designs at our leisure.

We began the actual construction of the inset by selecting the best place to cut out and remove the existing floor for the inset. We moved back from the front door to a place with the fewest short pieces of the old flooring and marked it off for Bill to make a straight cut from one wall to the other. Then we removed the pieces where the inset would go. Before installing the inset, Bill then "let down" a subflooring of plywood that was even with the top of the floor joists. This ensured that the inset would be level with the existing flooring and the plywood subfloor would make this area much stronger than the original floor.

After careful measurement, Bill cut and installed the outer rim of wide heart pine. He followed this by putting down the narrow, dark walnut border, and then added the inlaid floor of maple. He precisely mitered all of the corners. When it was completed the inset looked as if it had been assembled in a factory and installed when the house was built. After the entire flooring of the house was sanded and finished, the inset became a beautiful "accent" piece--one of the highlights of the entrance. I was grateful to have a "Master Carpenter" available to do this great looking piece of work!

On an earlier trip to Blacksburg, Bill Hartje and I had worked together trying to solve the problem of the large "hump" in the hallway floor. While we had easy access to the crawl space, we determined that the "hump" was being caused by a large, 4X4 concrete and brick pier that existed directly below the hump. We deduced that the hump was the result of the large pier remaining stable while the rest of the house was "settling" over the years. Therefore, after inspecting the area, we removed the top layer of brick from the pier, hoping the raised "hump" would eventually settle to the next layer of masonry.

By the time the water problem was solved and the hole in the floor permanently repaired, to our delight the raised part of the floor had settled down to the second layer of brick with no sign that a "hump" had ever been there! Things were beginning to look good to anyone entering 607 West Pine Street.

# CHAPTER 5

## Decision to Restore or Replace Entryway

WITH THE HOUSE now looking so much better, Bill Hartje and I debated the best way to enhance the beauty of the door entryway itself. Although not an eyesore, it no longer met the standards of the rest of the house. Consisting of a 3 foot door, sidelights, transom and frame, the entryway had suffered from exposure to the elements, settlement of the house and neglect. We considered several possibilities including: (1) contracting with a millworks shop to build an entirely new entryway; (2) trying to find another old entryway in better condition that could be modified to fit the existing space; or (3) repairing the original entryway. Both of us preferred the third option but the lack of proper tools and a workshop to do the work was a problem.

Then Bill came up with an idea that appealed to both of us. He suggested that we remove the entire old entryway, separate the parts so they could fit into his van, and he would take all the parts back to his Indiana shop which contained the tools he needed to restore the entire entryway. Meanwhile, the opening would be covered with plywood which would protect the property from the weather and unwanted visitors.

When Bill returned for his next visit, he brought the restored entryway parts and re-assembled them for re-installation. Since it would be hidden, he had built an entirely new frame from new treated wood and nailed that into place first. Then he re-installed the restored entryway which fit perfectly into its opening and looked better than new! He had cut out and replaced all the rotten or damaged areas and reglazed all the glass areas with insulated glass.

Bill had primed all the parts of the entryway and once installed, it was ready for a finish coat of paint. Without pictures of the entryway before it was primed, no one would have guessed that it had ever been exposed to the weather.

# CHAPTER 6
## A Beautiful but Unsound House

BY THIS TIME we knew for certain that the original builder had constructed a building that was magnificent from the street but was unsound and had been constructed as cheaply as possible. There were also many aesthetic deficiencies (some of which have already been mentioned) but much of this work had to await correction of the structural problems, which were many and serious.

Even after the major interior reconstruction was done, there was a time lag for much work needed to finish the interior. For example, the drywall which would replace the old rotting plaster could not be hung until the "rough in" of electrical, plumbing and HVAC was completed. And the trim around the windows, doors, and baseboard (assuming I could find the appropriate material) could not be installed until the new drywall was hung and finished.

However, I had not waited until the finishing stage to begin the search for authentic Greek Revival trim. My strenuous efforts over several months to find appropriate trim to replace the old trim had yielded no positive results. Finally I had exhausted all my resources and was beginning to think that I might have to get new trim made at a mill work shop--if I could find one willing and able to take on that job. That new work would be extremely expensive and not legitimately antique.

Then an incredible opportunity suddenly presented itself. While I was on a visit to Blacksburg from Indiana to check on construction and pay the contractor his "draw," I heard a rumor that the original Cash Mansion in nearby Gaffney (owned later by the Phillips family) was going to be bulldozed into the ground. The present owner, Mr. Jimmy Ruppe, who had purchased the Phillips/Cash house from sometime back had brought his heavy machinery onto the site and was ready to begin digging.

Upon hearing this, I made an immediate trip to Gaffney and located Mr. Ruppe who confirmed the rumor. He told me that he was planning to personally use his bulldozer to dig a large hole in the ground at the back of the property and push this wonderful example of a genuine Greek Revival mansion into the hole. Dismayed at the thought of this, I asked Mr. Ruppe if the property could not be moved and saved. He replied that the location of the house, which was completely surrounded by trailers and electrical and telephone poles, made it virtually impossible to move it to another location.

He explained that all possibilities of saving the property had already been considered and discarded. The possibility of moving it in parts by helicopter had even been explored but the problems of moving so many electrical, phone and other lines out of the way was too great and this effort was shelved. The only way he would delay digging the hole was if someone was willing to purchase salvage rights to the entire property.

I then asked Mr. Ruppe if he would let me take a look inside and he was willing to do so. When I entered the old mansion, I could hardly believe my eyes. Everywhere I looked I saw beautiful, authentic Greek Revival architectural materials. The trim around the doors and windows was exactly what I had been seeking. The baseboards were unlike any I had ever seen; they were in three pieces totaling more than 12 inches in height. A careful look around the Phillips house assured me that there was enough high quality architectural antique door and window trim to finish my entire house, and enough authentic baseboard and wainscoting material to finish at least the first floor and stairway of my house.

All of this was added to my "wish list." I had already purchased some very fancy, gold trimmed wainscoting salvaged from an Indianapolis mansion and if I could find some more to purchase, I would have enough antique wainscoting to do the entire Cash house.

Because I wanted the dining room to be the most elegant room in the house I would reserve the gold trim version as part of its interior trim. With the goal of making the dining room the centerpiece of the house, I had already designed a custom made plate rail to be installed about three feet below the ceiling. This custom piece would support a collection of R.S. Prussia deep bowls and other fancy collectibles that I owned and wanted to display in the Cash house. The plate rail would be one of the final finishing touches and I could take my time putting it together and installing it.

Since there was not enough special baseboard in the Phillips house to do my entire house, I had to figure out a way to disguise the difference. Ultimately, if I could fulfill my "wish list," I would use the Phillips house baseboard in the most visible places such as the living room, dining room and both hallways. And I would use 1X12 inch pine with some added trim for baseboard in less noticeable places such as bedrooms, the kitchen, butler's pantry, and the third level.

# CHAPTER 7
## A Plethora of Antique Artifacts

THE AMOUNT AND quality of antique material visible was almost overwhelming to someone with appreciation of such things. In addition to the Greek Revival trim, which I desperately needed, there were many more architectural antiques and collectibles (inside and outside) for someone who needed and could afford them. These included two beautiful heart pine stairways, fancy parquet flooring, two incredibly fancy fireplace mantels, numerous antique 6-panel doors, and many other desirable items. The Phillips house front entryway itself justified building an entire house around. It consisted of two solid walnut wood doors with large stained glass insets, plus matching stained glass side lights and transom.

Once you got past the entryway, you could see an entire interior wall consisting of matching antique stained glass! Finally, it was difficult to count the many antique light fixtures and other highly desirable items. The kitchen had been updated with 1950 "retro" appliances which had become fashionable in recent years, especially to the "boomer" generation.

When I went back outside to talk with Mr. Ruppe, I hoped to convince him to reconsider and sell me the door and window trim and some other architectural antiques. But he was adamant that he would not sell any of the parts piecemeal. It was "all or nothing." My heart sank at that point because I knew that I could not take on another major project while I was in the middle of one that was using up all of my resources. In addition, I did not need many of the architectural antiques available inside and outside the Phillips house.

Although very desirable, many of the beautiful antique items either did not fit my needs, the space in my house, *or for that matter, my budget*. For example, my existing front entry had been completely restored by Bill Hartje and was now a gleaming beauty. Also, I already owned a collection of antique stained glass and enough period light fixtures to equip my house. To use the elegant Phillips house entry with its stained side glass and transom would require completely redoing the entryway to my house. *The fact that I didn't need these items did not lessen my interest in seeing them saved for posterity!*

The thought of all these fine architectural antiques going to waste was heartbreaking to me and I began thinking about how they might be saved. Then I had an idea. I knew that my old friend, Les Roark of Shelby, NC shared my love for and appreciation of architectural antiques. Would he be interested in purchasing salvage rights of the Phillips House? I thought it was worth a try. I knew he had recently finished construction of a wonderful cabin in the mountains outside of Asheville utilizing much of the building material from the old Shelby High School which had been replaced with a new one. I knew that Les liked to stay busy and had long practiced the concept of saving antique architectural materials.

Although I didn't mention Les by name, I asked Mr. Ruppe's permission, to attempt to find someone who might be interested in buying all the salvage rights to the Phillips property. He thought about this for a few moments and then said he would hold back "digging the hole" a couple of weeks to see if I could find someone interested in buying salvage rights. I said goodbye to Mr. Ruppe and raced to Blacksburg where I immediately called Les. Fortunately Les answered the phone and I began extolling the virtues of the architectural antiques I had just seen in Gaffney.

I described the interior items mentioned above and also told him about the four enormous Greek columns out front, topped by large ionic capitals. I also mentioned the 11 smaller columns supporting a "wrap around" porch. These were also topped with similar but smaller capitals. I was desperately hoping that Les might consider taking on a new challenge or at least pointing me in the direction of someone who would be interested in saving these valuable symbols of the past.

Using every tool I had at my disposal, I also mentioned that this house had been built by relatives of W.J. Cash, famous but controversial Pulitzer Prize winning author, who wrote the highly acclaimed book, "The Mind of the South." A native of Gaffney, W.J. Cash was reputed to have spent much time visiting family members in both the original Gaffney home as well as the later Cash family home in Blacksburg. Although locally recognized for his fine writing as a columnist for the (now defunct) Charlotte News, he received national fame after his book was published in 1941.

Although the book helped him win the "Pulitzer Prize" and become nationally known, it brought him much criticism from many of his fellow Southerners. Cash's views were too liberal for the South at that time. When I mentioned the author's name to Les, he said that not only was he familiar with the works of W.J. Cash but greatly admired him. He said that in his opinion W.J. Cash was an excellent and courageous writer. He added that he had visited Cash's grave at Sunset Cemetery in Shelby.

My description of the wonderful architectural antiques which would soon be destroyed and mention of the connection of author W.J. Cash with the Cash homes in Gaffney and Blacksburg did the trick. In addition to his literary talents, Les was a successful businessman who quickly saw that acquisition of salvage rights to this historic property would not only save many antiquities about to be lost, but might also be a profitable venture. Les had successfully started (and sold) several businesses.

As soon as I finished describing the house and its historical importance, Les immediately expressed strong interest and wanted to see the property as soon as possible. I told him that if he could come to Blacksburg the following morning I would be glad to take him to see the house. He arrived the next morning and we headed to Gaffney.

When we arrived at the Phillips house, Mr. Ruppe had left the door unlocked so we could go right into the house. Like me, Les was overwhelmed when he saw the quantity and quality of the architectural antiques which would soon be buried in a large hole within a few days unless someone acted quickly. The two of us spent the next half hour admiring the interior architectural antiques of the Phillips house. Mr. Ruppe was waiting outside for us when we came back out. I introduced the two of them and then moved away so as not to interfere with their negotiations.

A few minutes later, Les rejoined me and said he had just arranged to pay Mr. Ruppe $5,000 for salvage rights to the property. He was also able to get an agreement from Mr. Ruppe to allow him up to six months to complete the salvage process. Naturally, I had already told Les that I wanted first pick--which was of course the trim I desperately needed. In addition to the trim, I later found the need to purchase other salvage items from Les. One of these was a set of stairway treads and risers which I used to make and install a full sized stairway from the second floor to the third floor of my house, i.e., the eventual Honeymoon Suite.

This normal sized stairway would replace the narrow stairway leading to the attic. At the time it was necessary to go up or down the old stairs sideways. Also, this new stairway would feature large bottom and top landings. Les also demonstrated his friendship by insisting that the two of us refinish all this material before transporting it to Blacksburg!

I also purchased quite a few six panel doors which Les had removed and stored in his mountain workshop. These doors matched those in the Cash house and were in better condition. I bought enough of them to replace a couple of damaged doors as well as to have matching doors for the bathrooms and closets to be added to my house. As a bonus, having these doors on hand allowed the carpenters to frame the openings precisely.

After my purchases, Les still possessed the most valuable interior and exterior items to sell at better prices than he was charging me. Such items included: the stained glass wall and the outstanding entryway with its matching stained glass transoms and sidelights and two walnut doors with stained glass insets. Other interior artifacts on the first floor included a spectacular half circular stairway with large landings at the bottom, midway, and top of the stairway; outstanding ceiling light fixtures; fancy parquet flooring; and two fireplace mantels fine enough to dress up any mansion. Although I never asked, I suspected (and hoped) that Les would make a tidy profit from the sale of these outstanding items. And of course this left him many valuable items (too much to describe) in second floor rooms and all the architectural items on the exterior.

I'm not certain how it happened but some members of the Phillips family, second owners of this grand mansion who now lived farther South, had learned about the fate of their former home. In any event, some out-of-town members of this family returned to Gaffney and purchased many of the most valuable artifacts from the mansion. In fact, while I was supervising the removal of the trim, some Phillips family members arrived with a huge transport truck and crane to remove the four huge outside columns to be transported and used on the front of a mansion they were building farther South (I believe either in Georgia or Alabama).

On a later visit I also saw their workers removing some of the fancy parquet flooring to be used in the interior of the house they were building. They may have bought other collectibles such as the light fixtures and mantels but I have no knowledge of that. In any event I was happy that some of the Phillips family were re-united with parts of their former home.

Although Les sold many items to the Phillips family (as well as to me) more of the items were purchased by a large architectural antiques business in Charlotte, NC. I stopped there soon afterward and was told that most of the Phillips house antiques, including many of the smaller columns had already been sold. The two or three remaining smaller columns were priced at several hundred dollars each. I did not ask the price of the items already sold. Based on what I observed none of the Cash/Phillips house architectural items went cheap.

Toward the end of Les's contract with Jimmy Ruppe, I stopped by and found him in the process of stripping off the aluminum siding which had been added (regrettably) sometime in the recent past. Les told me he had sold all of the remaining salvageable interior and exterior artifacts. But knowing Les, he was not going to let anything salvageable go to waste!

# CHAPTER 8
## Restoration Work Goes into High Gear

RETURNING TO MY own purchases, after I bought the trim I wasted little time hiring my brother-in-law Frank Ford and a friend of his, both retired carpenters, to take it down, pull the nails, and haul the trim to my back porch where it would be temporarily stored. I then built a large plywood vat in the backyard, filled the vat with water, added Red Devil Lye, and (wearing protective clothing) began stripping the trim of its many coats of old paint. Once this was completed and the trim had dried, I moved it back to the porch where I could patch and fill nail holes and do any needed sanding before adding a coat of primer. It would remain there until time to trim out the house.

Moving to the next project of my house, removing and replacing the front porch provided the contractor and me with an opportunity to see what was holding up the huge concrete pillars. Once the old rotten concrete front porch was removed, the first thing we did was scrape around the base of these columns. The contractor and I were appalled to see that only boulders with no concrete or mortar holding them together were supporting these huge concrete columns.

We agreed that the best solution was to frame for deep bases to go around the large columns, as well as to construct framing for a new front porch and patio. After that was completed, the entire framed area would be tied together with rebar and filled with concrete to strengthen support for the columns and tie everything together thus strengthening everything. This would not be done until the contractor scraped out all the loose dirt around the four columns and built 2X12 treated framing for all of it. *(You can bet that the porch floor this time would be sloped away from the house).* Once the concrete dried, framing was removed and the contractor used his skill as a mason to smooth the sides and tops of the cement.

My regular brick mason would later add a layer of solid brick as topping for the porch and front patio surfaces. The latter was to be used by guests as a temporary unloading area at the front of the house. It would be connected to the circular gravel driveway enlarged on one side to serve as a dedicated parking area for guests after they finished unloading their luggage.

On completion of this work, the concrete bases not only added strength, they greatly improved the looks of the entire front of the house. At that point, the contractor had a smooth level surface from which he could begin the work of replacing much of the wood siding which had deteriorated from lack of proper maintenance. The siding on the entire front of the house and areas of the sides and back was removed and replaced with new German siding that matched the existing original siding.

# CHAPTER 9

## Satisfying B&B Requirements Begins

IT WAS NOW time to figure out how to make the many changes required for a workable B&B as quickly and efficiently as possible without interfering too much with the structural reconstruction still going on. Starting with the kitchen, anyone could see that it was too small for a fine dining B&B. The kitchen was also handicapped, both space and appearance wise, by having a laundry room as part of it. Not wanting to put an addition onto the house, I could see two other choices for adding kitchen space: (1) incorporating the adjacent "butler's pantry" into the kitchen, or (2) "stealing" some space from the back porch.

Since the butler's pantry, located between the kitchen and formal dining room, was a distinctive part of the house, plus being large enough to comfortably serve up to four guests, I didn't want to change this attractive and convenient space. Therefore, I decided to keep this room "as is." Another thing that discouraged me from using this room as part of the kitchen was the fact that I already owned a rare, rustic, hand-made table with drawers which would fit perfectly in this space. It was reputedly left in Ohio by members of The Church of Jesus Christ of Latter Day

Saints (Mormons), led by Joseph Smith, as they fled to Utah to escape persecution. It would be supplemented with a primitive, Pennsylvania dry sink and four old matching chairs.

This left the back porch which ran almost completely across the back of the house as my best alternative for adding space to the kitchen. Thus, I decided to "steal" about 10X14 feet from the porch and add it to the kitchen. The porch already had a roof and flooring, reducing the effort to convert it to more kitchen space. It required only opening up part of the back kitchen wall to access the new space and enclosing the outside wall of the former porch space.

Before leaving this area, the contractor would make sure that the new part of the kitchen had proper finish flooring, insulation, electrical and plumbing, air conditioning and heating ductwork. This added space also had room for a commercial-sized washing machine and dryer, a second large refrigerator/freezer, an independent ice maker, and pantry space. Also, it offered a convenient place to install the 300 amp electric breaker box.

Moving the laundry function from the kitchen made room for a large peninsula which added greater counter space and turned out to be the perfect place to install a "downdraft" stove with interchangeable eyes and grille. Replacing two of the cooking eyes with a grille would make it easier to cook pancakes, omelets, or several eggs and meat at the same time. So I quickly made that change. Also, the countertop was designed with enough overhang to allow two or more bar stools. *The latter turned out to be a "mixed blessing" for the cook because guests often wanted to observe and converse while I was cooking breakfast!*

The re-designed kitchen with all new cabinetry provided space for double ovens, built-in microwave oven, double sink with garbage disposal, and the large main refrigerator/freezer. Also, I built and hung a shallow china cupboard (made from old heart pine) for the entry wall. This cupboard was handy for holding coffee cups and informal china but took up little of the visual or floor space. *The formal china and glassware were kept in the period walnut china cabinet in the dining room.* One big problem solved.

# CHAPTER 10
## Looking for a "Honeymoon Suite"

THE NEXT GREATEST problem to deal with was creating an impressive "honeymoon suite." After studying all seven bedrooms, none seemed adequate for this important function. Then I took a closer look at the third level, at that time a dark, dreary place that the Cash children used to "scare themselves" when their parents were not around. The only way to reach it then was to walk sideways up an 18 inch wide "make shift" stairway.

Despite its present appearance, I could see potential in the large open space with high ceiling. The first construction change needed to make the "scary" attic into a desirable suite was to remove the narrow existing stairway and replace it with a wide, attractive one with normal treads and risers. *Incidentally, I also knew Les still had one of the beautiful, antique heart pine stairways from the Phillips house which might be utilized!*

After removing the old stairway, the contractor enlarged the space at the top, and constructed a new standard width stairway with temporary risers and steps, and top and bottom landings. Once all the heavy work had been completed on that level, the temporary risers and steps would be replaced with the antique risers and steps now in Les' workshop. I still had enough wide boards of antique heart pine to cover the top and bottom landings. When all this work was completed, a "locking" door was installed at the bottom landing to ensure privacy for honeymooners. The contractor did such a good job of integrating the new stairway with the rest of the house that it looked as if it had always been there. Fortunately, both the downstairs and second floor hallways were 10 feet wide, thus the stairways at both levels did not appear crowded.

In order not to interfere too much with the main construction work being done by the contractor, I contacted my old friend and master carpenter Bill Hartje in Indiana and asked him to come down (when he had the time) to assist me with the attic renovation and some other jobs that needed his exceptional skills. I knew that Bill would take the time to make the attic area as attractive as the main house.

Once Bill arrived, we began laying out and building the "short" walls that would define the interior space of the suite. Then we replaced the three existing windows with new, larger, double-glazed dormer windows. Although the three new larger windows increased the light considerably, I decided to make the area even brighter by having three large skylights (which could be opened and closed) professionally installed while new roofing for the entire house was being done.

Before Bill left to return to Indiana, he also framed for a new bathroom in the suite and added a dropped ceiling which would be about ten feet tall when finished with drywall. We were able to utilize the space behind the short walls for closets; and we enclosed space under the windows (except of course for the bathroom window). With custom made cushions, the "window seats" not only provided comfortable seating but its frame hid the HVAC ductwork that went around the perimeter of the suite (again except for the bathroom).

With more space that needed to be heated and air conditioned, I consulted with HVAC installers who advised that these functions could be performed most efficiently by having two HVAC systems. One would be placed in the unused attic space to serve the two top floors and the second (an outside heat pump) would serve the main floor. That system worked beautifully in all types of weather. The downstairs heat pump was most efficient at providing warm air; and the upstairs system was most efficient at providing cool air. *(This of course follows the principle that heat rises and cold goes downward).*

Finally, I contracted with Gaffney Lumber Co. for its millworks specialist to measure, build and install stairway railing to match the existing stairway. A Gaffney cabinetmaker built and installed new custom cherry wood kitchen cabinets in the kitchen of the main house and in the honeymoon suite.

The suite had its own full size refrigerator, stove, and microwave oven. The bathroom was equipped with a tub-shower, lavatory, and commode. The large dormer windows (the only deviation from the matching double hung windows) could be opened to a bucolic view of acres of mature trees including beech, birch, pine, oak and poplar.

One of the last things Bill and I did we did was remove the old rough-sawn flooring, place soundproofing insulation between the joists, and replace the old boards with plywood subflooring. The rest of the work (including painting, wall-to-wall carpet installation, etc.) would be done concurrent with the rest of the house. *The insulation and carpeting ensured that those occupying the suite would not be bothered from noise below and vice-versa.*

# CHAPTER 11
## Private Baths and Closet Doors to Meet B&B Requirements

AFTER BILL LEFT for Indiana, I began to deal with the need to add private baths and closets for the guest bedrooms. One aspect of the construction of the house turned out to be an unexpected blessing in solving both of these problems. Space in each of the first and second floor existing bathrooms was very large. We took advantage of the large size to divide each into two good-sized bathrooms. On each floor, one of the bathrooms included the old clawfoot tub and the other included a modern tub/shower, commode and lavatory. *Note: before opening for guests, I added special order ceiling mounted oval brass shower rings for the old claw foot tubs so that guests who desired could take showers.*

Before this final work was done, workers had carried the two old clawfoot tubs outside and placed them upside down on saw horses. This made it easier for me to remove the claw feet and strip the tubs of their old exterior paint and rust. After this, I spray painted the exterior of the tubs black and painted the claw feet gold. All this work took time but the results made the work well worthwhile. Fortunately the inside porcelain of both tubs was in perfect condition, needing only thorough cleaning to remove some rust. When the refurbished clawfoot tubs were carried back inside the house and installed, along with special order iconic shower curtain rings hung from the ceilings, they became outstanding features of the house.

With the new bathroom added in the upstairs suite, I now had five full baths instead of two. And I had figured a way to add two more bathrooms if and when *needed. Over the succeeding years, I had a few instances where one of the bathrooms needed to be shared but these occurred in family situations and I never felt the need to add extra bathrooms.*

After installation of the three additional bathrooms, I was left with only two more major interior changes needed: the addition of bathroom and closet doors for each guest suite. The open construction of the house also made this easier. As mentioned earlier, I had two large chimneys and six fireplaces. Fortunately, the chimneys were free standing, i.e., the spaces between the rooms where the fireplaces were located had been left open. This left each guest bedroom with plenty of space for a closet once drywall was installed and finished.

All we had to do to create a closet was build a divider at the back and install a rod and one of the salvaged doors for each of the five guest closets. This small change made it possible for five of the guest rooms to have nice sized closets. I purchased two large, antique walnut wardrobes to serve as closets for bedrooms six and seven. I also placed two beautiful walnut wardrobes near the end of the second floor hallway for extra storage space for these bedrooms which could be used by the owner and family/friends.

# CHAPTER 12

## No Rest for This Owner

THROUGHOUT THE RESTORATION process my daytime hours were filled with tedious and time consuming jobs--things I could do largely on my own. In addition to restoring the clawfoot tubs, I spent days, weeks and months restoring decorative wood balusters, trim and other architectural antiques. Fancy wood balusters had once dressed up the porch railings but had been removed sometime in the past from the front porch, the second floor balcony, the porte cochere, the sun parlor, and the third level "widow's walk." Fortunately, most of these decorative parts had been saved for later restoration and re-installation.

I soon found that most of the fancy corbels which once decorated the roof line on the front, back and sides of the house had fallen or been removed and stored in the same leaky old metal building as the balusters. Thank goodness the old building gave these precious balusters and corbels enough protection that I was able to strip, patch missing chunks of wood, and refinish them. However, this work required much patience, time, and careful work.

*One early morning, a friend stopped by while I was working in the back yard on one of the corbels. He returned that afternoon and saw me still working on that corbel. "I can't believe that you're still working on that same corbel!" he exclaimed in disbelief. To further complicate this job, at the end I found I was missing a few corbels. Upon counting the corbels, I found that I needed a dozen or more of them. Since I did not have the equipment (or knowledge) to make new ones I took one of the refinished ones to Cleveland Mill Works and had them replicate enough to finish the job and have a few left over.*

When it was time to re-install the porch railings and corbels, the contractor had no serious problems completing those at ground level except for the fact the tops and bottoms of all of the porch railings were too rotten to support the balusters and needed to be replaced. The contractor used new treated wood to construct new top and bottom railings and posts. After being installed and painted, however, no one could spot the difference between the old and new. The contractor had to use his tallest ladders and scaffolding to complete these jobs around the roof and widow's walk. This was further affirmation that my decision to turn the major restoration work over to a professional contractor was the right one.

The contractor had told me that he had to use 100-300 ton jacks to level the floors in the house. After he had finished this work, a string level from front to back of the house showed that the floors were within half an inch of being perfectly level from front to back! I was amazed and happy about that. This thoroughly vindicated my decision to turn the major work over to a professional builder.

Meanwhile Bill and I made another trip from Indiana to check on the structural soundness of the house and take care of a few other projects. The house now seemed very structurally sound and installation of all new electrical wiring and plumbing, heat and air conditioning systems, and telephone, intercom and TV cable wiring had been "roughed in" and approved by the county inspectors.

At this point, Bill and I agreed that everything looked ready for dry wall installation and finishing, to be followed by completion of work by the sub-contractors listed above. This work would be followed by the trim work, final caulking, painting, and floor sanding and finishing. The contractor would be responsible for doing the trim work, but I would do needed caulking and contract with someone to do the interior and exterior painting, and hire a floor sanding and finishing contractor.

Once the drywall was installed and finished, the contractor began doing the trim work. Since I had stripped, filled nail holes, etc. and the trim pieces were already cut to size, the trim work was being done at a fast pace—almost like using new pre-cut trim. There were some places where the fit was not perfect but nothing I couldn't take care of with caulk. I was pleased with the fast pace and good work being done by the contractor. In fact he had almost finished this phase of the work when he approached with an expression I had not seen on his face previously. I sensed that something really bad had come up. I could not imagine what was wrong.

# CHAPTER 13
## An Unfortunate Ending to a Relationship

THROUGHOUT THE RESTORATION process, I thought the contractor had done an exceptional job and we had become good friends during this time. At least I had thought so. However, when I asked him what was wrong, he told me that he "was ashamed" of something he had done. When I asked him to explain, he said that the problem involved a sub-contractor he had urged me to hire, i.e. the electrical and HVAC installer.

*By way of background, I had received three bids for this job and told the contractor which one I preferred. He strongly objected to my choice and urged me to select one of the other bidders. In fact, he was so insistent that he said he would not work with my selection. I was taken aback by his apparent anger but not wanting to cause a rift between us, I agreed to his preference and soon forgot about the matter.*

I asked the contractor what he was ashamed of and he said he wanted to tell me about a problem he had, adding, "I want to tell you about it before you hear it from someone else." He then proceeded to tell me why he had pressured me to hire this particular electric/HVAC sub-contractor. "I did that because the HVAC in my own house went bad and I didn't have the money to get it fixed." He then explained that he had made a deal with this sub-contractor to raise his estimate by $1,000, and if he was able to persuade me to select this sub-contractor, he (the contractor) would receive $1,000 worth of work on his own defective system.

Now, the two of them had a disagreement over the amount of work to be done and the matter was going to be settled in court. My contractor knew that when the case went to court, it would become a matter of public record and he would no longer be able to hide his deception from me. He apologized to me again and offered to resign on the spot. Since I felt that, with this one exception, the contractor had always been fair with me, I told him he could continue and complete the work on my house.

But things didn't work out for us after that. Perhaps the guilt he felt was too much for him. In any event he began doing work not up to his (or my) standards. For example, I saw that he had failed to follow the common practice of installing the counter top before adding the back splash. Anyone with any knowledge of construction knows that the counter top goes on first and the back splash later to reduce the possibility of leakage. When I saw he had reversed this common practice, I called it to his attention.

Without saying a word, he packed up his tools and left. I didn't see him again for several days or until he came by to collect his final check. I removed the back splashes myself and waited for the people doing the kitchen cabinet work to complete the job properly.

After the contractor left with his tools, I decided I should take a closer look at other work he had done since his offer to resign. Upstairs, I immediately spotted another major flaw in his recent work. This was installation of baseboards in an upstairs bedroom where he had failed to level the floor. Instead, he had cut the 2X12 inch baseboards so they would be level at the top, but three inches out of level at the bottom. Anyone looking at the floor could see that the baseboard was 11 ½ inches at one end and 8 ½ inches on the other.

This and the other oversight made it obvious that the contractor had lost interest in doing the quality of work he did before his confession to me. This was a shame since we had worked so well together up to that point. In fact, after I thought about the last two jobs he had done for me, installing baseboards in a room with a very unlevel floor and permanently fastening kitchen counter backsplashes before the counters were installed, I was sorry I had not accepted his earlier offer to quit.

I was now faced with solving a major problem he had left behind and which should have been corrected during the deconstruction and reconstruction period--not after all the other leveling and installation of drywall had been completed. Now it was up to me to correct the unlevel floor since I could not live with it the way it was. I could think of only two ways to level the floor joists at that point: (1) use long shims that reached from one end of the room to the other or (2) "sister" a wide piece of wood to even the top of each existing joist. Of course neither of these could be done before removal of baseboard and the heart pine finish flooring.

# CHAPTER 14
## Hartje to the Rescue--Again

I REALIZED THAT I could not do this work by myself. Even if I could handle the removal work I didn't trust my ability to cut the long shims straight. If my decision was to use the "sister" option, I would need another someone to keep the "sister" joist level and in place while it was being fastened. So, I called old friend Bill Hartje and told him of my predicament and he loaded up his van and hurried to rescue me for perhaps the third or fourth time.

Once we had removed the baseboards and existing flooring, we discussed the two options mentioned above. After considering the pros and cons of each, we decided that the easiest and best way to correct this problem was to cut long shims and fasten them with screws and glue to the tops of the existing joists. We would use 16 foot 2X4's to make these shims. When they arrived, we placed them on saw horses in the hallway and Bill used his chalk line to mark a diagonal line from one corner to the other.

This cut would require a very steady hand to make a straight line cut with a hand held saw and I knew I was incapable of that. So, I held the wood in place while Bill made accurate cuts of each one. This process left us with two giant "shims" from one 2X4 which went from nothing to 3½ inches.

When he fastened each of the shims to a joist, we had a completely level area to install a plywood subfloor. Since I still needed some original flooring to make repairs to floors on the first and second floor levels, I decided to use the best of the flooring we had removed for that purpose while installing a subflooring of plywood covered by wall to wall carpeting in that one room.

Although I don't personally like wall to wall carpeting (and it would certainly not be acceptable in a true restoration) the fact is that many people actually prefer this floor covering--especially in bedrooms. It turned out that my B & B was rarely full and some guests actually chose this room over bedroom floors with the old, polished heart pine. *There's no explaining everyone's taste!* The bright side of the events above was that I ended up with a large amount of genuine old heart pine flooring to patch areas that needed it before calling for the floor sanding crew.

That was Bill Hartje's last trip down (except as a guest) and we used much of his time to repair that one unlevel floor and to carefully examine every part of the house for any flaws that needed correcting. Other than that one out-of-level-floor, we found very few serious flaws and used his remaining time to replace any of the old flooring that had the slightest flaw with the good flooring we had removed from the unlevel bedroom upstairs. Happily, we even had some good flooring left over in case I needed it later!

# CHAPTER 15
## Full Attention Now Devoted to Landscaping

UP TO THIS time, most of this narrative has been devoted to the building itself (other than work around the areas of the patio and driveway and grading to keep water away from the house). Now, more study and work needed to be done on landscaping the property. Old friend Les Roark had highly recommended a landscape architect from Shelby, NC. Les first introduced us by telephone and we had a gratifying conversation. Our first meeting in person at the site had to be delayed for a few days, because he was temporarily serving as escort for the head landscape architect for Buckingham Palace! I think that says enough about his qualifications.

When we had our first meeting at the house, the landscape architect took pictures of the entire grounds and house. While he was there, I asked if he required that his crew come to Blacksburg to do the actual plantings. He said that we could do this either way: (1) he would select and buy all plant materials and have his crew install it or (2) I could find and buy the plant materials on the detailed plan he (the architect) would provide and have someone local install it. He said it would no doubt be less expensive for me if I chose the second option. In either case, he would provide me with a detailed plan for the entire property and would be available for consultation by telephone or personal visit when and if needed.

Obviously, the second option was best for my dwindling bank account so I offered the planting job to Charles Rouse, who had done lots of planting in and around Blacksburg. Mr. Rouse accepted my offer and I began my search for the plant materials. I already knew that we were pretty much "starting from scratch" with the landscaping. We did have some nice trees, however, including two magnificent magnolia trees that framed the house, plus several established deadora cedars and centuries old hardwood and pine trees. The architect said that the only shrubs worth keeping were five, slow-growing Old English boxwoods. I'm sure there were six of these at one time but only five now remained.

The landscape architect said the five Old English boxwoods would make perfect foundation plants for the house, if I could find one more matching boxwood. He advised that if I could find a 50-year-old matching English boxwood to go with the five already there, the six should be placed in groupings of three on each side of the large center columns. He also advised that the boxwoods be supplemented with some specific perennials which he named on the plan. When I studied the plan, I found that it was outstanding, thorough, and even easy for a novice like me to understand.

With his experience, Charles would have no problem following the plan's instructions. So, I began buying the easily available plant materials and Charles began planting them. I could see that he was very capable, as well as likable and intelligent. He always took his time and made sure that he followed the plan, and that the plants were properly spaced and watered. Charles soon became my "right hand man," helping me in other ways as needed. *After the initial planting was completed, Charles remained as my yard maintenance person, doing all the pruning, grass cutting and replanting of annuals as long as I owned the property. Meanwhile, we became lifelong friends.*

Returning to the landscape plan, once we had obtained and planted readily available plant materials, I began to concentrate on finding the difficult to find plants. The first was finding the Old English boxwood of the proper look and age. I checked all the local nurseries and then began calling nurseries farther away but none had Old English boxwoods of the right age and size I needed. I was about give up and toss the five old boxwoods. Then as I was talking with my brother Bob's son, Keith, who lived in nearby Grover, NC, I asked him if he knew where I might find such a plant.

He exclaimed: "I think my Dad and Mom's vacant old house had some Old English boxwoods and if so, they would be about the right age. No one is living there and you can have any of the plants you want. Just help yourself." The next day I took Charles and a shovel to Grover and drove to my brother's deserted house. One of the first things we saw as we approached the house was one lone Old English boxwood that was almost identical to the five I had at my house. A few moments later, the boxwood was resting on some sacks in the back of my van on the way back to Blacksburg.

When we unloaded the new specimen and placed it among the other five, it was hard to tell the difference. Following the plan, Charles arranged them in a triangle on each side of the entrance along with a variety of flowering plants the architect had recommended. As the architect had predicted, these plantings served as a perfect beginning for the landscape plan.

Then, following the plan, Charles planted a row of low growing evergreen shrubs on the back side of the large brick patio (the stopping area for guests to unload luggage). The plan also recommended planting crape myrtles with the scientific name "Lagerstroemia Tuskegee" on each side of the row of evergreen shrubs. Finally, the plan had also suggested several other strategic placements of this same variety around the circular driveway along with some flowering dwarf cherry trees.

Since I was familiar with several nurseries in Upstate South Carolina as well as in nearby Cleveland County, NC, I had no difficulty locating most of the designated plant materials with the exception of the "Tuskegee" variety of crape myrtle. None of the nurseries I called were familiar with this variety and had no suggestions for finding them. Then I turned to the Internet to obtain telephone numbers of nurseries in the two states. I contacted many of these and got the same response: they did not have this particular species of crape myrtle.

After that I gave up looking and prepared to call the landscape architect for an alternative to that variety. Before I had a chance to contact him, however, I went to Gaffney's Wal-Mart store to purchase some more common plant materials. As I was browsing the garden area, I happened to look down at some small shrubs and saw the word "Tuskegee" on one tag. I looked closer and saw that there were at least 12 shrubs tagged with this name. I quickly abandoned my search for anything else, bought all of these plants, loaded them into my van and headed toward Blacksburg to find Charles.

Charles planted these rare plants the next day. They thrived beautifully and after a few years they became wonderful specimen trees that showed off The White House Inn to the degree that no other variety would have done! With these two difficult problems solved, I soon obtained and Charles planted all the plant materials appropriate for the period and house style.

In addition to recommendations for plants, the landscape architect had suggested that two large brick columns installed at each end of the circular driveway would add a stately touch to the landscaping and house. I agreed with him and also thought a heavy chain that attached to each brick column at night would discourage people from using my driveway as a "turn around." My favorite bricklayer, "Pop" Martin, soon made that a reality. I only fastened the chain a few times after all the guests had arrived, but it did its job and added class to the place.

By the time I was getting ready to open the White House Inn Bed and Breakfast, the landscape plan had been fully implemented, all of the recommended plants were in place and growing nicely. And the house itself was performing like a new house with its all new electrical, plumbing and HVAC systems fully operational.

# CHAPTER 16
## Friends Pitch in to Help Me Get Ready to Open

TWO OTHER ISSUES remained before I opened the Inn for business. One involved the need to serve superior food; the other was decorating the Inn and displaying my collectibles. Friends helped me deal with both of these finishing chores. Nephew Dan Turner was especially helpful with resolving these two issues. On the food side he was my best "taste tester." And as a former restaurant owner, along with wife, Carolyn, he was also a competent adviser in the kitchen.

Friends in Indiana and the Carolinas were generous in providing recipes they thought would be useful to me. Many were family recipes that could not be found in recipe books. Others were from "church recipe" books or slick, hardback "fine dining" recipe books.

As soon as I had an adequate working kitchen, I had begun practicing cooking breakfast foods and fancy snack foods for the 5 p.m. "wine and cheese" parties. Fortunately I had grown up in a house with a mother who thought her children should all be able to cook. As a youngster I followed her around the kitchen observing her cooking skill and providing help when she would let me. And since I had always liked to entertain in my various homes around the country (as well as prepare a variety of "libations,") I already had a rudimentary knowledge of providing good food. I had perhaps over-practiced mixing drinks.

I was also fully aware that if my B&B was to be a success I had to learn how to prepare and cook out-of-the-ordinary dishes that would leave guests with memories of gourmet food, e.g., Eggs Benedict, Eggs Florentine, cheese grits, and Shrimp and Grits. I would also need to be able to serve a variety of good breakfast casseroles, eggs cooked to order, pancakes and waffles. For the "cocktail hour," guests would be offered a variety of outstanding wines and brandies as well as exotic treats such as caviar. Serving simple wine and cheese would not be exactly memorable at cocktail hour.

And as a final touch, as they prepared to leave, I wanted every guest to receive an unexpected gift (the fancy word for that was "lagniappe"). In this case the "lagniappe" was a small jar of fine honey provided by my cousin Wofford Martin, a retired mill supervisor, and now an expert beekeeper, who also raised award winning Simmental cattle. The honey jar had both his brand name and the White House Inn name as a reminder of their visit to Blacksburg.

Since "practice makes perfect" (sometimes), I began a nightly routine of trying to prepare the best hollandaise sauce for Eggs Benedict. I also had to find the best meat (Canadian bacon or Virginia ham) for this same dish, and Tasso ham for shrimp and grits. When Tasso ham was not available, I substituted Mexican "chorizo sausage" to make the sauce for this dish.

Just as important, I'll always remember the quality time I spent with my nephew,

Dan. The memory of my almost nightly practice cooking and Dan's tasting and presence is as fresh as it was back then. We both gained unneeded weight during this time but it was worth it to spend these hours with Dan. Some other friends and relatives also served as occasional "taste testers" with strict instructions to be honest in their appraisals but Dan remained the chief encourager and friendly critic. *Sadly, he passed away several years ago, long before I began writing this memoir.*

Completing the decorating would be the final stage of getting the Inn ready to receive guests. As mentioned earlier, I had spent much of my spare time during my eight years in Indiana attending auctions and buying antiques and collectibles that would add elegance to The White House Inn. *(At the time I had no idea how I would use them but having them available turned out to be a blessing).*

Although I did most of the decorating myself, friends were always ready to give me a hand in hanging lace curtains, pictures, and paintings, and in placing the furnishings once all of it arrived. If I needed help with hanging more delicate, heavier items, volunteers such as Dan were always ready to assist. Of course final cursory examination might reveal the need to do some final "touch up" painting and the like after the furniture arrived and was put into place but I was positive I could get that and final decorating accomplished without too much effort.

I was feeling pretty comfortable with the house itself, as well as my cooking skills by this time. It should be noted that the major reconstruction, which began soon after I purchased the old mansion in 1989, was completed in late 1991, a period of about two years. The small finishing chores and decorating would continue until the Inn officially opened in early 1992 and will be described in more detail in the following Part 11. This may sound like a long and arduous period of time but it was well worth the effort to save and revitalize this wonderful old building.

Meanwhile, I had reached the point that I could spare friend Bill from further "rescue trips" from Indiana to Blacksburg. I realized that it had sometimes been an imposition on him to drop what he was doing in Indiana and head to South Carolina to give me a hand. I'll always be in debt to him for his willingness to do that. As a result, however, our friendship will remain while the two of us are alive.

One final word of advice to anyone contemplating restoration of an old house: unless you are a professional in this field, I advise you to find your own Bill Hartje when you run into unexpected trouble, which is likely to occur many times in a major restoration.

# PART 11

# SOON TO BE AN INNKEEPER

# CHAPTER 1
## Major Work on Inn Completed

IT'S 1991 AND I'm back in Blacksburg, SC, which I left about 50 years ago. After all those back and forth trips from Indiana to Blacksburg checking progress on restoration of the old Cash house, I'm now here to stay. However, I won't be living in the "lap of luxury" for awhile. Although I now had both hot and cold running water, AC and heat, and a fully functioning kitchen, most of my furniture remains stored in Indiana awaiting my call to have it delivered to 607 W. Pine Street. So, I'm "making do" with minimal furniture I brought down in my van.

Although the heavy construction work has been completed and all the appliances are now working, many small but vital finishing details must be done to turn the building into an elegant B&B. I could handle some critical finishing jobs by myself but with others I needed help to complete. One of the latter was installing a concrete floor for the porte cochere which had been and would continue to be used as a carport.

Nephew Dan Turner volunteered to help me with this job which included framing for the floor of the porte cochere and the short driveway leading from there to the circular driveway. A short brick wall to support the columns of the carport and a layer of rough gravel on the driveway already existed and helped speed up this job. Because of his long experience supervising such work at Duke Power (now Duke Energy), Dan marked the height of the floor for proper drainage and did the small amount of framing for the short driveway in a little over an hour. He also told me how much concrete to order. After it was poured, a local concrete finisher completed the job before nightfall.

Next came the installation of the plate rail for the dining room which also required help for several reasons, the most important of which was that much of the work required the use of ladders. My design for the plate rail consisted of three pieces of dimension trim from Cleveland Lumber Co. Long pieces of primed trim were now on site waiting to be cut to fit walls. I needed help leveling and holding them at proper height while they were nailed into place.

I enlisted the help of a young, local apprentice carpenter, a relative of my former contractor, to help me install the pieces that formed the plate rail. After we cut the trim pieces to fit the walls and installed them, I later filled the nail holes and put on a coat of finish paint. After the paint dried, the plate rail was ready to hold and display collectibles such as R.S. Prussia deep bowls, fine china, etc.

Other jobs that I could do on my own included: replacing the old, cheap, brass-plated door knobs with beautiful, antique knobs; fulfilling legal requirements needed for a business; requesting my professional sign company to finish and install a sign appropriate to the Inn and having my furniture and furnishings transported from Indiana to Blacksburg. Of course I would find places that needed touchup painting and other chores and I can do that myself.

I began replacing all the house's door knobs, installing keyed locks at exterior doors and guest room doors, and caulking and painting where needed. Why replace all the door knobs? Because many were either missing, damaged or were cheap, ugly knobs in the first place. I wanted to see period knobs that reflect the quality and beauty of a true Greek Revival mansion.

*With that goal in mind, I had scoured antique stores and malls, architectural antique salvage stores and yards, and flea markets around the Southeast and Midwest looking for "the real thing," i.e., old, matching glass or crystal door knobs removed from other fine old homes or mansions. By the time I needed them, I had accumulated enough quality antique knob sets that I could replace all of the old ones with proper ones. Incidentally, I had my best success finding these "jewels" at a large architectural antiques salvage store in Indianapolis, IN.*

I went to work and soon all the doors were equipped with beautiful antique door knobs. I sometimes had to make small adjustments and re-install some of the strike plates but most required little extra work. The only "fly in the ointment" was that the state suddenly required B&Bs to have modern "keyed locks" on guest room doors. After protesting that this harmed the vintage look we were seeking, most B&B owners (*including this one*) gave up and complied. I was pleased that we were still allowed to keep our vintage doorknobs.

Since I could not open for business until I received my local and State business licenses, that now became my top priority. I first went to the Blacksburg Town Hall and left a few minutes later with my town business license. I then drove to Spartanburg and found the office that issues state business licenses. When a license clerk approached, her first question was: "What is the name of your business?" Since I had not made a final decision on that, I hesitated for a moment and then stammered: "I'm calling it, The White House Inn Bed and Breakfast."

That may sound a bit pretentious for a new business but I thought it was appropriate since the owner's last name was White, the building itself was painted white, and many people described it as resembling a much larger building with a similar name in Washington, DC! In any event, a few minutes later I received my State business license and instructions regarding sales tax and other business matters.

With the Inn's name now official, I proceeded with final decisions on names for the guest rooms. I named them: The White Magnolia Room (which overlooked a magnificent magnolia tree); The Peach Room (to reflect this great peach growing area!); The Rose Garden Room (a downstairs bedroom with a view of a rose garden); the Green Apple Room (although it contained a real Lincoln bed I didn't dare call it the Lincoln Bedroom, so stuck with the color theme); and The Honeymoon Suite, for obvious reasons.

Also, now that I had an official name for my B&B, I called the sign company requesting them to finish the sign with the words: "The White House Inn Bed and Breakfast" followed in smaller letters: "Innkeeper Jim White." Since it was one of the first things that visitors would see upon arriving at the Inn, I had been willing to pay a large price for a sign that reflected the quality and beauty of the newly-restored building.

Once the sign company installed the sign, brick mason Pop Martin surrounded it with a short brick wall matching the brick columns at the entrances to the driveway. Charles Rouse filled and leveled the area with top soil and then planted ground cover and small, flowering plants inside the short walls. Finally, I had an electrician finish installing lights which would come on automatically at night.

Meanwhile, I had ordered and received new top-of-the-line mattresses and pillows for all of the beds, including a custom made mattress (six inches shorter than standard) to fit the antique Lincoln bed with fancy canopy. All guest beds would be outfitted with the highest thread count bed linens I could find. I ordered these from a company that specialized in supplying very high quality bed linens not readily available. My collection of antique Jacquard coverlets would serve as bed covers. All of these bed linens were stored in the appropriate bedrooms to be installed once the furniture arrived and was put into place.

After these chores were completed, I called the moving company in Indiana (which had stored my furniture since my house there was sold) and told them I was ready to have my furniture and furnishings delivered to Blacksburg. *By that time I was really tired of camping.* As mentioned earlier, I already owned enough antique and/or collectible furniture for much of the house, including the living room, dining room, sun parlor, hallways, butler's pantry, and three of the bedrooms. I drew a sketch for the moving crew to show them where to place the Persian rugs and individual pieces of furniture.

Things went smoothly with the move-in and I slept in my own bed that night. All that was left for me to do was to receive and place new furniture ordered for the other three bedrooms when it was delivered from the NC factories. Originally I offered six guest bedrooms but for reasons described later, I soon dropped it to five. I equipped the two extra bedrooms for my own use as well as for "non-paying" guests, i.e., family and friends.

# CHAPTER 2
## Final Finishing Touches

THE OFFICIAL OPENING of the Inn was fast approaching and it was vital to begin the final decorating phase of hanging all light fixtures, paintings, mirrors, antique stained glass and window curtains. I had delayed hanging many of these items for fear of damage by workers carrying ladders, long pieces of lumber, etc. Also, large pieces of furniture, e.g., mattresses and box springs being delivered posed a lesser but significant danger to such items as antique light fixtures.

With the heavy work done and most of the guest room furniture in place, I felt it was now safe to hang these vulnerable furnishings. In case you are wondering why all this concern, the fact is that some of these items were very valuable and irreplaceable. For example, the light fixtures I used in the downstairs hallway appeared to have been designed especially for this particular area of the inn. Although identical in design, one was slightly larger than the other. Therefore, the larger fixture was hung near the entrance where the hallway was a full 10 feet wide. The slightly smaller one was hung farther back where the space was smaller because of the stairway. And the largest and most impressive crystal chandelier was hung in the dining room.

Also, most of the stained glass was "one of a kind" and I would not have the time to try to find adequate replacements. Several of the oil paintings were by "listed artists," which meant they were very valuable and I no longer had money, time, or opportunity to replace them. Once it was safe to do so, all the mirrors, paintings, stained glass, chandeliers, and window treatments were put into place along with many collectibles throughout the Inn. The White House Inn was beginning to look like the upscale B&B I had envisioned.

*Note: I had purchased the stained glass and outstanding light fixtures at Indiana Auctions and stored them in the fourth level (a finished attic which had once been used for servant quarters) in my Lafayette home. At the time, I had no plans to use them but they were so desirable that I could not resist buying them. Perhaps fate had something to do with this! Whatever the reason, I was happy to already have these in my possession and ready for installation. An electrician friend in Indiana had already re-wired any that needed it and this proved very helpful in making them functional in a hurry. In describing the light fixtures, all were recognizable as being old and appropriate for the style and age of The White House Inn.*

Once it was known that restoration of the Inn was largely complete, I was besieged by telephone calls and "drop-by" visitors wanting a tour of the house. This took a heavy toll on the time I needed to complete the few but important finishing touches. All the wonderful publicity I had been receiving had whetted the appetite of local people. This interest in my Inn may seem like a good problem to have but not in this case since I was still spotting and correcting small problems--noticeable only to me.

Realistically, I suspected that few, if any, of the people telephoning and ringing my doorbell would ever be paying guests at the Inn. Most were just curious to see what people were talking about. This meant that my choices at the moment were to drop what I was doing and give them an escorted tour or risk angering them by refusing their requests. I did not like either of these options since I wanted and needed to retain good will in the community. Fearful that I was creating resentment by not giving everyone who called or dropped by a personal tour of the Inn, I decided that the best solution was to have a "grand opening" as soon as possible, ready or not. So, I scheduled that for Sunday, June 28, 1992.

This meant I needed to make decisions on who to invite and what to serve, and who and how many people I would need to serve as guides and/or tour leaders for the event. After all, I had too many valuables on display to allow mainly strangers to wander about the property unaccompanied. Since I had become a member of both the Gaffney and York Chambers of Commerce, I began by obtaining their membership lists and sending their members written invitations.

Then, despite my reservations but with contrary advice from many people, I decided to open the Inn to anyone who wanted to attend. With that decision, the local newspapers began writing more feature articles announcing that I was having an "Open House" and that anyone was welcome to attend during the hours of 1-4 p.m. at the designated time and date. *That answered the question of who (other than C of C members) to invite!*

In anticipation of the opening, the Cherokee Chronicle's Charles Wyatt wrote an almost full page article about the event. Under the heading: "White House Inn open for those looking for luxury," the article gave a brief history of the renovation, including the unusual coincidence of The Phillips House, which was facing demolition, providing the authentic trim needed to turn the Cash house into an elegant Greek Revival type mansion.

The article also contained a floor-by-floor description of the interior of the house, including guest bedrooms. It also included a photo of the front of the Inn as well as the dining room with caption describing it as "complete with real silver, crystal, and china." The writer also interviewed me about how paying guests could expect to be treated. In describing this process, Wyatt said, "After guests register, they can enjoy beverages and snacks and a tour of the home, or they can go directly to their appointed rooms to relax. Tours and refreshments are available to guests at any time except 5 p.m. which is set aside for wine and cheese." *No mention of caviar, thank goodness since it was sometimes difficult to find!*

In conclusion, the article said that before retiring for the night, guests would be encouraged to provide their breakfast preference and the time they would like to be served. (Note: this schedule proved to be difficult to maintain. Guests often failed to show up at the time they had indicated while others appeared as much as an hour earlier than they had indicated. Perhaps that was partially my fault because I provided them fresh coffee, juice and sweet rolls outside their doors an hour before breakfast time!)

Back to the upcoming "Open House," I solicited and received assistance as guides for the occasion from: Dan and Carolyn Turner; Sharon Turner, their daughter-in-law; Les and Dorothy Roark, old friends from Shelby; and Gary Stewart, flight attendant with U.S. Air. All of these gave me advice, served as greeters, and kept an eye on things. They were stationed at all three levels and served light refreshments and snacks provided by the Inn.

As a small token of thanks for their help and encouragement in the past, I invited my helpers, plus Mayor Hogue and his wife Cheryl to spend a free night at the Inn. For example, Nephew Dan Turner, who was a construction expert for Duke Energy, was always available to give me expert advice (and actual help as reflected by his work in completing the driveway to the garage); Les Roark made it possible for me to obtain many of the architectural antiques I needed to finish the structure properly (and even did some special painting himself); and Mayor Hogue had given me constant encouragement from beginning to end. He even gave me free space for directional signs to The White House Inn on property he owned a block away, as well as on town hall property.

# CHAPTER 3
## Grand Opening of the Inn

APPROXIMATELY 100 PEOPLE showed up for the first public showing of the Inn. Everyone who visited expressed awe at the transformation of the building, and the displays of various collections, including antique furniture and furnishings; bed and breakfast specialty items; country collectibles; forty rare "Jacquard" handmade woven coverlets on display on beds and stairways; and antique Persian rugs throughout the Inn. They also viewed many fine oil paintings, prints, and other artwork; fine china, crystal and glassware; plus a rare collection of R.S. Prussia bowls which lined two walls of the dining room.

After the last of the "lookers" left, I took my overnight guests to their rooms and invited them to relax for an hour, while I put the final touches to my first "official" 5 o'clock "Wine and Cheese" event. I spared nothing in "putting on a spread" for my first overnight guests. Hors d'oeuvres included caviar, egg salad, various breads and cheeses, deli meats and other snacks. I provided enough food that these special people would not need to go out for dinner. I offered a variety of beverages including several different types of wine, three different brandies, and fresh, hot coffee and dessert.

Before my guests went to their rooms for the night, I gave them breakfast choices of: Eggs Benedict; sausage, egg and cheese casserole; omelets or eggs prepared to their order; along with cheese grits and a platter of sausage, bacon, and liver mush. I had also offered breakfast in bed for anyone who wanted it. Only Les Roark took me up on this offer and I was glad to oblige.

I was totally exhausted by the open house and my first time to be a "bona fide" innkeeper. I went to bed early that evening, happy that the preliminaries had gone so well. The White House Inn had passed its first test and was now fully open for business as a licensed B&B.

Although I had spent much time improving my cooking skills and getting the Inn ready to receive guests, one thing was missing: actual experience as an innkeeper. It was hard to practice "innkeeping" without paying guests. That problem was easier to solve than I had expected. When word got out that my B&B was licensed to receive guests, my phone began ringing with requests for reservations. Surprise! Surprise! Several local people had been waiting to celebrate anniversaries and other such occasions at the Inn.

Even more surprising was the number of out-of-town people calling to make reservations. Several of these were Indiana friends who had followed the progress of the restoration and were anxious to see the finished product. Although I didn't really feel comfortable receiving these guests so soon (fearing that I would not meet their expectations) I didn't have the heart to say no. While some were "snow birds" who wanted to stop by on their way to vacations in the South, others were making the trip just to see the Inn.

Quite a few of the friends who wanted to visit had already sent me favorite family recipes. I had practiced cooking some of these dishes and they had turned out well, as verified by my "taste testers." Among the first of these out-of-town visitors were John and Martha Ervin, who lived just outside Indianapolis, IN. You may recall earlier mention of this couple who taught me how to bid at auctions and educated me to such things as antique hand-woven Jacquard coverlets, coin silver, unmarked R.S. Prussia and other collectibles, unfamiliar to me when I first met them.

Since both John and Martha were school teachers, they had spent time educating me about many things that turned out to be extremely useful as an innkeeper. By this time I was considered to be a serious collector of a variety of collectibles which were on display at the Inn. Along with the Ervins, I credit Virgil Scowden of Crawfordsville, IN, who supplied antiques to many Hollywood stars from Indiana, with helping teach me to recognize and buy quality antiques and collectibles. I attended Virgil's classes much of the time I was at Purdue University and he also gave me personal tours of several of his museums.

After John and Martha returned to Indiana, they sent me a copy of a column Martha wrote about their visit to Blacksburg. It had appeared in her regular "Cooking with M.E." column for "The Indy East" newspaper. The column said that she and John arrived in Blacksburg at night and the White House Inn "sparkled like a jewel." She went on to describe the layout of the Inn, "its beautiful facade and furnishings" and its "great breakfasts." She added: "Jim's southern hospitality immediately makes one feel right at home." She ended her column by printing two of the Inn's recipes: "White House Inn Grits" and "Jim White's Easy Eggs Benedict" in her column. *After urging from some of my reviewers, I included these recipes at the end of this document under "notes."*

Jo Ann Miller and her oldest son, Tim, his wife and three daughters from Indiana also were early visitors to the Inn. You may recall that Jo Ann was the lady I had dated in Lafayette and who had owned and operated a "fine dining" restaurant in the small town of Flora, IN. Purdue University professors were known to take out-of-town guests they wanted to impress to Jo Ann's restaurant and antique mall. She was now working at a newly opened Cracker Barrel Restaurant outside Lafayette where she served as "floor manager" and head of serving.

The Miller family had kept in touch during the past 2 ½ years of the restoration process and was anxious to see the finished product. I was equally anxious to see them and really looked forward to their visit. Since her son Tim was one of Indiana's top architects, I wanted his appraisal of the Inn's architectural changes and reconstruction. Also, I wanted Jo Ann's reaction and ideas for the furnishings and decorative schemes as well as for fine dining. Both praised the Inn's menu, architecture, furnishings, and elegance. Their reactions were confidence builders for me.

Another out-of-town couple, Bob and Debbie Price of West Columbia, SC visited soon after that. Although they were initially strangers, we quickly became friends. They said they were thinking about someday owning their own B&B. Soon we were thoroughly engaged in personal and business conversation. Needless to say, I served them my "Eggs Benedict" breakfast the next morning.

A few days after their visit, a package arrived containing a beautiful little "Sweet Heart" waffle maker. It was a gift from the Prices, who had noticed that my kitchen did not yet contain that cooking item. As our friendship deepened, this couple became one of my "guest innkeepers," along with Dan and Carolyn Turner, when I took a couple of days off. I used the waffle iron my remaining days as an innkeeper and still use it today.

In addition to the waffle iron, Bob and Debbie's visit provided another unexpected gift: favorable publicity for the Inn. A few days later, they sent me a copy of an article in the Columbia State Newspaper's "Travel Advisor" section. The heading was: "Great Finds: Retreat to Blacksburg Inn." The article, written by Bob and Debbie Price, lauded the Inn's nearby location, its bountiful supply of antiques, crystal chandeliers, and "gourmet breakfasts." It ended with: "Bob's favorite was "Jim's Eggs Benedict."

Soon afterward, the Inn received even more state-wide publicity when Dan Harmon, then managing editor of "Sandlapper Magazine" *(called The Magazine of South Carolina)* spent the night as part of the magazine's "Sandlapper Slept Here" series. The Cherokee Chronicle did a follow up of his visit with an article describing Dan's reaction to the Inn saying, "Harmon describes the Inn's sumptuous decor. As for antiques, think museum." Harmon was further quoted: "From unmarked R.S. Prussia deep bowls, to 300 year old French chairs, to a 19th century Sarouk rug, to White's fabulous art collection and chandeliers, your attention is diverted everywhere you turn. His collection of hand woven coverlets, some in perfect condition, date from 1835 to1868."

Dan's visit also began a life-long friendship. A talented musician as well as writer, when I first met him, Dan and his band were performing at clubs in and around Columbia. He and friends also hosted "musical parties" to which I was invited. In turn, when both of us had a free weekend, I reciprocated by inviting Dan and his band for musical weekends at the Inn. "Miller-Rowe Consort," an internationally known duo of Michael Miller (classical guitar) and Dr. David Rowe (hammered dulcimer) joined the party during the musical weekends. The two groups played separately and then combined for wonderful music. Miller-Rowe also recorded several of their albums at the Inn. *Update: I'm saddened to report that Dan Harmon recently lost his battle with cancer. This was a terrible loss to his friends, family, church and the world.*

Also, during this time my doorbell rang and when I opened the door, a well dressed stranger of middle age, asked, "Are you Jim White who worked for EPA?" I replied that I was, and then asked him how he knew about my background. He replied, "My name is Jerman Stein, owner of Stein Pest Control. Since I'm in the pest control business I need to remain familiar with all the Federal rules affecting my business. Therefore, I have frequently seen the name Jim White in the Code of Federal Regulations, regarding regulations that affect our business. I've also seen that name in connection with training needs for pesticide applicators who apply 'restricted use pesticides.' I received my Certified Applicator designation at Clemson University and knew that the training and testing were based on Standards prepared by a Jim White from EPA."

He then added that he stopped by the Inn to see if I was the same person he had read about. I told him that I was, then invited him into the house where we had a fairly long discussion about revisions to FIFRA, the law which resulted in many new rules affecting pesticides. He said he and some of his top people had attended training sessions at Clemson University where they gained the knowledge they needed to be "Certified."

Mr. Stein said I was widely recognized for my work at EPA, especially for my efforts to develop standards that would be acceptable to the states while ensuring the safe use of highly toxic pesticides. He added that he was also aware of my efforts to preserve the use of "chlordane," the best and safest method of protecting homes from termites when it was applied by ground treatment. *Soon after I left EPA, this wonderfully protective chemical was banned by the agency.*

I had noticed during my conversation with Mr. Stein that he had a slight Hispanic accent and when I commented on this, he explained that he was a native of Chile, and did not know any English when he entered the country at age 19. He said when he arrived in the U.S. he was directed to a Catholic organization in Hot Springs, NC, where he met and was befriended by Father Jeff Burton, a Jesuit priest. He said Father Jeff became his mentor and deserved much credit for his (Jerman's) business success.

Mr. Stein's visit resulted in the beginning of a long friendship with him, as well as Father Jeff, who always stayed at The White House Inn when he visited Blacksburg. Several years ago, Jerman returned to his native Chile to live but visits the U.S. at least once a year and always takes time to visit with me. We also stay in touch by telephone and emails. *Unfortunately, Father Jeff passed away several years ago and we both miss him.*

# CHAPTER 4

## A New Association and New Responsibilities

NEWS ABOUT THE White House Inn B&B apparently soon reached the ears of Ron Kay, Founding President of the new South Carolina Bed and Breakfast Association (SCBBA). Owner of the premier "Two-Suns Inn" B&B in Beaufort, SC, Ron called and urged me to attend the upcoming organizational meeting of SCBBA in Columbia, SC. I accepted his invitation realizing that this was a great opportunity to meet and learn from other, more experienced B&B owners and organization leaders.

The meeting was educational and had some unexpected results. I was surprised to learn that Ron Kay had arranged to have a private breakfast with me the following morning after the conference. During breakfast, I was startled when he offered to follow me to Blacksburg for an overnight visit to offer me personal advice on operating a successful B&B. I was puzzled but pleased at the attention I was getting from the new organization's first President.

Ron Kay followed me to Blacksburg and inspected the premises. Later, we sat down together and he expressed approval for most of my early efforts and also offered me lots of helpful advice. Our one disagreement was on the issue of allowing guests to smoke at a B&B. As a serious advocate of "non-smoking," I had planned not to allow any smoking inside or outside the Inn property. Ron, a smoker himself, insisted that I would alienate too many potential guests with this rigid rule. After thinking about it, I accepted Ron's advice and moderated my non-smoking rule by setting aside a small "smoking area" on my large back porch. This worked fine for those who desperately needed a smoke.

By now you probably suspect that there was a "catch" to all of this personal help. Just as he was getting ready to leave, Ron said that the organization badly needed a newsletter to serve its officials and members. He asked me if I would be willing to create and edit a newsletter with the tentative name of "SCBBA News." Obviously, Ron had done his homework and knew that I had been a professional journalist. I agreed to start the newsletter and serve as its first editor.

My acceptance of the job of creating and writing a SCBBA newsletter resulted in a Cherokee Chronicle headline: "Jim White Editor of B&B Newsletter." In the article, Charles Wyatt, stated: "Jim White is back behind the keyboard." He then announced that I had accepted the job of creating a newsletter for the fledgling B&B association and would be serving as its first editor. He also revealed that I had been elected to the SCBBA Board of Directors for Upstate SC. Both were for one year only at my request. More good publicity but also more work!

# CHAPTER 5

## Surprise! I Find Some Old Copies of Newsletter

IN THE COURSE of gathering material for this Memoir, I eventually came across single copies of the four (1993) issues of SCBBA News with my byline. This was somewhat of a surprise since over the years, I had rarely kept copies of things I had written. In the spring (or first) issue, I introduced the newsletter and revealed plans for future issues "which would include keeping members abreast of B&B activities within the state and around the nation." The newsletter said it "would also share new or unusual marketing ideas, report member honors and awards, and keep owners aware of tax implications for their businesses." I said the newsletter would maintain balance by reporting both positive and negative developments in the industry. I urged members to share story ideas about their interesting experiences as innkeepers.

Before turning my attention to the recent SCBBA conference at Myrtle Beach, SC, I reported that SCBBA had just been awarded the coveted "Bundy Award," for "Rural Tourism Development" at the Governor's Conference also recently held at Myrtle Beach. The award was represented by a 10 X 12 plaque to be "available for SCBBA members to display at special events such as Open Houses, Historical Tours, and the like." I opined that this award aptly reflected the major role that Parks, Recreation, and Tourism (PRT) had played in encouraging the growth of B&Bs in South Carolina. Much of the rest of this issue was devoted to coverage of the recent conference.

In reporting details of the Myrtle Beach event, I began with the election of officers and the decision to move the organization's office from Beaufort to Columbia. I thought the election of Bruce Earnshaw (Cassina Point Plantation at Edisto Island) as new president and the re-election of Peggy Waller (The Inn at Merridun, Union) as vice president were excellent choices. However, although I did not mention this in the newsletter, I was personally distressed that Ron Kay had been forced out as president because he refused to accept the members' action to move the SCBBA office from Beaufort to Columbia.

I felt moving the office could have been delayed for a year to allow Ron to finish out his "founding president" position. I thought Ron was owed this consideration for all he had done in creating the organization itself, and getting several rules favorable to B&Bs passed by the SC Legislature. Two of the most important rules for which he was largely responsible were: (1) B&Bs serving only breakfasts were not required to have "commercial kitchens" and (2) B&Bs with five or fewer guest bedrooms were not required to collect state sales tax--a good reason to change from six to five guest rooms, as I soon did!

Beyond the direct conference coverage, SCBBA News also began running what turned out to be an extremely well written and informative column by new president Bruce Earnshaw. In his first column titled "A View from Edisto," President Earnshaw began his column by urging all B&Bs to join SCBBA. He said that "even outsiders acknowledge that, though still in its infancy, SCBBA is larger, better organized, and more effective in promoting the industry than other state B&B organizations."

President Earnshaw also used the spring issue of his column to inform members that the first "SCBBA Directory" had gone to the printer and that the organization was looking at: (1) developing a "site visits" schedule with the purpose of ensuring that SC B&Bs meet acceptable standards), (2) finalizing the SCBBA Cookbook, and (3) planning the '94 Conference. He also revealed that American Classic Tea, the only tea grown in America (in Charleston SC), was available to SCBBA members at wholesale prices.

Other items mentioned in the newsletter included, "The SCBBA Exchange," which allowed a B&B to participate in a free "exchange program" with other B&B participants. *I immediately signed up for this program, which offered a chance to learn as well as to establish closer personal friendships with fellow innkeepers.* Finally, I used the spring issue to warn B&B owners to look out for a "con man" who was taking advantage of trusting innkeepers by stealing credit card numbers, blank checks and guests' names, addresses and phone numbers. I also warned B&B owners to be alert for people posing as "travel writers" in order to get a reduced or free rate.

*Post Script: In retrospect, I should have paid more attention to the two warnings, (1) being wary of con men and (2) those posing as travel writers, mentioned above in SCBBA News. I wish that I had taken my own advice since I had personal experiences with both of these types during my tenure as an innkeeper! These will be described in more detail later in this manuscript.*

I served out my terms as editor of the newsletter and member of the Board of Directors and gladly turned these responsibilities over to others. The only SCBBA highlight I remember participating in after that was SCBBA's hosting of an "International Conference on Bed and Breakfasts" at Hilton Head Island, SC. My major contributions to this event, which drew hundreds of people from around the world, were (1) arranging for The Miller-Rowe Consort musical duo to perform at the conference and (2) transporting a very large amount of Clemson University's famous blue cheese to the Conference. Both Miller-Rowe Consort and Clemson's blue cheese were highly appreciated by attendees. Miller-Rowe drew large crowds and there was no left over Clemson blue cheese for me to bring home. *Darn it!*

# CHAPTER 6
## My First Big Event as an Innkeeper

SOON AFTER MY "open house," I received a call from Hazel Ann Childers, a Gaffney business woman, married to a Gaffney businessman, both of whom I had recently met. Hazel Ann asked if I would be willing to prepare a special dinner for her Gaffney dinner club consisting of six or seven prominent couples. I knew that these club members were influential people in our area. Therefore, I wanted to get to know them better and wanted them to become familiar with my Inn. Although I liked Hazel Ann's idea, I was not sure that it was legal for me to prepare the entrée since I was licensed only to prepare breakfast and snack foods for guests.

I explained this to Hazel Ann and told her that, if she desired, I would do some checking on the legal aspects of this matter and get back to her. After discussing the situation with appropriate authorities, I found that I could legally prepare and serve the hors d'oeuvres and dessert provided someone licensed prepared the main course. I found a reputable caterer willing to prepare the entrée and side dishes and called Hazel Ann to give her the news. She was pleased at this and the two of us agreed on the date for the special dinner.

Since this would be the first big private event for the Inn to host, I wanted to make sure it was memorable. First, I asked my friend Gary Stewart if he would dress in his tuxedo and give me a hand with serving the group. He was not only willing to do this but also volunteered to bring a friend to help out. I knew that he and his friend were both knowledgeable about fine dining and was pleased that they were willing to help.

The three of us met to discuss plans for the dinner and I said that I wanted the hors d'oeuvres to include: caviar, egg salad and various other upscale appetizers but that I needed their ideas for the dessert. They suggested "Bananas Foster" and I whole heartedly agreed to their idea. Although both of them knew how to make this famous New Orleans dessert, they decided that Gary, more knowledgeable about the Inn, would assist me while his friend would be responsible for preparing the dessert.

The evening of the dinner, Gary and his friend arrived early wearing their tuxedos and looking very professional. We made our final arrangements before guests began arriving. Per our arrangement, the two of them would serve wine and appetizers while I offered tours to those interested in seeing the house--which was most of them. The caterer delivered the entrées and side dishes on time and Gary and I served the dinners and wine while Gary's friend was setting up to prepare the Bananas Foster which would be made on and served from the nearby buffet. All three of us pitched in to serve the dessert, coffee, and after dinner drinks.

Dinner went off without a hitch and we received high praise from the group. I made lots of photos of the group, provided attendees later with copies and kept one or two for my personal file. A copy of one of the most important of these will be displayed in the pictures.

# CHAPTER 7
## The Inn Becoming a "Place To Go"

AS I HAD hoped, The White House Inn soon became the place to go for special events in Blacksburg and to serve as an attractive alternative to local motels. This dream began to be a reality when local school officials started asking me to speak and offer guided tours of the Inn to high school classes interested in history and architecture. Student visits to the Inn became regular events.

One of these visits was featured in the Cherokee Tribune, published in Blacksburg. The article extolled the elegance of the Inn and included interior and exterior photos of the building with many of the students, chaperones, and teachers attending. The article ended: "Many of the students couldn't believe they were still in their home town of Blacksburg!"

Although these events initially provided no income to the Inn, they were important in establishing good will and countering the "dumb rich Yankee" description I had gained after purchasing the Cash property. This unflattering description of me began to change as word gradually got out that I was born on a nearby farm and had been a "sharecropper boy" until we moved to town when I was 14. Thus, the words "rich Yankee" were eliminated from my description. But the word "dumb" remained until after The White House Inn began receiving guests.

Somewhat to my surprise, the "free events" and interaction with the Cherokee County School system not only created good will but actually resulted in some unexpected business for the Inn. The business involved "educational consultants" assigned to visit county public schools (including Cherokee County) and offer advice about improving those schools. The consultants expressed the desire to stay at the Inn but the prices I had established exceeded the amount of per diem a state employee was allowed at that time. However, after discussions with these consultants, we reached an agreement that worked for both parties.

I agreed to give them a special rate, (i.e., the "per diem" they were allowed) on condition that I would not be required to provide them with my expensive, time consuming custom breakfasts. This allowed them to stay at a safe, luxurious place at a price covered by their per diem. The consultants were satisfied to receive a "continental breakfast" of coffee or tea, milk, orange juice and sweet rolls. Also, they were invited to attend the evening wine and cheese event.

In addition to the school events, other functions quickly followed. On two occasions I held receptions and book signings for old friend and author, Les Roark. The Cherokee Chronicle described the first such event as "a homecoming of sorts" for Roark and his first published book of poems entitled "It's A Matter of Time." The book received rave reviews from some other Carolina writers, including Kays Gary, superb columnist for The Charlotte (NC) Observer, and North Carolina Poet Laureate Sam Ragan. Columnist Kays Gary was quoted as saying, "Les Roark will forever astound me...this work dresses our memories with warmth and dignity." Ragan added "...a beautiful and moving book...Les Roark has taken exploration into Time further and deeper than anyone I know."

Another local reporter wrote: "Les Roark Gets Red Carpet Treatment at White House Inn." This was the headline of an article written by Jerry Phillips of the Cherokee Tribune. He explained that since Roark was born in the Mount Paran community of Cherokee County, "it seems legitimate for Blacksburg to claim him as its own."

As it happened, the event I sponsored for Les resulted in a similar affair in Shelby, NC. The Cherokee Chronicle reported that this event was sponsored by O. Max Gardner III, and his wife Victoria, owners of "The Inn at Webbley" on South Washington Street in Shelby. This Inn was the former home of O. Max Gardner Sr., who served North Carolina both as its Governor and as U.S. Senator, of course at different times. The present owners, who had inherited this fine home, visited my Inn to seek advice on holding a celebration and book signing for Les, similar to the one I had held for him.

The Shelby event celebrating the book described above was attended by Columnist

Kays Gary and Les' high school English teacher and mentor, Ed Hamrick, as well as several prominent political figures, including former U.S. Sen. Robert Morgan and former NC State Attorney General Lacy Thornburg. (Note: both of these men had employed Les during their political careers). The Chronicle article mentioned that "Les dedicated the book to Ed Hamrick and two other friends: the late John Elliott and Jim White, owner of the White House Inn."

Les Roark's next book, also celebrated at The White House Inn, was a memoir entitled "A Man Goes Back To Where The Boy Has Been." Like all of his writings, Les' book of "recollections" was beautifully written and illustrated. He demonstrated his poetic side with quotes such as: "Memories are what we see with our eyes closed," and "Times long ago and Places far away--Experienced now, only in the silence of warm memories." I was especially proud of Les' success as a writer since I had recommended him for his first two newspaper reporting jobs. This particular book contained 140 pages and covered the period of 1924-1942, i.e. from his birth until graduating from Grover (NC) High School and going into the Army Air Force. It is about his early life and cultural changes over the years.

Les gave me signed copies of both books. His memoir had this dedication: "To Jim White, my long-time friend and 'Charter Member' of our 'Recollection Club' of the last six or seven decades, with fond memories, Lester 'Les' Roark, March 9, 2002." As with his earlier book on "Time," proceeds from this book were donated to a Shelby High School Scholarship Fund.

On another personal note, Les and I both lived (at different times) in the same "tenant" farm house in the Holly Grove community near Blacksburg. During our childhood we sometimes spent nights with each other. Les' older brother, Sid, was also best friend of my brother, Frank. *Also, I would be remiss if I did not mention that shortly after I took the job at North Carolina State, Les visited me in Raleigh and I introduced him to Dorothy Mulder who later became Mrs. Dorothy Roark!*

Among other early special events hosted by the White House Inn was a reunion of Blacksburg band students from around the nation (as far away as Pennsylvania and California). The Inn was reserved for attendees of the reunion and was soon filled to capacity with out-of-town former band members. Many other attendees spent nights with local residents during the event.

The Spartanburg Herald Journal reported that "the event was a reunion of band members from the period of 1948-1958." Dean Ross of Gaffney was featured at the reunion for his stellar work in building a prize winning band at the small Blacksburg school. *The newspaper also revealed that Dean Ross was promised a Clemson scholarship while still attending Gaffney High School. After entering college in 1940, he accepted an offer to direct the school band. Sometime during that period he brought the "Tiger Rag" fight song to Clemson and it is still being played at sporting events there.*

The newspaper added that Ross was in his junior year when his entire class at Clemson was drafted to serve in World War II. *(At that time Clemson was a military school for male students only).* In describing Dean Ross' service in the war, the article mentioned that Ross fought in the "Battle of the Bulge," considered one of the critical battles of the war. After he was released from service, he returned to SC and established a notable career in education. *He also developed many friends and admirers over the years before passing away at age 92 in 2014.*

# CHAPTER 8
## Small B&Bs Not "Money Makers"

AS SUGGESTED ABOVE, The White House Inn achieved much recognition, but (like most small B&Bs) was never a big "money maker." After less than a year of being open, Sandlapper Magazine reported that the many guests hosted at the Inn included: one wedding couple; five couples spending their honeymoons there, and a couple married 33 years spending their vacation occupying the Inn's honeymoon suite. Although the Inn was rarely filled during those early days I rarely had more than a couple of days between guests. I was quickly learning that being an innkeeper is often a 24 hour per day job.

Despite appearances of success, from a financial standpoint my business stayed "in the red." This was largely my own fault, because I "spared no expense" to ensure that every single guest had a memorable time at the Inn. I thought that the worst thing that could happen was to have an unhappy guest so I never did anything "on the cheap." Based on guest responses, I think I achieved my goal of making stays at The White House Inn memorable.

Aside from the issue of profitability, small B&Bs offer the innkeeper a rich lifestyle of interaction with highly interesting people who appreciate historic buildings, the ambiance of period furniture and furnishings, gourmet breakfasts and personal attention from an attentive host. Before, during, and after I operated the White House Inn I was showered with praise and recognition I had never before anticipated. As a journalist, it had always been my job to write about and describe others. Suddenly I had become the subject rather than the writer of many stories.

One example of this was an article written by Jerry L. Phillips for the Cherokee Tribune. In a philosophical piece dated March 18, 1992, he wrote about the Inn and me. After relating some unflattering facts (e.g. gun fights in the streets) about early Blacksburg supplied by historian Bobby Moss, Phillips wrote: "History should never completely perish from society... recollecting the past makes one appreciate the present and might give direction to the future. One man here sees beauty in the old. He sees aesthetic beauty that could become extinct. He is Jim White, who, in a sense, is a deconstructionist. He has an obsession with reviving what others have dismissed as old, outdated, and worthless. One such endeavor was the complete restoration of the Cash House."

After describing the renovation effort, my work career, and the present elegance of the Inn, the writer concluded: "There are no longer gun fights in the street and criminal rings blatantly challenging the law, but will all the beauty disappear with the bad? Thanks to Jim White, some of it will stay with us for some time. He is this week's Who's Who in Cherokee County..."

# CHAPTER 9

## A "Win-Win" Business Arrangement Develops

DURING THE PERIOD of 1991-1996 when I operated the Inn, I had only one really lucrative business arrangement. It was with a New York company that employed "textile designers," most of whom were women. The story behind this arrangement involved women traveling alone on business and who had been physically attacked at motels where they were staying. Concerned about the possibility of this happening to its female employees, the company's headquarters in New York City decided that an owner-occupied small facility (e.g. a B&B with owner on site) offered a safer alternative for its female employees.

In this particular case, the company's female textile designers were required to visit a "textile finishing company" in nearby Gaffney where they installed their designs on a finishing company's looms. After some of its employees had reported having an enjoyable and secure stay at my Inn, an executive from the company called and suggested that they were willing to pay a monthly stipend to ensure that a room at the Inn was always available for their employees.

With this nice and unexpected "stipend" I assured the company that with sufficient notice, there would always be space available at the Inn for their employees visiting the area. Under the arrangement, I would also give them a discount for nights they used a room. However, the company excused me from serving my usual custom breakfasts. I was asked to provide a "continental breakfast," e.g., coffee, tea, milk or juice, and sweet rolls for its employees. Of course, like the educational consultants, they would be invited to participate in the 5 p.m. "wine and cheese" functions.

Also, as was the case with most of my guests, these women guests were universally nice and not overly demanding. They and I became quite comfortable with the arrangement. Although I required that they call ahead of time for a reservation, I ignored my usual "check-in-time" and provided them with a front door key so they could let themselves in at any time they arrived, whether I was there or not. They were also free to help themselves to drinks and snacks.

Revealing a secret never before told, some of the designers were so impressed by my colorful antique Jacquard coverlet collection that they asked permission to sketch or photograph the coverlets so they might use them as inspirations for their own designs. I was flattered that such talented people appreciated this lost art and did not hesitate to give them permission to photograph or copy at their will.

# CHAPTER 10
## Hollywood Arrives in Blacksburg

ALTHOUGH THE WHITE House Inn had received much favorable publicity during its reconstruction period, I was surprised to learn that Hollywood movie star and model, Andie MacDowell, a native of Gaffney, had been following the progress of restoration of the old Cash mansion into an upscale B&B. As a subscriber to The Cherokee Chronicle newspaper, she knew that the Inn was now open for business and told publisher Tommy Martin that she hoped to visit it someday.

This opportunity came sooner than expected when the City of Gaffney decided to name a street in her honor. My first word of this came when Tommy called me and asked, "Jim, how would you like to have Gaffney's famous movie star, Andie MacDowell, as a guest at your B&B? She has followed the development of your Inn by reading our newspaper and is anxious to see it and stay there." He also told me that Andie is known as "Rosie" in her Gaffney home town.

Although I was not then familiar with either Andie MacDowell or her movies ("Sex, Lies and Videotape"; "Short Cuts"; "Four Weddings and a Funeral"; "Groundhog Day," etc.), I knew that this chance for national exposure for the Inn was too good to pass up. So, I did not hesitate to agree to accommodate Andie, her father, Marion, and three sisters and their husbands for their weekend stay. (Note: since the educational consultants and New York designers were work-week guests, there was no conflict with them).

Andie was scheduled to arrive around noon on that Saturday. *(I made an exception of my "check-in" time of 3 p.m.).* However, my doorbell unexpectedly chimed at 10:30 a.m. that morning. When I opened the door, two women, one with a very tired look on her face, were at the front door. The tired looking one immediately stuck out her hand and said: "I'm Andie MacDowell, Jim, and this is my sister, Babs. I apologize for being here so early. But I'm dead tired from traveling by air all night and this morning and would really appreciate it if you let me go straight to my bed for a nap."

I welcomed Andie and took her straight to "The White Magnolia Room," which I thought would provide her with maximum quiet and privacy. Babs chose the Rose Garden Room for herself and husband who was to arrive later in the day. Then, about an hour and a half later, after rest and application of makeup, Andie came back downstairs and I was stunned to see just how beautiful she was! Obviously, that short rest and/or nap had overcome the tiredness and she more than met any expectations.

In addition to her beauty, Andie was gracious and modest. After visiting with me for a while and registering for the night, she returned to The White Magnolia Room to get ready for her noon and early afternoon activities. By noon I had completed registration of Andie's other family members and had shown them to their rooms. Then the MacDowells left for the street naming event, followed by a celebration at Hatcher Farm where country music star T. Graham Brown was to be the featured entertainer.

I could not leave the Inn to enjoy these festivities because a previously scheduled honeymoon couple was expected to arrive at 3 p.m. Also, I needed time to prepare for a late afternoon party for the MacDowells and their extended family. Right on the dot, the newlyweds rang my doorbell and I took them upstairs to the honeymoon suite which was well equipped with soft drinks and snacks. After inviting them to come downstairs later to join the party with Andie and relatives, I began getting ready for a very busy next 24 hours.

Later, I was told I missed a great celebration at Hatcher Farm where the crowd, attended by Dale Earnhardt's GM Goodwrench Racing Team, enjoyed music by country music star T. Graham Brown, accompanied by local entertainers, Kenneth Wright and Dede Upchurch. Unlimited barbeque, beer and soft drinks were available for participants. At the end of the Hatcher Farm celebration, some of the crowd trooped back to The White House Inn where they joined me, Sharon Turner and the newlyweds for a party designed to offer Andie's Gaffney friends and relatives a rare opportunity to spend time with this famous star.

I was happy that Charles Wyatt attended and also brought along country music star Brown to the party for the MacDowell family. This gave the Town of Blacksburg two celebrities visiting Blacksburg at the same time. I had an immediate connection with singer Brown and he asked me to give him a personal tour of the Inn. He was very complimentary of the Inn and said that he planned to incorporate some of my ideas into the house he was restoring in Nashville.

Meanwhile, Charles Wyatt was taking many photos at the party for a long illustrated "wrap up" article he planned to write for the next issue of the Chronicle fully covering Andie's visit back home. Charles also volunteered to take candid shots of Andie with relatives and friends, both individually and in groups. I helped set up the photo shoots and recorded names and addresses of those pictured so I could provide them later with copies of their pictures.

At breakfast the following morning, I seated Andie's father, Marion, at the head of the banquet table and Andie at the other end. Her sisters and their husbands filled the rest of the seats. I placed the honeymoon couple at a table for two near the front windows, close enough to the MacDowells that they could be part of the conversation. It was nice to see Andie and other MacDowell family members going out of their way to make the newlyweds feel comfortable by including them in their conversations.

Hosting the entire two day affair was costly because I provided free food and beverages for so many people, but I felt that it gave my Inn instant "celebrity status." This was publicity that I would never have been able to purchase. Andie herself could not have been more gracious. As she was leaving she offered to pay me for the accommodations I had supplied her and her family. I thanked her but said there would be no charge. She then slipped me an envelope with a generous gratuity. Also she and her family members wrote letters of appreciation to Tommy Martin and the Chronicle. In her letter, Andie lauded her "stay at The White House Inn and Innkeeper Jim White."

# CHAPTER 11
## Help Arrives from Indiana

ANOTHER HIGHLIGHT OF that time period: my friend Jo Ann Miller of Lafayette calling me and asking, "How would you like to have an assistant innkeeper?" I was startled by her question and asked, "What do you mean?" She explained, "My apartment lease is ending soon, and I thought that before I sign another lease, I would see if you need some help. If you'd like for me to move to Blacksburg, I could get my boys to bring me and some of my furnishings there at the end of my lease and give you a hand with your B&B. I know it's hard for one person to cook, serve, and make up beds, clean toilets and the like."

Since my number of guests had tripled by that time, I replied, "I could sure use your help but I don't think I can afford an assistant, especially one of your quality." She said, "It won't cost you anything. All I need is a place to sleep and I know you have extra bedrooms. I've already checked and found two Cracker Barrels in your area that would like to hire me. If I took a part time job with one of them, this would allow me to maintain my benefit program while earning some spending money. And as a 'part time' employee, I can arrange my schedule so that my time off coincides with your busiest time, which I suspect is early morning and later at Wine and Cheese."

Jo Ann's offer made sense to me. We had gotten along well in the past and I was fully aware of her love and knowledge of food service, especially fine dining, something I was still learning. I also knew she had boundless energy and loved working with people. Those attributes are essential if you are actively involved with a B&B. So I told her that I really wanted and needed her assistance, adding that I had two extra bedrooms and she could have her choice.

I also volunteered to drive her to the Cracker Barrel Restaurants she had contacted (one in Spartanburg and the other in Gastonia, NC). Each was within about 30 minutes of Blacksburg and she could make her decision of which one to select after visiting them and talking to their managers. After visiting both, she decided to accept the Gastonia NC Cracker Barrel job which was only about 20 minutes away.

After Jo Ann settled down at the Inn, my job became much easier and more enjoyable. I treated her like an equal partner to the extent that many people believed that we shared ownership. Right from the start, the personal and work relationship worked out nicely for both of us. I always tried to schedule my regular, paid housekeeper, Betty Gibson, to help get rooms ready between guests leaving and the next ones arriving. However, since Betty also had other clients, her schedule didn't always fit my needs. In those cases, it was up to me get rooms ready for the next guests and Jo Ann was almost always able to arrange her schedule so she could assist me with these chores. She also seemed to especially enjoy acting as hostess for special events and I turned the responsibilities for planning these events over to her.

One interesting event at the Inn involved the annual "Debutante Ball" which resulted in good publicity and, hopefully, good memories for these attractive young women. The Gaffney Ledger in an issue dated 3/26/93 introduced that year's event with the headline: "White House Inn site of Coke Party." The article then added: "The elegant White House Inn at Blacksburg was the site of the combined Blacksburg/ Gaffney 1993 Coke Party on March 7." The newspaper then explained that the "Coke Party" was part of a series of debutante season events which began Jan. 10 and culminated with the Debutante's Ball at the Armory in Gaffney.

After listing the parents and debutantes attending, the paper said "The White House Inn was decorated for the occasion in red, white and blue and the centerpiece was flanked by the honorees. The Inn served small, six-ounce bottled 'Cokes' with straws and various 'pick-ups.' " The article ended with: "Jo Ann Miller of The White House Inn served as hostess for the affair and Carolyn Turner conducted tours of the Inn and its many antiques and collectibles."

Years after the Inn closed, a lady whose daughter had been feted at one of the Debutante Balls was heard expressing fond memories of her visit to The White House Inn, commenting that The Inn and its furnishings "served as an attractive back drop" for these beautiful young ladies.

# CHAPTER 12
## Recognition from Outside Sources

IN ADDITION TO the excellent local publicity the Inn was receiving, it soon began receiving recognition from outside the area and in other media, especially books and magazines featuring articles about B&Bs. A major example of the latter was inclusion in a book called "Best Places to Stay--The South" by travel writer, Carol Timblin. I was pleased to be one of eight B&Bs in the state of South Carolina to be listed in this excellent book which contained about 900 pages.

In describing the Inn, author Timblin said "The White House Inn exudes opulence." In further describing it, Ms. Timblin mentioned that it "hosted movie star Andie MacDowell and her family and other celebrities" but added: "You don't have to be a star to get regal treatment at the White House Inn. Jim rolls out the red carpet for guests." She also lauded the Inn's wine and cheese reception; the morning's "full gourmet breakfasts (served) on china and silver. Caviar and Eggs Benedict are featured items at the Inn and snacks and beverages are available at all times."

The Inn was also mentioned in many other prestigious publications, including the book, "Hidden Carolinas, The Adventurer's Guide," written by Stacy Ritz, noted travel writer who wrote the award winning book *The New Key To Belize,* as well as *Disney World and Beyond.* She was a staff writer for *The Tampa Tribune* and had written for *Parents Magazine,* the *Washington Post,* the *Miami Herald* and others. *The reference to the White House Inn can be found on pg. 396 of "Hidden Carolinas" under the heading "Upcountry Lodging."*

Ms. Ritz introduced the Inn by writing: "About 30 miles east of Spartanburg in a funky railroad town of Blacksburg, The White House Inn is completely unexpected. (It is) a stately Greek Revival house in an ordinary Southern neighborhood. Pretty period pieces fill the five bedrooms, and a third floor suite is voluminous, modern, and private. Owner Jim White makes big breakfasts and serves afternoon tea." *Note: Stacy and I had lots of conversation the night she stayed at the Inn but I'm not sure where she got the idea that I served afternoon tea! But she got the rest of the story right.*

Favorable mentions in books such as those by Ms. Timblin and Ms. Ritz helped me achieve my goal of making the town of Blacksburg an "end destination." As a result of these favorable mentions, I began receiving new guests from many faraway places. Some said they wanted to experience the luxury of The White House Inn and were willing to drive hundreds of miles to spend a night in it.

# CHAPTER 13
## The Inn Goes International

I HAD BEEN very pleased that The White House Inn had gained national recognition and thought that hosting the Andie MacDowell family was the zenith of fame achievable in my lifetime. However, early in July, 1993, I received a call from the country of Scotland inquiring about the availability of the Inn for a documentary movie to be made in Blacksburg by British Broadcasting Company (BBC).

The caller was Eleanor M. (Elly) Taylor of "Taylored Productions, BBC Scotland," located in Glasgow. She would direct the movie which would be produced by the "Garfield Kennedy Co. of London, England." I would need to provide facilities for at least six people for an entire week which meant that it would be necessary to close the Inn to anyone other than the filming cast and crew during the period of their stay. Fortunately, none of my regulars, i.e. educational consultants and designers, were planning a visit to the Inn that week so there was no conflict.

After some detailed conversations and negotiations, Elly Taylor and I reached agreements covering issues of pricing of food and facilities. Our conversations also ended up with the possibility of my being an active participant in production of the movie. *I did participate but made no charge for that.*

When I asked Ms. Taylor for details about the film, she said the story involved a European jazz and blues singer, Suzanne Bonnar, who was known in Europe as "Scotland's Billie Holiday." She said the singer was the daughter of a white Scottish mother, Jill Bonnar, and a black father, a career U.S. Navy man by the name of James D. (J.D.) Wade, who was born and raised in Blacksburg, SC.

In an early article by the Spartanburg Herald-Journal, the newspaper explained that Suzanne had recently taken a five hour train ride from her home in Dunoon, Scotland, to Kings Cross, England, to meet her 68-year-old father for the first time. This meeting was so touching and successful that BBC decided to make a 29 minute documentary featuring Suzanne and her father visiting Blacksburg where Suzanne would have a chance to meet her U.S. black family members. The scenes of their first meeting in England would be included in the documentary filmed in Blacksburg and other nearby towns and sites.

J. D. Wade had retired from the Navy and now lived in London, England. The U.S. visit would give Suzanne a chance to meet her three half-brothers, plus cousins, aunts, uncles and other relatives for the first time. As noted by the Herald-Journal, she expected to "discover her American roots" in Blacksburg. Before their arrival, I had several long conversations with Elly Taylor and she sent me a "filming schedule" with the suggestion that, since I knew the areas in and around Blacksburg, she hoped I would be willing to serve as "scene locator" for several events. I studied the Filming Schedule showing filming locations that I would need to find and get commitments for their use before my guests arrived from Europe.

One scene was a slave quarters and another was a black night club where Suzanne Bonnar would perform before a black audience. It was easy to locate and get a commitment for the first; but it was extremely difficult to locate a black night club willing to let us use it for Suzanne's performance. The solution I came up with required Elly's approval. Results of the search for a suitable place for Suzanne to perform will be discussed in more detail later.

In keeping with the filming schedule, the crew members and Elly Taylor arrived late Friday, July 9, and settled in that evening at The White House Inn to recover from "jet lag." The next day, the cast (Suzanne and her father, along with Producer Garfield Kennedy) arrived in Blacksburg, stopped briefly at the Trinity AME Zion Church where Suzanne would sing with the choir on Sunday and then went to Carrie May Haines' house on Brugg Street, the site for a family reunion later that afternoon.

The reunion would offer Suzanne the first opportunity to meet her three half-brothers and dozens of other close relatives, many of whom had traveled long distances to meet their famous relative from Europe. It was a tearful meeting of Suzanne and her three half-brothers: James of Dorchester, MA, Kenneth of Roxbury, MA, and Kelvin of Randolph, NJ. All three of them turned out to be successful professional men. Suzanne also got lots of hugs from her many South Carolina relatives as well as those who had traveled from Dayton, OH, North Philadelphia, PA, Augusta, GA, and New York, NY. This reunion was not only filmed by BBC but also by television stations in Spartanburg and Columbia, SC.

After the party ended at around 7:30 p.m., J.D., Suzanne and Garfield joined the others to retire to The White House Inn to rest and prepare for the next day's activities. I don't recall the precise sleeping arrangements but if memory serves me right, Suzanne occupied the Honeymoon Suite, either alone or with Elly Taylor. After getting some rest, everyone gathered in the living room to relax and chat.

Then, as darkness approached, the doorbell rang. I opened the door and was shocked to see my old friend and former boss at both the Environmental Protection Agency (EPA) and the Department of Energy (DOE). William (Bill) Holmberg, was standing there with a lady friend. I had not seen nor talked with Holmberg since I had recovered from cancer many years ago. I welcomed them in and introduced them to the BBC cast and crew.

When Bill asked if I had a room available for that night, I had to tell him that every room at the Inn was occupied for the next few days but I arranged for the two of them to stay at a friend's B&B that night. I also invited Bill and his friend to return to Blacksburg the next day to attend the filming of the church services at Trinity AME Zion church where J.D. and Suzanne would be introduced to the congregation and Suzanne would be soloist with the 30 member choir.

Despite the fact that she had only one rehearsal (at 9:30 that morning) with the choir, the performances of both Suzanne and the choir were outstanding. There were few dry eyes at the end of her introduction and solo. This was my first time to hear Suzanne sing and I thought she fully lived up to her name of "Scotland's Billie Holiday." I voiced this opinion to Elly. Bill Holmberg and his friend agreed with this assessment and said they thoroughly enjoyed the musical performance and service that followed.

The two of them followed us back to the Inn where they chatted with the BBC cast and crew before Bill and I broke away to have our own little two person reunion before parting. During the few minutes we had alone, Bill told me he had left DOE after the election of President Reagan whose administration did not match Bill's environmental viewpoints on alternative energy and other environmental issues.

Bill told me he had been asked to moderate his environmental views but instead he told the Reagan administration representative where to "shove it" before leaving the Forestal Building. He said he was now working with one of the large environmental organizations. I thought this arrangement was a better fit for both him and the Reagan administration. I have not seen nor heard from him since that visit to Blacksburg. And although we disagreed on many issues, I remain grateful for his many kindnesses to me over the years.

# CHAPTER 14

## Filming Begins at First Location

BY PRE-ARRANGEMENT, FOLLOWING the next day's breakfast, the cast and crew drove to Great Falls, SC where Suzanne could visit her grandmother's grave at Camp Creek Cemetery. I spent this time with Jo Ann, making up the guest rooms and preparing for the next morning's breakfast. Assuming that all my British guests would be tea lovers, I had stocked up on specialty teas only to find out that not a single one wanted tea. All said they had looked forward to having great American coffee--something not easily found in Great Britain.

As for breakfasts, in line with the arrangement I had with Director Elly Taylor and Producer Garfield Kennedy, I was not expected to provide my usual individualized, fancy breakfasts, e.g., Eggs Benedict. They would be offered coffee or tea, juice, sweet rolls and a standard breakfast such as a breakfast casserole with bacon, sausage, or ham. Then I learned that one crew member wanted only beans for breakfast. So, I added that to the menu. Ugh!

Starting Monday, July 12, the schedule for me as "scene locater" kicked in. The assignment of finding slave quarters had been easy. Jo Ann and I had previously visited our friends, Jim and Peggy Waller, owners of "The Inn at Merridun," in Union, SC and had been shown the slave quarters which were once occupied by slaves working on a large plantation. The Wallers had purchased the plantation manor house and made it into an outstanding B&B. Fortunately they had preserved the old slave quarters for posterity. They had been more than willing to let it become part of the documentary.

The trip to Union had required about a 40 minute drive. Once there the scene footage showed an emotional Suzanne as she visited the slave quarters and the plantation house itself which had recently been restored by the Wallers. Her tears were for her black American ancestors who may have possibly been slaves there.

At the end of filming in Union we went to lunch at one of the town's small restaurants and then started back toward Blacksburg. We stopped once for filming of J.D.'s old, segregated school before returning to the Inn. The rest of the day's filming was of Suzanne and J.D. at the Inn, walking along the main street, and talking with local people.

After "wine and cheese time" later that day I invited any who wanted to join me on the shaded front porch to enjoy the nice breeze after enduring a hot summer day of filming. Before J.D. and Suzanne came outside, J.D. called me aside and asked if it might not "cause me trouble" if white townspeople passing by saw two black folks enjoying a glass of wine with me. I told him not to worry; that I had announced before opening the Inn that people of all colors would be welcomed as guests at The White House Inn. And I told him that I had already had black guests without incident.

Of course I understood J.D.'s reason for concern. After all, he probably recalled his younger days when Blacksburg was a thoroughly segregated town. I personally remembered when black folks were supposed to move off the town's sidewalks into the street to allow white folks to pass. After I explained the positive cultural changes in the South since he had left the area, JD and his daughter, along with Jo Ann and me, often enjoyed spending time together on the front porch. The Chronicle quoted me as describing J.D. as an "unforgettable person with the easy, sophisticated manner of someone who has seen and done it all--a world traveler. He is a highly-talented, intelligent person who captivates everyone with whom he comes in contact. He is someone to make Blacksburg proud."

*Note: I was told that the black community appreciated the fact that I was "black friendly." This was illustrated later when Charles was in the hospital and I needed temporary landscaping help. A young black man I did not know stopped by the Inn and said he understood that I needed help and he would like to work for me. I was planning to hire him until a black friend I knew well stopped by to warn me that this man was dangerous; that he had just been released from prison and was on parole after serving time for attacking and seriously injuring someone. I thanked the friend and didn't hire the parolee. Charles recovered from his illness and returned as my "indispensable" helper.*

Tuesday, July 13th, was spent mostly with a "shopping list" of scenes Elly wanted to film in and around Blacksburg and Gaffney, including a cotton field and peach orchard. Naturally she wanted to film Gaffney's famous "Peachoid." Late in the day, all of us went to "Our Place" just outside the town limits of Blacksburg where a night club scene with Suzanne singing would be filmed before a large audience of relatives, friends, and other black invitees that evening.

This brings up the interesting set of events that occurred in the course of locating a night club where Suzanne would perform. Elly and I had both assumed that the performance would be at a black night club, probably in Gaffney, since Blacksburg didn't have one at that time. I asked Kenneth Oglesby, a black musician friend, to accompany me for visits to select a night club. Since I had selected Ken to handle the music for the night club scene, it made sense to take him along.

Both Ken and I thought that the club owners or managers would jump at the chance to have an internationally known black singer perform at their club. So, at the first club we visited, we confidently made our pitch, emphasizing Suzanne's growing reputation in Europe. The manager listened to our pitch but when we asked him how much it would cost to rent the club for a few hours one evening he emphatically declined. In fact, he rather forcefully told us that he would not rent the club to us at any price. To our dismay, we received the same response at all the black clubs we visited. Not a single one would consider letting us rent their club for a few hours.

Then I had a crazy idea: I went to talk with Tommy Wilson, president of "Our Place" in Blacksburg, to see if he would consider letting us rent the club for Suzanne's performance before a black audience. The reason I thought my idea was "crazy" was that "Our Place" was exclusively a private "white" night club. This club occasionally had black entertainers but as far as I knew not a single black had ever requested to be a member. However, when I described the situation, Tommy smiled and said without hesitation, "I think we can work something out."

When I asked what the charge would be, he said, "It won't cost you anything if you let me and a few other white folks watch the performance. We'll sit in the back of the room and stay out of camera range if you would like." I was much relieved and relayed the idea to Elly Taylor for her reaction. She liked the idea and the price!

So, the afternoon of the performance that night, I took the crew to "Our Place" so they could set up the sound and filming for that evening. Meanwhile, we had become aware that the heavy schedule and emotional turmoil were taking a toll on Suzanne. In fact, at one point during the day of her scheduled night club performance, she almost collapsed and had to be helped to her room to rest. However, she readily went with us to "Our Place" for the evening performance.

The band of Ken Oglesby, Lloyd Williams and Tracy Littlejohn took the stage first, introduced themselves, and then Lloyd, acting as Master of Ceremony, introduced the featured performer with the words: "Tonight we are pleased to introduce Suzanne Bonnar, straight from Scotland, and known all over Europe as 'Scotland's Billie Holiday.' She is going to sing for us tonight. Come on up, Suzanne."

Instead of getting up, Suzanne lowered and shook her head "no." Despite being cued several times, Suzanne would not move from her seat. Seeing her despair, Jo Ann made her way through the crowd, took a seat beside Suzanne, and put an arm around her. Then, after realizing that Suzanne was not able to perform, Jo Ann helped her to her feet and, assisted by two men, brought her outside. I drove her to The White House Inn where Jo Ann took her to her room and stayed with her.

I returned to "Our Place" quickly and saw her irrepressible and talented father, J.D., on stage in his daughter's place. Showman that he was, he had not wanted to disappoint the audience or the movie makers so after a brief discussion with the band, he began singing. *In a previous conversation, J.D. had told me that he had sung professionally during and after his Navy career but had not sung before an audience in 20 or more years.* Despite his long absence from the stage, he still maintained a professional flair.

Then, Blacksburg's Belle Haines, J.D.'s niece, jumped up on stage and did a spirited dance with her uncle to the delight of the crowd. The night club scene was the final item on the filming schedule prepared by Director Taylor. It was filmed and recorded and appeared in the finished product. The next day we took Suzanne to a local doctor who prescribed something to calm her nerves. The doctor also suggested that when Suzanne returned home she should seek professional counseling to help her adjust to all the changes in her life. Suzanne had been supposed to go spend a couple of nights with her relatives before returning home but apparently meeting so many of them was too much for her and she insisted on staying at the Inn until she left the U.S.

# CHAPTER 15

## Saying "Goodbye" to Movie Crew

AS SCHEDULED, ELLY Taylor, cameraman Les Young, and sound man John Quinn, left for Europe the following morning. Because of Suzanne's fragile condition, producer Garfield Kennedy decided that he, Suzanne and her father, J.D. would remain in Blacksburg two more days to allow Suzanne additional time to recover. It should be mentioned that during the time the cast and crew stayed at The White House Inn, Jo Ann and Suzanne had formed a special connection. So, the last afternoon Suzanne was here, she and Jo Ann went on a shopping spree in Gaffney, which was fun for both.

Jo Ann and I regretted having to say goodbye to these fine British citizens with whom we had lived and worked during their stay in our town. Apparently, this sentiment was shared by our visitors. As he was getting ready to leave, Garfield Kennedy held on to my hand and told me how much everyone had enjoyed their stay at the Inn. He added that he hoped that someday he and his crew might be able to come back to our area to make another movie. If that happened they would want to stay at The White House Inn.

In his final statement to me Garfield explained that he and Elly were both greatly impressed by the music of the Trinity AME Zion church choir where Suzanne sang her solo. He said this had raised the possibility of their doing a documentary on "Southern black gospel music." I told him our area was blessed with the type of church music he had experienced at Trinity AME Zion. And I informed him that Blacksburg itself had a highly praised professional choral group of black male singers. I assured him that we would certainly welcome the group back to the Inn.

On the plane back to Europe, Garfield Kennedy hand-wrote a letter to Jo Ann and me expressing "gratitude for all the two of you did for us during these last few days." Soon after that I received a letter from Elly Taylor addressed to both of us saying, "I would like to thank you both for your kindness, help and participation in making the film about Suzanne. It goes without saying we couldn't have done it without your help."

She addressed me personally in her letter by saying: "Thank you, Jim, for your assistance in finding locations and musicians...You did a sterling job and your career in television is secured if you so wish it...and, Jim, you so rightly said I had a 'wee film' from the church footage alone..." She then added, "You will be glad to hear that Suzanne is making a good recovery now she is home and receiving counseling."

In later letters, Both Elly and Garfield wrote that, "Suzanne had a successful run at the Edinburgh Festival" adding that "she is currently performing in the Edinburgh Festival Show every night for three weeks." Both Elly and Garfield said they were very pleased with the quality of the film and sent me a copy. Elly Taylor also wrote the Cherokee Chronicle saying that: "I have visited the States several times, including New York, Las Vegas, Los Angeles and Boston, but I have never experienced the warmth that I received in Blacksburg, SC." I was certainly proud that our formerly racist town had progressed to the point that it had received such lavish praise from foreign visitors.

# CHAPTER 16
## A Dear Childhood Friend Remembered

AFTER THE EXCITEMENT wore off from the BBC movie, I received a call from a man saying that he and his fiancée wanted to reserve a room at the Inn. He said his name was Robert Love and he worked for the DuPont Co. in Wilmington, Delaware. I made the reservation and before getting off the phone asked, "You aren't connected to the Loves at Kings Creek are you?" He replied, "Yes, I am a member of the Kings Creek Love family. My father's name was Bascomb and his dad's name was John R. Love, rural mailman for that area."

I was momentarily speechless but soon regained my voice and said, "Bascomb Love was my best friend until he died in that horrible car accident. We were 'best little buddies' at Kings Creek School, and attended Blacksburg High School together until our junior year when my family moved to Shelby." I told Robert that as a result of the move we had lost contact and didn't see each other for many years. I related that in 1952 we reconnected in York, SC, where Bascomb had both a watch repair and car business and I was working as county-wide reporter for the Rock Hill Evening Herald at the time.

Robert then said: "When we meet, I hope you will tell me a lot about my Dad. I was just a child when he died and I have never heard a lot about his life as a boy and young man. So, I'm really looking forward to meeting you and learning more about my Dad." We chatted a few more minutes and Robert told me about his fiancée, Cindy Daut, who as I recall, was in the public relations business in New Jersey. Needless to say, I was looking forward to meeting Robert and Cindy and talking about my dear old friend, Bascomb.

When Robert and Cindy arrived at the Inn that first time, I was startled by the resemblance of Robert to his late father, Bascomb. In addition, although he was a child when his father died and he lived outside the South for many years, his voice retained much of the soft, southern sounds of Bascomb. Robert and Cindy made an extremely handsome couple.

We had a great time talking and I filled in lots of blanks about his father. I told him how his father and I met again after many years. The story: shortly after taking the job with the Rock Hill Evening Herald, I stopped at a downtown York drug store to get a cup of coffee. Soon after I was seated on a stool at the counter, a man took the stool next to me. I soon became aware that he was staring at me. Then the man asked: "Are you Jimmy White?" When I answered in the affirmative, he said, "I'm Bascomb Love."

I was completely taken aback but soon regained my composure and asked, "How did you happen to recognize me?" He replied: "I've been seeing the name 'Jim White' on articles in the Evening Herald and wondered if this person could be my old buddy from Kings Creek. Then, I was looking out the window of my watch business next door, saw you pass by and decided to follow you inside to see if you were the 'Jimmy White' I had gone to school with at Kings Creek and Blacksburg."

The two of us chatted awhile, and Bascomb invited me to walk next door to his watch shop where we continued to catch up on what had happened to us since we last saw each other back in 1940. After spending time together that day and succeeding days, we became even closer friends than we were as youngsters. When I was working in York, I would stop by his shop to see if he had time to go next door for a cup of coffee. Since he was self-employed, Bascomb usually could take a break and we would drink coffee and chat. Also, at the end of the work day, Bascomb would often stop by my garage apartment and we would talk for a while until he headed home to his family.

Also, I told Robert that when I could get away, I would sometimes accompany Bascomb to automobile auctions in the two Carolinas. This would give us quality time together and I could be useful in two areas: (1) If he purchased another car at the auction I could drive it back to his car lot in York, and (2) he began asking me to check out cars he was interested in and give him my opinion of their condition. As for the latter, Bascomb determined that for some reason (unknown to me) I had a special ability to spot whether or not a car had been in a wreck. Therefore, he often asked me to help him evaluate the condition of a car to be auctioned, or for that matter one he was considering buying or taking in a trade.

After we had exhausted personal conversation, Robert explained that, in addition to talking about his Dad, they had another reason for visiting the Inn. Robert said that although they were getting married in Delaware and having their main reception at the DuPont Country Club, they wanted to have a pre-marriage reception in South Carolina. This would give Cindy a chance to meet and become acquainted with Robert's local friends and relatives. A firsthand visit would give them a chance to see if The White House Inn would be suitable and available for them to hold their local reception.

After they arrived in Blacksburg and toured the Inn, the couple said they would very much like to have their local reception there. I replied that we would be honored to host the reception, provided it did not conflict with reservations already made for the Inn. After a quick check of my reservation book, I found there was no conflict for the weekend that Robert and Cindy wanted to have their reception. We then spent time working out a schedule and making decisions about such things as room assignments, food and beverages to be served, and who would be responsible for providing those items.

*On a personal basis, we also chatted about my cousin, Hayes Mitchell Faulkner. I had forgotten that Bascomb had built a home across the street from Hayes and her husband Hugh's home, and that the two families were great friends and neighbors for many years even after Robert moved to Delaware. I then recalled that Cousin Hayes had tracked me down to tell me that Bascomb had been killed in the car accident. Unfortunately, the news had not reached me in time to attend his funeral.*

Back to Robert and Cindy's wedding plans, Robert told me there were historic reasons why they were getting married (on April 23, 1994) in one of the oldest churches in America, the Immanuel Episcopal Church, New Castle, DE. He said the first rector of this church in 1703 was his Fifth Great Grandfather, the Rev. George Ross. He added that the pre-marriage rehearsal was to be held at the George Read House in New Castle, and that George Read was his Fifth Great Uncle-in-Law!

On the day of the reception at Blacksburg, the Inn was soon filled to capacity by members of the two families. As I recall, Cindy's parents and brother were present, while Robert's friends and relatives were there in great numbers. After much joyful mingling and conversation, most said their "goodbyes" and those spending the night adjourned to their rooms for rest and sleep after a long day and evening. Before leaving the Inn the following day, Robert and Cindy invited Jo Ann and me to attend their wedding at New Castle, DE and formal reception at the DuPont Country Club, at Wilmington, DE. We readily accepted the invitation.

The wedding ceremony at New Castle was beautiful and the reception at DuPont in Wilmington defied description. There were several "stations," as well as many watchful servers walking among attendees to supply their needs for food and drink. Unlimited offerings of a variety of hors d'oeuvres and beverages (from martinis to champagne) were available to suit every taste.

Then guests were invited to go to the buffet table for countless food entrées including unlimited steak and lobster tails and other fine dining selections. The DuPont Country Club put on the most elaborate reception I've ever attended, including several at the U.S. State Department. In addition there was live "Big Band" music from a large orchestra that soon drew Jo Ann and me to the dance floor! That was a memorable evening for both of us.

*Note: I lost touch with Robert and Cindy for several years while they were raising their fine son, Hugh, and I was fighting several near fatal illnesses. We regained touch while this Memoir was being written. Robert has been of great assistance to me in providing historic information and photos of both his family and mine. Unlike me, Robert was good at preserving news stories, and other information which he has freely shared with me. Many thanks, Robert!*

# CHAPTER 17

## Another Interesting Guest Arrives

ON A MONDAY morning in the fall of 1995, I received a call from the Assistant Pastor of Blacksburg's First Baptist Church. He wanted to reserve a room for a visiting evangelist who would be speaking at his church the following Sunday. The evangelist would be arriving on Saturday afternoon and would be checking out before church services on Sunday. He said the pastor's name was Rev. Barry Mayson and that the church would pay for his stay at my Inn.

The Rev. Mayson checked in early afternoon that Saturday and I noticed that his automobile parked at the front had a small enclosed trailer attached to it. We sat down for a brief conversation but he quickly asked if he could park his car and trailer behind the Inn. I'm sure I had a questioning look on my face but I replied, "Sure you can park it back there. It won't hurt the grass if you drive on it." He then added, "I'll explain the reason for this after I get the car and trailer containing my motorcycle out of sight."

A few minutes later Mayson came back inside and began telling this story: A few years earlier he had been head of the SC chapter of Hell's Angels, recognized as the most dangerous motorcycle club in the country. In that role, he went to California to attend the funeral of a California club member who had been murdered, supposedly by a rival motorcycle group. Mayson said that while he was in California, Hell's Angels top officials ordered him to eliminate some members of the rival East Coast motorcycle gang they suspected of being responsible for their member's death.

Mayson told me that his conscience would not allow him to follow this order and he left town in a hurry, knowing the California officials would not be happy with his refusal. As he feared, he soon learned that Hell's Angels had put a "contract on his life" for his failure to follow an order. Since then he had been taking precautions wherever he went. That was the reason he wanted to hide his motorcycle behind the Inn. As added protection he said he always requested churches and other organizations where he was to speak to send some rugged men to escort him to his destination.

Despite our different backgrounds, I made a connection with Barry that first night. We sat up talking for hours and established a friendship that lasted a long time. In fact, when Barry happened to be within a reasonable distance of Blacksburg, he would always try to arrange to stay at my Inn. On these occasions I learned more and more about him. During this time, he revealed the fact that his life was described in a book called: "Fallen Angel," with a sub heading of "Hell's Angel to Heaven's Saint."

When I expressed interest in his book, on his next visit he brought me a signed copy of it with the following inscription: "Oct. 12, 1995. Dear Jim, you have been a real friend to me while I stayed with you. God Bless you! Stay in Him! Col. 2: 6-10. Barry Mayson." The Biblical reference, Colossians 2: 6-10, says: "So then, just as you received Christ Jesus as Lord, continue to live in him, rooted and built up in him, strengthened in the faith as you were taught, and overflowing with thankfulness. See to it no one takes you captive through hollow and deceptive philosophy, which depends on human tradition and basic principles of this world rather than on Christ."

In Barry's book, his story begins: "My early childhood (in Georgia) was fairly normal, similar to that of thousands of other boys across the United States. I lived in a good home and was taught right from wrong. My childhood activities included attending a Baptist church with my parents. Like many others at the young and tender age of nine, I made a profession of faith in Jesus, and was baptized in water. But my life fell apart after my step father, an airline pilot, died when I was 16 years old."

He said that after his step father's death he became a troubled boy, deliberately failing at almost everything he did. Then he bought a motorcycle, learned to ride it, and ended up joining a small club called the "Rising Suns" which soon became his main interest in life. Lacking any restraint, the new freedom he was experiencing soon led to parties, fights, crime, and drugs. Eventually the police broke up the club and Barry was threatened with jail. He fled and ended up in Charleston, SC where he worked in night clubs.

There, he joined another motorcycle club called the Tribulaters. With this group, he thought he had it all---freedom to do what he wanted and growing popularity within the motorcycle community. In 1973 he came in contact with the Hell's Angels and soon became a member on the East Coast, eventually becoming president of the South Carolina chapter of Hell's Angels.

Then, the incidents on his California visit changed his life again, this time for the better. With urging from both his wife and mother, he began repenting for the bad life that he had lived. He told me he apologized to his wife and mother for the life he had been living. Then he said his mother began quoting scripture to him. saying: *"Jesus died for your sins 2000 years ago so that you could have 'eternal life' (John 3:16, For God so loved the world, that He gave His only begotten Son, that whoso-ever believeth in Him should not perish, but have everlasting life.)"* Barry said that he thought he had done so many bad things that Jesus would have nothing to do with him but his mother reminded him of Jesus' love and forgiveness. (Romans 8:32).

In one of the last times Barry stayed at my Inn, he told me: "Jim, I have surrendered my life to Jesus and I trust him to complete the good work that has started in my life. I have my mother, my wife, two sons and a daughter with me, and as I think about God's goodness and love, I know that we are growing together in him." He left and we lost touch.

*Post Script: In connection with this Memoir, I attempted to re-establish contact with Barry only to find that he had passed away in 2007. But on his web site, I learned that Barry had left a legacy of "doing good." He was the founder of "Heaven's Saints Motorcycle Ministry" as well as "The Barry Mayson Outreach" which the website said has been in operation for 31 years. And he left many who knew him and loved him, including me.*

# CHAPTER 18
## Too Many Women Guests Lead to Trouble

DURING THE PERIOD of 1993-95, the number of guests continued to increase. I was experiencing a steady stream of educational consultants as guests. Also, since I had signed the contract with the New York textile company design group, their number of visits to the Inn continued to grow. As far as I was concerned, these arrangements represented a win-win situation.

Despite this growth, my Inn was rarely full so I was happy to be receiving some guaranteed income from these two groups. At the same time, the ladies could stay in a beautiful, safe environment. It did not bother me (in fact I enjoyed it) that so many of my guests were women! But one day Jo Ann told me that this situation bothered her a lot. She added that, in her opinion, some of the women guests appeared overly fond of me. She accused one woman (by name) of openly flirting with me.

I was surprised by Jo Ann's reaction. Neither of us had ever demonstrated jealousy and I hardly knew how to respond. However, I did my best to reassure her that the woman she had accused of flirting with me was married and that nothing was going on between us or with any of the other women guests. I explained that what she was interpreting as "flirting" was nothing but friendly banter and teasing. I explained that it was natural that regular guests would become like part of the family. But she was not buying my reassurance.

In an attempt to mollify her I told her I would do my best to turn the relationship between innkeeper and guests into more of a business-like arrangement. Although my personality made it difficult for me to do this, I attempted and actually did create some distance between innkeeper and guests by trying to appear busy when one of them got a bit too close. Distancing myself from the women guests seemed to reassure Jo Ann that my relationship with the women guests was totally centered on friendship and making them feel comfortable in a "home like" atmosphere. Jo Ann's concern seemed to be lessening.

Then one day, after all the guests had gone and we were checking and making up the vacant rooms, Jo Ann angrily confronted me holding a pair of panties left by a woman guest--the one she had originally accused of flirting with me. Angrily shaking the panties toward me she said: "That woman left these deliberately! She thought I would see them and be jealous. I've decided that it's time for me to go back to Indiana for this reason as well as to be closer to my family."

I tried to convince her that leaving the panties behind was just an act of carelessness, but she could not be persuaded. She refused to discuss the matter further with me and immediately called her sons to bring a truck to move her and her belongings back to Indiana. I finally accepted the fact that since the situation was making Jo Ann unhappy, our friendship might be better preserved if she moved back to Indiana to be closer to her children and grandchildren.

In order to make the ordeal of her leaving less traumatic to both of us, I stayed away from the Inn until the Miller boys had loaded the truck with Jo Ann's things and headed toward Indiana, never to return. I missed her terribly for some time but finally decided that the move was probably best since we obviously did not share the same expectation for the future. Ironically, the woman who left the panties behind never returned to the Inn.

After waiting a few days for emotions to settle down for both of us, I called to thank her for her contributions and friendship as well as to say a proper goodbye.

After I finished saying these things, she lowered her voice and whispered: "Jim, as we were leaving the Inn, I realized I had made a terrible mistake but it was too late to do anything about it."

When I asked about her new living arrangement, she told me that she had signed a one-year lease on an apartment in Lafayette near her work but that she had asked her son, Tim, (the architect) to find a suitable modular home to be moved onto a nice wooded lot she owned within close walking distance to sons, Troy and Terry. This meant that three of the family would be living in the same neighborhood just a few miles outside of Lafayette.

The Cracker Barrel she previously worked for had taken her back, and she was head of the servers and assistant store manager for the restaurant. I was relieved that she was getting settled down quickly. And I thought her future plans to move into a house near two of her sons, was a very good idea. She said that after the modular home was moved onto her lot, Tim would ensure that it was customized to her taste. I had seen this lot and knew it would be a beautiful, safe environment for Jo Ann. And she would be among people she loved and who loved her deeply.

Meanwhile, our previous friendship began to return and continued over the years with telephone calls and several visits I made to Indiana to see her and other friends I had made while working for Purdue. *(More later about that).*

# CHAPTER 19
## A Whole Lot of Changes

LIKE THE OLD song by Gilbert O'Sullivan, with Jo Ann gone, I was "Alone Again Naturally" and doing most of the demanding household chores at The White House Inn myself. What made things even worse, my long-time friend and helper, Betty Gibson, told me she needed and wanted a full time job. Although her loss would complicate my life terribly, I volunteered to write an extremely complimentary reference letter that helped her to get a good job at the "Flying J Truck Stop and Restaurant."

She started as a server in the restaurant and was soon placed in charge of food preparation and the staff. I was happy for her because she certainly deserved more security than I could afford to provide. Since Betty was not available, I had to depend on others (when I could find them) to try to fill her shoes--although the word "depend" usually did not apply to her replacements. None of them was dependable. And as an unhappy coincidence, a growing lack of energy from my aging body was making it more difficult for me to climb stairs to complete the needed chores.

Also during this period my friend Gary Stewart (airline attendant) had become interested in restoring old houses after seeing The White House Inn rising "Phoenix-like from the ashes" of the Cash house. Consequently he had bought a little Victorian cottage on Carolina Street in Blacksburg with the idea of "bringing it back to life." I helped him when I had time and energy but Gary soon realized that house restoration was too time consuming and rigorous for someone with a regular, full time job. Also, he told me that he was not sure that Blacksburg represented the type of lifestyle that he was seeking. He thought that the town of York, which was now a bedroom community for the city of Charlotte, was a better fit for him.

After not being able to sell his house quickly, Gary was ready to walk away and lose his investment but I did not want to see that happen to a young friend. So, I agreed to buy it from him. I offered to pay him for his initial investment in the property plus the price of the materials he had bought. He quickly accepted my offer, turned the house over to me, and moved to York.

I had not expected to take on another renovation or restoration job. I thought those days were long past. However, the opportunity to help a friend save his investment as well as to salvage the work the two of us had already done was too compelling for me to resist.

Another reason, of course, was that I had already visualized that after total restoration with one major addition and the use of proper Victorian trim and paint scheme on the exterior, this plain cottage could be turned into a real little "jewel." Then I hired Mark Addy, the young man who helped with finishing touches of The White House Inn to begin work on the Carolina Street cottage. By that time, he had matured into a fully competent carpenter and needed the work.

So, I drew up a plan for a large addition that would extend across the back and got a building permit from the county. The new added space was large enough to allow for a new larger kitchen with a substantial eating area. Also, there was enough left over space in the new addition to enlarge the second bedroom into a "master suite" with room for a second bathroom. Most of the work was done by Mark with additional plumbing, electrical, and other help as needed. I mostly supervised and let more "able bodied" people do the heavy lifting.

The final house plan showed an entry from the front porch into a Victorian parlor, with two bedrooms (one a master) and two full bathrooms on the left side of the house and a great room between the parlor and new kitchen area to the right. While the walls were open, I had brick mason Pop Martin tear out the old fireplace and build a new one that was large enough for a "see through" fireplace that opened into both the parlor and the great room.

Coincidentally, as the electrical, plumbing and HVAC "rough in" work was completed and we were getting ready for dry wall installation, Nephew Dan Turner called and said, "Jim, I'm getting ready to tear down and bury the first of two old, falling down buildings on my property. The interior walls of one of these houses are covered with old, wide boards. I don't want any of this material and thought you might have a use for it." I said, "Dan, just stay there. Mark Addy and I are on the way to take a look at it."

When we arrived at the house to be demolished and entered it, I saw that all the interior walls were covered with wooden boards, 10-12 inches wide. The boards were so weathered from time and a leaky roof that I couldn't really tell by looking whether it was pine, oak or poplar but thought from its weight that it was pine. I could only dream that it might be "heart pine," one of my favorite woods. Anxious to find out, I decided to take a sample board back to town where I could run the board through my portable 12" planer.

Mark and I ran the board through the planer a couple of times and a beautiful "heart pine" pattern jumped out at us. We could already imagine how this would look with final planer work and finish sanding, so we headed back to begin taking down and transporting the remaining boards to the Carolina Street cottage. We would store them there until we could straighten, plane and sand them before installing them on all four walls of the great room. It took us two days to take down, and pull the nails from the boards, and another day to plane and finish all of them.

Once drywall was hung on the ceiling of the great room and ceilings and walls throughout the rest of the house, Mark and I installed the refinished heart pine boards around the walls of the great room. We stained crown and baseboard moldings to match. Fortunately, I had been able to save most of the original Victorian "bullet corner" type trim. Then, I acquired a small amount of matching trim from a similar "mill hill" cottage being torn down in Gaffney.

I had a cabinet maker design, make, and install custom kitchen and bathroom cabinetry. After upscale appliances were installed, the entire interior of the house painted, and heart pine floors sanded, the interior was pretty much finished and we were ready to concentrate on the exterior. As for the latter, I should mention that I had sent "pre-restoration" pictures of the Carolina cottage to an old friend, Bud Baugh, owner of Baugh & Reasor Hardware and Paint Store in Lafayette, IN. Bud was acknowledged to be Indiana's premier expert on Victorian trim and paint schemes and was consulted on many restorations of fine old homes in Indianapolis.

When I discussed the cottage with Bud, he requested that I send him photos so that he could give me some advice on finishing the exterior of the house. After studying the photos, Bud drew a sketch of the house, complete with suggested appropriate trim for a Victorian cottage along with a complete "numbered" exterior Benjamin Moore paint scheme and mailed it to me. He would not accept any money for his work saying that this work was "done out of friendship."

Meanwhile, I had already begun looking for vintage exterior Victorian cottage trim to either match or was similar to what Bud had recommended in his drawing. I had been successful enough in accumulating trim that Mark could begin installing it. By the time Mark finished this work I had found a painter I thought was capable and willing to faithfully follow the paint scheme designed by Bud Baugh. He did and suddenly the house was exactly like I had originally envisioned it.

Once all the work was completed, I called a real estate company which sent one of its agents to view the property, establish a price, prepare a proper listing contract and place a "For Sale" sign on the street. The listing agent was barely out of sight, when a young woman appeared at the cottage door, saying "I'm so glad to see that you're offering this beautiful house for sale. I've been driving by every day to look at this house since you've been working on it."

After giving her a tour of the completed interior I could see that she was in love with the house. She asked, "How much do you want for the house?" I told her the price and she said without hesitation, "Please hold the house until I can drive to the bank to get money for a deposit to buy it." A few minutes later she arrived with a bank check for the deposit. About a month later, I met her and her husband at their attorney's office in Spartanburg to complete the closing. When I entered the attorney's office, she and her husband embraced me and thanked me for allowing them to purchase my sparkling little Victorian cottage.

Although I made very little money on this project, it gave me great pleasure to see it go to people who loved it. Over the years since that time, when I visit Blacksburg I almost always try to drive past two very special houses: one a large, impressive Greek Revival which was once The White House Inn B&B and the other, a Victorian cottage that I consider to be a "little jewel." I'm especially pleased that Bud Baugh's paint scheme has been faithfully maintained.

# CHAPTER 20
## Getting Another Assistant Innkeeper

GOING BACK A few weeks, one night as I was sitting alone, the phone rang and it was Gene McKown, publisher of the Blacksburg Times on the line. He said, "Jim, I've heard that you lost your assistant innkeeper and might be able to use some help." I asked Gene what he had in mind. "Well, Jim, I've just hired a reporter who is down on his luck. He needs a place to stay and I can't afford to pay him enough to stay at your place as a regular guest. However, this man once owned a fine bed and breakfast on the Caribbean island of Saint Croix. He had to close his place there after being in a serious automobile accident that killed his son."

Gene added: "His name is Ray Bartness. I thought you guys might want to see if you could work out something whereby you could give him a reduced rate and he could help you with your B&B." I thanked Gene and asked him to send Ray to the Inn when he got off from work. Around 5 p.m. my doorbell rang and a nice looking man of about age 50 with a smile on his face said: "Hello Jim, I'm Ray Bartness." I invited him inside, noticing that the only sign of his recent injury was a slight limp.

Ray and I had a long conversation in which he told me he had graduated from Harvard Law School and was closely related to Leo Tolstoy, famous Russian author of War and Peace, and other great works. Ray also told me that he had operated his own B&B on the island of St. Croix. Naturally I had a hard time believing that a person with such qualifications would be willing to work for a small salary at the Blacksburg Times. I suspected he was inventing those credentials. So, I told him I needed to think about it and would get in touch with him later.

As a coincidence, Elly Taylor of BBC was back in South Carolina and had re-served two rooms at the Inn for the following night. The rooms were for herself and another BBC executive, Jim (don't recall his last name). As you may recall, Elly had recently directed a documentary about Suzanne Bonnar (known as "Scotland's Billie Holiday") in Blacksburg and the cast and crew stayed at my Inn. In letters to me and the Cherokee Chronicle, Elly had been very complimentary of the Inn and town of Blacksburg. She said she was thrilled to be back and so was I. The excitement that she and her crew brought to the Inn had been extremely stimulating.

After Elly and Jim checked in and went to their rooms to freshen up from their travel, they returned to the living room for conversation. We talked for a while about the movie Elly had recently directed in Blacksburg and we discussed Jo Ann's return-ing to Indiana leaving me to handle all of the Inn's business alone. Elly explained that she had arranged this visit to gather information in the hope that she could persuade the BBC to finance a documentary on "black Southern Gospel music." If she was successful, she would like for her and her crew to again stay at the White House Inn.

I was pleased with the prospect of getting to know Elly on a more personal basis and the possibility that the BBC cast and crew might again stay at my Inn. As director of a movie on a very tight schedule, I had seen her as a hard driving professional, de-termined to get the footage she needed to complete the documentary about Suzanne Bonnar. This would be a more leisurely visit. And the fact that she had brought a BBC employee with knowledge and interest in choral music with her gave me hope that Elly might be able to sell the idea for another documentary that would bring them back to Blacksburg.

This visit would also give me a chance to learn more about Jim and his major hobby of directing a large choral group in England. Jim said his work with BBC was not only fulfilling, it allowed him to meet and interact with fellow music lovers around the world.

During a pause in the conversation, I told the two of them about Ray and his background and the fact that he had just taken a job as a writer for the Blacksburg Times. I added that Ray wanted to help me with the Inn during his "off hours" in exchange for a reduced rate to stay at the Inn. I told them that I really did need some help since Jo Ann had left but that I had serious doubts about the veracity of the story Ray had told the Times publisher and me.

Before I had a chance to ask, Elly spoke up and said: "Jim, why don't you invite this fellow over? Jim and I will ask him some questions that might show whether he was telling the truth or not. And it might be fun to meet him." Elly's suggestion im-mediately sent me to the phone to call Ray and ask if he could get away long enough to come meet some visiting guests who worked for BBC and were spending the night at the Inn. Ray said, "I'll be right over." Five minutes later I opened the door for Ray and introduced him to Elly and Jim. I could see that he was enjoying the moment.

Elly led off the questioning by asking Ray if he, with his Russian background, was familiar with Galina Mezentseva, a famous ballet dancer from Russia. Ray immedi-ately responded that he was very familiar with this dancer and that he had followed her career in Russia and the United States. He said that he was aware that Galina was currently touring the United States teaching a particular type of dance that was being lost to posterity. She hoped to keep this style alive by tutoring young ballet dancers. He said he did not have her schedule but thought that she was currently in Alabama.

Ray's impromptu response and accurate knowledge about her friend struck a chord with Elly. They continued the conversation for a few more minutes and promised to keep in touch with each other. *After she returned to Scotland, Elly wrote me a letter saying, "As promised, I am enclosing a booklet for Ray which contains much background information about my friend Galina." Obviously, she didn't know the "rest of the story" when she wrote the letter.*

Jim then took up the questioning by asking Ray if he knew what had happened with the former Russian conductor of the National Symphony in Washington, DC. This famous man, Mstislav Rostropovich, conductor and master cellist, had recently resigned his position after many years as conductor of the symphony. Ray replied that he knew the conductor well and had spent time with him in Florida while visiting Leo Tolstoy's great granddaughter, Countess Vera Tolstoy who was living in New Smyrna Beach, FL. Then Ray excused himself to go to his car to fetch his briefcase.

When Ray returned a few moments later, he opened his briefcase and displayed an 8 X 10 photograph showing himself with conductor Rostropovich and Countess Vera Tolstoy. All were dressed formally and the photo removed any doubt by me, Jim, and Elly that Ray actually knew the famous conductor/cellist and Countess Vera Tolstoy.

Ray then explained that the reason Rostropovich left the National Symphony was that he was experiencing some age related memory problems that hampered his ability to remember the more intricate passages of symphonies the National Symphony Orchestra performed. Ray explained that the memory problem became so acute that Rostropovich had to resign from his job. Ray said that Rostropovich was now conducting for a less demanding symphony orchestra but didn't recall where. During this time Ray and Jim referred to the conductor by a "pet name" used only by relatives and close friends. Both knew the "pet name." As I recall it was "Slava."

After Ray excused himself to return to the newspaper office, both Jim and Elly agreed that Ray answered all their questions correctly. "We couldn't shake him," Elly declared. So the next evening I took Ray to his assigned room at The White House Inn. For the next few weeks, he helped me with every aspect of innkeeping (except cooking). Gene had so much confidence in him that Ray could set his own hours, as long as he produced good copy. Instead of a byline with his name, his articles initially included the words: (by Times Staff).

It did not take long for people to express surprise that the Blacksburg Times could afford to hire a writer of Ray's quality. And as a professional writer myself, I was amazed at his creative ability and wide range of knowledge. He downplayed his work to me and worried endlessly that I might find he had made a grammatical or spelling error. *(I never did!)*

While it lasted, I found it hard to believe that I had been able to find someone who was so helpful and interesting to have around. I listened to almost nightly stories about his life experiences, including getting a law degree from Harvard University. One fascinating story of his law career involved his (real or fabricated) representation of financier Robert Vesco and President Richard Nixon's nephew, Donald Nixon. He told me that in the 1970's, he accompanied Vesco when he fled the USA to escape charges of securities fraud.

According to Ray, they flew in a plane piloted by Donald Nixon. He said that they made a stop in Mexico and then flew on to Costa Rica. He said that Vesco was able to get a law passed in that nation to protect him from extradition. (That part is verified by internet). Ray stayed in Costa Rica for quite a while before returning to the U.S. after Vesco fell out of favor in Costa Rica. Vesco then moved to Cuba where he was also safe from extradition. After many legal troubles there, including crooked financial and drug dealing, Vesco died in Havana of lung cancer.

In addition to his storytelling ability, Ray was extremely helpful to me in keeping The White House Inn functioning. He quickly became aware that I was losing my physical capability and arranged his schedule to be available almost anytime I needed him. When I did not need him, he worked hard for the Times, developing and visiting his news sources and producing excellent copy. He composed much of his copy for the paper on my butler's pantry table.

When he was available, he did not need to be asked to help out. Once, when we had nothing special to do, I invited him to make the popular Russian dish, Borsch, for our evening meal. Despite the fact that he had none of his Russian recipes with him, he made a wonderful batch of Borsch for our supper.

A few days after Ray moved into the Inn, a family from Louisville, KY checked into the Inn. I cooked the food for breakfast and Ray helped me serve them. After they finished their meal, they invited Ray and me to join them for coffee and conversation. It turned out that the family owned powerful broadcast stations in and around Louisville. Ray knew the call letters of one of their largest radio stations and said that he had regularly listened to that station at his B&B in St. Croix. The broadcast station owner agreed with Ray, saying his family had vacationed at St. Croix and listened to their own radio station's broadcasts.

The owner then asked: "Have you guys ever attended the Kentucky Derby?" I replied that I never had but Ray responded quickly: "Yes, many times." The owner then asked Ray where he stayed while at the Derby. (It's difficult to find a place to stay in Louisville during Derby Week). Ray replied that he always stayed at the Kentucky estate of the Rockefeller family. They then asked Ray if he remembered which "guest suite" he occupied. Ray immediately got a piece of paper and drew a sketch of the suite. The guests said they recognized the suite from Ray's drawing and added that they had often occupied that same suite when visiting the Rockefellers. Passing this test convinced me that Ray was being truthful about the relationships he had with famous people.

By the time Ray moved into the Inn, the Carolina Street cottage was at the finishing stage and with Ray's obvious ability to handle the Inn, I was planning to make a vacation trip to Indiana to visit with Jo Ann and old friends and associates at Purdue. And it was also going to give me the chance to thank Bud Baugh personally for his gift.

Although I had guests at the time, I planned to leave Ray in charge of the Inn. These guests were all "long term" and did not require my daily presence. One of these was the Blacksburg "interim Postmistress" who was awaiting transfer to her home town in North Carolina. The others were from Texas, and they were staying at the Inn while completing work on cabinetry, etc. needed for a discount golfing business which would open in the nearly completed "Yellow Mall" outside the town of Gaffney.

Because of my failing health I was not actively seeking overnight guests but was happy to have the long term guests who required little from me. My health had been going down steadily and it had become obvious (to everyone except my Internist in Spartanburg) that something was wrong. My niece, Rachel Carpenter, an LGPN, now deceased, had become concerned about my health and was stopping by almost daily to take my vital signs. She was becoming alarmed because of my extremely low blood pressure and low heart rates which were now below 50.

On each visit, Rachel was recording these rates and asking me to give her notes to my doctor. He would take a quick look at Rachel's notes, smile, and remark that she was a nice young lady who liked to "play doctor." Then he would toss her notes into a waste basket. Future events made it obvious that she was "playing doctor" better than he was.

Despite my deteriorating condition, with assistance from Ray and my arrangement with the long term guests, things were functioning quite well at the Inn. At the request of my Texas guests, I had given them permission to use the Inn's kitchen to prepare their own Tex Mex food (as long as I could share it with them!). Under our arrangement, these guests were expected to provide their own meals and make up their own beds, thus sparing me the effort of climbing stairs to make up rooms and fix breakfasts.

Also, I had a similar arrangement with my lone lady postmaster guest. I had placed a hot plate, small refrigerator and microwave oven in her room. This meant she could be largely self-sufficient. Since all my guests were on a monthly rate schedule, I had no worries about being away from the Inn for a week or two, especially since I had Ray to keep an eye on things.

Then, the week before I left for Indiana, I was nailing a final piece of trim at the Carolina Street house when I heard the front door open and someone enter. I saw that my visitor was Wayne Elder, the Blacksburg Chief of Police. I was surprised and said, "Hi Wayne, what's up?" He said, "Jim I wanted you to be the first to know that I just arrested your assistant innkeeper at The White House Inn."

I asked Wayne to explain, and he said, "Jim I've been watching this guy since he arrived in town and planned to keep gathering information, until I heard you were leaving town on vacation and leaving him in charge of your Inn. I decided I needed to arrest him now because I was afraid your place would be stripped of its valuables while you were gone. I had him taken to the Cherokee County Jail in Gaffney."

"What did he do wrong and why were you suspicious of him?" I asked. He answered, "I became suspicious when his first stop in town was the police station where he introduced himself, told us he was going to work at the Blacksburg Times, which is across the street from us, and asked for directions to the newspaper office. I thought this was a ruse to gain our confidence and cover his tracks so I contacted the FBI and learned he was 'wanted' in more than 40 states."

"What was he wanted for?" I asked Wayne. He replied: "I have a list of the states and charges supplied by the FBI in my office. I can let you read the lists but I can't legally give you a copy. I can tell you that most of the crimes involved theft of money, credit cards, blank checks, and forgery, mostly petty crimes. He stole almost anything of value he could put his hands on. Posing as a former owner of a fine bed and breakfast, he thought B&B owners were easy targets. When we finish at my office, I think that you should go take a close look at your blank check books," adding, "Go to the middle of your checks because thieves usually remove blank checks from the middle where it is harder to detect those missing."

Chief Elder then said, "Jim, I have his car keys and briefcase in my car outside. The briefcase is locked but on suspicion that he has stolen some of your blank checks, if you will follow me to my office to serve as a witness, I can legally force the briefcase open to see what, if anything, he might have stolen from you. Also, while you're there I can let you look at and make notes from the FBI lists." So, I followed the chief to his office.

Looking back, I had observed how protective Ray had been of his briefcase, always carefully locking it, even when he was inside the Inn. Suspecting that he might be the "con man" I had warned members about in the first issue of the SCBBA News, I accompanied Chief Elder to the Blacksburg Police Station, where the chief forced open the briefcase. I was shocked at what we found. In looking through the items, we found many things of interest including four different social security cards with different names, numbers and dates of birth; a copy of a birth certificate with the name Ray Baker Lynn, date of birth, 10/02/44, with the father's name of E. O. Lynn and mother's name, Myrtice (McLain) Lynn.

We also found copies of two obituaries, one each for E. O. Lynn and Myrtice (McLain) Lynn, presumably the father and mother of the man we thought was "our Ray" who had been going under the name of Ray Bartness. We also spotted the 8X10 photo of Ray with the Countess Vera Tolstoy and the Russian conductor Rostropovich.

However, a quick reading of the obituaries created more questions than answers. The father's obit showed two surviving sons, Robert Lynn and Ray Lynn. The mother's later obit showed only Robert Lynn as a surviving son, which raises the question, "What happened to the other son, Ray?" Did Ray Lynn just disappear or was he another family's son, whose name was stolen by "our Ray?" We may never know but thought that Ray Bartness was really "Ray Lynn" and that his name was omitted from the mother's obit for unknown reasons.

Chief Wayne Elder showed me the list of charges and names used in the crimes. He said these were supplied by the FBI and that for "legal reasons" he could not give me a copy but I could look at his copies. While reading the list of crimes I jotted them down: ITSP (Interstate Transportation of Stolen Property), bad checks, violation of parole, simple assault, resisting arrest, attempting to pass bad checks or ones with insufficient funds, flight to avoid prosecution, several counts of grand larceny, and swindling innkeepers. *He sounded like the guy I warned about in the newsletter!*

As for names and aliases used in committing crimes, many of them gave Ray as a first name but sometimes used Raymond, Gary, Bryan, Blair, Robert etc. Last names used included Lynn, Bartness (in Blacksburg), Bartiness, Livingston, Blair, Baker, Parsons and Vartiness. He apparently admired the name Livingston (with whom he claimed friendships) and often used full names, e.g. Gary Allen Livingston, Gerard Cornelius Livingston, and Ray Moncrieft Livingston. I'm sure there were others but these were the ones I was able to jot down.

Chief Elder also told me he had checked the car Ray had been driving. In the glove compartment he found a printed statement giving Ray permission to drive the car, which was owned by a man in Georgia. The owner had stated his name, date, and mileage when it left Georgia. He did not include the date the car must be returned. The present mileage was several hundred miles more than the original, leading us to wonder where Ray had driven before arriving in Blacksburg.

Chief Elder told me that I would probably be the first person Ray called and he was right. Later that day, Ray did call and asked me to call his friend in Georgia (who lent him the car) so that he could come to retrieve it at the Inn; and he inquired about his briefcase. I agreed to call his Georgia friend as soon as I returned home. I told him that his briefcase was in the hands of the police. Ray also urged me to visit him at the jail. He said that he had no money even to buy a coke, and that a $20 bill would really be helpful to him.

As soon as I arrived back home, I called Ray's Georgia friend to tell him about Ray's troubles and where to come get his automobile. His friend, who owned one or more pizza restaurants, appeared shocked to learn that Ray was in jail. He said that Ray had worked for him and that they had become great friends. He said he had lent Ray his car because he trusted him to return the car once he had settled into his new job in Blacksburg.

The friend said he had initially questioned whether Ray was truthful with all his stories about being friends with prominent people until he accompanied Ray to Florida. He said that while they were in the Palm Beach to Miami area, they stopped at the homes of several famous and wealthy people. He added that, although it was summer and the owners were at cooler locations, Ray was invariably greeted joyfully by the staffs and invited into the large, impressive homes.

He said one of these homes where they were welcomed was in the Kennedy compound. His Georgia friend told me that after the Florida trip he never had any reason to doubt Ray's veracity. I ended the call by telling the Georgia man where he could retrieve his car and we never talked again.

The next day I visited Ray at the County Jail and told him that his Georgia friend would come to Blacksburg to pick up his car at the Inn. I also gave Ray the $20 bill he requested. The interesting thing was that Ray was already working as an educator to fellow prisoners. He was giving them history lessons and helping them write letters (correcting misspelled words and grammar). One of two "special students" he introduced me to said, "Ray has changed my life for the better."

The last time I saw Ray in Gaffney, he urged me to keep in touch with these two men "to help them stay on the 'straight and narrow path' he had shown them." *Note: I did not follow this advice since I didn't need any more ex cons in my life!*

Ray almost always used his daily phone call to contact me. After a few days both Ray and Chief Elder called to inform me that Ray was being extradited to Clearwater, Florida, to face charges there. As soon as he arrived at Clearwater, Ray began writing me letters. He also wrote letters to Gene McKown and his assistant Linda Northey and asked them to share these letters with me. Gene told me that Ray had offered to write a weekly column for the Times and that he was seriously considering the offer. Linda told me that the letters and phone calls made her nervous and she didn't encourage Ray to continue them.

Naturally, I had no idea what Ray's fate would be and never expected to see him again. However, son Mitch was interested in establishing a tennis training center in Florida and about two weeks later he drove the two of us to explore the area around Tampa for possibilities. One day we were driving past Clearwater and decided to stop and see if we could visit with Ray at the prison. Mitch had briefly met Ray at the Inn and thought it might be interesting to stop by and see what he had to say.

We stopped at the prison, asked to visit with Ray Lynn, and he was quickly brought to us in the visiting area. Ray seemed quite cheery under the circumstances. After conversing a while, it was obvious that Ray had taken a liking to Mitch. Ray said he was going to do a weekly column for the Blacksburg Times and asked if it would be o.k. for him to address his column to "Dear Mitch" under the heading: "letter to a young friend." My son of course gave his permission. Ray appeared touched by our visit and urged Mitch to "take care of your Dad; I'm concerned about his health."

After we said goodbye to Ray, we returned to our original quest. Mitch told me that he was quite impressed with Ray's intellect and personality. We both wondered aloud why someone with his talents and intelligence would take such a wrong turn in life. Others who had met him in Blacksburg had similar feelings. The best example was his former boss, Gene McKown, who expressed the hope that someday Ray would clear up his legal problems and come back to Blacksburg. But none of us ever saw him again.

During his stay at my Inn, Ray had told me that he and Gene had discussed the idea of his becoming Gene's "estate executor." He also said that Gene had asked him if he would be willing to assume the position of Publisher of his three newspapers. He said that Gene "was tired and in poor health and that he had no relatives interested in taking over this demanding job." All of this might have been "wishful thinking" on Ray's part. However, after Ray failed to return, Publisher McKown soon announced that he was selling or closing the Chesnee Tribune, the Cowpens/Pacolet

Tribune, and the Blacksburg Times within 90 days. So, perhaps there was some validity to Ray's account of the depth of his friendship with McKown. Sadly, Publisher McKown passed away a few years later in 1999.

In almost daily letters to me from the Florida prison, Ray expressed great sorrow that his chance to straighten out his life was snatched away by his arrest. In almost every letter, he expressed his thanks to me and Mr. McKown for being so kind to him during his brief stay in Blacksburg. However, in one of his letters, he blamed Blacksburg's Police Chief Wayne Elder for his lost chance for a new life. I replied to this letter by writing that Chief Elder was just doing his job and that he (Ray) was responsible for his situation.

Finally, a few weeks later I received word that Ray had been discharged from the Florida prison and was now at an unknown location. I also learned that none of the other states with charges against Ray had been willing to pay the cost of extraditing him. I just hope that he had finally learned that he could use his many talents in a positive way.

*Post Script: The last I heard about Ray came from Robert Love, my friend who worked for DuPont in Delaware. Earlier, Robert had commented about the fine quality of several feature articles and columns he had read in the Blacksburg Times published with no byline. He asked me who the author of these articles was. I told him that these articles were written by Ray Bartness (or Lynn), who was now in jail for crimes he had allegedly committed in many states. I told Robert that the person writing the columns and news articles claimed to be related to Leo Tolstoy, but that I had serious doubts about this relationship.*

At that time, if Ancestry.com existed I was unaware of it. However, Robert had his own resources and told me he was going to do some checking on the Tolstoy family to try to find a Ray Bartness. Robert later called to tell me that in his research he found that there were many "legitimate" Tolstoy family members living in this country, including Countess Vera Tolstoy, Leo's granddaughter of New Smyrna, FL, and two sisters living in New York. He also said Vera had a son, Serge, who lived in Washington, DC. Ray had claimed that Serge was his uncle! Robert said he had found no Ray Bartness connected to the Tolstoy family. And Harvard University had no record of Ray's ever attending classes there.

Robert gave me telephone numbers for several of the Tolstoys living in the U.S. I called the number for Serge and a guttural voice with heavy Russian accent answered the phone. When I asked if this was Serge Tolstoy, he said, "Yes, what can I do for you?" I told him I was calling about a Ray Bartness or Ray Lynn who claimed to be his nephew. Serge laughed loudly and said, "This guy is a con man; he is not related at all to the Tolstoy family." I asked him how Ray knew so much about the family and he told me that Ray hung around the home of Countess Vera Tolstoy (Serge's mother) who was then age 92. He added that Ray helped her in and out of her limousine and was courteous and helpful to her.

Serge said that because Ray was so kind to the Countess, she returned his kindness by allowing Ray to live in her home as a friend and employee. Serge explained how Ray managed to accumulate so much information about the Tolstoy family, as well as other famous people and events. He said that Ray was very intelligent, read books and asked questions about the family, their many friends and their lifestyles. "His brain was like a sponge and he memorized enough about our family to begin passing himself off as a Tolstoy descendant and he memorized enough information about other famous people that he could fool most people." Serge concluded by saying that Ray had stolen some of his personal papers.

As much as I had liked and admired Ray and had hoped that he was being truthful, my conversation with Serge helped me accept the fact that I had been dealing with a very good confidence man. It made me sad that he did not choose to use his many talents for good. But there was no doubt that Ray was one of the most interesting people ever to spend time at the White House Inn. And I remained fond of him even after he was arrested and I had read the FBI report showing the many crimes with which he was charged.

# CHAPTER 21
## Delayed Trip to Indiana

WITH ALL THE things happening with Ray and my own health problems, I had postponed my planned trip to Indiana. By this time I was no longer able to climb stairs and had almost stopped taking overnight guests. Also, just before I was to leave, I made another visit to my doctor in Spartanburg. For the first time, he expressed concern about my heart rate being so slow. So, while I was in his office, he called a cardiologist and relayed his concerns. Then my doctor said he thought it would be o.k. for me to drive to Indiana with the provision that upon my return, he would make an appointment for me to visit the cardiologist in person and get some tests done.

Deciding that it would be best if I made a two-day trip to Indiana rather than to drive it in one day, I called a motel in Williamsburg, KY to make reservations for an overnight stay. I said goodbye to my long term guests and got an early start in my Dodge Voyager. Getting the early start allowed me to make a leisurely drive to reach Williamsburg before dark. However, as I approached the exit to my motel, the minivan's transmission began to lose power badly. I did not expect this since my minivan had recently had its transmission rebuilt and checked at a well-known transmission repair garage in Spartanburg. It struggled to reach the top of the grade at the exit but I was able to coast down the hill onto motel property.

After I completed my room registration, I found the room's telephone directory and began looking for the nearest Dodge-Chrysler dealership. Fortunately, I found a dealership nearby and called them for an appointment. Since it was late afternoon by then, the dealer suggested that we wait until morning when they would send a tow truck to take the minivan to the dealership rather than to risk further damage by trying to drive it there. Once the dealership had placed my minivan on the lift and checked the transmission, they gave me the bad news: the transmission required rebuilding or replacing. The dealer said they could rebuild it but it would take several days and cost almost as much as a new transmission. If I decided on the latter, it could be ready to drive in a couple of days. So, with yesterday's experience with a rebuilt transmission it was an easy choice for me to opt for the new one.

A bit of good news: my warranty for the rebuilt job was still good; I made sure that the dealership wrote down the current mileage on the van. Then I rented a small Toyota and headed on to Indiana with Jo Ann's apartment the first stop in Lafayette. For the next couple of days, although tired and lacking energy, I visited Purdue friends and antique shops operated by friends. I slept restlessly each night in Jo Ann's spare bedroom, thinking about my car and an upcoming meeting with Internal Revenue Service people in connection with an audit of my B&B business.

*I had learned that IRS was launching an effort to charge a large number of inactive B&B owners who were operating their B&Bs as a "hobby" or a "tax write off." However, with a comprehensive "marketing plan" and hundreds of clippings testifying to my efforts to build a profitable business, no one in the state expected The White House Inn to be subject to an audit. But the good ole IRS ignored several B&B owners who closed their inns for much of the year and actually discouraged guests, while they chose to target my inn.*

On the third day, a call to the Williamsburg Chrysler dealership told me that my minivan was ready, so Jo Ann and I headed south to turn in the Toyota car to the rental agency and retrieve my car with its newly installed transmission. Jo Ann and I drove back to Lafayette where I planned to finish my vacation. Upon our return to Jo Ann's apartment, I slept better than usual that night but after awakening, I suddenly passed out. Jo Ann saw what was happening and shook me slightly. I regained consciousness but knew something was badly wrong with me.

Jo Ann checked my pulse which was barely at 30 beats per minute. She helped me walk around the apartment trying to speed up my heart rate, but it never got beyond 30 beats. We knew it was time to get me to a hospital. At that point, Jo Ann helped me into her car and drove me to the emergency room at St. Elizabeth Hospital.

It took some time but eventually a room opened up and I was admitted. After several tests, it was determined that I needed to consult with a cardiologist. I called my friend, Dr. John Osmun, and asked him to recommend someone. He recommended the cardiologist who had supervised his (Osmun's) successful open heart surgery. The cardiologist came to the hospital to give me more tests that revealed that my heart's mitral valve was bad and needed replacement. Also, at that time I was told that tests showed my heart had actually stopped earlier when I fainted.

Later that day, I was visited by the heart surgeon who would perform the actual surgery to implant an artificial heart valve. I asked what my options were and the surgeon told me that my only options were: (1) replacing my faulty mitral valve with a mechanical valve or (2) replacing it with a pig valve. I asked what were the "pros" and "cons" of each. He said that the mechanical valve would last indefinitely but that it would require me to take a blood thinner for the rest of my life. The pig valve had a life span of 8-10 years but did not require a blood thinner.

I asked the surgeon what he would do if he were in my situation and without hesitation he said "I would choose the mechanical valve and not risk having my chest cut open again at around age 80 for another valve replacement." I agreed with the heart surgeon and said: "Let's do the mechanical valve." He performed the surgery the next day and the valve is still "clicking along" 20 plus years later. But I still have to get my finger pricked once or twice a month to determine if my INR level is correct or whether the blood thinner, Coumadin, needed to be increased or decreased.

While preparation for my heart surgery was going on, Jo Ann was attempting to get in touch with Mitch; she finally reached him and he told her that he and his fiancée, Jeannette Lee, would catch the first plane headed to Indiana. They arrived around 2 a.m. and stayed at my bedside until I went for my surgery at 7 that morning. A few hours later the surgery was complete, and I awoke briefly in the recovery room before being transferred to a private room. The next day hospital personnel attempted to walk me down the hallway. I was so weak that they almost had to carry (or drag) me the first few attempts. Mitch and Jeannette stayed until assured that I was "going to make it" before flying back to Washington.

A few days later I was placed in the rehab unit where I stayed for about two weeks. During the time I was there, Dr. Osmun stopped by to visit me almost every day carrying a small vase and a flower of some kind. Two weeks later I was discharged from rehab and two of the Miller boys almost carried me up the stairs into Jo Ann's apartment.

Perhaps because the surgery had to be performed on an emergency basis, I was forced to continue rehabilitation for three months before I was able to return home. Jo Ann looked after me the entire time while I regained strength. After work, she would drive me to large stores or malls where I would walk and rest; and walk and rest. Finally, the doctors gave me clearance to travel by air. I was taken on board the plane by wheelchair and taken off the same way in Charlotte, NC.

My oldest nephew, Howard White Jr., a Charlotte, NC, city police captain, met my plane and transported me back to The White House Inn. It was another three months before I could return to Indiana to get my minivan. Nephew Dan Turner drove me up and I followed him back to Blacksburg. Meanwhile, The White House Inn had survived quite well while I was gone. During my long absence, the Postmistress who had been occupying the White Magnolia Room had collected the rent money each month and turned it over to my friend-minister, Dr. David Rowe who placed it in my bank account.

David had also kept an eye on the place and convinced the IRS to postpone our scheduled meeting. Apparently IRS was ready to throw the book at me. They refused to take the word of David over the telephone that I really was recovering from emergency open heart surgery in Indiana and was not using this as a ruse to avoid meeting with them to discuss my case. He had to drive to Spartanburg to present his credentials to prove he was my minister.

Incidentally, upon my return, after I laboriously put together more records, my CPA took over my representation and appealed my case to a higher level IRS person in Charlotte. This official after reviewing the evidence, exclaimed: "Looking at the information provided by Mr. White, I don't know why he was subjected to an audit in the first place." He ended the case against me.

I spent several more months recovering from the "near death" heart experience. During the period I was away, the Postmistress had moved to that position in her home town, and the people from Texas had completed work on the Golf Outlet Store at the Yellow Mall and were back in Texas. So, all my long term guests were now gone.

In addition, during my long absence I had lost my frequent, pleasant, and non-demanding guests, i.e., the education consultants and textile designers from New York. The consultants had been forced to find other accommodations during my long absence and the textile designers lost their reason to come to Gaffney because the Cherokee Finishing Company had closed its doors. That left me the option of starting over or closing down my B&B business. Since I was still facing a long recovery period, I was leaning toward the latter.

While mulling over these options I received a call from someone claiming to be a travel writer. He wanted me to provide him and his wife a free night at my inn, in exchange for writing a favorable article about it. I told him I did not think I needed any articles because I was probably going to close down the Inn shortly. However, he said he was from Washington, DC and dreaded the thought of having to spend the night at a motel. Since I was alone that night, I thought it might be interesting to have a guest with whom I could exchange information about the area where I had spent so many years as a resident. I finally agreed to register the couple for a one-night stay.

He asked if there were any restaurants nearby that I could recommend. Kelly's Steak House was closed on Sundays so I had no restaurant to recommend. I gave him the names of some good chain restaurants in Gaffney that would be on the way to the Inn but he sneered at the idea of eating in a chain restaurant. He also wanted to make sure that mine was a smoke-free business and I assured him that there was no smoking allowed inside my B&B.

I never knew where this couple ate, but they arrived at the Inn as darkness set in. They were not particularly friendly and I was kicking myself in the rear for not following my first instinct: to say I had no available rooms. I poured them a glass of wine and then showed them to their room. The next morning they ate their breakfasts of Eggs Benedict and I breathed a sigh of relief when they left. An hour or so later, as I was gathering strength to climb the stairs to remake the White Magnolia Room, I realized that a bird was flying around the downstairs ceiling. After about an hour of effort I was finally able to get the bird out through the front door. When I was able to climb the stairs to the second floor, I discovered several disgusting bird droppings and then went into the room just vacated by the "so called" travel writer.

As I entered the suite, I got a slight smell of smoke; I continued on to the bathroom where the smell was much stronger. At that point, I found that the window (including screen) was open. This, of course, was what allowed the bird to enter. Apparently he (or they) opened the window and tried to blow out the smoke and then left the window open. The bird left several "calling cards" on furniture and floors on two levels of the Inn. Fortunately, the door to the third floor honeymoon suite was closed so the bird could not make any deposits there.

My biggest regret is that the bird didn't fly over my obnoxious guest's bed while he was in it and release a load. That was the unhappy end of my "innkeeping experience." However, I have many good memories of my guests and events at The White House Inn during the five year period I was the innkeeper.

---

PART 12

# LIFE AFTER CLOSING THE INN

---

# CHAPTER 1

## A Stranger Stops By

ONE EVENING SHORTLY after I closed the Inn to overnight guests, I was enjoying a quiet time alone when my doorbell rang. I went to the door and a stranger, accompanied by a very attractive woman, stood there. I asked if I could help them. (Even when the Inn was open I didn't ordinarily accept "drop in" guests without reservations. However, I was always courteous to them). The man then introduced himself as Leon Rippy, and his wife, Carol. Seeing that I was not familiar with the name, Mr. Rippy explained that, although he was born in Rock Hill, SC, he was now a Hollywood actor working with Mel Gibson (who I was familiar with) on a movie called "The Patriot" being filmed in the Rock Hill area. I invited them in and he said that he and his wife were currently staying at a small farm he owned outside of Grover, NC.

He explained that he was showing his wife the area and happened to pass by the Inn. He said they were so impressed with its beauty that they drove past a couple of times before they had the nerve to enter the driveway for a closer look, hoping they might be invited to see the interior.

At that, I gave them a quick tour of the house and as they prepared to leave, I asked if they would like to have a drink with me. They quickly accepted the invitation and we went to the kitchen where we shared adult beverages and conversation for two or three hours. Leon volunteered that he had inherited the farm outside of Grover from his late grandfather and had the house restored for a "getaway" from Hollywood and the movie business. He said he employed a full time person to live there and take care of the property.

*Leon Rippy turned out to be a very interesting, modest man and a person of many talents and interests. During our conversation that evening, I asked him many questions about his background and life in Hollywood. He also asked me about my life experiences, which I was glad to share. Modesty aside, I'm afraid my life experiences did not come close to matching his.*

He told me that he once worked in a circus and at another time was foreman of a cattle ranch. Also, at one time, as hard as it is to believe, he was once considered an accomplished ballet dancer. He said his acting career followed appearances in college and regional theatrical productions, and he eventually founded and operated two theatrical companies. His first professional acting job was in The Lost Colony where he received $25 weekly.

As a Hollywood "character actor," he has appeared in countless movies such as The Alamo, The Life of David Gale, Beyond the Law, Star Gate, The Tracker and Young Guns II, to name a few. Moreover, he became part of numerous television series. Among these were Deadwood, Saving Grace, StarTrek: The Next Generation, Quantum Leap, and Walker, Texas Ranger.

After going to Hollywood, Leon met Mel Gibson and the two of them became close friends over the years. He said that Gibson often gave him acting jobs in films in which he was involved, such as his current role in The Patriot. He was playing the part of Gibson's best friend, John Billings, whose young son was a soldier in the South Carolina Militia fighting the Redcoats. Early in the film, John found his wife and son dead, killed by the British. He then put a pistol to his head and pulled the trigger.

Leon said his role in The Patriot was a distinct change in character for him. He was usually cast as a villain or as a mean, uncaring military officer or government authority, because of his swarthy features and ugly teeth. He said that his crooked teeth made it easy to appear "villainous." He added that when people asked him why he did not get his teeth fixed, he replied, "Because these teeth have made me millions of dollars!"

Before they left the Inn, Leon pulled out a card and wrote down a special phone number which he said would ensure a response from him. Then he invited me to a "cast party" he was hosting two weeks later at his home in Grover, NC, for the actors in The Patriot. He said he would like to introduce me to Mel Gibson who would be at the party.

I told him I didn't think I could get away for the party, but he urged me to call him at the special number he had just given me if I wanted to get in touch with him either about the party or at any other time. I didn't call nor go to Rippy's party since I'm not a celebrity seeker. However, the brief time I spent with Leon and Carol Rippy was enjoyable and memorable to me. *One question: Was it a blessing or a curse that I was born with nice, straight teeth?*

# CHAPTER 2

## Update on Mitch

AS MENTIONED EARLIER, Hurricane Hugo wiped out my son Mitch's growing tennis business in Charleston by destroying the outdoor tennis courts. Soon afterward, he moved back to his place of birth, Washington, DC. During the period of 1990-94 he served as Director of Tennis at Chantilly National Country Club where he had received his first tennis lessons. Then he left Chantilly to start his own business, Topspin Unlimited, a professional and club management company.

Having his own business allowed him the freedom to work with and train touring tennis pros, taking some of them to Florida where he did intensive one-on-one training with them for up to a month before they returned to the pro tennis tour. During his trips to Florida and back, he would usually stop by the Inn for a short visit with me. In addition, he sometimes came down from DC for longer visits. Often he was accompanied by beautiful ladies of different nationalities, e.g., Australian,

Asian, Canadian, and others I don't remember. Also, during this period while he was conducting a clinic for junior players he met a beautiful American Korean woman, Jeannette Lee, whose son, Charlie, was one of his junior students.

Jeannette owned her own IT company, Sytel, based in Bethesda, MD. They began dating and when they both came to Indiana to be with me for my open heart surgery, I realized that this was a serious relationship. I did not know just how serious it was, however, until 1998 when Mitch called to tell me that he and Jeannette were planning to get married. He then asked if they could be married at the Blacksburg Associate Reformed Presbyterian (ARP) Church by Pastor David Rowe, a friend of mine and of Mitch. I contacted Dr. Rowe on behalf of the couple and he said he would arrange to reserve the church and would be glad to perform the ceremony. Mitch and Jeannette wanted a low key ceremony with just a few close friends and relatives, including Jeannette's parents and Mitch's parents and maternal grandmother.

Mitch and I discussed sleeping accommodations for my ex-wife and his mother, Gwen, and his grandmother, Dorothy. I told Mitch that they would be welcome to stay at the Inn, but if Gwen preferred otherwise, I would make reservations for her and her mother at Jolly Place in Gaffney. This was a very nice B&B owned and operated by Henry Jolly, a friend of mine and mayor of Gaffney. Gwen told Mitch she would be more comfortable staying at a place other than The White House Inn so I arranged with Henry for her and her mother to stay at his place.

Although I had not had contact with Gwen in many years, I still had strong feelings for her and hoped I would be able to control my emotions upon seeing her. Mitch met his mother and grandmother at the Charlotte Airport and took them directly to Jolly Place, so my first view of her was at the church just before the ceremony began. It was probably to my emotional advantage that I was serving as "best man" and my attention was devoted to that function, rather than to the 20 plus years of marriage to Gwen. However, I could not help but notice that she was still beautiful.

The marriage of Mitch and Jeannette went smoothly with the couple glowing with love. Jeannette's little son, Charlie, then about 9-10 years old, acted as "sound man" in playing Miller-Rowe Consort music from the "M-R" wedding album at appropriate times. It took Charlie, an extremely bright little boy, just a few minutes to become acquainted with the church's sound system and he handled this duty with aplomb.

Immediately after the wedding, the small wedding party adjourned to the White House Inn for an informal reception with beverages and snacks. David Rowe brought his hammered dulcimer musical instrument and provided background music during the reception. My only close contact with Gwen occurred when she asked me to give her a tour of the Inn. She was very complimentary of the décor and beauty of the house. However, during this time together she remained very tense and never once looked me in the eye. I was not surprised at that because that had been the pattern in previous times when we had been together after our separation.

When we returned to join the others at the reception, Gwen devoted the rest of her time there watching and listening to David play the hammered dulcimer. The reception ended and Mitch drove his mother and grandmother back to Gaffney. Meanwhile, new bride Jeannette was preparing delicious, homemade Korean food for those of us staying at the Inn. This began my love affair with Korean food.

Mitch drove Gwen and her mother to the airport in Charlotte the following morning, so I did not see Gwen again until the big reception for Mitch and Jeannette which was held at a famous Georgetown (DC) waterfront restaurant, called "The Sequoia." Jo Ann joined me for this event. When Jo Ann and I arrived we were startled to learn that Mitch and his new wife, Jeannette, had rented the entire restaurant for this occasion which involved about 100 friends and relatives from the Washington, DC area. The event began with the cocktail hour, which was held in late afternoon on the celebrated outdoor terraced patio bar of the Sequoia. Hors d'oeuvres and a variety of beverages were served as recording star and jazz pianist Bill Harris entertained.

At the scheduled time, everyone went into the elegant dining room with its curving white marble and granite bar, floor-to-ceiling windows and dramatic starburst chandeliers. A well known restaurant critic made this assessment: "This glamorous restaurant takes full advantage of its sweeping Potomac River views from the majestic dining room." The restaurant was noted for its fine service and seafood oriented menu. All guests were soon enjoying delicious food to the music of Tony Gil's orchestra which played "Big Band" music for dancing. *Note: Tony is a highly talented singer who sounds like a blend of Frank Sinatra and Tony Bennett.*

When we entered the dining room, I noted that Mitch and Jeannette had seated ex-wife Gwen far from our table. We avoided eye contact during much of the meal except for one brief moment when I was giving a humorous toast to the couple. She kept a stone faced expression while everyone else was laughing. We exchanged not a word despite the fact that we were celebrating a wedding for the son we shared.

Soon after the meal ended, dancing began and Jo Ann and I wasted little time in taking to the floor. Although my dancing was pretty "rusty," Jo Ann was in great dancing shape since she had been recently competing in dance contests in Indiana. She carried me along until some of the rust in my dancing prowess was removed. However, at best there was no resemblance to the college boy who served as the designated "stag" at women's colleges in North Carolina during his college days. However, as a couple we were still good enough to receive acclaim from the younger attendees not as familiar as we were with "Big Band" type dance music.

# CHAPTER 3
## Time to Sell Large B&B House and Furnishings

FOR A FEW months after closing the Inn, I enjoyed the freedom and solitude of living alone in what had been The White House Inn B&B. It was nice that I still owned a place large enough to accommodate guests at Mitch and Jeannette's wedding and reception. However, living alone in a 7 bedroom, 5½ bath home of about 5,000 square feet made no sense, certainly not on a permanent basis.

I had moved into the first floor guest room (the Rose Garden Room) so that my need to climb stairs to the second and third floors was reduced. But the upkeep was burdensome since I no longer had Betty Gibson to do the housekeeping chores for me. After mulling the situation over, I contacted my friend, Don Wilkins, a top real estate broker, for his advice and to see if he wanted to handle the listing and sale of the Inn.

After reflecting, Don said, "Jim, to be honest with you, the economy in this area would make it almost impossible to sell your property for what it is worth. As much as I would like to handle this for you, I know the market here and I advise you to consider utilizing the Internet, which will reach the type of people able and willing to pay the price you need and deserve for this fine property." I left Don's office disappointed but appreciative of his honesty; I contacted my friend, David Rowe, and explained the situation to him. I knew that David was knowledgeable about computer technology and the Internet. He immediately volunteered to help me when or if I decided to go in that direction.

Asking David to hold that thought, I told him that I first wanted to try to find a good auction company to sell most of the furnishings while retaining enough to furnish a small house for myself. I thought that if anyone interested in buying the building saw the furnishings in place, they would make their offer contingent upon inclusion of the furnishings, either free or at a very low price. Because of the high value of the antiques and collectibles, I thought (perhaps erroneously) that I would get a better price if the house and furnishings were sold separately.

Then I began the search for that "perfect" auction company, i.e., one that was honest, knowledgeable about fine antiques and collectibles, and which would make the necessary effort to get the best prices for my valuable auction items. This search proved to be more difficult than expected. Over the years as a frequent purchaser at auctions, I had learned to avoid auctions conducted by those wearing Texas hats and boots and answering to "Colonel." Unfortunately, most of the auction companies who visited the Inn met that description.

However, I asked all of those who visited to estimate the value of my auction items. The estimates ranged from $300,000 to $600,000 but I knew the real value would be determined by the number, type, and knowledge of potential buyers as well as the people conducting the auction. So far, none of the auction companies who visited had convinced me that they were capable of attracting enough of the type of bidders I needed. I talked with Doug Davies, a very knowledgeable and honest auctioneer in Indiana, about coming south to conduct the auction. He was willing to handle my auction when and if it could be fitted into his schedule.

Before I could make the out-of-state arrangements, however, an auction company from Spartanburg with some impressive looking credentials came to visit. The owner and his top assistant were both wearing dress suits and neckties (no cowboy boots or hats) and appeared to be both knowledgeable and professional. In addition to appearance, I was pleased that these auction company representatives quickly recognized a variety of extraordinary collections and pieces accumulated over the years. For example, when I took them into the dining room, one of them immediately looked up and asked, "Are all of those bowls R.S. Prussia?" When I replied "Yes," they shook their heads in disbelief.

*Note: Although my bowls displayed were unsigned, R.S. Prussia experts know that they are just as valuable as signed ones, provided the buyers and sellers recognize "the signs" of legitimate R.S. Prussia.* Some obvious signs are: "blown out" edges, lightness of the piece, quality of the art work and other less visible features. I had learned to recognize unmarked R.S. Prussia from years in Indiana while taking classes from Virgil Scowden, an acknowledged expert, and from attending auctions with R.S. Prussia collector friends.

In addition to their recognition of quality antiques and collections, I was impressed by the expertly produced samples of auction brochures they had prepared for upscale auctions in Upstate SC. I was also pleased that this company would supply a large tent to ensure that an auction could be held on the scheduled date, i.e. "rain or shine." Weighing these factors convinced me that this was the right auction company and I signed the contract for this company to conduct my auction.

I lived to regret that action. Although this may sound like just an excuse for bad judgment, let me remind you that at this time I had not completely recovered from my recent near fatal heart problem that resulted in open heart surgery. My usual self would have been more cautious and would have done more investigative work before signing that contract. But concerns about my health problems, past, present, and future caused me to want to simplify my life as quickly as I could. Those concerns caused me to abandon my usual cautious nature and make a mistake that cost me dearly.

But, unaware of the mistake at that time, David Rowe and I began preparing a color brochure needed before the auction took place. David, who is not only a great musician, pastor, and talented artist, volunteered to help me with the selection of items to be photographed and the layout of the brochure. David took the lead in how these articles were presented in the brochure and I took the photos and wrote the text. We would supply all of the artwork and text and the auction company would handle production of the brochure.

*Incidentally, the auction company strongly advised me (and I finally agreed) to offer the building and grounds for auction at the same time, but with a "reserve" or minimum price, on the building.* Their reasoning was that offering both the real estate and furnishings for sale at the same time, would attract more people interested in one or the other, or both. They also advised me that the furnishings, artwork, etc. should be sold at "absolute auction," i.e. to the highest qualified bidder with no limiting conditions or reserve. Again, I agreed to that provision which proved to be another costly mistake on my part!

The finished brochure was beautiful by any standard. The front of the brochure showed a fabulous front view of the Inn in all its glory. The front text also explained the sale and touted the quality of the auction company. The two inside pages featured color photos of David Rowe's artistic arrangements of the most beautiful and outstanding items. The 12 complete settings of "Flow Blue" china dominated the inside of the brochure since "Flow Blue" is usually sold by the piece. The last page of the brochure presented the rear image of the house and its porch plus details about "terms of sale," directions, etc.

Before the auction, I asked for a meeting to discuss the marketing that was being done by the auction company but for which I was paying. Although in general I agreed with their efforts, I had one serious complaint: the town of Shelby, NC, recognized as a "hot bed" of auctions, had not been included in the advertising despite being less than 30 minutes from the auction site. On the other hand, the auction company had done costly advertising in Charleston, several hours away from Blacksburg. *This aroused my suspicion that the auction company was more interested in enhancing its reputation than it was in attracting buyers to my auction.* Although I knew it was too late to completely correct this oversight, I personally made sure that a small "last minute" ad for my auction appeared in the Shelby Daily Star.

On the day of the auction, the day was bright and clear, and the number of items to be sold totaled over 3,000. In one case a complete set of antique silver constituted one item! I was disappointed at the relatively small crowd present but the auction company assured me that a great many of these were dealers prepared to spend big money. I also learned that an auctioneer from Fort Mill, SC, would do most of the auctioning and that he had drawn a relatively large group of antique dealers who were "regulars" at his auctions. I had assumed that one of the auction company's own auctioneers would be calling the signals.

Although not up to full strength, I decided to take a back row seat to get a feel for how the auction would proceed. The first offering was for the real estate and the bidding failed to reach the reserve, which didn't surprise me at all. In my experience, fine real estate was not often sold at auctions for a reasonable price. Often auctions are employed in a "desperate to sell" situation. So, I had no great expectations about selling the real estate and only agreed to include it in the auction after much urging by the auction company.

Then the auction for the furnishings began. The first item held up to be auctioned was an R.S. Prussia deep bowl with an estimated value of about $300. The auctioneer took a look at the bottom of the bowl and said: "There's no signature on this but it looks like R.S. Prussia. However, since it's not signed we're selling it as a "R. S. Prussia type deep bowl." The bowl was quickly "knocked down" (i.e. sold) for $35 to one of the 20 dealers sitting as a group on the front row. I should have stopped the auction to note that I was considered by many as an expert in recognizing unmarked R. S. Prussia. If the auctioneer disagreed, I should have removed my collection of unsigned R.S. Prussia deep bowls. But I didn't know what I could do legally and feared that my heart would not withstand a big hassle.

However, this event told me that I was probably going to be "screwed" and not wanting to witness this in person I retired to the kitchen for the rest of the auction. Since I was still recuperating from the heart surgery, I did not want to risk the stress that was likely to occur. After the auction was over, the auction company executive proudly told me that the record showed that the sale of each item averaged 10 seconds. I did not see that as a source of pride. Friends who attended the auction told me that most of the items were "knocked down" to one of the dealers before other potential bidders had a chance to lift their bid cards.

This viewpoint was confirmed by Dr. James Jacubchek of Spartanburg, a well known eye doctor and collector of "flow blue" and other fine china. He visited me the following day and said that he was rarely able to get the auctioneer's attention as he frantically waved his bid card. He added that in almost all cases the auctioneer avoided looking his way before saying "sold." "Dr. J," as he was known, told me he finally stood up and shouted at the auctioneer trying to get him to take his bid. It was apparent to him and others that the auctioneer was favoring his front row dealer friends and often said "sold" at their first bid.

As the auction company personnel prepared to leave, the executive who handled the paperwork asked me to come to Spartanburg the next day to pick up my check for $65,000, a fraction of what it should have been. A few months later I became friends with another auctioneer who auctioned my "leftovers" (only a fraction of the number and quality of the original auction). At the conclusion of the later auction, I received a check for $21,000 for the much smaller sale of fewer and less valuable items. I have no doubt that if I had contracted with this auctioneer (who I did not know at the time) the proceeds from the first auction would have been quite different.

# CHAPTER 4
## Trying a New Way (for me) to Sell a House

ONCE I RECOVERED from the auction fiasco, I knew it was time to follow Don Wilkins' advice and turn to the Internet with its huge national audience to sell the Inn. I told David Rowe that I was now ready to put the Inn property online and he sent the necessary information to "B&B Online." He also helped me prepare a more detailed package that I could email to prospective buyers. *Note: although I had owned a computer for years, I had not had time to familiarize myself with the Internet. And I never learned how to prepare "websites," etc. David Rowe, who engineered the recording process of Miller-Rowe Consort albums before having them reproduced in volume by a professional reproduction company, was an expert at many things!*

It turned out that (and I cannot explain how) David Rowe tied the "for sale information" about my Inn to his own "Miller-Rowe Consort" website. As a result of his fine work, within a few days I began receiving responses by telephone and email from people all over the country. Most wanted more detailed information. Eventually, these inquiries totaled about 200. Of these, about 75 indicated serious interest in buying the Inn. I answered their questions over the telephone and sent them the email package showing interior and exterior scenes and interior room dimensions.

During the next few weeks, calls and emails about my property continued and several individuals and couples actually visited the Inn. Of these, three couples showed strong interest and indicated they would be making purchase offers. Although all of these potential buyers seemed nice, a couple from Breckenridge, Colorado, immediately stood out as my favorite and I prayed they would be the ones making the best offer.

The couple I favored were Tony Krysiak, an airline pilot, and his wife, Pat, a pretty former flight attendant. These two were warm, open people, and I felt an immediate connection with them. It was obvious that both were in love with the house, which warmed my heart. In line with my wishes, the Krysiaks made the first and best offer. I happily accepted their offer even though it was contingent on the sale of their house in Breckenridge. This was no big problem for me at the time since I had no mortgage on the property and no immediate need for the relatively large amount of money involved.

I was very pleased that my lovely B&B was going to people who obviously loved it. I knew that the Krysiak property in the popular winter resort of Breckenridge would not stay on the market long. In anticipation of the sale of my Inn and knowing I would need a new place to live, I had purchased an old, dilapidated house about a mile outside of Blacksburg. As you can see, I still retained a need to do some limited house renovation. *As an interesting sidelight, I traded a restored classic Jaguar as a down payment on this house, which was owned by Blacksburg Mayor David Hogue. He had been born and raised in the house.*

At that time it consisted of two small bedrooms, one bath, and a small kitchen. I knew this place needed a total renovation and additional space to make it livable for me but it was located on a nice one acre lot and I could see potential in the large lot and the house itself. Obviously, *since the Inn was sold and my farm house was definitely not yet even close to being habitable, I needed a place to live immediately. Fortunately, a Blacksburg ARP Church friend offered me the use of a small, furnished guest apartment behind her home in town. This gave me a comfortable place to live while the little farm house was being rehabilitated.*

I began the renovation by hiring an itinerant carpenter and we started the process of expanding the house by incorporating some areas that had served as porches in its past. We also began gutting the structure to allow installation of additional insulation and new electrical, plumbing, and central air conditioning and heating systems. I gained some space by removing and moving some walls. Finally, I decided that the house still needed more space and I gained that by making one fairly large addition and several smaller ones to add more functional space.

By enclosing what had once been a side porch, we were able to create a new, larger kitchen area with new custom cabinets and all new appliances plus room for a dining area. I was able to find enough wide, heart pine boards to beautifully finish the three interior walls of the dining area. *David Rowe helped me plane and refinish the boards which were then installed vertically by the carpenter. This became the most dramatic feature of the little house.*

Finally, after several weeks of hard work (mostly by the carpenter), I was able to move into a completely renovated home with two bedrooms, one a master suite with bath, and the second one adjacent to a new bathroom created from what had been part of another porch. We had also incorporated a small brick building adjacent to the master suite, utilizing the space to enlarge the bathroom and provide space for a large walk in closet for the master suite.

After the initial excitement of moving to a new place, I gradually began to realize that the smaller space and its isolation in the countryside made it less appealing to me than I had thought. I had become used to the larger space and activity at the Inn. Also, I was surprised at how much I missed the Inn and the little town of Blacksburg. So, I pretty quickly knew that 327 York Road would not be my permanent address. But it would be a comfortable place to live until I found something better fitted to my new lifestyle.

# CHAPTER 5

## Overcoming a Tragedy

AS MENTIONED EARLIER, Jo Ann and I had fully restored our friendship by the time I moved into my little house. In fact, I had visited her in Indiana twice and we talked by telephone frequently. One night, soon after my move to the farm house, she called to tell me that she had just received the results from her annual health checkup and we were both pleased that the test results showed that she was in excellent health. Since I had known her as always being healthy and full of energy, I was not surprised to get this news. I expected her to outlive me by many years. But life is not always predictable.

The day after that call, I received a shocking call from her family. The caller said when a family member dialed Jo Ann's number that morning, she failed to answer the phone. When her son Troy went next door to check on her she was lying unconscious on the floor. The caller then said that the family immediately called for an ambulance that took her to the hospital where the doctors examined her and said that she had had a very bad stroke.

Later that day, her son Tim called to tell me that the doctors at St. Elizabeth Hospital had determined that Jo Ann's stroke was so massive and there was so much damage to her brain that she would never recover. He added that her condition had triggered her living will and that the family would like for me to come to Indiana to be with them during Jo Ann's last days on this earth. I immediately agreed to do this and early the next morning set out for Indiana.

After driving all day, I reached Lafayette and checked into a nearby motel before going to the hospital. When I arrived at Jo Ann's room I was shocked at her appearance. She no longer resembled the vigorous, youthful looking person I had known for many years. That evening, Tim called me aside and said that his family wanted me to cancel my reservation at the motel and move into their home in Noblesville for the remainder of Jo Ann's life. He also hoped I would remain with them until after her funeral. I agreed with his requests and moved out of my room at the motel. Then I followed them back to their home in Noblesville, IN.

Jo Ann lived for two or three more days but never regained consciousness, at least to the extent that she acknowledged my presence. However, her family believed that unconsciously she knew I was there. I was holding one of her hands and Tim was holding the other when she breathed her last breath. I sat with the family at Jo Ann's funeral and grieved along with them.

The loss of Jo Ann and my declining health (again) meant that I was having a hard time keeping my morale up. Not having inn-keeping duties did provide me with some positive benefits. One of these was that I had more time to worship at my church. It also gave me more time to spend with my family members and begin to get to know my younger relatives better. Some of these grew up while I was living many miles away. Regrettably, my career pursuit resulted in neglect of family and the little church I attended as a youngster. I had not been in it for too many years.

Although being slightly depressed and missing the Inn more than I expected, the fact that I had become close friends with the Krysiaks helped me maintain touch with the place I had worked so hard to save and preserve. I was often invited to visit and share a cocktail and food with them. For example, soon after re-opening the inn, and still using its original name, Pat invited me to have breakfast with a guest celebrity who had said he wanted to meet me. The guest was Hollywood movie star Jack Palance. Pat explained that Mr. Palance was staying at the Inn while working on a commercial for a national furniture company.

Pat said that Mr. Palance was so impressed with the Inn that he wanted to meet the person responsible for its beauty. I did not want to impose on Pat's kindness and declined the breakfast invitation but agreed to come by for coffee with Jack Palance. Like my earlier actor visitor, Leon Rippy, Palance had an interesting history before becoming a well known, successful character actor. When I asked about his life and background, Jack told me that he was born in a Pennsylvania coal town called Lattimer Mines in the year 1919 and at a young age followed his Ukrainian immigrant father into the mines. His father, an anthracite miner, died of black lung disease.

However, Jack used his athletic prowess to escape the mines. He won a football scholarship to the University of North Carolina where he played fullback. After he tired of football and dropped out of the University he became a professional boxer. Since Jack was modest to an extreme degree, I had to turn to the Internet to learn that fighting under the name "Jack Brazzo," he won his first 15 fights, 12 by knockouts, before losing a decision to future heavyweight contender, Joe Baksi, on Dec. 17, 1940. The Internet told me that Palance continued to box until 1942 when he joined the Army Air Force and became a bomber pilot. He participated in many bombing raids before his plane crashed, causing serious injuries and burns which required him to have facial reconstructive surgery.

His injuries from the crash ended his career as a bomber pilot. He left the service as a hero with many awards including the Purple Heart. Although it's sad to think of all the pain he must have suffered and the change in his appearance caused by facial injuries and burn scars, the resourceful young man was able to turn this potential tragedy to his advantage in Hollywood.

No longer possessing the looks of a romantic leading man, Palance concentrated on being an archetypal villain with his glare, intimidating stance and killer smile. *As it was with Leon Rippy, I had to pry information from him. Both of these famous people wanted to know more about me and my life than to tell me about theirs.* Obviously my life was infinitely less interesting than theirs but I was glad to oblige them. I genuinely enjoyed my time with each of them.

# CHAPTER 6
## Start of Another SC Coastal Venture.

DESPITE THESE NICE happenings, I was bored living in Blacksburg and restless for more adventures. *You may have noted by now that this has been a pattern of my life.* The town of Beaufort, SC had always captured my attention as a nice place to vacation and possibly to live some day. Since I had moved into my little house and with time on my hands, I had made several trips to Beaufort, always staying with Ron Kay and his wife, Carrol, at the Two Suns Inn. I mentioned to the Kays how much I regretted selling the house located on "The Point," still an exclusive part of Beaufort and now very expensive.

Sensing that I might want to return to this historic city, Ron invited a realtor friend, Mike McFee, over to meet me. Mike and I got along well and he offered to pick me up early the next day to do some "house looking." He took me to see properties in downtown Beaufort, Lady's Island, and Dataw, Fripp and Distant Islands, plus the town of Port Royal. We found nothing in my price range that I liked enough to make an offer. As I was getting ready to return to Blacksburg, Mike called me and said, "Jim, I have some friends who are thinking about placing their house for sale and I will be the listing agent if they do so."

He added that the property that "might be for sale" was within 10 minutes of downtown and in my price range. He said if I liked, he would call the owners and see if they would allow me to be the first potential buyer to look at it before it went on the market. If they agreed, he would try to arrange for me to see the property before I left town.

I told Mike I liked the idea of being the first to look at the property and a few hours later he called to tell me that the owners had definitely decided to sell and that they would delay showing the house to anyone else until I had a chance to see it. Mike picked me up the following day, drove over the Battery Creek Bridge, just across the highway from Parris Island Marine Base and the interesting little town of Port Royal and turned right at a small development, stopping at the last house on the street.

The view of the property was very appealing from the entry road. The lot itself was quite large with a small stream and row of trees separating the house from another development upstream, making the lot appear even larger. I noted that the front yard was beautifully landscaped with mature trees and traditional Spanish moss, as well as mature azaleas and other perennial plantings. A two car garage (with workshop space) was to the left and a few feet away from the house which had a "killer view" of Battery Creek.

*Note: This creek may sound like a small stream. However, Battery Creek bears no resemblance to the small streams called creeks in other parts of SC. It is the same body of water which is deep and wide enough for ocean going ships to dock at Port Royal nearby. Even at low tide the water level of the main channel was as large or larger than many "rivers" in the upstate.*

The house itself was contemporary style from the outside. That theme was also repeated to a lesser degree in the interior. The entrance opened to a center hallway with a "step down" formal living room with cathedral ceiling and "see-through" fireplace that opened to both the living and dining rooms. The hallway ended at the entrance to the dining room, kitchen, and great room. The latter, which joined the kitchen, had almost an entire glass wall overlooking Battery Creek. A powder room was near the entrance to the master bedroom with full bath, which took up the remainder of the first floor. The second floor contained two bedrooms, a second full bath, and a stairway to the third level (or loft). This level was currently being used as an office and study. Because of its height, however, the third level offered the best view of Battery Creek, the marsh, and the natural beauty of the place.

I was favorably impressed with the location, layout of the property and its beautiful setting. Therefore, I returned to the Two Suns Inn to discuss the property with Ron and Carrol, both of whom were familiar with the location. They urged me to leave an offer with Mike to submit to the owners. A few days later, he called to tell me that my offer had been accepted. In order to spare me another long trip to Beaufort so soon, Mike arranged to have the "closing" without my presence. *This allowed me to bring enough furniture in my van to sleep there the first night.*

That house became my "vacation home" for the next three years. I even thought that it might someday become my permanent retirement home. Although it was on what was considered "marsh land," even at low tide the main channel was deep and wide enough for fairly large boats to travel to and from a large lake farther upstream. With the idea that this might become my permanent home, I acquired a permit from the county to build an overhead walkway to the main channel where I could have a dock built. When the dock was completed it would provide access to deep water even at low tide.

Even without the dock, at high tide the water reached the bottom step of the back deck of the house, bringing with it hundreds of small water creatures (e.g. fiddler crabs) which remained until they scuttled back with the receding water. Once, at low tide I saw an orca beating the water while chasing a school of fish headed up the channel toward the large lake upstream. That was a sight to behold.

I might still own that beautiful property except that once, while I was vacationing there, the National Weather Service issued warnings that a mighty hurricane was headed directly toward Beaufort. The prediction was that if it continued on its projected course, "there would no longer be a city of Beaufort, SC." City officials issued "mandatory evacuation" orders, and I headed back to Blacksburg with bumper to bumper traffic. This congestion of people fleeing from the hurricane lasted all the way to Columbia.

Early the following morning, I received a telephone call from Ron Kay (who had defied evacuation orders) telling me that the hurricane had turned away from Beaufort at the last minute and that the town and my house had escaped serious damage from it. However, he said that when he went to check on my property, he found that vandals had broken through my glass wall facing the water and had ransacked the house. *Further checking by Ron revealed that almost every house in the neighborhood backing up to Battery Creek suffered the same fate.*

Ron said that "with my permission" he would have some workers seal the broken glassed-in area with plywood to temporarily secure the place until I could get back down there to supervise permanent repairs. I gave my permission to secure the back of the house and expressed my appreciation to Ron for checking on my property. A few days later, I drove back to Beaufort to check on damage and find someone to make permanent repairs. When I arrived, I found many of my valuables strewn around the floor. All the silver plate was still there but the sterling silver could not be found. This told me that the thieves knew what they were doing.

However, the thieves were dumb in another sense. They had taken most of the stolen goods to a nearby pawn shop and were promptly caught and jailed by police. They must have hidden or disposed of my sterling silver because when I looked at the stolen goods at police headquarters none of it was there. However, I was eventually paid for my losses by the thieves themselves through a special State "Restitution Law for Victims of Crime" that requires thieves to agree to repay their victims as part of their sentencing, even if the victim does not request it. This program worked well in my case thanks to the police and the law enforcers.

Despite restitution of my stolen treasures and insurance company payment for my needed repairs, the entire experience left a bad taste in my mouth. I had the same reaction I had when Hurricane Hugo hit the towns of Mt. Pleasant/Charleston, SC several years earlier. I knew my nervous system did not respond well to threats of hurricanes and that I should give up my love affair with coastal property. Mike McFee handled the sale of my Beaufort property and for the first time in my real estate dealings, I made a nice profit.

# CHAPTER 7

## The Mountains Beckon

WHILE RETURNING TO Blacksburg to live full time at my little farm house, I still yearned to have a place to "get away." Although not initially thinking about purchasing mountain property, I had made trips to the Boone/Blowing Rock area over the years. More recently I had spent time with Alyce Bright, widow of my Catawba College roommate, Bob Bright. I hasten to add that our relationship was not a romantic one. My friendship with the couple had begun and grown with the two of them over the years, even continuing when I lived in Illinois, Washington, DC, and Indiana. And my friendship continued with Alyce after Bob passed away.

Every time I talked with Alyce, she urged me to consider the Boone/Blowing Rock area as a place to vacation, or even as a place to live. She said that she and Bob had never regretted buying their house in Blowing Rock despite owning a large, well maintained, home in Statesville, NC. At her urging, I began seriously thinking about buying some mountain property.

Since I already knew that I could not afford to buy anything substantial in the town of Blowing Rock, I suggested we explore the Boone/Banner Elk area as a possibility. The difference in prices aside, this area of beautiful mountains and ski slopes really piqued my interest and I became increasingly interested in finding a home or cabin there. And of course I had money from the sale of the Beaufort house with which to make a large down payment.

In our exploration, we drove up and down Hwy. 105 looking for something that appealed to me and that I could afford. I almost bought a nice place on Sugar Mountain but did not act quickly enough and it was sold on the day before I arrived with my offer. I also came close to buying a house at Valle Crucis on 1½ acres with a wonderful stream running through it. The only thing that kept me from buying it was the sloppy restoration work done by a previous owner. I knew I could not live with this bad workmanship. It would have required undoing the previous work and starting over again. I thought about it overnight and decided I did not want to undertake another project that demanding.

However, it was a sad day when I left that unique little community of Valle Crucis, featuring the Mast General Store, recognized by the National Register of Historic Places as one of the best remaining examples of old general stores. The Mast store is still the center of the community, offering many items unavailable at modern businesses. It still had coffee for 5 cents a cup on the honor system. Alyce and I spent many enjoyable days browsing the store and having lunch at picnic tables on the banks of the lively stream behind the Mast Store.

After regrettably saying goodbye to Valle Crucis, we resumed cruising down 105 looking for other possibilities. Then one day near the village of Foscoe, we saw a "For Sale" sign at the entrance to a small development we had not noticed before. It was called "The Ponds." We drove through the entrance and saw a "For Sale" sign in front of a neat cabin across the street from the larger of two ponds. This pond would be considered a lake in other parts of the state.

The cabin for sale had a front porch close enough to the water to cast a fishing line into it. This body of water contained an abundance of crappie, bream, bass, and trout. Just up the street was a smaller pond, which was set aside to contain only trout. But because both ponds received most of their water from the Watauga River (which ran alongside the back of the Ponds property), other freshwater fish encroached and grew rapidly by eating food being fed to the trout.

I was impressed enough with the quiet beauty of this place to contact the listing realtor, and ask that she arrange an appointment for Alyce and me. After we met at the house, the realtor rang the door bell and we entered the house. We were shocked by the disarray. The house must have contained 100 children's toys scattered around the floor. We had to walk carefully to avoid stepping on toys. When we tried to look at the downstairs bathroom, our view was blocked by toys which literally filled up the bathtub.

Finally I asked the owner what the deal was with all the toys. He said, "When I was a little boy my parents did not have enough money to buy toys and I vowed that when I had children of my own and money, I would make up for this by buying them lots of toys."

Despite the over-abundance of toys, plus house cats and a large bloodhound dog (who thankfully was tied up on the back deck), we were impressed by the house, its location, and design. About half of the first floor featured a cathedral ceiling over the great room with fireplace, the dining area and kitchen, plus an open stairway to the upstairs. The rest of the downstairs had a regular height ceiling with two bedrooms, plus a full bath and a powder room. The second floor consisted of a very large bedroom, full bath, and large storage area.

Even with the unkempt nature of the house and its smell of cats and dog I was still impressed with the house. So, after a night to think it over, I made an offer that was accepted and with Alyce's help, I began the process of cleaning the place. That job was even worse than I expected because so much had been hidden by the toys and furniture of the previous owners.

In attempting to get rid of the cat and dog smells, I discovered that animal urine (and maybe more) had actually penetrated the floor covering in the kitchen. No amount of cleaning would solve that problem. So, I contracted with a flooring company to take the flooring up and replace it with new. To accomplish this, the contractor had to remove all of the appliances and place them in another part of the house. They then removed the top layer of the flooring and installed a complete new kitchen floor before moving the appliances back to the kitchen. This took care of about 90 percent of the bad smells but many other areas required repeated scrubbings before the house became clear of pet odors.

Not wanting to face the task of moving furniture from Blacksburg up the mountains, I decided to try to find enough locally to furnish the mountain cabin. I perused ads in the local newspapers and found what seemed like much of what I needed was "for sale" by a couple who were moving from the mountains to Hilton Head Island, SC. Climbing the mountain to see the furniture turned out to be a difficult endeavor for me. I made the first attempt in my car, with Alyce sitting in the passenger seat, but the height and narrow curving road got to me. I turned around and went back down to my house.

Then Alyce, who was used to the narrow curving roads and height, took over. She coaxed me into her car and drove up the mountain and eventually found the house where the furniture was for sale. I hesitated to go into the house, which appeared to be hanging dangerously on the side of the mountain but finally got my nerves under enough control to enter the house to look at the furniture. I was amazed by the quantity and fine quality of the furniture.

Much of the furniture was exactly what I needed to furnish my little cottage. The bedroom furniture contained a queen bed, large dresser with two mirrors, and lamp table. In addition, there was a matching hutch I knew was perfect for the dining area. Finally, there was a chiffarobe type storage cabinet with shelves above and drawers below which I thought would make a good entertainment center for the great room. All of this furniture was made with solid pine by a well known NC furniture maker. I decided to purchase most of this furniture. I paid a reasonable price in advance for this furniture because I planned not to see it again until it was unloaded at my newly-acquired house. I would never experience this climb again.

When I returned to "terra firma," I contracted with "Two Men and a Truck" and gave them precise directions of how to reach the location of the house containing my newly purchased furniture. Obviously, the local movers were more acclimated to such terrain than I. They found the correct cabin, loaded and delivered the furniture to my cottage, then unloaded and put the pieces in place without a scratch or expression of concern.

In another stroke of good luck, Alyce's son, Jeff Bright, had a managerial job with an upscale NC furniture company, and he volunteered to supply me with all needed upholstered pieces at wholesale prices. This included a new sofa, two new easy chairs, a variety of cushions and pillows and a suitable coffee table. I purchased an outstanding Persian rug for this room at an auction. So, within a two week period my great room and master bedroom were furnished attractively and comfortably. This left only the two guest bedrooms and eating area still needing furniture.

I went to garage sales, flea markets, antique malls and used furniture stores to obtain the furniture needed for the two guest bedrooms. I also bought a nice small dining room set including six chairs, and some fine lamps from a couple going into a retirement home. Finally, at a huge quilt outlet in nearby Tennessee, I bought quilts handmade by a famous quilt maker from Kentucky for beautiful bed coverings. Those quilts and the lamps continue to be part of the furnishings of the White household.

The Ponds was an ideal place to spend time in the summer season. The cool mountain air meant that the use of air conditioning was not needed most of the time. And The Ponds was a wonderful place to enjoy this weather. The development contained a large outdoor covered cedar structure that was great for fish fries and picnics held by residents on a regular basis. These development-wide events were well organized. The best fishermen were responsible for catching enough trout for everyone, while another group took care of cleaning and frying the fish. The women brought salads, desserts and other dishes to complete the meals.

*Note: I was not a good enough fisherman to be designated as one of the trout fishermen. I tried to make up for this lack of fish catching talent by bringing some tasty dishes to the cookouts.*

Although the mountain trout was the featured food item at our fish fries, my taste buds really preferred either crappie or bream and I mentioned this to the head fisherman who looked after both ponds. After that, he saw to it that bream caught inadvertently from the trout pond were cleaned and cooked for me rather than tossed into the larger pond. The almost weekly "fish fry" was the "mixer" of our neighborhood and a way to get to know all of the neighbors. This was not a difficult job since there were only about a dozen houses and two or three townhouses.

My friend Cliff Nunally, who had moved from Virginia to Blacksburg, SC, often came to visit me in the mountains. He taught me to cast (and decent guy that he is) also cleaned the fish, a skill I did not really want to learn. However, I used knowledge obtained as the chef at the Inn, to handle all the food preparation. We ate well over the summer months, both at the fish fries and at my house. Also, I introduced him to my attractive friend, Barbara Looman, who owned the Foscoe antique mall, and they later became man and wife.

# CHAPTER 8
## Friendships Keep Me Going

ALTHOUGH MY LIFE was considerably less stimulating than it was when I operated the Inn, I was grateful that friends and relatives rallied around me. Chief among these were Pat and Tony Krysiak. I had reached the point that I was comfortable around their dog, Pearl, and took care of her when the Krysiaks needed a break from innkeeping. They also demonstrated their friendship by keeping in close touch with me to make sure I was all right. Their friendship and kindness were demonstrated in many other ways. An extreme example was the time I was at my mountain cabin and became very sick, very quickly.

In fact, during one night I was there, I became so ill that I could not walk but had to crawl downstairs. Once I got downstairs, I called Alyce Bright and told her what was happening. Having trained and worked at high level jobs as a nurse, Alyce raced to my assistance and with her help I was able to get into her car. She then drove me to the emergency room at the Boone Hospital.

After some tests, the doctors said I had a serious condition and would be out of action for several months. They advised me to call my hometown doctor for an immediate appointment upon my return. When I called Dr. Nazarino in Gaffney and described my situation, she said she would see me as soon as I arrived. I was taken to Alyce's car on a stretcher and she drove me to Gaffney. Apparently Dr. Nazarino was alerted to my arrival because almost simultaneously an ambulance arrived at her office to transport me to the nearby hospital.

I stayed at that hospital for a few days while numerous tests were made. Meanwhile, Alyce had returned to her home in Blowing Rock while Pat had become my caretaker. Deciding that I needed more care than I could receive at this small hospital, Dr. Nazarino sent my test results to Spartanburg Regional Hospital and made an appointment for me to see a noted doctor there.

Pat drove me to Spartanburg where I had a brief meeting with the doctor who said, "Mr. White, you don't look that sick but based on the tests I've just reviewed you need to be hospitalized right now." I asked, "Can't I go home and get pajamas and some toiletries first?" He promptly said "no" and called for an immediate private hospital room for me. At that, Pat said, "Jim, don't worry. I'll go get you some new pajamas and toilet articles."

I was placed on a stretcher, taken to a room, and, to my surprise, was immediately placed under quarantine. By the time Pat returned, she was required to put on a protective mask before entering my room. The same applied to all my visitors. As I recall, doctors told me I had a contagious bacterial infection called "C difficile" or "C diff." The doctors speculated that my body was still weakened by the heart surgery and that my age and other health issues had made me more susceptible to this potentially fatal disease.

As an indication of its seriousness, doctors supervising my transportation for further tests and/or treatment asked if I had a "living will." I replied that I did, told Pat where it was located, and that it stated "no resuscitation." I said that I wanted that provision respected. When I said that, Pat and Alyce (who had returned from Blowing Rock) both winced and said, "No, Jim." They were "tearing up" as the stretcher left with me. Although provisions of the living will never kicked in, my condition continued to worsen for the next few days.

At my lowest point during my illness, Dr. Nazarino called my son, Mitch, and told him, "If you want to see your father alive, you need to get here in a hurry." He stopped what he was doing and drove to Spartanburg immediately and spent several days with me. During this illness, I was repelled by the sight of food and was rapidly losing weight to the point that the hospital's dietician personally visited my room and said, "Mr. White, you're starving yourself to death. Tell me what you will eat and I'll have it prepared for you. That includes steak or lobster tail or any food you desire." I replied, "Thanks, but I can't stand the thought of food."

The hospital brought me various types of liquid and I was gradually able to keep enough down to slow down my weight loss. My recovery slowly began and about two weeks later tests revealed that the "C diff" was gone and that I was no longer contagious. I asked to be transported to my little farm house but Pat was having none of that. "Jim, you're coming back to stay at The White House Inn where I can take care of you until you're completely well." I stayed there for another 10 days and really appreciated her good care.

However, I knew that preparing special food and managing my medication was too much of a burden and against Pat's wishes, I drove myself back to my home. I was able to do that because old friend Cliff Nunnally had someone drive him to my mountain cottage so he could drive my car back to Blacksburg and park it at the Inn.

It took me some time to regain enough strength even to walk slowly with a cane. I recall Nephew Dan Turner taking me to his home during this time so I could take a shower. I wasn't strong enough to get into the shower by myself and Dan had to lift me in and out. I was lucky to have someone strong enough and willing to do that for me.

As I began slowly to gain some strength an old friend, Caroline Martin, was very helpful. Caroline and her husband, John, had owned and operated a restaurant in Blacksburg until John passed away. One late afternoon, Caroline stopped at my house and said "Jim, I want to get you out among people again and I'm taking you with me to a Parents Without Partners (PWP) dinner/dance tonight in Spartanburg." I protested that I had difficulty even walking without assistance and certainly would not have the strength to dance.

She agreed but explained that it would be helpful to me to be around people and listen to some live music. She said that everyone brought enough food to satisfy themselves and others at PWP dinner dances. That's exactly what Caroline did that night and for several other nights until I was strong enough to do some cooking and bring food myself.

Although I didn't dare get on the dance floor that first night, I enjoyed the food, company and music by a live band. This became a pattern for the next few weeks and months. About the third or fourth week, a lady approached me as the dancing started and said, "I think you're ready to begin dancing again." I replied, "If you will hold me up, I'll give it a try." Within the next three weeks, I had gained enough strength to dance a couple of slow dances without the need to be held up by my partner.

A few weeks later I was able to dance to most of the slow dance music. Then, one night I asked one of the women out and that was the start of my dating after the loss of Jo Ann. I dated a few of the women at PWP, but made no serious connections with any of them. With this experience, however, I began thinking that it was about time that I become serious about finding a woman to connect with on a long range (and dare I say, even permanent) basis.

# CHAPTER 9
## Time to Face Some Facts

I HAD REACHED the age that I did not want to be a lonely old man with no one to share the last years of my life. The main problem was that I was still a romantic even though I was in my 70's. Therefore, I would not settle for a relationship based just on companionship. I was still looking for love and was planning to wait until I found romantic love. The only woman who had made my heart flicker in many years was one of the attendees at the special dinner for a Gaffney dinner club shortly after I opened The White House Inn for business 10 years previously. Since she was married at the time, I assumed this was a lost cause. *But I kept only two of the photos taken at the dinner and she was featured in both.*

Since the already married Gaffney lady was the only local woman who had attracted me and I had met no one of serious interest at PWP Spartanburg, I knew that I had to broaden my horizon if I were ever to find that special woman with whom I might share a future. I began to investigate possible ways to do that while continuing to live in Blacksburg. I had heard there were private clubs in Gastonia and Charlotte that (for a big price) would attempt to connect you with someone that fit your personality, desires and background. I heard that such a club existed in Charlotte but that it was expensive to join.

After checking this club out, I decided to join despite its high price. Initially, the club did seem to take seriously its job of putting together people with similar likes and dislikes. For example, it required an extensive interview, complete with video, to help them determine the type of person that would best suit the needs of each. After completing their requirements, I awaited their call with anticipation. Finally, they called to tell me that they had found the "perfect match" for me. They gave me a name and telephone number and suggested I call the woman for a date. I called this "perfect match," we talked for awhile, and then agreed on a date and time to meet. A few days later, I went to her apartment, picked her up, and drove us to a restaurant nearby.

Although the woman was nice looking and intelligent, I soon found out we had absolutely nothing in common. She was trained in opera and sometimes performed that music genre. I am a jazz lover and she despised jazz. We both struggled to find some shared interest but failed miserably. The clincher was that I had no romantic and few common interests with her and hoped she would not expect me to kiss her goodnight. As soon as I could tactfully end the date, I suggested I had a busy day tomorrow and needed to head back home.

A few nights later, she called and said, "Since I haven't heard from you I assume you don't want to pursue this relationship." I replied that I thought she was a nice lady but didn't think we shared enough interests to make things work out for us. We said goodbye and I said goodbye to the club. I could not believe that after all the preliminary "research," the club thought that we would be a "perfect match."

After that fiasco, I decided to try one of the online dating sites. I began with eHarmony which I had been told had a good reputation for matching up people. On my first telephone conversation with eHarmony, I was impressed by their criteria so I paid my fee and supplied them the necessary photos and profile information. Soon after my photo and profile appeared on eHarmony, I was inundated by lonely women from California, New York City, Singapore, China, and other faraway places. The few I received within driving distance ranged in age from 35 to 45 rather than the 60 plus I had specified that I wanted to meet.

Out of courtesy, I responded to a few of these, saying that I was flattered that they wanted to meet me but that I was much too old for them. Most replied that age didn't matter to them and was just a number. I found it was useless to respond and stopped further contact with them. I also called eHarmony to tell them that I would appreciate it if they didn't forward emails to me from women 30-40 years younger than I. The dating service replied that their system did not recognize age as one of their criteria. So I gave up on eHarmony.

As my final effort to find love on the Internet, I signed up with Match.com, hoping they might magically find a woman who matched my needs and age, excited me, and was within a reasonable driving distance to my home. Soon after sending my photos and profile to Match.com, I began receiving responses. Unfortunately, most of these were located far from Blacksburg, SC. However, a few were within driving distance and reasonably close in age to mine.

I checked some of these out but usually found that the photos they had put online appeared to be their college or even high school pictures. Without the red carnation, I would not have recognized them from their profile photo! One of these was actually from Cherokee County and I met her at Hardee's in Blacksburg. Beside the fact that she was at least 30 years older than her photo suggested, we talked through one coffee and a refill and I found we had nothing in common. However, the next day she called and asked me if I wanted to see her again. I explained that we did not share enough likes and dislikes to establish a workable relationship and wished her the best.

In another case, Match.com sent me a profile of an attractive retired English teacher and I thought that she might be a real possibility for a relationship. After all, I was an English major in college and had a career in journalism. Also, another favorable factor was that she lived between Salisbury and Charlotte, about an hour and a half away. However, the appearance of the photo with my profile ruined that chance. The retired teacher could not believe that a man in his 70's still had good teeth and a reasonably full head of hair. She did not believe that my profile picture was made within the past six months at the Shelby Walmart photo studio. She insisted that the photo must have been taken years ago or that I was one of those young male predators on the Internet who preyed on older women.

I was somewhat flattered by her appraisal of my picture and tried to convince her that my full head of hair was the result of good genes and that I had spent a great deal of money taking care of my teeth. But she was not persuaded. Finally,

I gave up on her as a possibility without ever meeting her in person. Match.com did succeed in introducing me to one attractive woman of the right age and with similar interests.

Although she lived in Augusta, GA, at least two hours away, I thought that the match up of our profiles might justify the longer distance. We corresponded several times and she volunteered to drive to our first meeting. She made it to Blacksburg in little more than an hour, driving her expensive Lexus coupe/convertible at speeds that must have far exceeded speed limits. We met at the local Hardee's in sight of I-85. After enjoying a cup of coffee there, she followed me to my little restored farm house a mile away and we spent most of the rest of the day getting to know each other. I found her to be highly intelligent, attractive and fun to be around. We also shared common interests in several areas including reading and writing. *In fact, she had written and published a work of fiction.*

Before leaving for Augusta, we made another date and I would drive this time. After informing me that she had another condominium adjoining the one she lived in, she suggested that I stay over the weekend. I was pleased that I would not have to drive to and back from Augusta the same day and readily agreed to her suggestion. Of course, with my more cautious nature, it took me much longer to make that trip than it took her.

When I arrived at her condo, she immediately took me to her guest condo which was beautifully furnished with all the amenities including coffee maker, coffee, several types of creamers, and a refrigerator stocked with snacks and beverages of all descriptions. It had all the features of home. At that time I also met her two German Shepherds which shared her condo with her. Having two large dogs in the condo with her, helped explain why she had a separate condo for guests—if you had that kind of money to spend.

After several hours of conversation, both of us and the Shepherds were ready for dinner and she said she had already planned that. The four of us would go to dinner in her car with the two big dogs in the back seat and the two of us in front. She took us to a steak house she favored and before we went into it, she placed a sign on the windshield telling anyone concerned that she had deliberately left the engine running so that she could leave the air conditioning on to keep her dogs comfortable.

I thought all of this was rather strange, but then I was not a dog owner and this was none of my business. After seeing that the dogs were comfortable, we headed into the restaurant where we enjoyed a glass of wine, and conversed while our steak dinners were being prepared. Dinner was wonderful but halfway through our meal, my date asked the server to have the chef cook a very large porterhouse steak and cut it in two pieces. That was my clue that the "take out" steak was for the German Shepherds. She explained that this was the dogs' favorite food; that she had offered them fried chicken once but the dogs held up their noses and refused to eat it. *Although I suspect that the hound dogs on our tenant farm would not have been that picky, I can't prove it!*

Despite coming from different backgrounds, this Augusta lady and I had some good times together. When she came to Blacksburg, I could only offer a private bedroom and bath but she never complained about having to put up with these lower standards. In addition to a shared enjoyment of reading and writing we had fun playing word games. *I still had a reasonably good vocabulary and memory at that time.*

Despite the interesting times I had with this lady, our relationship was "off and on" for about a year. Not too surprising, she turned out to be quite temperamental and would suddenly break up with me and then come running back with apologies. We would resume dating until the next temperamental fit.

Finally, I had enough and said, "Let's make it final this time." I returned all the pictures she had given me but she kept all of mine for some strange reason. I was a bit relieved by our final breakup since one of her close relatives had called to warn me that the lady in question had emotional problems that had distanced her from her own family. On her good behavior she could be a wonderful companion. I hope she conquered the "demons" that caused her periodic emotional problems.

# CHAPTER 10
## The Email I've Been Waiting For

AFTER SEVERAL UNHAPPY dating situations, I was ready to give up trying to meet someone on the Internet until I opened my email one morning to read that Match. com had found a 99.7% "match" for me. I read the woman's profile and looked at her photo and found her quite attractive. I was also interested because her profile showed quite a few common interests (including a liking for Thai food) and even more importantly, her profile showed she lived in Spartanburg, SC, less than an hour away from Blacksburg. So, I responded to this lady's profile, feeling I would be able to live with that .3% deficiency.

At this point, I should explain that under Match.com rules no names, addresses or phone numbers were shared until both parties were ready to reveal them. Therefore, I had no idea who she was when I responded to Match's information about her. Imagine my surprise the next morning when I opened my email to be greeted with the words, "Hi Jim." Then I quickly realized that this was Gloria Humphries, the woman I had pined for over the past 10 years! The photo did not do her justice in my opinion. I was pleased that she had recognized my picture. *Since the picture flattered me a bit, I've always suspected that she recognized me from the text of my profile rather than my picture.*

In my opinion, however, there was also a bit of duplicity on her part. I found out that she still lived in Gaffney where she owned and operated her real estate business. Obviously, showing the Spartanburg address represented an effort to disguise the fact that she was on an online dating site! In any event, I wasted no time in calling and inviting her to have dinner with me at Thai Taste Restaurant in Spartanburg. She accepted and after we arrived at the restaurant, I ordered a huge bowl of Tom Yum Gai Thai spicy soup. When it came and I started trying to transfer some of it to two smaller bowls, she saw that my right hand was shaking and volunteered to take over the serving duties.

She later told me she thought I was very nervous about our date. Then I told her that I am afflicted with "essential tremor," sometimes mistaken for Parkinson's disease. In my mother's (Mitchell) family, the ailment often occurs with male family members. Mitchell women relatives don't seem to have this problem. In my home area, it was prevalent enough in my family that it was often referred to as the "Mitchell shake." *Confession: I hereby admit that I* <u>*was*</u> *really a little bit nervous about finally having a date with the one woman who had touched my heart at our only other meeting 10 years previously.*

After that first "ice breaker," Gloria and I soon began dating on a regular basis. Early on, our dating was restricted to the Gaffney area because of Gloria's heart-felt Christian beliefs regarding unmarried couples being together alone overnight. What would her family think if she and a male companion spent a night alone, even in separate bedrooms? The Hatcher family, to which Gloria belonged, was prominent and proper, and we were not about to besmirch that name. In addition, I had enough respect for Gloria's beliefs that I was not about to suggest doing anything that conflicted with her own strong ethical standards. However, it pained me that we had to restrict ourselves to going places where we had to go and return the same day, since both of us had wonderful vacation spots.

By the time we met, Gloria was already part owner of a very nice 3 bedroom, 3 bath condo overlooking the Atlantic Ocean at North Myrtle Beach and of course I owned a nice cabin located on a small lake in the mountains. Therefore, we had two excellent vacation places which we could not use because of the reasons cited above. Fate eventually solved this problem in a strange way. Gloria's sister, Dorcas, had a Sunday luncheon at her home and invited the two of us and a couple from Spartanburg named Jean and Dale Ogden. Jean had been a close friend of the Hatcher family since she was a little girl and was best friends with Dorcas. She had even accompanied the Hatcher family on a cross country trip to California where they visited a Gaffney friend married to a famous Hollywood actor (Bob Cummings).

At this luncheon, I was seated next to Dale Ogden and we had an animated conversation during the meal and afterward. Dale and I shared many interests. Both of us liked sports, reading books (the Ogdens also sold books on the Internet) and both Dale and I had served in the military. I was in the U.S. Navy when WWII ended and Dale had been a career Air Force Master Sergeant. One final connection was the state of Illinois. Dale was born and reared in that state and I had attended graduate school at the University of Illinois. So we had plenty of conversational topics and were solid friends by the time the dinner party broke up.

I don't recall who suggested it, but the idea of the four of us vacationing together quickly caught on. In addition to the nice vacation spots available to Gloria and me, the Ogdens owned two Marriott time shares at Hilton Head Island. With the Ogdens serving as chaperones, we were suddenly able to spend nights and weekends together at three different fine vacation spots while assuring the most suspicious persons that no "hanky panky" was going on.

We went on many vacations together for some time and had great fun. I had only one problem with the arrangement: Dale took his chaperoning duties too seriously. The Ogdens always went to bed earlier, leaving Gloria and me alone for awhile. Then, as I was preparing to give Gloria a goodnight kiss, Dale would invariably become thirsty and would enter the kitchen to get a glass of water. He would usually stay and chat until Gloria and I went to our separate bedrooms.

All joking aside, we really enjoyed our time with the Ogdens. We made many vacation trips as a foursome, going back and forth to North Myrtle Beach, Hilton Head, and the mountains. During all this time Gloria was insisting that she would never get married again and I didn't pressure her on that point. This meant that the Ogdens always got the master suite while we occupied lesser bedrooms. Separately, of course.

Believing Gloria's protestations about never getting married again, the Ogdens bought an expensive set of king sized bed linens to accommodate the king sized bed in the master suite at Gloria's Myrtle Beach property. Having their own linens allowed them to strip the bed and take the linens home to wash and dry them at their leisure.

On a personal basis, there was just one problem with my mountain cabin. Unless Gloria and the Ogdens were with me, the mountains could be a lonely place from October to May. That's the period that my neighborhood friends went south for the winter. Since they had to spend more than six months a year in Florida to qualify as a resident for tax purposes, it made sense for them to spend their winters in that state and their summers enjoying the cool mountain air of North Carolina. Incidentally my friend Alyce Bright left the mountains during that same period because of allergies caused by some sort of "tree blight" present there at certain times of the year.

This left me with only a couple of mountain friends, Todd Wright and Barbara Looman, and both of them had very busy business lives, leaving me with too much time on my hands when I went to the mountains in the fall and winter. Todd, a great musician and head of Jazz Studies at Appalachian State University in Boone, had his hands full, serving as a department head and performing with his band all over the state. Barbara owned and managed a very busy antique mall in the area. Finally the Ogdens had busy lives of their own and were not always available for "chaperone duty." And since Gloria still owned her real estate company with its demands on her time, during the winter months the cabin usually remained vacant.

That situation made me decide to place my mountain cabin for sale. Now clean with no toys on the floor, it sold quickly. *Had I known that I would someday get married again, I would probably still own the Foscoe mountain cabin. With a loving wife to keep me company it might have been fun to sit by the fireplace and watch the snow fall outside.*

# CHAPTER 11

## A Private Dinner for Two and a Surprise

SEVERAL MONTHS LATER, when Gloria and I were at her North Myrtle Beach condo with the Ogdens, the two of us went out alone for dinner at a fine dining restaurant nearby. I decided that after dating for a year, it was time to test just how serious Gloria was about never getting married again. I had brought an engagement ring with me and tipped off the restaurant staff that I was going to offer it to my girlfriend that evening. As we were finishing our dinner, I pulled the ring out of my coat pocket and handed it to Gloria. Although the ring was too small she gamely forced it on her ring finger and then asked, "Did I put it on the right finger?"

I assured her that she had put it on the correct finger and signaled the wait staff at the restaurant to pop the cork on the champagne. They surrounded our table and took turns looking at and admiring the ring. The event became an unplanned party/reception with many hugs and expressions of joy.

*On the way home, I told Gloria that I had already contacted my jeweler friend and told him that I might (and hoped) I would need him to order the proper size setting for her ring. When we returned to the Upstate, we visited the jeweler who measured and provided the size of ring setting she needed.*

We thoroughly enjoyed our engagement time. Gloria had just recently started making homemade wine and I began helping her with the process. Her wine was not the overly sweet wine usually associated with the homemade variety. Hers was like the best commercial varieties, except better. We enjoyed the process of making and drinking batches of 30 bottles of delicious wine. In addition to wine making we enjoyed many great trips with our chaperones, the Ogdens, and began making plans for the future.

On August 13, 2005, we were married at the Blacksburg ARP Church by Pastor David Rowe. We had determined that only close relatives would be invited to the wedding but hinted we wouldn't mind if we had a few "wedding crashers." Dale and Jean Ogden were two of the "wedding crashers." The third one was old friend, Jerman Stein, who has since returned to his own native Chile. We were happy to have these non-family members at our wedding.

At a reception hosted by Gloria's sister, Dorcas, immediately after the wedding, Gloria and Dorcas sprang an unusual surprise for the guests. The two of them had set up a "take away" table on the front lawn. At our age, we did not want or need gifts because we had double and triple of everything needed for a household. Guests attending the reception were at first hesitant to take anything from the "take away" table. But they soon warmed up to the idea and after a while they were bartering with each other over items. The table was empty before the party ended.

Despite our best efforts to avoid it, our car was decorated with "Just Married" signs and cans tied to the back bumper as we left for Greenville to spend our wedding night at the beautiful Westin Poinsett Hotel.

P.S. Although the Ogdens were happy about our marriage, it meant they lost the privilege of automatically getting the master suite at Gloria's condo when we vacationed there as two married couples. The Ogdens were gracious enough to donate the nice, slightly used, king sized bed linen to us and we made good use of this gift while at the beach place.

# CHAPTER 12
## Another Real Estate Venture

SHORTLY AFTER OUR engagement but before our marriage, the Krysiak's house in Colorado sold and they paid me in full for The White House Inn. I now had extra money which I needed to invest. After an earlier losing effort with stock market investing, (Remember "Black Monday"?) I wasn't about to do that again. Then, I learned that a new upscale housing development called Sterling Lakes was being built around three small lakes near Gaffney. Despite my own usually profitless real estate dealings, I still had a love of real estate and thought I should investigate Sterling Lakes as a possible investment.

It didn't take long for me to learn that I knew (and trusted) all three of the partners involved with Sterling Lakes. I contacted one of the partners, looked at the map of the unsold lots, and spotted three prime lots, side-by-side, and asked about the price. When I found out the price for one, I then asked if I could get a reduced cash price for all three of them. The three partners then got together, discussed this possibility, and decided that the sale of these three lots, even at a reduced rate, would allow them to complete the road system for the development. So they accepted my offer.

With my adventuresome spirit in full sway, I then decided to design and build a large home on one of these lots. I knew the home needed to be large enough to meet the Sterling Lakes requirements and to justify the relatively high prices of the lots. So, I decided to design and build a house that would be nice to live in and easy to sell. Since all the lots sloped downward toward the middle lake it made sense to design a three level house. All three levels would have 9 foot ceilings. When completed, the heated space would have over 4,000 square feet and six bedrooms and the possibility of more if needed. It would have six full baths and a powder room.

As soon as the house design was completed, I put the blueprints for my house design out for bids and selected a builder from Blacksburg. I had been able to view several of his finished products at a nearby upscale development so I knew he was a quality builder. He was also the low bidder on the project.

Starting from the basement (or 1st floor level) this space would have a huge great room and fireplace, plus one bedroom, a full bath, work room and a kitchenette designed with an extremely large sink and cabinets large enough to accommodate "carboys" and other wine making storage space. This, of course, was made for our "little winemaker, Gloria."

The second (or entry) level contained a large kitchen space equipped with upscale appliances and a window "greenhouse." That floor would also have a pantry/computer room, a formal dining room, a large great room with a kitchen eating area, window wall with large deck for lake viewing, and corner fireplace. Finally, it would contain a master bedroom with small library that led to a balcony with another lake view, large master bathroom with Jacuzzi, and large walk in closet; plus a smaller full bath with shower.

The main part of the third level contained another master suite with master bath and walk-in closet, plus two more bedrooms and another bath. The space over the three car garage contained one bedroom and full bath, plus a third great room with the best view of the lake. This space could also accommodate additional bedrooms and bathrooms if needed, since the double HVAC and plumbing and electrical systems were designed to serve all three levels.

As the house neared completion, I decided to move into it to complete a few things that needed to be done but were not part of the builder's contract. A friend, Billy Wilson, owner of Custom Specialties Inc., an auto supply company in Gaffney, volunteered to bring a couple of his employees and a big truck to move me from one house to the other. He refused to accept payment saying this was for "friendship." He also gave me a card with his private number and said: "If you ever need me, even if it's midnight, call me at that number and I will be there for you." *And I knew he meant it!* I've been blessed with many friends in my lifetime and Billy Wilson certainly is among those at the top of that list.

*Before leaving the subject of Billy Wilson, I want to briefly leave continuity to explain his success as a businessman. As a young man especially interested in automobiles and motorcycles, he aspired to turn his hobby into a business but lacked money to do so. However, he thought he might gain enough money to start the business by getting a job within the racing car business, e.g. NASCAR. With no experience at that level, he used his ingenuity to devise a plan to get that needed experience by rigging up his own system that allowed him to practice how to change tires quickly.*

His intelligence and hard work paid off big time and he was soon able to get a job at a NASCAR race. His first race turned out to be at the great Daytona International Speedway. He worked long enough at various NASCAR races to earn the money he needed, saved it, and started his business. The rest is history. In my opinion he is the type of person who represents the best of this nation.

Moving to the house nearing completion helped me spot other work that needed my special attention. It was especially helpful for spotting areas needing retaining walls and walkways. Pop Martin, my long time brick mason friend, handled these jobs. One outstanding example of his work was building a stone walkway from the basement area down to the lake. He also built an attractive short brick wall to define the automobile parking area extending from the garage. As usual Pop's work was professional and reasonably priced.

Moving into the house early really helped take care of little finishing tasks (such as installing blinds) and custom work. Getting settled into the new house also revealed things I had not observed before. For example, some large poplar trees were partially blocking the view of the lake and I made the decision to have several of them cut down. I then had the logs hauled to a sawmill where they were cut into lumber. This lumber was then hauled to Ellis Lumber Company in Shelby where it was made into tongue and groove, dried and planed before being brought back to Sterling Lakes.

Although this was an expensive endeavor, it provided beautiful material for custom work such as enclosures for fireplaces and cabinetry for the wine making area. People familiar with poplar know that it is a hardwood that takes stain well, especially cherry. I like the natural look of poplar so I used no stain to change its color. My cousin, Campbell Martin, a highly talented cabinet maker, used this natural poplar to construct custom cabinet work which became special features of the house. Also, from a historical viewpoint, it was nice to use material from trees that once graced these acres. There were enough boards to complete the custom work at the Sterling house as well as to have some left over.

# CHAPTER 13

## Several More Moves

SINCE I HAD been living in the Sterling Lakes house for a full year, this made it easy for me to supervise several modifications to accommodate Gloria's wine making hobby. She had rented her house and we moved into our new home after returning from our honeymoon. As expected, when we combined furniture and furnishings, we had far too much and contracted with an auctioneer we knew and trusted. This auction went well, as described earlier.

We enjoyed living at Sterling Lakes for the next two years. Gloria immediately planted small vegetables in the kitchen's window "greenhouse" and a variety of plant materials on an outside "raised" garden. We also put out bird feeders, including several finch feeders. Our finch feeders attracted many different varieties, including house finches and goldfinches and one greenish colored finch that we could not identify until friends from Virginia, Dennis and Anne Avery, came to visit. Dennis is an old friend I worked with at the U.S. Department of Agriculture and his wife, Anne is an avid "bird watcher" and dog rescuer.

While we were doing lake and bird watching, Anne spotted the greenish colored finch and exclaimed, "That is the variety that I went to Mexico to see!" She later wrote to tell me that she had done some research and found that two colonies of these green finches had relocated to South Carolina (the Upstate and Charleston areas). Mexico could no longer claim exclusivity for this variety.

Although we enjoyed the lakeside location, our advancing age, climbing stairs, and other factors led us to decide to move after two years. The age factor came into play because my house had three levels (with two sets of stairs) and had an extremely large lawn with grass that required lots of care. Since Charles was not nearby and it was difficult to find good help, the burden was a bit too much for my aging body.

Our new house had many attractive features but its large size on lots of land made it difficult to maintain. As mentioned earlier it was not designed to be our permanent home. However, I needed to live in it for two more years in order to take advantage of the "three out of five year" tax provision. I also needed to protect my investment in the three expensive lots I had purchased before our marriage. So, when we reached the three year mark, I listed it for sale and it sold after two weeks on the market. This allowed us to move to Gloria's excellent large ranch house located in the town of Gaffney.

Gloria's house had many advantages over my house at the lake. First, it was on one level, plus small basement, and had been designed for seniors, with wide doors and level entrances for wheel chairs. In fact it had a full range of handicap features. Also, we needed to live in Gloria's house for at least one more year in order for her to benefit from the same tax provision I had used for my house. Why this emphasis on the tax provision? We were preparing for full retirement and needed to plan for it. I had retired at a relatively high grade but after only about 20 years of government service. The shortness of my career reduced my retirement income significantly. And at age 75, Gloria had sold her business to her daughter, Gloria Geary.

Not wanting to reduce Gloria's pleasurable wine making hobby, I asked my cousin Campbell Martin to build custom cabinets in the walkout basement with the "leftover" poplar lumber. Also, fearing that she might slip on the grass while walking down to the basement, I called Pop Martin to build brick steps from top to bottom. This enabled anyone to walk to the basement safely. You may be getting the idea that I was very much in love with this beautiful lady I found again after more than 10 years of looking. You would be right.

Again, we initially enjoyed living in Gloria's excellent house with one exception: Gloria's house was located on a very large lot with much grass to cut and at least three rose gardens to tend. Anyone familiar with rose gardens knows that maintaining one rose garden is a demanding job. At my age and with several serious physical ailments, I was not much help and it was becoming increasingly hard to hire dependable help. Thus the work to maintain this outside property pretty much fell to my 75 year-old wife. For anyone over 70 to do this hard work alone seemed risky to the extreme. I simply could not imagine living alone again, after finally meeting and marrying my "dream girl." So, at my urging, we soon began looking at retirement communities in which to spend the rest of our days.

Gloria was not at all happy about the prospect of moving from the home we had worked so hard to remodel and enhance. At my urging, however, we visited several retirement communities in Columbus, NC as well as Rock Hill and Spartanburg, SC. All were very nice but, with one exception, were too expensive or had other factors we did not like.

Then one day, when Gloria had other plans, I drove to Spartanburg alone and visited the former "model home" at Summit Hills Retirement Community. I liked the floor plan of the first vacant house I was shown but had some concerns about its closeness to the entry gate. Then, the lady representing Summit Hills said, "The house next door is also available and I can show you that house." We walked down the street and I was immediately impressed with the floor plan of this house. I liked its location about 100 steps from the dining room, and its privacy on a very large lot. The rear of the house featured large, mature trees that suggested a deep forest behind us. *In this case, the large lot was not a problem but an asset since Summit Hills took care of both interior and exterior maintenance.*

When we entered the second house, I thought that this place might be ideal for us. The one thing missing was a fireplace, something we almost considered a requirement. I asked the sales lady if it would be permissible to add a gas fireplace in the back left corner of an extremely large great room. She said, "Yes, a gas fireplace would be allowable." As I was leaving, she must have sensed that I was a real prospect since she handed me a key to the house and suggested that I might want to show this house to my wife.

That evening I told Gloria about the house and suggested we go see it together the next day. However, Gloria again had plans so I drove to Spartanburg alone for the second time. When I reached the house, a pickup truck was parked in the driveway so I didn't need a key to enter. Imagine my surprise when I saw workmen building a fireplace in the very corner I had asked about! I went back to the sales office, negotiated with the sales person, and made the down payment on the house, figuring that with the new corner fireplace the house would "get away" before I could show it to Gloria. I was assured that I could get my down payment back if my wife did not approve of the deal.

Gloria was understandably upset that I had made this much of a commitment without her presence. I tried to convince her that the price and layout of this particular house was perfect for us and that I was fearful someone else would buy it before she had a chance to see it. I also told her that Summit Hills was in the process of building a modern, fully equipped "wellness center" with fitness pool for residents and that this particular feature might ensure that we had a long, healthy, and happy lifestyle for our remaining years. I used all the salesmanship in my arsenal and she finally agreed to go with me to see the house.

Although still somewhat disgruntled, Gloria agreed that this house had potential and I finally convinced her to put her house on the market. With all the upgrades we had made to her house, it sold quickly. As a matter of fact she received cash for the house one day less than the two weeks she had been promised. And we moved to Summit Hills on Sept. 16, 2008. Summit Hills was having a dinner dance that evening and someone took a picture of us in our formal outfits.

# CHAPTER 14

# Life in Retirement and Discovery of Unknown Family Members

WE HAVE CONSIDERED it a privilege to live in a community containing so many great people, both residents and staff members. Although there is a great variety of residents, including former doctors, lawyers, college professors, business tycoons and a former coal mine worker, all are uniformly nice. As part of this book, I started listing resident couples and individual residents who are special friends but stopped and deleted the list before finishing it since the number of special couples and individuals at Summit Hills we consider friends would require writing another book. Staff members, such as the maintenance people, servers and kitchen help, transportation people, and courtesy officers would also be listed as friends.

One of the first persons we encountered at Summit Hills was Joan Gibson, who not only was an early friend of Gloria's but was born the same week in the same hospital as Gloria. They took piano lessons from the same teacher and were fast friends until Joan's family moved to Charleston where her father took a job with a company producing materials for the WWII war effort. Joan was and still is active in Summit Hills affairs and was extremely helpful to us in adjusting to the active lifestyle here. *And, oh yes, she is older than Gloria by three days.*

Tim and Peggy Brackett were the first new friends we made at Summit Hills. They were in the process of moving into their brand new home at about the same time we were moving into our older but well maintained home. Tim is younger than I but we share memories of the Shelby, NC area where each of us grew into adulthood.

Over the years here I have become friends with many other residents including Russell Blackburn, Don Winslow, and Ade O'Neal. It turned out that the four of us had a connection with the Island of Okinawa during WWII or soon after it ended. Russ and I were "amphibious" sailors already on board Landing Ship Tanks (LSTs) awaiting the signal to invade Japan. Don was in the Army along with Ade O'Neal who had participated in the fierce and costly battle that succeeded in securing Okinawa. Don said he later joked with Ade that he saw him in the landing craft but all that he really saw were helmeted soldiers.

*Unfortunately, since I wrote this, Ade O'Neal passed away and there are now only three of us. Apparently, God has not been in a big hurry to take us survivors since we're all in our 90's and enjoying life at Summit Hills.*

I must mention one other person by name at Summit Hills. Although not a blood relative, this lady turned out to have an unexpected family connection with me. It happened this way: One day Gloria and I were about to sit down for lunch in the dining room when an elderly lady approached and said, "Jim, my name is Louise Beckett and I've been wanting to talk to you." We invited her to sit with us for lunch and the first thing she asked me was, "Jim, do you have male siblings? If so, what were their names?" Puzzled by this question, I nevertheless replied that I had once had three brothers named Frank, Robert and Howard but that all were deceased.

Before I could ask her any questions, Louise said, "Along with your name, those are the same names as my relatives in Illinois. My grandfather's name was Jim White and I had uncles named Robert and Frank (or Francis). This White family helped establish the town they lived in and although I lived with my parents in Pennsylvania, I spent many summers with Grandfather Jim White and his family in Marissa, Illinois." I replied that I had heard that some members of my White family had moved west because of the "slave issue" but I did not know who they were or where they went. *Could these be my long lost relatives?*

I had never had much interest in genealogy but some time earlier had received a package from a niece, Kay Blackwell, who said the package contained some White family history. Not very interested, I had set this material aside to read later. At the time she sent it to me she said she had used this information to get Marvin, her husband (my nephew) into an organization called "Sons of the American Revolution" or "SAR," which is the male version of "Daughters of the American Revolution," or "DAR." Later, Kay used much of the same material she sent me to help make me eligible for membership in SAR. Although not a "joiner" I thought this membership would give me an opportunity to spend more time with my nephew and his family so I paid a small fee to join.

In any event, after lunch with Louise Beckett, I returned to our cottage and retrieved the package that Kay had sent me. After flipping through some pages I found what I was looking for: confirmation that the White family that Louise Beckett mentioned which had settled in Marissa, Illinois were part of my family that sailed from Belfast, Ireland aboard the ship called the "Earl of Donegal" on Oct. 2, 1767 and arrived at Charleston, SC, on Dec. 22, 1767.

The document Kay sent me said that the "root stock" of the White family arriving in America from Ireland consisted of John White, age 47, and his wife Ann Garner White, age 40, plus their six children: William, 14; Margaret, 11; Helen, 9; Isabel, 7; Janet, 5; and Victoria, 3. The document further stated that the John White family settled about three miles south of the town of Chester, SC on the Chester-Great Falls highway, one third mile west of the highway and 200 yards north of a large spring which was still in use when this was written. The land came to them by way of a grant from King George III of England.

Space in this memoir does not permit me to include the genealogy of all branches and generations of the White family. However, it was especially interesting to learn that successive generations of this family used the names of James, Frank, Robert and William for male members and Isabel, Margaret, Jane, Victoria and Elizabeth for female members. That was why Louise asked me for the names of my siblings. As already indicated three out of four of those names were used for the male members of my own family. Also, my oldest sister was named Isabel and a niece, Victoria.

*In order to reduce the details of the genealogy of our family in this memoir, I shall henceforth use the prefix "later" to indicate repetitive names from the original ones.*

Other information contained in the material Kay had sent me showed that the original John White and wife Ann Garner became active and solid citizens of the Chester county area that included several other families who arrived from northern Ireland and settled in the Chester/Lancaster area. I also learned that John White was killed in a skirmish with the Cherokee Indians who frequently came across the North Carolina border and raided the Catawba Indians who lived in the vicinity of Rock Hill, SC. Although not well documented, it is believed that because of the distance and lack of transportation, John's body was not returned to Chester for burial and that his remains were buried in the Old Concord cemetery near what then was known as Youngsville but now is known as Woodward.

*Many other deceased members of the White family are buried at Purity Cemetery, outside of Chester. Gloria and I visited there along with Earl and Sue Ritch (my nephew and niece).* Despite John's death the remainder of the White family expanded and prospered with plantations and slaves mostly in the Chester/Lancaster area. However, some bought land in York County and lived in the towns of York and Clover.

By way of background, during at least some of these encounters, the white settlers joined forces with the Indians of the Catawba tribe, and as a result of such cooperation on the part of the settlers, the Indians became fast friends of their white neighbors. *It is interesting to note that a remnant of the Catawba Indians still exists near Rock Hill, SC where the SC government has set aside a reservation for those Indians and provides a pension from the state.*

During this period, some of the Brownlow family, friends of the White family in Ireland, also immigrated to the U.S. and settled on land nearby. There, William, John White's only son, resumed his friendship with Jane Brown, daughter of Sir John Brownlow. Eventually this friendship turned to love. William and Jane were married in 1778. The two of them had eight sons and one daughter. They named their only daughter Jane. Their sons were named: John, James, Samuel, Abraham, Hugh, William, Frank, and Garner. Note that the names of both males and females of the William White family follow the familiar White family pattern of borrowing names from previous generations.

Since I brought up the Brownlow name, it seems appropriate to provide a brief summary of information about the maternal side of our family. The fact is that Jane Brown brought some "royal blood" to the White family through her father, Sir John Brownlow. The reason she had the surname of Brown, rather than Brownlow? It appears that her parents had failed to find proper mates and Sir John married his cousin Eleanor Brownlow. *I hasten to add that intermarriage was not that unusual in those days because of the small gene pool. However, the fact that they used the names Brownlow, Brownlee and Brown (as in Jane) may have been an attempt to disguise this intermarriage.*

Among his titles (too many to mention) Sir John Brownlow was a Member of Parliament (M.P.) for Grantham and Lincolnshire. He was also 1st Baron Charleville, Co.

Cork and 1st and last Viscount Tyrconnel (Ireland). He was invested as a Knight, Order of the Bath (K.B.) in 1725. According to the Ipswich Society, the Brownlow family lived in their own castle (called Belton House) for over 300 years. Located in County Antrim, it is now part of the "Tour of Historic Castles" in Ireland. *I've read that my great grandfather, William White and his wife, Jane Brown White, lived in Belton House for some time after they married. My name is listed as fifth great grandson of Sir John, by Ancestry.com.*

Louise Beckett made me aware that Jane and William White were featured in a book written by Elizabeth F. Ellet, called "Women of the American Revolution." According to the book (which I retrieved from the Internet), William and Jane White "were married and had one child when hostilities commenced in the South." The book said William and his future brother-in-law, Robert Miller, quickly enlisted on the Patriot side. It mentioned their role in several smaller battles between the Patriots and the Redcoats and then addressed the battle of Kings Mountain saying that William and Robert were "rushing up the mountain together at full speed to join in the fighting." The book said Miller fell, badly wounded, and William White carried him to a secure area before joining the fight.

The book continued, "After the battle was won by the Patriots, White and 19 of his comrades ventured home to find his wife and sisters in the field with baskets of wheat, which they were beginning to plant. It turned out that Jane White had been busy attending to their home and business while having to contend with Tories who visited to steal from her." Although she was defenseless and had to give much of her produce to the Redcoats, the book said that, along with her goods, she gave them serious "tongue lashings."

*More details about William White's exploits during the Revolutionary War can be found in the book, "The Patriots At Kings Mountain" by Dr. Bobby Gilmer Moss, a local historian and Professor Emeritus of Limestone College in Gaffney, SC. Dr. Moss has written many books of regional and local interest. (Note: I offered Dr. Moss' books for sale at my Inn).*

Life in the U.S. was good for the White family which continued to expand in South Carolina. Then in the mid 1800's, tensions over the "slavery issue" grew in the South and North, as well as within families who had emigrated from Ireland and settled in the Chester County area. On his deathbed, a later John White, who had strong convictions about slavery, called his family together, and requested that his wife and family move west out of the slave holding area.

After his death and the plantation sold and the slaves freed, his wife, Margaret and daughters, Catherine Boyd White (Nelson), Jane Brown White (Wilson). Elizabeth White (Johnson), sons, Francis (Frank) White and John Kennedy White moved west and settled in the town of Marissa, IL. As years went by their family expanded and played a strong role in the development of Marissa. *It makes me sad that I knew none of this history when I attended graduate school at the University of Illinois and traveled near Marissa, doing research on my Master's Thesis. What a missed opportunity to meet my relatives, some of whom still live there and operate the family lumber and millworks business.*

My branch of the family emanated from William White (another son of the above mentioned John White), who did not move with the rest of the family. This William was already married to Isabella Armstrong of York Co. SC. They had children of their own and were living on land owned by his father-in-law, Francis Armstrong, and later they bought land in York County. Among their children was Andrew Jackson White, my great grandfather, who produced among others, Andrew White, my grandfather, who produced my father, Haskell Howard White, who married my mother, Macie Mitchell White.

In case you're wondering how Louise Beckett was connected to the White family, it began when some White family members from Marissa, IL went to Key West, FL or the nation of Cuba (neither Louise or I have been able to establish which) with the purpose of rescuing a "Cuban orphan." The young orphans were marched across the stage, and my family members pointed and said, "We want that one!" The chosen orphan was Clara Louisa Moraleda, who was brought to Marissa and grew up as part of the White family. When grown, Clara Louisa met and married a young Pennsylvania minister named Dr. Vincent D. Beckett. They had three children, Joe, Ruth and Louise.

Personally, I consider Louise a member of my family. *She accompanied Gloria and me to the last two White reunions where she got to meet some other members of the White family whose ancestors stayed in South Carolina.* Louise and I call each other "Cousin" and Gloria and I sit with her at Sunday School and church services at Skylyn Dr. (ARP) Church. Now in her mid 90's, Louise still retains a vivacious personality, sense of humor, and love of music and singing. Although losing her eyesight, her memory is so good she needs no hymn book at church. If the minister asks the congregation to sing verses two and four, she doesn't miss a beat.

Louise recently moved from Independent to Assisted Living at Summit Hills. Shortly after she arrived there, the staff had a "Name This Tune" contest for residents. I wasn't surprised to hear that Louise won the contest hands down. She not only named every tune but sang their lyrics. At the sound of music, look around and you'll spot Louise. *Sadly, just days after she celebrated her 98th birthday, Louise passed away. She was much loved by Gloria and me as well as fellow residents of Summit Hills, plus the pastor and members of our church, and will be greatly missed by all of us.*

Soon after we arrived at Summit Hills, we were surprised and saddened to learn that after seven years of marriage, son Mitch and his wife, Jeannette, were getting a divorce. Fortunately, the divorce was amicable. Continuing the update on Mitch, he pursued his business career by traveling back and forth between the U.S. and Korea. Several years later, he met a beautiful and intelligent woman of Italian descent named Natalie whom he later married.

In 2010, they moved from the DC area to Charleston SC where he had invested in a small, natural snack manufacturing company. The move allowed Mitch to take a more active role in the business and to gain more experience in the subject of healthy eating. They also began jointly raising two boys and a girl that Natalie had by an earlier marriage. Eventually, largely by his hard work and business sense, Mitch's little company was getting its products into stores throughout the U.S., including Whole Foods. Natalie was also succeeding by becoming co-owner of a company that used the Internet to sell its goods.

Then disaster struck them. Apparently, Natalie had hidden the fact she was having some serious health problems. Then one morning these symptoms could no longer be hidden. After Mitch left the bedroom to walk their dogs, she had to crawl to the bathroom where she threw up repeatedly. Mitch came back into the house, saw her on the floor, carried her to the car and rushed to a hospital emergency room. Hours later the doctors trying to find the cause of her problem said they thought it was probably Multiple Sclerosis (MS) and put her on steroids. Two weeks and many steroids later a neurologist confirmed that Natalie had MS. A doctor explained that MS was incurable and there was no drug protocol to heal it.

Doctors said that Natalie's treatments would require multiple daily injections at the cost of about $40,000 a year, and that the treatment would not relieve her of all the terrible symptoms. They said at best the treatments would slow down the decline but that eventually she would be in a wheelchair or bedridden. Greatly distressed by this prognosis, they began the search for a better one. About two weeks later Mitch called to tell me they had read about a doctor who had created a food protocol that healed her own MS 20 years earlier.

Natalie began following this protocol and six months later Mitch called to say that following this program religiously had reversed almost all of Natalie's symptoms. Mitch added that he himself had decided to follow the protocol hoping that it might help him reverse tissue damage from tennis as well as to improve his declining eyesight. Both began a program of eating a clean, autoimmune protocol based diet. Both soon claimed that they were the healthiest either of them had been in 20+ years. Natalie is now essentially free of MS symptoms (unless she violates protocol) and Mitch's eyesight has improved 30%.

*I have personal evidence of Mitch's physical improvement. Once when I was visiting him at his home in Potomac, MD, he met my car at the curb and apologetically said: "Dad, I'm sorry that I can't carry your bag upstairs to the guest bedroom. My knees won't let me climb stairs." More recently when I visited him in Charleston, I was shocked to see him running up and down the stairs like a youngster. His present diet and lifestyle have also resulted in him almost regaining his tennis playing weight. He is now also back in tennis, his first love, and is co-directing a successful junior tennis academy in Mount Pleasant. More evidence later about the benefit of healthy eating.*

Many people voice the opinion that retirement centers are "a place to die." We and many others think of Summit Hills as "a place to live." Although we had to give up dancing when I reached age 90 *(it's not very glamorous to see a man with a walker trying to dance!)* Gloria and I continue to exercise regularly and attend many fun events here and away. Since Gloria is just 88, she is still extremely active with water aerobics, balance, and other planned exercise classes. Also, she wears a "fitbit" and almost always makes her goal of 5,000 steps a day. Occasionally, she exceeds her goal by doing 9-10 thousand steps. She is also an excellent bridge player, gardener, and cook.

After coming to Summit Hills, she also achieved fame as one of "The Hatcher Sisters" trio. By way of background, Gloria and her sisters, Dorcas and Annie, had performed as a song and dance trio at family (but not public) functions. At ages ranging from 75 to 85, their first public performance was here at a "Ladies Luncheon." This happened after the person responsible for supplying the speaker or entertainer for an event failed to find anyone suitable. In desperation she asked Gloria and her sisters to perform. At the end of their performance people lined up to request them to perform at their churches and other venues.

Thus, "The Hatcher Sisters" trio was born. Although they disclaimed any real talent, their "fun" act became so popular that they had to restrict their performances to one a month. The highlight of their new career was at a charitable event where they were the only entertainment. They drew a large crowd and raised $10,000 for charity. Unfortunately for the world, the lead singer decided that at age 90+ her voice was no longer acceptable (to her) and they disbanded.

I may be a bit prejudiced but I think Gloria, although now in her late 80's, retains the beauty she had in 1962 when she won the title of "Mrs. South Carolina." I have no doubt she would have won the title of "Mrs. America" had the icing on the cake she baked not melted from the heat of the TV cameras. She had used whipped cream for the icing! Obviously, she is not a baker!

Reviewers of this manuscript have insisted that I include the description of one other important event, i.e. being invited to participate in an "Honor Flight" for veterans who served in a "war zone" during World War II. This event involved a one day flight to Washington, DC to visit the relatively new World War II Memorial. *On an earlier trip we had tried to visit this Memorial but when our bus arrived, the place was so crowded there was no place to park.*

This time that was not a problem because special accommodations had been arranged for members of various "Honor Flights" from around the nation. Such flights are sponsored by the "Honor Flight Network," a non-profit organization created for the purpose of transporting America's veterans to the nation's capital to visit the memorial dedicated to honoring the service and sacrifices of themselves and their fellow veterans. Top priority for these "Honor Flights" is given to World War II survivors, along with other veterans who may be terminally ill.

According to the Department of Veterans Affairs, an estimated 640 WWII veterans die each day. The organizers of Honor Flights recognize that time for expressing thanks to these survivors is fast running out.

Our particular flight for upstate SC war veterans began and returned to Greenville-Spartanburg (GSP) Airport. Our group of veterans from Summit Hills joined a flight of about 200 other SC veterans. A band already on hand and playing patriotic music greeted our arrival and departure. A large crowd of "well wishers" were on hand to shout and wave goodbye. When our flight arrived at Reagan Airport, another band

and hundreds of people were on hand to greet us. Also, in my case at least, a young sailor in full dress uniform was waiting to be my escort while we were visiting the World War II Memorial and other sites honoring veterans.

Although I was still able to walk, I was provided a wheel chair to ease the strain on my elderly body. Among the greeters from South Carolina was Junior Senator Tim Scott who spent considerable time with us. We were amazed that when we were being transported from one spot to another, all other traffic stopped and officers waved us through traffic lights. All of our needs were anticipated and taken care of by the Honor Flight organizers.

Our return to GSP Airport was again greeted by a band playing patriotic music and a huge number of greeters, including a busload from Summit Hills. I was amazed when I viewed this large group but especially thrilled when I saw my wife, Gloria, and son, Mitch, smiling and waving to me from the crowd.

My only regret was that my two older brothers were never given this opportunity because they both passed away at relatively young ages. Frank, with his heart damaged as a boy by rheumatic fever and after 42 months in battle, died at age 38. Bob, with some serious health problems aggravated by his service, died at age 55. Life is not always fair and my life, along with thousands of others, may have been spared by the ending of the war because of the development and use of the atomic bomb. And I was fortunate to be able to use the GI Bill to get a college education while my brothers were not.

As I near the end of this long memoir, I've passed the age of 92 and God has saved me from four death sentences. The first was in 1978 when I was diagnosed with Stage 4 cancer and my oncologist gave me just a few months to live. The second incident was in 1997 when my heart stopped beating for a short time requiring me to have emergency open heart surgery; the third was in 2001 when I was diagnosed with "C difficile" or "C diff" and my doctor called Mitch to tell him that he needed to "come to Spartanburg if you want to see your father alive." The fourth came after we moved to Summit Hills and I suffered a blood infection. Mitch was again heavily involved in that event and deserves a lot of credit for my recovery. A brief discussion of that follows:

After a week at Spartanburg Regional, the doctors there said that they had been unable to find the source of my infection and that I needed to be transferred to their Restorative Care Center where I would receive two strong antibiotics on a 24 hours per day basis. The doctors hoped that these antibiotics might overcome the infection, which would result in a clear blood sample. After two weeks of this treatment, there had been no improvement. Mitch, fearing the worst, had come from Charleston to spend time with me.

Shortly after his arrival, he, Gloria, and I were chatting in my room when three doctors converged to say, "Mr. White, after a sufficient time for the 24 hour per day antibiotic treatment to work, we've been unable to get a single clear blood sample. Although we don't know for sure, we suspect that the infection is coming from one or both of your artificial heart valves. The only option we have left is to remove both of your heart valves and replace them. And because of your advanced age, no surgeon would agree to perform such an operation. We're sorry to inform you that we've run out of options." *In other words I was going to die!*

With that news Mitch stood up and said, "Dad I'm not going to sit here and see you die. If you agree, I'll draw up a plan to replace your regular diet with the 'clean' diet Natalie and I have been on for the past year." I turned to the doctors and asked for their opinion of this approach. One said immediately, "Mr. White, I would give that a try because you have nothing to lose." The others agreed and said they would continue to keep me on the 24 hour antibiotic regimen.

The doctors left the room and Mitch asked Gloria if she was willing, with his guidance, to prepare special meals for me every day. She agreed and the two of them left the room to go shopping for the equipment and healthy, organic food items needed for my special "clean" diet. Once this was completed, Mitch returned to Charleston and Gloria, who was spending nights in the second bed of my room, had coffee with me before leaving to prepare my special meals for each day. *We got a big laugh from the nurses who saw us enjoying our coffee together in my little hospital bed!* The hospital continued to bring her meals so that she could eat without leaving me alone for long periods of time.

A few days after I began this regime I got a clear blood sample. Obviously God (with Mitch's help) had not been ready to take me and I recovered from my fourth death sentence. *("Recover" might be an overstatement since I now require a walker to get around).* But my brain is still reasonably active. After these commutations, I asked God for one more favor: to give me time to finish the memoir I began writing at age 89. I assume that He listened to me, since after three years of searching my memory and writing the memoir, it is finished except for printing/publishing details. And I'm still here.

As for my future, with this massive amount of writing completed, I would like to take it easy for awhile. I'll have more time to read, relax, try to get in better shape, participate in more activities with my "super active" wife and spend more time with other members of my family while awaiting what God has (or doesn't have) for us to do.

When Gloria and I were contemplating getting married at our advanced ages (I was 79 and she was 75), we agreed that if we could have five reasonably healthy, happy years together, our marriage would be worthwhile. Now, we have 14 years under our belt and are going for 15!

Did someone say, how about 20?

The End

# Reconstruction of Cash House which became
## The White House Inn B&B

Master carpenter Bill Hartje at work repairing exterior wall damage in 1990.

In March 1990, exterior work included renovated front entrance work and re-installation of front entry door by Bill Hartje. Note how front porch was raised to prevent water damage. Work was also being done to increase strength of balcony.

View of third floor (as found, originally).

View of 3rd floor restored as Honeymoon Suite by Bill Hartje and Jim.

**White House Inn interior before.**

**White House Inn interior after.**

Restoration complete and White House Inn B&B ready for business, 1991.

The White House Inn roadside welcome sign.

**Actress Andie MacDowell (center) talks with country music star T. Graham Brown.**

**White House Inn formal dining room with Andie MacDowell family.**

**Miller-Rowe Consort performing at the Inn.**

**Dining room ready for guests.**

**White House family reunion; surviving sibling, Edith Ford, at front beside me.**

**My favorite guests, Robert and Cindy Love, at their wedding.**

**Party for Gaffney dinner club; Gloria in center.**

**White House Inn formal sitting room and sunroom.**

**Sisters Nell (on left) & Edith (on right).**

Jim with son Mitch (on far right), and friends Jerman (on left) and Father Jeff.

Singer Suzanne Bonnar and Jim's colleague at EPA and
Department of Energy Bill Holmburg.

Suzanne Bonnar, James Wade (father) and
BBC director Elly Taylor during filming at The White House Inn.

Gloria cuts cake at our wedding reception and we prepare to leave on our
honeymoon.

We attend a formal dance our first night at
Summit Hills.

The big White House Inn auction fiasco.

Wife Gloria and friend Fred Oates.

Two happy endings: Gloria and I at a Summit Hills function;
and son Mitch with the love of his life, Natalie.

The photo above is part of the Marissa, Ill. White family that moved out of the South over the slavery issue. My branch of the family continued to live in South Carolina, and I was not aware that I had relatives in Illinois until I met Louise Beckett at our retirement community. Louise is pictured as a little girl on the lap of an aunt (third from left).

Louise Beckett (now deceased) shown here with my wife, Gloria.

Belton House built for and occupied for many years by the Brownlow family, (i.e., the maternal side of the White family). It is now part of Ireland's "Castle Tour." My 5th great grandmother, Jane Brown, grew up here and then married my 5th great grandfather, William White. Both of them are featured in a book about the American Revolution.

# Note about White House Inn Recipes

SEVERAL GUESTS AT the Inn requested copies of my favorite recipes: Jim White's Eggs Benedict, Shrimp and Grits and a variety of breakfast casseroles. One guest, a columnist for an Indiana newspaper, printed my Eggs Benedict recipe as part of her weekly column. As lovers of this dish know, it normally consists of poached eggs, either Canadian bacon or a high quality ham, on toasted English muffin, topped by hollandaise sauce, accompanied by either a twist of orange slice or slice of fresh tomato.

Since the hollandaise sauce is probably the single most important part of this tasty breakfast dish, I spent most of my mealtime "practice sessions" to perfect this ingredient. Initially, I tried making the hollandaise sauce from "scratch" but thought the result was too time consuming and too bland. So I abandoned that effort and began experimenting with commercial products. Finally, I found that Knorr's Hollandaise Sauce was quite good when made by directions on the package. Then I thought I could make it better by adding lemon or lime juice and a small amount of hot sauce. These additions took the Eggs Benedict to another level attested to by many people who expressed their opinion on the subject

*Note: In years since I closed the Inn, I've ordered Eggs Benedict from other bed and breakfasts, as well as some restaurants. In two of the latter, one in Spartanburg and the other in Blowing Rock, NC, I thought the sauce tasted like the sauce I made and used at my Inn. I mentioned this to the owners and both said that they followed the same course as the one I described and ended up with the same sauce I had served.*

An interesting sidelight about food: Soon after I opened my B&B, I was visited by a Jewish couple who were spending a week at the Inn. I offered Eggs Benedict as one of the breakfast options. The wife said my Eggs Benedict would be fine since she and her husband were not "kosher." She then volunteered an alternative, "Eggs Florentine," which she said would be suitable for "kosher" Jews. The only difference from the original was that the meat was omitted and replaced with spinach. She recommended that the spinach be the frozen kind but I've used it from the can and it was difficult to tell the difference.

"Shrimp and Grits" was not offered on the menu but I was willing to make it for guests who requested this dish. For those not familiar with this dish, it consists of shrimp cooked lightly (or heated) in a sauce made from Tasso ham which, along with the shrimp, would go on top of the grits. Because of the difficulty in finding the Italian made Tasso ham, I experimented by substituting Mexican chorizo sausage, which is readily available. I thought that the sauce made with chorizo was just as good as that made with Tasso ham. *Sometime later, I watched a TV cooking show featuring famous chef Emeril Legasse, and he made the same substitution so I thought I was in good company. I made one further change by using cheese grits rather than plain grits.*

In addition to the above items, I offered pancakes or waffles, omelets or eggs cooked to order, along with ham, bacon, or sausage (or all three if requested). And finally I offered a variety of breakfast casseroles, including ham or bacon, cheese, eggs, and seasoning. I also dressed them with either orange or tomato slices. Serving a casserole as the entrée made things easier for the cook since it could be made in advance and frozen until needed.

# Acknowledgments

TO GLORIA WHITE: First of all I owe the largest debt to my wife, Gloria. Since we were married, she has urged me to write a memoir. Finally, her gentle prodding paid off. When I reached age 89, I decided it was "now or never" for this project. She has been a source of encouragement throughout this effort. She has read every word of this memoir and offered helpful insights that I needed and appreciated.

To Maureen Johannigman: I cannot find words adequate to describe the help I've received from my friend and main editor, Maureen Johannigman. Maureen was an English Major in college and taught this subject at the high school level. She has kept me going with her editing, correction of grammar and spelling and in helping to organize this long document. And just as importantly, when my resolve and spirit began to slip away (along with my ability to write coherently), she has always encouraged me to keep going. I've thought of "throwing in the towel" on many occasions but Maureen always managed to help me regain enough energy and resolve to keep working. Thank you Maureen for all you have done for me.

To Bill Hartje: I can never repay my friend and master carpenter, Bill Hartje, of Indiana. His expertise and faithfulness to quality work was responsible for turning my formerly "falling down old house" into a superb specimen of a Greek Revival style mansion. Any time I had a crisis during the restoration effort, he dropped whatever he was doing in Indiana to come to my rescue. Even these many years later, when I contacted Bill about dates and events I had failed to record and that I needed for the memoir, he was not only able to produce receipts showing precise dates, he described the reasons for his visits to Blacksburg and what was accomplished during his stays there.

In addition, Bill even provided "before and after" photos which were used in this book to illustrate some of the restoration work being done. His contributions helped overcome my failure to document the process. Receiving this information helped bring order and authenticity to this document.

To Kay Blackwell: Although she has long been deceased, I will always be grateful for the work she did in providing the early history of my branch of the White family, i.e. those who chose to remain in South Carolina. Because Ancestry.com was not available at that time (as far as I knew) much of Kay's early work required visiting graveyards and searching for and reading old books and archives in courthouses around the state. Her research work was accepted by experts at the Sons of the American Revolution (SAR) making it possible for her husband, Marvin Blackwell, my late nephew, and me to become SAR members.

To Earl and Sue Ritch: Earl took up where Kay Blackwell stopped with genealogical research on the White and Mitchell families. Married to my niece, Martha Sue White, he used Ancestry.com to reach back to the 1600's in Ireland to uncover early White history which included a touch of "royalty" on the maternal side of the Whites who immigrated to this country. In addition, Gloria and I accompanied Earl and Sue on trips to graveyards at Chester, Hickory Grove, and Union, gathering information about the White, Brownlow, and Mitchell families.

To Robert Love: When I met you at The White House Inn back in 1995 I almost felt that I was in the presence of my old best friend, Bascomb Love. You looked and sounded like him reincarnate. Since then I've gotten to know you better in your own persona, i.e., Robert Love, one of the top officials at DuPont in Wilmington, DE. I can't thank you enough for the tremendous help you've given me with research on Ray Lynn as well as the Love, Mitchell and White families. The research you did on the Tolstoy family in attempting to see if Ray Bartness (or Lynn) was related to any of the Tolstoy family as he claimed was an incredible piece of work!

Also, Robert your ability to find and send me copies of old newspaper articles, photos, etc. on family members that I never knew existed, has lent needed authenticity to this document. Your help and friendship would make Bascomb proud. Your efforts on my behalf helped cement a lifelong friendship.

To Lester Roark: I owe tremendous debts of gratitude to the late Lester Roark who was an inspiration to me as a book author. We maintained close contact with each other as our careers progressed over the years. I also appreciate his active help in the restoration of the old Cash House into The White House Inn. Like Kay Blackwell and many close friends and relatives, Les has passed away but our long friendship will always be remembered and cherished.

To members of my White family, both those who went to Marissa, IL and those who stayed in SC, thanks for your acceptance of me when I returned to my home area after almost 50 years absence. When I was making a decision on where to retire, I didn't even think of Blacksburg. Why would I want to return to the area where I had been born and mostly raised as a "dirt poor, sharecropper boy?" Thinking of those days was not always pleasant. I was reminded of hoeing and picking cotton, and working in fields during scorching summer days. In addition, I still remember our large family living in small tenant houses without heating, cooling, electricity, running water or indoor toilets.

Those unhappy memories quickly dissipated after I returned to my home area under very different circumstances. I now realize that despite the earlier harsh conditions, I was blessed by growing up in a loving, functional family. As the only surviving direct member of the H.H. and Macie Mitchell White family, my memories now revolve around how much I miss Mom, Dad and all of my brothers and sisters. Of my siblings, only Nell Turner and Edith Turner still remained when I came back but I spent lots of quality time with them and their children and grandchildren before they passed.

Although my family members are too numerous to mention, I would be remiss not to say a special "thanks" to a few of them, starting with sister Faye White Shillinglaw. She and husband, Alfonso, better known as "Shilly," found summer jobs for me during high school and invited me to live with them in Asheville for two summers. Also, their daughter Sue, who was a baby during that time, played a large role in getting me back and re-introducing me to my old home town, Blacksburg.

I mentioned Sue's role in bringing me back to Blacksburg by calling Sister Nell about the Cash House that faced demolition if someone didn't take action to save it. But I also owe Sue a big debt for urging me to come back to the Blacksburg ARP Church that I had attended as a child. That was where I met Pastor David Rowe who was not only a fine minister but a great musician. David became my best friend and I became a "groupie" for Miller-Rowe Consort consisting of David, who played the hammered dulcimer, and Michael Miller, who played the classical guitar. These two excellent musicians performed internationally and played on a regular basis at such venues as Biltmore Estate and Colonial Williamsburg. David became such an influential person in my life that he seemed more like a brother than a friend. Miller-Rowe recorded some of their albums at the Inn and I stocked their albums for sale

I should also mention nephew Blair Turner (son of my sister Edith and her husband, R.B. Turner). We've had a close relationship since his birth in Gastonia, NC. Blair overcame great odds, starting when he was barely beyond the babyhood stage. *Background: During the 20ᵗʰ century, especially in the 1940s and 1950s, polio became epidemic in the United States and the world.* As a toddler, Blair was stricken with this terrible disease. He was never expected to walk again but with special help from his aunt, Edna Jane Turner, a young nurse who moved into the house to give him special care, he made a remarkable recovery and as an adult became a strapping, 6 ft. plus athletic man.

Blair's successful efforts to succeed in life are illustrated by the fact that as a young boy of 13, he began working with a Gastonia neighbor who was an electrical contractor. By the time he went to high school, he knew how to wire a house! This knowledge and his willingness to learn made it possible for him to work his way through NC State in Raleigh largely on his own. Since I was on the staff of NC State at the time, I often encountered him as he went around campus doing electrical work. After he graduated from college he served with the U.S. Air Force and then took a job with the National Security Agency where he rose to the senior executive level. Since I also worked in Washington, our families often visited each other. Today we still keep in close touch by telephone and email.

One final note about nephew Blair and wife, Chee Chee: they served as great examples for their two children, Kathy and Roger to follow. Kathy, with her good looks could have perhaps had a career as a model. Instead, along with her husband, Stew Mitchell, she concentrated on raising her three fine sons and when they were grown, had a successful business career in real estate "staging" properties and she later worked in the county school system in the counseling office. Son Roger, as a Marine, served several tours of duty in Iraq and Afghanistan. Now, as a Brig. General, he is currently serving as Commanding General of the Marine Corps Air Ground Combat Center and Marine Air Ground Task Force Training Command, located at 29 Palms, California.

Once I made the decision to retire to Blacksburg, sister Nell Turner's son, Dan and family, also were especially helpful in making my return comfortable and in being able to complete the transition of the "falling down old house" into the elegant and award winning White House Inn.

During the renovation, Dan contributed by helping me deal with construction problems and also as a faithful (almost nightly) "taste tester" as I practiced my skills as a chef. I knew I had to learn much before being able to prepare praiseworthy breakfasts including eggs Benedict, shrimp and grits, and various casseroles that would appeal to guests expecting gourmet breakfasts at the Inn. He and Carolyn were always willing to serve as "guest innkeepers" when I needed to get away. Carolyn also served as "house tour guide" at many large events.

More close relatives who were exceedingly helpful to me both during my days as an innkeeper and later included the Wofford Martin family, consisting of Wofford, his wife Lois, and son Campbell. *Our mothers were sisters, Macie and Bessie Mitchell, before they were married to their respective husbands.* When I began visiting Blacksburg and after I moved here, I had a chance to renew my friendship with Wofford and Lois. They would often invite me to dinner at their house and to accompany them to dances in Gaffney and other nearby towns.

One of Wofford's several serious hobbies was beekeeping. He planted many special bushes around his property so that his bees could easily dine and produce exceptionally tasty honey. At one time he maintained 55 hives of bees and became a sought out lecturer on beekeeping. Wofford's hobby of beekeeping gave me an idea for the Inn. I wanted to provide departing guests with a little, unexpected gift to commemorate their stay. The fancy way to say this was the French word "lagniappe." I knew that anything Wofford did had to be perfect so I mentioned my idea to Wofford and he agreed to make a supply of small containers of his excellent honey with the names of his beekeeping business and The White House Inn displayed. As they were leaving the Inn, each guest received a jar of this honey to take with them. The only problem I had was Wofford's generosity; I had to force him to accept payment for the honey I used for "lagniappes."

Wofford has long since departed but I remember his many kindnesses to me. Distance caused us to lose contact with each other for many years. Our only personal contact during this period was when I was a newspaper reporter covering an event in York County where the entertainment was supplied by the "Wofford Martin Dance Team." I especially enjoyed the performance but had no idea that my cousin Wofford loved and excelled at dancing and once had his own dance team. With Wofford's passing, only my dear cousin, Hayes Mitchell Faulkner, and I remain to represent our generation of the Mitchell family.

Wofford and Lois's son, Campbell Martin, a retired postman, shares many of his father's good qualities. He is also a great dancer and is multi talented like his father. One of the latter is his skill as a cabinet maker. He exhibited this skill by doing some fine cabinet work at the large home I had built at Sterling Lakes and at Gloria's house in Gaffney. As an example of both of his parents' generous spirit, he remains in close contact with his mother, Lois, and looks after his late father's farm, especially the herd of Simmental cattle which was Wofford's pride and joy.

Bob and Debbie Price of Columbia, SC, who were among the first of my "paying guests" at the Inn, also deserve special thanks. After their first visit, they wrote an article published in the Columbia State Newspaper praising the beauty of the Inn as well as the quality of the breakfasts. This helped my Inn achieve statewide recognition. Thereafter, they would drive almost 200 miles roundtrip to serve as "guest innkeepers." And they presented me with a great little "Sweet Heart" waffle maker that I still use.

In recent years, I've had the chance to become closer to other members of the family, some of whom were born and grew up while I was away. Chief among these is Dianne White Wilson, youngest daughter of my oldest brother, Howard. I hardly knew her until Gloria and I moved to Spartanburg. A pretty redhead, she often spent time with me when Gloria was visiting her daughter and grandsons in Gaffney. Some fellow residents questioned why I would be having dinner with a much younger, very pretty woman by asking, "Where is Gloria?" I would reply, "Gloria has gone away and this is my new girlfriend!" Seeing the difference in our ages and appearances, residents at our retirement community knew that I was joking and chuckled appropriately.

I don't see as much of Dianne these days since she has remarried. However, our relationship has not suffered because she is married to one of the nicest persons that anyone could meet. The Wilsons always invite us to their "hobby farm" outside of Forest City, NC for family reunions and holiday meals. At age 93, I no longer venture to drive far from Spartanburg. Therefore, the Wilsons and brother Howard's youngest son, Boyce and his wife Martha, always make sure that we are picked up and driven to Forest City where both Dianne and Boyce live. After feasting on wonderful home cooked food, we are returned to Summit Hills Retirement Community.

A resounding thanks to Thelma Easley, a retired school principal now living at Summit Hills and Jean Ogden, who is author of an exceptionally fine memoir of growing up in Gaffney, as well as long time friend Joan Gibson, for their willingness to take on the task of doing the last reading of this large document.

Also, a special thanks to Bill Crotzer of Gaffney, whose imaginative drawing of the farm scene adorns the front cover of the memoir.

Both Gloria and I are eternally grateful for our acceptance and love from members at the Spartanburg ARP church. Friend and former pastor, David Rowe helped make the transition from my "home church" in Blacksburg to Spartanburg ARP church easier by personally driving me to Spartanburg to meet Pastor Peter Waid.

And I thank God often that this "sharecropper boy" decided to "come back home."

CPSIA information can be obtained
at www.ICGtesting.com
Printed in the USA
LVHW070818021121
701904LV00008B/41